Oracle Database 11g Oracle Real Application Clusters Handbook

Second Edition

K Gopalakrishnan

McGraw-Hill

New York   Chicago   San Francisco
Lisbon   London   Madrid   Mexico City
Milan   New Delhi   San Juan
Seoul   Singapore   Sydney   Toronto

The McGraw·Hill Companies

Cataloging-in-Publication Data is on file with the Library of Congress

McGraw-Hill books are available at special quantity discounts to use as premiums and sales promotions, or for use in corporate training programs. To contact a representative, please e-mail us at bulksales@mcgraw-hill.com.

Oracle Database 11g Oracle Real Application Clusters Handbook, Second Edition

1234567890   DOC DOC   10987654321

ISBN   978-0-07-175262-6
MHID   0-07-175262-5

Sponsoring Editor	**Technical Editors**	**Composition**
Wendy Rinaldi	Arup Nanda	Newgen Publishing
Editorial Supervisor	Sandesh Rao	and Data Services
Patty Mon	John Kanagaraj	**Illustration**
Project Manager	**Copy Editor**	Newgen Publishing
Aloysius Raj,	Bart Reed	and Data Services
Newgen Publishing	**Proofreader**	**Art Director, Cover**
and Data Services	Paul Tyler	Jeff Weeks
Acquisitions Coordinator	**Indexer**	**Cover Designer**
Stephanie Evans	Jack Lewis	Pattie Lee
	Production Supervisor	
	George Anderson	

Dedicated to
My parents and my beloved country

About the Author

K Gopalakrishnan (Gopal) is an award-winning author (*Oracle Magazine*'s "Oracle Author of the Year 2005") of the bestselling *Oracle Wait Interface: A Practical Guide to Performance Diagnostics & Tuning* book (Oracle Press/McGraw-Hill, 2004). He has also authored *Oracle Database 10g Real Application Clusters Handbook* (Oracle Press/McGraw-Hill, 2006). He has published articles in various international magazines, and Oracle Technology Network (OTN) recognizes him as Oracle ACE.

Gopal has architected and implemented a few of the biggest and busiest databases on the planet and has deep experience in the performance management and tuning of very large online transactional databases. One of his core competencies is the design and deployment of scalable database solution architectures that support extreme performance, high availability, and manageability.

Gopal is a recognized expert in Oracle RAC and Database Internals and has used his extensive expertise in solving many vexing performance issues all across the world for telecom giants, banks, financial institutions, and universities in over 30 countries across five continents.

Gopal is currently working with Engineered System Services at Oracle Corporation, focusing on architecting solutions around Oracle Exadata Database Machine and Real Application Clusters.

About the Contributing Author

Harish Kumar is an independent Oracle consultant at ORAXperts Pty Ltd., based in Australia. Prior to ORAXperts, Harish worked with Oracle Australia in Oracle Advanced Customer Services, supporting enterprise customers in Oracle RAC, database performance tuning, and high availability. He is an active contributor on Oracle Forums and blogs on his website at www.oraxperts.com. He can be contacted at harish.kumar@oraxperts.com.

About the Technical Editors

John Kanagaraj is an IT Architect at Cisco Systems, Inc., where he specializes in application and database performance management. He has been working with various flavors of Unix and Oracle since 1984 as a developer, DBA, and system administrator. John is a frequent presenter at Oracle OpenWorld, IOUG, OAUG, and local user group conferences. He has co-authored *Oracle Database 10g: Insider Solutions*, published by Sams and has served as a technical editor for various books, including the award winning *Oracle Wait Interface: A Practical Guide to Performance Diagnostics & Tuning*. John also serves as the executive editor of IOUG's *SELECT Journal*, and in that capacity is always looking forward to developing and mentoring new authors. John and his family reside in the Bay Area in sunny California. You can e-mail him at ora_apps_dba_y@yahoo.com.

Arup Nanda has been working exclusively as an Oracle DBA for the last 15 years, covering everything from performance tuning to disaster recovery. He is the global head of database architecture for a New York–area multinational company. He has co-authored four books on Oracle Database, written 300+ articles in many publications, including *Oracle Magazine* and OTN, and presented 150+ sessions at conferences such as Oracle Open World and IOUG Collaborate. He also publishes a blog (arup.blogpsot.com), conducts training sessions, and builds tools for effective database administration. He is an Oracle ACE Director, a member of the Oak Table Network, an editor for *SELECT Journal* (a publication of IOUG), and a member of the Board of Directors of Exadata SIG. In 2003, he was awarded "DBA of the Year" by Oracle.

Sandesh Rao runs the RAC Assurance Development Team within RAC Development at Oracle Corporation, specializing in developing customer best practices for Grid/Cloud deployments and Exadata Database Machines. With 13 years of experience in the HA space and having worked across different versions and application stacks, he is a recognized expert in the Grid Stack. He is also responsible for supporting customer escalations. Prior to RAC Assurance, Sandesh managed the Database, Enterprise Manager, and Languages BDE (Bugs Diagnostics and Escalations). Sandesh has more than a decade of onsite and back-office experience and more than six years of management experience in running Support and Development organizations. He is backed by a degree in Computer Science from the University of Mumbai, India.

Contents

PART I
High Availability Architecture and Clusters

v

PART III
Oracle RAC Administration and Management

PART IV

Advanced Concepts in Oracle RAC

PART VI
Appendixes

Foreword

Oracle Real Application Clusters (RAC) is the best-selling Oracle Database option, and has been since its introduction in 2001. Why has this option been so successful? Because it provides clear value to companies—value that has evolved over time as their IT environments have evolved.

Take a look at the data center in the post-mainframe era. Traditionally, IT has built dedicated silos of hardware and software for each application. This made it easy to provide predictable service levels, unless of course there were wild peaks in load. However, it also meant over-provisioning hardware and software to meet peak demand. It was difficult to scale as the application demand grew, often requiring forklift updates and the associated downtime. Because IT tended to over-provision, companies paid more than they needed to for hardware, software, and maintenance. And, of course, each silo was independently managed, which drove up costs further. Yet, companies weren't yet focused on the inefficiencies of this model. Rather, they needed a way to increase availability. Downtime costs money, and as more and more critical business processes moved online, availability was the most important business driver. Oracle RAC, soon after its introduction, became the premier solution for database high availability.

Once companies solved their availability issues, they started to take a closer look at reducing costs. They had built large, scalable high-availability systems using expensive symmetric multiprocessing (SMP) servers. The lines of business paying the bills began to push for cost reductions. Forward-thinking leading IT managers, those who use technology to build competitive advantages, looked for a more cost-efficient architecture. They found it in commodity servers connected in a scale-out cluster, able to deliver service levels at a fraction of the cost of large, expensive SMP servers. How does a database run in such an environment? You use Oracle RAC to scale your database across multiple servers. Thus, Oracle RAC had evolved to address the new challenges facing IT.

Reducing costs by moving to lower-cost servers only temporarily satiated the hunger of the business to wring out costs. Next, IT looked to ways to use its resources more efficiently, to improve utilization, and to achieve more with less. In 2004, Oracle introduced Oracle Database 10*g* and the Enterprise Grid Computing architecture. This helped reduce costs by consolidating to a shared architecture, where peak and failover capacity could be shared by multiple applications. Oracle RAC provided the key features to unlock this architecture, by providing the flexibility for workloads to scale and shrink their footprint as load increased and decreased. Oracle Database 10*g* also introduced Automatic Storage Management, which extended the grid architecture to the storage tier.

Today, this trend to consolidate to a shared architecture continues. Companies now want to increase their agility and reduce their time to market. They are looking to cloud computing to help move to the next step. Clouds improve upon grids by providing rapid provisioning of resources, enabling databases to be easily created on demand, and to satisfy new initiatives in a timely manner. However, take a close look at the characteristics of the cloud, and you'll see exactly the same capabilities that Oracle RAC has been providing for the past decade. The cloud highlights the principles that have guided Oracle products since the early days of relational databases. Oracle has long advocated consolidating work into a shared pool of computing resources, network access has always been a critical component of its solutions, and rapid provisioning of computing resources with minimal management effort has been built directly into Oracle Database products.

To fully appreciate how Oracle RAC helps companies build database clouds, it's useful to look at a database cloud more closely. In general, clouds are pools of resources—that is, hardware, software, and storage—into which you can deploy applications. The resources are pooled and shared across multiple applications. This pooling of resources ensures enough resources are available to meet quality of service requirements, even in the face of demand spikes and resource failures. Resources in a cloud appear to be elastic—they can grow and shrink as required, appearing infinitely scalable. Often this is achieved through rapid provisioning, generally via a self-service or automatic infrastructure. This makes it simple to quickly deploy applications, test beds, and development platforms, thus increasing an organization's agility. Management costs are kept low via centralized management and features to automate meeting quality of service objectives. End users need not be concerned with managing the resources— rather they interact with managed services that allow them to focus on their core business.

Although many well-known infrastructure clouds are built using server virtualization, server virtualization is not a requirement of a cloud. A database cloud need not be deployed in a server virtualization environment. Oracle RAC has for years had the ability to abstract a database service from the underlying physical hardware and storage hosting it, providing its own virtualization capabilities. This enables multiple deployment models for the database cloud, which allow for deployment in both physical and virtual environments.

A database cloud helps to facilitate consolidation, but not all forms of consolidation yield the same benefits. To maximize ROI, companies need to understand the various forms of consolidation and their impact on the bottom line. The easiest form of consolidation is to consolidate at the server level, often using server virtualization. This is easy, and provides immediate and visible payback. Whereas you once had 100 underutilized database servers, you now have 10 fully utilized servers, albeit still running 100 operating systems and databases. You save on floor space, power, cooling, capital expenditures, and your hardware admin is freed from managing 100 servers. However, your system, storage, database, and application administrators don't see any savings. To improve your ROI even more, you should consolidate higher in the stack. Consolidate your storage to reduce your storage costs. Consolidate your operating systems, your databases, and even your workloads. As you move up the stack, consolidation requires a little more thought. However, the paybacks are huge. Those 100 servers, 100 storage volumes, 100 operating systems, 100 databases, and 100 schemas could be consolidated into a very small number of items, dramatically reducing the number of items you need to manage.

As you consolidate into clusters of servers and ultimately into fewer larger databases, Oracle RAC becomes the critical component of these database cloud solutions. Oracle RAC provides the flexibility to deploy databases to a clustered pool of servers and storage, to span servers, and to perform online rebalance work across the nodes in the cluster. Oracle RAC is critical in supporting large consolidated databases, because these databases must now scale across multiple low-cost commodity servers to meet the aggregate demand of the consolidated database.

Oracle Real Application Cluster is now over 10 years old. In the past 10 years, Oracle has continued to develop additional technologies that today enable the database cloud. Here are a few notable examples: Oracle 10g introduced Dynamic Database Services, which allows IT to control workloads running in a shared cluster environment. Automatic Storage Management extends the benefits of the database cloud to the storage layer, providing elastic storage for databases that can be provisioned online with no downtime. Instance caging provides isolation between instances in a shared OS deployment, thus facilitating OS consolidation. Oracle 11g brought Server Pools and Quality of Service Management, which are key for meeting service levels in a consolidated environment. Oracle Exadata broke new ground by changing the procurement and deployment model of the cloud, providing a cloud in a box. It also introduced key performance improvements such as Hybrid Columnar Compression, smart flash cache, and smart scans.

All these technologies may sound advanced, and you may be unsure of how to get started leveraging them. I encourage you to read this book, to learn more, and to use Oracle RAC to give your company the competitive edge necessary to thrive in the twenty-first century.

Bob Thome
Senior Director of Product Management
Oracle Corporation

Acknowledgments

'Tis never good to let the thought of good things done thee pass away.

Writing a book is not just simply about the author putting down thoughts or sharing knowledge via the printed material. It is like directing an orchestra. Many musicians have to come together and play their individual instruments in tune in an orchestra under the guidance of a good conductor in order to sound melodious. In the same way, a great team has to work together and help the author create a book. When a stellar team comes together this way, the result is a book that is both pleasurable to read and simple to comprehend. As the author of this book, I am greatly indebted to this team who stood behind me and helped me create this book.

First and foremost, my sincere thanks to my long-term friend, philosopher and guide John Kanagaraj for his support in every project I start. John, an Oracle author himself, has been an inspiration from the very beginning. I salute him for his patience and guidance. John kept my spirits up whenever I was running low.

A special thanks to my contributing author Harish Kumar Kalra. Harish has contributed immensely to the book, especially in the administration chapters, and helped me throughout the book in various forms. He has made available his support in a number of ways, and without Harish it would have been very tough sailing for me.

I am thankful to everyone who contributed to this book either directly or indirectly. During the past few years, I have learned a lot from many people, and my special thanks go to Steve Adams, Jonathan Lewis, Vijay Lunawat, Scott Gossett, Scott Heisey, Gaja Vaidyanatha, and James Morle. A favor conferred in the time of need, though it be small (in itself), is (in value) much larger than the world!

It is an honor for me to work with some of the smartest minds in Oracle Corporation and I would like to show my sincere gratitude to Kotaro Ono, Sarr Maoz, Roderic Manalac, Nitin Vengurlekar, Sudhi Vijayakumar for their help. I am thankful to my colleagues

Sreekanth Krishnavajjala, Sathish Natarajan, Ganesh Rajamani, and Kirti Deshpande for their initial reviews.

I would also like to extend my sincere thanks to my managers Michael Erwin, Inderpal Tahim, at Oracle Engineered Systems Services and Shankar Jayaganapathy at Oracle Enterprise Solutions Group for supporting and encouraging me in this effort. Without their help and guidance, I am afraid that I would not have found time to work on this book. I also thank Jerry Rickers, Angelo Prucino, Sheila Capreo, and Sohan Demel, also from Oracle Corporation, for their help and support at various stages.

I am truly indebted to my esteemed clients. They not only posed challenges, but also were willing to implement my solutions in their systems. They played a big role in the knowledge acquisition and enhancement that I shared in this book.

It was great working with the awesome people at McGraw-Hill: Lisa McClain, Wendy Rinaldi, Stephanie Evans, Aloysius Raj, and Bart Reed. Thank you all very much for being so patient with me, and for making sure that this book project stayed on track and on time.

Last but not the least, I wish to thank again my technical editors and reviewers John Kanagaraj, Arup Nanda, and Sandesh Rao, whose great efforts are reflected in the rich content and timely completion of the book.

—K Gopalakrishnan

Introduction

Whatever is heard from whosever's mouth,
Wisdom will rightly discern its true meaning.
(Kural 423: Thiruvalluvar)

I work as a consultant and visit many sites for Oracle RAC implementations around the globe. My regular work involves answering simple questions such as what platform to choose for RAC as well as working on very complex performance problems. Most of the customers I met complained that there is no definite text available on the subject, and many of them still treat RAC as a "black box." This is true even for seasoned database administrators who have been working on Oracle databases for many years! Customers who had previously implemented Oracle Parallel Server (OPS) also wanted to know how RAC works and how it is different from OPS.

Although a number of other books on the market are devoted to Oracle RAC, I have not seen a single book that covers the complete spectrum of topics related to RAC. As a result, there is a significant gap in knowledge about RAC internals and nuances in the public domain. My failure in finding any such book was the impetus to write this book. I was also emboldened as my other book (*Oracle Wait Interface: A Practical Guide to Performance Diagnostics & Tuning*) was a great success and even fetched me *Oracle Magazine's* Editor's Choice "Oracle Author of the Year" Award in 2005.

As in my previous book, my goal in this book has been to explain how to implement and use RAC in the most efficient manner rather than providing a theoretical overview about the grid. If you look at the contents, you will find that we have not discussed anything about the grid technologies or grid architecture. Similarly, you will not find any details about grid management, including the Enterprise Manager or Grid Control and any of the fancy technical concepts. I have carefully avoided topics that are not suitable for a wider audience.

I believe in the proverb "Give a man a fish, you feed him for a day. Teach a man to fish, you feed him for life." Thus, the purpose of the book is to provide a solid background and fundamentals of Oracle Real Application Clusters rather than providing a heap of commands and syntax that are readily available in the standard documentation and other Oracle texts. Although this book covers the spectrum of topics related to RAC, it is still by no means complete—it's just the start of a long and exciting journey. The expectation is that you can use this book as a reference and concepts guide (with a long shelf life) rather using it for a specific release. I also don't intend to provide quick-fix solutions and commands. However, a few chapters contain best-practice techniques and design considerations relevant to Oracle Database 11*g*.

Some of the concepts discussed here are truly complex, and I would recommend that you skip them during the first read. Once you are done reading the book, revisit these chapters a few times until you obtain a clear understanding of the concepts. Note that a few of the concepts discussed here are applicable only to current versions of Oracle, unless noted otherwise.

You may also notice that some of the technical topics are treated very lightly. So, as a DBA, you just need to have a basic but solid understanding about the architecture of Oracle and the way it works. I believe that discussions about some deep technical aspects are impractical and not really required everywhere. For example, the inner workings of Cache Fusion and distributed lock managers cannot be explained in a single chapter. In my opinion, each deserves an independent book on its own. Therefore, be aware that the discussions are modeled according to the context of this title.

The book is organized in five distinct parts.

Part I deals with the history and architecture of the high availability clusters and compares the various clustering architecture. It also dives deep into Oracle clustering architecture, including Oracle Parallel Server and the evolution of the Oracle clustering technologies. We also discuss the architecture of Real Application Clusters and Oracle kernel components that make RAC a working solution.

Chapter 1 talks about high availability architecture and clusters. Here, we will learn the most common techniques used for availability and see the impact of planned and unplanned downtime for the business. We also discuss the most common solutions used to achieve high availability and scalability. Hardware clustering is the most commonly used method to achieve high availability and "on-demand" scalability.

Chapter 2 introduces users to the rich history of RAC with some details about the basics of clustering technologies and a discussion on the early days of Oracle Parallel Server. We also discuss the intrinsic limitations of Oracle Parallel Server and how RAC overcomes those limitations with the new techniques. You then learn some basics about Distributed Lock Manager (DLM) locking too.

Chapter 3 introduces Oracle RAC architecture and the components that make it work. We will cover why global coordination is required for RAC and also briefly discuss RAID, because shared storage is the key in the RAC infrastructure. The Automatic Storage Management (ASM) and the new 11*g*-related technologies, such as Oracle Grid Infrastructure (GI), are also introduced.

Part II of this book deals with the installation of Real Application Clusters software and ASM. It provides basic details of preparing the hardware for Real Application Clusters and installing RAC in generic Unix and Linux environments. The fundamentals of Automatic Storage Management are also introduced here.

Chapter 4 is about preparing the hardware for RAC installation. A proper and sound preparation of the hardware for the RAC installation tasks is the key to a successful deployment.

Oracle Grid Infrastructure is the Oracle Clusterware, which logically binds the servers at the operating system level, and we discuss installing the Oracle Clusterware here.

Chapter 5 deals exclusively with installation of RAC on the cluster. We use the screenshot process for RDBMS installation and RAC database configuration. We also use the new cluster verify utility to validate the integrity of the installation.

Chapter 6 is on Automatic Storage Management. ASM is the new database file system from Oracle, and you'll learn how to manage disk groups and administer disk groups in the ASM environment. You also learn the new enhancements in ASM, such as ASM Cluster File System (ACFS) and various command-line tools. The Oracle-provided utility ASMLIB is also briefly discussed in this chapter.

Part III discusses the generic administration of the RAC databases. It has notes on the basic administration of a RAC database and lists the similarities and differences between single-instance management and Real Application Clusters database management. The RAC performance management chapter introduces the most common problems, issues, and wait scenarios in 11g RAC, along with potential solutions where applicable. In addition to advanced administration, this chapter introduces service management in RAC.

Chapter 7 talks about administering an Oracle RAC database from a DBA's perspective. Administering RAC is similar to administering the single-instance database, with some changes. We look at the considerations for RAC database administration and also cover the administration topics for Oracle Cluster Ready Services and voting disks.

Chapter 8 deals with administering services in the RAC environment. "Services" is still a relatively new concept in databases that simplifies resource management and workload distribution and provides high availability to the workload. Also Oracle Clusterware command-line interfaces are discussed in detail in this chapter.

Chapter 9 talks about backup and recovery concepts for RAC as well as the concepts of instance and database recovery in Real Application Clusters. We do not discuss the commands and syntaxes involved in the backup and recovery procedures. This chapter delves deep into the architecture of recovery in a single instance and provides good insight into the different types of recovery in an Oracle RAC database.

Chapter 10 deals with performance management in RAC. Managing and achieving good performance in any system is probably the primary objective, and this is more so in RAC. Performance tuning of Real Application Clusters needs a few extra considerations when compared to single-instance tuning because of the additional instances accessing the same set of resources. A few additional considerations should be taken into account while designing and tuning the Real Application Clusters database, and we discuss them in detail in the performance-tuning topics of this chapter. The Oracle Wait Interface is enhanced in 11g, and we discuss events specific to it in fine detail. This chapter also offers advice on tuning those events.

Part IV of this book is intended for advanced topics. We get in to the resource management aspect of a Real Application Cluster environment and discuss how the resources are shared and managed in the RAC environment. We discuss the Global Cache Services and Global Enqueue Services and their inner workings. We also discuss the Cache Fusion topics in more detail. This includes a complete overview of how things worked in the past and how Cache Fusion has changed the dynamics of data sharing between the instances.

Chapter 11 provides a detailed discussion of global resource directory and what it does. You learn about the different locking and serialization mechanisms as well as their importance and relevance in operating an Oracle RAC database. You should note that the discussions are quite deep in nature, so you should plan to read the chapter a few times to grasp its contents effectively. The global resource directory and resource-mastering issues are discussed in this chapter.

Chapter 12 provides most of the details you'll need to know about Cache Fusion. We look at how Cache Fusion *really* works, with examples and demonstrations. This is the most important chapter in the book, and understanding it will help you appreciate the intelligence built into this component. It will also help you significantly in designing a scalable RAC solution and debugging most complex performance problems. You learn some of the exciting internal techniques of how RAC works in Oracle 11g, and a well-documented example is provided to help you understand the facts easily.

Chapter 13 introduces workload management from Oracle's perspective. You also learn about Transparent Application Failover (TAF) and how to implement it. Oracle 11g has enhanced Fast Application Notification (FAN) and has taken service-based management to the next level. This chapter talks about them and their usage.

Chapter 14 discusses RAC troubleshooting—one of the least-known RAC topics. This chapter provides you with some methods you can use to quickly troubleshoot a misbehaving RAC instance. This chapter talks about troubleshooting from an operational perspective and introduces performance diagnosis as well troubleshooting instance recovery.

Part V covers deploying RAC, including extending RAC to a geo-cluster environment and common application development best practices. The most common RAC application development techniques are discussed here.

Chapter 15 is on Extended RAC and discusses extending RAC in a WAN environment. Oracle RAC is most commonly used as a scalability and availability solution. However, in specific cases, it could also be used as a disaster recovery solution. This configuration is known as Extended RAC Clustering, and we will be discussing the most common issues related to this topic.

Chapter 16 introduces some of the best practices in application development for RAC. We have tried to cover some of the most commonly found issues in an Oracle RAC environment and provide some best-practice methods for overcoming those challenges.

The most useful and commonly used V$ views are explained in Appendix A. The dynamic performance views are grouped together based on their use. Appendix B discusses adding and removing nodes to and from the cluster. Appendix C lists the texts used during the production of this book.

By no means have we attempted to cover all aspects of Oracle RAC. I believe this book is just the beginning.

As an author, I would like to hear from you about how you liked the book and what could be done to improve it. Please feel free to contact me at kaygopal@yahoo.com with whatever comments you have on this book.

—K Gopalakrishnan

PART

I

High Availability Architecture and Clusters

CHAPTER

1

Introduction to High Availability and Scalability

n today's fast-paced world, data and application *availability* can make or break a business. With access to these businesses granted via the ubiquitous and "always-on" Internet, data availability is an extremely important component in any business function.

Database systems are growing at an enormous rate in terms of the number of simultaneously connected and active users as well as the volume of data they handle. Even though the servers used to store huge, active databases have also improved in performance and capacity, a *single* server, powerful though it may be, is frequently unable to handle the database load and capacity requirements for these active databases. This factor makes it necessary to scale the processing capacity or scale the hardware or software to accommodate these requirements.

High Availability

When availability is crucial for a business, extremely high levels of disaster tolerance must allow the business to continue in the face of a calamity, without the end users or customers noticing any adverse consequences. The effects of global companies conducting business across time zones spanning "24 × 7 × forever" operations, e-commerce, and the challenges associated with today's "flat world" all-drive businesses to achieve a level of disaster tolerance capable of ensuring continuous survival and profitability.

Different businesses require different levels of risk with regard to loss of data and potential downtime. A variety of technical solutions can be used to provide varying levels of protection with respect to these business needs. The ideal solutions would have no downtime and allow no data to be lost. Although such solutions do exist, they are expensive, and hence their costs must be weighed against the potential impact of a disaster and its effects on the business.

Because computers are capable of working at faster and faster rates, the businesses that depend on them are placing more and more demands on them. As a result, the various interconnections and dependencies in the computing fabric, consisting of different components and technologies, are becoming more complex every day. The availability of worldwide access via the Internet is placing extremely high demands on businesses as well as the IT departments and administrators that run and maintain these computers in the background.

Adding to this complexity is the globalization of businesses, which ensures that there is no "quiet time" or "out-of-office hours" so essential to the maintenance requirements of these computer systems. Hence, businesses' computer systems—the lifeblood of the organization—must be available at all times: day or night, weekday or weekend, local holiday or workday. The term *24 × 7 × forever* effectively describes business computer system availability and is so popular that this term is being used in everyday language to describe non-computer–based entities such as 9-1-1 call centers and other emergency services.

The dictionary defines the word *available* as follows:

1. Present and ready for use; at hand; accessible.

2. Capable of being gotten; obtainable.

3. Qualified and willing to be of service or assistance.

When applied to computer systems, the word's meaning is a combination of all these factors. Thus, access to an application should be present and ready for use, capable of being accessed, and qualified and willing to be of service. In other words, an application should be available easily for use at any time and should perform at a level that is both acceptable and useful. Although this is a broad, sweeping statement, a lot of complexity and different factors come into play before true high availability is achieved and sustained.

HA Terminology

The term *high availability (HA),* when applied to computer systems, means that the application or service in question is available all the time, regardless of time of day, location, and other factors that can influence the availability of such an application. In general, it is the ability to continue a service for extremely long durations without any interruptions. Typical technologies for HA include redundant power supplies and fans for servers, RAID (Redundant Array of Inexpensive/ Independent Disks) configuration for disks, clusters for servers, multiple network interface cards, redundant routers for networks, and even multiple datacenters within the same metro area to provide an extremely high level of availability and load balancing.

Fault Tolerance

A *fault-tolerant* computer system or component is designed so that, in the event of component failure, a backup component or procedure can immediately take its place with no loss of service. Fault tolerance can be provided with software, embedded in hardware, or provided by some combination of the two. It goes one step further than HA to provide the highest possible availability within a single datacenter and within a single application execution environment such as a database.

Disaster Recovery

Disaster recovery (DR) is the ability to resume operations after a disaster—including destruction of an entire datacenter site and everything in it. In a typical DR scenario, significant time elapses before a datacenter can resume IT functions, and some amount of data typically needs to be reentered to bring the system data back up to date.

Disaster Tolerance

The term *disaster tolerance (DT)* is the art and science of preparing for disasters so that a business is able to continue operation after a disaster. The term is sometimes used incorrectly in the industry, particularly by vendors who can't really achieve it. Disaster tolerance is much more difficult to achieve than DR because it involves designing systems that enable a business to continue in the face of a disaster, without the end users or customers noticing any adverse effects. The ideal DT solution would result in no downtime and no lost data, even during a disaster. Such solutions do exist, but they cost more than solutions that have some amount of downtime or data loss associated with a disaster.

Planned and Unplanned Outages

So what happens when an application stops working or stops behaving as expected, due to the failure of even one of the crucial components? Such an application is deemed *down* and the event is called an *outage*. This outage can be planned for—for example, consider the outage that occurs when a component is being upgraded or worked on for maintenance reasons.

Whereas planned outages are a necessary evil, an unplanned outage can be a nightmare for a business. Depending on the business in question and the duration of the downtime, an unplanned outage can result in such overwhelming losses that the business is forced to close. Regardless of the nature, outages are something that businesses usually do not tolerate. There is always pressure on IT to eliminate unplanned downtime totally and to drastically reduce, if not eliminate, planned downtime. We will see later how these two requirements can be effectively met for at least the Oracle database component.

Note that an application or computer system does not have to be totally down for an outage to occur. It is possible that the performance of an application degrades to such a degree that it is unusable. In this case, although the application is accessible, it does not meet the third and final qualification of being willing to serve in an adequately acceptable fashion. As far as the business or end user is concerned, this application is down, although it is available. We will see later in this book how Oracle Real Application Clusters (RAC) can provide the horizontal scalability that can significantly reduce the risk of an application not providing adequate performance.

An End-to-End Perspective

From the start, you should be clear that high availability is not just dependent on the availability of physical components such as hardware, system software (operating system and database), environment, network, and application software. It is also dependent on other "soft" resources such as experienced and capable administrators (system, network, database, and application specialists), programmers, users, and even known, repeatable business processes.

It is entirely possible that a business installs and configures highly available "hard" components but does not employ competent administrators who are able to maintain these systems properly. Even if the administrators are competent, availability can be adversely affected when a business process, such as change control, is not followed properly, and incorrect, untested changes are made that could bring such a system down. High availability therefore needs to be seen with an end-to-end perspective that covers all aspects.

Having said this, we should now define the *single point of failure (SPOF)*—any single component that can bring down the entire system as a result of failure. For example, in a computer system that has a single controller interfacing with the disk subsystem, a hardware failure of this controller will bring the whole system down. Although the other components are working, this one *single* component has caused a failure. Identification of and protection against SPOFs are crucial tasks of providing HA.

It is not possible to cover all aspects of HA in an Oracle-specific book such as this. We will cover only how HA can be achieved specifically in the area of the Oracle RDBMS, which is an important component of the HA picture. We will also equip you—the database administrator, programmer, or architect—with techniques that will enable you to achieve HA in this area.

What's more, HA is not something that can be achieved simply by installing HA-aware hardware and software components, employing competent administrators, creating proper procedures, and walking away from it all. The HA process needs continual adjustment, evolution, and adaptation to changing circumstances and environments. Also, this uphill battle occurs on a continual basis—so be prepared!

Cost of Downtime

As hinted at earlier, there is a cost to downtime, just as there is a cost to ensuring that downtime is drastically reduced or even completely eliminated. The trick is to build your systems so that they never go down, even though you *know* that they *will* go down at some time or another. Making downtime the last option will ensure HA. Of course, most companies cannot continue to throw large sums of money at this issue. At some point in time, the additional money spent will return only marginal benefits. Therefore, it is essential to price out your downtime and then use that figure to determine how much you can afford to spend to protect against planned/unplanned downtime. With some effort and experience, this expense can be determined, and you might want to use this information while providing various options and scenarios to management.

The cost of being down usually amounts to lost user productivity, and the actual cost is mostly dependent on what work the users perform when accessing the affected systems. For example, if your development server went down for one hour during prime office time, and 10 developers sat idle for that hour waiting for the server to come up, and each developer costs $100 per hour, then the downtime has effectively cost $100 × 10 × 1 = $1,000. However, if the server that went down served a major shopping site on the Internet during a holiday gift-buying season, you might count the losses in millions of dollars, even if the downtime was brief, because shoppers may move away to a competing site rather than wait for yours to become usable. Figure 1-1 shows a sample chart comparing downtime to cost.

The potential cost of downtime is also dependent on various factors such as time of day and duration of the downtime. For example, an online stock brokerage firm cannot afford to be down even for seconds during business hours. On the other hand, it could go down for hours during nontrading hours without any consequences. Cost of downtime is not linearly dependent on the duration of the downtime. For example, a two-hour outage may not necessarily cost the same as two one-hour downtime periods.

One helpful trick used with balancing the cost of downtime versus the cost of ensuring against downtime is the "availability curve." The more you spend on HA components, the higher you move up the curve. However, the incremental costs of moving from one level to the next increase as you move up the curve.

Here are the four distinct levels of system availability components on the curve:

- **Basic systems**   These are systems with no protection or those that employ no special measures to protect their data and accessibility. Normal tape backups occur at scheduled intervals, and administrators work to restore the system from the last known good backup if and when it breaks. There is no extra cost for HA.

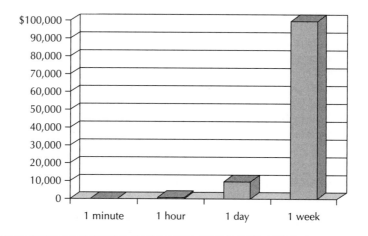

FIGURE 1-1   *Cost of downtime*

- **Redundant data** Some level of disk redundancy is built into the system to protect against loss of data due to disk failures. At the most basic level, this is provided by RAID 5 or RAID 1–based disk subsystems. At the other end of the scale, redundancy is provided by storage area networks (SANs) that have built-in disk-protecting mechanisms such as various RAID levels, hot-swappable disks, "phone home"-type maintenance, and multiple paths to the SAN. The cost of such protection includes procurement of the SAN, attendant SAN fabric and controllers, as well as extra sets of disks to provide RAID protection.

- **System failover** In this case, two or more systems are employed to do the work of one. When the primary system fails, the other, usually called the "secondary" system, takes over and performs the work of the primary. A brief loss of service occurs, but everything quickly works as it did before the failure. The cost of this solution is more than double that of basic systems. Usually, a SAN needs to be employed to make sure that the disks are protected and to provide multiple paths to the disks from these servers.

- **Disaster recovery** In this case, in addition to the systems at the main site (which in themselves may incorporate the previous highest level of protection), all or part of these systems are duplicated at a backup site that is usually physically remote from the main site. You must develop ways of replicating the data and keeping it up to date. The costs are more than double that of the previous level, because you will also have to duplicate an entire site, including datacenters, real-estate facilities, and so on.

As you can easily see, higher and higher levels of availability equate to escalating costs. When faced with even a rough estimate of cost, business leaders (and especially accounting staff) are quick to adjust their levels of expectancy.

Underpinning every aspect, of course, is the fact that you are monitoring, measuring, and recording all this uptime (or downtime, as the case may be). It is a given that you cannot quantify what you do not measure. Nevertheless, many organizations that demand 100-percent uptime do not even have basic measurement tools in place.

Five Nines

The phrase "five nines" is usually thrown about during discussions of high availability, and you need to understand what this means before agreeing (as an administrator or system architect) to provide such a level of availability. A user or project leader will invariably say that 100-percent availability is a necessity, and barring that, at least five nines availability must be maintained—that is, 99.999-percent availability.

To make this concept a bit clearer, Table 1-1 compares uptime and downtime percentages to real-time figures. As you study this table, keep in mind that the cost of providing higher and higher levels of uptime becomes progressively (and sometimes prohibitively) expensive. As you work with management, understanding this can help you provide a clear explanation of these terms and what they mean when translated to actual downtime and attendant costs.

Building Redundant Components

High availability is made possible by providing availability in multiple layers of the technical stack. The inclusion of redundant components that reduce or eliminate SPOFs is the primary key in achieving high availability. For example, more than one host bus adaptor (HBA), a controller for communicating with remote disks, is usually present in each server that connects to a SAN.

Percent Uptime	Percent Downtime	Downtime per Year	Downtime per Week
98	2	7.3 days	3 hours, 22 minutes
99	1	3.65 days	1 hour, 41 minutes
99.8	0.2	17 hours, 30 minutes	20 minutes, 10 seconds
99.9	0.1	8 hours, 45 minutes	10 minutes, 5 seconds
99.99	0.01	52.5 minutes	1 minute
99.999	0.001	5.25 minutes	6 seconds

TABLE 1-1 *Uptime Percentage with Real-Time Figures*

These HBAs, in turn, are able to connect into two or more network adaptor switches to which the SANs are themselves connected. This way, the failure of one HBA or even one network switch will not bring down the server and the application hosted on that server. *Multihosting* (the ability to attach multiple hosts to a single set of disks) and *multipathing* (the ability to attach a single host to its set of disks via more than one path) are common ways of introducing redundancy in such HA systems.

Redundant components exist in the software layers as well. For example, multiple web servers can be front-ended by a load balancer that directs all web requests to a bank of web servers. In this case, when one web server fails, existing connections migrate over to surviving web servers, and the load balancer connects new requests to these surviving web servers.

Redundancy is not restricted to hardware and software, however. Redundancy also includes building physical, environmental, and other elements into the framework. Most of the major Internet datacenters or Internet exchange points now have complete redundancy in terms of power, air conditioning, and other factors, so that the failure in any one of the provider's resources won't affect the operation.

In New York City, for example, two telecommunication systems were strategically placed in the erstwhile World Trade Center complex—one in each tower—with the assumption that the probability of both buildings collapsing was close to zero. However, unfortunately, that assumption was proved wrong. Now, companies are building redundant datacenters that are geographically separated across state or even country boundaries to avoid natural or other catastrophic events. Availability of dark fibers and the improvements in technology such as dense wavelength division multiplexers (DWDMs) make this possible.

Redundancy in the network layer is achieved through the redundant hardware engines in a chassis, a redundant network through multiple chassis, or a combination of the two. Host protocols such as ICMP Route Discovery Protocol (IRDP), Cisco's Hot Standby Routing Protocol (HSRP), and Virtual Router Redundancy Protocol (VRRP) help choose the best next-hop router to reach if one of the routers is unavailable from the server's perspective. In the routing level, Non-Stop Forwarding (NSF) protocol suites combined with millisecond timers reduce the failure or switchover time in case of primary hardware switching engine failure.

In the transport level, physical layer redundancy can be achieved by SDH/SONET self-healing, which restores the traffic in an alternate path in case of fiber link failure. During early 2000, a major transport provider experienced a fiber cut in its long-haul, coast-to-coast transport network in the United States and rerouted the traffic through Europe without most of the end users knowing that the rerouting even took place.

Also, it is now possible to provide redundant database services via the Oracle RAC, and you will see this in detail in subsequent chapters. Suffice it to say at this time that redundancy in database services is an important part of providing HA in the organization, and Oracle RAC enables such a provision.

Of course, adding redundancy into the system also increases its cost and complexity. We hope that the information contained in this book can help you understand that complexity and ease your fears about managing such a complex environment.

Common Solutions for HA

Depending on your budget, you can arrive at a number of solutions for providing high availability. Clustering servers has been a common way to build a highly available and scalable solution. You can provide increasing levels of HA by adopting one of the higher levels of protection described earlier. In most current datacenters, RAID disks, usually in SANs, provide at least a basic level of disk protection. Failover servers at the third level provide some protection from server failure. At the highest level, the disaster recovery site protects against drastic site failure.

Oracle technology can be used to provide all these levels of protection. For example, you can use Automatic Storage Management (ASM) to provide protection at the disk level, Oracle RAC to provide failover protection at the database level (in addition to database-level load balancing), and Oracle standby and Oracle replication to provide site protection failure. Of course, all this requires varying levels of support at the hardware, network, and software layers.

Cluster, Cold Failover, and Hot Failover

Although we will be dealing with clustering in detail in subsequent chapters, we will define it here. A *cluster* is a set of two or more similar servers that are closely connected to one another and usually share the same set of disks. The theory is that in the case of failure of one of the servers, the other surviving server (or servers) can take up the work of the failed server. These servers are physically located close to one another and connected via a "heartbeat" system. In other words, they check one another's heartbeats or live presence at closely defined intervals and are able to detect whether the other node is "dead" within a short period of time. When one of the nodes is deemed nonresponsive to a number of parameters, a failover event is initiated and the service of the nonresponsive node is taken over by other node(s). Additional software may also allow a quick takeover of one another's functions.

Clusters can be implemented in many configurations. When one or more servers in a cluster sit idle, and takeover from another server (or servers) occurs only in the case of a failure, a *cold failover* occurs. When all servers in a cluster are working, and the load is taken on by the surviving server (or servers), this is called a *hot failover*. Assuming that all the servers in the cluster are similar in configuration, in a cold failover, the load carried by the surviving server is the same. In case of a hot failover, however, the load taken on by the surviving server may be more than it can handle, and thus you will need to design both the servers and the load carefully.

There are three general approaches to system failover. In order of increasing availability, they are *no failover, cold failover,* and *hot failover.* Each strategy has a varying recovery time, expense, and user impact, as outlined in Table 1-2.

Variations on these strategies do exist: For example, many large enterprise clients have implemented hot failover and also use cold failover for disaster recovery. It is important to

Approach	Recovery Time	Expense	User Impact
No failover	Unpredictable	No to low cost	High
Cold failover	Minutes	Moderate	Moderate
Hot failover	Immediate or in seconds	Moderate to high	None*

TABLE 1-2   *Failover Approach and Impacts*

differentiate between failover and disaster recovery. *Failover* is a methodology used to resume system availability in an acceptable period of time, whereas *disaster recovery* is a methodology used to resume system availability when all failover strategies have failed.

No Failover

If a production system fails due to a hardware failure, the database and application are generally unaffected. Disk corruption and disk failures, of course, are an exception. Therefore, disk redundancy and good backup procedures are vital to mitigate problems arising from disk failure.

With no failover strategy in place, system failures can result in significant downtime, depending on the cause and your ability to isolate and resolve them. If a CPU has failed, you replace it and restart, while application users wait for the system to become available. For many applications that are not business critical, this risk may be acceptable.

Cold Failover

A common and often inexpensive approach to recovery after failure is to maintain a standby system to assume the production workload in the event of a production system failure. A typical configuration has two identical computers with shared access to a remote disk subsystem.

After a failure, the standby system takes over the applications formerly running on the failed system. In a cold failover, the standby system senses a heartbeat from the production system on a frequent and regular basis. If the heartbeat consistently stops for a period of time, the standby system assumes the IP address and the disk formerly associated with the failed system. The standby can then run any applications that were on the failed system. In this scenario, when the standby system takes over the application, it executes a preconfigured start script to bring the databases online. Users can then reconnect to the databases that are now running on the standby server.

Customers generally configure the failover server to mirror the main server with an identical CPU and memory capacity to sustain production workloads for an extended period of time. Figure 1-2 depicts server connections before and after a failover.

Hot Failover

The hot failover approach can be complicated and expensive, but it comes closest to ensuring 100-percent uptime. It requires the same degree of failover used for a cold failover but also

---

* To be precise, saying there is no user impact in a hot failover scenario is inaccurate. Very few systems are truly "hot" to the point of no user impact; most are somewhat "lukewarm," with a transient brownout.

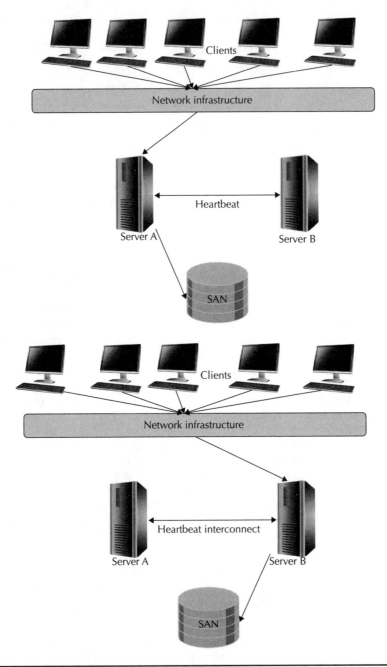

FIGURE 1-2 *Server connections before (top) and after (bottom) a failover*

requires that the state of a running user process be preserved to allow the process to resume on a failover server. One approach, for example, uses a three-tiered configuration of clients and servers. Hot failover clusters are normally capable of client load balancing. Oracle RAC supports hot failover configuration by transparently routing the incoming connections to the services in surviving nodes.

Table 1-3 shows load distribution of a 3,000-user workload in a three-node cluster. During normal operation, all nodes share approximately an equal number of connections; after failover, the workload from the failed node will be distributed to surviving nodes.

The 1,000 users on servers A and C are unaware of server B's failure, but the 1,000 users who were on the failed server are affected. However, systems A, B, and C should be appropriately configured to handle the additional load during unexpected node failures. This is one of the key elements during the capacity planning for clusters.

Table 1-4 summarizes the most common aspects of cold failover versus hot failover.

State	A	B	C
Normal	1,000 users	1,000 users	1,000 users
B fails	1,000 users	0 users	1,000 users
B users log on again	1,500 users	0 users	1,500 users

TABLE 1-3 *Workload Distribution During Cluster Failovers*

Aspects	Cold Failover	Hot Failover
Scalability/number of nodes	Scalability limited to the capacity of the single node.	Because nodes can be added on demand, it provides infinite scalability. High number of nodes supported.
User interruption required	Required up to a minimal extent. The failover operation can be scripted or automated to a certain extent.	Not required. Failover is automatic.
Transparent failover of applications	Not possible.	Transparent application failover will be available where the sessions can be transferred to another node without user interruption.
Load balancing	Not possible; only one server will be used.	Incoming load can be balanced between both nodes.
Usage of resources	Only one server at a time; the other server will be kept idle.	Both the servers will be used.
Failover time	More than minutes because the other system must be cold started.	Less than a minute; typically within a few seconds.

TABLE 1-4 *Cold Failover vs. Hot Failover*

HA Option Pros and Cons

Each HA option has its own advantages and disadvantages. Costs of setup and running the service are important to consider when deciding which HA option to use. At the end of the day, as an administrator or system architect, you are responsible for costing out the various options and helping management decide what is best. What's more, you will need to figure in the additional complexity of maintaining various configurations, remembering that as you add more redundancy into the system, you are also increasing the options for failure when handling these now complex configurations. In addition, employing consultants or engaging third-party vendor professional services to set up these complex configurations, deploy additional hardware and software, and maintain these systems can also quickly add to the basic costs.

Scalability

As mentioned at the beginning of the chapter, even powerful servers cannot always handle database load and capacity requirements. Server scalability can be improved using one or more of the following methods:

■ Increase the processor count on the system, or *scale up* the computing resources.

■ Increase the amount of work done in a given time via application tuning or *speed up* the processing.

The most common view of scaling is that of hardware scaling, which has at least as much to do with the software components as with the hardware. But what do you do when you cannot increase the processor count because you have reached the maximum capacity for that line of servers, or when you have tuned all the workloads as best you can and no more tuning opportunities exist?

Initial solutions to these problems include the use of multiple application copies and databases, but these result in data-sync problems and other process issues. The best solution, of course, is the use of clustered servers that can collectively perform much better than a single server for many applications. In other words, we can use clusters of servers to *scale out* (also known as *horizontal scalability*) rather than *scale up* (also known as *vertical scalability*). It is in the provision of horizontal scalability where Oracle Real Application Clusters (RAC) excels.

Oracle Real Application Clusters Solution

Oracle Corporation introduced database clustering with Oracle version 6.2 exclusively on the DEC VAX/VMS. We will deal with many details of Oracle RAC in later chapters and see how it provides for high availability and scalability.

Essentially, Oracle RAC provides the ability for multiple servers to consistently access a single copy of the data. Theoretically, as the requirement to access this single copy increases, you keep adding nodes to the cluster. This ability to provide consistent access is not simple—the process requires a lot of coordination between the various nodes in the cluster. Oracle RAC does this efficiently, and we will see how exactly this occurs in later chapters.

Although Oracle RAC scales well, there is an upper limit on horizontal scalability. In general, application scalability is based on how good the application works in a single instance. If the SQL statements executed by the application are efficient and use an expected and reasonable amount of resources (usually measured by Logical I/O and/or Physical I/O counts), you can generally expect this to scale well. In other words, you might compare Oracle RAC to a stereo amplifier: If the quality of the recording, whether on an audio tape or a digital device, is bad, placing even the best amplifier in front of it will not solve the problem. Instead, it will amplify the problem and make the situation unpleasant. This is also applicable for Oracle RAC or any other scalability solution. Hence, you will need to make sure application-level tuning is performed to remove bottlenecks before using clustering to scale out.

With the constant downward pressure on improving Total Cost of Ownership (TCO), businesses have chosen to move away from "Big Iron," monolithic servers to smaller sets of lower-cost "commodity" servers, And this is where Oracle RAC has truly come into its element because it helps businesses realize this paradigm shift by enabling large workloads to run on clusters of lower-cost servers rather than single, monolithic boxes. Also, such servers are able to scale up or down to the workload easily. Many new features in Oracle Database 11*g* RAC, such as server pools and SCAN (Single Client Access Names listeners, discussed in later chapters) provide the ability to perform this scaling seamlessly without interruption to the business.

Along with near-linear scalability, Oracle RAC–based systems can be configured to eliminate SPOF as far as the database layer is concerned. When database servers fail, applications based on Oracle RAC systems simply keep running. When designed and coded properly, this application failover is mostly transparent to users.

When combined with Oracle Data Guard, Oracle RAC is protected from major site failures. Oracle RAC enables horizontal scalability and thus the ability to support large, global, single-instance computing that hosts thousands of users. When protected via various HA options, such single global instances significantly reduce costs via consolidation in terms of servers, datacenters, software licenses, and skilled staff to maintain them.

Emerging Trends

Businesses today need to not just scale up but also to scale back—and to perform such scale-ups and scale-downs quickly, in a matter of a few hours or even minutes. This has placed an enormous demand on IT and datacenters to provide infrastructure not in a matter of days or weeks, but in terms of minutes. In other words, IT organizations should be able to commission and decommission computing services on the fly—something that was a pipe dream a few years ago.

IT organizations and vendors are now able to provide this scaling quickly and easily using a combination of first "virtualizing" computing resources and then building the ability to expose these resources in a metered and controlled fashion (namely "cloud computing"). This is achieved first by carving out virtual machines (VMs) from physical servers and presenting them as a service to both internal and external consumers.

IT vendors today are able to virtualize environments using products such as Oracle Virtual Servers (a hypervisor based on open-source Xen technology) to spin up computing resources on demand. Prime examples of the ability of vendors to provide cloud computing includes Amazon's Elastic Cloud Computing (EC2) and SalesForce.com's Sales Cloud 2. The former has quickly become sophisticated to the extent that they are now even able to provision complete Oracle E-Business Suite environments in minutes.

On the backend database side, this means that Oracle technologies should be able to scale database services as well. Oracle RAC plays a key role here because it provides scalability. However, the challenge is to perform this scaling dynamically without any interruption to the availability.

Oracle 11*g* Solutions

Oracle Database 11*g* RAC takes this challenge head on. The key requirement for dynamic provisioning is that the technology should be able to support resource movement and reassignments easily and dynamically from a pool, along with support for such functionality at all layers and components. We will dive into more detail in later chapters, but briefly, Oracle ASM provides the total abstraction at the storage layer, allowing multiple hosts to see not just database storage but share disk files as well, and dynamically adjust them to changing requirements. Oracle ASM also provides a complete suite of fully functioning Dynamic Volume Manager and File System for Oracle storage needs.

Also, server pools in the Oracle Grid Infrastructure foundation provide the capability of dynamically allocating resources within a Grid of Oracle RAC environment, thus providing flexibility at the database layer. SCAN IP provides a way to access a cluster using a single IP address, thus simplifying naming and administration.

In the latest version (namely Oracle Database 11*g*R2), Oracle provides the ability to spin up single, non–Oracle RAC instances for smaller loads and yet provide the high availability and "hot failover" to another node using RAC One. Edition-based Redefinition completes the high availability scenario because this feature can be used to provide application transparency during software changes as well—that is, online hot patching, the holy grail of downtime optimizations.

In a Nutshell

Modern business requirements have great impact on database and application availability, and vice versa. With ever-growing requirements and extreme dependence on information availability, the information systems are expected to remain fully functional and survive all external failures. The key to designing highly available systems relies on eliminating single-point failures in all critical components.

Oracle technologies are always a leap ahead on the current trends, making sure the enterprise requirements are met. Current versions of Oracle Clustering and Oracle Grid Infrastructure components allow us to increase and shrink the capacity on demand seamlessly. Oracle ASM and ACFS completely virtualized the storage infrastructure for the datacenter and have components built in to support continuous availability and transparent scalability.

Clusters provide an enterprise with uninterrupted access to their business-critical information, enabling the nonstop functions of the business. Clusters can be configured with various failover modes, depending on the requirements of the business. When designed and implemented judiciously, clusters also provide infinite scalability to business applications.

CHAPTER
2

Clustering Basics
and History

s defined in Chapter 1, a *cluster* is a group of interconnected nodes that acts like a single large server capable of growing and shrinking on demand. In other words, clustering can be viewed logically as a method for enabling multiple standalone servers to work together as a coordinated unit called a *cluster*. The servers participating in the cluster must be *homogenous*—that is, they must use the same platform architecture, operating system, and almost identical hardware architecture and software patch levels—as well as independent machines that respond to the same requests from a pool of client requests.

From another perspective, clustering can also be viewed as host virtualization in the modern cloud computing architectures—the end-user applications do not specifically connect to "a server," but rather connect to a logical server that is internally a group of physical servers. The clustering layer wraps the underlying physical servers and only the logical layers are exposed externally, thus offering the simplicity of a single node to the outside world.

Traditionally, clustering has been used to scale up systems, to speed up systems, and to survive failures.

Scaling is achieved by adding extra nodes to the cluster group, thus enabling the cluster to handle progressively larger workloads. Clustering provides horizontal on-demand scalability without incurring any downtime for reconfiguration.

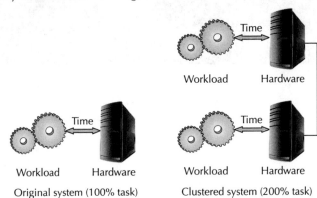

Speeding up is accomplished by splitting a large workload into multiple smaller workloads and running them in parallel in all the available CPUs. Parallel processing provides massive improvement in performance for jobs that can be run in parallel. The simple "divide and conquer" approach is applied to the large workloads, and parallel processing uses the power of all the resources to get work done faster.

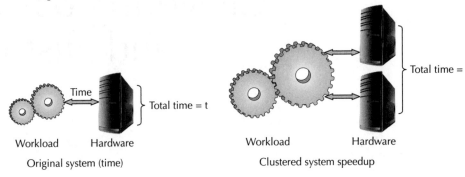

Because a cluster is a group of independent hardware nodes, failure in one node does not halt the application from functioning on the other nodes. The application and the services are seamlessly transferred to the surviving nodes, and with proper design the application continues to function normally as it was functioning before the node failure. In some cases, the application or the user process may not even be aware of such failures, because the failover to the other node is transparent to the application.

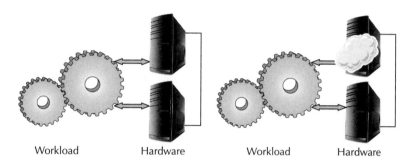

| Workload | Hardware | Workload | Hardware |

When a uniprocessor system reaches its processing limit, it imposes a big threat to scalability. Symmetric multiprocessing (SMP)—the use of multiple processors (CPUs) that share memory (RAM) within a single computer to provide increased processing capability—solves this problem. SMP machines achieve high performance by *parallelism,* in which the processing job is split up and run on the available CPUs. Higher scalability is achieved by adding more CPUs and memory.

Figure 2-1 compares the basic architectural similarities between symmetric multiprocessing and clustering. However, the two architectures maintain cache coherency at totally different levels and latencies.

Grid Computing with Clusters

Clustering is part of Oracle's grid computing methodology, by which several low-cost commodity hardware components are networked together to achieve increased computing capacity. Scalability on demand is achieved by adding additional nodes and distributing the workload to the available machines.

Scalability and application performance improvement can be done via three methods:

- By working harder
- By working smarter
- By getting help

Working harder means adding more CPUs and more memory so that the processing power increases to handle any amount of workload. This is the usual approach and often helps as additional CPUs address the workload problems. However, this approach is not quite economical, because the average cost of the computing power does not always increase in a linear manner. Adding computing power for a single SMP box increases the cost and complexity at a logarithmic scale. Also, the performance (and scalability) is often constricted by the bottlenecks in the infrastructure layer, such as the available bandwidth and speed of the wires connecting storage to servers.

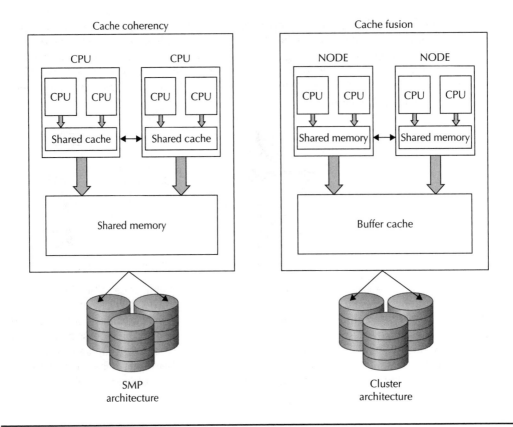

FIGURE 2-1 *SMP vs. clusters*

Working smarter is accomplished by employing intelligent and efficient algorithms at either the application layer or storage layer. By introducing "smartness" in the storage layer, you can greatly reduce the total amount of work to be done to achieve the desired results. Working smarter at the application layer often requires rewriting the application or changing the way it works (or sometimes changing the application design itself), which is quite impossible for a running application and requires unacceptable downtime. This option sometimes becomes almost impossible for a third-party vendor and packaged applications, because getting everyone onboard can become a tedious and time-consuming task.

Working smarter at the storage layer is accomplished by introducing intelligent storage servers, where the storage servers offload some amount of processing. This requires specially designed storage servers such as Oracle Exadata Storage Servers (used in Oracle Database Machine) to process some amount of critical workload close to storage. Processing the workload close to where it is stored greatly enhances the performance of the application because it largely limits the number of roundtrips between the storage and hosts as well as limits the size of data transferred to the database cluster infrastructure.

Getting help can be as simple as using other machines' computing power to do the work. In other words, getting help simply involves clustering the hardware, using the spare processing capacity of the idle nodes, and combining the processing transaction results at the end. More

Oracle Exadata and Smart Scans

The newly introduced Oracle Exadata storage servers rightly fit into the "working smarter" method of improving performance and scalability. Traditional database implementations use the storage as a plain container to dump and retrieve data, and the storage containers are relatively "dumb" about the data they often store. All the database processing is handled in database host memory, and often this involves transferring huge amounts of data from the storage to host machines that do the actual number crunching. The summarized results are then passed to the upper layers of end-user applications. An extremely large volume of raw data is processed to validate the required business intelligence operations by applying filtering conditions on the column-level data.

Special-purpose storage servers are built with additional intelligence at the storage layer where the storage is fully "aware" of the data that is stored in the disks. While processing the complex business intelligence reports, the host machines talk to the storage servers and provide additional information about the dataset being requested from the storage servers. The storage servers filter the data in the storage (known as "smart scan" processing) and pass the records matching the conditions specified by the host machines. Some amount of the processing is handled in the storage layer, and the database host machines do not need to process the huge amount of raw data to process the queries.

In a traditional storage-hosted database, the SQL query processing is handled at the database server. The data stored in the disks is retrieved as blocks to the database server and loaded in database buffer cache memory for processing. The following illustration shows the table scans processing in the conventional storage architecture.

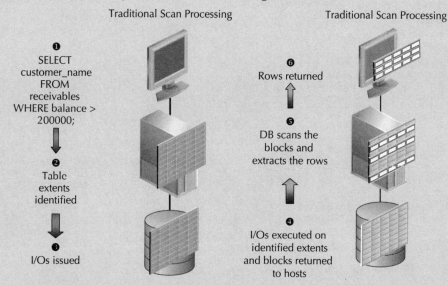

1. The application layer (end user client) issues a SQL query. For simplicity, we assume this is a SELECT statement with a WHERE condition.

2. The database kernel queries the data dictionary and identifies the file and extents where the table data is stored.

3. The database kernel issues I/O calls to read all the physical blocks from the disk.

4. The physical data blocks from disk are loaded to the database server's memory (buffer cache in the SGA).

5. The database server reads the memory buffers and filters the rows satisfied by the predicate (WHERE condition).

6. The matching rows are returned to client.

The traditional SQL processing works better if the tables are relatively small and well indexed. But for complex business intelligence queries involving multiples of larger tables, the reading of all the data from disk and transferring it to host memory is a very expensive task. It requires a huge amount of raw data transferred between storage to host memory over the network. Moreover, the records that do not meet the filter conditions are simply discarded at the host level. This is a totally unproductive I/O operation that impacts dearly the query response time. In this case, we often read multiple times the data required to match the filter conditions; poorly constructed queries put unnecessary overhead on the storage subsystem and affect the total system performance.

However, in the Exadata smart scan model the entire workflow is handled very intelligently and totally different. The queries that perform the table scans are offloaded to the Exadata storage server, and only records meeting the filter criteria are returned to the database server. Tasks such as row filtering, column filtering, and some amount of join processing are performed in the storage server. Also Exadata uses a special kind of highly efficient unbuffered direct-read mechanism for scanning the tables. This is similar to Oracle parallel query operations. The following illustration shows the operation.

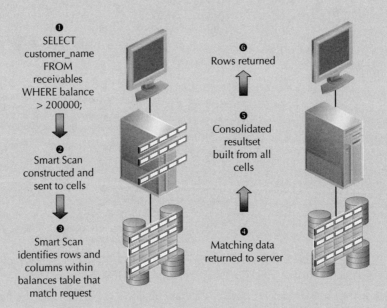

1. The application layer (end user application) issues a SELECT query.

2. When the database server detects exadata, it builds an exadata construct (known as an iDB command) representing the SQL and sends this to Exadata storage server. iDB is a data-transfer mechanism based on the infiniband protocol (low latency, high bandwidth) used between an Exadata storage server and database server communications.

3. The Exadata storage servers perform a "smart scan" on the tables and extract the rows of interest by applying the WHERE conditions directly on the storage.

4. The resultset is transferred directly to the database instance. The resultset is the query result and not the blocks satisfying the filter condition. This is sent directly to the Progam Global Area (PGA) of the user session and is not cached in System Global Area (SGA).

5. Matching rows are returned to the client.

Offloading SQL processing to the Exadata server tremendously increases the speed of the query processing and frees up the CPU cycles in the database server. Also, processing the data closer to the storage eliminates a massive amount of unproductive I/O and improves the scalability of the storage subsystem.

importantly, this approach does not require any changes to the application because it is transparent to the application. Another advantage to using this approach is that it allows on-demand scalability—you can choose to get help whenever required, and you do not need to invest in massive hardware.

Shared Storage in Clustering

One of the key components in clustering is shared storage. Storage is accessible to all nodes, and all nodes can read and write in parallel to the shared storage, depending on the configuration of the cluster. Some configurations allow the storage to be accessible by all the nodes at all times; some allow sharing only during failovers.

More importantly, the application will see the cluster as a single system image and not as multiple connected machines. The cluster manager does not expose the system to the application, and the cluster is transparent to the application. Sharing the data among the available nodes is a fundamental concept in scaling and is achieved using several types of architectures.

Types of Clustering Architectures

Clustering architecture can be broadly categorized into three types, based on how storage is shared among the nodes:

- Shared nothing architecture
- Shared disk architecture
- Shared everything architecture

Table 2-1 compares the most common functionalities across the types of clustering architectures and lists their pros and cons along with implementation details with examples. Shared disks and shared everything architecture slightly differ in the number of nodes and storage sharing.

Function Shared	Shared Nothing	Shared Disks	Shared Everything
Disk ownership/ sharing	Disks are owned by individual nodes and are not shared among any of the nodes at any time.	Active nodes usually own disks and the ownership is transferred to the surviving node during failure of the active node—that is, disks are shared only during failures.	Disks are always shared and all instances have equal rights to the disks. Any instance can read/write data to any of the disks because no nodes exclusively own any disk.
Number of nodes	Typically very high number.	Normally two nodes, with only one node active at any time.	Two or more, depending on the configuration. The number of nodes is sometimes limited by the cluster manager or distributed lock manager (DLM) capacity when vendor-supplied clusterware is used.
Data partitioning	Strictly partitioned—one node cannot access the data from the other nodes. Local nodes can access data local to that node.	Data partitioning is not required because only one instance will access the complete set of data.	No data partitioning is required because the data can be accessed from any nodes of the cluster.
Client coordinator	External server or any group member.	No coordinator is required because the other node is used only during failover.	Not required. Any node can be accessed for any set of data.
Performance overhead	No performance overhead because no external coordination is involved or required.	No performance overhead.	No overhead after three nodes. Very negligible overhead up to three nodes.
Lock manager	Not required because data is not shared among the members.	Not required.	DLM is required for managing the resources.
Initial/on-demand scalability	Initially highly scalable, but limited to the capacity of the individual node for local access. On-demand scalability is not possible.	Not very scalable. Scalability is limited to the computing capacity of the single node.	Infinitely scalable because nodes can be added on demand.
Write access	Each node can write but only to its own disks. One instance cannot write to the disks owned by another instance.	Only one node at a time. One node can write to all the disks.	All nodes can write to all disks simultaneously because the lock manager controls the orderly writes.
Load balancing	Not possible.	Not possible because there is only one active node at any point in time.	Near perfect load balancing, and a variety of configuration choices is offered.

TABLE 2-1 *Functionalities of Clustering Architectures*

Function Shared	Shared Nothing	Shared Disks	Shared Everything
Application partitioning	Strictly required because the member nodes only see a subset of data.	Not required because only one node is active at any time.	Not required, but can be configured if required.
Dynamic node addition	Not possible.	Possible, but does not make any sense because only one node will be active at any time.	Very much possible. This is a key strength of this architecture type.
Failover capacity	No failover because the nodes/disks are tied to specific nodes.	Can be failed over to other nodes, with minimal loss of service.	Very capable. Often it is transparent.
I/O fencing	Not required.	Not required.	Provided by the DLM and cluster manager.
Failure of one node	Makes a subset of data inaccessible momentarily: 100/N% of the data is inaccessible, with N being the number of nodes in the cluster. Then the ownership is transferred to the surviving nodes.	Data access momentarily disrupted, until the applications are failed over to the other node.	As connections spread across all the nodes, a subset of sessions may have to reconnect to the other node and total data is accessible to all the nodes. No data loss due to node failures.
Addition of nodes	Requires complete reorganization as redeployment of the architecture.	Not possible because the addition of nodes does not help anything.	Nodes can be added and removed on the fly. Load balancing is done automatically during reconfiguration.
Examples	IBM SP2, Teradata, Tandem NonStop, Informix OnLine XPS, Microsoft Cluster Server	HP M/C ServiceGuard, Veritas Cluster Servers	Oracle Parallel Server/Real Application Clusters, Oracle Exadata Database Machine

TABLE 2-1   *Functionalities of Clustering Architectures* (continued)

Shared Nothing Architecture

Shared nothing architecture is built using a group of independent servers, with each server taking a predefined workload (see Figure 2-2). If, for example, a number of servers are in the cluster, the total workload is divided by the number of servers, and each server caters to a specific workload. The biggest disadvantage of shared nothing architecture is that it requires careful application partitioning, and no dynamic addition of nodes is possible. Adding a node would require complete redeployment, so it is not a scalable solution. Oracle does not support the shared nothing architecture.

In shared nothing clusters, data is typically divided across separate nodes. The nodes have little need to coordinate their activity because each is responsible for different subsets of the overall database. But in strict shared nothing clusters, if one node is down, its fraction of the overall data is unavailable.

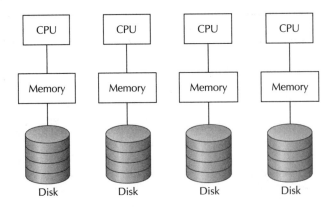

FIGURE 2-2   *Shared nothing clusters*

The clustered servers neither share disks nor mirror data—each has its own resources. Servers transfer ownership of their respective disks from one another in the event of a failure. A shared nothing cluster uses software to accomplish these transfers. This architecture avoids the distributed lock manager (DLM) bottleneck issue associated with shared disks while offering comparable availability and scalability. Examples of shared nothing clustering solutions include Tandem NonStop, Informix OnLine Extended Parallel Server (XPS), and Microsoft Cluster Server.

One of the major issues with shared nothing clusters is that they require very careful deployment planning in terms of data partitioning. If the partitioning is skewed, it negatively affects the overall system performance. Also, the processing overhead is significantly higher when the disks belong to the other node, which typically happens during the failure of any member nodes.

The biggest advantage of shared nothing clusters is that they provide linear scalability for data warehouse applications—they are ideally suited for that. However, they are unsuitable for online transaction processing (OLTP) workloads, and they are not totally redundant, so a failure of one node will make the application running on that node unavailable. Still, most major databases, such as IBM DB2 Enterprise Edition, Informix XPS, and NCR Teradata, do implement shared nothing clusters.

NOTE
Some shared nothing architectures require data to be replicated between the servers so that it is available on all nodes. This eliminates the need for application partitioning but brings up the requirement of a high-speed replication mechanism, which is almost always impossible to attain, compared to high-speed memory-to-memory transmission.

Shared Disk Architecture
For high availability, some shared access to the data disks is needed (see Figure 2-3). In shared disk storage clusters, at the low end, one node can take over the storage (and applications) if

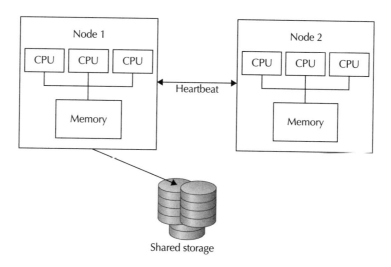

FIGURE 2-3   *Shared disk cluster*

another node fails. In higher-level solutions, simultaneous access to data by applications running on more than one node at a time is possible, but typically a single node at a time is responsible for coordinating all access to a given data disk and serving that storage to the rest of the nodes. That single node can become a bottleneck for access to the data in busier configurations.

In simple failover clusters, one node runs an application and updates the data; another node stands idle until needed, and then takes over completely. In more sophisticated clusters, multiple nodes may access data, but typically one node at a time serves a file system to the rest of the nodes and performs all coordination for that file system.

Shared Everything Architecture

Shared everything clustering utilizes the disks accessible to all computers (nodes) within the cluster. These are often called "shared disk clusters" because the I/O involved is typically disk storage for normal files and/or databases. These clusters rely on a common channel for disk access because all nodes may concurrently write or read data from the central disks. Because all nodes have equal access to the centralized shared disk subsystem, a synchronization mechanism must be used to preserve coherence of the system. An independent piece of cluster software, the DLM, assumes this role.

In a shared everything cluster, all nodes can access all the data disks simultaneously, without one node having to go through a separate peer node to get access to the data (see Figure 2-4). Clusters with such capability employ a cluster-wide file system (CFS), so all the nodes view the file system(s) identically, and they provide a DLM to allow the nodes to coordinate the sharing and updating of files, records, and databases.

A CFS provides the same view of disk data from every node in the cluster. This means the environment on each node can appear identical to both the users and the application programs, so it doesn't matter on which node the application or user happens to be running at any given time.

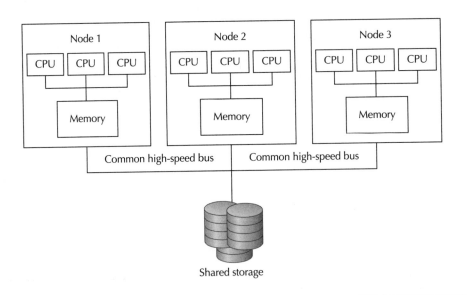

FIGURE 2-4 *Shared everything cluster*

Shared everything clusters support higher levels of system availability: If one node fails, other nodes need not be affected. However, higher availability comes at a cost of somewhat reduced performance in these systems because of the overhead in using a DLM and the potential bottlenecks that can occur in sharing hardware. Shared everything clusters make up for this shortcoming with relatively good scaling properties.

Oracle RAC is the classic example of the shared everything architecture. Oracle RAC is a special configuration of the Oracle database that leverages hardware-clustering technology and extends the clustering to the application level. The database files are stored in the shared disk storage so that all the nodes can simultaneously read and write to them. The shared storage is typically networked storage, such as Fibre Channel SAN or IP-based Ethernet NAS, which is either physically or logically connected to all the nodes.

History of Oracle RAC

The ever-hungry vagabonds of the Silicon Valley pioneered the concept of massive parallel processing (MPP) and christened the same as "clustering." Digital, IBM, and Cray were some of the pioneers in the field of clustering. The first success toward creating a clustering product, ARCnet, was developed by DataPoint in 1977.

ARCnet, though a good product in the research labs and a darling in the academic world (for university-based research groups, departments, and computer cluster resources for an entire university), was not a commercial success and clustering didn't really take off until Digital Equipment Corporation (DEC) released its VAX cluster product in the 1980s for the VAX/VMS operating system. The ARCnet and VAX cluster products not only supported parallel computing, but they also shared file systems and peripheral devices. They were intended to provide the advantage of parallel processing while maintaining data atomicity.

Oracle's cluster database was introduced with Oracle 6 for the Digital VAX cluster product and on nCUBE machines, and Oracle was the first commercial database that supported clustering at the database level. Oracle created the lock manager for VAX/VMS clusters, as the original lock manager from Digital was not very scalable for database applications, and a database requires fine-grained locking at the block level. Oracle 6.2 gave birth to Oracle Parallel Server (OPS), which used Oracle's own DLM and worked very well with Digital's VAX clusters. Oracle was the first database to run the parallel server.

In the early 1990s, when open systems dominated the computer industry, many UNIX vendors started clustering technology, mostly based on Oracle's DLM implementation. Oracle 7 Parallel Server (OPS) used vendor-supplied clusterware. OPS was available with almost all UNIX flavors and worked well, but it was complex to set up and manage because multiple layers were involved in the process.

When Oracle introduced a generic lock manager in version 8, it was a clear indication of the direction for Oracle's own clusterware and lock manager for future versions. Oracle's lock manager is integrated with Oracle code with an additional layer called OSD (Operating System Dependent). Oracle's lock manager soon integrated with the kernel and became known as the IDLM (Integrated Distributed Lock Manager) in later versions of Oracle.

Oracle Real Application Clusters version 9*i* used the same IDLM and relied on external clusterware. Oracle provided its own clusterware for Linux and Windows in Oracle 9*i* and for all operating systems starting from 10*g* and enhanced tremendously with Oracle 11*g* with the introduction of server pools and additional APIs to manage third-party applications. Oracle Clusterware is the de facto clusterware and an absolute must for running Oracle RAC. Table 2-2 lists the most common clusterware for various operating systems.

Oracle Parallel Storage Evaluation

Along with the cluster software infrastructure, another key component, which grew along with Oracle RAC, is the development of parallel storage management systems. Earlier versions of Oracle clusters (known as Oracle Parallel Servers until Oracle 8*i*) depend on third-party software for parallel storage management. Cluster file systems such as Veritas Cluster File

Operating System	Clusterware
Solaris	Sun Cluster, Veritas Cluster Services
HP-UX	HP MC/ServiceGuard, Veritas Cluster Services
HP Tru64	TruCluster
Windows	Microsoft Cluster Services
Linux	Oracle Clusterware
IBM AIX	HACMP (High Availability Cluster Multiprocessing)

TABLE 2-2 *Common Clusterware for Various Operating Systems*

Systems (VxFS) and RAW disk partitions were used as foundations for parallel storage in Oracle RAC.

The unavailability of general-purpose clusterware and a cluster-wide file system was hampering the adaptation of Oracle RAC. Oracle provided generic clusterware with Oracle 9i RAC called Oracle Cluster Manager (OraCM) for Linux and Windows. Along with the clusterware, Oracle also developed a cluster file system called Oracle Cluster File System (OCFS), which was used to build the shared storage for Linux and Windows environments. The newly provided OraCM with OCFS has significantly advanced the adaptation of Oracle RAC. However, OCFS has inherent limitations and was not very scalable for larger numbers of cluster nodes. Moreover, OCFS was only ported for Linux and Microsoft Windows.

Oracle introduced another similar product in Oracle database 9i Release 2 called Oracle Disk Manager (ODM) for Solaris operating systems. ODM was capable of handling file management operations (which were handled outside Oracle prior to this, including creating and destroying files), and file identifiers in ODM replaced file descriptors. ODM file identifiers were cached in the SGA, reducing the kernel overheads for file lookups and file I/O operations.

With the success and wisdom gained from Oracle Disk Manager, Oracle was ready for a fully functioning cluster-aware database file system called Automatic Storage Management (ASM). Starting with Oracle Database 10g, Oracle introduced ASM for mainline storage and promoted extensively for the use of ASM. Oracle ASM was even mandated as required storage to run Oracle RAC on the Standard Edition. Oracle ASM quickly gained traction in the market and performed flawlessly in Oracle benchmarks and large customer environments.

While Oracle ASM was being used as mainline storage for data, there was still a requirement for additional shared storage (outside ASM) for some of the Oracle RAC components used to house the cluster configuration details as well as special-purpose storage used during cluster configurations commonly known as "voting disks." The initial versions of ASM lack the capacity to store the cluster components (like OCR and Voting Disks) inside ASM, as clusterware should be started to access the data stored inside ASM managed storage. The current versions of ASM implement an intelligent trick to access the ASM data, and details of the ASM are discussed in the later chapters of this book.

Custom applications built using the Oracle database and even some of commercial applications (such as Oracle E-Business Suite) used a wide variety of external files during data extraction and loading. A classic example is processing Call Data Records (CDR) in a telecom billing application or output files in Oracle Applications concurrent manager processing. Database applications similar to these required a scalable cluster-wide file system so that all the data could be accessed concurrently among the nodes.

To address the requirement for a cluster-wide file system, Oracle ASM was enhanced further to serve as a general-purpose file system called ASM Cluster File System (ACFS). ACFS offered a seamless way to provide access to non-database files across the nodes and was used widely to store the database binaries, log files, and non-data files used in the Oracle database. The application programming interfaces (APIs) built on Oracle ASM allowed the use of ACFS volumes like traditional network file system (NFS) mount points across the servers.

Oracle ASM with ACFS addresses the total storage solution for parallel storage requirements for Oracle Clusterware and eliminates the need for expensive third-party file systems or maintenance-heavy raw devices. Oracle ASM also provides volume manager and file system functionalities for an Oracle database and is an integrated part of the Oracle clusterware architecture.

Oracle Parallel Server Architecture

An Oracle parallel or cluster database consists of two or more physical servers (nodes) that host their own Oracle instances and share a disk array. Each node's instance of Oracle has its own System Global Area (SGA) and its own redolog files, but the data files and control files are common to all instances. Data files and control files are concurrently read and written by all instances; however, redologs can be read by any instance but written to only by the owning instance. Some parameters, such as db_block_buffers and log_buffer, can be configured differently in each instance, but other parameters must be consistent across all instances. Each cluster node has its own set of background processes, just as a single instance would. Additionally, OPS-specific processes are also started on each instance to handle cross-instance communication, lock management, and block transfers.

Figure 2-5 shows the architecture of OPS. It is important to understand the inner workings of OPS to understand Oracle RAC because this provides a solid foundation to visualize the under-

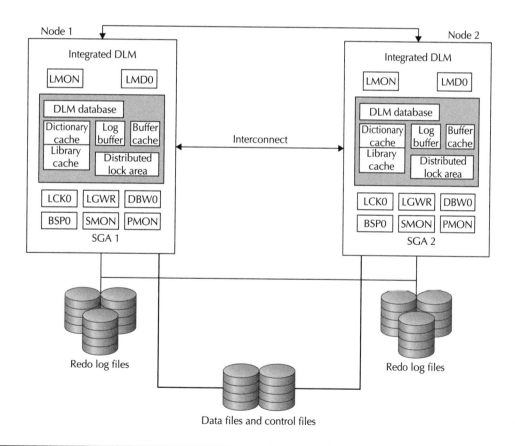

FIGURE 2-5 *OPS architecture*

the-hood operations of Oracle RAC. Although this is not mandatory knowledge to manage Oracle RAC, a deeper understanding of the OPS components makes you an expert in Oracle RAC because Oracle RAC is evolved from an OPS foundation.

Components of an OPS Database

On every instance of an Oracle 8i Parallel Server database, the following components can be found:

- Cluster manager, which is OS vendor specific (except Windows), including a node-monitoring facility and failure detection mechanism
- Distributed lock manager (DLM), including deadlock detection and resource mastering
- Cluster interconnect
- Shared disk array

NOTE
Vendor-specific cluster manager software is not discussed here and is mentioned only for completeness. The vendor product is the basic cluster software that is mandatory before installing and configuring OPS and some variants of earlier versions of RAC. This is generally termed as the Cluster Manager (CM), which has its own group membership services, node monitor, and other core layers.

Cluster Group Services (CGS)

One of the key "hidden" or lesser-known components of OPS is the Cluster Group Services (CGS), which was formally known as the Group Membership Services (GMS) in Oracle 8. CGS has some OSD components (node monitor interface), and the rest of it is the GMS part that is built into the Oracle kernel. CGS holds a key repository used by the DLM for communication and network-related activities. This layer in the Oracle 8i kernel (and beyond) provides some key facilities without which an OPS database cannot operate:

- Internode messaging
- Group membership consistency
- Cluster synchronization
- Process grouping, registration, and deregistration

Some cluster components were still OS specific, so an OSD layer had to be developed and implemented. Certain low-level cluster communications can be done only by this OSD layer, which communicates with the Oracle kernel using Oracle-specified APIs. These OSD components are included with the Node Monitor (NM) that is part of the CGS.

A whole set of cluster communication interfaces and APIs became an internal part of the Oracle code in OPS 8i. GMS provided many services, such as member status, node evictions, and so on, that were external in Oracle 8 but were made internal in Oracle 8i. GMS, now CGS in

Oracle 8*i* (8.1.6), basically includes the GMS as well as the NM component of cluster management. Below this layer is the cluster monitor, or the cluster software provided by an OS vendor (such as TruCluster, Veritas Cluster Services, HP MC/ServiceGuard, and so on).

Oracle 8*i* also introduced network redundancy, in which problems or breakdowns of the network path were communicated up to the cluster monitor level (part of CGS) and allowed for the instance to be shut down or provided for a failover of the network path using redundant network hardware. Until OPS version 8*i,* network problems would cause an indefinite hang of the instance.

Distributed Lock Manager (DLM)

The DLM is an integral part of OPS and the RAC stack. As mentioned, earlier Oracle versions relied on OS vendors to provide this component, which coordinated resources globally and kept the system in sync. Data consistency and integrity are maintained by this layer in all versions of Oracle OPS from 7 to 11*g.* Any reference to DLM from Oracle 8/8*i* onward pertains to the Integrated DLM (IDLM), which was introduced with Oracle 8 and integrated into the Oracle OPS kernel. The terms *DLM* and *IDLM* are used to describe a single entity and are one and the same.

In versions prior to version 8, the DLM API module had to rely on external OS routines to check the status of a lock (because DLM functions were provided by the OS vendor). This communication was done using UNIX sockets and pipes. With IDLM, the required data is in the SGA of each instance and requires only a serialized lookup using latches and/or enqueues (see the next section) and may require global coordination, the algorithm for which was built into the Oracle kernel code.

With OPS 8*i,* the IDLM has undergone significant development and stabilization. IDLM holds an inventory of all the locks and global enqueues that are held by all the instances in the OPS database. Its job is to track every lock granted to a resource. The coordination of requests from various instances for lock acquisition and release is done by the DLM. The memory structures required by DLM to operate are allocated out of the shared pool. The lock resources, messages buffers, and so on are all in the shared pool of each instance. DLM is designed such that it can survive node failures in all but one node of the cluster.

The DLM is always aware of the current holders or requestors of locks and the grantee. In case locks are not available, the DLM queues the lock requests and informs the requestor when a lock resource becomes available. Some of the resources that the DLM manages are data blocks and rollback segments. Oracle resources are associated with the DLM locks by instance, using a complex hashing algorithm. The lock and enqueue functionality in OPS is the same as in a single-instance RDBMS server, except that OPS takes a global view.

DLM relies on the core RDBMS kernel for locking and enqueues services. These established and already proven techniques and functionalities need not be rewritten in the DLM layer. The DLM coordinates locking at the global level, and this is a service that the core layers don't provide. To make things simpler, the locking and enqueues kernel services in Oracle 8*i* OPS and Oracle RAC are kept separate from the DLM functionality.

Locking Concepts in Oracle Parallel Server

In an OPS database, a user must acquire a lock before he can operate on any resource. This is also applicable in a single-instance scenario. In pure DLM terminology, a *resource* is any object accessed by users, and a *lock* is a client operational request of certain type or mode on that resource.

A new concept in OPS called *Parallel Cache Management (PCM)* means that coordination and maintenance of data blocks exists within each data buffer cache (of an instance) so that the data viewed or requested by users is never inconsistent or incoherent. The access to data is controlled using the PCM framework using data blocks with global coordinated locks. In simple terms, PCM ensures that only one instance in a cluster can modify a block at any given time. Other instances have to wait.

Broadly speaking, locks in OPS are either PCM locks or non-PCM locks. PCM locks almost exclusively protect the data blocks, and non-PCM locks control access to data files, control files, data dictionary, and so on. PCM locks are static in OPS, and non-PCM locks are dynamically set using the init.ora settings of certain parameters. Locks on PCM resources are referred to as "lock elements" and non-PCM locks are called "enqueues." DLM locks are acquired on a resource and are typically granted to a process. PCM locks and row-level locks operate independently.

PCM Lock and Row Lock Independence

PCM locks and row locks operate independently. An instance can disown a PCM lock without affecting row locks held in the set of blocks covered by the PCM lock. A row lock is acquired during a transaction. A database resource such as a data block acquires a PCM lock when it is read for update by an instance. During a transaction, a PCM lock can therefore be disowned and owned many times if the blocks are needed by other instances.

In contrast, transactions do not release row locks until changes to the rows are either committed or rolled back. Oracle uses internal mechanisms for concurrency control to isolate transactions so modifications to data made by one transaction are not visible to other transactions until the transaction modifying the data commits. The row lock concurrency control mechanisms are independent of parallel cache management: Concurrency control does not require PCM locks, and PCM lock operations do not depend on individual transactions committing or rolling back.

IDLM lock modes and Oracle lock modes are not identical, although they are similar. In OPS, locks can be local or global depending on the type of request and operations. Just as in a single instance, locks take the form

   <Type, ID1, ID2>

where *Type* consists of two characters and *ID1* and *ID2* are values dependent on the lock type. The ID is a 4-byte, positive integer.

Local locks can be divided into latches and enqueues. These could be required for local instance-based operations. A shared pool latch is a simple example of a local latch, irrespective of whether OPS is present or not. Enqueues can be local or global. They take on a global role in an OPS environment and remain local in a single instance. A TX (transaction) enqueue, control file enqueue (CF), DFS (Distributed File System) enqueue lock, and a DML/table lock are examples of a global enqueues in an OPS database. The same enqueue is local in a single-instance database. Similarly, data dictionary and library cache locks are global in an OPS environment.

Local locks provide transaction isolation or row-level locking. Instance locks provide for cache coherency while accessing shared resources. GV$LOCK and GV$LOCK_ELEMENT are important views that provide information on global enqueues and instance locks.

In Oracle 8*i*, two background processes—Lock Manager Daemon (LMD) and Lock Monitor (LMON)—implement the DLM (see Figure 2-5). Each instance has its own set of these two processes. The DLM database stores information on resources, locks, and processes. In Oracle 9*i*, the DLM has been renamed Global Cache Services (GCS) and Global Enqueue Services (GES).

Although some of the code has changed, the basic functionality of GES and GCS remain the same as the prior versions of the DLM.

DLM Lock Compatibility Matrix

Every resource is identified by its unique resource name. Each resource can potentially have a list of locks currently granted to users. This list is called the "Grant Q." Locks that are in the process of converting or waiting to be converted from one mode to another are placed on the "Convert Q" of that resource. For each lock, a resource structure exists in memory that maintains a list of owners and converters. Each owner, waiter, or converter has a lock structure, as shown in Table 2-3.

Every node has directory information for a set of resources it manages. To locate a resource, the DLM uses a hashing algorithm based on the name of the resource to find out which node holds the directory information for that resource. Once this is done, a lock request is done directly to this "master" node. The directory area is nothing but a DLM memory structure that stores information on which node masters which blocks.

The traditional lock naming conventions (such as SS, SX, X) are provided in Table 2-4 along with the DLM mode.

Note that in this table, NL means null mode; CR/SS means concurrent read mode; CW/SX means concurrent write mode; PR/S means protected read mode; PW/SSX means protected write mode; and EX/X means exclusive mode.

Lock	NL	CR	CW	PR	PW	EX
NL	Grant	Grant	Grant	Grant	Grant	Grant
CR	Grant	Grant	Grant	Grant	Grant	Queue
CW	Grant	Grant	Grant	Queue	Queue	Queue
PR	Grant	Grant	Queue	Grant	Queue	Queue
PW	Grant	Grant	Queue	Queue	Queue	Queue
EX	Grant	Queue	Queue	Queue	Queue	Queue

TABLE 2-3   *DLM Lock Compatibility Matrix*

Conventional naming	NL	CR	CW	PR	PW	EX
DLM naming	NL	SS	SX	S	SSX	X

TABLE 2-4   *Conventional Naming vs. DLM Naming*

Lock Acquisition and Conversion

Locks granted on resources are in the Grant Q (as discussed previously). Locks are placed on a resource when a process acquires a lock on the Grant Q of that resource. It is only then that a process owns a lock on that resource in a compatible mode.

A lock can be acquired if there are no converters and the mode the Oracle kernel requires is compatible with the modes already held by others. Otherwise, it waits on the Convert Q until the resource becomes available. When a lock is released or converted, the converters run the check algorithm to see if they can be acquired.

Converting a lock from one mode to another occurs when a new request arrives for a resource that already has a lock on it. *Conversion* is the process of changing a lock from the mode currently held to a different mode. Even if the mode is NULL, it is considered as holding a lock. Conversion takes place only if the mode required is a subset of the mode held or the lock mode is compatible with the modes already held by others and according to a conversion matrix within the IDLM.

Processes and Group-Based Locking

When lock structures are allocated in the DLM memory area, the operating system process ID (PID) of the requesting process is the key identifier for the requestor of the lock. Mapping a process to a session is easier inside Oracle, and the information is available in V$SESSION. However, in certain clients, such as Oracle multithreaded servers (MTS) or Oracle XA, a single process may own many transactions. Sessions migrate across many processes to make up a single transaction. This would disable identification of the transaction and the origin of the same. Hence, lock identifiers had to be designed to have session-based information where the transaction ID (XID) is provided by the client when lock requests are made to the DLM.

Groups are used when group-based locking is used. This is preferred particularly when MTS is involved, and when MTS is used the shared services are implicitly unavailable to other sessions when locks are held. From Oracle 9i onward, process-based locking no longer exists. Oracle 8i OPS (and later) uses group-based locking irrespective of the kind of transactions. As mentioned, a process within a group identifies itself with the XID before asking Oracle for any transaction locks.

Lock Mastering

The DLM maintains information about the locks on all nodes that are interested in a given resource. The DLM nominates one node to manage all relevant lock information for a resource; this node is referred to as the "master node." Lock mastering is distributed among all nodes.

Using the Interprocess Communications (IPC) layer, the distributed component of the DLM permits it to share the load of mastering (administering) resources. As a result, a user can lock a resource on one node but actually end up communicating with the LMD processes on another node. Fault tolerance requires that no vital information about locked resources is lost irrespective of how many DLM instances fail.

Asynchronous Traps

Communication between the DLM processes (LMON, LMD) across instances is implemented using the IPC layer across the high-speed interconnect. To convey the status of a lock resource, the DLM uses asynchronous traps (AST), which are implemented as interrupts in the OS handler routines. Purists may differ on the exact meaning of AST and the way it is implemented (interrupts or other blocking mechanism), but as far as OPS or Oracle RAC is concerned, it is an interrupt. AST can be a *blocking* AST or an *acquisition* AST.

When a process requests a lock on a resource, the DLM sends a blocking asynchronous trap (BAST) to all processes that currently own a lock on that same resource. If possible and necessary, the holder(s) of the lock may relinquish the lock and allow the requester to gain access to the resource. An acquisition AST (AAST) is sent by DLM to the requestor to inform him that it now owns the resource (and the lock). An AAST is generally regarded as a "wakeup call" for a process.

How Locks Are Granted in DLM

To illustrate how locking works in OPS's DLM, consider a sample two-node cluster with a shared disk array:

1. Process p1 needs to modify a data block on instance 1. Before the block can read into the buffer cache on instance 1, p1 needs to check whether a lock exists on that block.

2. A lock may or may not exist on this data block, and hence the LCK process checks the SGA structures to validate the buffer lock status. If a lock exists, LCK has to request that the DLM downgrade the lock.

3. If a lock does not exist, a lock element (LE) has to be created by LCK in the local instance and the role is local.

4. LCK must request the DLM for the LE in exclusive mode. If the resource is mastered by instance 1, DLM continues processing. Otherwise, the request must be sent to the master DLM in the cluster.

5. Assuming the lock is mastered on instance 1, the DLM on this instance does a local cache lookup in its DLM database and finds that a process on instance 2 already has an exclusive (EX) lock on the same data block.

6. DLM on instance 1 sends out a BAST to DLM on instance 2 requesting a downgrade of the lock. DLM on instance 2 sends another BAST to LCK on the same instance to downgrade the lock from EX to NULL.

7. The process on instance 2 may have updated the block and may not have committed the changes. The Dirty Buffer Writer (DBWR) is signaled to write out the block to disk. After the write confirmation, the LCK on instance 2 downgrades the lock to NULL and sends an AAST to DLM on the same instance.

8. DLM on instance 2 updates its local DLM database about the change in lock status and sends an AAST to DLM on instance 1.

9. The master DLM on instance 1 updates the master DLM database about the new status of the lock (EX) that can now be granted to the process on its instance. DLM itself upgrades the lock to EX.

10. DLM on instance 1 now sends another AAST to the local LCK process informing it about the lock grant and that the block can be read from disk.

Cache Fusion Stage 1, CR Server

OPS 8*i* introduced Cache Fusion Stage 1. Until version 8.1, cache coherency was maintained using the disk (ping mechanism). Cache Fusion introduced a new background process called the Block Server Process (BSP). The major use or responsibility of BSP was to ship consistent read (CR) version(s) of a block (or blocks) across instances in a read/write contention scenario. The shipping was done using the high-speed interconnect and not the disk. This was called Cache Fusion Stage 1 because it was not possible to transfer all types of blocks to the requesting instance, especially with the write/write contention scenario.

Cache Fusion Stage 1 laid the foundation for Oracle RAC Cache Fusion Stage 2, in which both types of blocks (CR and CUR) can be transferred using the interconnect, although a disk ping is still required in some circumstances.

Oracle 8*i* also introduced the GV$ views, or "global views." With the help of GV$ views, DBAs could view cluster-wide database and other statistics sitting on any node/instance of the cluster. This was of enormous help to DBAs because earlier they had to club or join data collected on multiple nodes to analyze all the statistics. GV$ views have the instance_number column to support this functionality.

Block Contention

Block contention occurs where processes on different instances need access to the same block. If a block is being read by instance 1 or is in the buffer cache of instance 1 in read mode, and another process on instance 2 requests the same block in read mode, *read/read* contention results. This situation is the simplest of all cases and can easily be overcome because there are no modifications to the block. A copy of the block is shipped across by BSP from instance 1 to instance 2 or read from the disk by instance 2 without having to worry about applying an undo to get a consistent version. In fact, PCM coordination is not required in this situation.

Read/write contention occurs when instance 1 has modified a block in its local cache, and instance 2 requests the same block for a read. In Oracle 8*i*, using Cache Fusion Stage 1, instance locks are downgraded, and the BSP process builds a CR copy of the block using the undo data stored in its own cache and ships the CR copy across to the requesting instance. This is done in coordination with DLM processes (LMD and LMON).

If the requesting instance (instance 2) needs to modify the block that instance 1 has already modified, instance 1 has to downgrade the lock, flush the log entries (if not done before), and *then* send the data block to disk. This is called a "ping." Data blocks are pinged only when more than one instance need to modify the same block, causing the holding instance to write the block to disk before the requesting instance can read it into its own cache for modification. Disk ping can be expensive for applications in terms of performance.

A *false ping* occurs each time a block is written to disk, even if the block itself is not being requested by a different instance, but another block managed by the same lock element is being requested by a different instance.

A *soft ping* occurs when a lock element needs to be down converted due to a request of the lock element by another instance, and the blocks covered by the lock are already written to disk.

Write/Write Contention

This situation occurs when both instances have to modify the same block. As explained, a disk ping mechanism results where the locks are downgraded on instance 1 and the block is written to disk. Instance 2 acquired the exclusive lock on the buffer and modifies it.

Limitations of Oracle Parallel Server

OPS's scalability is limited on transactional systems that perform a lot of modifications on multiple nodes. Its scalability is also limited to I/O bandwidth and storage performance.

Oracle Parallel Server requires careful and clear application partitioning. For example, if two different applications require two logical sets of data, the application should be configured in such a way that one node is dedicated to one application type, and no overlapping of the connections occurs on the other node. Hence, the scalability is also restricted to the computing capacity of the node. Because of this "application partitioning" limitation, OPS is of limited suitability for packaged applications.

On-demand scalability is also limited, because we cannot dynamically add the nodes in an OPS cluster. Sometimes adding nodes will require careful analysis of the application partitioning and sometimes application repartitioning. This greatly limits true scalability.

An OPS does require careful setup and administration—a third-party cluster manager is necessary for clustering, requiring additional cost to the total application deployment. In other words, OPS is not cheap in any context.

Lock Configuration

OPS also requires a highly skilled database architect for tuning and initial configuration. OPS supports many types of locks, and each needs to be carefully analyzed; the number of locks is also limited by physical memory. DLM requires additional memory for lock management, and careful analysis is necessary before fixed/releasable/hash locks are configured.

Another important issue with OPS was the lack of a diagnosable framework. Operating systems, the cluster manager, and the database are integrated, and diagnosing the errors in this stack is quite complex, even for experienced support staff. Deadlock detection, lock tracing, and cluster-wide statistics are inadequate in OPS. These features or functionalities are difficult to implement or expensive to run, and customers are usually not cooperative enough to understand the complexities involved in dealing with the technical challenges, difficulties, or requirements.

For example, to diagnose an application locking problem or a deep-rooted OPS issue, a cluster system state dump of all the instances is required. In a four-node OPS cluster, this task *will consume time*. This is not a limitation but a requirement. Dumping the contents of the entire SGA, all its lock structures, and so on, is an expensive task. Oracle 9*i* RAC has come a long way in its diagnostics capability, and Oracle 11*g* RAC has improved on those capabilities with the introduction of the Automatic Diagnostic Repository (ADR) and incident reporting.

Manageability

OPS requires RAW partitions for almost all operating systems. RAW devices are complex to set up and manage for novice DBAs. A RAW device does not support dynamic file extensions, and there are some limitations in the number of RAW partitions an operating system can support. RAW device backup and recovery is different from normal file system backup, and extra care should be taken for RAW device management. Reconfiguration of a DLM takes a lot of time, and cluster availability (as well as database availability) is compromised due to the enormously heavy OSD-level API calls when a node crash is noticed by OPS. The RDBMS kernel has to make calls to many APIs to communicate with the OS cluster software, and the DLM has to wait for OS clusterware to finish its job before doing its own configuration. In Oracle 9*i*, tightly integrated code in the kernel for cluster communication has reduced this time lag.

The Oracle RAC Solution

Oracle RAC is a natural evolution of OPS. The limitations of the OPS are addressed through improvements in the code, the extension of Cache Fusion (discussed in detail later in the book), and dynamic lock remastering. Dynamic lock remastering allows the frequently used database objects to be managed in the local instance, and this greatly reduces the interconnect traffic and increases performance. Oracle 11*g* RAC also comes with an integrated clusterware and storage management framework, removing the dependency of the vendor clusterware and providing ultimate scalability and availability for database applications.

Availability

Oracle RAC systems can be configured to have no single point of failure, even when running on low-cost, commodity hardware and storage. If a monolithic server fails due to any reason, the applications and databases running on the server are completely unavailable. With Oracle RAC, if any of the database servers fail, applications simply keep running and the services are continuously available through the remaining servers. The underlying clusterware makes sure the services are relocated to other running servers, and failover is frequently transparent to applications and occurs in seconds.

Oracle RAC has proven time and again in all "near death" situations that it can hold the honor of the hour with its controlled reliability. The paradigm has shifted from reliability to maximum reliability. Analyzing and identifying the subsystem and system failure rates in accordance with the appropriate standard ensures reliability, which is a key component in the Oracle RAC technology.

Scalability

Oracle RAC allows multiple servers in a cluster to manage a single database transparently and without any interruptions to database availability. Additional nodes can be added when the database is up and running. With dynamic node addition and effective workload management, Oracle RAC allows database systems to scale out in both directions with an ability to run an increased workload by increasing the number of nodes and also with the ability to reduce the amount of time to complete a workload. This means that the previous ceilings on scalability have been removed. Collections of servers can work together transparently to manage a single database with linear scalability.

Oracle RAC requires no changes to existing database applications. A clustered Oracle RAC database appears to applications just like a traditional single-instance database environment. As a result, customers can easily migrate from single-instance configurations to Oracle RAC without needing to change their applications. Oracle RAC also requires no changes to existing database schemas.

Affordability

Oracle RAC allows organizations to use collections of low-cost computers to manage large databases rather than needing to purchase a single large, expensive computer. Clusters of small, commodity-class servers can now satisfy any database workload. For example, a customer needing to manage a large Oracle database might choose to purchase a cluster of eight industry-standard servers with four CPUs each, rather than buying a single server with 32 CPUs.

Oracle RAC allows clusters of low-cost, industry-standard servers running Linux to scale to meet workloads that previously demanded the use of a single, larger, more expensive computer. In the scale-up model of computing, sophisticated hardware and operating systems are needed to deliver scalability and availability to business applications. But with Oracle RAC, scalability and availability are achieved through functionality delivered by Oracle above and beyond the operating system.

In a Nutshell

Clustering is great solution to scale up and speed up the database workload processing with extreme availability. Because the storage is shared among the nodes, all the members of cluster node can concurrently access the storage, which helps the system be available during node failures. Oracle databases implement the shared everything architecture to achieve on-demand scalability and ultimate availability.

Infinite scalability on demand and uninterrupted availability can be achieved by the right clustering technology. Oracle databases have a good history on clusters with the OPS and its successor, Oracle RAC. The previous limitations of OPS are addressed in the current versions of RAC, with the introduction of the Cache Fusion framework. Oracle 11g has further improved Cache Fusion with the introduction of the read-only and read-mostly locking framework.

Oracle Parallel Storage technology has grown a lot along with clustering technologies. With the introduction of the Grid Infrastructure in Oracle 11g, Oracle integrates the Automatic Storage Management, a true volume manager and file system for the Oracle database infrastructure. This totally eliminates the requirement of having any third-party volume manager of file systems for the Oracle infrastructure. Oracle RAC 11g provides enormous scalability, availability, and flexibility at a low cost. It makes the consolidation of databases affordable and reliable by leveraging scale across the architecture.

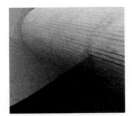

CHAPTER
3

Oracle RAC
Architecture

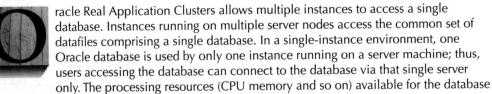 racle Real Application Clusters allows multiple instances to access a single database. Instances running on multiple server nodes access the common set of datafiles comprising a single database. In a single-instance environment, one Oracle database is used by only one instance running on a server machine; thus, users accessing the database can connect to the database via that single server only. The processing resources (CPU memory and so on) available for the database work are limited to the single server's processing resources. In an Oracle RAC environment, more than one instance can use the same database. This scenario presents multiple processing resources for database users.

NOTE
An instance *is a set of memory structures in a machine associated with the database. A* database *is a collection of physical files. Database and instance share one-to-many relationships. A database can be concurrently mounted by more than one instance in Oracle RAC, and at any point, one instance will be part of only one database.*

The nonvolatile storage for datafiles comprising the database is equally available to all the nodes for read and write access. Oracle RAC needs to coordinate and regulate simultaneous data accesses from multiple server nodes. Hence, an efficient, reliable, and high-speed private network must exist among the nodes of the cluster for sending and receiving data. Figure 3-1 shows the configuration of a single-instance database and an Oracle RAC database.

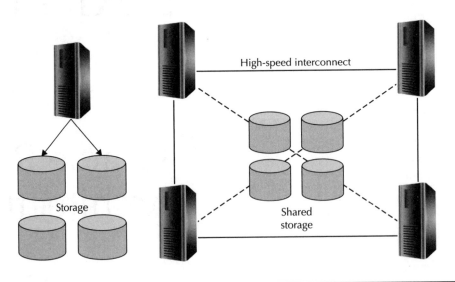

FIGURE 3-1 *Single-instance database and an Oracle RAC setup*

Single-Instance vs. Oracle RAC Environment

Similar to in a single-instance environment, each instance in an Oracle RAC environment has its own System Global Area (SGA) and background processes. However, all the datafiles and control files are equally accessible to all the nodes, so these files must be placed on a shared disk subsystem. Each instance also has its own dedicated set of online redo log files. The online redo log files can be written to only by the instance to which they belong. However, these files must be readable by other instances during instance crash recovery. This requires that online redo log files reside on a shared disk subsystem and not on a node's local storage, because the files would be lost if the node crashed.

Table 3-1 compares single-instance components to components of an instance in an Oracle RAC environment.

Instances in an Oracle RAC environment share the data because the same set of data might be needed by multiple instances simultaneously. There is no danger in multiple instances reading the same data simultaneously; however, data integrity issues may arise if one instance modifies (via insert or update) while another instance(s) reads or multiple instances modify the same data concurrently. This concurrent read/write or write/write behavior, if not coordinated correctly,

Component	Single-Instance Environment	RAC Environment
SGA	Instance has its own SGA.	Each instance has its own SGA.
Background processes	Instance has its own set of background processes.	Each instance has its own set of background processes.
Datafiles	Accessed by only one instance.	Shared by all instances, so must be placed on shared storage.
Control files	Accessed by only one instance.	Shared by all instances, so must be placed on shared storage.
Online redo log file	Dedicated for writing and reading to only one instance.	Only one instance can write, but other instances can read during recovery and archiving. If an instance is shut down, log switches by other instances can force the idle instance redo logs to be archived.
Archived redo log	Dedicated to the instance.	Private to the instance, but other instances will need access to all required archive logs during media recovery.
Flash recovery log	Accessed by only one instance.	Shared by all the instances, so must be placed on shared storage.
Alert log and other trace files	Dedicated to the instance.	Private to each instance; other instances never read or write to those files.
ORACLE_HOME	Multiple instances on the same machine accessing different database can use the same executable files.	Same as single instance, but can also be placed on shared file system, allowing a common ORACLE_HOME for all instances in an Oracle RAC environment.

TABLE 3-1 *Components of Single-Instance vs. Oracle RAC*

might lead to data corruption or inconsistent representation of the data. Single-instance Oracle already ensures that readers never block writers and that "dirty" reads are never allowed.

Oracle RAC ensures that all the instances across the clusters see a consistent image of the database. The Distributed Lock Manager (or DLM; called the Global Resource Directory, or GRD, beginning with version 9i) coordinates resource sharing among the instances.

Oracle RAC Components

The Oracle Database 11g RAC stack is slightly different from previous versions of Oracle because the clustering software is totally integrated into the RDBMS kernel in the latest version. In earlier versions of Oracle RAC the third-party vendors (except for Linux and Windows ports, where Oracle started shipping its own clusterware) provide the underlying clustering functionality. Starting from Oracle 11g Release 2, Oracle Clusterware stack is known as *Oracle Grid Infrastructure*.

The major components of Oracle RAC are

- Shared disk system
- Oracle Clusterware
- Cluster interconnects
- Oracle kernel components

Figure 3-2 shows the basic architecture.

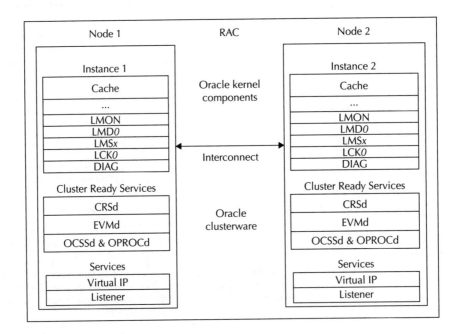

FIGURE 3-2 *Oracle 11g architecture*

Shared Disk System

Scalable shared storage is a critical component of an Oracle RAC environment. Traditionally, storage was attached to each individual server using SCSI (Small Computer System Interface) or SATA (Serial ATA) interfaces local to the hosts. Today, more flexible storage is popular and is accessible over storage area networks (SANs) or network attached storage (NAS) using regular Ethernet networks. These new storage options enable multiple servers to access the same set of disks through a network, simplifying provisioning of storage in any distributed environment. SANs represent the evolution of data storage technology to this point.

Traditionally, in single-instance client/server systems, data was stored on devices either inside or directly attached to the server. This kind of storage is known as *directly attached storage devices (DAS)*. Next in the evolutionary scale came network attached storage (NAS), which removed the storage devices from the server and connected them to the network. SANs take the principle a step further by allowing storage devices to exist on their own separate networks and communicate with each other over very fast media, such as a high-speed Fibre Channel network. Users can gain access to these storage devices through server systems that are connected to the local area network (LAN) and SAN.

In shared storage, database files should be equally accessible to all the nodes concurrently. Generic file systems do not allow disks to be mounted in more than one system. Also, the regular UNIX file systems (UFS) do not allow the files to be shared among the nodes because of the obvious file-locking (inode locks) issues and unavailability of a coherent file system cache. One option is to use the Network File System (NFS), but it is unsuitable because it relies on a single host (which mounts the file systems) and for performance reasons. Because the disks in such an implementation are attached to one node, all the write requests must go through that particular node, thus limiting the scalability and fault tolerance. The total available I/O bandwidth is dependent on the bandwidth provided by that single host through which all I/O can be serviced. Because that node may become a single point of failure (SPOF), it is another threat for the high-availability (HA) architecture.

The choice of file system is critical for Oracle RAC deployment. Traditional file systems do not support simultaneous mounting by more than one system. Therefore, you must store files in either raw volumes without any file system or on a file system that supports concurrent access by multiple systems.

Thus, three major approaches exist for providing the shared storage needed by RAC:

- **Raw volumes**   These raw devices require storage that operates in block mode, such as Fibre Channel SANs or Internet SCSI (iSCSI). This was the preferred and only available option in releases previous to Oracle 9*i*.

- **Cluster File System**   One or more cluster file systems can be used to hold all Oracle RAC datafiles. Oracle provides the Oracle Cluster File System (OCFS) for Oracle RAC for Microsoft Windows and Linux operating systems. It is not widely used, so we will not be discussing it in great detail.

- **Automatic Storage Management (ASM)**   ASM is a portable, dedicated, and optimized cluster file system for Oracle database files, introduced in Oracle 10*g*. ASM is the only supported storage if you use Oracle Standard Edition with Oracle RAC. ASM is discussed in Chapter 6.

Performance Benefits of RAW Partitions

Oracle's database cache algorithms, based on the touch count of the buffers, are more sophisticated than the traditional operating system algorithms. Most operating systems just keep the *most recently used* buffers rather than the *most frequently used* buffers. Also the OS cache is not as optimized for usage for database buffers because it makes no distinction between database blocks and file inodes, which lie on the same page cache.

Buffering the data blocks in the file system cache wastes precious main memory, and two versions of the blocks are cached in two different places. Leaving the unwanted file system cache to the OS will provide additional memory to Oracle or the operating system and may improve performance because the OS can resort to paging of non-database files under memory pressure.

Avoiding double buffering greatly increases the I/O performance because data doesn't need to be written in two locations. Oracle's log writer process writes small pieces of change records to the file system cache, and then the cache writes back to the redo log files. In RAW partitions, the log writer directly writes the change records to the log files, which dramatically increases the performance of the online transaction processing (OLTP) systems.

Of course, additional administrative overhead is necessary if RAW partitions are used, because normal RAW partitions cannot be grown on demand, like file systems, without third-party volume management software. A limitation on the number of RAW partitions on a few operating systems curbs the use of raw devices for the packaged applications, which requires numerous datafiles and tablespaces. Another limitation in the raw device is that because it is not visible to the operating systems, a rookie system administrator may ruin the RAW partitions, thinking that they are unused partitions.

The use of raw devices has been the traditional approach for sharing files across nodes. Some experts even recommend the use of raw devices for single-instance systems for performance reasons. The RAW partition avoids the double buffering in the file system cache, and data is read into the Oracle database buffer cache, thus avoiding the operating system buffer cache altogether. A lot of storage vendors these days offer file systems whose performance comes close to that of raw devices.

RAID

Any discussion about storage choices would be incomplete without including RAID, which is a foundation for highly available storage systems because uninterrupted access to storage is one of the key aspects in a highly available solution. Redundant Array of Independent (or Inexpensive) Disks, affectionately known as RAID, is key in high-performance storage systems.

Numerous varieties of RAID implementation mechanisms are available, depending on the standards, and few vendor-specific implementations are also on hand, such as Auto RAID from HP. We will discuss common RAID concepts and most common RAID implementations, as well as the pros and cons of each of them.

Conceptually, RAID uses two or more physical disks to create a single logical disk, where the physical disks operate in tandem to provide greater size and more bandwidth. Before delving deeper into RAID, you need to be clear about terminology, especially the terms *striping, mirroring,* and *parity.* Striping yields better I/O performance, mirroring provides protection, and parity (when applicable) is a way to check the work. Using these three aspects of RAID, you can achieve scalable, protected, and highly available I/O performance.

Striping is the process of breaking down data into pieces and distributing it across multiple disks that support a logical volume. This often results in a logical volume that is larger and has greater I/O bandwidth than a single disk. Most volume managers stripe the data across all of the devices (either RAID or disks) based on a stripe width. The stripe width is generally set to a value based on the number of streams of I/O and the I/O request size such that all of the devices can be in use. The goal is to keep all of the disks busy to achieve parallelism on all the devices.

By creating a single volume from pieces of data on several disks, you can increase the capacity to handle I/O requests in a linear fashion, by combining each disk's I/O bandwidth. When multiple I/O requests for a file on a striped volume are processed, they can be serviced by multiple drives in the volume because the requests are subdivided across several disks. This way, all drives in the striped volume can engage and service multiple I/O requests in a more efficient manner.

Mirroring is the process of writing the same data simultaneously to another member of the same volume. Mirroring provides protection for data by writing exactly the same information to every member in the volume. Additionally, mirroring can provide enhanced read operations because the read requests can be serviced from either member of the volume.

Parity is error checking. Some implementations of RAID (such as RAID 5) perform calculations when reading and writing data. The calculations primarily occur on write operations. However, if one or more disks in a volume are unavailable, then depending on the level of RAID, even read operations would require parity operations to rebuild the pieces on the failed disks. Parity is used to determine the write location and validity of each stripe that is written in a striped volume.

Parity is implemented on those levels of RAID that do not support mirroring. Parity algorithms contain error correction code (ECC) capabilities, which calculate parity for a given stripe or chunk of data within a RAID volume. The size of a chunk is OS and hardware specific. The codes generated by the parity algorithm are used to re-create data in the event of disk failure(s). Because the algorithm can reverse this parity calculation, it can rebuild data lost as a result of disk failures.

Types of RAID

RAID can be software based, where the control software is usually bundled with the OS, or in the form of an add-on, such as Veritas Volume Manager. This type of RAID, also known as *host-based* RAID, imposes a small overhead, as it consumes memory, I/O bandwidth, and CPU cycles on the host where it is implemented. Normally, this overhead is not alarming, but it should be factored into the resource capacity plans of the host.

RAID implemented by hardware is in the form of micro-code present in dedicated disk controller modules that connect to the host. These controllers are internal to the host where RAID is implemented. This type of RAID is also known as *embedded controller-based RAID.*

RAID can also be implemented using controllers that are external to the host where it is implemented. This implementation is called *bridge based* and is not preferred because it can incur longer service times for I/O requests due to the longer I/O paths from the disks to the host. This type of implementation is usually typical of I/O subsystems that are half fiber and half SCSI. It is also common to see this implementation on storage systems that support multiple hosts running multiple operating systems. The "bridges" also have a tendency to become saturated when the system is busy with I/O requests. Hardware-based RAID should be preferred over software-based or host-based RAID, which is preferred over bridge-based RAID.

RAID Levels

Initially, RAID was a simple method of logically joining two or more disks, but like all things in our industry, more choices were needed to meet different requirements. Today, RAID levels usually range from 0 to 7, and because of the peculiar way that we count in our world, this offers us more than eight choices. The differences among the various levels are based on varying I/O patterns across the disks. These patterns by their inherent nature offer different levels and types of protection and performance characteristics:

- **RAID 0** A "normal" file system with striping, in which data loss is imminent with any disk failure. Simply put, it is data striped across all the available disks. This level provides good read/write performance but no recoverability.

- **RAID 1** Provides mirroring and thus full data redundancy; often called a *mirrored disk*. In most cases, the volume the operating system sees is made up of two or more disks. However, this is presented to an application or a database as a single volume. As the system writes to this volume, it writes an exact copy of the data to all members in the volume. This level requires twice the amount of disk storage as compared to RAID 0. Additionally, some performance gains can be reaped from parallel reading of the two mirror members. RAID 1 doubles the capacity of processing read requests from the volume when compared to not having mirrored members. There are no parity calculations involved in this level of RAID.

- **RAID 0 + 1** This level stripes first and then mirrors what was just striped. It combines levels 0 and 1 (striping and mirroring) and provides good write and read performance and redundancy without the overhead of parity calculations. On disk failure(s), no reconstruction of data is required because the data is read from the surviving mirror. This level is the most common RAID implementation for write-intensive applications and is widely used. The most common complaint is the cost because it requires twice as much space. To justify this, you will have to spend some time understanding the performance requirements and availability needs of your systems. Note that if one of the pieces becomes unavailable due to a disk failure, the entire mirror member becomes unavailable. This is a very important consideration because the loss of an entire mirror member reduces the I/O servicing capacity of the volume by 50 percent.

- **RAID 1 + 0** This level mirrors first, then stripes over what was mirrored. This level has the same functionality as RAID 0 + 1 but is better suited for high availability because upon the loss of one disk in a mirrored member, the entire member of a mirrored volume does not become unavailable. Note that the loss of one disk of a mirrored member does not reduce the I/O servicing capacity of the volume by 50 percent. This is the preferred method for configurations that combine striping and mirroring, subject to hardware limitations.

- **RAID 2** Incorporates striping and redundancy/protection provided through parity. This method requires less disk space compared to RAID 1, but the need to calculate and write parity will make writes slower. This level was one of the early implementations of "striping with parity" using the famous hamming code technique, but it was later replaced by RAID 3, 5, and 7. This level of RAID is rarely implemented.

- **RAID 3** The error correction code (ECC) algorithm calculates parity to provide data redundancy as in RAID 2, but all of the parity is stored on one disk. The parity for this level is stored at the bit/byte level as opposed to the block/chunk level. RAID 3 is slowly gaining popularity but is still not widely used. It is best suited for data mart/data warehouse applications that support a few users but require sequential bulk I/O performance (data-transfer intensive). When full table scans and/or index range scans are the norm for a given application and the user population is small, RAID 3 may be the ticket.

- **RAID 4** The same as RAID 3 but with block-level parity. This level is rarely implemented.

- **RAID 5** This level is by far one of the most common RAID implementations today. Data redundancy is provided via parity calculations as in RAID 2, 3, 4, and 7, but the parity is stored along with the data. Hence, the parity is distributed across the number of drives configured in the volume. RAID 5 is attractive for many environments, because it results in minimal loss of disk space to parity values, and it provides good performance on random read operations and light write operations. RAID 5 caters better to Input Output Per Second (IOPS) with its support for concurrently servicing many I/O requests. It should not be implemented for write-intensive applications because the continuous process of reading a stripe, calculating the new parity, and writing the stripe back to disk (with the new parity) will make writes significantly slower.

- **RAID 6** Parity is calculated using a more complex algorithm, and redundancy is provided using an advanced multidimensional parity method. RAID 6 stores two sets of parity for each block of data and thus makes writes even slower than RAID 5. However, on disk failures, RAID 6 facilitates quicker availability of the drives in the volume (after a disk failure), without incurring the negative performance impact of resyncing the drives in the volume. This level of RAID is rarely implemented.

- **RAID 7** This level is a better implementation of RAID 3. Because read and write operations on RAID 3 are performed in a synchronous fashion, the parity disk can bottleneck during writes; RAID 7 allows asynchronous reads and writes, which inherently improves overall I/O performance. RAID 7 has the same characteristics as RAID 3, where all of the parity is stored on a dedicated drive. RAID 7 is relatively new in the market and has potential to be a great candidate for implementations that historically have chosen RAID 3. With RAID 7, you can "have your cake and eat it too" because you can reap the data-transfer benefits of RAID 3 and not lose the transactional I/O features that RAID 7 offers.

- **RAID-S** If you are using EMC storage arrays, this is your version of RAID 3/5. It is well suited to data mart/data warehouse applications. This level of RAID should be avoided for write-intensive or high-volume transactional applications for the same reasons as any RAID 5 implementation. EMC storage solutions are usually configured with large write caches, but generally speaking, these write caches are not large enough to overcome the additional overhead of the parity calculations during writes.

- **RAID-DP** This is Network Appliance's (NetApp's) implementation of block-level parity with two parity disks. RAID 4 and RAID 5 slightly differ in the implementation of parity drives. RAID 4 has a dedicated parity, whereas in RAID 5 the parity is stored along with data. NetApp uses two drives dedicated to parity, thus eliminating the issue of a hot parity disk. Also, NetApp uses a slight differential layout for data known as Write Anywhere File Layout (WAFL), which writes the data to the first available free space and thus provides slightly better write performance over traditional RAID 5 volumes.

- **Auto RAID** As implemented by HP, the controller along with the intelligence built within the I/O subsystem dynamically modifies the level of RAID on a given disk block either to RAID 0 + 1 or RAID 5, depending on the near historical nature of the I/O requests on that block. The recent history of I/O patterns on the disk block is maintained using the concept of a *working set* (a set of disk blocks). For obvious reasons, there is one working set each for reads and writes, and blocks keep migrating back and forth between the two sets, based on the type of activity. A disk block in this context is 64KB in size.

Said in a different way, a RAID 5 block can be dynamically converted into a RAID 0 + 1 block if the "intelligence" determines and predicts that the block will be accessed primarily for writes. The controller can also perform the converse of the previous operation, namely converting a RAID 0 + 1 block into a RAID 5 block, if it determines and predicts that the block will be primarily accessed for reads. To support this configuration, all the drives in the array are used for all RAID volumes configured on that array. This means that physical drive independence across volumes cannot be achieved.

Table 3-2 summarizes the various levels of RAID with their descriptions and implementation issues.

Level	Description	Comments
RAID 0	Plain striping	No recoverability; provides read/write performance without recoverability.
RAID 1	Plain mirroring	Recoverability; excellent write performance because writes can go parallel.
RAID 0 + 1 or 1 + 0	Combination of 0 and 1—stripe and then mirror or mirror and then stripe	Recoverability; provides read and write performance, very widely used; 1 + 0 is better than 0 + 1 for availability.
RAID 2	Early implementation of striping with parity	Uses the hamming code technique for parity calculations and was replaced by RAID 3, 5, and 7. Rarely implemented.
RAID 3	Striping with bit/byte-level parity, dedicated parity disk	Recoverability; good read performance for bulk sequential reads; not widely used but gaining popularity.
RAID 4	Striping with block-level parity	Dedicated parity disk, recoverability, rarely implemented.
RAID 5	Striping with block-level parity, distributed parity across the number of disks in the volume	Recoverability; provides better read performance for random reads that are small in nature; widely used.
RAID 6	Striping with block-level multidimensional parity	Recoverability; slower writes than RAID 5; rarely implemented.
RAID 7	Same as RAID 3, but with better asynchronous capability for reads and writes	Significantly better overall I/O performance when compared to RAID 3, but also significantly more expensive than RAID 3.
RAID-S	EMC's implementation of RAID 3/5	Provides better write performance when used with cache at the storage array level.
RAID-DP	NetApp's implementation of RAID 6 (striping with dual parity)	Provides better read performance due to striping, and dual parity provides redundancy.
Auto RAID	HP's automatic RAID technology	Automatically configures the I/O system based on the nature and type of I/O performed on the disk blocks within the RAID array.

TABLE 3-2   *Levels of RAID*

Oracle Clusterware

Oracle Clusterware is portable software (which is now an integrated part of Oracle Grid Infrastructure). It consists of several background processes that perform different functions to facilitate cluster operations. Oracle Clusterware is a mandatory piece of software required to run the Oracle RAC option. It provides the basic clustering support at the OS level and enables Oracle software to run in clustering mode. Oracle Clusterware can run as a standalone cluster service or with vendor-supplied clusterware such as Sun Cluster or TruCluster—although care should be taken when Oracle Clusterware is installed on top of a vendor clusterware, as discussed a bit later in this chapter.

The background processes and services that comprise Oracle Clusterware are CRSd, OCSSd, OPROCd, EVMd, and ONS. The CRSd process further spawns dedicated RACGIMON for each database instance. The operating system's init daemon starts these processes by using the Oracle Clusterware wrapper scripts, which are installed by Oracle Universal Installer during the installation of Oracle Clusterware. Oracle installs three wrapper scripts: init.crsd, init.evmd, and init.cssd. These are configured with the respawn action so that they will be restarted whenever they fail, except that the init.cssd wrapper script is configured with the *fatal* parameter, causing the cluster node to reboot to avoid any possible data corruption, which is explained later in this chapter.

Oracle Clusterware Components

Oracle Clusterware software enables nodes to communicate with each other and forms the cluster that makes the nodes work as a single logical server. Oracle Clusterware is managed by Cluster Ready Services (CRS) using the Oracle Cluster Registry (OCR), which records and maintains the cluster and node membership information, as well as the voting disk, which acts as a tiebreaker during communication failures. Consistent heartbeat information from all the nodes is sent to the voting disk when the cluster is running.

CRS has five components—namely the Process Monitor daemon (OPROCd; obsolete in 11,2), the CRS daemon (CRSd), the Oracle Cluster Synchronization Service daemon (OCSSd), the Event Volume Manager daemon (EVMd), and the Oracle Notification Service (ONS)—and each handles a variety of functions. Failure or death of the CRSd can cause node failure, and it automatically reboots the nodes to avoid data corruption because of possible communication failure among the nodes. The CRSd runs as the superuser *root* in the UNIX platforms and runs as a background service in Microsoft Windows platforms.

Cluster Ready Services

The Cluster Ready Services daemon (CRSd) process is spawned by the init.crsd wrapper script and provides the high-availability framework for Oracle Clusterware and manages the states of cluster resources by starting, stopping, monitoring, and relocating the failed cluster resources on to the available cluster nodes within the cluster. A cluster resource can be a network resource such as a virtual IP, database instance, listener, database, or any third-party application, such as a web server and so on. The CRSd process retrieves the cluster resource's configuration information stored in the Oracle Cluster Registry (OCR) before taking any action on the cluster resource. CRSd also uses OCR to maintain the cluster resource profiles and statuses. Every cluster resource has a resource profile, which is stored in the Oracle Cluster Registry.

The CRSd process runs as a root operating system user and spawns one dedicated RACGIMON process per instance to monitor the database and ASM instances. CRSd also provides Real Application Cluster Guard Infrastructure (RACG) and can spawn more temporary processes such as *racgvip, racgmdb, racgchsn,* and *racgeut* to take actions on standard Oracle cluster resources that start with ora.*.

Here's a list of the functionalities of CRS:

- CRS is installed and run from a different Oracle home known as GRID_HOME (known as ORA_CRS_HOME in earlier versions), which is independent from ORACLE_HOME.

- CRSd manages resources such as starting and stopping the services and failovers of the application resources. It spawns separate processes to manage application resources.

- CRSd has two modes of running during startup and after a shutdown. During a planned clusterware startup, it is started in reboot mode. It is started in restart mode after an unplanned shutdown. In reboot mode, CRSd starts all the resources under its management. In restart mode, it retains the previous state and returns the resources to their previous states before shutdown.

- CRS manages the Oracle Cluster Registry (OCR) and stores the current known state in the OCR.

- CRS runs as *root* on UNIX and LocalSystem on Windows and automatically restarts in case of failure.

- CRS requires a public interface, private interface, and the virtual IP (VIP) for operation. Public and private interfaces should be up and running and should be pingable to each other before the CRS installation is started. Without this network infrastructure, CRS cannot be installed.

Oracle Cluster Synchronization Services

OCSSd provides synchronization services among the nodes. It provides the access to the node membership and enables basic cluster services, including cluster group services and cluster locking. It can also run without integrating with vendor clusterware. Failure of OCSSd causes the machine to reboot to avoid a "split-brain" situation (when all the links of the private interconnect fail to respond to each other, but the instances are still up and running; each instance thinks that the other instance is dead and tries to take over ownership). This is also required in a single instance if Automatic Storage Management (ASM) is used. (ASM is discussed in detail in Chapter 6.) OCSSd runs as the *oracle* user.

The Oracle Cluster Synchronization Services daemon (OCSSd) process is spawned by the init.cssd wrapper script and runs as a non-*root* operating system user with real-time priority and manages the configuration of the Oracle Clusterware by providing Node Cluster and Group membership services. OCSSd provides these services by two types of heartbeat mechanisms: network heartbeat and disk heartbeat. The main objective of the network heartbeat is to check the viability of the Oracle cluster, whereas the disk heartbeat helps to identify the split-brain situation. Due to this fact, it is very important that OCSSd is always running; hence, the init.cssd wrapper script is configured with *fatal* parameter. Failure of OCSSd causes the machine reboot to avoid a split-brain situation. This is also required in the single instance if Automatic Storage Management (ASM) is used.

OCSSd uses vendor cluster software Group Services using the SKGXN library when Oracle Clusterware is installed with third-party vendor cluster software. SKGXN libraries link the OS-dependent network components with Oracle software.

The following list summarizes the functionalities of OCSSd:

- CSS provides basic Group Services support. Group Services is a distributed group membership system that allows applications to coordinate activities to archive a common result.

- Group Services use vendor clusterware group services when available. However, it is capable of working independently if no vendor clusterware group services are available.

- Lock Services provides the basic cluster-wide serialization locking functions. It uses the First In, First Out (FIFO) mechanism to manage locking.

- Node Services uses OCR to store data and updates the information during reconfiguration. It also manages the OCR data, which is otherwise static.

Event Manager Process

The third component in OCS is called the Event Management Logger, which runs the daemon process EVMd. The daemon process spawns a permanent child process called *evmlogger* and generates the events when things happen. The evmlogger spawns new children processes on demand and scans the callout directory to invoke callouts. It will restart automatically on failures, and the death of the evmd process does not halt the instance. EVMd runs as the *oracle* user.

Oracle Event Manager Process evmd is spawned by the init.evmd wrapper script and runs as a root operating system account. The evmd daemon process starts the evmlogger child process, which scans the callout directory and, on demand, starts the racgevt process to execute the callouts from the callout directory. The evmd process receives the FAN events posted by clients and distributes the FAN events to the clients that have subscribed to them. The evmd process will restart automatically on failures, and the death of the evmd process does not halt the instance. The evmd process runs as the *oracle* user. Imagine an Oracle cluster composed of two cluster nodes: Node A and Node B. When Node B leaves the cluster, the ocssd process on Node A posts a leave FAN event, which the evmd process on Node A publishes to the crsd process on Node A because the CRS process is the subscriber for the leave FAN event. Oracle provides the evmwatch and evmget utilities to view the FAN events on the standard output. These utilities are also useful to test the functionality of the *evmd* process.

Oracle Process Monitor

The Oracle Process Monitor daemon (OPROCd) provides the I/O fencing solution for Oracle Clusterware. The prime objective of the OPROCd process is to identify potential cluster node hangs and reboot the hanged node so that processes on the hung node cannot write to the storage. OPROCd uses the hang check timer or watchdog timer (depending on the implementation) for cluster integrity. OPROCd is locked in memory and runs as a real-time process. It sleeps for a fixed time and runs as the *root* user. Failure of the OPROCd process causes the node to restart.

The OPROCd process uses the operating system signal handle SIGALRM to set the interval timer. Oracle writes messages in the system messages log whenever the OPROCd process is causing a cluster node to reboot. The OPROCd process is so important that Oracle Clusterware uses another OCLSOMON process to monitor the OPROCd process and causes a cluster node to reboot if the OPROCd process is hung. Oracle does not start the OPROCd process when third-party cluster software is used; instead, it uses the OCLSVMON process to know the synchronization problems from the third-party cluster software.

I/O Fencing

Fencing is an important operation that protects processes from other nodes modifying the resources during node failures. When a node fails, it needs to be isolated from the other active nodes. Fencing is required because it is impossible to distinguish between a real failure and a temporary hang. Therefore, we assume the worst and always fence. (If the node is really down, it cannot do any damage; in theory, nothing is required. We could just bring it back into the cluster with the usual join process.) Fencing, in general, ensures that I/O can no longer occur from the failed node. Raw devices using a fencing method called STOMITH (Shoot The Other Machine In The Head) automatically power off the server.

Other techniques can be used to perform fencing. The most popular are reserve/release (R/R) and persistent reservation (SCSI3). SAN Fabric fencing is also widely used both by Red Hat Global File System (GFS) and Polyserv. Reserve/release by its nature works only with two nodes. (That is, one of the two nodes in the cluster upon detecting that the other node has failed will issue the reserve and grab all the disks for itself. The other node will commit suicide if it tries to do I/O in case it was temporarily hung. The I/O failure triggers some code to kill the node.)

In general, in the case of two nodes, R/R is sufficient to address the split-brain issue. For more than two nodes, the SAN Fabric fencing technique does not work well because it would cause all the nodes but one to commit suicide. In those cases, persistent reservation, essentially a match on a key, is used. In persistent reservation, if you have the right key, you can do I/O; otherwise, your I/O fails. Therefore, it is sufficient to change the key on a failure to ensure the right behavior during failure.

All of the Oracle clients that are I/O capable can be terminated by the CSS before it takes a node out, which avoids the I/Os from going through because they will be intercepted and not completed. Hence, the database will not treat those transactions as committed and errors will be returned to the app; for those that did get committed and did not make it to the datafiles, the database will recover them on startup of the same or another instance that is running.

Oracle Notification Services

The Oracle Notification Services (ONS) process is configured during the installation of Oracle Clusterware and is started on each cluster node when CRS starts. Whenever the state of a cluster resource changes, the ONS process on each cluster node communicates with one another and exchanges the HA event information. CRS triggers these HA events and routes them to the ONS process and then the ONS process publishes the HA event information to the middle tier. To use ONS on the middle tier, you need to install ONS on each host where you have client applications that need to be integrated with FAN. Applications use these HA events for various reasons, especially to quickly detect failures. The whole process of triggering and publishing the HA events is known as Fast Application Notification (commonly known as FAN in the Oracle community). Alternatively, the HA events are called FAN events.

These FAN events alone are of no use until applications do not have the logic to respond to the FAN events published by the ONS process. The best way to receive and respond to these FAN events is by using a client that is tightly integrated with FAN, such as Java Database Connectivity

(JDBC) Implicit Connection Cache, Universal Connection Pool for Java, and database resources. Using a user-defined callout script is another way to publish these FAN events to the AQ (Advance Queue) tables. FAN events will contain important information, such as event type, reason, and status, and users can write their own callout scripts to act upon certain types of events instead of taking action on each FAN event.

Table 3-3 summarizes the details of the various CRS processes and their functionalities.

Cluster Ready Services

The Oracle Grid Infrastructure uses CRS for interaction between the OS and the database. CRS is the background engine for the Oracle 11g RAC high availability framework, which provides the standard cluster interface for all platforms. The functionality was previously handled by vendor clusterware based on the platform. In this discussion, we use the Oracle Grid Infrastructure and Oracle Clusterware interchangeably.

The Oracle Grid Infrastructure must be installed in a separate Oracle home before the standard RAC installation. This separate Oracle home is known as GRID_HOME. The Oracle Grid Infrastructure is a mandatory component for Oracle 11g RAC and can run either alone or on top of vendor-supplied clusterware such as Veritas Cluster Server, Sun Cluster, or HP Serviceguard. However, if third-party clusterware is used for OS clustering, Oracle Clusterware components in the Oracle Grid Infrastructure should be integrated on top of them.

When Oracle Clusterware is installed on the cluster where third-party clusterware is integrated, CRS relies on the vendor clusterware for the node membership functionality and just manages Oracle services and resources. If CRS is the only clusterware in the cluster, it manages the node membership functionality along with managing regular RAC-related resources and services.

CRS Process	Functionality	Failure of the Process	Runs as
Cluster Ready Services daemon (CRSd)	Resource monitoring, resource failover, and node recovery	Process restarted automatically depending on the startup mode. Node reboot if it is running in reboot mode. Does not cause node restart when running in restart mode.	root
Cluster Synchronization Services daemon (CSSd)	Basic node membership, Group Services, and basic locking	Node restart.	oracle
Oracle Notification Service (ONS)	Used to extend the HA notification to clients	Restarts automatically during failures.	oracle
Event Management daemon (EVMd)	Spawns a child process event logger and generates callouts	Automatically restarted; does not cause node reboot.	oracle
Oracle Process Monitor daemon (OPROCd)	Provides basic cluster integrity services	Node restart.	root

TABLE 3-3 *CRS Processes and Functionalities*

Cluster Membership Decisions

Oracle Clusterware contains logic for determining the health of other nodes of the cluster and whether they are alive. After a certain period of inactivity of a node, Oracle Clusterware declares the node dead and evicts it. If a new node needs to be added, it is allowed to join immediately.

In the presence of vendor clusterware, Oracle Clusterware limits its view of the cluster to those nodes that the vendor also sees. Oracle Clusterware allows new nodes to join as soon as the vendor clusterware reports that the new node is up, and it waits to evict a node until vendor clusterware is certain that the remote node is dead. However, if Oracle Clusterware cannot communicate with a node for 10 minutes, and vendor clusterware maintains that the node is still alive, Oracle Clusterware will forcibly evict the remote node to prevent an indefinite hang at the Oracle layer.

This delay is set so that if vendor clusterware is taking a long time to resolve network splits, Oracle does not end up killing the nodes on the wrong side of the split. This dueling clusterware scenario can otherwise yield a full cluster outage if this timeout is too low.

Resource Management Frameworks

Resources represent applications or system components (both local and remote to the cluster) whose behavior is wrapped and monitored by a cluster framework. Thus, the application or system component becomes highly available. Correct modeling of resources stipulates that they must be managed by only one cluster framework. Having multiple frameworks managing the same resource can produce undesirable side effects, including race conditions in start/stop semantics.

Consider an example in which two cluster frameworks manage the same shared storage, such as a raw disk volume or cluster file system. In the event that the storage component goes down, both frameworks may compete in trying to bring it back up and may decide to apply totally different recovery methods (for example, restarting vs. using a notification for human intervention, or waiting before restarting vs. retrying in a tight loop).

In the case of single application resources, both frameworks may even decide to fail over the component to a totally different node. In general, clusterware software systems are not prepared to handle resources that are managed by multiple HA frameworks.

Starting and Stopping Oracle Clusterware

When a node fails, Oracle Clusterware is brought up at boot time via the init daemon (on UNIX) or Windows Service Management (on Windows). Therefore, if the init process fails to run on the node, the OS is broken and Oracle Clusterware does not start.

Oracle Clusterware can be manually started, stopped, enabled, and disabled using the following commands (which must be run as the superuser):

```
crsctl stop crs    # stops Oracle Clusterware
crsctl start crs   # starts Oracle Clusterware
crsctl enable crs  # enables Oracle Clusterware
crsctl disable crs  # disables Oracle Clusterware
```

The commands to start and stop Oracle Clusterware are asynchronous, but while it is stopped, a small wait time may occur before control is returned. Only one set of CRSs can be run on one cluster.

Starting with Oracle Database 10g Release 2, the Oracle Clusterware APIs are documented. Customers are free to use these programmatic interfaces in their custom or non-Oracle software to operate and maintain a coherent cluster environment. To start and stop Oracle resources named with "ora.", you must use SRVCTL. Oracle does not support third-party applications that check Oracle resources and take corrective actions on those resources. Best practice is to leave Oracle resources controlled by Oracle Clusterware. For any other resource, either Oracle or the vendor clusterware (not both) can manage it directly.

Clusterware Startup Process in Oracle 11*g* R2

Oracle introduced Oracle High Availability Service daemon (OHASd) in Oracle 11*g* Release 2, which starts all other Oracle Clusterware daemons. During installation of Oracle Grid Infrastructure, Oracle adds an entry into the /etc/inittab file, as shown here:

```
h1:35:respawn:/etc/init.d/init.ohasd run >/dev/null 2>&1 </dev/null
```

The /etc/inittab file executes the /etc/init.d/init.ohasd control script with the *run* argument that spawns the ohasd.bin executable. The cluster control files are stored at the same location (/etc/oracle/scls_scr/<hostname>/root) as of 11*g* Release 1. The /etc/init.d/init.ohasd control script starts the OHASd based on the value of the ohasdrun cluster control file. The value *restart* causes Oracle to restart the crashed OHASd using $GRID_HOME/bin/ohasd restart. The value *stop* indicates a scheduled shutdown of the OHASd, and the value *reboot* causes Oracle to update the ohasdrun file with a value of *restart* so that Oracle will restart the crashed OHASd.

The OHASd uses cluster resources to start other Clusterware daemons. The OHASd will have one cluster resource for each Clusterware daemon, and these resources are stored in the Oracle Local Registry, which is explained further in this book. These daemon resources use agents to manage the Clusterware daemons, such as starting, stopping, and monitoring the Clusterware daemons. These agents are multithreaded daemons that manage multiple resource types and spawn new processes for different users. There are four main agents: oraagent, orarootagent, cssdagent, and cssdmonitor. These agents perform start, stop, check, and clean actions on their respective Clusterware daemons. As with internal agents, Oracle allows you to have application agents.

So to put it into context, in Oracle 11*g* Release 2 onward, the OHASd will start all other Clusterware daemons and will replace the init scripts used in pre-11*g* Release 2 to start the Clusterware daemons. Once started, OHASd will start the daemon resources, and daemon resources using their respective agents will start the underlying Clusterware agents.

Cluster Repositories

The cluster repository on Microsoft Cluster Service (MSCS) is called the Cluster Configuration Database (CCD). This is where the cluster bootstrap information resides. The CCD contains information about the physical and logical entities in a cluster. MSCS exposes a registry-like interface (API) that can be used by cluster-aware applications to retrieve and store data from the CCD. A Configuration Database Manager (CDM) resides on every node and is responsible for keeping the CCD consistent.

The cluster repository for Sun Cluster is called the Cluster Configuration Repository (CCR) and is a distributed database for storing cluster configuration and state information. Information is stored in flat ASCII files. Each node maintains its own independent copy of this database and uses a two-phase commit to ensure the consistency of the contents of CCR. One or more files on the cluster file system (CFS) act as the cluster repository.

Oracle Cluster Registry

Oracle Clusterware uses Oracle Cluster Registry to store the metadata, configuration, and state information of all the cluster resources defined in Oracle Clusterware. Oracle Cluster Registry (OCR) must be accessible to all nodes in the cluster, and Oracle Universal Installer fails to install all nodes in the installer that does not have proper permissions to access the Oracle Cluster Registry files, which are binary files and cannot be edited by any other Oracle tools. The OCR is used to bootstrap the CSS for port information, nodes in the cluster, and similar information. The Cluster Synchronization Services daemon (CSSd) updates the OCR during cluster setup, and once the cluster is set up, OCR is used for read-only operations. Exceptions are any change in a resource status which triggers an OCR update, services going up or down, network failovers, ONS and change in application states, and policy changes.

OCR is the central repository for the CRS and keeps the details of the services and status of the resources. OCR is the registry equivalent of Microsoft Windows, which stores name/value pairs of information, such as resources that are used to manage the resource equivalents by the CRS stack. Resources with the CRS stack are components that are managed by the CRS and need to store some basic demographic information about the resources—the good state, the bad state, and the callout scripts. All such information makes it into the OCR. The OCR is also used to bootstrap CSS for the port information, nodes in the cluster, and similar information. This is a binary file and cannot be edited by any other Oracle tools.

Oracle Universal Installer gives the option to mirror the OCR file during installation of Oracle Clusterware. Although this is important, it is not mandatory. The OCR file should be mirrored if the underlying storage does not guarantee continuous access to the OCR file. The mirror OCR file has the same content as the primary OCR file and must be stored on shared storage, such as a cluster file system or raw device. Oracle stores the location of the OCR file in a text file called ocr.loc, which is located in different places depending on the operating system. For example, on Linux-based systems the ocr.loc file is placed under the /etc/oracle directory, and for UNIX-based systems the ocr.loc is placed on /var/opt/oracle. Windows systems uses the registry key Hkey_Local_Machine\software\Oracle\ocr to store the location of the ocr.loc file.

Oracle Universal Installer (OUI) also uses OCR during installation time. All the CSS daemons have read-only access during startup. Oracle uses an in-memory copy of OCR on each cluster node to optimize the queries against the OCR by various clients, such as CRS, CSS, SRVCTL, NETCA, Enterprise Manager, and DBCA. Each cluster node has its own private copy of the OCR, but to ensure the atomic updates against the OCR, no more than one CRSD process in a cluster is allowed to write into the shared OCR file.

This master CRSd process refreshes the OCR cache on all cluster nodes. Clients communicate with the local CRSd process to access the local copy of the OCR and contact the master CRSd process via the local CRSd process for any updates on the physical OCR binary file. OCR also maintains the dependency hierarchy and status information of the cluster resources defined within the cluster. For example, there is a service resource that cannot be started until the dependent database resource is up and running, and OCR maintains this information.

The Cluster Synchronization Services daemon (CSSd) updates OCR during the cluster setup. Once the cluster is set up, OCR will be used by read-only operations. During node addition or deletion, CSS updates the OCR with the new information. The CRS daemon will update the OCR about the status of the nodes during failures and reconfiguration. Other management tools such as NetCA, DBCA, and SRVCTL update the services information in the OCR as they are executed. OCR information is also cached in all nodes, and the OCR cache will benefit more of the read-only operations.

The OCR file is automatically backed up in the OCR location every four hours. These backups are stored for a week and circularly overwritten. The last three successful backups of OCR (a day old and a week old) are always available in the directory $ORA_CRS_HOME/cdata/<*cluster name*>. The OCR backup location can also be changed using the ocrconfig command-line utility. Oracle Clusterware 11*g* allows taking manual backup of the OCR binary file using the ocrconfig-manualbackup command, provided that the Oracle Clusterware is up and running on the cluster node. The user running the ocrconfig command must have administrative privileges. The ocrconfig command can also be used to list the existing backup of the OCR and the backup location, as well as to change the backup location.

Oracle Local Registry

Oracle 11*g* Release 2 introduces the concept of the Oracle Local Registry, similar to the Oracle Cluster Registry, but it only stores information about the local node. The OLR is not shared by other nodes in the cluster and used by the OHASd while starting or joining the cluster. The OLR stores information that is typically required by the OHASd, such as the version of Oracle Clusterware, the configuration, and so on.

Oracle stores the location of the OLR in a text file named /etc/oracle/olr.loc. This file will have the location of the OLR configuration file $GRID_HOME/cdata/<hostname.olr>. Oracle Local Registry is similar to OCR in terms of internal structure because it stores information in keys and the same tools can be used to either check or dump the data of OLR.

Voting Disk

A *voting disk* is a shared disk that will be accessed by all the member nodes in the cluster during an operation. The voting disk is used as a central reference for all the nodes and keeps the heartbeat information between the nodes. If any of the nodes is unable to ping the voting disk, the cluster immediately recognizes the communication failure and evicts the node from the cluster group to prevent data corruptions. The voting disk is sometimes called a "quorum device" because the split-brain resolution is decided based on the ownership of the quorum device.

The voting disk manages the cluster membership and arbitrates the cluster ownership during communication failures between the nodes. Oracle RAC uses the voting disk to determine the active instances of the cluster, and inactive instances are evicted from the cluster. Because the voting disk plays a vital role, you should mirror it. If Oracle mirroring is not used for the voting disk, external mirroring should be used.

Voting is perhaps the most universally accepted method of arbitration. It has been used for centuries in many forms for contests, for selecting members of government, and so forth. One problem with voting is plurality—the leading candidate gains more votes than the other candidates, but not more than half of the total votes cast. Other problems with voting involve ties. Ties are rare, and the node contained in the master subcluster will survive. In 11.2.0.2, we can evict the specific subcluster that has the smaller number of nodes all the time rather than guess based on the voting map.

Occasionally, voting is confused with a quorum. They are similar, but distinct. A *vote* is usually a formal expression of opinion or will in response to a proposed decision. A *quorum* is defined as the number, usually a majority of officers or members of a body, that, when duly assembled, is legally competent to transact business. Both concepts are important; the only vote that should ratify a decision is the vote of a quorum of members. For clusters, the quorum defines a viable cluster. If a node or group of nodes cannot achieve a quorum, they should not start services because they risk conflicting with an established quorum.

Oracle Virtual IP

Virtual IP is required to ensure that applications can be designed to be highly available. A system needs to eliminate all single points of failure. In Oracle, clients connected to an Oracle RAC database must be able to survive a node failure. Client applications connect to the Oracle instance and access the database through the instance. Therefore, a node failure will bring down the instance to which the client might have connected.

The first design available from Oracle was Transparent Application Failover (TAF). With TAF, a session can fail over to the surviving instances and continue processing. Various limitations exist with TAF; for instance, only query failover is supported. Also, to achieve less latency in failing over to the surviving node, Oracle tweaked the TCP timeout (platform dependent; defaults to 10 minutes in most UNIX ports). It wouldn't be a good idea to design a system in which a client takes 10 minutes to detect that there is no response from the node to which it has connected.

To address this, Oracle version 10*g* introduced a new feature called *cluster VIPs*—a cluster virtual IP address that would be used by the outside world to connect to the database. This IP address needs to be different from the set of IP addresses within the cluster. Traditionally, listeners would be listening on the public IP of the box and clients would contact the listeners on this IP. If the node dies, the client would take the TCP timeout value to detect the death of the node. In 10*g*, each node of the cluster has a VIP configured in the same subnet of the public IP. A VIP name and address must be registered in the DNS in addition to the standard static IP information. Listeners would be configured to listen on VIPs instead of the public IP.

When a node is down, the VIP is automatically failed over to one of the other nodes. During the failover, the node that gets the VIP will "re-ARP" to the world, indicating the new MAC address of the VIP. Clients who have connected to this VIP will immediately get a reset packet sent. This results in clients getting errors immediately rather than waiting for the TCP timeout value. When one node goes down in a cluster and a client is connecting to the same node, the client connection will be refused by the down node, and the client application will choose the next available node from the descriptor list to get a connection. Applications need to be written so that they catch the reset errors and handle them. Typically for queries, applications should see an ORA-3113 error.

NOTE
In computer networking, the Address Resolution Protocol (ARP) is the method of finding the host's hardware addresses (MAC address) when only the IP address is known. The hosts use ARP when they want to communicate with each other in the same network. It is also used by routers to forward a packet from one host through another router. In cluster VIP failovers, the new node that gets the VIP advertises the new ARP address to the world. This is typically known as gracious-ARP, and during this operation, the old hardware address is invalidated in the ARP cache, and all the new connections will get the new hardware address.

Application VIP

Oracle uses Virtual IP to allow Oracle database clients to rapidly recognize that a node has died, thus improving the reconnect time, and Oracle Database 10*g* Release 2 extends this capability to user applications. Application VIP is a cluster resource to manage the network IP address.

Application VIP is mostly used by an application that is accessed over the network. When an application is built dependent on Application VIP (AVIP), whenever a node goes down; the Application VIP fails over to the surviving node and restarts the application process on the surviving node.

The steps to create an application VIP are the same as creating any other cluster resource. Oracle supplies the standard action program script usrvip, which is located under the <GIRD_HOME>/bin directory. Users must use this action script to create an application VIP in Oracle Cluster. DBAs always wonder what is the difference between a normal VIP and an application VIP. Upon failover to a surviving node, normal VIP does not accept connections and forces clients to reconnect using another address, whereas application VIP remains fully functional after it is relocated to another cluster node and it continuously accepts connections.

Single Client Access Name

SCAN (Single Client Access Name) is a single network name that resolves to three different IP addresses registered either in DNS or GNS. During installation of Oracle Grid Infrastructure, Oracle creates three SCAN listeners and SCAN VIPs. If GNS (Grid Name Server) is not used, then SCAN must be registered in DNS before installation of the Oracle Grid Infrastructure. Oracle fails over SCAN VIP and the listener to another node in case of failure. Each database instance registers itself to the local listener and SCAN listener using the database initialization parameter REMOTE_LISTENER because this is the only way the SCAN listener knows about the location of the database instances. The SRVCTL utility can be used to manage and monitor the SCAN resources in the cluster.

SCAN allows users to connect to the database in the cluster using the EZconnect or jdbc thin driver, as shown here:

```
sqlplus system/password@my-scan:1521/oemdb
jdbc:oracle:thin:@my-scan:1521/oemdb
```

SCAN eases the client connection management because there is no need to change the client connection strings even if the client's target database is moved to a different node in the cluster. With more and more customers deploying Oracle RAC and building shared database services, there's always a demand to simplify the client connect management and failover capabilities between moved database instances. For example, prior to Oracle 11g Release 2, there was no way except modifying the service to notify the client connection that the database instance it is intending to connect to using the Oracle RAC service has been moved to another cluster node. SCAN allows failover to the moved database instances without modifying the Oracle RAC service. The following steps explain how a client connects to the database in a cluster using SCAN:

1. The TNS layer retrieves the IP address of the SCAN from the Domain Name Server or Grid Name Server; it then load balances and fails over across the IP address.

2. The SCAN listener is now aware of databases in the cluster and will redirect the connection to the target database node VIP.

Also with 11g Release 2, Oracle provides self-management of the network requirements of the cluster by supporting DHCP for private interconnect and virtual IP addresses. Oracle needs an optimized way to resolve the IP address to a name; hence, it developed its own Grid Name Service, which is linked to the Domain Name Service and allows users to connect to the cluster and the databases in the cluster. Oracle uses a dedicated subdomain and a virtual IP GNS (aka

GNS VIP) that is registered in the DNS. Each cluster will have its own GNS, GNS virtual IP, and a dedicated subdomain, and the subdomain will forward all requests for addresses in the subdomain to the GNS virtual IP. Oracle fails over the GNS and GNS virtual IP to another node in case of node failure.

When using GNS and DHCP, Oracle obtains the virtual IP address from the DHCP server and configures the SCAN name during cluster configuration. Oracle dynamically obtains new IP addresses from the DHCP server and configures the cluster resource whenever a node joins the cluster. Oracle does not use DHCP for the GNS VIP for obvious reasons—it must be known to the cluster prior to installing the Oracle Grid Infrastructure. There are significant changes in Oracle 11*g* Release 2 in terms of starting the GNS service as well as other Oracle Grid Infrastructure daemons.

Networking Stack Components

The Oracle Grid Infrastructure requires fast communication over the public and private networks between the cluster nodes; hence, all the network components enabling this communication between the cluster nodes are very important, and it is not possible to build the Oracle Real Application Cluster database without these network components.

Network Interface Cards

Oracle requires each cluster node to have at least two network interface cards—one for the public network and one for the private network. Four are preferred when bonded and for HA. Otherwise, single interfaces are a point of failure unless one creates a VLAN on the two interfaces bonded and exposes it as a separate interface name associated with each network. The interface cards must be the same on all cluster nodes in an Oracle cluster. The network interface card for the public network must support TCP/IP and must have a valid IP address and an associated hostname registered in the domain name server.

You can complete the Oracle Grid Infrastructure installation by just registering the hostname in the /etc/hosts file; however, it is *strongly* recommended for an associated hostname to be registered in the domain name server. The network interface card for the private network must support UDP (User Data Program). Performance of the Oracle Real Application Cluster depends on the speed of the private network; hence, a high-speed network interface card such as Gigabit or higher is recommended.

Network IP Addresses

The public network interface on each cluster node must have a valid public IP address to identify the cluster node on the public network, and the public IP address must be associated with a hostname registered in the Domain Name Service (DNS). Sometimes more public IP addresses are required depending on the redundancy technology used to team or bond network interface cards. For example, IPMP on the Solaris operating system would require three public IP addresses.

Each cluster node must have assigned an unused virtual IP address associated with a virtual hostname registered in DNS. Oracle will configure this virtual IP address during installation of the Oracle Grid Infrastructure. This virtual IP address must have the same subnet as the public IP address configured for the public network interface card.

Each cluster node must have a private IP address for the private interface card. It is recommended that the private IP address be from a nonroutable private network. Oracle does not require a private hostname and IP address to be registered in DNS because this private IP address must be known to cluster nodes only, so a private hostname can be registered in the /etc/hosts file of each cluster node. An Oracle cluster requires three IP addresses for SCAN that have the same subnet as the public IP address.

Cluster Interconnects

Cluster interconnect is another important component in Oracle RAC. It is a communication path used by the cluster for the synchronization of resources and is also used in some cases for the transfer of data from one instance to another. Typically, the interconnect is a network connection that is dedicated to the server nodes of a cluster (and thus is sometimes referred to as a *private* interconnect) and has a high bandwidth and low latency. Different hardware platforms and different clustering software have different protocol implementations for the high-speed interconnect.

Oracle RAC is all about scalability and high availability, so every effort must be made to configure redundant hardware components to avoid and single point of failure. Therefore, it is highly recommended to configure redundant network interface cards for private and public networks. Different technologies are available to bond network interface cards together, such as teaming on Linux and IPMP on the Solaris operating system. Active/Passive teaming of the network interface cards works fine but users can configure the redundant network interface cards in Active/Active configuration, where each network interface card transmits and receives network packets.

Table 3-4 lists the various interconnects used by the implementations based on the clusterware used and network hardware. Using vendor-specific interconnects is often discouraged by Oracle because they make troubleshooting more complex than with the standard open-system protocols.

Network Bonding

At the network level, a failure in a NIC can cause an outage to the cluster, especially if the failure occurs at the interface on which the interconnect is configured. To achieve high availability at this layer, network bonding is recommended. Bonding allows a node to see multiple physical NICs as a single logical unit.

The Linux kernel includes a bonding module that can be used to achieve software-level NIC teaming. The kernel-bonding module can be used to team multiple physical interfaces to a single logical interface, which is used to achieve fault tolerance and load balancing. The bonding driver is available as part of the Linux kernel version 2.4 or later. Because the bonding module is delivered as part of the Linux kernel, it can be configured independently from the interface driver vendor (different interfaces can constitute a single logical interface).

Various hardware vendors provide different types of NIC bonding solutions for the network interconnect resiliency. Typically, bonding offers the following benefits:

- **Bandwidth scalability**   Adding a network card doubles the network bandwidth. It can be used to improve aggregate throughput.

- **High availability**   Provides redundancy or link aggregation of computer ports. Failure of a network interface card (NIC) does not induce a cluster outage because the traffic is routed through the other network.

- **Load balancing**   Port aggregation supports true load balancing and failure recovery capabilities as well as distributes traffic evenly across the aggregated links.

Operating System	Clusterware	Network Hardware	RAC Protocol
HP OpenVMS	HP OpenVMS	Memory Channel	TCP
HP OpenVMS	HP OpenVMS	Gigabit Ethernet	TCP
HP Tru64	HP TruCluster	Memory Channel	RDG
HP Tru64	HP TruCluster	Memory Channel	UDP
HP Tru64	HP TruCluster	Gigabit Ethernet	RDG
HP Tru64	HP TruCluster	Gigabit Ethernet	UDP
HP-UX	Oracle Clusterware	Hyper fabric	UDP
HP-UX	Oracle Clusterware	Gigabit Ethernet	UDP
HP-UX	HP Serviceguard	Hyper fabric	UDP
HP-UX	HP Serviceguard	Gigabit Ethernet	UDP
HP-UX	Veritas Cluster Server	Gigabit Ethernet	LLT
HP-UX	Veritas Cluster Server	Gigabit Ethernet	UDP
IBM AIX	Oracle Clusterware	Gigabit Ethernet (FDDI)	UDP
IBM AIX	HACMP	Gigabit Ethernet (FDDI)	UDP
Linux	Oracle Clusterware	Gigabit Ethernet	UDP
MS Windows	Oracle Clusterware	Gigabit Ethernet	TCP
Sun Solaris	Oracle Clusterware	Gigabit Ethernet	UDP
Sun Solaris	Fujitsu Primecluster	Gigabit Ethernet	ICF
Sun Solaris	Sun Cluster	SCI Interconnect	RSM
Sun Solaris	Sun Cluster	Firelink interconnect	RSM
Sun Solaris	Sun Cluster	Gigabit Ethernet	UDP
Sun Solaris	Veritas Cluster Server	Gigabit Ethernet	LLT
Sun Solaris	Veritas Cluster Server	Gigabit Ethernet	UDP

TABLE 3-4   *Interconnects Based on Clusterware and Hardware*

■ **Single MAC address**   Because port-aggregated networks share a single, logical MAC address, there is no need to assign individual addresses to aggregated ports.

■ **Flexibility**   Ports can be aggregated to achieve higher performance whenever network congestion occurs.

Interconnect Switch

A private network between cluster nodes must be configured using a high-bandwidth network switch (Gigabit or higher) that supports TCP/IP. The Oracle requirement is to have a high-bandwidth nonroutable private network between the cluster nodes. Generally, big organizations share the network switches and are mostly reluctant to have a dedicated network switch for the Oracle Real Application Cluster databases. Users can use the shared network switches for the private interconnect and can follow the given guidelines to choose the right private interconnect:

- Oracle prefers using a dedicated high-bandwidth network switch such as Gigabit network switch.

- If you're using the shared network switch, then use a dedicated untagged private nonroutable VLAN. VLANs should not span the switchblades. Using a VLAN may have lots of advantages, but it is not superior to a dedicated switch. An overloaded backplane or processor on the physical switch will adversely impact the performance of the Cache Fusion traffic over the private network; this is why Oracle prefers using the dedicated physical switch for private interconnects.

- Always configure the network interface card on the fastest PCI bus available on the cluster nodes.

- Make sure that network interface cards are switched to autonegotiate and are configured for the maximum supported bandwidth.

- Jumbo frames can be configured for private network interface cards provided the private interconnect switch supports the jumbo frames.

- Consider configuring redundant network switches for interconnect because failure in a network switch can bring the whole Oracle RAC database down.

The basic requirement of an interconnect is to provide reliable communication between nodes, but this cannot be achieved by a crossover cable between the nodes. However, using a crossover cable as the interconnect may be appropriate for development or demonstration purposes. Substituting a normal crossover cable is not officially supported in production Oracle RAC implementations for the following reasons:

- Crossover cables do not provide complete electrical insulation between nodes. Failure of one node because of a short circuit or because of electrical interference will bring down the surviving node.

- Using crossover cables instead of a high-speed switch greatly limits the scalability of the clusters because only two nodes can be clustered using a crossover cable.

- Failure of one node brings down the entire cluster because the cluster manager cannot exactly detect the failed/surviving node. Had there been a switch during split-brain resolution, the surviving node could easily deduct the heartbeat and take ownership of the quorum device and node failures could be easily detected.

- Crossover cables do not detect split-brain situations as effectively as a communication interface through switches. Split-brain resolution is the effective part in cluster management during communication failures.

Node Time Synchronization
Time on each cluster node must be synchronized because different time stamps on the cluster nodes can lead to false node eviction in the cluster. All operating systems provide a Network Time Protocol feature, which must be configured and used before the Oracle Grid Infrastructure is installed.

Split-Brain Resolution

In the Oracle RAC environment, server nodes communicate with each other using high-speed private interconnects. The high-speed interconnect is a redundant network that is exclusively used for inter-instance communication and some data block traffic. A *split-brain* situation occurs when all the links of the private interconnect fail to respond to each other, but the instances are still up and running. So each instance thinks that the other instances are dead, and that it should take over the ownership.

In a split-brain situation, instances independently access the data and modify the same blocks, and the database will end up with changed data blocks overwritten, which could lead to data corruption. To avoid this, various algorithms have been implemented.

In the Oracle RAC environment, the Instance Membership Recovery (IMR) service is one of the efficient algorithms used to detect and resolve the split-brain syndrome. When one instance fails to communicate with the other instance, or when one instance becomes inactive for some reason and is unable to issue the control file heartbeat, the split brain is detected and the detecting instance will evict the failed instance from the database. This process is called *node eviction*. Detailed information is written in alert log and trace files, and this is also discussed in detail in Chapter 14.

Oracle Kernel Components

The Oracle kernel components in the Oracle RAC environment are the set of additional background processes in each instance. The buffer cache and shared pool become global in the Oracle RAC environment, and managing the resources without conflicts and corruptions requires special handling. The new background processes in the Oracle RAC environment, along with those normal background processes that usually exist in single instances, manage the global resources effectively.

Global Cache and Global Enqueue Services

In Oracle RAC, as more than one instance is accessing the resource, the instances require better coordination at the resource management level. Otherwise, data corruption may occur. Each instance will have its own set of buffers but will be able to request and receive data blocks currently held in another instance's cache. Buffer manipulation in the Oracle RAC environment is quite different from a single-instance environment because at any time only one set of processes may be accessing the buffer. In Oracle RAC, the buffer cache of one node may contain data that is requested by another node. The management of data sharing and exchange in this environment is done by the Global Cache Services (GCS).

Global Resource Directory

All the resources in the cluster group form a central repository of resources called the Global Resource Directory (GRD), which is integrated and distributed. Each instance masters some set of resources and together all instances form the GRD. The resources in the cluster group are equally distributed among the nodes based on their weight. The GRD is managed by two services called Global Cache Services (GCS) and Global Enqueue Services (GES). GCS and GES together form and manage the GRD (called the DLM in prior cluster releases such as Oracle Parallel Server, and often still referred to as such in some Oracle documentation).

When one instance departs the cluster, the GRD portion of that instance needs to be redistributed to the surviving nodes. Similarly, when a new instance enters the cluster, the GRD portions of the existing instances must be redistributed to create the GRD portion of the new instance. The components of the GRD and management issues are discussed in Chapter 11.

Oracle RAC Background Processes

Oracle RAC databases have two or more instances with their own memory structures and background processes. Other than the normal single-instance background processes, some additional processes are started to manage the shared resources. Thus, the Oracle RAC database has the same structure of the single-instance Oracle database plus additional processes and memory structures that are specific to Oracle RAC. These processes maintain cache coherency across the nodes.

Maintaining cache coherency is an important part of an Oracle RAC. *Cache coherency* is the technique of keeping multiple copies of a buffer consistent between different Oracle instances (or disjoint caches) on different nodes. Global cache management ensures that access to a master copy of a data block in one buffer cache is coordinated with the copy of the block in another buffer cache. This ensures the most recent copy of a block in a buffer cache contains all changes that are made to that block by any instance in the system, regardless of whether those changes have been committed on the transaction level.

The Importance of Coordination

You must understand why inter-instance cache coordination is necessary in an Oracle RAC environment. Consider a two-instance environment without any cache coordination and communication among the instances, as shown in Figure 3-3:

1. Referring to Figure 3-3, consider at time t1, instance A reads a block in its buffer cache and modifies row 1 in it. The modified block is still in its buffer cache and has not yet been written to disk.

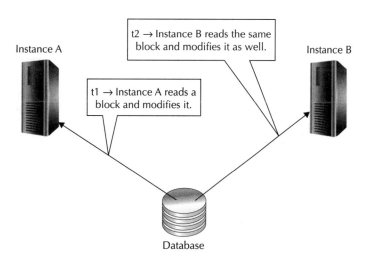

FIGURE 3-3 *Instances read a block without any coordination.*

2. Sometime later at time t2, instance B reads the same block in its buffer cache and modifies another row in that block. Instance B also has not written the block to disk, thus the disk still contains the old version of the block.

3. Now at time t3, instance A writes the block to disk. At this stage, modifications from instance A are written to disk (see Figure 3-4).

4. Later at time t4, instance B writes the block to disk. It overwrites the block written by instance A in step 3. As you can easily infer, the changes made to the block by instance A are lost (see Figure 3-5).

This scenario and many other similar situations require that when data is simultaneously accessed by multiple machines, the read and especially the write activities must be coordinated

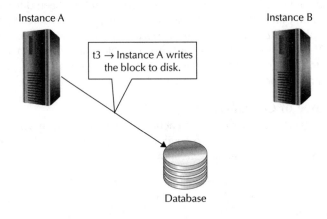

FIGURE 3-4   *Instance A writes the block to disk without coordination.*

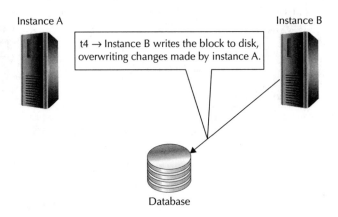

FIGURE 3-5   *Instance B overwrites the changes made by instance A.*

among these machines or else data integrity problems will result, which may manifest as data corruption.

Now let's repeat the preceding operation sequence in the presence of coordination (more details later in this chapter):

1. At time t1, when instance A needs a data block with an intent to modify, it reads the block from disk. However, before reading, it must inform the GCS (DLM) of its intention to do so. GCS keeps track of the lock status of the block being modified by instance A by keeping an exclusive lock against the block on behalf of instance A.

2. At time t2, instance B wants to modify the same block. Before doing so, it must inform the GCS of its intention to modify the block. When GCS receives the request from instance B, it asks the current lock holder instance A to release the lock. Thus, GCS ensures that instance B gets the latest version of the block and also passes on the write privilege to it (exclusive lock).

3. At time t3, instance B gets the latest (current) version of the block that has the changes made by instance A and modifies it.

4. At any point in time, only one instance has the current copy of the block. Only that instance can write the block to disk, thereby ensuring that all the changes to the block are preserved and written to disk when needed.

The GCS thus maintains data coherency and coordination by keeping track of the lock status of each block that is read and/or modified by the server nodes in the cluster. GCS guarantees that only one copy of the block in memory can be modified and that all the modifications are written to disk at the appropriate time. It maintains the cache coherence among the nodes and guarantees the integrity of the data. GCS is an in-memory database that contains information about the current locks on blocks and also keeps track of instances that are waiting to acquire locks on blocks. This is known as *Parallel Cache Management (PCM)* and has been a central feature of Oracle clustered databases since the introduction of Oracle Parallel Server (OPS) in the early 1990s.

PCM uses distributed locks on the resources to coordinate access to resources by different instances of an Oracle RAC environment. The GRM helps to coordinate and communicate the lock requests from Oracle processes between instances in the Oracle RAC environment.

Each instance has a buffer cache in its SGA. To ensure that each Oracle RAC database instance obtains the block that it needs to satisfy a query or transaction, Oracle RAC instances use two processes: the GCS and the GES. The GCS and GES maintain records of the lock status of each datafile and each cached block using a GRD. The GRD contents are distributed across all of the active instances.

Hence, it is good to increase the SGA size by a factor but not more than 5 percent of the total SGA size. Tests have found that the larger your block size, the lower the memory overheads for the extra GCS, GES, and GRD components in the SGA. For large SGAs that exceed 20GB, it has been noted that the overhead is dependent on the block size used and could be around 600MB to 700MB for a 16KB block–sized database.

The *cost* (or overhead) of cache coherency is defined as the need to check with other instances if a particular access is permitted before granting any access to a specific shared resource. Algorithms optimize the need to coordinate on each and every access, but some overhead is incurred. Cache coherency means that the contents of the caches in different nodes are in a well-defined state with respect to each other. Cache coherency identifies the most up-to-date copy of a resource, also called the "master copy." In case of node failure, no vital information is lost (such as committed transaction state) and atomicity is maintained. This requires additional logging or copying of data but is not part of the locking system.

A *resource* is an identifiable entity—that is, it has a name or reference. The entity referred to is usually a memory region, a disk file, or an abstract entity. A resource can be owned or locked in various states, such as exclusive or shared. By definition, any shared resource is lockable. If it is not shared, no access conflict will occur. If it is shared, access conflicts must be resolved, typically with a lock. Although the terms *lock* and *resource* refer to entirely separate objects, the terms are sometimes (unfortunately) used interchangeably.

A *global resource* is visible and used throughout the cluster. A *local resource* is used by only one instance. It may still have locks to control access by the multiple processes of the instance, but no access to it occurs from outside the instance. Data buffer cache blocks are the most obvious and most heavily used global resource. Other data item resources are also global in the cluster, such as transaction enqueues and database data structures. The data buffer cache blocks are handled by the Global Cache Service (GCS), also called Parallel Cache Management (PCM).

The nondata block resources are handled by Global Enqueue Services (GES), also called Non-Parallel Cache Management (Non-PCM). The Global Resource Manager (GRM), also called the Distributed Lock Manager (DLM), keeps the lock information valid and correct across the cluster.

All caches in the SGA are either global and must be coherent across all instances, or they are local. The library, row (also called dictionary), and buffer caches are global. The large and Java pool buffers are local. For Oracle RAC, the GRD is global in itself and also used to control the coherency.

After one instance caches data, in some cases other instances within the same cluster database can acquire a block image from another instance in the same database faster than by reading the block from disk. Therefore, Cache Fusion moves current copies of blocks between instances rather than re-reading the blocks from disk under certain conditions. When a consistent block is needed or a changed block is required on another instance, Cache Fusion can transfer the block image between the affected instances. RAC uses the private interconnect for inter-instance communication and block transfers. GCS manages the block transfers between the instances.

The GRD manages the locking or ownership of all resources that are not limited to a single instance in Oracle RAC. The GRD comprises GCS, which handles the data blocks, and GES, which handles the enqueues and other global resources.

Each process has a set of roles, and we will study them in detail in the following sections. In Oracle RAC, the library cache and shared pool are globally coordinated. All the resources are managed by locks, and the key background process also manages the locks. GCS and GES use the following processes to manage the resources. These Oracle RAC–specific processes and the GRD collaborate to enable Cache Fusion:

- **LMS**   Global Cache Services process
- **LMON**   Global Enqueue Services Monitor
- **LMD**   Global Enqueue Services daemon
- **LCK0**   Instance Enqueue process
- **DIAG**   Diagnostic daemon

The LMON and LMD processes communicate with their partner processes on the remote nodes. Other processes may have message exchanges with peer processes on the other nodes (for example, PQ). The LMS process, for example, may directly receive lock requests from remote foreground processes.

LMS: Global Cache Services Process

LMS is a process used in Cache Fusion. The acronym is derived from the Lock Manager Server process. It enables consistent copies of blocks to be transferred from a holding instance's buffer cache to a requesting instance's buffer cache without a disk write under certain conditions. It also retrieves requests from the server queue queued by LMD to perform requested lock operations.

It also rolls back any uncommitted transactions for any blocks that are being requested for a consistent read by the remote instance. LMS processes also control the flow of messages between instances. Each instance can have up to 10 LMS processes, though the actual number of LMS processes varies according to the amount of messaging traffic between nodes. The hidden parameter _lm_lms can also be used manually to control the number of LMS processes. This is no longer an underscore parameter with recent releases, although it is not advocated except when running on systems that display threads as cores. If this parameter is not set manually, the number of LMS processes automatically started during instance startup is a function of the CPU_COUNT of that node and is usually adequate for most types of applications. It is only under special circumstances that you may need to tweak this parameter to increase the default number of LMS processes.

LMS processes can also be started dynamically by the system based on demand, and this is controlled by the parameter _lm_dynamic_lms. By default, this parameter is set to FALSE. In addition, LMS processes manage Lock Manager Server requests for GCS resources and send them to a service queue to be handled by the LMS process. It also handles global lock deadlock detection and monitors for lock conversion timeouts.

LMON: Global Enqueue Services Monitor

LMON is the Lock Monitor process and is responsible for managing the Global Enqueue Services (GES). It maintains consistency of GCS memory in case of process death. LMON is also responsible for the cluster reconfiguration and locks reconfiguration when an instance joins or leaves the cluster. It also checks the instance death and listens for local messages. The LMON process also generates a detailed trace file that tracks instance reconfigurations.

The background LMON process monitors the entire cluster to manage global resources. LMON manages instance deaths and the associated recovery for any failed instance. In particular, LMON handles the part of recovery associated with global resources. LMON-provided services are also known as Cluster Group Services (CGS).

LMD: Global Enqueue Services Daemon

LMD is the daemon process that manages Enqueue Manager Service requests for the GCS. The acronym *LMD* refers literally to the Lock Manager Daemon, the term used for the process in OPS. The resource agent process manages requests for resources to control access to blocks. The LMD process also handles deadlock detection and remote resource requests. Remote resource requests originate from another instance.

LCK0: Instance Enqueue Process

The Lock (LCK) process manages instance resource requests and cross-instance call operations for shared resources. It also builds a list of invalid lock elements and validates lock elements during recovery. An instance can use only a single LCK process because primary functionality is handled by the LMS process.

DIAG Process

DIAG is a lightweight daemon process for all the diagnostic needs of an instance in an Oracle RAC environment. Although several debugging and diagnostic tools are available, they do not provide a single interface for a cluster environment and are not cluster-ready, making diagnosis across multiple instances difficult.

To solve the cluster-related debugging, the DIAG framework was introduced with the DIAG daemon. This framework does not interfere with or affect the normal operation of the system. DIAG works independently from an instance and relies only on services provided by the underlying operating system. This is integrated with the RDBMS kernel for startup and shutdown and its need to access the SGA for trace buffers. This framework implements clusterwide debugging using the oradebug utility.

Process Monitor (PMON) restarts a new DIAG process to continue its service if the DIAG process dies. The DIAG daemon also monitors the health of the local Oracle RAC instance. On failure of an essential process, the DIAG in the local instance can capture the system state and other useful information for later diagnosis and then notify DIAG on the other instances to capture similar information. This provides a snapshot view of the entire cluster environment. DIAG will be responsible for monitoring the liveliness of operations of the local Oracle RAC instance and performing any necessary recovery, if an operational hang is detected.

In a Nutshell

This chapter introduced the various building blocks of Oracle RAC. Oracle Grid Infrastructure provides the foundation for Oracle RAC scalability and availability. Because storage is shared across all the nodes, it is very important to establish redundancy at the disk level, and the RAID technologies help to build a very scalable and highly available storage subsystem.

Next, the storage the network components play a vital role in building the cluster. We also looked into the different options available for storage and interconnects, which are key to the systems in supporting scalability and availability. Bonded network interfaces at the operating system level provide the redundancy and required scalability for cluster operations. Redundant network switches should also be part of high-availability architecture.

You should understand the importance of resource coordination and the kernel components involved in the clusterwide operations. Global Cache Services and Global Enqueue Services ensure the resources are properly queued and synchronize the database operations. With this background in mind, we will begin preparing the hardware to install Oracle RAC in the next chapter.

PART
II

Installation, Configuration, and Storage

CHAPTER
4

Oracle Grid
Infrastructure
Installation

his chapter focuses on installing the Oracle Grid Infrastructure, which includes preparing the hardware, storage, and networking layer components for clustering, along with the cluster software install. The Oracle Grid Infrastructure must be installed and running before you install the RDBMS software. Figure 4-1 shows the installation process for the Oracle 11g RAC. The term *Grid Infrastructure* is new in Oracle 11g Release 2 and meant for Oracle Clusterware and ASM. This was known as Oracle Clusterware in Oracle 11g Release 1 and earlier versions.

The first step involves configuring the operating system and hardware for the Oracle Grid Infrastructure and RDBMS software. Each server in the cluster will have at minimum one public network interface and one private network interface. The *public network interface* is the standard network connection that connects the server to all of the other computers in your network. The *private network interface* is normally a nonroutable private network connection shared by only the servers in the cluster. Some servers have additional network interfaces for management framework, and they are not critical for the installation or functioning of the Oracle Grid Infrastructure. The Oracle Grid Infrastructure and Oracle RAC software use the private network interface to communicate with the other servers in the cluster.

Another important step is the decision about shared storage. The *shared storage* for datafiles is an important step in hardware preparation. As a fundamental requirement for high availability, all the database files in the cluster will be stored on shared storage that is separate from the server nodes in the cluster. The shared storage allows multiple database instances, running on different servers, to access the same database information and ensures that if one or more server nodes fail, all remaining nodes will continue to have access to all database files.

After the shared storage for the datafiles is defined, the next step is installing the Oracle Grid Infrastructure, which logically binds multiple servers into a cluster. During the Oracle Grid

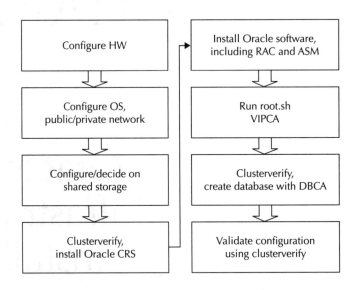

FIGURE 4-1   *Oracle RAC installation flowchart*

Infrastructure install, you specify the location at which to create two Oracle Grid Infrastructure components: a voting disk to record node membership information and the Oracle Cluster Registry (OCR) to record cluster configuration information. Starting with Oracle 11*g* Release 2, the voting disk and OCR can be stored inside the Oracle ASM. However, a local copy of OCR known as Oracle Local Registry (OLR) is stored along with the Oracle Grid Infrastructure binaries. The Oracle Grid Infrastructure install is performed on one server and will be automatically installed on the other servers in the cluster during the remote operation phases of the Oracle Universal Installer.

At the end of the Oracle Grid Infrastructure install, Oracle configures the virtual IP (VIP) addresses, ASM, the local listener, and the SCAN listeners for the servers in the cluster. Clients use a single client access name to connect to the database service in the cluster. The SCAN is a domain name that resolves to three IP addresses from the same subnet of the public network in round-robin fashion. Because the SCAN is not associated with any particular server in the cluster, there is no need to reconfigure the clients if a server is added or removed from the existing cluster.

Prior to Oracle 11*g* Release 2, clients connecting to the database using a virtual IP required reconfiguration if the connecting database service was moved onto another server in the cluster. Clients can still connect to the database service using a virtual IP, but this is not a preferred way to connect to a database service in Oracle 11*g* Release 2 RAC.

After the Oracle Grid Infrastructure is installed, if you use ASM for shared storage, you will create additional disk groups using the ASM Configuration Assistant to store the Oracle datafiles; then you will install the Oracle Database 11*g* Release 2 RAC database software and create the cluster database. The installer will recognize that the Oracle Grid Infrastructure has already been installed. Like the Oracle Grid Infrastructure install, the Oracle RAC database install is performed on one server, and the software is automatically installed on the other servers in the cluster.

After the database software is installed, you will create a cluster database using the Database Configuration Assistant (DBCA). The last step is to install the Enterprise Manager Agent. The Enterprise Manager Agent connects to the Enterprise Manager Grid Control, where you administer the Oracle RAC environment. Like the previous installs, the agent install is performed on one node in the cluster and automatically installed on the other nodes.

This chapter uses the 64-bit Linux operating system, and Oracle Database 11*g* Release 2 (11.2.0.2) is the installation. Also, this chapter assumes that the cluster servers have the minimum required hardware. Port-specific documentations and installation guides should be consulted during installation. This chapter is *not* intended to replace the Oracle installation guide, and it is always recommended that you consult the support notes from Oracle Support. However, this chapter can be used in parallel with the installation manuals.

Preinstallation Tasks

Installing the Oracle Grid Infrastructure starts with some hardware preparation steps, such as configuring network names and addresses, updating relevant configuration files, and setting up specific operating system users, groups, and privileges. Installation of the Oracle Grid Infrastructure will be smooth sailing when the required prerequisites are configured correctly.

Configuring the Network

The preinstallation tasks start with configuring the network. Multicast communication must be enabled for the private network. This is a new requirement in Oracle Grid Infrastructure 11*g* Release 2 (11.2.0.2) to provide redundancy for the cluster interconnect (private network interfaces) without using any OS-specific teaming or bonding drivers. Oracle uses multicast communication on the private network to establish initial communication with the peer servers in the cluster and later on switches to unicast communication once the communication is established. Therefore, it is very critical that you enable multicast network communication for the private network for a successful install or upgrade of Oracle Grid Infrastructure 11*g* Release 2 (11.2.0.2). Oracle has published My Oracle Support Note 1212703.1, which provides scripts to test and verify that the servers in the cluster can communicate with each other using multicasting on the private network.

NOTE
In computer networking, unicast routing is the communication protocol used for sending messages between a single sender (tx) and single receiver (rx) over a network. Multicast, on the other hand, is communication between a single sender and multiple receivers. Point-to-point communication is unicast communication, and point-to-multipoint is multicast communication.

Large installations and organizations generally use IGMP snooping to monitor the multicast traffic. If IGMP is not properly configured, it may interfere with the server's communication over the private network and break the whole Oracle RAC system.

The public and private interfaces on all cluster servers must have the same name. For example, in a two-node Oracle RAC, if the public interface name on node 1 is eth0, then the public interface name on node 2 should also be eth0.

You need to register three IP addresses in the DNS for the single client access name resolving to a domain name in round-robin fashion. Register one virtual IP for each cluster node in the DNS as well. The virtual IP must be unplumbed because the Oracle Grid Infrastructure will configure the virtual IP during the installation process.

You also need to configure the /etc/hosts file, which contains the Internet Protocol (IP) host names and addresses for the local host and other hosts in the Internet network. This file is used to resolve a name to an address (that is, to translate a host name into its Internet address). When your system is using a domain name server (DNS) for address resolution, this file is accessed only if the name server cannot resolve the host name. Oracle Grid Infrastructure 11*g* Release 2 allows you to assign IP addresses dynamically using the Oracle Grid Naming Service (GNS), which requires a DHCP service running on the public network to provide one IP address for each cluster server's VIP and three IP addresses for the single client access name addresses. For simplicity and better explanation of the whole installation and configuration process, this chapter uses manual assignment of the IP addresses.

Following is a sample hosts file. The command ping (which stands for Packet Internet Grouping) can be used to verify the configuration. Except for the VIP interface, all other interfaces, including SCAN (Single Client Access Name), should be up and running at this time. Do *not* register the SCAN name in the /etc/hosts configuration file because doing so will not allow SCAN to resolve with three different IP addresses.

```
127.0.0.1        localhost.localdomain   localhost
#Public Host Names
10.1.1.161       alpha1.us.oracle.com alpha1
10.1.1.171       alpha2.us.oracle.com    alpha2
10.1.1.181       alpha3.us.oracle.com    alpha3
10.1.1.191       alpha4.us.oracle.com    alpha4
#Private Host Names
192.168.1.161    alpha1-priv.us.oracle.com    alpha1-priv
192.168.1.171    alpha2-priv.us.oracle.com    alpha2-priv
192.168.1.181    alpha3-priv.us.oracle.com    alpha3-priv
192.168.1.191    alpha4-priv.us.oracle.com    alpha4-priv
#Virtual Host Names
10.1.1.61        alpha1-vip.us.oracle.com     alpha1-vip
10.1.1.71        alpha2-vip.us.oracle.com     alpha2-vip
10.1.1.81        alpha3-vip.us.oracle.com     alpha3-vip
10.1.1.91        alpha4-vip.us.oracle.com     alpha4-vip
```

In this entry, the IP address is specified in either dotted decimal or octal format, and the host name is specified in either relative or absolute domain name format. If you specify the absolute domain name, the portion of the name preceding the first period (.) has a maximum length of 63 characters and cannot contain blank spaces. For both formats of the name, the total number of characters cannot exceed 255 characters, and each entry must be contained on one line. Multiple host names (or aliases) can be specified.

After the hosts file is configured properly on one of the nodes, copy it to the other nodes so that they are exactly the same. The hosts file on each node needs to contain the private, public, and virtual IP (VIP) addresses and node names of each node in the cluster.

You need to edit the /etc/sysconfig/ntpd configuration file of the NTP service on each cluster node to use the slewing option to synchronize the time on each cluster node, as shown next. It is very important that the system time on all servers in the cluster is synchronized to avoid false node evictions.

```
OPTIONS="-x -u ntp:ntp -p /var/run/ntpd.pid"
```

Oracle 11g introduced the Cluster Time Synchronization Service, which will start the CTSSd in exclusive mode if NTP is not started on the cluster nodes. If the NTP service is configured and running on all nodes in the cluster, the CTSSd will run in observer mode.

Setting Up the Groups and Users

In typical Oracle RAC installations, the operating system user *oracle* will own the RDBMS binaries and all Oracle-related files. Normally this user will be the part of the DBA group. Any user who is part of the DBA group and has sysoper/sysdba privileges can connect to the *oracle* instance without supplying a password. This is called *operating system authentication*. This privileged user can also start up and shut down instances.

Oracle RAC allows using different operating system users to own different components of Oracle RAC so that people with different job responsibilities and accountabilities can manage their respective components of the whole Oracle RAC system. For example, the system admin team may use the operating system account *grid* to manage the Oracle Grid Infrastructure, whereas the database team may use the *oracle* user to manage the databases. We will use different operating system accounts in the installation process explained in this chapter. Oracle products use an operating system group called *oinstall* that is associated with the central inventory. All operating system accounts used for Oracle product installation will have *oinstall* as a primary group so that Oracle central inventory is shared by all Oracle product owners. You will create the following operating system users and groups on each cluster node before installing the Oracle Grid Infrastructure and RDBMS software:

```
#/usr/sbin/groupadd -g 501 oinstall
#/usr/sbin/groupadd -g 502 dba
#/usr/sbin/groupadd -g 504 asmadmin
#/usr/sbin/groupadd -g 506 asmdba
#/usr/sbin/groupadd -g 507 asmoper
#/usr/sbin/useradd -u 501 -g oinstall -G asmadmin,asmdba,asmoper grid
#/usr/sbin/useradd -u 502 -g oinstall -G dba,asmdba
```

Verify that the attributes (uid and gid) of the users and groups created here are identical on all cluster nodes. Internal to the operating system and cluster layer, the UIDs are compared to the UIDs of the member nodes while authorizations and permissions occur. Therefore, it is important to keep the user IDs and group IDs consistent across the nodes.

```
# id oracle
uid=502(oracle) gid=501(oinstall) groups=502(dba),501(oinstall)
# id grid
uid=501(grid) gid=501(oinstall) groups=501(oinstall),504(asmadmin),506(asmdba),
507(asmoper)
```

Configuring Shared Storage

If you decide to use Automatic Storage Management (ASM) as shared storage for the datafiles, you should configure partitions on the external shared disks. ASM requires raw disks for storage because file systems cannot be used as ASM devices. The disk partitions are without any file systems and initially owned by the *root* user. You should only create one partition per disk presented to the ASM, and each ASM disk should be of the same size for better I/O performance.

System vendors use the logical volume manager to present the external shared storage to the servers in the form of logical volumes to properly utilize the available storage space; however, using logical volumes for Oracle ASM to be used with Oracle RAC is not supported because logical volumes encapsulate the physical disk architecture and do not allow Oracle ASM to optimize the I/O on the available physical devices.

NOTE
Oracle does not support raw or block devices as shared storage for Oracle RAC in Oracle 11g Release 2 and onward. This is only supported if you are upgrading from the previous release.

Oracle provides ASM libraries to ease the management of the storage devices. The ASMLib library provides persistent paths and permissions for storage devices used with ASM. Once the ASMLib library is installed and configured on all cluster nodes, there is no need to update udev or any other device label files that typically store device paths and permissions. Oracle supplies ASMLib for each Linux distribution, which can be downloaded from the Oracle Technology Network website (www.oracle.com/technetwork/topics/linux/asmlib/index-101839.html).

ASMLib

ASMLib is a support library for Automatic Storage Management. This library provides a layer of abstraction for the devices used by ASM. The ASMLib library also allows an Oracle database using ASM more efficient access to the disk groups it is using.

Download the ASM library oracleasmlib-2.0, the Oracle ASM utility oracleasm-support-2.0, and the ASM kernel module oracleasm from the aforementioned web location and install them on each cluster node as the *root* user. Here is an example of installing ASM libraries on a Linux machine:

```
# rpm -ivh oracleasm-support-2.1.3-1.el5x86_64.rpm \
oracleasmlib-2.0.4-1.el5.x86_64.rpm \
oracleasm-2.6.18-92.1.17.0.2.el5-2.0.5-1.el5.x86_64.rpm
```

You will have to configure the Oracle ASM library driver on all nodes in the cluster. While configuring this, choose the *grid* user and the *asmdba* group as the owner of the ASM driver because the *grid* user will own the Oracle Clusterware and ASM components of the Oracle RAC. Oracle loads and runs the ASM driver on system startup according to this configuration. Here is an example of configuring ASM on a Linux machine:

```
#/etc/init.d/oracleasm configure
Configuring the Oracle ASM library driver.
This will configure the on-boot properties of the Oracle ASM library driver.
The following questions will determine whether the driver is loaded on boot
and what permissions it will have. The current values will be shown in
brackets ('[]'). Hitting <ENTER> without typing an answer will keep
that current value. Ctrl-C will abort.
Default user to own the driver interface []: grid
Default group to own the driver interface []: asmdba
Start Oracle ASM library driver on boot (y/n) [n]: y
Scan for Oracle ASM disks on boot (y/n) [y]: y
Writing Oracle ASM library driver configuration: done
Initializing the Oracle ASMLib driver: [ OK ]
Scanning the system for Oracle ASMLib disks: [ OK ]
```

Repeat this step on each cluster node. If this step is not performed, the oracleasm service will not start on the cluster node and you will not be able to use Oracle ASM as shared storage for the Oracle RAC database.

The next step after configuring the Oracle ASM driver on each cluster node is marking the shared disk partitions on the first cluster node and scanning the marked disk partitions on the other nodes in the cluster. Marking a shared disk partition is also called "creating the Oracle ASM device."

You will perform the following step on the first cluster node only to mark all candidate disk partitions to be used with Oracle ASM. This ensures the disk headers are wiped clean because ASM will not select the devices as candidates if it finds the Volume Table of Contents (VTOC) information of any volume manager or file system.

```
#dd if=/dev/zero of=/dev/sda1 bs=1M count=10
10+0 records in
10+0 records out
10485760 bytes (10 MB) copied, 0.400074 seconds, 26.2 MB/s
# dd if=/dev/zero of=/dev/sdb1 bs=1M count=10
10+0 records in
10+0 records out
10485760 bytes (10 MB) copied, 0.431521 seconds, 24.3 MB/s
# dd if=/dev/zero of=/dev/sdc1 bs=1M count=10
10+0 records in
10+0 records out
10485760 bytes (10 MB) copied, 0.414814 seconds, 25.3 MB/s
```

Once the disk headers are wiped clean, the next step is to stamp the ASM header information on the devices. The following sequence of operations mark the devices as ASM disks:

```
# /usr/sbin/oracleasm init
Creating /dev/oracleasm mount point: /dev/oracleasm
Loading module "oracleasm": oracleasm
Mounting ASMlib driver filesystem: /dev/oracleasm
[# /usr/sbin/oracleasm createdisk DISK1 /dev/sda1
Writing disk header: done
Instantiating disk: done
[# /usr/sbin/oracleasm createdisk DISK2 /dev/sdb1
Writing disk header: done
Instantiating disk: done
# /usr/sbin/oracleasm createdisk DISK3 /dev/sdc1
Writing disk header: done
Instantiating disk: done
```

Once all the candidate disk partitions are marked as candidate disks for Oracle ASM, scan the newly marked disks on the other nodes in the cluster because there is no need to mark the candidate disk partitions on each cluster node. Here is an example to scan the marked disks on other nodes in the cluster:

```
# /usr/sbin/oracleasm scandisks
Scanning system for ASM disks [ OK ]
# /usr/sbin/oracleasm scandisks
Reloading disk partitions: done
Cleaning any stale ASM disks...
Scanning system for ASM disks...
```

```
# /usr/sbin/oracleasm listdisks
DISK1
DISK2
DISK3
```

NOTE
When using Oracle ASM devices on multipath devices, update the ORACLEASM_SCANORDER and ORACLEASM_SCANEXCLUDE variables in the /etc/sysconfig/oracleasm file on all nodes in the cluster with the expected scan ordering and exclusion of the multipath devices. You should refer to My Oracle Support Note 394956.1, which explains this process in detail.

Secure Shell and User Limits Configuration

Oracle Universal Installer (OUI) installs the binaries in one node and then propagates the files to the other nodes in the cluster. The installer primarily uses the ssh and scp commands in the background during installation to run remote commands and copy files to the other nodes in the cluster.

This requires non-interactive file copying across the nodes. You must configure ssh so that these commands do not prompt for a password. Setting up scp can enable this across the nodes. You also need to turn off the banner for ssh. Unlike in previous releases of Oracle RAC, there is no need to manually configure the user equivalence for the Oracle software owners because Oracle allows you to set this up during installation of the Oracle Grid Infrastructure.

The default hard limits for Oracle software owners are not sufficient to install and configure the Oracle Grid Infrastructure. You should edit the /etc/security/limits.conf file as shown here:

```
grid soft nproc 2047
grid hard nproc 16384
grid soft nofile 1024
grid hard nofile 65536
oracle soft nproc 2047
oracle hard nproc 16384
oracle soft nofile 1024
oracle hard nofile 65536
```

You will also need to add the following line to the /etc/pam.d/login configuration file if it has not already been added:

```
session     required     pam_limit.so
```

This configuration causes the user login process to load the pam_limits.so module of PAM to further enforce/set the hard limits for the login user as defined in the /etc/security/limits.conf configuration file, because /etc/security/limits.conf is the configuration file of the pam_limits.so module of PAM.

Pluggable Authentication Module (PAM)
PAM was invented by Sun, and in the Linux operating system it provides library modules to supply a flexible authentication mechanism. Programs such as *login* and *su* can use these modules for authentication. The updated authentication schemes can be added into the PAM modules rather than changing the programs that depend on the authentication. Each PAM module has its own text configuration file, and PAM consults with these text configuration files before taking any security-related action for the application. In a nutshell, PAM provides account, authentication, and session management.

Configuring the Kernel Parameters

As the *root* user, update the kernel parameters in the /etc/sysctl.conf file on *both* nodes. If these settings are already configured, make sure they are at least set to the following values (it is OK if the values are set higher):

```
kernel.shmmni = 4096
kernel.sem = 250 32000 100 128
fs.file-max = 512 x processes (for example 6815744 for 13312 processes)
net.ipv4.ip_local_port_range = 9000 65500
net.core.rmem_default = 262144
net.core.rmem_max = 4194304
net.core.wmem_default = 262144
net.core.wmem_max = 1048576
```

NOTE
You should always refer to Oracle My Support Note 169706.1 for the latest information on the updated prerequisites (kernel, memory, swap, OS packages, and so on) prior to installing Oracle databases. Oracle regularly updates this My Oracle Support note, which covers the system and software requirements for each platform supported with the Oracle RAC database.

Oracle Validated Configuration RPM

Oracle provides a RedHat Package Manager (RPM) file for Oracle Enterprise Linux and Red Hat Linux users, which can automatically complete most of the preinstallation tasks. In a nutshell, Oracle Validated Configuration RPM can perform the following tasks:

■ Install missing operating system packages required for Oracle Grid Infrastructure

■ Configure kernel parameters and user parameters in the */etc/sysctl.conf* file

■ Create Oracle software owner, inventory, and dba group. This RPM only creates *oracle* user; if you are installing the Oracle Grid Infrastructure then you may need to create additional users manually.

You will need to register your cluster servers with Oracle Unbreakable Linux Network to use the latest enterprise channel for your operating system and hardware. Oracle uses these channels to download updates and additional software. You should navigate to http://linux.oracle.com for complete details of Oracle Unbreakable Linux Network.

Running the Cluster Verification Utility

Deploying Oracle RAC is a multistage operation, and components can malfunction at any stage due to the various dependencies at each layer.

Testing and verification are required at each stage before proceeding to the next stage. Oracle provides a tool you can use to verify the cluster setup at every stage: the cluster verification utility, or cluvfy.

The cluvfy is a standalone utility used to verify a well-formed Oracle RAC cluster. It can be used at any stage—preinstallation, configuration, or operation—because it verifies the entire cluster stack and does not perform any configuration changes on cluster or Oracle RAC operations. It can be used to verify the stage-by-stage progress during Oracle RAC installation as each stage comprises a set of operations during Oracle RAC deployment. Each stage has its own set of entry (prechecks) and/or exit (postchecks) criteria. Oracle internally runs this utility during the installation process to verify the prerequisites and provide the fix-up scripts for the fixable issue. It is good to run this utility to verify the prerequisites prior to the installation of the Oracle Grid Infrastructure, but this is not compulsory.

Cluster Verification Utility Stages

Following are the 14 stages in the Oracle RAC deployment where the cluster verification utility can be run. Note that the utility automatically checks all nodes that are specified, so it is necessary to run the utility from only one node. This utility is available in the Oracle Grid Infrastructure software media and is named runcluvfy.sh.

```
$./runcluvfy.sh stage -list
USAGE:
cluvfy stage {-pre|-post} <stage-name> <stage-specific options>  [-verbose]
Valid Stages are:
      -pre cfs          : pre-check for CFS setup
      -pre crsinst      : pre-check for CRS installation
      -pre acfscfg      : pre-check for ACFS configuration
      -pre dbinst       : pre-check for database installation
      -pre dbcfg        : pre-check for database configuration
      -pre hacfg        : pre-check for HA configuration
      -pre nodeadd      : pre-check for node addition
      -post hwos        : post-check for hardware and operating system
      -post cfs         : post-check for CFS setup
      -post crsinst     : post-check for CRS installation
      -post acfscfg     : post-check for ACFS configuration
      -post hacfg       : post-check for HA configuration
      -post nodeadd     : post-check for node addition
      -post nodedel     : post-check for node deletion
```

At the first stage in preparing the hardware for Oracle RAC installation, you can use clusterverify to check the hardware for basic network connectivity and most common operating system requirements. It also checks the software owner privileges and access to shared storage from both the nodes. It can be invoked by using the following command-line option. The output text (edited for clarity and simplicity) will be similar to the following:

```
$ ./runcluvfy.sh stage -post hwos -n alpha1,alpha2,alpha3 -verbose
Performing post-checks for hardware and operating system setup
Checking node reachability...
Check: Node reachability from node "alpha1"
 Result: Node connectivity check passed
<<output trimmed>>

Checking for multiple users with UID value 0
Result: Check for multiple users with UID value 0 passed
Check: Time zone consistency
Result: Time zone consistency check passed
Shared storage check was successful on nodes "alpha1,alpha3,alpha2"
Post-check for hardware and operating system setup was successful.
```

Note that the cluster verification utility can also be used to verify the components level. An individual subsystem or a module of the Oracle RAC cluster is known as a *component* in the utility. Availability, integrity, liveliness, sanity, or any other specific property of a cluster component can be verified. Oracle has enhanced the cluster verification utility to include almost all components of Oracle Grid Infrastructure 11*g* Release 2.

The following components are listed in the cluster verification utility:

```
$ ./runcluvfy.sh comp -list
Valid Components are:
        nodereach     : checks reachability between nodes
        nodecon       : checks node connectivity
        cfs           : checks CFS integrity
        ssa           : checks shared storage accessibility
        space         : checks space availability
        sys           : checks minimum system requirements
        clu           : checks cluster integrity
        clumgr        : checks cluster manager integrity
        ocr           : checks OCR integrity
        olr           : checks OLR integrity
        ha            : checks HA integrity
        crs           : checks CRS integrity
        nodeapp       : checks node applications existence
        admprv        : checks administrative privileges
        peer          : compares properties with peers
        software      : checks software distribution
        acfs          : checks ACFS integrity
        asm           : checks ASM integrity
        gpnp          : checks GPnP integrity
        gns           : checks GNS integrity
        scan          : checks SCAN configuration
        ohasd         : checks OHASD integrity
        clocksync     : checks Clock Synchronization
```

```
    vdisk              : checks Voting Disk configuration and UDEV settings
    dhcp               : checks DHCP configuration
    dns                : checks DNS configuration
```

Once the hardware, operating system, and network are verified, the cluster is ready for the Oracle Grid Infrastructure installation. Oracle Cluster Ready Services is the foundation for the Oracle Grid Infrastructure and using the following option in the cluster verification utility can check the readiness for the CRS installation. It should be invoked as the OS user *grid* and the nodes should be listed as command-line parameter arguments. The resulting output is edited for clarity.

```
$ ./runcluvfy.sh stage -pre crsinst -n alpha1,alpha2,alpha3
Performing pre-checks for cluster services setup
Checking node reachability...
Node reachability check passed from node "alpha1"
Checking user equivalence...
User equivalence check passed for user "grid"
Checking node connectivity...
Checking hosts config file...
Verification of the hosts config file successful
Node connectivity passed for subnet "10.1.1.0" with node(s)
alpha1,alpha3,alpha2
TCP connectivity check passed for subnet "10.1.1.0"
Node connectivity passed for subnet "192.168.1.0" with node(s)
alpha1,alpha3,alpha2
TCP connectivity check passed for subnet "192.168.1.0"
Interfaces found on subnet "10.1.1.0" that are likely candidates for VIP are:
alpha1 eth0:10.1.1.161
alpha3 eth0:10.1.1.181
alpha2 eth0:10.1.1.171
Interfaces found on subnet "192.168.1.0" that are likely candidates for a
private interconnect are:
alpha1 eth1:192.168.1.161
alpha3 eth1:192.168.1.181
alpha2 eth1:192.168.1.171
Node connectivity check passed
Checking ASMLib configuration.
Check for ASMLib configuration passed.
Total memory check passed
Available memory check passed
Swap space check passed
Free disk space check passed for "alpha1:/tmp"
Free disk space check passed for "alpha3:/tmp"
Free disk space check passed for "alpha2:/tmp"
Check for multiple users with UID value 54321 passed
User existence check passed for "oracle"
Group existence check passed for "oinstall"
Group existence check passed for "dba"
Membership check for user "oracle" in group "oinstall" [as Primary] passed
Membership check for user "oracle" in group "dba" passed
Run level check passed
```

```
Hard limits check passed for "maximum open file descriptors"
Soft limits check passed for "maximum open file descriptors"
Hard limits check passed for "maximum user processes"
Soft limits check passed for "maximum user processes"
System architecture check passed
Kernel version check passed
<<output trimmed>>
Check for multiple users with UID value 0 passed
Current group ID check passed
Starting Clock synchronization checks using Network Time Protocol(NTP)...
NTP Configuration file check started...
NTP Configuration file check passed
Checking daemon liveness...
Liveness check passed for "ntpd"
Check for NTP daemon or service alive passed on all nodes
NTP daemon slewing option check passed
NTP daemon's boot time configuration check for slewing option passed
NTP common Time Server Check started...
PRVF-5408 : NTP Time Server "128.59.59.177" is common only to the following
nodes "alpha1"
PRVF-5408 : NTP Time Server "207.171.7.152" is common only to the following
nodes "alpha3,alpha2"
Check of common NTP Time Server passed
Clock time offset check from NTP Time Server started...
Clock time offset check passed
Clock synchronization check using Network Time Protocol(NTP) passed
Core file name pattern consistency check passed.
User "grid" is not part of "root" group. Check passed
Default user file creation mask check passed
Checking consistency of file "/etc/resolv.conf" across nodes
File "/etc/resolv.conf" does not have both domain and search entries defined
domain entry in file "/etc/resolv.conf" is consistent across nodes
search entry in file "/etc/resolv.conf" is consistent across nodes
All nodes have one search entry defined in file "/etc/resolv.conf"
The DNS response time for an unreachable node is within acceptable limit on
all nodes
File "/etc/resolv.conf" is consistent across nodes
Time zone consistency check passed
Starting check for Huge Pages Existence ...
Check for Huge Pages Existence passed
Starting check for Hardware Clock synchronization at shutdown ...
Check for Hardware Clock synchronization at shutdown passed
Pre-check for cluster services setup was successful on all the nodes.
```

When the cluster verification utility does not report any errors, you have successfully set up the cluster for the Oracle Grid Infrastructure installation. If errors are reported, you must fix them before starting the Oracle Grid Infrastructure installation. If the cluster verification utility is successful, the next step will be installing the Oracle Grid Infrastructure on the cluster nodes. The Oracle Grid Infrastructure installation uses OUI, and the steps are common across all of the operating systems.

Oracle Grid Infrastructure Installation

The Oracle Grid Infrastructure installation is the foundation for the Oracle RAC database installation. The Oracle Grid Infrastructure is the backbone of the remainder of the installation, because more than one database can share the same Oracle Grid Infrastructure foundation. OUI is run from one node, preferably as the *grid* operating system user, in the cluster under an *X* environment, and the files will be propagated to the other nodes using the scp commands.

The installer works in the background and appears to be hanging in the foreground. For those who are interested in knowing the undercover operations of the installer, we will trace the installer using the options discussed next.

Tracing the Universal Installer

OUI is a simple Java program that copies the files from the staging area and relinks with the operating system libraries to create and update the Oracle inventory. The staging area can be the CD-ROM/DVD or a local mount point in the file system.

OUI puts minimum details about the installation's options and progress in the installations_ <timestamp>.log. This log file will be typically stored in the $ORACLE_HOME/orainventory directory. However, this log does not contain a detailed level of operations to debug the installation issues.

Starting from Oracle 10*g*, OUI can be invoked using the DTRACING (or Java tracing) option in the command line. The following invokes the installer with tracing in Oracle 11*g* Release 2:

```
$ runInstaller -debug  -J-DTRACING.ENABLED=true -J-DTRACING.LEVEL=2
-DSRVM_TRACE_LEVEL=2
```

Optionally, you can redirect the tracing output to a file. (I always start the installer with tracing on so that I don't need to restart the installer if any failures occur.). Here is an example of redirecting the output of the tracing to an output file:

```
$ script /tmp/install_screen.`date +%Y%m%d%H%M%S`.out
$ runInstaller -debug -J-DTRACING.ENABLED=true -J-DTRACING.LEVEL=2
-DSRVM_TRACE_LEVEL=2
```

Once the installation is complete, simply type **exit** to close the output file. This tracing option is useful during installation of Oracle RAC, where the files are copied to the remote nodes using the scp command. Tracing tells you what the installer is doing at any point in time by providing detailed traces to the install actions. However, the limited information is also written to the trace file <installations_timestamp>log.

This information is very "high level" and does not get into the actual problems faced by the installer.

Tracing DBCA/NetCA

Because OUI is invoked from the command line, you can easily set the tracing to that program. But in Windows, the platform installer is called by another program, setup.exe, and this program calls most of the other programs, such as dbca and NetCA. To trace these programs, you need to add the tracing codes inside the respective batch files. For example, the dbca utility invokes the dbca.jar file, and you should add the tracing information in the JAR file to get the tracing of the other packaged programs.

The following procedure illustrates dbca tracing in a Windows environment. Here you need to customize the file dbca.bat (under the $ORACLE_HOME/bin directory). You need to add the tracing option inside the batch file and save the batch file with a different name; in this case, we'll change dbca to cdbca (customized dbca). To do so, simply add the following line before the -classpath argument:

```
-DTRACING.ENABLED=TRUE   -DTRACING.LEVEL=2 - DSRVM_TRACE_LEVEL=2
```

(I always customize the required batch files before any installation and use the customized startup files for the installation.)

```
**dbca.bat file** after customization . cdbca.bat
if "%args%"=="" goto with_no_args
"C:\oracle\product\11.2.0\db_1\jdk\jre\BIN\JAVA"
-Dsun.java2d.noddraw=true  -DORACLE_
HOME="%OH%" -DJDBC_PROTOCOL=thin -mx64m -DTRACING.ENABLED=TRUE
-DTRACING.LEVEL=2 DSRVM_TRACE_LEVEL=2
-classpath "%JRE_CLASSPATH%;%I18N_CLASSPATH%;%DBCA_CLASSPATH%;
%ASSISTANTS_COMMON_
CLASSPATH%;%EWT_CLASSPATH%;%BALISHARE_CLASSPATH%;%SWING_CLASSPATH%;
%ICE_BROWSER_CLASSPATH%;%HELP_
CLASSPATH%;%KODIAK_CLASSPATH%;%XMLPARSER_CLASSPATH%;%GSS_CLASSPATH%;
%EM_CLASSPATH%;%SRVM_CLASSPATH%;%NETCFG_
CLASSPATH%;%JDBC_CLASSPATH%;%ORB_CLASSPATH%;%ORACLE_OEM_CLASSPATH%;
%INSTALLER_CLASSPATH%"
oracle.sysman.assistants.dbca.Dbca  %args%
goto end
:with_no_args
"C:\oracle\product\11.2.0\db_1\jdk\jre\BIN\JAVA"
-Dsun.java2d.noddraw=true -DORACLE_
HOME="%OH%" -DJDBC_PROTOCOL=thin -mx64m -DTRACING.ENABLED=TRUE
-DTRACING.LEVEL=2 DSRVM_TRACE_LEVEL=2
-classpath "%JRE_CLASSPATH%;%I18N_CLASSPATH%;%DBCA_CLASSPATH%;
%ASSISTANTS_COMMON_CLASSPATH%;%EWT_CLASSPATH%;%BALISHARE_CLASSPATH%;
%SWING_CLASSPATH%;%ICE_BROWSER_CLASSPATH%;%HELP_CLASSPATH%;%KODIAK_CLASSPATH%;
%XMLPARSER_CLASSPATH%;%GSS_CLASSPATH%;%EM_CLASSPATH%;%SRVM_CLASSPATH%;
%NETCFG_CLASSPATH%;%JDBC_CLASSPATH%;%ORB_CLASSPATH%;%ORACLE_OEM_CLASSPATH%;
%INSTALLER_CLASSPATH%"
oracle.sysman.assistants.dbca.Dbca
**dbca.bat** file after customization
```

When you involve the dbca after customization, it will show all the tracing information on the screen. Optionally, you can redirect the output to a trace file and use it for offline diagnosis, as in the following example, in which the output is moved to a new trace file called cdbca.out:

```
C:> cdbca >cdbca.out
Sample Tracing output:
[main] [1:4:45:401] [NetworkUtils.getOneLocalListenerProtocolAddress:2594]
returning bestSoFar=(ADDRESS=(PROTOCOL=IPC)(KEY=EXTPROC))
[main] [1:4:45:401] [NetworkUtils.getOneLocalListenerProtocolAddress:2461]
```

```
bestSoFar=(ADDRESS=(PROTOCOL=IPC)(KEY=EXTPROC))
 [main] [1:4:45:401] [NetworkUtils.getOneLocalListenerProtocolAddress:2461]
bestSoFar=(ADDRESS=(PROTOCOL=IPC)(KEY=EXTPROC))
[main] [1:4:45:401] [NetworkUtils.getOneLocalListenerProtocolAddress:2474]
host=null hostParam=IBM-0B84C585AB2
[main] [1:4:45:401] [NetworkUtils.getOneLocalListenerProtocolAddress:2534]
returning bestAddrSoFar=(ADDRESS=(PROTOCOL=TCP)(HOST=IBM-0B84C585AB2)
(PORT=1521))
[main] [1:4:45:401] [NetworkUtils.getOneLocalListenerProtocolAddress:2594]
returning bestSoFar=(ADDRESS=(PROTOCOL=TCP)(HOST=IBM-0B84C585AB2)(PORT=1521))
[main] [1:4:45:401] [NetworkUtils.getOneLocalListenerProtocolAddress:2594]
returning bestSoFar=(ADDRESS=(PROTOCOL=TCP)(HOST=IBM-0B84C585AB2)(PORT=1521))
[main] [1:4:45:401] [NetworkUtils.getOneLocalListenerProtocolAddress:2594]
returning bestSoFar=(ADDRESS=(PROTOCOL=TCP)(HOST=IBM-0B84C585AB2)(PORT=1521))
[main] [1:4:45:401] [NetworkUtils.getLocalListenerAddresses:881]
listener[0]=LISTENER address=null
[main] [1:4:45:851] [DBCAWizard.removePageFromList:1238]  DBCAWizard-
>removePageFromList: The page to be removed = NetworkConfPage
[main] [1:4:45:851] [DBCAWizard.removePageFromList:1238]  DBCAWizard-
>removePageFromList: The page to be removed = NetworkConfPage
```

From this trace file, you can see that tracing is enabled for the customized dbca and that it outputs detailed information about the activities at every millisecond. This detailed tracing is quite enough to find and diagnose the most common problems expected during the runtime of the database configuration utility.

Cloning Process and OUI
OUI uses the parameter file oraparam.ini, which is included in the directory where setup.exe or runinstaller.sh is located. For example, in Solaris systems, the file is under /Disk1/install/solaris/ OraParam.ini, and in Windows, it's under \Disk1\install\ win32\OraParam.ini.

OUI verifies that all the conditions are set in the oraparam.ini file and begins the installation. Most of the prerequisite checks are specified in the installer parameter file, and you normally don't need to modify the contents. Under certain conditions, you can modify the parameter file to install the components or to skip certain conditions for testing purposes.

OUI also supports a few command-line parameters during the installation. The runInstaller help command will show the full list of command-line options and their descriptions, as well as command-line variables usage.

OUI also sends the exit codes after the installation. This can be used in an unattended installation. The following table summarizes the OUI exit codes and relevant descriptions.

Code	Description
0	All installations were successful.
1	All installations were successful, but some optional configuration tools failed.
−1	At least one installation failed.

Installing the Oracle Grid Infrastructure

The Oracle Grid Infrastructure installation is simple and straightforward once the prerequisites are met. It can be installed from the installation media (CD-ROM or DVD) or from the staging area if the software is dumped to the disk. Oracle has introduced lots of new features in Oracle RAC 11g Release 2 that are also reflected in the way you install and configure the Oracle RAC database using the Oracle Universal Installer. If you are familiar with Oracle RAC database installation in prior releases of Oracle RAC, you will find lots of changes installing the Oracle RAC database in Oracle RAC 11g Release 2 and onward. One of the major changes is that you can install the latest version of the Oracle Grid Infrastructure without applying any incremental patchset because, starting with Oracle Grid Infrastructure 11g Release 2, each patchset includes a complete set of binaries. Oracle has introduced the Out-Of-Place upgrade option in Oracle Grid Infrastructure 11g Release 2, which allows you to install Oracle Grid Infrastructure 11g Release 2 in a separate home on the same cluster node to minimize the overall downtime required to upgrade the Oracle RAC database.

Run the following in an X client on only the first node in the cluster:

```
$ cd /u01/stage/11gR2/grid
$ ./runInstaller
```

The OUI will display the Download Software Updates screen, shown in Figure 4-2.

This screen allows you to specify Oracle My Support login details so that OUI can download the required software updates, such as any new installation requirement, known patchset update (PSU), and so on, from Oracle My Support automatically before starting the Oracle Grid

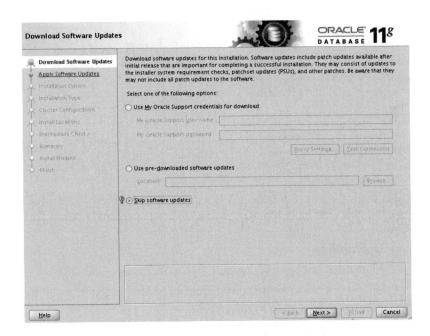

FIGURE 4-2 *The Oracle Universal Installer Download Software Updates screen*

Infrastructure software installation. This is a new feature from the Oracle Grid Infrastructure 11g Release 2 (11.2.0.2) patchset. Most large organizations' database servers are behind firewalls, and it is a common practice to restrict Internet access on these servers. Therefore, you will rarely use this option. This screen also allows you to specify a storage location where these software updates are pre-downloaded. We will select Skip Software Updates on this screen because we don't want to download software updates during this installation.

Click Next in the Download Software Updates screen to open the Select Installation Option screen (see Figure 4-3), where you specify the required installation and configuration option for the current install. This screen provides the following four installation options:

- **Install and Configure Oracle Grid Infrastructure for a Cluster** This option (the default) installs and configures the Oracle Grid Infrastructure for the current installation.

- **Configure Oracle Grid Infrastructure for a Standalone Server** This option installs and configures the Oracle Grid Infrastructure on a standalone server. This option is useful if you want to create an Oracle RAC One Node database because it requires Oracle Grid Infrastructure up and running on the server before it can be installed and configured.

- **Upgrade Oracle Grid Infrastructure or Oracle Automatic Storage Management** This option upgrades the existing Oracle Grid Infrastructure installed on the cluster nodes.

- **Install Oracle Grid Infrastructure Software Only** This option installs the Oracle Grid Infrastructure binaries on the current node only. This option is rarely used because it will not perform remote operations or any other cluster configurations, such as configuring virtual IPs, the local listener, and SCAN listeners.

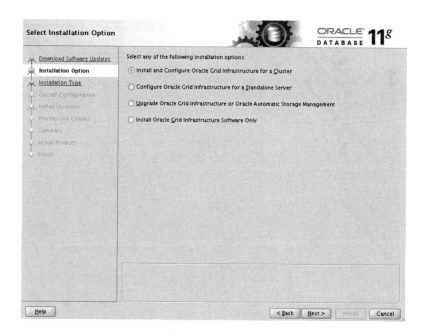

FIGURE 4-3 *The Select Installation Option screen*

Select the Install and Configure Grid Infrastructure for a Cluster option on this screen.

After specifying the installation option, click Next. In the Select Installation Type screen (see Figure 4-4), you can choose between Typical Installation and Advanced Installation. This is a new feature in Oracle Grid Infrastructure 11g Release 2. With the Typical Installation, Oracle will install and configure Oracle Grid Infrastructure with the recommended defaults, providing fewer options to customize the Oracle RAC system. The Advanced Installation, on the other hand, is more flexible and provides more options for configuring/using Grid Plug and Play, shared storage, Grid Naming Services, and the Intelligent Platform Management Interface (IPMI). Select the Advanced Installation option on this screen.

After specifying the type of installation in the Select Installation Type screen, click Next. In the Select Product Languages screen (see Figure 4-5), select the required product language. By default, Oracle uses English for all Oracle products.

After selecting the product language in the Select Product Languages screen, click Next. In the Grid Plug and Play Information screen (see Figure 4-6), you can specify configuration details for Grid Plug and Play functionality, which is introduced in Oracle 11g Release 2 Grid Infrastructure. On this screen, you specify the name of your cluster, SCAN, the port number to be used by the SCAN listeners, and the Grid Naming Services (GNS) information. You should uncheck the Configure GNS check box on this screen because we will not configure GNS in this installation.

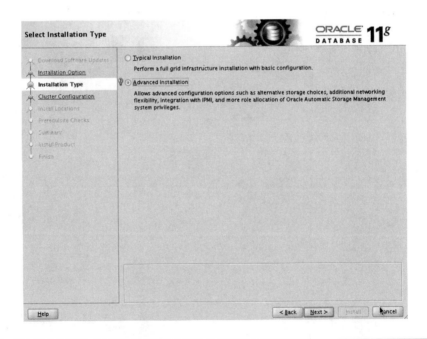

FIGURE 4-4   *The Select Installation Type screen*

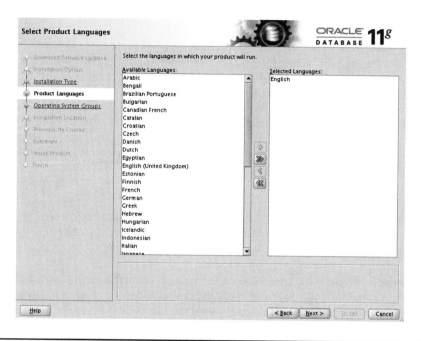

FIGURE 4-5   *The Select Product Languages screen*

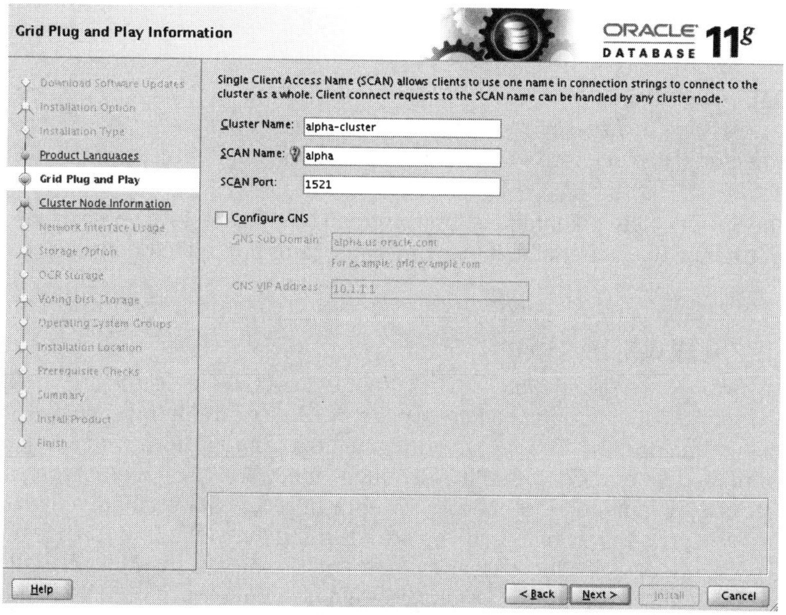

FIGURE 4-6   *The Grid Plug and Play Information screen*

Grid Plug and Play

Grid Plug and Play is a new feature of Oracle Grid Infrastructure 11g Release 2 that eases the management of large grid systems by providing the ability to add and remove cluster nodes dynamically. Oracle requires a dynamic naming scheme to implement this feature; hence, it uses GNS (Grid Naming Services). GNS provides such a naming scheme by using a DHCP server to assign virtual IPs dynamically. Because GNS provides virtual IP assignments dynamically and also resolves the server names, this eliminates any manual configuration of IPs and server names before a node is added or removed from the existing cluster.

NOTE
Please ensure that the cluster name is unique in your network because Oracle Grid Control will not discover and allow you to add the cluster if another cluster with the same name exists in the network.

Now you will see the Cluster Node Information screen (shown in Figure 4-7), where you can specify the names of the cluster and the participating nodes. For each node, you must specify the name of the public and the virtual node name. You can click the Add, Edit, or Remove button to add, modify, or remove node names. Optionally, you can use the cluster configuration file with the same information. The cluster configuration file is useful when you have to specify many nodes. It is not required to specify a private node name in Oracle Grid Infrastructure 11g Release 2 and onward. On this screen, you can configure the passwordless connectivity for the Oracle Grid software owner by clicking the SSH Connectivity button. After specifying the cluster node names, click Next.

NOTE
Oracle assigns a virtual IP and virtual node name automatically if GNS is configured and selected in the Grid Plug and Play screen.

In the Specify Network Interface Usage screen (see Figure 4-8), you can specify the planned usage of each network interface. If many network cards are in the nodes, you can instruct the

Highly Available IP (HAIP)

Highly Available IP is a private virtual IP that Oracle Grid Infrastructure configures to provide redundancy for private interconnect in Oracle Grid Infrastructure 11g Release 2 (11.2.0.2) and onward. Oracle can configure up to four HAIPs per cluster server for private network redundancy. Oracle utilizes IP range 169.254.0.0 and multicasting on the private network to implement this redundancy; hence, it is very important that multicasting is enabled on private interfaces and you are not using the 169.254.0.0 range on your network. Otherwise, the Oracle Grid Infrastructure install or upgrade to 11g Release 2 (11.2.0.2) and onward will fail. Please refer to My Oracle Support Bulletin 1212703.1 (Grid Infrastructure Install or Upgrade May Fail Due to Multicasting Requirement) for additional details and a test program to validate the requirement.

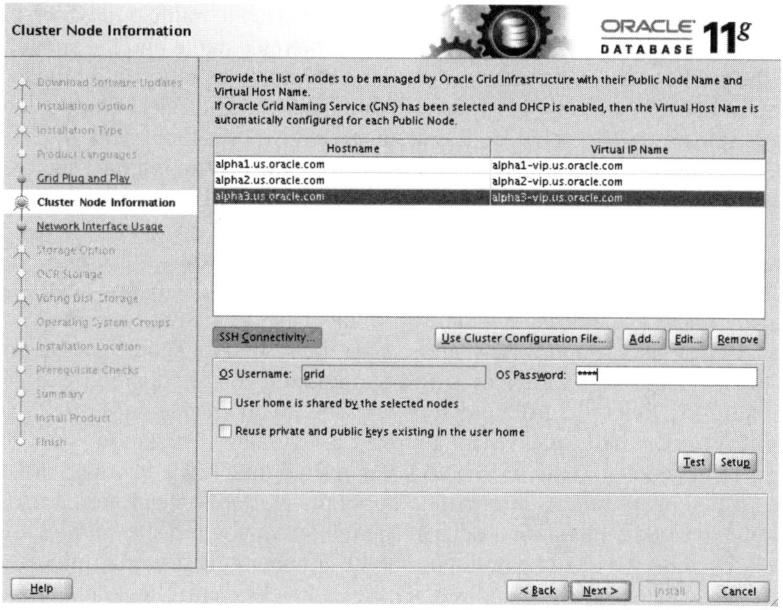

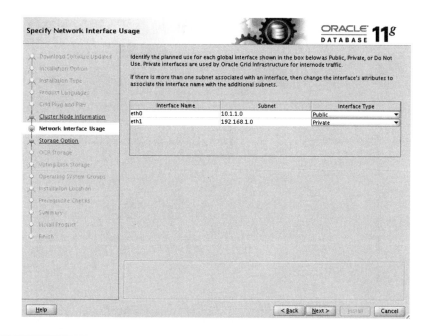

FIGURE 4-7   *The Cluster Node Information screen*

FIGURE 4-8   *The Specify Network Interface Usage screen*

Oracle Grid Infrastructure about which one to use for public traffic and which one to reserve for private network traffic. Here, you can specify the interface name and the subnet. You will also specify the public and private networks, and the VIP interface must be set to Do Not Use. If you don't want Oracle to use a specific network interface, you can select Do Not Use. If the network IP address starts with *10.x* or *192.x*, it is assumed to be a private network by default. Starting with Oracle 11g Release 2 (11.2.0.2), you can select multiple private interfaces and Oracle will automatically configure private interconnect for redundancy by using Highly Available IP (HAIP) cluster resources. Once the correct network is selected, click Next.

You'll now see the Storage Option Information screen (shown in Figure 4-9). This screen shows that Oracle Universal Installer does not allow you to specify raw devices for shared storage because in Oracle 11g Release 2 and onward, raw devices are not supported with Oracle RAC database. Oracle only supports ASM and cluster file system for shared storage to be used with Oracle RAC. The use of raw devices is only supported if you are upgrading to Oracle Grid Infrastructure 11g Release 2 from previous releases. If you choose ASM on this screen, Oracle will start ASMCA (Automatic Storage Management Configuration Assistant) in the Create ASM Disk Group screen to configure the ASM before it can store the OCR and voting disk inside the ASM.

The OCR contains critical information about the cluster configuration, including the public and private network configuration details. The minimum advised size of the OCR and voting disk is 280MB, because the reconfiguration of the OCR and voting disk may affect the entire cluster, although the actual information in these files is relatively small. The voting disk is used by the Cluster Synchronization Service (CSS) to resolve network splits, commonly referred to as *split brains*. It is used as the final arbiter on the status of configured nodes, either up or down, and to

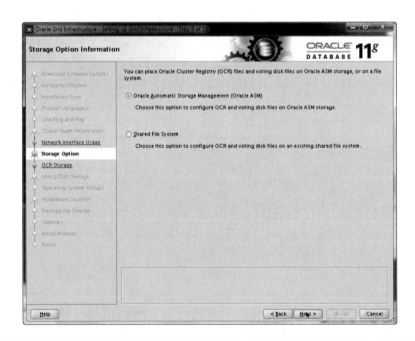

FIGURE 4-9   *The Storage Option Information screen*

deliver eviction notices. It contains the kill block, which is formatted by the other node during the node eviction.

Oracle allows mirroring of the OCR and voting disk. If you decide to choose mirroring, select Normal Redundancy and provide the location of the mirror device. Otherwise, choose External Redundancy. The OCR location can be either a clustered file system or ASM. If you use ASM to store the OCR and voting disk, Oracle decides the number of the OCR and voting disks based on the configuration of the ASM disk group being used to store the OCR and voting disk. The number of voting disks in an ASM disk group is based on the redundancy level of the ASM disk group. Oracle allocates three voting disks in normal redundancy and five voting disks for a high-redundancy ASM disk group. The OCR file is treated like any other database file in the ASM; hence, no special care is required. Specify the location(s) of the voting disk and the OCR as Automatic Storage Management on this screen and click Next.

NOTE
Storing the OCR file and voting disks in an ASM disk group created with five ASM disks of 1GB each is sufficient for normal to medium-size grid environments. Oracle has improved the node fencing in Oracle Grid Infrastructure 11.2.0.2 and onward as it tries to kill the processes capable of performing I/O operations and stopping the Oracle Grid Infrastructure on the failed node rather than rebooting the failed node as the first thing to stop the failed node issuing any I/O requests to the database files. This is also known as rebootless node fencing.

In the Create ASM Disk Group screen (see Figure 4-10), Oracle creates the ASM disk group to be used to store the OCR and voting disks. Oracle Universal Installer internally executes the ASMCA to create and configure the ASM disk group. The Add Disks section on this screen lists all candidate disks that can be used to create an ASM disk group. You can type the name of the ASM disk group; choose the required redundancy for this ASM disk group and select the candidate disks for this ASM disk group on this screen. Specify **DATA** as the disk group name, choose normal redundancy, select three candidate disks to create the DATA disk group, and then click Next.

NOTE
ASMCA, by default, sets the discovery string to /dev/raw/raw* so you may need to change the discovery string by clicking Change Discovery Path button on this screen. Oracle also verifies the minimum number of candidate disks selected to create the ASM disk group for the OCR and voting disks and would not allow you to create the ASM disk group if the number of selected candidate disks is less than three or five for the ASM disk group with normal redundancy or high redundancy, respectively.

In the Specify ASM Password screen (see Figure 4-11), you can specify the password for SYS and ASMSNMP users. Select Use Same Passwords for These Accounts because we will use the same password for these users. The ASMSNMP user is required to monitor the ASM targets in the Oracle Grid Control, also known as OEM. Enter the password and click Next.

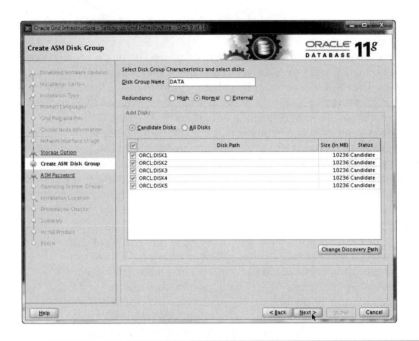

FIGURE 4-10   *The Create ASM Disk Group screen*

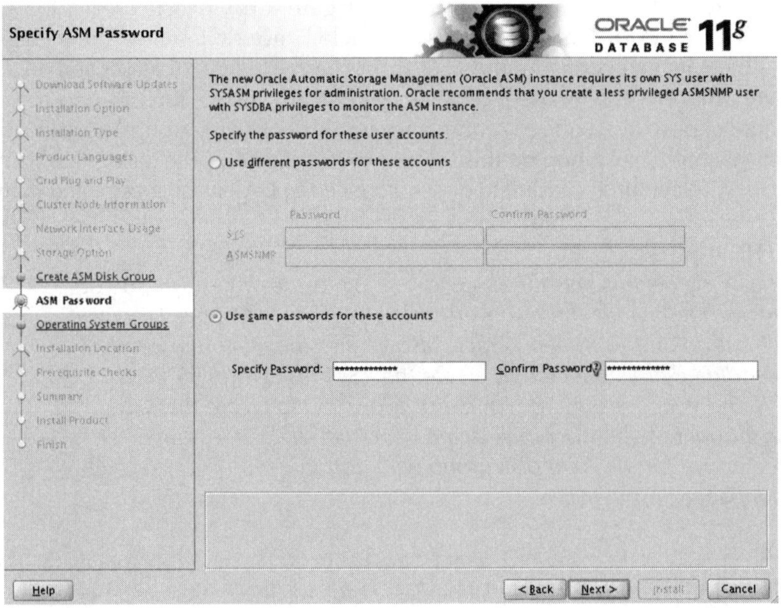

FIGURE 4-11   *The Specify ASM Password screen*

In the Failure Isolation Support screen (see Figure 4-12), you can specify the IPMI credentials if you want Oracle to utilize IPMI on the cluster servers to shut down the cluster servers in the event of a failure. Oracle requires IPMI drivers and a Baseband Management Controller on each cluster server to integrate Oracle Grid Infrastructure with IPMI. We will not use IPMI in this installation, so select Do Not Use Intelligent Platform Management Interface on this screen and then click Next.

In the Privileged Operating System Groups screen (see Figure 4-13), you can select the operating systems groups to be used for operating system authentication for ASM. Select asmdba for the OSBDA group, asmoper for the OSOPER group, and asmadmin for the OSASM group on this screen and then click Next.

In the Specify Installation Location screen (see Figure 4-14), you will specify the storage location for Oracle base and software installation. You should use a separate location for Oracle base for each software owner. For example, you can use /u01/app/grid as the Oracle base for the grid software owner and /u02/app/oracle for the database software owner. You must ensure that the software location is not inside the path specified for the Oracle base; the software location should be in a path that can be owned by the *root* user. Specify the Oracle base and software location for the Oracle Grid Infrastructure software owner on this screen and then click Next.

You will now see the Perform Prerequisite Checks screen (shown in Figure 4-15), where the Oracle Universal Installer verifies the minimum requirements for installing the Oracle Grid Infrastructure. Oracle Universal Installer internally executes the cluster verification utility to verify the operating system and hardware prerequisites. Based on the results of the verification tests performed by the cluster verification utility, Oracle displays the failed prerequisites on this screen. Staring with Oracle Clusterware 11*g*, Oracle also provides the fix-up scripts to fix the failed but

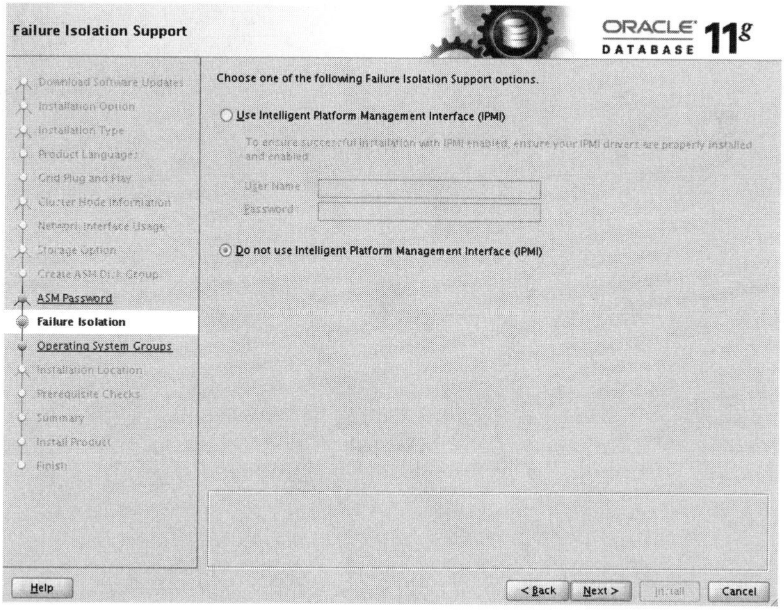

FIGURE 4-12 *The Failure Isolation Support screen*

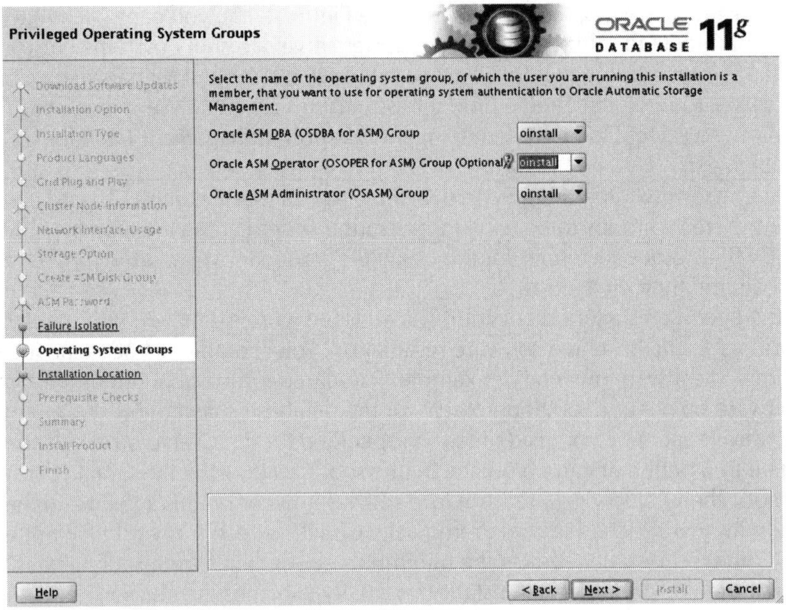

FIGURE 4-13   *The Privileged Operating System Groups screen*

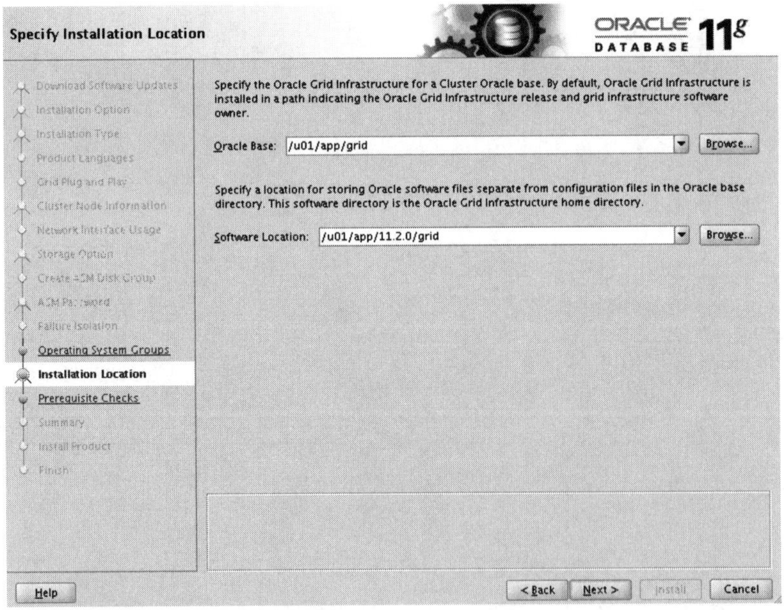

FIGURE 4-14   *The Specify Installation Location screen*

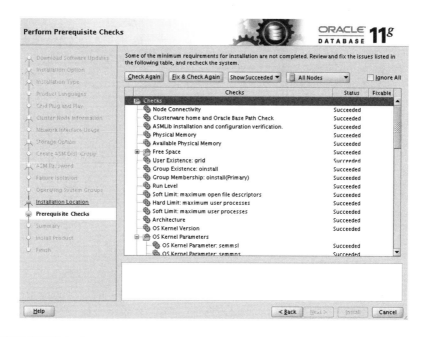

FIGURE 4-15 *The Perform Prerequisite Checks screen*

fixable prerequisite requirements. Oracle marks each failed prerequisite with a fixable status of Yes, which is also displayed on the screen. You can select the failed prerequisites with a fixable status of Yes and then click the Fix & Check Again button on this screen to fix and verify the prerequisites again. Once the installer verifies the required prerequisites successfully, click Next to continue.

In the Summary screen (see Figure 4-16), Oracle will display the installation information. You should verify this information. If the information displayed is correct, click Finish to start the software installation.

Installation of the Oracle Grid Infrastructure may take up to 30 minutes, depending on the hardware configuration. The installer will copy all the required files to the Oracle Gird Infrastructure home directory and link the files with the operating system libraries. Once the installation and linking is done at the local node, the installer will copy the files to the remote node. During the entire process, you can view the status in the progress bar of the Install Product screen (see Figure 4-17), which shows the percentage completion.

You will be instructed to run the installation scripts as the superuser *root*. You need to open a new terminal window and run orainstRoot.sh and root.sh as the superuser on the first node first and then you can run these scripts in parallel on the other cluster nodes, except the last cluster node. Once these scripts are executed successfully on other cluster nodes, run them on the last cluster node. The first script, orainstRoot.sh, sets the inventory settings. The second script, root.sh, sets the permission for the files inside the Oracle Grid Infrastructure home, configures the cluster, and starts Oracle Clusterware on the cluster node. The root.sh script internally calls other configuration scripts such as rootmacro.sh, rootinstall.sh, and rootcrs.pl. The rootcrs.pl script does the majority of the post-installation configuration. The root.sh script will also set the write

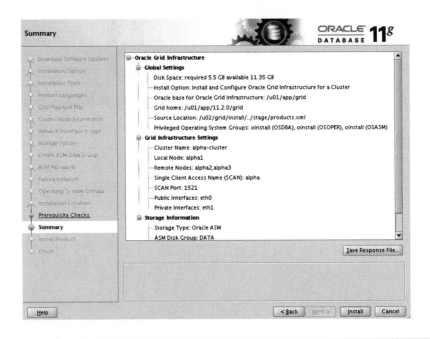

FIGURE 4-16 *The Summary screen*

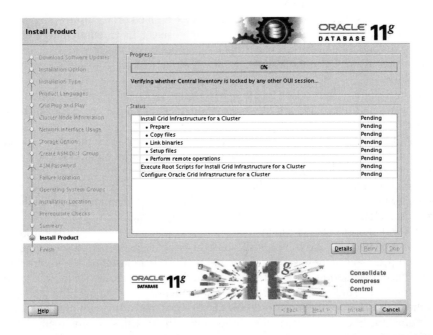

FIGURE 4-17 *Oracle Grid Infrastructure installation progress*

permission on the parent directory of the $GRID_HOME to the *root* user only. This is the reason it was advised in previous sections to use a separate storage location for the Oracle Grid Infrastructure home. The orainstRoot.sh script creates the /etc/oracle directory and the oratab file entries. These entries are used by the Oracle Grid Infrastructure agents, which are executed during startup and shutdown of the operating system. Once the scripts are run, click Next to see the Finish screen (shown in Figure 4-18).

Changes in root.sh script in Oracle Grid Infrastructure 11.2.0.2

Starting with Oracle Grid Infrastructure 11.2.0.2, there is no need to deconfigure the cluster nodes prior to restarting the root.sh script on a failed cluster node because it can be restarted after the issue on the failed cluster node is fixed. Oracle internally records the checkpoint of the root.sh execution and uses these checkpoints to know the starting point of the root.sh script execution when it is restarted. Oracle has also enabled the ability to execute the root.sh script in parallel on the cluster nodes, except for the first and the last cluster node in the cluster.

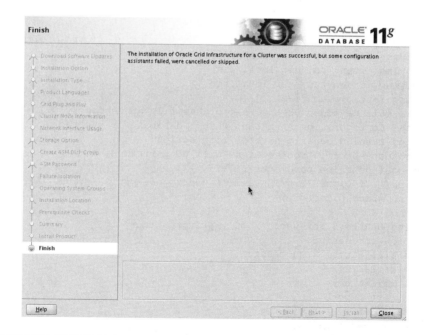

FIGURE 4-18 *End of installation*

```
[root@alpha1 oraInventory]# ./orainstRoot.sh
Changing permissions of /u01/app/oraInventory.
Adding read,write permissions for group.
Removing read,write,execute permissions for world.
Changing groupname of /u01/app/oraInventory to oinstall.
The execution of the script is complete.
[root@alpha1 oraInventory]# ssh alpha2 /u01/app/oraInventory/orainstRoot.sh
root@alpha2's password:
Changing permissions of /u01/app/oraInventory.
Adding read,write permissions for group.
Removing read,write,execute permissions for world.
Changing groupname of /u01/app/oraInventory to oinstall.
The execution of the script is complete.
[root@alpha1 oraInventory]# ssh alpha3 /u01/app/oraInventory/orainstRoot.sh
root@alpha3's password:
Changing permissions of /u01/app/oraInventory.
Adding read,write permissions for group.
Removing read,write,execute permissions for world.
Changing groupname of /u01/app/oraInventory to oinstall.
The execution of the script is complete.

/u01/app/11.2.0/grid
[root@alpha1 grid]# ./root.sh
Running Oracle 11g root script...
The following environment variables are set as:
    ORACLE_OWNER= oracle
    ORACLE_HOME=  /u01/app/11.2.0/grid
Enter the full pathname of the local bin directory: [/usr/local/bin]:
    Copying dbhome to /usr/local/bin ...
    Copying oraenv to /usr/local/bin ...
    Copying coraenv to /usr/local/bin ...
Creating /etc/oratab file...
Entries will be added to the /etc/oratab file as needed by
Database Configuration Assistant when a database is created
Finished running generic part of root script.
Now product-specific root actions will be performed.
Using configuration parameter file:
/u01/app/11.2.0/grid/crs/install/crsconfig_params
Creating trace directory
LOCAL ADD MODE
Creating OCR keys for user 'root', privgrp 'root'..
Operation successful.
OLR initialization - successful
  root wallet
  root wallet cert
  root cert export
  peer wallet
  profile reader wallet
  pa wallet
  peer wallet keys
  pa wallet keys
```

```
        peer cert request
        pa cert request
        peer cert
        pa cert
        peer root cert TP
        profile reader root cert TP
        pa root cert TP
        peer pa cert TP
        pa peer cert TP
        profile reader pa cert TP
        profile reader peer cert TP
        peer user cert
        pa user cert
Adding daemon to inittab
ACFS-9200: Supported
ACFS-9300: ADVM/ACFS distribution files found.
ACFS-9307: Installing requested ADVM/ACFS software.
ACFS-9308: Loading installed ADVM/ACFS drivers.
ACFS-9321: Creating udev for ADVM/ACFS.
ACFS-9323: Creating module dependencies - this may take some time.
ACFS-9327: Verifying ADVM/ACFS devices.
ACFS-9309: ADVM/ACFS installation correctness verified.
CRS-2672: Attempting to start 'ora.mdnsd' on 'alpha1'
CRS-2676: Start of 'ora.mdnsd' on 'alpha1' succeeded
CRS-2672: Attempting to start 'ora.gpnpd' on 'alpha1'
CRS-2676: Start of 'ora.gpnpd' on 'alpha1' succeeded
CRS-2672: Attempting to start 'ora.cssdmonitor' on 'alpha1'
CRS-2672: Attempting to start 'ora.gipcd' on 'alpha1'
CRS-2676: Start of 'ora.cssdmonitor' on 'alpha1' succeeded
CRS-2676: Start of 'ora.gipcd' on 'alpha1' succeeded
CRS-2672: Attempting to start 'ora.cssd' on 'alpha1'
CRS-2672: Attempting to start 'ora.diskmon' on 'alpha1'
CRS-2676: Start of 'ora.diskmon' on 'alpha1' succeeded
CRS-2676: Start of 'ora.cssd' on 'alpha1' succeeded
ASM created and started successfully.
Disk Group DATA created successfully.
clscfg: -install mode specified
Successfully accumulated necessary OCR keys.
Creating OCR keys for user 'root', privgrp 'root'..
Operation successful.
CRS-4256: Updating the profile
Successful addition of voting disk 770cf8c87bf84fbdbfe14be9b3966c55.
Successfully replaced voting disk group with +DATA.
CRS-4256: Updating the profile
CRS-4266: Voting file(s) successfully replaced
##  STATE    File Universal Id                 File Name Disk group
--  -----    ----------------                  --------- ---------
 1. ONLINE   770cf8c87bf84fbdbfe14be9b3966c55 (ORCL:DISK1) [DATA]
Located 1 voting disk(s).
CRS-2672: Attempting to start 'ora.asm' on 'alpha1'
CRS-2676: Start of 'ora.asm' on 'alpha1' succeeded
```

```
CRS-2672: Attempting to start 'ora.DATA.dg' on 'alpha1'
CRS-2676: Start of 'ora.DATA.dg' on 'alpha1' succeeded
ACFS-9200: Supported
ACFS-9200: Supported
CRS-2672: Attempting to start 'ora.registry.acfs' on 'alpha1'
CRS-2676: Start of 'ora.registry.acfs' on 'alpha1' succeeded
Configure Oracle Grid Infrastructure for a Cluster ... succeeded
```

Running root.sh on the first cluster node will start the Oracle Grid Infrastructure daemons and ASM as well as mount the DATA disk group. Successful execution of the root.sh script is very important to complete the installation of the Oracle Grid Infrastructure.

```
[[root@alpha2 grid]# ./root.sh
Running Oracle 11g root script...
The following environment variables are set as:
    ORACLE_OWNER= oracle
    ORACLE_HOME=  /u01/app/11.2.0/grid
Enter the full pathname of the local bin directory: [/usr/local/bin]:
The contents of "dbhome" have not changed. No need to overwrite.
The contents of "oraenv" have not changed. No need to overwrite.
The contents of "coraenv" have not changed. No need to overwrite.
Entries will be added to the /etc/oratab file as needed by
Database Configuration Assistant when a database is created
Finished running generic part of root script.
Now product-specific root actions will be performed.
Using configuration parameter file:
/u01/app/11.2.0/grid/crs/install/crsconfig_params
LOCAL ADD MODE
Creating OCR keys for user 'root', privgrp 'root'..
Operation successful.
OLR initialization - successful
Adding daemon to inittab
ACFS-9200: Supported
ACFS-9300: ADVM/ACFS distribution files found.
ACFS-9307: Installing requested ADVM/ACFS software.
ACFS-9308: Loading installed ADVM/ACFS drivers.
ACFS-9321: Creating udev for ADVM/ACFS.
ACFS-9323: Creating module dependencies - this may take some time.
ACFS-9327: Verifying ADVM/ACFS devices.
ACFS-9309: ADVM/ACFS installation correctness verified.
CRS-2672: Attempting to start 'ora.mdnsd' on 'alpha2'
CRS-2676: Start of 'ora.mdnsd' on 'alpha2' succeeded
CRS-2672: Attempting to start 'ora.gpnpd' on 'alpha2'
CRS-2676: Start of 'ora.gpnpd' on 'alpha2' succeeded
CRS-2672: Attempting to start 'ora.cssdmonitor' on 'alpha2'
CRS-2672: Attempting to start 'ora.gipcd' on 'alpha2'
CRS-2676: Start of 'ora.gipcd' on 'alpha2' succeeded
CRS-2676: Start of 'ora.cssdmonitor' on 'alpha2' succeeded
CRS-2672: Attempting to start 'ora.cssd' on 'alpha2'
CRS-2672: Attempting to start 'ora.diskmon' on 'alpha2'
CRS-2676: Start of 'ora.diskmon' on 'alpha2' succeeded
```

```
CRS-2676: Start of 'ora.cssd' on 'alpha2' succeeded
Preparing packages for installation...
cvuqdisk-1.0.9-1
Configure Oracle Grid Infrastructure for a Cluster ... succeeded
```

You can exit the installer and look for the installActions.log file in the oraInventory home. If you enabled installer tracing, you also get more information on the installer actions with finer details.

Verifying the Oracle Grid Infrastructure Installation

After the installation, exit the installer. Optionally, you can use the clusterverify utility, as shown next, to verify the Oracle Grid Infrastructure installation. This stage is automated, starting in version 10.2, because the installer runs the cluster verification utility at both the start and the end of the install.

```
$ ./runcluvfy.sh stage -post crsinst -n alpha1,alpha2,alpha3
Performing post-checks for cluster services setup
<<output truncated>>
Post-check for cluster services setup was successful
```

The other way to verify whether the Oracle Grid Infrastructure is installed successfully is to display the cluster resources status. You should see that the cluster resources are started and that their status is ONLINE. Here is a sample display of cluster resources using the CRSCTL utility:

```
[grid@alpha1]$ ./crsctl stat res -t
-------------------------------------------------------------------------
NAME            TARGET  STATE      SERVER          STATE_DETAILS
-------------------------------------------------------------------------
Local Resources
-------------------------------------------------------------------------
ora.DATA.dg
                ONLINE  ONLINE     alpha1
                ONLINE  ONLINE     alpha2
                ONLINE  ONLINE     alpha3
ora.LISTENER.lsnr
                ONLINE  ONLINE     alpha1
                ONLINE  ONLINE     alpha2
                ONLINE  ONLINE     alpha3
ora.asm
                ONLINE  ONLINE     alpha1          Started
                ONLINE  ONLINE     alpha2
                ONLINE  ONLINE     alpha3
ora.gsd
                OFFLINE OFFLINE    alpha1
                OFFLINE OFFLINE    alpha2
                OFFLINE OFFLINE    alpha3
ora.net1.network
                ONLINE  ONLINE     alpha1
                ONLINE  ONLINE     alpha2
                ONLINE  ONLINE     alpha3
```

```
ora.ons
                ONLINE   ONLINE        alpha1
                ONLINE   ONLINE        alpha2
                ONLINE   ONLINE        alpha3
ora.registry.acfs
                ONLINE   ONLINE        alpha1
                ONLINE   ONLINE        alpha2
                ONLINE   ONLINE        alpha3
--------------------------------------------------------------------------
Cluster Resources
--------------------------------------------------------------------------
ora.LISTENER_SCAN1.lsnr
      1         ONLINE   ONLINE        alpha1
ora.alpha1.vip
      1         ONLINE   ONLINE        alpha1
ora.alpha2.vip
      1         ONLINE   ONLINE        alpha2
ora.alpha3.vip
      1         ONLINE   ONLINE        alpha3
ora.cvu
      1         ONLINE   ONLINE        alpha1
ora.oc4j
      1         ONLINE   ONLINE        alpha1
ora.scan1.vip
      1         ONLINE   ONLINE        alpha1
```

In a Nutshell

Oracle Grid Infrastructure is the foundation of the Oracle Real Application Clusters deployment, and the installation process is quite simple and straightforward when the underlying storage and network components are configured appropriately. High availability of the infrastructure is obtained by configuring redundant components at the network and storage layers.

The Oracle-provided clusterverify utility helps a lot in preparing and validating the Oracle Grid Infrastructure and provides a lot of options to validate the installation process at various stages. The installer also provides fix-up scripts to help in reconfiguring the kernel parameters and the required settings, thus eliminating mundane tasks and human errors in the preparation of the cluster nodes during the installation.

Oracle Grid Infrastructure 11*g* Release 2, especially 11.2.0.2, has made significant improvements in the installation and configurations with the new Grid Plug and Play, the Typical Installation type, and restartable root scripts. Oracle Universal Installer performs the prerequisite checks and provides a fix-up script for fixable issues, which makes Oracle Grid Infrastructure installation even easier for the end user. In the next chapter we will be installing the Oracle 11*g* Release 2 (11.2.0.2) database with the Oracle RAC option.

CHAPTER
5

Oracle RAC Installation

n this chapter we walk through the Oracle 11*g* (11.2.0.2) RAC database installation process in detail. Most of the required groundwork for installation was completed in the preinstallation stages in the previous chapter; installing the Oracle RAC software will be similar to performing a single-instance installation. Even internally, the Oracle Universal Installer (OUI) installs the binaries in a single node and uses the underlying file transfer mechanisms to propagate the files to other nodes, relinking them with the respective operating system binaries.

Oracle has introduced few changes in the Oracle 11*g* Release 2 database, especially in the 11.2.0.2 patchset. We will discuss the important changes in this section; changes and features introduced in Oracle RAC 11*g* Release 2 will be marked appropriately in this book for better readability. Starting with Oracle 11*g* Release 2, the database patchset will include the software binaries and support out-of-place database upgrades, thus avoiding installation of Oracle base release binaries and then upgrading to the latest patchset.

Oracle RAC One Node is another important feature introduced in Oracle RAC 11*g* Release 2. Oracle RAC One Node is a single-instance Oracle RAC database that runs on a single machine preconfigured with Oracle Grid Infrastructure. Also, with this release onward, the maintenance of TIMESTAMP with TIMEZONE data is simplified via DBMS_DST PL/SQL packages, which can transparently upgrade the TIMESTAMP with TIMEZONE data without requiring clients to patch their time zone datafiles.

Oracle RAC One Node

Oracle RAC One Node is a single-instance Oracle RAC database running on a single node preconfigured with Oracle Grid Infrastructure. By utilizing the clustering technology, the Oracle RAC One Node database allows on-demand migration of database instances to other servers, conversion to Oracle RAC without any downtime, and rolling patches for single-instance databases. Oracle RAC One Node also provides high availability for single-instance databases. Oracle provides the OMOTION utility to migrate Oracle RAC One Node database instances to other servers in the cluster online without any downtime.

Oracle internally uses transaction shutdown to migrate single instances online without impacting the current transactions, but Oracle ensures that two servers do not provide the same services at the same time. This is really a welcome change in Oracle 11*g* Release 2 because it allows large organizations to consolidate smaller single-instance databases in one place and at the same time allows them to standardize the deployment of Oracle databases within the organization with the option to increase the scalability of single-instance databases by upgrading them to Oracle RAC databases without any downtime.

NOTE
*Oracle Support has published Note 1189783.1, which explains the important changes introduced in the Oracle 11*g* Release 2 (11.2.0.2) patchset. Detailed information about new features in Oracle 11*g* Release 2 can be found in the New Feature Guide available on the Oracle Technology Network website, which can be accessed directly from the following web page: http://download.oracle.com/docs/cd/ E11882_01/server.112/e17128/toc.htm.*

Although it is not required, the Cluster Verification Utility (cluvfy) can also be used for the pre–database installation check. You can run the Cluster Verification Utility in preinstallation mode to verify the basic node reachability and integrity of Oracle Clusterware. This also checks the basic kernel parameters and required operating system libraries. At the end, the utility checks the status of the Oracle Clusterware daemons and the network infrastructure issues. To confirm the install readiness on the hardware, run cluvfy as shown here:

```
$ ./runcluvfy.sh stage -pre dbinst -n alpha1,alpha2,alpha3 -osdba dba
Performing pre-checks for database installation
<<output truncated>>
Pre-check for database installation was successful on all the nodes.
```

That is it! Now you are ready to start the installation of RAC after deciding the storage location for the datafiles. Oracle only supports the use of RAW devices with Oracle 11g Release 2 RAC if you're upgrading the Oracle RAC database from a previous release; otherwise, you can only use a supported cluster file system, NFS, or Oracle ASM.

Unlike the prior release of Oracle RAC, there is no need to install and configure the ASM using Oracle database binaries before the database install because ASM is installed and configured with Oracle Grid Infrastructure. Because we will be using Oracle ASM to build this Oracle RAC database, you will need to create Oracle ASM disk groups to store the Oracle data and backup.

Before installation, you can adjust the environment settings for your favorite shell and start the installer with the tracing option (discussed in detail in the previous chapter) turned on. Tracing will help you get the current stage of the installer and debug the installation in case of failure and/or hang.

Oracle Real Application Clusters Installation

Oracle Universal Installer is used to install Oracle RAC binaries. OUI will install Oracle RAC binaries on the first node and then copy them onto the other servers in the cluster.

The cluvfy utility can be used for the pre–database configuration check, as shown next. You must run the utility as the user oracle. It is not mandatory to run the cluvfy utility to check the prerequisites because the Oracle Universal Installer will run cluvfy internally to verify all prerequisites before installing Oracle RAC 11g Release 2.

```
$ ./runcluvfy.sh stage -pre dbcfg -n alpha1,alpha2,alpha3 -d
<<output truncated>>
Pre-check for database configuration was successful on all the nodes.
```

As mentioned earlier, the Oracle RAC installation is as simple and straightforward as a single-instance environment once the prerequisites are correctly set. It can be installed from the installation media (CD-ROM or DVD) or from the staging area if the software is dumped to the disk.

Run through the following steps in an X client on only the first node in the cluster:

1. Begin by running the following code:

    ```
    $ cd /u01/stage/11gR2/database
    $ ./runInstaller
    ```

The OUI will display the Configure Security Updates screen (see Figure 5-1), which allows you to specify your e-mail address registered with Oracle My Support and the password so that Oracle can notify you whenever a new security update is available. Note that this requires the database servers to be connected to the Internet, and most datacenters do not expose their database servers to the public network for security reasons. Uncheck the box labeled "I wish to receive security updates via My Oracle Support" on this screen.

2. Click Next. This brings you to the Download Software Updates screen (see Figure 5-2), which allows you to specify Oracle My Support login details so that OUI can download the required software updates—such as any new installation requirements, known patchset updates (PSUs), and so on—from My Oracle Support automatically before starting the Oracle RAC software installation. This screen also allows you to specify a storage location where these software updates are predownloaded. We will select skip software updates on this screen because we don't want to download software updates during this installation.

3. Click Next in the Download Software Updates screen to open the Select Installation Option screen (see Figure 5-3), where you specify the required installation and configuration option for the current install. This screen provides the following three installation options:

   ■ **Create and configure a database** This option is the default installation option, which installs Oracle RAC binaries and creates a database based on a preconfigured template. This option is useful especially for beginners because Oracle provides separate templates for different types of workloads, such as for OLTP and decision support systems.

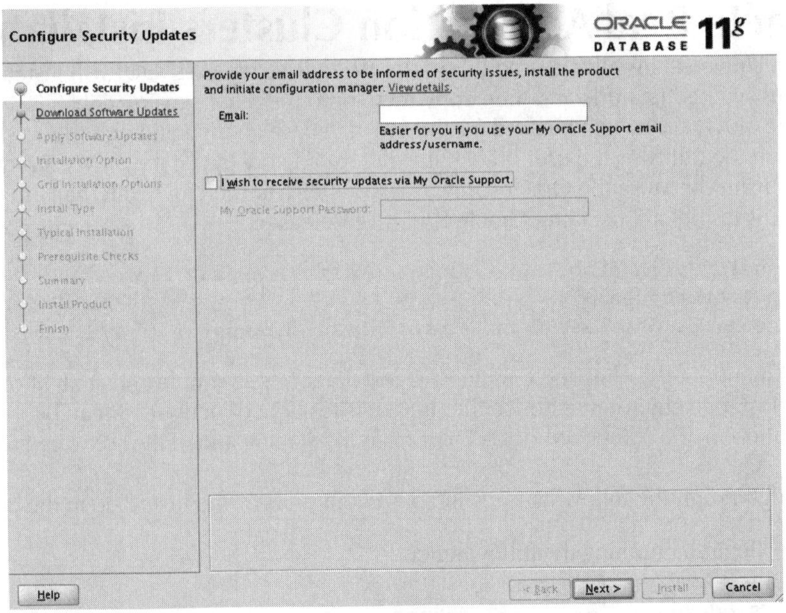

FIGURE 5-1 *The Configure Security Updates screen*

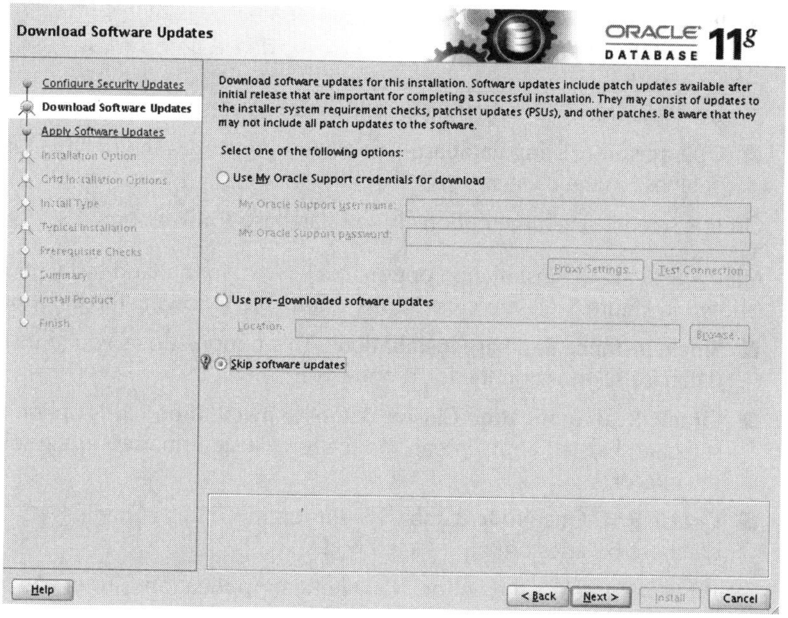

FIGURE 5-2   *The Download Software Updates screen*

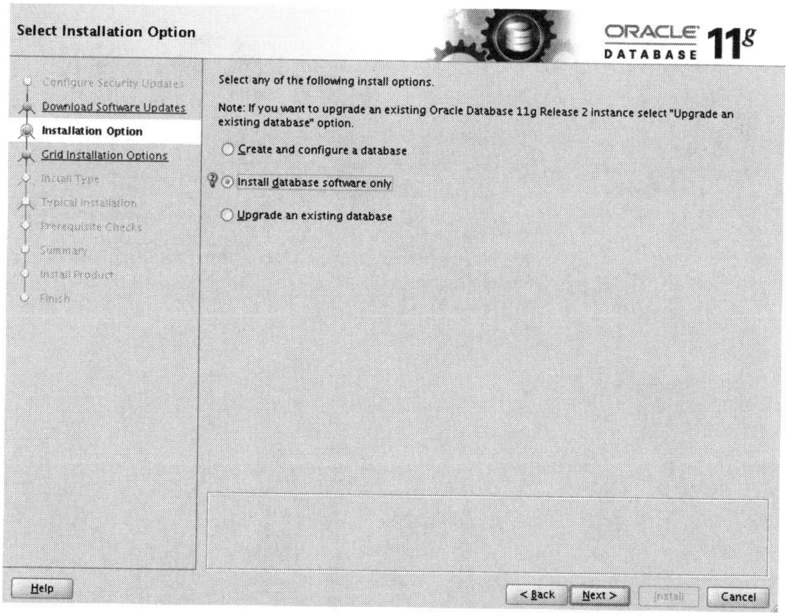

FIGURE 5-3   *The Select Installation Option screen*

- **Install database software only**   This option installs only the Oracle RAC software on all the servers in the cluster. Database administrators mostly use this option, which allows them more flexibility while creating the database using the Database Configuration Assistant once Oracle RAC binaries are installed.

- **Upgrade an existing database**   This option upgrades the existing Oracle RAC database in the cluster.

   On this screen, select the option "Install database software only."

4. After specifying the installation option, click Next. In the Grid Installation Options screen (shown in Figure 5-4), you can choose among the following three options:

   - **Single instance database installation**   This option allows you to install single-instance database software on the local node only.

   - **Oracle Real Application Cluster database installation**   This option allows you to select and install Oracle Real Application Cluster binaries on the selected nodes in the cluster.

   - **Oracle RAC One Node database**   This option installs Oracle RAC One Node database binaries on the selected node.

   On this screen, select the option "Oracle Real Application Cluster database installation."

5. After selecting the grid installation option, you will be taken to the Select Product Languages screen (see Figure 5-5), where you choose the installation language (English is selected by default). You can choose the required languages from the list available in the table.

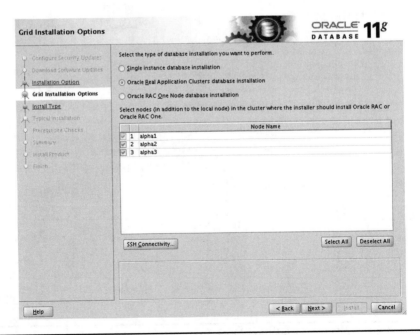

FIGURE 5-4   *The Grid Installation Options screen*

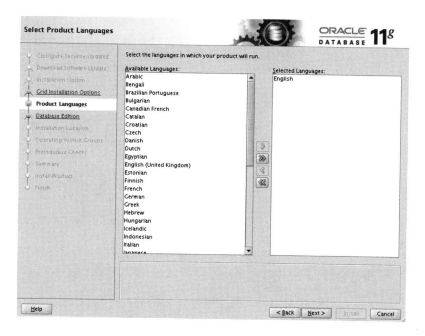

FIGURE 5-5 *The Select Product Languages screen*

6. After the Select Product Languages screen, you will be taken to the Select Database Edition screen (see Figure 5-6), where you can choose between the Enterprise and Standard Edition of the Oracle RAC database. Select the option on this screen carefully based on the purchased licenses.

7. Next, in the Specify Installation Location screen (see Figure 5-7), you will specify the storage location for ORACLE_BASE and ORACLE_HOME. If you are upgrading in place from a previous version (for example, 11.2.0.1), Oracle will allow you to choose the existing ORACLE_HOME; otherwise, the storage location for ORACLE_HOME will always be unique.

8. In the Privileged Operating System Groups screen (see Figure 5-8), select the database administrator and the database operator OS groups from the provided list of values. You should ensure that you are selecting the correct operating system group on this screen because a wrong selection may interfere with operation of the Oracle RAC database software.

9. In the Perform Prerequisite Checks screen (see Figure 5-9), Oracle Universal Installer verifies the minimum requirements for installing the Oracle RAC database software. Oracle Universal Installer internally executes the Cluster Verification Utility to verify the operating system and hardware prerequisites. Based on the results of the verification tests performed by the utility, Oracle displays the failed prerequisites on this screen. Because we have run the Cluster Verification Utility before starting the installer, we do not expect any surprises at this stage.

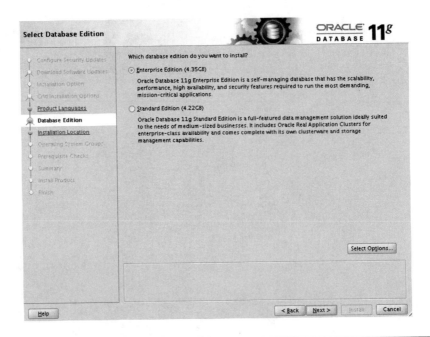

FIGURE 5-6 *The Select Database Edition screen*

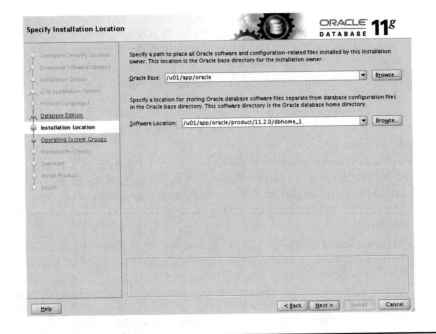

FIGURE 5-7 *The Specify Installation Location screen*

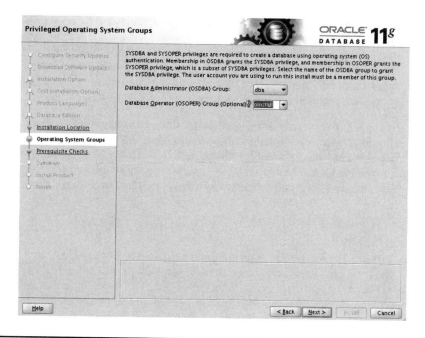

FIGURE 5-8   *The Privileged Operating System Groups screen*

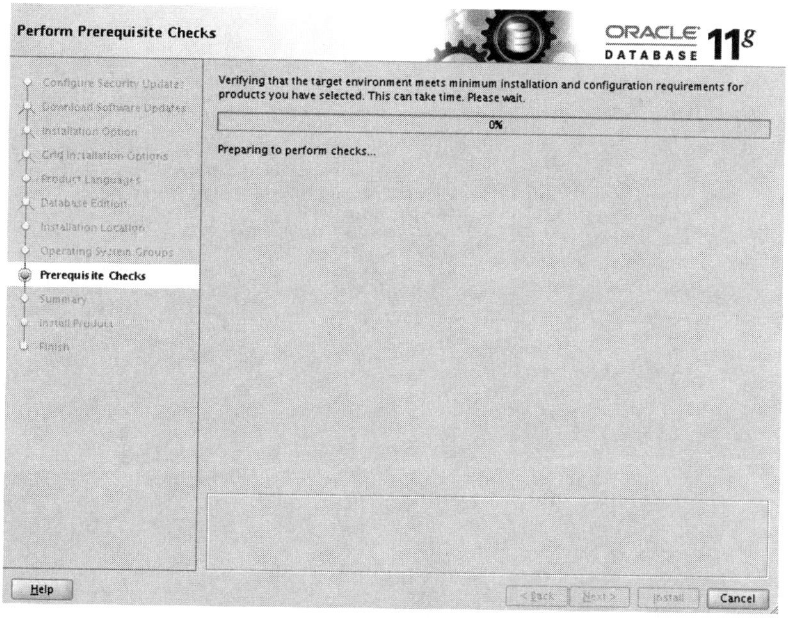

FIGURE 5-9   *The Perform Prerequisite Checks screen*

Starting with Oracle Database 11g, OUI also provides the fix-up scripts to fix the failed but fixable prerequisite requirements. Oracle marks each failed prerequisite with a fixable status of Yes if it can be fixed by a fix-up script, which is also displayed on the screen. You can select the failed prerequisite with a fixable status Yes and click the Fix and Check Again button on this screen to fix and verify the prerequisites again. Once the installer verifies the required prerequisites successfully, click Next to continue.

10. In the Summary screen (see Figure 5-10), Oracle displays the installation information. You should verify this information. You can also save this as a response file to use it for mass deployment with the silent install method. Refer to the *Oracle Universal Installer Guide* for running Oracle Universal Installer with a response file for automated deployment. Our step-by-step install process is known as an interactive installation process.

Oracle Silent Installation

The silent installation method is used for mass deployment of Oracle products because using the interactive method to install Oracle software multiple times on multiple machines is time consuming and error prone. Also, silent install provides an option to have a uniform deployment pattern across the organization. This ensures multiple users in the organization use a standard installation option to install their Oracle products. This greatly helps the internal Oracle support teams because they already know what components and options are installed on each server and their environment settings, including locations of various trace files.

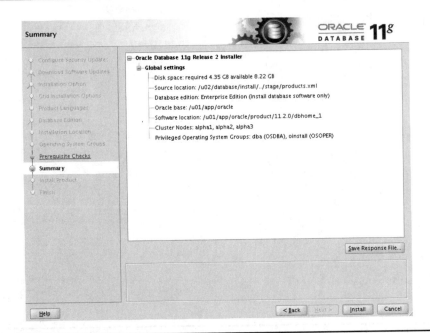

FIGURE 5-10 *The Summary screen*

11. If the information displayed is correct, click Finish to start the software installation. Installation of Oracle RAC software may take up to 30 minutes, depending on the hardware configuration. The installer will copy all the required files to the Oracle database home directory and link the files with the operating system libraries. Once the installation and linking is done at the local node, the installer will copy the files to the remote node. During the entire process, you can see the status in the progress bar of the Install Product screen (see Figure 5-11), which shows the percentage completion.

12. You will be instructed to run the installation script as the superuser root. You need to open a new terminal window and run the root.sh script as the superuser on all nodes in the cluster (see Figure 5-12). This script creates the oraenv and oratab files under /etc and sets the Oracle executable permissions to the owner and group levels. The location of the file for the oratab entry is platform specific and normally found in either the /etc or /var/opt/oracle directory. This root.sh script must be run as the superuser root.

13. After root.sh is run, go back to the installer and click the OK button to display the Finish screen (see Figure 5-13).

14. Click the Close button in the Finish screen to close the Oracle Universal Installer.

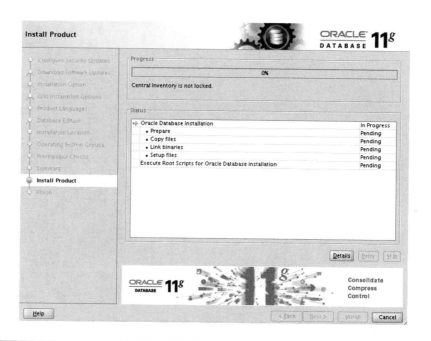

FIGURE 5-11 *The Install Product screen*

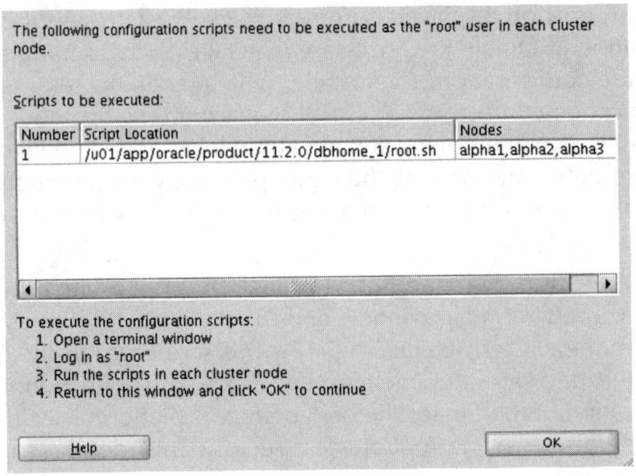

FIGURE 5-12 *The root.sh screen*

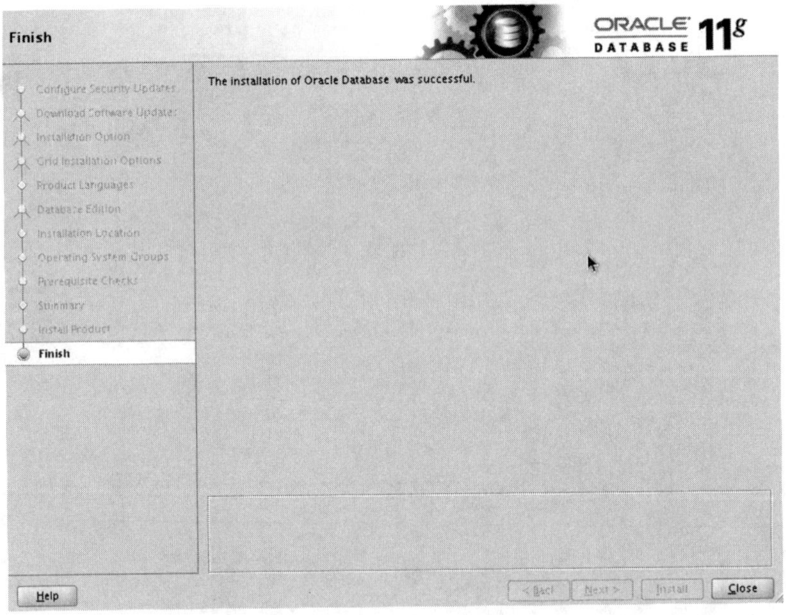

FIGURE 5-13 *The Finish screen*

Creating the Oracle RAC Database

Creating the RAC database in an Oracle RAC environment is as simple as creating the database in a single-instance environment. The only change in the creation process using DBCA is to select the nodes in the Database Identification screen. Optionally, you can generate the scripts using DBCA and run them later.

To create a database using ASM for datafiles, walk through the following steps. (The number of steps may vary a bit if different storage choices are used. However, the database-creation process is the same as creating the database in the ASM environment.)

1. Create the ASM disk groups that will be used to store the datafiles. Starting with Oracle 11g Release 2, the DBCA cannot be used to create the ASM disk groups. Instead, Oracle has introduced a dedicated configuration assistant called the Automatic Storage Management Configuration Assistant (also known as ASMCA) to create and manage the ASM instances, volumes, cluster file system, and disk groups. ASMCA can be launched from $GRID_HOME/bin as the grid user in the same way we will execute DBCA in the next step. We will use the DATA disk group created as part of the Oracle Grid Infrastructure installation in the previous chapter, but the typical steps for creating an ASM disk group include marking disks to be used by ASM and then creating the ASM disk group using any ASM client, such as ASMCA, ASMCMD, or SQL*Pus. We will discuss this in detail in the next chapter.

2. Start the Database Configuration Assistant (DBCA) as the user oracle. Navigate to the $ORACLE_HOME/bin directory. If you want to enable tracing, you need to customize the Java runtime environment as discussed in Chapter 4 to get the trace information.

   ```
   $ ./dbca
   ```

   DBCA enables you to create, configure, or delete a cluster database and manage database templates. If you are creating the first database in the cluster, only the Create a Database option and the Manage Template option are allowed. In the Welcome screen (see Figure 5-14), select the Oracle Real Application Clusters (RAC) Database option to create an Oracle RAC database using DBCA. Click Next.

3. In creating an Oracle RAC database, you'll select the participating nodes, whereas in a single-instance environment, the node from where DBCA is invoked is the default node for database creation. In the next screen (see Figure 5-15), choose Create a Database. Click Next.

NOTE
Starting with Oracle RAC 11g Release 2, DBCA can be used to create an Oracle RAC One Node database. The SRVCTL utility is also integrated with the Oracle RAC One Node database and can be used to relocate the Oracle RAC One Node database to another server. In Oracle RAC 11g Release 2, you create an Oracle RAC One Node database by creating and converting the newly created Oracle RAC database.

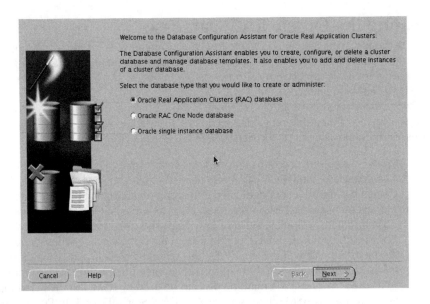

FIGURE 5-14 *The Welcome screen*

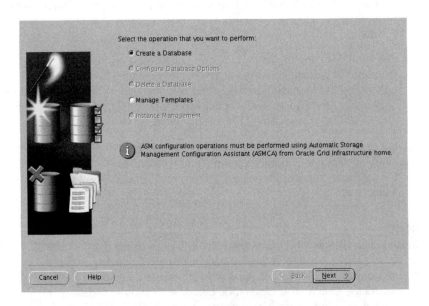

FIGURE 5-15 *The Operations screen*

4. Predefined database configuration templates are available to make the process easier. In the Database Templates screen (see Figure 5-16), Oracle provides predefined templates that can be used to create a new database based on the expected type of workload. These templates come with datafiles, but you can use these templates without datafiles if you want to customize database attributes such as block size. This screen displays three options: General Purpose or Transaction Processing, Custom Database, and Data Warehouse. Each option provides preconfigured parameters/attributes for the new database, and Custom Database allows you to decide these attributes and parameters. Regardless of your choice on this screen, you can still customize the database in later steps. Choose the General Purpose or Transaction Processing option on this screen and click Next.

5. In the Database Identification screen (see Figure 5-17), you select the global name of this cluster database and a prefix to be used for the database service identifier. Starting with Oracle RAC 11g Release 2, Oracle has introduced two different configuration schemes for the cluster database. On this screen, you choose between an admin-managed and policy-managed configuration for this database. These different configurations allow you to further improve the resource utilization in the Oracle RAC database. If Oracle Clusterware is up and running, the Database Configuration Assistant will automatically detect the cluster and the number of nodes in the cluster and then populate the node names in this screen. Select the Admin-Managed option and enter **RAC** in the Global Database Name and SID Prefix fields on this screen. The local node is selected by default, so click Select All and then click Next.

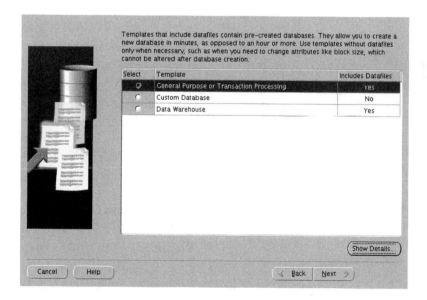

FIGURE 5-16 *The Database Templates screen*

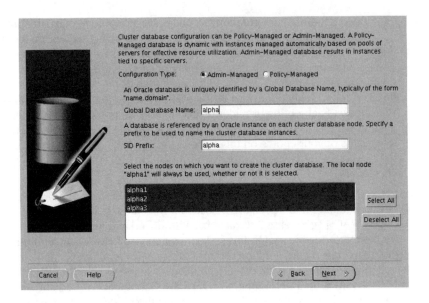

FIGURE 5-17 *The Database Identification screen*

NOTE
The Global Database Name and SID Prefix values must start with an alphabetical character but can be followed by alphanumeric characters.

Admin-Managed and Policy-Managed Oracle RAC Database

An admin-managed Oracle RAC database is a traditional configuration approach where you can specify the servers in the cluster that will run the Oracle RAC database instances. You can also decide the preferred and available Oracle RAC database instances for a given database service. In a policy-managed Oracle RAC database, you don't have flexibility to decide which server in the cluster will run the Oracle RAC database instance. Oracle will start the number of Oracle RAC database instances on servers in a server pool based on the cardinality of the Oracle RAC database.

In an admin-managed RAC database, there is a relation/association between the database service and the Oracle RAC database instance, whereas in a policy-managed Oracle RAC database, there is a relation between a database service and the server pool because Oracle will automatically decide the RAC database instance, which will serve a given database service. A server pool is a pool of different servers in the cluster, which Oracle uses to automatically host database instances. You should always have a number of servers in the server pool greater than the number of Oracle RAC database instances specified in cardinality. The CRSCTL and SRVCTL utilities can be used to create and manage server pools in an Oracle RAC database.

6. You can use the Oracle Enterprise Manager to manage the database. In the Management Options screen (see Figure 5-18), if you would like to use the Enterprise Manager to manage this database, check Configure Enterprise Manager. If the Oracle Grid Control agent is running on the local node and the Oracle Grid Control is installed and working in your network, you can register and manage this database with the Oracle Grid Control environment. Alternatively, you can use Oracle Database Control for Local Management. You have options to configure notification and backups using the database control as well. Uncheck the Configure Enterprise Manager option on this screen and click Next.

7. In the next screen, you are asked to enter the passwords for the SYS, SYSTEM, DBSNMP, and SYSMAN accounts (see Figure 5-19). In earlier Oracle versions, the SYS and SYSTEM accounts used a default password (for SYS, it was change_on_install, and for SYSTEM, it was manager). Because no default passwords for these administrative accounts exist in Oracle Database 10g and onward, select the Use the Same Password for All Accounts option, enter and confirm the password, and click Next. Optionally, you can use different passwords for these administrative accounts by choosing the Use Different Administrative Passwords option.

8. In the next screen, specify the storage type and database file location for the database (see Figure 5-20). The available storage types are Cluster File System and Automatic Storage Management, which can be selected from the Storage Type drop-down list. Starting with Oracle 11g Release 2, RAW devices are not supported. Choose Automatic Storage Management from the Storage Type drop-down list because we will be using ASM for this cluster database. In this screen, Oracle allows you to select database files location from a template; you can store the database file onto a common location or you can let Oracle manage these database files for you using the Oracle-Managed Files mechanism. Select the Use Oracle-Managed Files option for the storage location and then click Next.

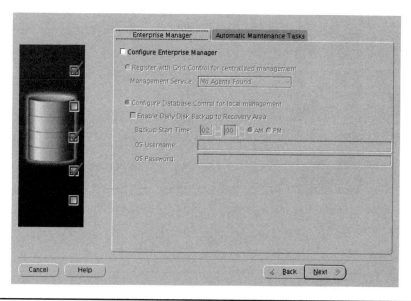

FIGURE 5-18 *The Management Options screen*

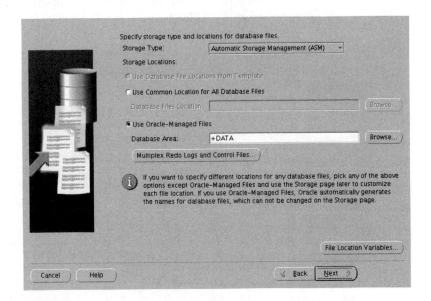

For security reasons, you must specify passwords for the following user accounts in the new database.

○ Use Different Administrative Passwords

User Name	Password	Confirm Password
SYS		
SYSTEM		

● Use the Same Administrative Password for All Accounts

Password: `*************`

Confirm Password: `*************`

Cancel   Help   ‹ Back   Next ›

FIGURE 5-19   *The Administrative Passwords screen*

Specify storage type and locations for database files.

Storage Type: Automatic Storage Management (ASM) ▼

Storage Locations:

○ Use Database File Locations from Template

○ Use Common Location for All Database Files

Database Files Location: [   ] Browse...

● Use Oracle-Managed Files

Database Area: +DATA   Browse...

[Multiplex Redo Logs and Control Files...]

ⓘ If you want to specify different locations for any database files, pick any of the above options except Oracle-Managed Files and use the Storage page later to customize each file location. If you use Oracle-Managed Files, Oracle automatically generates the names for database files, which can not be changed on the Storage page.

[File Location Variables...]

Cancel   Help   ‹ Back   Next ›

FIGURE 5-20   *The Database File Location screen*

9. In the next screen, you specify the FastRecovery Area used to store Oracle database backup files, including archive and flash logs (see Figure 5-21). You can specify the size of the Fast Recovery Area in the Fast Recovery Area Size field. Oracle will not use more space in the ASM disk group than the Fast Recovery Area size. In this screen, you can also enable redo log archiving by selecting the Enable Archiving check box. We will not use Fast Recovery Area and archiving in our installation process, so uncheck Specify Fast Recovery Area and Enable Archiving on this screen and then click Next.

Fast Recovery Area

Fast Recovery Area (also known as Flash Recovery Area in previous database releases) is a dedicated storage location Oracle uses to store all database backup-related files so that in an event of database recovery Oracle can quickly restore backup pieces from this dedicated storage location rather than fetching from the slow tape libraries. This storage is configured using two database initialization parameters: DB_RECOVERY_FILE_DEST and DB_RECOVERY_FILE_DEST_SIZE. Oracle manages this storage area and automatically purges obsolete backups based on the backup retention policies.

10. In the Database Content screen, you can choose to create sample schemas—a set of schemas that can be used for training purposes (see Figure 5-22). These include the

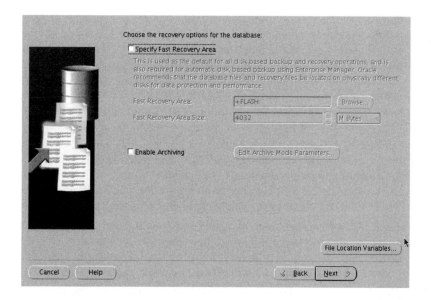

FIGURE 5-21   *The Recovery Configuration screen*

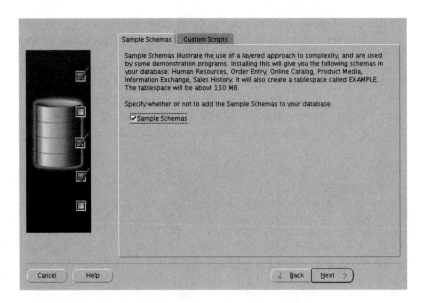

FIGURE 5-22 *The Database Content screen*

infamous EMP and DEPT tables. In the Custom Scripts tab, you can select your custom scripts to be run as part of the database creation process. Click Next.

11. In the Initialization Parameters screen, you can specify the initialization parameters that control the memory used by the Oracle database (Figure 5-23). Most of the tuning parameters can be changed later. In the Character Sets tab, along with the character set you can select the default language and date format for this database. In the Connection Mode tab, you can specify the connection mode for the database. By default, Oracle uses the Dedicated Server mode. The only important thing you must be aware of at this stage is the character set and block size for the database. Choose the appropriate character set and block size and leave the rest of the initialization parameters set to their defaults. You can refine these later.

12. Click Next to open the Database Storage screen (see Figure 5-24). Here you can specify the locations for the datafiles, control files, and redo log groups. File location variables for datafiles and redo logs can also be specified. Once you have specified the locations for the datafiles, control files, and redo log groups, you are ready to create the database. You can create a database immediately or generate scripts for database creation.

13. If you create the database immediately, it is a good practice to generate the scripts to be able to see what is being run and to have these scripts available for future reference. You can choose the location of the scripts in any local directory. By default, they are stored under $ORACLE_BASE/admin directory, as shown in Figure 5-25.

14. Click Finish to view the Summary screen (see Figure 5-26). This screen contains the selected options for the installation. Click OK. After the database is created, click Exit to start the database instances.

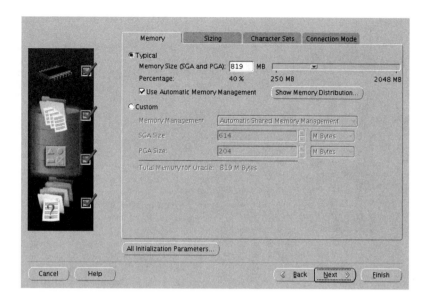

FIGURE 5-23   *The Initialization Parameters screen*

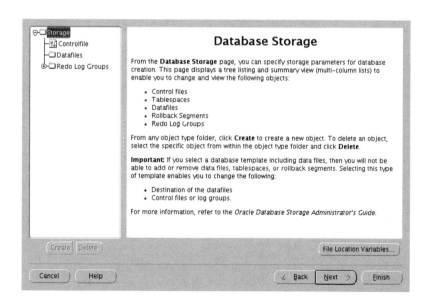

FIGURE 5-24   *The Database Storage screen*

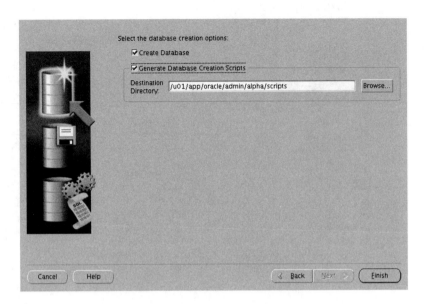

FIGURE 5-25 *The Creation Options screen*

FIGURE 5-26 *The Summary screen*

In a Nutshell

This chapter covered the installation process of Oracle Database 11g Release 2 RAC in detail. The number of steps in the installation may vary slightly depending on the options and configurations selected. We walked through the important changes that Oracle has introduced in Oracle RAC Database 11g Release 2, such as Oracle RAC One Node and the admin- and policy-managed configurations of the Oracle RAC database.

Oracle RAC One is a newly introduced option that helps build a single-database infrastructure that's ready for the high-availability features provided by Oracle Grid Infrastructure. Instance failures are detected by Oracle Clusterware and automatically restarted in another server in the server pool, which ensures failover protection for Oracle RAC One Node.

Unlike previous releases of Oracle RAC, there is no need to install and configure ASM separately because ASM is part of Oracle Grid Infrastructure and configured during Oracle Grid Infrastructure installation and configuration. In the next chapter, we discuss ASM architecture and explore its functionalities in detail.

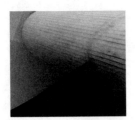

CHAPTER
6

Automatic Storage
Management

anaging storage is one of the most complex and time-consuming tasks of a DBA. Data growth occurs at an exponential pace due to consolidation of databases and high-velocity business growth. Business requirements demand the continuous availability of database storage systems, and the maintenance window for storage is shrinking from hours to minutes. Legal requirements add even more baggage because data has to be retained for an extended period of time. (I know some sites that store hundreds of terabytes of active data for seven years or more!) The average storage size managed by a DBA has grown from a few terabytes (TB) to close to a petabyte (PB).

Figure 6-1 shows the management gap between disk capacities to management capacity per DBA.

Other than the challenge posed by the external entities, storage management always involves many internal operational organizations. It involves the participation of system administrators, network administrators, and storage (or SAN) administrators, along with the operational DBA team. To eliminate complexities and interdependence with various entities, all this data is required to be stored in one place and, more importantly, administered by the same operational group.

New technologies help DBAs easily manage huge volumes of data without a considerable amount of administrative overhead. New tools are being developed that work closely with the RDBMS kernel to make data management and data consolidation easier. Automatic Storage Management (affectionately called *Awesome Storage Management*) is one of those revolutionary solutions from Oracle. Oracle introduced Automatic Storage Management in Oracle 10*g*, which has been enhanced to a great extent in Oracle 11*g* to provide a complete volume manager built into Oracle database software. Oracle ASM and file system are highly optimized to provide raw disk performance by avoiding various types of overhead associated with a conventional file system.

Facts about Automatic Storage Management

ASM is a storage solution that provides a volume manager and file system capabilities that are tightly integrated and optimized for Oracle databases. It is implemented via three key components: ASM instance, ASM Dynamic Volume Manager (ADVM), and ASM Cluster File System (ACFS). The ASM Dynamic Volume Manager provides the functionality of a volume

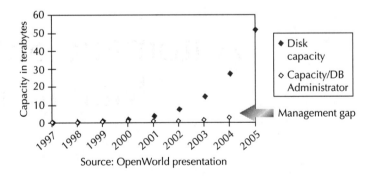

FIGURE 6-1 *Storage growth and management gap*

manager for the ASM Cluster File System. ASM Cluster File System is only available in Oracle Grid Infrastructure 11g Release 2 and onward.

ACFS helps customers in reducing overall IT budget costs because it totally eliminates the need for third-party cluster file systems, which is the most common requirement for clustered applications. Because ACFS is built as a true cluster file system, it can be used for non-Oracle enterprise applications as well. ASM simplifies storage management by enabling you to do online reconfiguration and rebalancing of the ASM disks. ASM is highly optimized for the Oracle database because it distributes I/O operations onto all available disks in a disk group and provides raw disk performance.

In short, the ASM environment provides the performance of raw disk I/O with the easy management of a file system. It simplifies database administration by eliminating the need to manage potentially thousands of Oracle database files in a direct manner.

Physical Limits of ASM

The number of datafiles per database has consistently increased since Oracle version 7, in which only 1,022 datafiles per database could be used. Current Oracle versions support 65,533 datafiles per tablespace, and managing thousands of files in a multidatabase environment is a challenge. ASM simplifies storage management by enabling you to divide all available storage into disk groups. You can create separate disk groups for different performance requirements. For example, an ASM disk group can be created with low-performance hard disks to store archive data, whereas an ASM disk group with high-performance disks can be used for active data.

You manage a small set of disk groups, and ASM automates the placement of the database files within those disk groups. With ASM you can have 63 disk groups with 10,000 ASM disks in it, where each ASM disk can store up to 2TB of data. A disk group can handle one million ASM files. The maximum supported file size for a datafile in Oracle Database 11g is 128TB, whereas ASM supports up to 140PB with external redundancy, 42PB with normal redundancy, and 15PB with high redundancy. Figure 6-2 compares the traditional data storage framework to that of ASM.

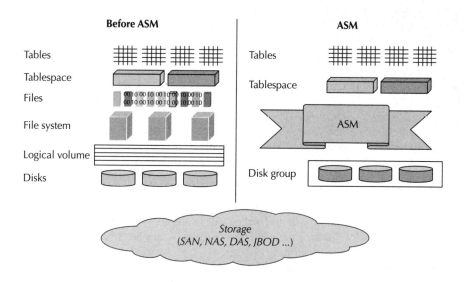

FIGURE 6-2 *Traditional framework vs. ASM*

ASM in Operation

ASM divides a file into pieces and spreads these pieces evenly across all the disks, unlike other volume managers, which spread the whole volume onto the different disks. This is the key difference from the traditional striping techniques that use mathematical functions to stripe complete logical volumes independent of files or directories. Striping requires careful capacity planning at the beginning, because adding new volumes requires rebalancing and downtime.

With ASM, whenever new storage is added or removed, ASM does not restripe all the data. It just moves an amount of data proportional to the amount of storage added or removed to redistribute the files evenly and maintain a balanced I/O load across the disks. This occurs while the database is active and is totally transparent to the database and end-user applications.

ASM supports all files to be used with an Oracle database (with an exception of pfile and password files). Starting with Oracle 11*g* Release 2, ACFS can be used for non-Oracle application files. ASM also supports Oracle Real Application Clusters (Oracle RAC) and eliminates the need for a cluster Logical Volume Manager or a third-party cluster file system. Another key fact about ASM is that it is integrated with Oracle Clusterware and can read from a mirrored data copy in an extended cluster and improve I/O performance when used in an extended cluster. (An *extended cluster* is special-purpose architecture in Oracle RAC where the nodes are geographically separated. More details on the design and implementation are discussed in Chapter 15.)

ASM is available in both the Enterprise Edition and Standard Edition installations and is automatically installed with Oracle Grid Infrastructure. ASM code was tightly integrated with RDBMS code, and it was part of the RDBMS installation until version 11.1. Starting with Oracle Database 11*g* Release 2, ASM is integrated with Oracle Grid Infrastructure.

SQL is the interface to the database, and ASM provides the SQL interface for creating database structures such as tablespaces, controlfiles, redo logs, and archive log files. You specify the file location in terms of disk groups; ASM then creates and manages the associated underlying files for you. Other interfaces interact with ASM as well, such as ASMCMD, OEM, and ASMCA. SQL*Plus is the most commonly used tool to manage ASM among DBAs. However, system and storage administrators tend to like the ASMCMD utility for managing ASM.

ASM Striping and Mirroring

Striping is a technique used for spreading data among multiple disk drives. A big data segment is broken into smaller units, and these units are spread across the available devices. The unit at which the data is broken is called the *data unit size* or *stripe size*. Stripe size is also sometimes called the *block size,* referring to the size of the stripes written to each disk. The number of parallel stripes that can be written to or read from simultaneously is known as the *stripe width*. Striping can speed up operations that retrieve data from disk storage as it extends the power of the total I/O bandwidth. This optimizes performance and disk utilization, making manual I/O performance tuning unnecessary.

ASM supports two levels of striping: fine striping and coarse striping. Fine striping uses 128KB as the stripe width, and coarse striping uses 1MB as the stripe width. Fine striping can be used for files that usually do smaller reads and writes. For example, online redo logs and controlfiles are the best candidates for fine striping when the reads or writes are small in nature. Current Oracle versions do not support other striping options.

ASM mirroring is more flexible than operating system mirrored disks because ASM mirroring enables the redundancy level to be specified on a per-file basis rather than on a volume basis. Internally, mirroring takes place at the extent level. If a file is mirrored, depending on the redundancy level set for the file, each extent has one or more mirrored copies, and mirrored copies are always kept on different disks in the disk group.

The following table describes the available mirroring options that ASM supports on a per-file basis:

ASM Redundancy	Mirroring Level	Description
External	No mirroring	No mirroring from ASM. Can be used when mirroring is implemented at the storage or disk level.
Normal	Two-way mirroring	Each extent has one mirrored copy in the different failure groups.
High	Three-way mirroring	Each extent has two mirrored copies in different failure groups.

In summary, ASM does not require external volume managers or external cluster file systems for disk management; these are not recommended because the functionalities provided by the ASM will conflict with the external volume managers. ASM extends the power of Oracle-managed files that are created and managed automatically for you, but with ASM you get the additional benefits of features such as mirroring and striping.

Stripe and Mirror Everything

Stripe and Mirror Everything (SAME) is a simple and efficient technique used in managing a high volume of data. ASM implements the Oracle SAME methodology, in which all types of data are striped and mirrored across all available drives. This helps the I/O load to be evenly distributed and balanced across all disks within the disk group. Mirroring provides the much-required fault tolerance for the database servers, and striping provides performance and scalability to the database. ASM implements the SAME methodology to strip and mirror files inside the ASM dynamic volume.

Character Devices and Block Devices

Any direct attached or networked storage device can be classified as a *character device* or a *block device*. A character device holds only one file. Normally, raw files are placed on character devices. The location of the raw devices is platform dependent, and they are not visible in the file system directory. A block device is a type of character device, but it holds an entire file system. If ASMLib is used as a disk API, ASM supports block devices. ASM presents an ASM dynamic volume device file as a block device to the operating system.

Storage Area Network

A *storage area network (SAN)* is the networked storage device connected via uniquely identified host bus adapters (HBAs). The storage is divided into logical unit numbers (LUNs), and each LUN is logically represented as a single disk to the operating system.

In Automatic Storage Management, the ASM disks are either LUNs or disk partitions. They are logically represented as a raw device to the ASM. The name and path of the raw device is dependent on the operating system. For example, in the Sun operating system, the raw device has the name *cNtNdNsN*:

- **cN** is the controller number.
- **tN** is the target ID (SCSI ID).

- *dN* is the disk number, which is the LUN descriptor.

- *sN* is the slice number or partition number.

So when you see a raw partition in Sun listed as *c0t0d2s3,* you'll know that the device is the third partition in the second disk connected to the first controller's first SCSI port. HP UX does not expose the slice number in the raw device.

HP uses the *cNtNdN* format for the raw partitions. Note that there is no concept of slice designation, because HP/UX does not support slices. (HP/UX Itanium does have slice support, but HP does not support the use of this feature.) The entire disk must be provided to ASM.

A typical Linux configuration uses *straight disks*. RAW functionality was an afterthought. However, Linux imposes a limit of 255 possible RAW devices, and this limitation is one of the reasons for the development of Oracle Cluster File System (OCFS) and the use of ASMLib. Raw devices are typically stored in /dev/raw and are named raw1 to raw255. ASMLib is discussed later in the chapter.

ASM Building Blocks

ASM is implemented as a special kind of Oracle instance with the same structure and its own System Global Area (SGA) and background processes. Additional background processes in ASM manage storage and disk-rebalancing operations. The components discussed next can be considered the building blocks of ASM.

ASM Instance

An *ASM instance* is an Oracle instance that manages the metadata for disk groups, ADVM (ASM Dynamic Volume), and ACFS (ASM Cluster File System). All metadata modifications are done by an ASM instance to isolate failures. Database instances connect to an ASM instance to create, delete, resize, open, or close files, and database instances read/write directly to disks managed by the ASM instance. Only one ASM instance is possible per node in a cluster. Sometimes this can be a disadvantage for a large Oracle RAC cluster (such as an eight-node Oracle RAC, where eight separate instances need to be maintained for ASM in addition to eight "user" instances). An ASM instance failure kills attached database instances in the local node.

An ASM instance is just like an Oracle database instance, which consists of System Global Area and background processes. Just like the buffer cache in an Oracle database instance, an ASM instance has a special cache called *ASM cache* to read and write blocks during rebalancing operations. Apart from ASM cache, an ASM instance's System Global Area has a shared pool, large pool, and free memory area. Oracle internally uses Automatic Memory Management, and you will hardly need to tune an Oracle ASM instance.

An Oracle ASM instance does not maintain a data dictionary, so you can only connect to an ASM instance through system privileges SYSDBA, SYSADM, and SYSOPER, which are implemented by operating system groups for the Oracle Grid Infrastructure owner provided to the Oracle Universal Installer during the installation of Oracle Grid Infrastructure.

ASM Listener

The *ASM listener* is also like the database listener, a process that is responsible for establishing a connection between database server processes and the ASM instance. The ASM listener process *tnslsnr* is started from the $GRID_HOME/bin directory and is similar to Oracle Net Listener. The ASM listener also listens for database services running on the same machine, so there is no need to configure and run a separate Oracle Net Listener for the database instance. Oracle will, by default, install and configure an ASM listener on port 1521, which can be changed to a nondefault port while Oracle Grid Infrastructure is being installed or later on.

Disk Groups

A *disk group* is composed of disks that are managed together as a single unit of storage. As the primary storage unit of ASM, this collection of ASM disks is self-describing, independent of the associated media names. Oracle provides various ASM utilities such as ASMCA, SQL statements, and ASMCMD that create and manage disk groups, their contents, and their metadata. Disk groups are integrated with Oracle managed files and support three types of redundancy: external, normal, and high. Figure 6-3 shows the architecture of the disk groups.

The disks in a disk group are referred to as *ASM disks*. In ASM, a disk is the unit of persistent storage for a disk group. The disk group in a typical database cluster is part of a remote shared-disk subsystem, such as a SAN or network-attached storage (NAS). It can be accessed via the normal operating system interface and must be accessible to all nodes. Oracle must have read and write access to all the disks, even if one or more servers in the cluster fails. On Windows operating systems, an ASM disk is always a partition. On all other platforms, an ASM disk can be a partition of a logical unit number (LUN) or any NAS device.

NOTE
Oracle does not support raw or block devices as shared storage for Oracle RAC in Oracle 11g Release 2 and onward. However, in our examples we have used raw devices as the database was migrated from Oracle 10g. Raw devices are only supported if you are upgrading from a previous release.

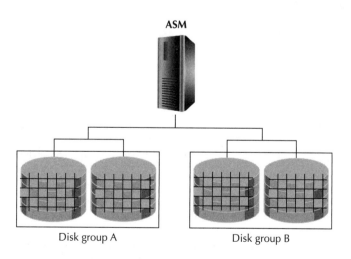

FIGURE 6-3 *Disk groups in ASM*

Allocation Unit

ASM disks are divided into a number of units or storage blocks that are small enough not to be hot. The allocation unit of storage is large enough for efficient sequential access. The allocation unit defaults to 1MB in size and is sufficient for most configurations. ASM allows you to change the allocation unit size, but that is not normally required unless ASM hosts a very large database (VLDB). You cannot change the size of an allocation unit of an existing disk group.

Significance of 1MB in ASM

Various I/O clients and their usage models are discussed in this section to provide insight into I/O block size and parallelization at the Oracle level. The log writer writes the very important redo buffers into log files. These writes are sequential and synchronous by default. The max size of any I/O request is set at 1MB on most platforms. Redo log reads are sequential and issued either during recovery or by LogMiner or log dumps. The size of each I/O buffer is limited to 1MB in most platforms. There are two asynchronous I/Os pending at any time for parallelization.

DBWR is the main server process that submits asynchronous I/Os in a big batch. Most of the I/O request sizes are equal to the database block size. DBWR also tries to coalesce the adjacent buffers in the disk up to a max size of 1MB whenever it can and submits them as one large I/O. The Kernel Sequential File I/O (ksfq) provides support for sequential disk/tape access and buffer management. The ksfq allocates four sequential buffers by default. The size of the buffers is determined by the dbfile_direct_io_count parameter, which is set to 1MB by default. Some of the ksfq clients are Datafile, Redologs, RMAN, Archive log file, Datapump, Oracle Data Guard, and the File transfer package.

Volume Allocation Unit

Like the allocation unit of the ASM disk group, the volume allocation unit is the smallest storage unit that ASM allocates for space inside the ASM dynamic volume. ASM allocates space in multiples of the volume allocation units. The size of the volume allocation unit is related to the size of the allocation unit of the ASM disk group. By default, ASM creates a volume allocation unit of 64MB inside the ASM disk group created with a default allocation unit size of 1MB.

Failure Groups

Failure groups define ASM disks that share a common potential failure mechanism. A failure group is a subset of disks in a disk group dependent on a common hardware resource whose failure must be tolerated. It is important only for normal or high redundancy configurations. Redundant copies of the same data are placed in different failure groups. An example might be a member in a stripe set or a set of SCSI disks sharing the same SCSI controller. Failure groups are used to determine which ASM disks should be used for storing redundant copies of data. By default, each disk is an individual failure group. Figure 6-4 illustrates the concept of a failure group.

For example, if two-way mirroring is specified for a file, ASM automatically stores redundant copies of file extents in separate failure groups. Failure groups apply only to normal and high redundancy disk groups and are not applicable for external redundancy disk groups. You define the failure groups in a disk group when you create or alter the disk group.

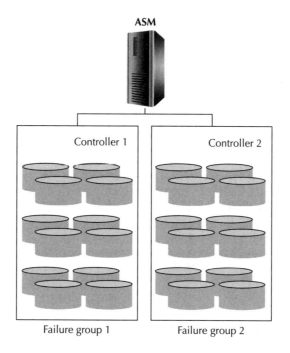

FIGURE 6-4 *Failure groups*

ASM Files

Files written on ASM disks are called *ASM files*. ASM file names normally start with a plus sign (+). Although the names are automatically generated by ASM, you can specify a meaningful, user-friendly alias name (or alias) for ASM files. Each ASM file is completely contained within a single disk group and evenly divided throughout all of the ASM disks in the group. An ASM file is a collection of data extents, where each data extent is a collection of allocation units. You cannot change the data extent size because Oracle will automatically increase the size of the data extent when an ASM file increases in size.

The extent allocation is similar to the locally managed tablespace extent sizes when an auto allocate mode is used. First, 20,000 data extents are allocated as one allocation unit per extent and thereafter the data extent size for the next 20,000 data extents is eight allocation units. When the ASM file is larger than 40,000 data extents, the data extent size for data extents above 40,000 is 64 allocation units per extent. Starting with Oracle 11g Release 2, Oracle ASM can store all types of Oracle database files.

Disk Partners

Disk partners limit the possibility of two independent disk failures losing both copies of a virtual extent. Each disk has a limited number of partners, and redundant copies are allocated on partners. The disk partner is automatically chosen by ASM, and partners are placed in different failure groups. Partner disks should be the same in size, capacity, and performance characteristics.

ASM Dynamic Volume Manager and ASM Cluster File System

Oracle ASM Dynamic Volume Manager is the foundation for ASM Cluster File System (ACFS). ACFS is a general-purpose cluster file system and supports non-Oracle applications.

The ASM disk group is the basic element in creating ACFS because the disk group contains the ASM dynamic volume device files, which ADVM (ASM Dynamic Volume Manager) presents to the operating system. Once these files are presented to the operating system, the traditional mkfs utility can be used to build and mount the ASM Cluster File System on the ASM dynamic volume device files, which are block devices. ADVM supports ext3, ACFS, and NTFS file systems, and users can use the advmutil utility on Windows systems to build the file system on ADVM.

ADVM is installed in the Oracle Grid Infrastructure home as part of the Oracle Grid Infrastructure installation, and Oracle Clusterware loads the oracleadvm, oracleoks, and oracleacfs modules automatically on system reboot. These are important to provide ADVM and ACFS functionalities of Oracle ASM. These ACFS modules are not reloaded automatically on system reboot when ACFS is used with Oracle Restart in a single-instance environment, and you must load them and mount the ACFS file system manually.

ASM tools such as ASMCA, ASMCMD, Oracle Enterprise Manager, and SQL*Plus can be used to create ASM dynamic volumes. ASMCA is new to 11gR2 and can be used for all ASM management operations.

There are some restrictions in terms of ACFS usage; for example, ACFS cannot be used to create a root or boot directory because ACFS drivers are loaded by Oracle Clusterware. Similarly, you cannot use ACFS to store Oracle Grid Infrastructure software. ACFS is a general file system, and you can perform I/O on an ACFS as you do on any other third-party file system. Operating system tools and APIs such as ioctl can access ACFS; hence, ACFS supports any standard file access protocols such as NAS.

Oracle ACFS is integrated with Cluster Synchronization Services; in case of failure, Cluster Synchronization Services will fence the failed cluster node from the active cluster to avoid any possible data corruption. Needless to say, Oracle uses various background processes to provide ADVM. These processes are explained in "ASM Background Processes" in this chapter.

ACFS Snapshots

Another exciting feature bundled with ACFS is the ability to create snapshots of the ASM dynamic volume; this allows users to recover from the deleted files or even to point in time in the past. ACFS snapshots are point-in-time copies of the ACFS file system, which is read-only and taken online. To perform point-in-time recovery or even to recover deleted files, you need to know the current data and changes made to the file. When you create a snapshot, ASM stores metadata such as the directory structure and the name of the files in the ASM dynamic volume. Along with the metadata, ASM stores the location information of all the data blocks of the files that have never had any data and the actual data blocks with data.

Once the snapshot is created, to maintain the consistency of the snapshot, ASM updates it by recording the file changes. The ASM Cluster File System supports POSIX and X/Open file system APIs, and you can use traditional UNIX commands such as cp, cpio, ar, access, dir, diff, and so on. ACFS supports standard operating system backup tools, Oracle secure backup, and third-party tools such as storage array snapshot technologies.

NOTE
Starting with Oracle Grid Infrastructure 11.2.0.2, ACFS is renamed Oracle Cluster File System–Cloud Edition and is supported on the

*Linux, Solaris, AIX, and Windows operating systems. Oracle has also
introduced new features for Oracle Cluster File System–Cloud Edition,
such as tagging, replication, and encryption.*

ASM Administration and Management

Administering an ASM instance is similar to managing a database instance but with fewer tasks.
An ASM instance does not require a database instance to be running for you to administer it. An
ASM instance does not have a data dictionary, because metadata is not stored in a dictionary.
ASM metadata is small and stored in the disk headers. SQL*Plus can be used to perform all ASM
administration tasks in the same way you work with a normal RDBMS instance.

NOTE
*To administer ASM with SQL*Plus, you must set the ORACLE_SID
environment variable to the ASM SID before you start SQL*Plus.
The default ASM SID for a single-instance database is +ASM, and
the default SID for ASM on Oracle RAC nodes is +ASMnode#. ASM
instances do not have a data dictionary, so you must use operating
system authentication and connect as SYSASM or SYSOPER. When
connecting remotely through Oracle Net Services, you must use a
password file for authentication.*

ASM Instance Management

An ASM instance is designed and built as a logical extension of the database instances; they share
the same mechanism of instance management. Similar to the database instance parameter file, an
ASM instance also has a parameter file called a registry file that's stored in the <cluster name>/
ASMPARAMETERFILE directory of the ASM disk group specified to store the OCR and vote disk
during installation of Oracle Grid Infrastructure. Oracle uses reserved file number 253 for the ASM
parameter file. The SID for ASM defaults to +ASM for a single-instance database and +ASMnode#
for Oracle RAC nodes. The rules for filenames, default locations, and search orders that apply to the
database initialization parameter files also apply to the ASM initialization parameter files. However,
they have a separate set of initialization parameters that cannot be set in the database instance.

Administering the ASM Instance

ASM instances are started similarly to Oracle database instances; as with connecting to the
instance with SQL*Plus, you must set the ORACLE_SID environment variable to the ASM SID. The
initialization parameter file, which can be a server parameter file also known as an ASM
parameter file, must contain the parameter INSTANCE_TYPE = ASM to signal the Oracle
executable that an ASM instance is starting and not a database instance. Apart from the disk
groups specified by the ASM_DISKGROUPS initialization parameter, ASM will automatically
mount the disk groups used to store the voting disk, OCR, and ASM parameter file.

The STARTUP command starts the instance with the set of memory structures and it
mounts the disk groups specified by the initialization parameter ASM_DISKGROUPS. If ASM_
DISKGROUPS is blank, the ASM instance starts and warns that no disk groups were mounted.
You can then mount disk groups with the ALTER DISKGROUP MOUNT command (similar to
the ALTER DATABASE MOUNT command).

The following table describes the various startup modes of the ASM instance:

Startup Mode	Description
NOMOUNT	Starts up the ASM instance without mounting any disk groups.
MOUNT	Starts up the ASM instance and mounts the disk groups.
OPEN	Mounts the disk groups and allows connections from the database. This is the default startup mode.
FORCE	Starts up MOUNT after a SHUTDOWN ABORT.

Other startup clauses have comparable interpretations for ASM instances as they do for database instances. For example, RESTRICT prevents database instances from connecting to this ASM instance. OPEN is invalid for an ASM instance. NOMOUNT starts up an ASM instance without mounting any disk group.

An ASM instance does not have any data dictionary, and the only possible way to connect an ASM instance is via operating system privileges such as SYSDBA, SYSASM, and SYSOPER. You specify the operating system groups OSASM, OSDBA, and OSOPER during installation of Oracle Grid Infrastructure, and these operating system groups implement the SYSASM, SYSDBA, and SYSOPER privileges for the Oracle ASM instance. Oracle allows password base authentication to connect to an ASM instance, which requires that the ASM initialization parameter REMOTE_LOGIN_PASSWORDFILE be set to a value other than NONE.

By default Oracle Universal Installer will create a password file for an ASM instance and new users will automatically be added to the password file; users can then connect to an ASM instance over the network using Oracle Net Services. Oracle connects as SYSDBA to an ASM instance when connecting via ASMCMD. You can use SQL*Plus to connect to the instance and run simple SQL commands such as "show sga" and "show parameter <parameter name>." Here's an example:

```
$ sqlplus / as sysdba
SQL*Plus: Release 11.2.0.2.0 Production on Fri Jan 14 11:09:38 2011
Copyright (c) 1982, 2010, Oracle.  All rights reserved.
Connected to:
Oracle Database 11g Enterprise Edition Release 11.2.0.2.0 - 64bit Production
With the Real Application Clusters and Automatic Storage Management options
SQL> show sga
Total System Global Area  283930624 bytes
Fixed Size                  2225792 bytes
Variable Size             256539008 bytes
ASM Cache                  25165824 bytes
```

You can query the V$PWFILE_USERS dynamic view to list users in the password file. Another possible way to list users in the password file is to use the lspwusr command from the ASMCMD command prompt. ASMCMD can be used to create and manage a password file manually.

ASM instance shutdown is similar to a database instance shutdown. The database instances using the ASM instance must be shut down before the ASM instance is shut down. When a NORMAL, IMMEDIATE, or TRANSACTIONAL shutdown is used, ASM waits for any in-progress SQL to complete. Once all ASM SQL is completed, it dismounts all disk groups and shuts down the ASM instance in an orderly fashion. If any database instances are connected to the ASM instance, the SHUTDOWN command returns an error and leaves the ASM instance running.

When SHUTDOWN ABORT is used, the ASM instance is immediately terminated. It does not dismount the disk groups in an orderly fashion. The next startup requires recovery of ASM—similar to RDBMS recovery—to bring the disk groups into a consistent state. The ASM instance also has components similar to undo and redo (details are discussed later in the chapter) that support crash recovery and instance recovery.

If any database instance is connected to the ASM instance, the database instance aborts because it does not get access to the storage system that is managed by the ASM instance.

In Oracle 11g Release 2, an ASM instance can also be started and stopped by the ASMCA, ASMCMD, and SRVCTL utilities. SRVCTL uses startup and shutdown options registered in the OCR to start or stop an ASM instance. The following are examples of starting and stopping the ASM instance +ASM1 on cluster node racnode01 using the SRVCTL utility.

Use the following command to start the ASM instance on racnode01 cluster node:

```
$srvctl start asm -n racnode01
```

Use the following command to stop the ASM instance on racnode01 cluster node:

```
$srvctl stop asm -n racnode01
```

Similar to SQL*Plus, the ASMCMD command-line utility can be used to start and stop the ASM instance with the available startup/shutdown options with different syntax. Here are examples of starting and stopping an ASM instance using ASMCMD.

Use the following command to start the ASM instance in a mount state:

```
$asmcmd
ASMCMD> startup --mount
```

Use the following command to shut down the ASM instance immediately:

```
$asmcmd
ASMCMD> shutdown --immediate
```

NOTE
You cannot start or shut down an ASM instance alone in the Oracle RAC database system if the OCR and voting disks are stored inside the ASM disk group. You must use the crsctl command to start or stop the CRS, which will start/stop the ASM instance also.

Although ASM does not have a data dictionary, it provides dynamic performance views stored inside memory that can be used to extract metadata information from an ASM instance. Here are short descriptions of the important dynamic performance views. By all means, this is not a complete list of performance views. Therefore, you should refer to Oracle documentation available on the Oracle Technology Network website for a complete list of the ASM dynamic performance views.

- **V$ASM**   This view displays the instance information of the ASM instance you are connected to.
- **V$ASM_DISKGROUP**   This view lists the disk groups created inside the ASM along with metadata information such as free space, allocation unit size, and the state of the disk group.

- **V$ASM_FILE**   This view lists the files created within the disk groups listed in the V$ASM_DISKGROUP view.

- **V$ASM_ALIAS**   This view lists the user-friendly name of the ASM files listed in the V$ASM_FILE view. This view is useful to identify the exact name of the ASM file because the V$ASM_FILE view only lists the file number.

- **V$ASM_DISK_IOSTAT**   This view lists the disk I/O performance statistics for each disk listed in the V$ASM_DISKGROUP view.

- **V$ASM_ACFSVOLUMES**   This view lists the metadata information of the ASM dynamic volumes.

- **V$ASM_OPERATION**   This view displays the current operations, such as any rebalancing happening on the disk groups listed in the V$ASM_DISKGROUP view. This view is useful to monitor the rebalancing operation in ASM.

ASM Background Processes

Because ASM is built using the RDBMS framework, the software architecture is similar to that of Oracle RDBMS processes. The ASM instance is built using various background processes, and a few of these processes specific to the ASM instance manage the disk groups, ASM Dynamic Volume Manager, and ASM Cluster File System in ASM. The following listing shows the background processes of the ASM instance having an SID of ASM:

```
grid     23405     1   0   2010  ?       00:00:25 asm_o000_+ASM1
grid     25753     1   0  21:37  ?       00:00:00 asm_pz99_+ASM1
grid     27524     1   0   2010  ?       00:00:53 asm_pmon_+ASM1
grid     27526     1   0   2010  ?       00:00:01 asm_psp0_+ASM1
grid     27530     1   0   2010  ?       00:00:00 asm_vktm_+ASM1
grid     27534     1   0   2010  ?       00:00:00 asm_gen0_+ASM1
grid     27536     1   0   2010  ?       00:00:02 asm_diag_+ASM1
grid     27538     1   0   2010  ?       00:01:06 asm_ping_+ASM1
grid     27540     1   0   2010  ?       00:21:59 asm_dia0_+ASM1
grid     27542     1   0   2010  ?       00:08:59 asm_lmon_+ASM1
grid     27544     1   0   2010  ?       00:16:53 asm_lmd0_+ASM1
grid     27546     1   1   2010  ?       11:14:44 asm_lms0_+ASM1
grid     27550     1   0   2010  ?       00:00:00 asm_lmhb_+ASM1
grid     27552     1   0   2010  ?       00:00:00 asm_mman_+ASM1
grid     27554     1   0   2010  ?       00:00:02 asm_dbw0_+ASM1
grid     27556     1   0   2010  ?       00:00:00 asm_lgwr_+ASM1
grid     27558     1   0   2010  ?       00:00:04 asm_ckpt_+ASM1
grid     27560     1   0   2010  ?       00:00:00 asm_smon_+ASM1
grid     27562     1   0   2010  ?       00:05:55 asm_rbal_+ASM1
grid     27564     1   0   2010  ?       00:00:00 asm_gmon_+ASM1
grid     27566     1   0   2010  ?       00:00:00 asm_mmon_+ASM1
grid     27569     1   0   2010  ?       00:00:00 asm_mmnl_+ASM1
grid     27576     1   0   2010  ?       00:00:01 asm_lck0_+ASM1
grid     27680     1   0   2010  ?       00:01:11 asm_asmb_+ASM1
grid     30118     1   0   2010  ?       00:00:39 asm_o001_+ASM1
```

Look at the background processes closely, and you will see that the background processes used in RDBMS instance management are similar to smon and pmon. However, additional processes, such as rbal and gmon, are specific to ASM instances. Let's take a closer look at the ASM-specific processes. You will see additional background processes such as VDBG, VBG*n*, and VMB when ASM dynamic volumes are created in the ASM instance. Some important ASM background processes are explained here:

- **RBAL** This is the Rebalancing background process. It is responsible for the rebalancing operation and also coordinates the ASM disk discovery process.

- **GMON** This is the Group Monitor background process. It manages disk groups by marking a disk group "offline" or even by dropping the disk group.

- **ARB*n*** Whereas RBAL coordinates the rebalancing of disk groups, ARB*n* actually performs the rebalancing operations.

- **VMB** This is the Volume Membership Background process, which is responsible for cluster membership with the ASM instance. The ASM instance starts this background process when ASM dynamic volumes are created.

- **VDBG** This is the Volume Driver background process. It works with the Dynamic Volume Driver to provide the locking and unlocking of volume extents. This is a vital process and will shut down the ASM instance if killed unexpectedly.

- **VBG*n*** This is the Volume Background process. VBG from the ASM instance communicates with operating system volume drivers. It handles messaging between ASM to the operating system.

- **XDMG** This is the Exadata Automation Manager. XDMG monitors all configured Exadata cells for state changes, such as a bad disk getting replaced. Its primary tasks are to watch for inaccessible disks and cells and, when they become accessible again, to initiate the ASM ONLINE operations.

ASM Processes in the Database Instance

Each database instance using ASM has two background processes: ASMB and RBAL. The ASMB background process runs in a database instance and connects to a foreground process in an ASM instance. Over this connection, periodic messages are exchanged to update statistics and to verify that both instances are healthy. All extent maps describing open files are sent to the database instance via ASMB. If an extent of an open file is relocated or the status of a disk is changed, messages are received by the ASMB process in the affected database instances.

During operations that require ASM intervention, such as a file creation by a database foreground, the database foreground connects directly to the ASM instance to perform the operation. Each database instance maintains a pool of connections to its ASM instance to avoid the overhead of reconnecting for every file operation.

A group of slave processes in O001 to O010 establishes a connection to the ASM instance, and these slave processes are used as a connection pool for database processes. Database processes can send messages to the ASM instance using the slave processes. For example, opening a file sends the open request to the ASM instance via a slave. However, slaves are not used for long-running operations, such as those for creating a file. The slave connections eliminate the overhead of logging into the ASM instances for short requests. These slaves are automatically shut down when not in use.

Communication Between a Database and ASM Instance

ASM is like a volume manager for the Oracle database that provides the file system for Oracle database files. When you create a new tablespace or just add a new datafile to an existing tablespace, the Oracle database instance requests an ASM instance to create a new ASM file that the Oracle database instance can use. Upon receiving a new file creation request, the ASM instance adds an entry into the Continuing Operation Directory and allocates space for the new file in the ASM disk group. ASM creates extents and shares the extent map with the database instance; in fact, the ASMB background process in the database instance receives this extent map process.

Once the database instance opens the file successfully, the ASM instance commits the new file creation and removes the entry from the Continuing Operation Directory because new file information is now stored in the disk headers. Here is one important concept to understand: Most people see database I/O being redirected to the ASM instance and the ASM instance performing I/O on behalf of the database instance; however, this is incorrect. The Oracle database instance performs I/O directly onto the ASM files, but it has to reopen the newly created ASM file once for when the ASM instance confirms with the database instance that the new file has been committed. The ASM instance uses two data structures—known as Active Change Directory (ACD) and Continuing Operations Directory (COD)—to manage the metadata transactions it contains.

Active Change Directory (ACD)

Active Change Directory (ACD) is a journaling mechanism that provides functionalities similar to redo logs in an Oracle database. Active Change Directory records all the metadata changes in the ASM instance required to decide to roll forward in an event of unexpected failures—either due to operation failures or an instance crash. ACD is stored as a file (42MB in size) in one of the ASM disks. ASM metadata is triple-mirrored (high redundancy) and can grow within the disk group when new instances are added. Transaction atomicity for ASM is guaranteed by ACD.

Continuing Operations Directory (COD)

Continuing Operations Directory (COD) is a memory structure in the ASM instance that maintains the state information of the active ASM operations and changes, such as rebalancing, new disk addition, or disk deletion. Also, file creation requests from clients such as the RDBMS instance use COD to protect the integrity. COD records are either committed or roll backed upon success or failure of the ASM operation. COD is similar to rollback segments (or undo tablespace) of an Oracle database.

Initialization Parameters

Just like a database instance, an ASM instance requires mandatory and optional parameters. Initialization parameters can be set in both database and ASM instances, but some parameters are only valid for an ASM instance. The following initialization parameters can be set in the ASM instance. Parameters that start with "ASM_" cannot be used in database instances. It is strongly recommended that you store these parameters in the ASM parameter file (also known as SPFILE or registry file).

- **INSTANCE_TYPE** This parameter instructs the Oracle executables about the instance type. By default, the Oracle executables assume the instance type is a database instance. This is the only mandatory parameter in an ASM instance. All other parameters have suitable default parameters when not specified.

- **ASM_POWER_LIMIT** Sets the power limits for disk rebalancing. This parameter defaults to 1. Valid values are 0 through 11. This parameter is dynamic. More details on rebalancing are provided later in the chapter.

- **ASM_DISKSTRING** A comma-separated list of strings that limits the set of disks that ASM discovers. This parameter accepts wildcard characters. Only disks that match one of the strings are discovered. The string format depends on the ASM library in use and the operating system. The standard system library for ASM supports glob pattern matching. If you are using ASMLib to create ASM disks, the default path will be ORCL:*.

- **CLUSTER_DATABASE** This parameter must be set to TRUE if the ASM instance on the cluster nodes wants to access the same ASM disk. This parameter actually enables clustered storage. You must ensure that this parameter is set to the same value on all ASM instances in the cluster.

- **ASM_DISKGROUPS** A list of the names of disk groups to be mounted by an ASM instance at startup, or when the ALTER DISKGROUP ALL MOUNT statement is used. If this parameter is not specified, no disk groups are mounted except the ASM disk groups that store the SPFILE, OCR, and voting disk. This parameter is dynamic, and when a server parameter file (SPFILE) is used, altering this value is not required.

- **ASM_PREFERRED_READ_FAILURE_GROUPS** This parameter is introduced in Oracle 11g and allows an ASM instance in extended cluster configuration, where each site has its own dedicated storage, to read data from the local disks rather than always reading data from the primary. Prior to Oracle 11g, ASM always read data from the primary copy regardless of the same extent being available on the local disks. This is a welcome enhancement in Oracle 11g, which is very useful for performance in Oracle extended clusters. You should choose the number of failure groups carefully when configuring ASM for extended cluster because this will have a direct impact on ASM read performance.

- **LARGE_POOL_SIZE** The internal packages used by ASM instances are executed from the large pool, and therefore you should set the initialization parameter LARGE_POOL_SIZE to a value greater than 8MB. Regarding other buffer parameters, you can use their default values.

Creating a Disk Group Manually

Oracle provides different ASM tools such as ASMCA, ASMCMD, Oracle Grid Control, and SQL*Plus to create and manage disk groups inside the ASM instance. It is very important to understand the performance and availability requirements for an ASM disk group before creating the ASM disk group (for example, the redundancy level for the ASM disk group). If the underlying storage is not protected by a RAID configuration, you should use ASM mirroring by choosing the correct redundancy for the ASM disk group. ASMCA is a GUI tool that's self-explanatory and does not require much expertise, but you should click on the Show Advance options to change the different attributes of the ASM disk group. ASMCM uses XML-style tags to specify the ASM disk group name, disk location, and attributes. These XML tags can be specified as inline XML, or you can create an XML file that can be used with the mkdg command inside the ASMCMD.

In SQL*Plus, the CREATE DISKGROUP command is used to create a disk group in an ASM instance. Before creating a disk group, the ASM instance will check that the disk/RAW partition being added in a disk group is addressable. If the disk/RAW partition is addressable and not being used by any other group, ASM writes specific information in the first block of the disk or RAW partition being used to create the disk group. Starting with Oracle 11*g*, you can specify different attributes for an ASM disk group that impact the performance and availability of the ASM disk group. Attributes specified while creating the ASM disk group can be queried from the V$ASM_ATTRIBUTE dynamic performance view. Following is a list of important ASM disk group attributes that you will mostly use:

- **AU_SIZE**   Used to specify the allocation unit size of the ASM disk group being created. You cannot change the allocation unit of an existing disk group, so make sure you specify the correct allocation unit size while creating an ASM disk group. By default, Oracle uses 1MB for the allocation unit.

- **DISK_REPAIR_TIME**   This attribute is related to the performance and availability of the disk group. This attribute specifies the amount of time ASM will wait for an offline ASM disk to be dropped and the disk group to be rebalanced.

- **COMPATIBLE.ADVM**   This attribute is required if the intended disk group will be used to create an ASM dynamic volume and can be used only in Oracle Grid Infrastructure 11*g* Release 2 and onward.

- **CELL.SMART_SCAN_CAPABLE**   This attribute is only valid for Oracle Exadata Grid disks and it enables smart scan predicate offload processing.

ASM mounts the disk group automatically when the CREATE DISKGROUP command is executed, and a disk group name is also added in the ASM_DISKGROUPS parameter in the SPFILE so that whenever the ASM instance is restarted later, only this newly created disk group will be mounted.

If you want ASM to mirror files, define the redundancy level while creating the ASM disk group. Oracle provides two redundancy levels: normal redundancy and high redundancy. In normal redundancy, each extent has one mirrored copy; in high redundancy, each extent has two mirrored copies in different disk groups.

Disks in a disk group should be of a similar size with similar performance characteristics. It's always advisable to create different disk groups for different types of disks. Disks in disk groups should be of the same size to avoid wasting disk space in failure groups. All disks that will be used to create disk groups must be in line with the ASM_DISKSTRING parameter to avoid disk discovery issues.

Creating a Disk Group

In the following example, we create a disk group named DGA with two failure groups, named FLGRP1 and FLGRP2, using four raw partitions—namely, /dev/raw/raw3, /dev/raw/raw4, /dev/raw/raw5, and /dev/raw/raw6:

```
SQL> CREATE DISKGROUP DGA NORMAL REDUNDANCY
  2   FAILGROUP FLGRP1 DISK
  3 '/dev/raw/raw3',
  4 '/dev/raw/raw4',
  5   FAILGROUP FLGRP2 DISK
  6 '/dev/raw/raw5',
  7 '/dev/raw/raw6',
```

After creating a disk group, you may need to alter the disk group depending on your business requirements. Oracle allows you to perform create, drop/undrop, resize, rebalance, and mount/dismount operations on disk groups after they've been created.

Adding Disks to a Disk Group

Whenever disks are added into a disk group, Oracle internally rebalances the I/O load. The following example shows you how to add disks to an existing disk group. Oracle uses the ADD clause to add disks or a failure group to an existing disk group. In this example, raw partition /dev/raw/raw7 is being added to the existing group DGA:

```
ALTER DISKGROUP DGA ADD DISK
   '/dev/raw/raw7' NAME disk5;
```

No failure group is defined in the statement, so the disk will be assigned to its own failure group.

Dropping Disks in a Disk Group

Oracle provides the DROP DISK clause in conjunction with the CREATE DISK GROUP command to drop a disk within a disk group. Oracle internally rebalances the files during this operation. Oracle fails the DROP operation if other disks in the disk group don't have enough space. If you are adding and dropping disks from a disk group, it is advisable that you add first and then drop, and both operations should be performed in a single ALTER DISKGROUP statement, because this reduces the time spent on rebalancing. Oracle also provides force options to drop a disk within a disk group even if ASM can't read or write to those disks. This option can't be used with external redundancy disk groups.

In this example, we drop /dev/raw/raw7 from the DGA disk group:

```
ALTER DISKGROUP DGA DROP DISK '/dev/raw/raw7';
```

Resizing the Disks

Oracle provides a RESIZE clause that can be used in conjunction with the ALTER DISKGROUP command to resize the disk, resize any specific disk, or resize the disks within a specific failure group.

Resizing is useful for reclaiming disk space. For example, if the SIZE defined for the disks was less than the disk size when the disk group was created and later on you want to claim the full size of the disk, you can use this option without giving any SIZE so that Oracle will take SIZE as returned by the operating system:

```
ALTER DISKGROUP DGA RESIZE DISK '/dev/raw/raw6' SIZE 500M;
```

Administering the ACFS

ASM tools such as ASMCA, ASMCMD, OEM, and SQL*Plus can be used to create and manage ACFS. Creating ACFS is just like creating a file system with any traditional volume manager. In a traditional volume manager, you first create a volume group and then the volumes. Finally, you create the file system and then mount the file system.

Just like an allocation unit in the ASM disk group, Volume Allocation Unit is the smallest storage unit that can be allocated in an ASM dynamic volume. ASM allocates stripes in each Volume Allocation Unit, where each stripe is the equivalent of the volume extent size, which is directly related to the allocation unit size of the underlying ASM disk group. By default, the size of one volume extent is 64MB for a 1MB allocation unit size disk group. When you create an ASM dynamic volume, you specify the number of stripes (also known as stripe columns) and the width of each stripe because Oracle internally uses the SAME approach to stripe and mirror data. Oracle will then distribute the file being stored inside the ACFS into chunks, with a strip width size of 128KB (the default stripe width) on each volume extent.

For example, if you create an ASM volume of 400MB and store a 1MB file initially with default settings, Oracle will create a volume extent size of 64MB and each Allocation Volume Unit will be of 256MB (the number of stripes multiply by the volume extent size). Because Oracle allocates space in multiples of Volume Allocation Unit, it will allocate 512MB for the ASM dynamic volume although you requested 400MB. The ASM dynamic volume can be extended later on. ASM will distribute the file into eight chunks of 128KB and store them on volume extents. ASM stripes the volume extents in the same way on the available disks inside the ASM disk group; hence, it provides very efficient I/O operations. You can use the V$ASM_ ACFSVOLUMES and V$ASM_FILESYSTEM dynamic performance views of the ASM instance to display the ACFS file system information on the connected ASM instance.

Setting Up ACFS

Follow the steps given next to create the ASM Cluster File System:

1. Create an ASM disk group with the attribute COMPATIBLE.ADVM set at to a minimum value of 11.2.0.0.0, because setting this attribute tells ASM that this disk group can store ASM dynamic volumes. If this attribute is not set, you cannot create a dynamic volume in this ASM disk group. The minimum value for the attribute is 11.2.0.0.0 because ACFS is introduced in Oracle 11*g* Release 2 and cannot be used in prior releases of Oracle Clusterware. You can use either ASMCA, ASMCMD, OEM, or SQL*Plus to create the ASM disk group. If you are using ASMCA, you can set the disk group attribute by clicking on the Show Advance Options button. Other ASM tools allow you to specify the attribute at the command line.

2. Once the ASM disk group is created, you need to create the ASM dynamic volume in the ASM disk group created in the previous step.

3. Create the required OS directory structure to mount the newly created ASM dynamic volume.

4. Once you have created the directory, you need to create the ACFS file system using the operating system command mkfs. Make sure you use the following syntax to create the ACFS-type file system on the ASM dynamic volume:

```
mkfs -t acfs /dev/asm/<your asm dynamic volume>
```

5. Now mount the newly created file system using the mount operating system command. Make sure you use the ACFS file system type to mount the file system.

Creating the ACFS Snapshot

ASM tools are used to create and manage ACFS snapshots. The ASMCMD command acfsutil can be used to create and managed snapshots via a command-line interface. Here is an example of creating the ACFS snapshot:

```
acfsutil snap create acfs_snap_01 /app/oracle/myfirstacfs
```

The snapshot creation process will create a hidden directory (.ACFS) and a directory structure of snaps/<snapshot name> inside the hidden directory. In our example, ASM will create the following directory structure:

```
.ACFS/snaps/acfs_snap_01
```

With all the exciting features of ACFS, it comes with some restrictions, which you must be aware of before using the ACFS. Although you can create other file systems on an ASM dynamic volume, Oracle only supports ACFS as a cluster file system on an ASM dynamic volume. Partitioning of an ASM dynamic volume is not supported, so you cannot use the fdisk command to partition an ASM dynamic volume device. Apart from this, you should not use ASMLib over an ASM dynamic volume because Oracle does not support this configuration. You can use multipath devices to create an ASM disk group, but using multipathing on ASM dynamic volumes is prohibited.

ASM Fast Mirror Resync

Prior to Oracle 11*g*, whenever ASM was not able to write the data extent to the ASM disk, it took the ASM disk offline. In addition to this, further reads on this disk were prohibited and ASM would re-create the extents from the mirror copies stored on the other ASM disks. When you added the disk back to the disk group, ASM would perform this rebalancing operation again to reconstruct all the data extents. This rebalancing operation is very time consuming and also has an impact on the response time of the ASM disk group.

Oracle 11*g*, on the other hand, does not drop the offline ASM disk and waits and tracks the data extents modified up to the time specified by the ASM_DISK_REPAIR attribute of the associated disk group. When the failure is repaired within this timeframe, ASM will reconstruct the modified data extents only, rather than requiring a complete rebalancing of the whole disk group, thus resulting in an overall faster and more efficient rebalancing operation.

ASM Rebalancing

ASM does not require any downtime during storage configuration and reconfiguration—that is, you can change the storage configuration without having to take the database offline. ASM automatically redistributes file data evenly across all the disks of the disk group after you add or drop disks from a group. This operation is called *disk rebalancing* and is transparent to the database.

A rebalancing operation evenly spreads the contents of every file across all available disks in that disk group. The operation is driven by space usage in the disks and not based on the I/O statistics on those disks. It is invoked automatically when needed, and no manual intervention is required during the operation. You can also choose to run the operation manually or change a running rebalancing operation.

Increasing the number of background slave processes responsible for the operation can speed up the rebalancing operation. The background process ARBx is responsible for disk rebalancing during storage reconfiguration. To increase the number of slave processes dynamically, you use the init.ora parameter ASM_POWER_LIMIT. It is recommended that you perform rebalancing using only one node when running in Oracle RAC. Shutting down any unused ASM instances can do this. Figure 6-5 shows the rebalancing functionality.

If the POWER clause is not specified in an ALTER DISKGROUP command, or when adding or dropping a disk implicitly invokes a rebalance, the rebalance power defaults to the value of the ASM_POWER_LIMIT initialization parameter. You can adjust this parameter dynamically. The

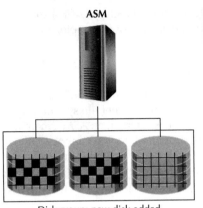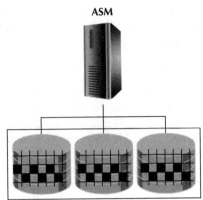

FIGURE 6-5 *ASM rebalancing*

higher the limit, the faster a rebalancing operation may complete. Lower values cause rebalancing to take longer but consume fewer processing and I/O resources. This leaves these resources available for other applications, such as the database. The default value of 1 minimizes disruption to other applications. The appropriate value is dependent on your hardware configuration as well as the performance and availability requirements.

If a rebalance is in progress because a disk is manually or automatically dropped, increasing the power of the rebalance shortens the window during which redundant copies of that data on the dropped disk are reconstructed on other disks.

The V$ASM_OPERATION view provides information that can be used for adjusting the ASM_POWER_LIMIT and the resulting power of rebalancing operations. The V$ASM_OPERATION view also gives an estimate in the EST_MINUTES column of the amount of time remaining for the rebalancing operation to complete. You can see the effect of changing the rebalance power by observing the change in the time estimate.

Manually Rebalancing a Disk Group

You can manually rebalance the files in a disk group using the REBALANCE clause of the ALTER DISKGROUP statement. This would normally not be required, because ASM automatically rebalances disk groups when their composition changes. You might want to perform a manual rebalancing operation, however, if you want to control the speed of what would otherwise be an automatic rebalancing operation.

The POWER clause of the ALTER DISKGROUP...REBALANCE statement specifies the degree of parallelization, and thus the speed of the rebalancing operation. It can be set to a value from 0 to 11. A value of 0 halts a rebalancing operation until the statement is either implicitly or explicitly reinvoked. The default rebalance power is set by the ASM_POWER_LIMIT initialization parameter.

> **NOTE**
> *ASM automatically disables the rebalancing feature when you create a disk group with REBALANCE POWER 0. If you add more disks to this disk group, ASM will not distribute data to the newly added disks.*

Also, when you remove disks from this disk group (DROP DISK),
the status of the disk group remains DROPPING until you change
REBALANCE POWER to greater than 0.

Entering the REBALANCE statement with a new level can change the power level of an ongoing rebalancing operation. The ALTER DISKGROUP...REBALANCE command by default returns immediately so that you can issue other commands while the rebalancing operation takes place asynchronously in the background. You can query the V$ASM_OPERATION view for the status of the rebalancing operation. Starting with Oracle 11*g*, you can use the lsop command on the ASMCMD command prompt to list the ASM operations. Here is an example of using the lsop command:

```
ASMCMD> lsop
Group_Name  Dsk_Num  State  Power
data        RBAL     REAP   2
```

If you want the ALTER DISKGROUP...REBALANCE command to wait until the rebalancing operation is complete before returning, you can add the WAIT keyword to the REBALANCE clause. This is especially useful in scripts. The command also accepts a NOWAIT keyword, which invokes the default behavior of conducting the rebalancing operation asynchronously. You can interrupt a rebalance running in wait mode by pressing CTRL-C on most platforms. This causes the command to return immediately with the message "ORA-01013: user requested cancel of current operation," and to continue the rebalance operation asynchronously.

Additional rules for the rebalancing operation include the following:

- The ALTER DISKGROUP...REBALANCE statement uses the resources of the single node upon which it is started.
- ASM can perform only one rebalance at a time on a given instance.
- Rebalancing continues across a failure of the ASM instance performing the rebalance.
- The REBALANCE clause (with its associated POWER and WAIT/NOWAIT keywords) can also be used in ALTER DISKGROUP commands that add, drop, or resize disks.

The following example manually rebalances the disk group dgroup2. The command does not return until the rebalancing operation is complete:

```
ALTER DISKGROUP dgroup2 REBALANCE POWER 5 WAIT;
```

V$ASM_DISK_STAT and V$ASM_DISKGROUP_STAT can be used to query performance statistics. The following query can be used to get the performance statistics at the disk group level. These views, along with V$filestat, can provide greater information about the performance of the disk groups and datafiles.

```
SELECT PATH, READS, WRITES, READ_TIME, WRITE_TIME,
READ_TIME/DECODE(READS,0,1,READS) "AVGRDTIME",
WRITE_TIME/DECODE(WRITES,0,1,WRITES) "AVGWRTIME"
FROM V$ASM_DISK_STAT;
PATH             READS    WRITES  READ_TIME WRITE_TIME  AVGRDTIME  AVGWRTIME
--------------- -------- -------- ---------- ---------- ---------- ----------
ORCL:DISK1         50477    67683      20.86 724.856718 .000413258 .010709583
ORCL:DISK2        418640   174842    100.259 802.975526 .000239487 .004592578
```

Backup and Recovery in ASM

An ASM instance is *not* backed up because an ASM instance itself does not contain any files but rather manages the metadata of the ASM disks. ASM metadata is *triple mirrored,* which should protect the metadata from typical failures. If sufficient failures occur to cause the loss of metadata, the disk group must be re-created. Data on the ASM disks is backed up using RMAN. In case of failure, once the disk groups are created, the data (such as database files) can be restored using RMAN.

Each disk group is self-describing, containing its own file directory, disk directory, and other data such as metadata logging information. ASM automatically protects its metadata by using mirroring techniques, even with external redundancy disk groups. An ASM instance caches the information in its SGA. ASM metadata describes the disk group and files, and it is self-describing as it resides inside the disk group. Metadata is maintained in the blocks, and each metadata block is 4KB and triple mirrored.

With multiple ASM instances mounting the same disk groups, if one ASM instance fails, another ASM instance automatically recovers transient ASM metadata changes caused by the failed instance. This situation is called *ASM instance recovery* and is automatically and immediately detected by the global cache services.

With multiple ASM instances mounting different disk groups, or in the case of a single ASM instance configuration, if an ASM instance fails while ASM metadata is open for update, the disk groups that are not currently mounted by any other ASM instance are not recovered until they are mounted again. When an ASM instance mounts a failed disk group, it reads the disk group log and recovers all transient changes. This situation is called *ASM crash recovery.*

Therefore, when using ASM clustered instances, it is recommended that you have all ASM instances always mounting the same set of disk groups. However, it is possible to have a disk group on locally attached disks that are visible only to one node in a cluster, and have that disk group mounted only on the node where the disks are attached.

ASM supports standard operating system backup tools, Oracle Secure backup, and third-party backup solutions such as storage array snapshot technologies to back up the ACFS file system.

ASM Tools

The new ASM tools, such as the ASM command-line interface and the ASM file transfer utilities, emulate the UNIX environment within the ASM file system. Even though ASMCMD internally uses the SQL*Plus interface to query the ASM instance, it greatly helps system administrators and storage administrators because it provides the look and feel of a UNIX shell interface.

ASMCA: The ASM Configuration Assistant

ASM Configuration Assistant is a GUI tool, introduced in Oracle 11*g*, that can be used to install and configure an ASM instance, disk groups, volumes, and ACFS. Like the DBCA, ASMCA can also be used in silent mode. Oracle Universal Installer internally uses ASMCA in silent mode to configure ASM disk groups to store OCR and voting files. ASMCA is capable of managing the complete ASM instance and associated ASM objects. Starting with Oracle 11*g*, DBCA does not allow creating and configuring ASM disk groups, and Oracle's future directions are to promote the use of ASMCA because it is a complete ASM management tool.

ASMCMD: The ASM Command-Line Utility

Oracle introduced ASMCMD as a new option to access the ASM files and related information via a command-line interface, which makes ASM management easier and handy for DBAs. This new option can be used on Oracle 10*g* and onward, but is available by default only from Oracle 10*g* Release 2 and onward. Oracle has enhanced this tool to provide more management features so that users can now manage an ASM instance and ASM objects such as disk groups, volumes, and an ASM cluster file system from this command-line interface.

ASMCMD provides the DBA with a similar look and feel as well as the privileges of most UNIX-flavor systems, with commands such as cd, ls, mkdir, pwd, lsop, dsget, and so on. Starting with Oracle 11*g*, lots of new commands have been added to manage the complete ASM instance and its objects. It is now possible to completely manage an ASM instance from the command-line interface, including starting/stopping; managing the disk groups, volumes, and the ASM cluster file system; backing up and restoring metadata; and even accessing the GPnP profile and ASM parameter file within ASMCMD. You should refer to the command-line help for an explanation and sample usage of specific ASMCMD commands because the ASMCMD command-line help provides sufficient information for these commands.

ASM FTP Utility

Oracle 11*g* ASM supports ASM FTP, by which operations on ASM files and directories can be performed similarly to conventional operations on normal files using conventional File Transfer Protocol (FTP). A typical use of such access to an ASM file can be to copy ASM files from one database to another.

The Oracle database leverages the virtual folder feature of XML DB that provides a way to access the ASM files and directories through XML DB protocols such as FTP, Hypertext Transfer Protocol (HTTP), and programmatic APIs. An ASM virtual folder is mounted as /sys/asm within the XML DB hierarchy. The folder is called "virtual" because nothing is physically stored in XML DB. All operations are handled by underlying ASM components.

The virtual folder is created by default during the installation of XML DB. If the database is not configured to use automatic storage, this virtual folder will be empty and no operation will be permitted. The /sys/asm virtual folder contains folders and subfolders in line with the hierarchy of the ASM fully qualified naming structure. Figure 6-6 shows the hierarchy of an ASM virtual folder.

As shown in Figure 6-6, the virtual folder contains a subfolder for each mounted disk group in an ASM instance. Each disk group folder contains a subfolder for each database using that disk group subfolder, the database folder contains a file type subfolder, and the file type subfolder contains ASM files, which are binary in nature. Although we can access the ASM files as we can access normal files in a conventional FTP application, some usage/access restrictions are in place. DBA privilege is a must to view the contents of the /sys/asm virtual folder.

The next example demonstrates accessing ASM files via the virtual folder. In this example, we assume that we are in the home directory of user *oracle*, which is /home/oracle, and we are connecting to the server, using FTP, where the ASM instance is hosted. The ASM instance is hosted on the racnode01 server. The disk group name is DGA, and the database name is *dba* using the DGA disk group.

First, we open the FTP connection to i3dl045e and pass on the login information. Only users with the DBA privilege can access the /sys/asm folder. After connecting, we change our directory to the /sys/asm virtual folder and list the contents of the /sys/asm folder. A subfolder named DGA is used for the DGA disk group. Then we change to the DGA directory and see another subfolder

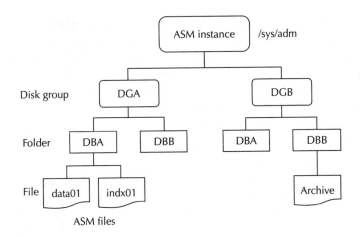

FIGURE 6-6 *ASM virtual folder hierarchy*

with a database name, which is *dba* in our case. Then we list the contents of the dba directory that contains the ASM binary files related to the dba database. Finally, we download the file data01.dbf to our local directory, which is /home/oracle.

```
ftp> open racnode01 7777
ftp> use system
ftp> passwd manager
ftp> cd /sys/asm
ftp> ls
DGA
ftp> cd DGA
ftp> ls
dba
ftp> ls
data01.dbf
indx01.dbf
ftp> bin
ftp> get data01.dbf
```

ASMLib

ASMLib is the storage management interface that helps simplify the operating system–to–database interface. The ASMLib API was developed and supported by Oracle to provide an alternative interface for the ASM-enabled kernel to identify and access block devices. The ASMLib interface serves as an alternative to the standard operating system interface. It provides storage and operating system vendors the opportunity to supply extended storage-related features that provide benefits such as improved performance and greater integrity than are currently available on other database platforms.

Installing ASMLib

Oracle provides an ASM library driver for the Linux OS. With the advent of this library, steps such as raw device binding become unnecessary. The ASM library driver must be installed prior to installing any Oracle Database software. In addition, it is recommended that any ASM disk devices required by the database be prepared and created before the OUI database installation.

The ASMLib software is available on the Oracle Technology Network (OTN) for free download. Go to http://otn.oracle.com/tech/linux/asmlib/ and chose the link for your version of the Linux platform.

Three packages are available for each Linux platform. The two essential rpm packages are the oracleasmlib package, which provides the actual ASM library, and the oracleasm-support package, which provides the utilities to configure and enable the ASM driver. Both these packages need to be installed. The third package provides the kernel driver for the ASM library. Each package provides the driver for a different kernel. You must install the appropriate package for the kernel you are running.

Configuring ASMLib

After the packages are installed, the ASMLib can be loaded and configured using the configure option in the /etc/init.d/oracleasm utility. For Oracle RAC clusters, the oracleasm installation and configuration must be completed on all nodes of the cluster. Configuring ASMLib is as simple as executing the following command:

```
[root@racnode01/]# /etc/init.d/oracleasm configure
    Configuring the Oracle ASM library driver.

    This will configure the on-boot properties of the Oracle ASM library
    driver. The following questions will determine whether the driver is
    loaded on boot and what permissions it will have.  The current values
    will be shown in brackets ('[]'). Hitting  without typing an
    answer will keep that current value.  Ctrl-C will abort.

    Default user to own the driver interface []: oracle
    Default group to own the driver interface []: dba
    Start Oracle ASM library driver on boot (y/n) [n]: y
    Fix permissions of Oracle ASM disks on boot (y/n) [y]: y
    Writing Oracle ASM library driver configuration        [  OK  ]
    Creating /dev/oracleasm mount point                    [  OK  ]
    Loading module "oracleasm"                             [  OK  ]
    Mounting ASMlib driver filesystem                      [  OK  ]
    Scanning system for ASM disks                          [  OK  ]
```

Note that the ASMLib mount point is not a standard file system that can be accessed by operating system commands. Only the ASM library to communicate with the ASM driver uses it. The ASM library dynamically links with the Oracle kernel, and multiple ASMLib implementations could be simultaneously linked to the same Oracle kernel. Each library would provide access to a different set of disks and different ASMLib capabilities.

The objective of ASMLib is to provide a more streamlined and efficient mechanism for managing disks and I/O processing of ASM storage. The ASM API provides a set of interdependent functions that need to be implemented in a layered fashion. These functions are dependent on the backend storage implementing the associated functions. From an implementation perspective, these functions are grouped into three collections of functions.

Each function group is dependent on the existence of the lower-level group. *Device discovery functions* are the lowest-layer functions and must be implemented in any ASMLib library. *I/O processing functions* provide an optimized asynchronous interface for scheduling I/O operations and managing I/O operation completion events. These functions, in effect, extend the operating system interface. Consequently, the I/O processing functions must be implemented as a device driver within the operating system kernel.

The *performance and reliability functions* are the highest-layer functions and depend on the existence of the I/O processing functions. These functions use the I/O processing control structures for passing metadata between the Oracle database and the backend storage devices. The performance and reliability functions enable additional intelligence on the part of backend storage. This is achieved when metadata transfer is passed through the ASMLib API.

Device Discovery
Device discovery provides the identification and naming of storage devices that are operated on by higher-level functions. Device discovery does not require any operating system code and can be implemented as a standalone library invoked and dynamically linked by the Oracle database. The discovery function makes the characteristics of the disk available to ASM. Disks discovered through ASMLib do not need to be available through normal operating system interfaces. For example, a storage vendor may provide a more efficient method of discovering and locating disks that its own interface driver manages.

I/O Processing
The current standard I/O model imposes a lot of OS overhead, due in part to mode and context switches. The deployment of ASMLib reduces the number of state transitions from kernel to user mode by employing a more efficient I/O schedule and call-processing mechanism. One call to ASMLib can submit and reap multiple I/Os. This dramatically reduces the number of calls to the OS when I/O is performed. Additionally, one I/O handle can be used by all the processes in an instance for accessing the same disk. This eliminates multiple open calls and multiple file descriptors.

One of the critical aspects of the ASMLib I/O interface is that it provides asynchronous I/O interface-enhancing performance and enables database-related intelligence on the backend storage devices. As for additional intelligence in the backend storage, the I/O interface enables passing metadata from the database to the storage devices. Future developments in the storage array firmware may allow the transport of database-related metadata to the backend storage devices and will enable new database-related intelligence in the storage devices.

In a Nutshell
Automatic Storage Management is one of the best frameworks for managing data storage for the Oracle database. ASM implements the Stripe and Mirror Everything (SAME) methodology to manage the storage stack with an I/O size equal to the most common Oracle I/O clients, thus providing tremendous performance benefits.

Oracle has enhanced and improved ASM to a level that it is supported with non-Oracle enterprise applications to store application data. ASM provides the GUI tools ASMCA and OEM for management of the ASM instance and its associated objects. The ASM Cluster File System is a true cluster file system built on ASM foundations, and it eliminates the need for third-party cluster file systems in enterprise cluster applications. ACFS also comes with rich functionalities such as snapshots and encryption.

Command-line tools such as SQL*Plus, ASMFTP, and ASMCMD are also available to provide a command-line interface to design and build provisioning scripts. With the added features of the ACFS and ACFS snapshot, managing a huge amount of storage is no longer a complex task that involves lots of planning and day-to-day administration issues.

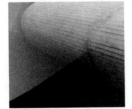

PART

III

Oracle RAC Administration and Management

CHAPTER
7

Oracle RAC Basic Administration

racle Real Application Clusters database administration is similar to single-instance database administration. Accomplishing tasks such as managing users, datafiles, tablespaces, controlfiles, and undo tablespaces is similar to managing those aspects in a single-instance environment. The information in this chapter assumes that you are familiar with single-instance database administration and focuses on aspects of Oracle RAC that are different from those of a single instance. This chapter covers the tasks of administering an Oracle RAC database in an Oracle RAC instance and administering an Oracle RAC database and database objects.

Initialization Parameters

Oracle is a highly flexible, function-rich RDBMS that can be used on a laptop by a single user or used on the world's most powerful computer systems and accessed by thousands of users. How does Oracle offer such flexibility? How does an end user choose which functions to use and optimize the database for the intended use? The answers lie in Oracle's parameter file, which contains a set of parameters that allow an end user to customize and optimize an Oracle database instance. When an Oracle instance starts, it reads these parameters, which in turn define the features the database uses, the amount of memory an instance uses, how users interact with the database, and other important information.

Prior to Oracle version 9*i*, parameters used by an instance could be stored only in a text file (frequently referred to as init.ora). Its name was somewhat operating system dependent, however—for example, on a UNIX-based system, the parameter file's default name was init<sid>.ora. A DBA could use a nondefault parameter file by specifying the pfile clause of the startup command. The text file used during startup was never referred to by the Oracle instance again, and the only means of updating it was by editing it through a text editor.

Starting with Oracle 9*i*, Oracle introduced the server parameter file (or SPFILE). This binary file can be updated only by Oracle. SPFILE offers the following advantages over the traditional init .ora text file:

- Any changes made to an instance's parameter can be persistent through shutdown and startup. A DBA can control whether the change is intended for the current life of the instance (by specifying `SCOPE=MEMORY`), should be permanent (by specifying `SCOPE=SPFILE`), or should be immediate and permanent (by specifying `SCOPE=BOTH`).

- When used, an Oracle instance remembers which SPFILE was used to start the instance. The SQL command `show parameter spfile` can be used to display the SPFILE used to start the instance. Oracle does not remember the name of the traditional parameter file (init.ora, known as pfile) used to start the instance.

- An instance will update the SPFILE whenever the DBA uses the `alter system` command with `SCOPE=SPFILE` or `SCOPE=BOTH`. The DBA does not need to remember the file used to start the instance, and there is no need to edit the file manually.

In an Oracle RAC environment, a DBA can use a parameter file shared by all the instances, or each instance can have its own dedicated parameter file. Using a shared SPFILE for managing instances in an Oracle RAC environment is highly recommended.

NOTE
In an Oracle RAC environment, SPFILE is recommended to be shared and should be placed on a shareable disk subsystem—that is, either on a raw device, a clustered file system, or Automatic Storage Management (ASM). The typical size of an SPFILE need not be more than few kilobytes, so if you are using a raw device, allocating 5MB is more than adequate.

Oracle instance parameters for the Oracle RAC environment can be grouped into three major categories:

- **Unique parameters**   These parameters are unique to each instance. Parameters in this category identify resources to be used by an instance exclusively. Some examples of this type of parameter are instance_name, thread, and undo_tablespace.

- **Identical parameters**   Parameters in this category need to be the same on all the instances in an Oracle RAC environment. Parameters defining the database characteristics, interinstance communication characteristics, and so on, fall into this category. The parameters max_commit_propagation_delay, db_name, and control_file belong to this category. Beginning with Oracle 10g, you can use the ISINSTANCE_ MODIFIABLE column of the v$parameter view to see a list of such parameters:

```
select name, ISINSTANCE_MODIFIABLE
from v$parameter
where ISINSTANCE_MODIFIABLE='FALSE'
order by name;
```

- **Neither unique nor identical parameters**   Parameters that do not fall into either of the preceding two categories are included here. Those that define performance characteristics of an instance generally fall into this section. Some examples of this type of parameter are db_cache_size, large_pool_size, local_listener, and gcs_server_ processes.

Unique Parameters

The following parameters are unique to each instance.

instance_name

This parameter defines the name of the Oracle instance. Although not required, this parameter is generally chosen to be the same as the ORACLE_SID environment variable defined at the operating system level. The default value for this parameter is also the value of the environment variable ORACLE_SID. In a single-instance environment, the instance name is usually the same as the database name. In an Oracle RAC environment, the instance name is constructed by appending a suffix to each instance of the database (for example, for a database named "prod," instance names could be prod1, prod2, prod3, and so on).

Generally the value of this parameter is not set in the parameter file, thus leaving it at its default value of SID. We strongly recommend not specifying this parameter and leaving it at its default setting.

Note that some of the dynamic performance views (more than 30 of them) that contains the column instance_name or inst_name derives the value from the environment variable ORACLE_SID and *not* from this parameter.

The following SQL session demonstrates the parameter behavior:

```
$echo $ORACLE_SID
PROD1
$grep instanace_name initPROD1.ora
instance_name=xyz
. . .
SQL>
SQL> select instance_name from v$instance ;
INSTANCE_NAME
----------------
PROD1
SQL> show parameter instance_name
NAME                                 TYPE         VALUE
------------------------------------ -----------  ----------------
instance_name                        string       xyz
```

instance_number

This is a unique number greater than 0 (zero) and smaller than the max_instance parameter specified when the database was created. Oracle uses it internally to identify the instance. The INST_ID column in GV$ corresponds to the value of this parameter for that instance. Generally, the value of this parameter is kept equal to the value of the thread parameter to make administrative tasks simple.

If Manual Segment Space Management is used (as opposed to Automatic Segment Space Management), Oracle uses the instance number to map the instance to the freelist group.

The following example sets instance_number to 1 for instance prod1:

```
prod1.instance_number=1
```

thread

This parameter specifies the set of redo log files to be used by the instance. All thread values default to 1 if the thread parameter is not specified. Therefore, only the first instance will start.

To simplify administrative tasks, it is highly recommended that you use the same thread number for an instance. Also, as mentioned, the value of the parameter instance_number should be the same as the value of thread. The following example assigns a thread value of 2 to instance prod2:

```
prod2.thread = 2
```

undo_tablespace

This parameter specifies the name of the undo tablespace to be used by an instance. An instance uses its own undo tablespace to write the undo data for its transaction; however, it can read other instances' undo tablespaces. The following line specifies undo tablespace UNDOTBS1 to the instance prod1:

```
prod1.undo_tablespace='UNDOTBS1'
```

For more information on managing the undo tablespace, refer to the "Administering Undo" section of this chapter.

rollback_segments

It is highly recommended that you use Automatic Undo Management. If, due to any reason, an older method of rollback segments is being used, this parameter is used to specify a list of rollback segments. For the best practices on using rollback segments and further details, refer to the Oracle 8*i* documentation.

The following line assigns rollback segment "rbs1, rbs2" to instance prod1:

```
prod1.rollback_segments = (rbs1, rbs2)
```

cluster_interconnects

This optional parameter is used only when the Oracle instance is not able to pick the correct interconnect for interinstance communication automatically. This parameter can also be used to specify multiple networks' interconnect to be used for Oracle RAC traffic. Use this parameter to specify the IP address of the network to be used for Cache Fusion traffic. In the following example, 10.0.0.1 is the IP address of the private interconnect to be used for the cluster traffic:

```
prod1.cluster_interconnects = "10.0.0.1"
```

The following example specifies two IP addresses for Oracle RAC network traffic:

```
prod1.cluster_interconnects = "10.0.0.1:10.0.0.2"
```

When multiple networks cards/interconnects are to be used for Oracle RAC traffic, it is advisable that you use OS-level techniques to configure for the desired failover and traffic-sharing features.

In Oracle Database Release 11*g*, you can specify a private interconnect during installation and therefore do not need to use this parameter. Oracle 11*g* should also automatically detect the network to be used for the private interconnect, and generally you do not need to use this parameter. Use this parameter as a last resort to specify network interconnects.

NOTE
Specifying multiple interconnects by using the cluster_interconnets parameter enables Cache Fusion traffic to be distributed on all the interconnects. However, if any one of the interconnects is down, Oracle will assume the network is down; thus, it does not provide redundancy and high availability.

asm_preferred_read_failure_groups

This optional parameter specifies the name of the preferred failure disk groups so that disks in the failure groups become the preferred read disks in order for the instance to read from disks closer to it. This is an instance-specific parameter. The preferred read failure group is used in a special type of cluster configuration called *extended clusters* or *metro clusters*. Implementation consideration and installation strategies of extended clusters are discussed in Chapter 14.

Identical Parameters

Using the following query, you can determine that more than 100 parameters fall into the identical parameters category:

```
select name, ISINSTANCE_MODIFIABLE
from v$parameter
where ISINSTANCE_MODIFIABLE='FALSE'
order by name;
```

However, we will restrict our discussion to commonly used parameters. For information on other parameters, refer to the *Oracle Database Reference Manual*.

In this book, parameters are divided into the following groups:

- Oracle RAC–specific parameters.
- Database characteristic parameters (parameters that are alike across instances). Here's an example:

```
*.cluster_database = TRUE
```

Oracle RAC–Specific Parameters

Following are the Oracle RAC–specific parameters.

cluster_database

The possible values of this Boolean parameter are TRUE and FALSE. The value of this parameter should be set to TRUE for all the instances. The TRUE value directs the instance during startup to mount the controlfile in shared mode. If an instance starting first has this parameter set to FALSE, it will be able to mount the controlfile in exclusive mode. However, this will prevent all subsequent instances from starting up.

During the following maintenance activities, you must start up an instance using `cluster_database = FALSE`:

- Converting from no archive log mode to archive log mode, and vice versa
- Enabling the flashback database feature
- During upgrades
- Performing a media recovery on a system tablespace
- Converting to a single-instance database from Oracle RAC database, and vice versa

The default value for this parameter is FALSE. To start up instances in an Oracle RAC environment, this parameter must be set to TRUE.

cluster_database_instances

This parameter specifies the number of instances that will be accessing the database. For administrator-managed cluster databases, the default value for this parameter is based on the number of database instances configured in the cluster database, whereas for policy-managed cluster databases, the default value for this parameter is 16 (you should set the value for this parameter higher than 16 if you are expecting more than 16 database instances in this cluster database). Oracle uses the value of this parameter to compute default values of some other parameters such as large_pool_size.

The value of this parameter should be set equal to the maximum number of instances to join the cluster.

dml_locks

This parameter specifies the number of Data Manipulation Language (DML) locks for that instance. (A DML lock is obtained on a table that is undergoing a DML operation, such as insert, update, or delete.) If this parameter is set to 0 on the instance starting first, it must be set to 0 on all other instances. However, if the value of this parameter is set to any positive number, it can be set to different values for different instances. The default value for this parameter is derived from the transaction parameters.

Leave this parameter at its default value unless the application requires a different setting. Errors such as ORA-00055 require this parameter to be set higher.

In an Oracle RAC environment, you might get marginal performance improvement by setting dml_locks to 0. However, note that setting dml_locks to 0 will prevent users from executing some of the Data Definition Language (DDL) commands. For example, a user can create a table and never be able to drop the table. Therefore, it is better to disable the table locks using the following command than to set dml_locks to 0:

```
ALTER TABLE DISABLE TABLE LOCK
```

gc_files_to_locks

This parameter allows you to specify the number of global locks to a datafile. Oracle recommends you not set this parameter. Setting this parameter disables the Cache Fusion mechanism for the specified datafile and uses the disk ping mechanism to transfer contentious blocks. The following example allocates 100 locks to file number 5:

```
gc_files_to_locks = "5:100"
```

max_commit_propagation_delay

This is an Oracle RAC–specific parameter, and its value influences the mechanism Oracle uses to synchronize the system commit numbers (SCNs) among all instances accessing a database. Its default value is 700 and should not be changed unless necessary. For a default value of this parameter, Oracle uses the Lamport scheme for SCN propagation.

NOTE
This parameter has been deprecated in Oracle Database 10g Release 2, and by default the Broadcast on Commit method is used for SCN propagation.

In situations when application sessions connected to one instance need to read the data recently modified/inserted by another instance and do not find the most recent data, it might be necessary to set max_commit_propagation_delay to 0. Setting this parameter to 0 will direct Oracle to use the Broadcast on Commit scheme to generate SCNs. An Oracle instance decides the SCN generation scheme at startup and logs it in the alert.log as follows:

```
This instance was first to open
Picked Lamport scheme to generate SCNs
```

Several packaged applications such as SAP and the Oracle Collaboration Suite recommend that the value of this parameter be set to 0. Review Chapter 10 for information on the performance impact of setting this parameter to a nondefault value.

instance_groups
This parameter allows you to specify multiple parallel query execution groups and assigns the current instance to those groups.

parallel_instance_group
This parameter specifies the group of instances to be used for parallel query execution. Oracle will spawn parallel query slaves only on the instances specified by this parameter. This parameter can be set to a group name—usually the group defined by the INSTANCE_GROUPS parameter or a valid service name. It is specifically useful when a parallel query workload should not take away resources intended for other purposes—for example, online transaction processing (OLTP) work.

By default, Oracle spawns parallel query slaves on all active instances. When this parameter is specified, Oracle spawns the parallel slaves on the instances running the service specified by this parameter or the cluster database instances, which are part of the group specified by this parameter. You must be careful while setting this parameter because if the service or the group name specified by this parameter does not exist, Oracle will execute the expected parallel query in serial, which may impact the overall response time of the query.

Consider a three-node Oracle RAC environment consisting of instances prod1, prod2, and prod3. The following scheme can be used to restrict execution of a parallel query on instances prod2 and prod3, thereby leaving resources on instance prod1 for other purposes:

```
prod2.instances_groups = group23
prod3.instance_groups = group23
prod2.parallel_instance_group = group23
```

When a parallel query is initiated on instance prod2, it will spawn query slaves only on instances prod2 and prod3.

Parameters Specifying Database Characteristics (Alike Across Instances)
The following parameters specify database characteristics that need to be alike across all instances. These parameters behave exactly the same as in a single-instance environment; refer to the Oracle Database 11*g* R2 reference manual for more information about these parameters.

```
archive_lag_target
compatible
control_files
db_block_size
db_domain
db_files
db_name
license_max_users
parallel_execution_message_size
remote_login_passwordfile
spfile
trace_enabled
undo_management
undo_retention
```

Instance-Specific Parameters

Following are the initialization parameters whose influence is generally limited to the local instance's performance characteristics. These parameters can have any value, depending on the workload the instance is serving or the capacity of the machine on which the instance is running. For example, one instance could be serving an OLTP workload, and another instance might be serving a data warehouse (DW) workload; in these situations, a DBA is free to choose different values for the parameters, such as db_cache_size to optimize the instance performance with respect to the workload it is executing.

These parameters behave in exactly the same way that they do in a single-instance environment; refer to the appropriate Oracle documentation for more information about these parameters.

gcs_server_processes

This parameter specifies the number of Lock Manager Server (LMS) background processes used by the instance for the Cache Fusion traffic. Its default value is 2 and can be set between 1 and 20, as appropriate, for different instances. However, the number of LMS processes need to be the same on the instances to allow for proper balanced communication across the cluster.

remote_listener

This instance-specific parameter is used to register the instance with listeners on remote nodes, generally in a clustered environment. Incoming connection requests received by the Transparent Network Substrate (TNS) listener on a node are directed to the instance running on the least loaded node, thereby distributing the workload among all available nodes. Here is an example of how to specify the parameter in a three-node environment:

```
prod1.remote_listener = listener_prod2, listener_prod3
```

Here, listener_prod2 and listener_prod3 are valid tnsnames.ora entries, specifying the listeners on node2 and node3.

NOTE
If Single Client Access Name (SCAN) is used, then this parameter must be set to the value "scan" and the scan listener port number, as shown here:

```
*.remote_listener=prod-scan:1701
```

Managing the Parameter File

In the Oracle RAC environment, a DBA can use a parameter file shared by all instances, or each instance can have its own dedicated parameter file. Following is the syntax for a shared parameter file containing parameters for multiple instances:

```
<instance_name>.<parameter_name>=<parameter_value>
```

An asterisk (*) or no value in place of an *instance_name* implies that the parameter value is valid for all the instances. Here's an example:

```
inst1.db_cache_size = 1000000
  *.undo_management=auto
```

If a parameter appears more than once in a parameter file, the last specified value is the effective value, unless the values are on consecutive lines, in which case values from consecutive lines are concatenated.

The "ALTER SYSTEM SET" command is available to change initialization parameters for an Oracle instance using SPFILE. Following is the complete syntax of the command:

```
alter system set <parameter>=<value>
    scope=<memory/spfile/both>
    comment=<'comments'>
    deferred
    sid=<sid, *>
```

- **scope=memory**   Indicates that the parameter should be changed only for the current instance; these changes are lost upon instance restart. If a parameter can be modified only for the local instance, the following error is signaled: "ORA-32018: Parameter cannot be modified in memory on another instance."

- **scope=spfile**   Indicates that the changes are to be made only in the file, and new values of the changed parameter will be effective upon instance restart. The current incarnation of the instance is not affected by this change. If an instance was not started using an SPFILE and you try to use this option, the following error is signaled: "ORA-32001: Write to SPFILE requested but no SPFILE specified at startup."

- **scope=both**   Means that the intended parameter change will be effective for the current incarnation of the instance and is persistent through instance restarts.

- **comment**   Allows you to specify comments to be associated with the parameter change.

- **deferred**   Indicates that the changes are effective only for the sessions that are spawned after the command is issued. The sessions that are already active are not affected.

- **sid**   Allows specifying the name of the instance the parameter change is intended for. An asterisk (*) implies that the change is to be made across all the instances. This is the default value as well. Generally in an Oracle RAC environment, you can change parameter values for remote instances, with some restrictions depending on the status of the remote instance and the static/dynamic nature of the parameter.

Here is an example:

```
alter system set db_2k_cache_size=10m scope=spfile sid='prod2';
```

Whenever a parameter is changed using the "alter system" command, Oracle logs the command in the alert.log file.

When the Database Configuration Assistant (DBCA) is used to create an Oracle RAC database, by default it creates an SPFILE on the shared disk subsystem used for the database. If due to any reason SPFILE is not being used, the "create spfile..." command can be used to create an SPFILE from a parameter file.

Starting and Stopping Instances

An Oracle instance can be started automatically at system boot time. In an Oracle RAC environment, you need to ensure that the cluster software is started before database instances can be started. Starting with Oracle Database 10g R1, DBCA configures database instances to be started automatically by Cluster Ready Services (CRS) at system boot time.

Using srvctl to Start/Stop Instance(s)

The srvctl command is a convenient and highly recommended way to start/stop multiple instances in an Oracle RAC environment. Use the following command to start all instances associated with a database:

```
srvctl start database -d prod
```

In this example, the database name is prod. This command can be executed from any of the nodes. The command also starts listeners on each node if not already running. This command also starts the services defined for the prod database.

To shut down all instances associated with the prod database, you can use the following command:

```
srvctl stop database  -d prod
```

This command shuts down only instances and services; the listeners are not stopped because they might be serving other database instances running on the same machines. You can use the –o option to specify startup/shutdown options. Srvctl invokes CRS Application Program Interfaces silently to perform start/stop operations. Options specified by –o are directly passed on as command-line options for start/stop commands. For example, to stop all the instances with the "immediate" option, use the following command:

```
srvctl stop database -d prod -o immediate
```

Similarly, to initiate startup force for all the instances, use the following command:

```
srvctl start database -d prod -o force
```

To perform a normal shutdown of instance prod3, use the following command:

```
srvctl stop database -d prod -i instance prod3
```

Using SQL*Plus to Start/Stop Instances

Similar to a single-instance environment, you can use SQL*Plus to start/stop instances individually:

```
$sqlplus '/ as sysdba'
>shutdown immediate;
. . .
$ sqlplus '/ as sysdba'
. . .
>startup
```

Note that connecting as "/ as sysdba" requires OS authentication and needs the logged-in user to be a member of the OSDBA group. Refer to the appropriate *Oracle Database 10g Administrator's Guide* for more information about the OSDBA group.

Registering a Single-Instance Database in OCR Using SRVCTL

A single-instance database can now be registered and managed by Oracle Clusterware, but older versions of single-instance databases should be registered with Oracle Cluster Registry manually using the SRVCTL utility. Oracle will automatically start all dependent resources for a single-instance database.

Here's how to add single-instance database prod11g:

```
$ srvctl add database -d prod11g -o /u01/app/oracle/product/11g/db -x node-a -p
+ASMDATA1/spfilePROD11g.ora -r primary -s open -t immediate -y automatic -a
ASMDATA1,ASMFRA1
```

Administering Undo

Oracle stores the original values of the data called before an image in undo segments. The data stored in an undo segment is used to provide read consistency and to roll back uncommitted transactions. Starting with Oracle 10*g*, the flashback feature also makes use of undo data.

Oracle provides two methods of undo management: automatic undo management and manual undo management.

Automatic Undo Management

Automatic undo management was introduced in Oracle Database 9*i* R1 and is highly recommended. In this method an Oracle instance uses a tablespace of type "undo" to store undo/rollback data. The instance creates the required number of undo segments in the dedicated tablespace and allocates them to transactions to store the undo data; these operations are totally transparent to the DBA and the end user.

Starting with Oracle 9*i*, DBCA automatically configures the database to use automatic undo management. The following initialization parameters enable automatic undo management:

```
undo_management = "auto"
undo_tablespace = undo_tbs1
```

Another parameter related to automatic undo management is undo_retention_time. Its default value is 900, which means that an Oracle instance will make the best effort not to overwrite (reuse) an undo block for 900 seconds after the transaction has been committed. This ensures that transactions/queries that are running for 15 minutes are not likely to get ORA-1555 (the "snapshot too old" error). If the instance is executing longer-running transactions/queries, the DBA needs to size the undo tablespace accordingly. You can use the average undo generation rate to calculate the required size of the undo tablespace.

In the Oracle RAC environment, each instance stores transaction undo data in its dedicated undo tablespace. The DBA can set the undo tablespace for each instance by setting the undo_tablespace parameter. The following lines will set undo_tablespace for instance prod1 to undo_tbs1 and for instance prod2 to undo_tbs2:

```
prod1.undo_tablespace= undo_tbs1
prod2.undo_tablespace=undo_tbs2
```

All the instances in an Oracle RAC environment are required to use either automatic undo management or manual undo management, and the parameter undo_management needs to be the same across all the instances. Note that the undo tablespace can't be shared among the instances, so the parameter undo_tablespace must be unique for each instance.

Either of the following methods can be used to increase the size of an undo tablespace:

- Add another datafile to the undo tablespace.
- Increase the size of the existing datafile(s) belonging to the undo tablespace.

You can change the undo tablespace for an instance. Create the new undo tablespace as follows:

```
create undo tablespace undotbs_big
datafile '/ocfs2/prod/undotbsbig.dbf' size 2000MB;
```

Here's how to instruct the instance to use the newly created undo tablespace:

```
alter system set undo_tablespace=undotbs_big scope=both;
```

The instance will start using the new undo tablespace for newer transactions; however, transactions that were active before the new undo tablespace was assigned will continue to use the older undo tablespace until completed. An original undo tablespace can be dropped or taken offline when all the active transactions using it are committed and undo retention time has expired.

Manual Undo Management

The manual method of undo management requires the DBA to create rollback segments. The initialization parameter rollback_segments is used to indicate rollback segments to be used by an instance. The DBA can create rollback segments in any desired tablespace; however, the following are recommended:

- Use manual undo management only if you have a very good reason for not using automatic undo management.
- Do not create other objects such as tables, indexes, and so on in the tablespace used for rollback segments.
- Create one rollback segment for every four concurrent transactions.

Administering a Temporary Tablespace

Oracle uses a temporary tablespace as a "scratch pad" area to perform sort operations that cannot be done in the memory. Oracle also uses the temporary tablespace to create TEMP tables. Any user who is not assigned a temporary tablespace explicitly will use the default temporary tablespace. Starting with Oracle Database 10g R1, DBCA automatically creates a default temporary tablespace. When you're creating a database with a locally managed system tablespace, a default temporary tablespace must be specified.

Starting with Oracle Release 10g, you can define a temporary tablespace group that can be used wherever a temporary tablespace is used. The use of a temporary tablespace group in an Oracle RAC environment is similar to that of a single-instance environment. We recommend the use of a temporary tablespace group in an Oracle RAC environment, because different temporary tablespaces are assigned to the sessions when more than one user connects to the database using the same username. This allows different sessions to use different tablespaces for sort activities—a useful feature when you're managing packaged applications such as Oracle applications.

In an Oracle RAC environment, a user will always use the same assigned temporary tablespace irrespective of the instance being used. Each instance creates a temporary segment in the temporary tablespace it is using. If an instance is running a big sort operation requiring a large temporary tablespace, it can reclaim the space used by other instances' temporary segments in that tablespace. The default temporary tablespace cannot be dropped or taken offline; however, you can change the default temporary tablespace. Follow these steps to do this:

1. Create a new temporary tablespace:

```
create temporary tablespace temp2
tempfile '/ocfs2/prod/temp2.dbf' size 2000MB
autoextend on next 1M maxsize unlimited
extent management local uniform size 1M;
```

2. Make a new temporary tablespace as the default temporary tablespace:

```
alter database default temporary tablespace temp2;
```

3. Drop or offline the original default temporary tablespace.

The following v$ views contain information about temporary tablespaces:

- **gv$sort_segment**   Use this view to explore current and maximum sort segment usage statistics.

- **gv$tempseg_usage**   Use this view to explore temporary segment usage details such as username, SQL, and so on.

- **v$tempfile**   Use this view to identify temporary datafiles being used for a temporary tablespace.

NOTE
You can use the gv$sort_segment and gv$tempseg_usage views to determine the temporary tablespace used by each instance. Use the column INST_ID to separate the data per instance.

In an Oracle RAC environment, all instances share the same temporary tablespace. The size of the tablespace should be at least equal to the concurrent maximum requirement of all the instances. If an instance needs a larger sort space, it will ask other instances to release space. In turn, when other instances need more sort space, they will ask this instance to release the sort space. Frequent requests to release temporary space by other instances may impact performance. Pay attention to the columns FREED_EXTENTS and FREE_REQUESTS of V$SORT_SEGMENT; if they grow on a regular basis, consider increasing the size of the temporary tablespace.

Administering Online Redo Logs

Oracle uses online redo log files to log any changes to data blocks. Each instance has its own set of online redo log files. A set of redo logs used in a circular manner by an instance is known as a *thread.* A thread contains at least two online redo logs. The size of an online redo log is independent of other instances' redo log sizes and is determined by the local instance's workload and backup and recovery considerations.

Each instance has exclusive write access to its own online redo log files. An instance can read another instance's current online redo log file to perform instance recovery if that instance has terminated abnormally. Thus, an online redo log needs to be located on a shared storage device and cannot be on a local disk.

Operations such as add, delete, and mirror performed on redo log files are similar to those operations performed on a single-instance environment.

Use the dynamic views V$LOG and V$LOGFILE to explore which log files are allocated to each thread, their sizes, names, and other characteristics.

Enabling Archive Logs in the Oracle RAC Environment

As mentioned, online redo log files are reused by Oracle in a circular manner. To facilitate media recovery, Oracle allows you to make a copy of the online redo log files before they are reused. This process is called *archiving.*

DBCA allows you to enable archiving at the time of database creation. If the database has been created in "no archive log" mode, use the following process to change to archive log mode:

1. Set cluster_database to false for the instance:

   ```
   alter system set cluster_database=false scope=spfile sid= 'prod1';
   ```

2. Shut down all the instances accessing the database:

   ```
   srvctl stop database -d prod
   ```

3. Mount the database using the local instance:

   ```
   SQL> startup mount
   ```

4. Enable archiving:

   ```
   SQL> alter database archivelog;
   ```

5. Set the parameter cluster_database to true for the instance prod1:

   ```
   alter system set cluster_database=true scope=spfile sid='prod1'
   ```

6. Shut down the local instance:

   ```
   SQL> shutdown ;
   ```

7. Bring up all the instances:

   ```
   srvctl start database -d prod
   ```

Once in archive log mode, each instance can archive redo logs automatically.

Enabling the Flashback Area

Oracle Database 10g Release 1 introduced the flashback area to roll back the database to a time in the recent past. A flashback log is different from an archive log and is kept in a separate location specified by flashback log location.

The procedure for enabling the flashback is similar to the procedure for enabling the archiving log mode—it requires the database to be mounted in the exclusive mode. If you attempt to enable flashback while mounted/open in shared mode, Oracle will signal an error.

The following steps enable the database's flashback mode. This can be done from any node.

1. Verify that the database is running in archive log mode (if not already enabled, use the preceding procedure to enable archive log mode):

    ```
    SQL> archive log list
    Database log mode       Archive Mode
    Automatic archival      Enabled
    Archive destination     /u01/app/oracle/11g/dbs/arch
    Oldest online log sequence 59
    Next log sequence to archive    60
    Current log sequence 60
    ```

2. Set the cluster_database parameter to false for the instance to perform this operation:

    ```
    alter system set cluster_database=false scope=spfile sid= 'prod1';
    ```

3. If not already done, set the parameters DB_RECOVERY_FILE_DEST_SIZE and DB_RECOVERY_FILE_DEST. The DB_RECOVERY_FILE_DEST parameter should point to a shareable disk subsystem because it needs to be accessible to all the instances. The value of the DB_RECOVERY_FILE_DEST_SIZE parameter should be the same for all the instances.

    ```
    alter system set DB_RECOVERY_FILE_DEST_SIZE=200M scope=SPFILE;
    alter system set DB_RECOVERY_FILE_DEST='/ocfs2/flashback' scope=SPFILE;
    ```

4. Shut down all instances accessing the database:

    ```
    srvctl stop database -d prod
    ```

5. Mount the database using the local instance:

    ```
    SQL> startup mount
    ```

6. Enable the flashback by issuing the following command:

    ```
    SQL> alter database flashback on;
    ```

7. Set the parameter cluster_database back to true for the instance prod1:

    ```
    alter system set cluster_database=true scope=spfile sid='prod1'
    ```

8. Shut down the instance:

```
SQL> shutdown;
```

9. Start all the instances:

```
$srvctl start database -d prod
```

NOTE
You can optionally turn on or off the flashback logging for a particular tablespace as shown here:
SQL> alter tablespace user_data flashback on;
SQL> alter tablespace user_data flashback off;

Managing Database Configuration with SRVCTL

SRVCTL, or the server control utility, is a command-line utility. The functions performed by SRVCTL can be divided into two major groups:

- Database configuration tasks
- Database instance control tasks

Oracle stores database configuration information in a repository. In Oracle 9*i*, the repository is located in a file stored as srvConfig.loc. The file itself should be located on a shared storage device so that it can be accessed from all the nodes. In Oracle 10*g*, the repository information is stored in the Oracle Cluster Registry (OCR) that is created while CRS is being installed and must be located on shared storage. In Oracle 11*g* R2, there is another repository that stores a local copy of OCR data. It is known as the Oracle Local Repository (OLR).

Type **srvctl** without any command-line options to display the usage options:

```
$ srvctl
Usage: srvctl <command> <object> [<options>]
    commands: enable|disable|start|stop|relocate|status|add|remove|modify|
    getenv|setenv|unsetenv|config
    objects: database|instance|service|nodeapps|vip|asm|diskgroup|listener|
    srvpool|server|scan|scan_listener|oc4j|home|filesystem|gns
For detailed help on each command and object and its options use:
  srvctl <command> -h or
  srvctl <command> <object> -h
```

As indicated in this output, use the –h option of the srvctl command to display detailed help. The following sample output is from a 11.2.0 database:

```
[oracle@node3 ~]$ srvctl -h
```

Let's have a look at some of the sample commands. To display the databases registered in the repository, you can run the following command. Ensure that you invoke srvctl from the grid infrastructure home; otherwise, srvctl may not report the cluster resources.

```
$srvctl config database
prod
test
```

Here's how to display the configuration details of the prod database:

```
$ srvctl config database -d prod
Database unique name: PROD
Database name: PROD
Oracle home: /u01/app/oracle/product/11.2.0/db
Oracle user: oracle
Spfile: +ASMDAT1/PROD/spfilePROD.ora
Domain:
Start options: open
Stop options: immediate
Database role: PRIMARY
Management policy: AUTOMATIC
Server pools: PROD
Database instances: PROD1, PROD2, PROD3
Disk Groups: ASMDATA1,ASMFRA1
Services: prod_batch, prod_oltp
Database is administrator managed
$
```

To change policy of database prod from automatic to manual, use the following command:

```
$ srvctl modify database -d PROD -y MANUAL
```

Here's the command to change the startup option of the database prod from open to mount:

```
$ srvctl modify database -d PROD -s mount
```

To display the status of the database prod, use the following command:

```
$ srvctl status database -d prod
Instance prod1 is running on node node_a
Instance prod2 is running on node node_b
Instance prod3 is running on node node_c
```

Here's how to display the status of services running in the database prod:

```
$ srvctl status service -d prod
Service prod_batch is running on instance(s) PROD1
Service prod_oltp is running on instance(s) PROD1
```

And here's how to relocate the prod_batch service of the database prod from instance PROD1 to PROD2:

```
$ srvctl relocate service -d PROD -s prod_batch -i PROD1 -t PROD2
```

Finally, use the following command to check nodeapps running on a node:

```
$ srvctl status nodeapps
VIP node1-oravip is enabled
VIP node1-oravip is running on node: node_a
VIP node2-oravip is enabled
VIP node2-oravip is running on node: node_b
VIP node3-oravip is enabled
VIP node3-oravip is running on node: node_c
Network is enabled
Network is running on node: node_a
Network is running on node: node_b
Network is running on node: node_c
GSD is disabled
GSD is not running on node: node_a
GSD is not running on node: node_b
GSD is not running on node: node_c
ONS is enabled
ONS daemon is running on node: node_a
ONS daemon is running on node: node_b
ONS daemon is running on node: node_c
eONS is enabled
eONS daemon is running on node: node_a
eONS daemon is running on node: node_b
eONS daemon is running on node: node_c
```

Although mostly transparent to the end user and the DBA, CRS (introduced in Oracle 10*g)* has changed the mechanism SRVCTL uses to interface with the database. In Oracle 10*g* onward, OCR is used to store all the information, including the database configuration information used by the SRVCTL utility. SRVCTL uses CRS to communicate and perform startup and shutdown functions on other nodes. On Oracle 9*i,* SRVCTL uses the Global Services Daemon (GSD) to perform instance startup and shutdown operations. GSD should be started before SRVCTL can be used. SRVCTL stores database information in a repository known as the Server Control Repository, which must reside on shared storage because it is accessed from all the nodes. SRVCTL can also be used to define the dependencies while you are registering older versions of databases in an Oracle 11*g* Grid Infrastructure cluster.

Managing Database Objects

Managing database objects in an Oracle RAC environment is similar to managing them in a single-instance environment. In this section, we point out particular items to which you should pay special attention in the Oracle RAC environment.

Managing Tablespaces

To alleviate any concern for contention in an Oracle RAC environment, you should use all tablespaces with Automatic Segment Space Management (ASSM). ASSM was introduced in Oracle 9*i* and eliminates the need to define freelists, freelist groups, and so on, in an Oracle RAC environment.

Use the following SQL command to verify whether all your tablespaces are using ASSM:

```
SQL> select tablespace_name, SEGMENT_SPACE_MANAGEMENT
  2  from dba_tablespaces ;
TABLESPACE_NAME                   SEGMENT
------------------------------    -------
SYSTEM                            MANUAL
UNDOTBS1                          MANUAL
SYSAUX                            AUTO
TEMP                              MANUAL
USERS                             AUTO
UNDOTBS2                          MANUAL
EXAMPLE                           AUTO
UNDOTBS3                          MANUAL;
```

By default, the "create tablespace" command creates a tablespace with ASSM. All you need to do is *not* use the MANUAL clause.

ASSM characteristics cannot be specified at the object level. For an object to use ASSM, create the object in an ASSM tablespace.

Managing Sequences

It is good practice to increase the cache values for the sequences that are used by multiple concurrent sessions in multiple instances. This will eliminate the possibility of contention on sequences. The default value for a cache sequence is 20. However, depending on the frequency of use, cache values as high as 2000 could be acceptable. The disadvantage of using a very high cache value is that the unused sequence numbers are lost in the event of an instance's crash or when a shared pool is flushed.

Managing Tables

The Oracle RAC environment does not require specific treatment for tables. Best practices, such as partitioning very large tables and avoiding "hot" I/O spots by putting active tables on different spindles that are followed in a single-instance environment, are sufficient for Oracle RAC as well.

Managing Indexes

Avoiding contention on B-tree index blocks is a huge challenge in designing highly scalable systems. A good application design—whether it is for a single-instance environment or for Oracle RAC—should use all available techniques for avoiding index block contention. Using partitioned indexes and reverse key indexes are the two most commonly used techniques available to avoid index block contention.

Scope of SQL Commands

Although administration of an Oracle RAC database is similar to a single-instance database, you must be cautious about the scope of the commands being executed. Some commands affect the specific instance, whereas others may affect the whole database. For example, the RECOVER command affects the whole database, whereas the STARTUP and SHUTDOWN commands affect only the connected instance. On the same note, some ALTER SYSTEM commands only affect the connected instance; for example, ALTER SYSTEM SWITCH LOGFILE will switch the log file on the connected or local instance, whereas ALTER SYSTEM SWITCH LOG CURRENT will switch the current log file on all instances.

Database Connections

Oracle 11g introduced Single Client Access Name (SCAN) to further simplify the database connection in an Oracle RAC database because all databases in the same cluster can now connect to the Oracle RAC database by using the SCAN name in the connection string instead of listing all virtual IPs of the cluster nodes running the cluster database instance. Applications connecting to an Oracle 11g RAC database using SCAN require a JDBC driver version greater than 11.1.0.6 because using an older version of the JDBC driver is not certified with the Oracle 11g RAC database. The JDBC drivers can be downloaded from the Oracle Technology Network website at www.oracle.com/technetwork/database/features/jdbc/index-091264.html.

Oracle 11g provides different ways of connecting with an Oracle RAC database. Following are examples of connection strings for the database prod.

Here's how to connect to the database prod using a conventional TNS alias:

```
prod =
(DESCRIPTION =
(ADDRESS = (PROTOCOL = TCP)(HOST = prod-scan)(PORT = 1701))
(CONNECT_DATA =
(SERVER = DEDICATED)
(SERVICE_NAME = PROD_OLTP)
)
)
```

In the preceding connection string, users can connect to the database 'prod' using SCAN name 'prod-scan' on port 1701 listening and providing service as 'PROD_OLTP'.

Here's a sample connection JDBC string for database prod:

```
jdbc:oracle:thin:@(DESCRIPTION=(ADDRESS=(PROTOCOL=tcp) (HOST=prod-scan)
(PORT=1701))(CONNECT_DATA=(SERVICE_NAME=PROD_OLTP)))
```

Oracle introduced EZConnect—another easy way to connect a database without looking for service names in the conventional tnsnames.ora file. EZConnect does not use any naming or directory system. A sample EZconnect connection string for the database prod is shown here:

```
$ sqlplus username/password@prod-scan:1701/PROD_OLTP
```

In a Nutshell

Administering the Oracle RAC database is similar to managing a single-instance Oracle database. Because more than one instance is accessing the same set of database objects, a little caution is required while you are managing the Oracle RAC database.

Managing the initialization parameter file (SPFILE) requires some special handling in Oracle RAC databases because the parameters have a database-wide effect. A few database parameters should be set the same across Oracle RAC instances, and instance-specific parameters can be set to different values for Oracle RAC instances. Using a common SPFILE is highly recommended with SID-prefixed instance-specific parameters. This is the best practice in managing the parameter file.

The server control utility (SRVCTL) helps manage the Oracle RAC database efficiently and can be used as a central management tool to manage the Oracle RAC instances. An Oracle RAC instance depends on the Oracle Cluster Ready Services, and we will discuss the administration of Oracle Clusterware in the next chapter.

CHAPTER
8

Oracle RAC Advanced
Administration

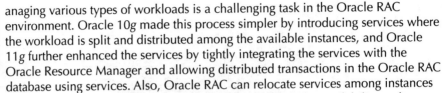 anaging various types of workloads is a challenging task in the Oracle RAC environment. Oracle 10*g* made this process simpler by introducing services where the workload is split and distributed among the available instances, and Oracle 11*g* further enhanced the services by tightly integrating the services with the Oracle Resource Manager and allowing distributed transactions in the Oracle RAC database using services. Also, Oracle RAC can relocate services among instances in response to planned and unplanned outages, which greatly extends the availability and scalability of Oracle RAC environments.

Understanding Services

Services are used to manage the workload in an Oracle RAC environment. They provide a logical approach to group a workload so that users employing the same set of data, functionalities, and service-level requirements can be grouped together to use the same services. For example, an online transaction processing (OLTP) service can be defined for the users who execute small, short-lived transactions; a BATCH service can be defined for users executing long-running batch transactions; a data warehousing (DW) service can be defined for users using data warehousing features; and so on. Another useful way to group users could be according to the type of functionalities used, such as sales, human resources, order entry, and so on.

Services in Oracle 11*g* Release 2 RAC database can be defined for both admin- and policy-managed databases, but there are some restrictions while creating services for a policy-managed database. Services in a *policy-managed* database are assigned to a server pool and can be defined as a SINGLETON or UNIFORM service. A SINGLETON service runs on only one database instance in its server pool and the user does not have control over which instance will serve the service. In case of failover, Oracle will automatically relocate the SINGLETON service to another available database instance within the same server pool. A UNIFORM service runs on all database instances in its server pool. The *administrator-managed* database uses the conventional method of assigning services to preferred and available database instances, which is discussed further in this chapter.

Following are some of the important features of services:

■ Services are used to distribute the workload. The Oracle RAC Load Balancing Advisory provides workload execution efficiency and system resource availability information to listeners and mid-tier servers to route the incoming workload in an optimal manner.

■ Services can be configured to provide high availability. You can configure multiple instances to provide the same services. If an instance or a node failure occurs, the workload can be relocated to another existing instance.

■ Services provide a transparent way to direct workload. In many cases, users may not even notice the instance, node, or the machine from where the services are being provided.

■ Services can be defined for both policy-based and administrator-based databases.

■ Services are tightly integrated with Oracle Resource Manager and consumer groups are automatically assigned to sessions based on a session's service.

■ Services are tightly integrated with the scheduler, which allows better workload management of the work done by the scheduler.

■ Services allow capturing various metrics about the workload, thus making it possible to measure the amount of resources used for that workload or application. These are exposed in the dynamic views V$SERVICEMETRIC and V$SERVICE_STATS.

Service Characteristics

The v$services view contains information about services that have been started on that instance—that is, services being currently served by that instance. Here is sample output from v$services:

```
SQL> SELECT NAME,NETWORK_NAME, CREATION_DATE, GOAL, DTP, AQ_HA_NOTIFICATION,
CLB_GOAL FROM V$SERVICES;

NAME              NETWORK_NAME      CREATION_ GOAL          D AQ_ CLB_G
---------------   ---------------   --------- ------------  - --- -----
prodXDB           prodXDB           10-AUG-09 NONE          N NO  LONG
prod              prod              10-AUG-09 NONE          N NO  LONG
SYS$BACKGROUND                      30-JUN-09 NONE          N NO  SHORT
SYS$USERS                           30-JUN-09 NONE          N NO  SHORT
SQL> SELECT NAME,NETWORK_NAME, CREATION_DATE, GOAL, DTP, AQ_HA_
NOTIFICATION,CLB_GOAL FROM V$SERVICES;

NAME    NETWORK_NAME      CREATION_ GOAL          D AQ_ CLB_G
------  ---------------   --------- ------------  - --- -----
PROD_BATCH        PROD_BATCH        23/AUG/10 NONE          N NO  LONG
PROD_OTLP         PROD_OLTP         23/AUG/10 NONE          N NO  LONG
PRODXDB           PRODXDB           20/AUG/10 NONE          N NO  LONG
PROD              PROD              20/AUG/10 NONE          N NO  LONG
SYS$BACKGROUND                      15/AUG/09 NONE          N NO  SHORT
SYS$USERS                           15/AUG/09 NONE          N NO  SHORT
```

Note that services that have not been started on the instance are not shown in the view. The characteristics of services are briefly described here, and many of these concepts are explained in detail in Chapter 13.

Load Balancing

An Oracle service in Oracle RAC databases allows load balancing at two different levels: namely, client-side load balancing and server-side load balancing. Client-side implements the basic load balancing methods by distributing the workload using a simple round-robin approach within the available servers, whereas the server-side load balancing method uses the Load Balancing Advisory to redirect the database connection to the least loaded database instance or the best database instance meeting the service-level requirements.

Goal

The service-level goal must be configured to implement the server-side load balancing feature so that Oracle Net Services is redirected to the best database instance. The type of a service goal suggests the type of workload an Oracle Net Service is required to serve—or in simple terms, a service goal suggests the nature of a database connection.

Oracle Net Services can have one service goal: either LONG or SHORT. A LONG service goal is for long-lived connections, where a database connection is assumed to be active for a time and actively processing in the Oracle database instance, such as Oracle Form sessions or sessions in the database connection pool.

A SHORT service goal, as the name suggests, is for short-duration database connections such as an application accessing the metadata from the master tables. Oracle balances the workload based on the goal of a service. Oracle uses the Load Balancing Advisory for services defined with a SHORT goal, whereas for a LONG goal service, Oracle balances the connection per instance using a session count per service.

Users must use the SRVCTL utility to implement server-side load balancing. For example, the following srvctl command implements a SHORT goal for the PROD_OLTP service on the PROD database:

```
$srvctl modify service -s prod_oltp -d prod -j SHORT
```

Distributed Transaction Processing

Starting with Oracle 11*g*, the distributed transaction can span across the database instances in a cluster database. Prior to Oracle 11*g*, customers did not have the liberty to fully utilize the Oracle RAC database if their applications used distributed transactions, which is no longer a bottleneck in the Oracle 11*g* RAC database. There is no need to configure a service to run only on one instance because distributed transactions are tightly integrated with the Oracle 11*g* RAC database.

Oracle introduced a new background process called global transaction process (GTX*n*), where *n* is the number of the Oracle Global Transaction process. The number of global transaction processes are controlled by the Oracle database initialization parameter GLOBAL_TXN_ PROCESSES. Setting this parameter to 0 disables the XA support for the Oracle RAC database. Oracle sets this parameter to a default value of 1 so that, by default, Oracle RAC databases span distributed transactions across the available database instances.

Oracle 11*g* still allows users to add a singleton DTP service in case they observe some performance degradation with the distributed transaction. Users can direct all branches of the distributed transactions to one database instance, similar to Oracle singleton services in prior releases of Oracle RAC databases.

DTP (Distributed Transaction Processing) services ensure that all globally distributed transactions performed have their tightly coupled branches running on a single Oracle RAC instance. By default DTP is disabled on a singleton service, but a singleton service can be modified by setting the DTP parameter of the service to true. Here is an example that changes the singleton service PROD_SERVICE to a DTP-enabled service:

```
$ srvtl modify service -d PROD -s PROD_SERVICE -x TRUE
```

Preferred and Available Instances

Preferred instances for a service are instances in which the service will be started, and these instances will serve the users. *Available* instances are the backup instances; the service will be started on these instances in the event of failure of preferred instances.

To view a service's high availability (HA) characteristics, you can use the srvctl command:

```
[oracle@alpha3 ~]$ srvctl config service -s PROD_OLTP -d PROD
Service name: PROD_OLTP
Service is enabled
Server pool: PROD_PROD_OLTP
```

```
Cardinality: 1
Disconnect: false
Service role: PRIMARY
Management policy: AUTOMATIC
DTP transaction: false
AQ HA notifications: false
Failover type: NONE
Failover method: NONE
TAF failover retries: 0
TAF failover delay: 0
Connection Load Balancing Goal: LONG
Runtime Load Balancing Goal: NONE
TAF policy specification: NONE
Preferred instances: PROD1
Available instances: PROD2, PROD3
```

NOTE
Users can specify the available and preferred database instances for administrator-managed databases only.

Management Policy
Oracle 11g allows specifying the management policy for each server. The management policy specifies whether Oracle Clusterware should start an Oracle Net Service automatically when a database starts. Management policy can be set to either manual or automatic. Prior to Oracle 11g, all Oracle Net Services are defined as manual. In some special occasions, such as troubleshooting, the DBA may want to start the database services manually. The SRVCTL utility can be used to specify the management policy for an Oracle Net Service.

Transparent Application Failover
The transparent application failover (TAF) feature of the Oracle RAC database allows database connections to automatically relocate to another database instance in case the database instances serving the database connection fail or simply shut down. Oracle services implement this feature by specifying a TAF policy. Oracle TAF restarts the failed query on the new database instance, but the DML transactions (INSERT, UPDATE, and DELETE) are not supported by Oracle TAF. Applications will have to roll back and reissue the transaction.

A TAF configuration specified on a service always overrides a TAF configuration on the client side. The Oracle RAC database in 11g can be either administrator or policy based. The Oracle TAF feature only applies to administrator-managed databases. Users can choose from three TAF policies available in Oracle 11g, which are NONE, BASIC, and PRECONNECT. The NONE policy is similar to not having any TAF policy. The BASIC policy restarts the failed query on the new database instance upon failover. The database reconnection is established at failover time. The PRECONNECT method is the same as the BASIC method, except that Oracle anticipates connection failure and creates a shadow connection to the other instance, which is always available on the available instance to improve the failover time.

Here's how to change the TAF policy of the PROD_BATCH service of the PROD database to PRECONNECT:

```
$srvctl modify service -d PROD -s PROD_BATCH -P PRECONNECT
```

AQ_HA_Notifications

When AQ_HA_Notifications is set to TRUE, information about an instance being up or down (or about similar events) will be sent to the mid-tier servers via the advance queuing mechanism. Some applications such as .NET applications cannot use FAN events, and in such cases AQ notifications are useful. You may need to enable the AQ HA events for services while configuring client failover in an Oracle Data Guard environment for OCI applications using these services.

Resource Management

Oracle Database Resource Manager is tightly integrated with Oracle Net Services in Oracle 11*g*. Oracle Database Resource Manager binds the services to the respective consumer groups and accordingly prioritizes the services within the database instance. When users connect to the database using a service, Oracle transparently assigns a database session to a consumer group mapped with the connected database service at runtime.

For example, suppose you have two services named HIGHPRI and LOWPRI that are assigned to high-priority and low-priority resource consumer groups. Oracle will prioritize the sessions connecting using the HIGHPRI service over those that connect using the LOWPRI service.

Use the DBMS_RESOURCE_MANAGER package to assign a resource group to a service.

Using Services with Oracle Scheduler

Services can be assigned to jobs created in the scheduler so that Oracle can efficiently manage the workload and so that the same jobs can utilize the full benefits of Oracle RAC. When a service is assigned to a job, Oracle identifies the work of the scheduler for workload management.

Administering Services

The following tools are available for administering services:

- **Database Creation Assistant (DBCA)**   An easy and intuitive GUI tool for creating and modifying services.

- **Oracle Enterprise Manager/Grid Control (OEM/GC)**   An easy and intuitive GUI tool for managing services.

- **Server control (SRVCTL)**   A comprehensive command-line Oracle RAC administration tool. DBCA and OEM, in turn, call this tool.

Oracle highly recommends the use of SRVCTL and OEM for managing services.

NOTE
It is not recommended that you use the DBMS_SERVICE package to modify a service that requires persistence across restarts. Service modifications using DBMS_SERVICE do not update the attributes of the cluster resources in the Oracle Cluster Registry (OCR). Oracle Clusterware updates the service updates stored in the cluster resources, and the changes made by the DBMS_SERVICE package will be lost. SRVCTL is the recommended tool for administering and managing services.

Creating Services

During installation of the Oracle RAC database, Oracle automatically creates a database service that has the same name as the Oracle RAC database and is available to all database instances in the Oracle RAC database. In addition to the default database service, Oracle also employs the following two internal services:

- **SYS$BACKGROUND**   This service is used by an instance's background processes only.
- **SYS$USERS**   When users connect to the database without specifying a service, they use this service.

These two internal services are available on all the instances all the time as long as the instance is up. You cannot relocate or disable these two services.

Creating a Service Using Enterprise Manager

Oracle Enterprise Manager (OEM) provides another GUI for managing services. The Create Service page provides all the parameters used to create a service. This page can be located by navigating to the Manage Cluster Database Service page from the Cluster Database Maintenance home page.

Oracle Enterprise Manager (OEM) provides a GUI for managing cluster services. The Create Service page provides all the parameters used to create a service. This page can be located by navigating to the Cluster Database home page and then to the Cluster Managed Database Services page. Click on Create Service on the Cluster Managed Database Services page. This Create Service page allows you to configure various attributes of the Oracle service explained in the previous sections.

Creating a Service Using the Server Control Utility

The following is the syntax for creating a service using the server control utility:

```
$srvctl add service -d database_name -s service_name -r
preferred_instance(s)-a available_instance(s) -y
[AUTOMATIC or MANUAL] [-P TAF_policy]
```

For example, the following command creates a service named *test* that defines instances prod1 and prod2 as the preferred instances, instances prod3 and prod4 as available instances, and basic TAF policy, as well as configures the service to start automatically using automatic management policy:

```
$srvctl add service -d prod -s test - r prod1, prod2 -a prod3,
prod4 -P  basic -y AUTOMATIC
```

The following example creates a singleton service test for policy-managed database ORCL using server pool SRVPL1:

```
$srvctl add service -d prod -s test  -g SRVPL1 -c singleton -y AUTOMATIC
```

For the service to be available for client connections, the service needs to be started as follows:

```
$srvctl start service -d prod -s test
```

Service Thresholds

Service-level thresholds are useful for comparing the achieved service level with the minimum configured/accepted service levels. Setting appropriate service-level thresholds allows you to predict a system capable of achieving the required service levels. You can use the DBMS_SERVER_ALERT package to set service-level thresholds.

Application Contexts

Oracle collects important statistics for the work done by a service, which is further enhanced in Oracle 11*g*, and now user applications can qualify a service by action or module name to easily identify transactions within a service. It is strongly recommend that you set module and action names because this allows you to identify the culprit transactions or application code while optimizing the database or application. The DBMS_APPLICATION_INFO package can be used to set module and action names for the application programs.

For example, suppose we are creating a table called tab1 and have inserted a record into the table and then updated the same record from two different sessions at the same time. Therefore, we will set application context information on another session where the update statement is expected to wait and showcase how we can query the V$SESSION dynamic performance view for additional application information of the problematic session.

```
CREATE TABLE TAB1 (COL1 VARCHAR2 (10));
INSERT INTO TAB1 VALUES ('FIRST');
UPDATE TAB1 SET COL1 = 'SECOND'
```

From another database session, let's try to update the recently inserted record. However, before executing the DML, let's set the module name, action name, and client info using the DBMS_APPLICATION_INFO package.

```
exec DBMS_APPLICATION_INFO.SET_MODULE
( MODULE_NAME => 'UPDATE RECORD', ACTION_NAME => 'UPDATE TAB1');
exec DBMS_APPLICATION_INFO.SET_CLIENT_INFO ( CLIENT_INFO => 'SUNRAY');
UPDATE TAB1 SET COL1 = 'UPDATED';
```

This session will appear to hang (waiting forever) because the same row is being updated by another session and not committed. Because we set the application context using the DBMS_APPLICATION_INFO package, we can easily identify the problematic code location via a simple query to the V$SESSION dynamic performance view:

```
SELECT SID,EVENT,MODULE,ACTION,CLIENT_INFO
FROM V$SESSION WHERE STATE='WAITING' AND
WAIT_CLASS='Application';
SID EVENT                            MODULE        ACTION       CLIENT_INFO
388 enq: TX - row lock contention    UPDATE RECORD UPDATE TAB1  SUNRAY
```

As shown here, V$SESSION exposes the application context information set in the DBMS_APPLICATION_INFO package, which can be quite handy while troubleshooting application performance issues.

Refer to *Oracle Database PL/SQL Packages and Types Reference* for details and more examples using this wonderful package that can make your life a lot easier, especially when you are troubleshooting custom code.

Administering SCAN

Oracle 11*g* Release 2 introduced Single Client Access Name, which is explained in Chapter 3. SCAN simplifies the administration and management of client network connection files with the change in cluster database configuration.

To display the status of SCAN VIPs:

```
[root@alpha2 bin]# $GRID_HOME/bin/srvctl status scan
SCAN VIP scan1 is enabled
SCAN VIP scan1 is running on node alpha3
SCAN VIP scan2 is enabled
SCAN VIP scan2 is running on node alpha2
SCAN VIP scan3 is enabled
SCAN VIP scan3 is running on node alpha1
[root@alpha2 bin]#
```

To display the status of SCAN listeners:

```
[root@alpha2 bin]# $GRID_HOME/bin/srvctl status scan_listener
SCAN Listener LISTENER_SCAN1 is enabled
SCAN listener LISTENER_SCAN1 is running on node alpha3
SCAN Listener LISTENER_SCAN2 is enabled
SCAN listener LISTENER_SCAN2 is running on node alpha2
SCAN Listener LISTENER_SCAN3 is enabled
SCAN listener LISTENER_SCAN3 is running on node alpha1
[root@alpha2 bin]#
```

To display the existing configuration of SCAN:

```
[root@alpha3 bin]# ./srvctl config scan
SCAN name: prod-scan, Network: 1/172.16.194.144/255.255.255.240/bond0
SCAN VIP name: scan1, IP: /172.16.194.157/172.16.194.157
SCAN VIP name: scan2, IP: /172.16.194.156/172.16.194.156
SCAN VIP name: scan3, IP: /172.16.194.155/172.16.194.155
[root@alpha2 bin]#
```

To add a SCAN:

```
[root@alpha3 bin]# $GRID_HOME/bin/srvctl add scan -n prod-scan
```

To remove a SCAN:

```
[root@alpha3 bin]# $GRID_HOME/bin/srvctl remove scan
```

Users can use the -f option with the preceding command to remove SCAN forcefully.

To modify a SCAN:

```
[root@alpha3 bin]# $GRID_HOME/bin/srvctl modify scan -n new-scan
```

To add a SCAN listener:

```
[root@alpha3 bin]# $GRID_HOME/bin/srvctl add scan_listener
```

This command will add a listener with a default port, but users can use the -p option to specify a nondefault port for the listener.

To remove a SCAN listener:

```
[root@alpha3 bin]# $GRID_HOME/bin/srvctl remove scan_listener
```

Users can use the -f option to remove the SCAN listener forcefully.

To modify a SCAN listener port:

```
[root@alpha3 bin]# $GRID_HOME/bin/srvctl modify scan_listener -p <port_number>
```

Users can use the -u option to reflect changes to the current SCAN listener only.

Administering Cluster Ready Services

Cluster Ready Services (CRS) is Oracle's cluster software included since Oracle 10*g*. Oracle CRS can coexist with vendor-supplied clusterware, although third-party clusterware is not required for Oracle RAC (except for the HP True64 platform, for which vendor-supplied clustering software is required, even with CRS).

NOTE
The Oracle Support (http://support.oracle.com) "Certification and Availability" section on the Web contains information on operating system, clusterware, and RDBMS version certification and compatibility.

Clusterware Startup Process (Oracle 11*g* R1)

During the installation of Oracle Clusterware (Oracle Grid Infrastructure), Oracle Universal Installer installs three wrapper scripts—inti.crsd, init.cssd, and init.evmd—on each cluster node. These wrapper scripts set the required environment variables and start the daemons, depending on the user action and auto startup configuration of Oracle Clusterware. Oracle places one entry each for these wrapper scripts in the /etc/inittab file on UNIX and Linux systems, and the operating system init daemon starts these wrapper scripts:

```
h1:35:respawn:/etc/init.d/init.evmd run >/dev/null 2>&1 </dev/null
h2:35:respawn:/etc/init.d/init.cssd fatal >/dev/null 2>&1 </dev/null
h3:35:respawn:/etc/init.d/init.crsd run >/dev/null 2>&1 </dev/null
```

These wrapper scripts are very important for Oracle Clusterware startup and must always be running on the cluster node. Therefore, these wrapper scripts are configured with the respawn action so they will be restarted whenever they die. The init.cssd wrapper script is passed with fatal arguments, causing a cluster node to reboot on failure. The following diagram shows the chart of the startup flow from the inittab file.

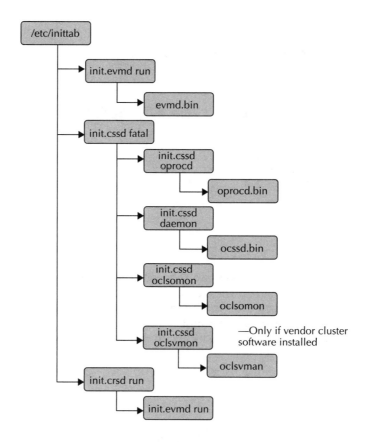

Oracle Clusterware can be started either manually upon user request or automatically when a cluster node starts. Oracle Clusterware uses cluster control files to maintain the state and runtime information of different Oracle Clusterware daemons. Oracle stores these cluster control files under the <scls_dir>/root directory on each cluster node. The <scls_dir> directory is OS dependent. For instance, in HP-UX, it is located under the /var/opt/oracle/ directory.

Clusterware Starting Sequence

As just discussed, the wrapper scripts run continuously and are responsible for starting the Oracle Clusterware daemons. Therefore, it is very important to understand the flow of these wrapper scripts. Oracle calls the init.cssd wrapper script with startcheck and runcheck in all wrapper scripts. During 'startcheck', Oracle checks the run status of the wrapper scripts; presence of vendor cluster and dependencies of file systems. 'Runcheck' is intended to check the run status for any of the run or fatal scripts (evm/crs/css) as initialized by the automatic startup or manual startup routines. This check is supposed to be very fast and silent because it will be invoked regularly while the system is up. The following diagram illustrates the startup sequence of the clusterware.

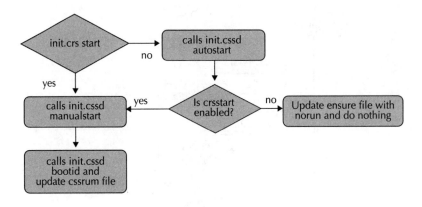

EVMd Process Startup

The operating system's init daemon executes the init.evmd wrapper script with the run parameter, which internally calls the init.cssd wrapper script with the startcheck parameter. Upon success of the init.cssd startcheck, Oracle starts the EVMd daemon. Oracle disables the respawn of the init .evmd wrapper script if boot time or the hostname of the cluster node before starting the EVMd daemon is not the same as after starting the EVMd daemon. The following diagram illustrates the startup sequence of the EVMd process.

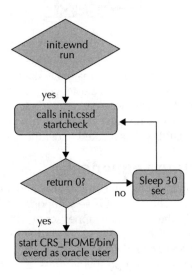

CRSd Process Startup

The operating system's init daemon executes the init.crsd wrapper script with the run parameter, which internally calls the init.cssd wrapper script with the startcheck parameter. Upon success of the init.cssd startcheck, Oracle compares the actual boot time of the cluster node with the boot timestamp stored in the crsdboot cluster control file.

If the boot timestamp is not the same, Oracle stores the current boot timestamp in the crsdboot cluster control file and starts the CRSd daemon with the reboot start flag; otherwise, the CRSd daemon is started with the restart start flag. Oracle sets "stopped" in the crsdboot cluster control file if the CRSd daemon does not start successfully

The following diagram illustrates the startup sequence and the associated validations during the CRSd startup.

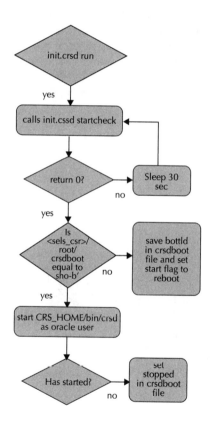

CSSd Process Startup

The operating system's init daemon executes the init.cssd wrapper script with the fatal parameter, which internally calls the init.cssd wrapper script with the startcheck parameter. This script is responsible for starting four different daemons: CSSd, OPROCd, OCLSOMON, and OCLSVMON. Upon success of the init.cssd startcheck, Oracle creates three cluster control files—noclsvmon, noclsomon, and noprocd—under the <scls_dir>/root directory to disable the OCLSVMON,

OCLSOMON, and OPROCd daemons. Later, Oracle removes the noclsomon file because the OCLSOMON daemon runs regardless of whether the vendor cluster is used or not.

During startup, the startup process also compares the actual boot time of the cluster node with the boot timestamp stored in the cssfboot cluster control file. If the boot timestamp is the same, it is highly possible that the other daemons are already running because the operating system's init daemon has respawned this wrapper script. Oracle extracts the pid of the running daemons from the clsvmonid, clsomonpid, daemonpid, and oprocpid files and stores them in memory (environment variables). If the boot timestamp is not the same, Oracle stores the new boot timestamp in the cssfboot cluster control file and removes the noprocd file if OPROCd is enabled and no vendor cluster is installed.

If the vendor cluster is installed, Oracle removes the noclsvmon file because Oracle requires the OCLSVMON daemon to monitor the vendor cluster. Oracle removes the noclsomon file to ensure that the OCLSOMON daemon starts during startup. Oracle checks the content of the cssrun cluster control file and if this file contains "norun," the init.cssd fatal script completes successfully without starting the daemons, assuming that this is a clean shutdown of the Oracle Clusterware. If the cssrun file does not contain "norun," Oracle starts the OPROCd if it is enabled, starts OCLSVMON if the vendor cluster is installed, starts OCLSOMON if it's not running, and finally starts the CSSd by calling the init.cssd daemon wrapper script again. The following diagram illustrates the sequence of actions in the CSSd.

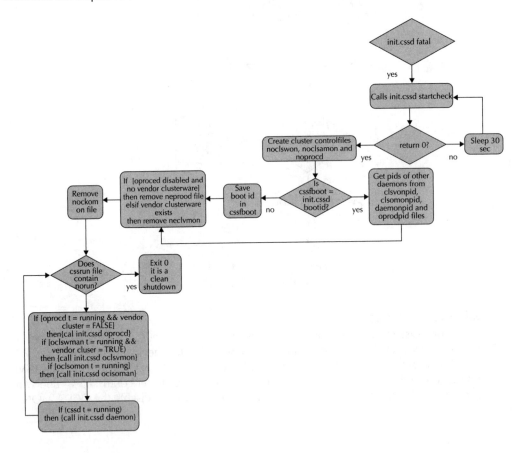

Regardless of the method used to start Oracle Clusterware, Oracle uses the wrapper scripts described. Different Oracle Clusterware startup methods set the cluster control files differently to queue the Oracle Clusterware startup and wrapper scripts, read these cluster control files, and take the appropriate action to start different daemons.

Oracle Clusterware Auto Startup

The operating system init process calls init.crs start upon operating system startup, which internally calls the init.cssd wrapper script with the autostart parameter. Oracle first checks the content of the crsstart cluster control file to determine whether auto startup for Oracle Clusterware is enabled. If the crsstart file contains the "enable" string, Oracle will call the init.cssd wrapper script with the manualstart parameter, identify the full timestamp of the "/proc" file system, and set this information in the cssrun file and queue the startup for Oracle Clusterware.

Oracle Clusterware Manual Startup

Oracle calls the init.cssd wrapper script with the manualstart parameter upon manual startup of Oracle Clusterware. Oracle identifies the full timestamp of the "/proc" file system and sets this information in the cssrun file stored under the <scls_dir>/run directory.

The operating system's init daemon starts the clusterware processes by using the Oracle Clusterware wrapper scripts, which are installed by Oracle Universal Installer during the installation of Oracle Clusterware. Oracle installs three wrapper scripts—init.crsd, init.evmd, and init.cssd—that are configured with the respawn action so that they will be restarted whenever they fail (except the init.cssd wrapper script, which is configured with the fatal parameter, causing the cluster node to reboot to avoid any possible data corruption, as explained later in this chapter).

Starting and Stopping CRS (Oracle 11g R2)

Oracle CRS is started automatically at system boot time. Manually starting and stopping CRS is generally not required, except in the following rare situations:

- Applying a patchset to Oracle Grid Infrastructure
- OS/system maintenance
- Debugging CRS problems

In Oracle Database 11g R2, CRS can be started and stopped using the following commands.
To start CRS:

```
# $GRID_HOME/bin/crsctl start crs
[root@alpha2 bin]# ./crsctl start crs
CRS-4123: Oracle High Availability Services has been started.
[root@alpha2 bin]#
```

To stop CRS:

```
# $GRID_HOME/bin/crsctl stop crs
[root@alpha2 bin]# ./crsctl stop crs
CRS-2791: Starting shutdown of Oracle High Availability Services-managed
resources on 'alpha2'
```

```
<<OUTPUT TRIMMED>>
CRS-2673: Attempting to stop 'ora.gipcd' on 'alpha2'
CRS-2677: Stop of 'ora.diskmon' on 'alpha2' succeeded
CRS-2677: Stop of 'ora.gipcd' on 'alpha2' succeeded
CRS-2793: Shutdown of Oracle High Availability Services-managed resources on
'alpha2' has completed
CRS-4133: Oracle High Availability Services has been stopped.
[root@alpha2 bin]#
```

To stop all cluster resources running in all nodes:

```
# $GRID_HOME/bin/crsctl stop cluster -all
```

To start all cluster resources across all nodes:

```
# $GRID_HOME/bin/crsctl start cluster -all
```

Verifying CRS

The following commands can be used to verify the status of the cluster and related CRS daemon processes.

To check the current status of a cluster:

```
[root@alpha2 bin]# $GRID_HOME/bin/crsctl check cluster
CRS-4537: Cluster Ready Services is online
CRS-4529: Cluster Synchronization Services is online
CRS-4533: Event Manager is online
[root@alpha2 bin]#
```

To check the current status of CRS:

```
[root@alpha2 bin]# $GRID_HOME/bin/crsctl check crs
CRS-4638: Oracle High Availability Services is online
CRS-4537: Cluster Ready Services is online
CRS-4529: Cluster Synchronization Services is online
CRS-4533: Event Manager is online
[root@alpha2 bin]#
To check current status of OHASD daemon:
[root@alpha2 bin]# $GRID_HOME/bin/crsctl check has
CRS-4638: Oracle High Availability Services is online
[root@alpha2 bin]#
```

Disabling and Enabling CRS

By default, CRS will restart on system reboot. If system maintenance is being done, and CRS needs to be prevented from starting on system reboot, you can disable it. Also, the enable and disable CRS commands are effective only for future reboots of the node and do not impact the availability of the currently running CRS and its components.

In Oracle 11g, you can use the following commands to enable/disable CRS and its daemons.

To disable all CRS daemons:

```
#$GRID_HOME/bin/crsctl disable crs
```

To enable all CRS daemons:

```
#$GRID_HOME/bin/crsctl enable crs
```

CRS Utilities

All CRS utilities are present in the $GRID_HOME/bin directory. Some of the CRS utilities are also available in ORACLE_HOME; however, you should always use CRS utilities from the $GRID_HOME/bin directory only. Do not put $GRID_HOME/bin in your path, but execute these utilities by specifying the full pathname. Oracle has consolidated most of the utilities into one CRSCTL utility, but you may still find all utilities mentioned in the following table under $GRID_HOME/bin. Most of the utilities have been deprecated in Oracle 11*g* Release 2, which is documented in the following table also. Some of the functionalities for managing resources (such as crs_profile and crs_register) are merged with the SRVCTL utility.

Table 8-1 briefly describes the CRS utilities.

Utility	Description
crs_stat	Queries or displays the status of various resources controlled by CRS. Deprecated in Oracle 11*g* Release 2. This functionality is still available for backward compatibility.
crsctl	CRS control utility used to check, start, stop, get status, enable, and disable CRS components and resources controlled by CRS. Also used for managing OCR and voting disks and debugging various CRS components.
crs_profile	Creates an application resource profile. Deprecated in Oracle 11*g* Release 2.
crs_register	Registers an application in OCR. Deprecated in Oracle 11*g* Release 2.
crs_unregister	Unregisters an application from OCR. Deprecated in Oracle 11*g* Release 2.
crs_start	Starts an application resource controlled by CRS. Deprecated in Oracle 11*g* Release 2.
crs_stop	Stops an application resources controlled by CRS. Deprecated in Oracle 11*g* Release 2.
crs_getparam	Finds the permissions associated with a resource. Deprecated in Oracle 11*g* Release 2.
crs_setparam	Sets permissions for a resource. Deprecated in Oracle 11*g* Release 2.
crs_relocate	Relocates application resources controlled by CRS. Deprecated in Oracle 11*g* Release 2.
cemutlo	Cluster name check utility.
clsfmt	Cluster formatting utility. Also called while managing voting disks. Called implicitly as part of root.sh.
diagcollection.pl	Oracle cluster diagnostic collection tool.
oifcfg	Oracle interface configuration utility. Used by Oracle Universal Installer during installation.
clscfg	Oracle cluster configuration utility.

TABLE 8-1 *CRS Utilities*

CRSCTL

The CRSCTL utility is used to control the clusterwide operations in Oracle Clusterware. Oracle 11*g* Release 2 introduced some cluster-aware commands that can be used to take action on cluster resources on all cluster nodes. Oracle 11*g* Release 2 also consolidated most of the CRS utilities into the CRSCTL utility. This section explains some important commands that replace the old CRS utilities.

To display the status of cluster resources:

```
# $GRID_HOME/crsctl stat res -t
[root@alpha2 bin]# ./crsctl stat res -t
NAME    TARGET  STATE         SERVER     STATE_DETAILS
Local Resources
ora.ASMCCF1.dg
                ONLINE  ONLINE        alpha1
                ONLINE  ONLINE        alpha2
                ONLINE  ONLINE        alpha3
ora.ASMDAT1.dg


........ output truncated


#
```

This command displays cluster resources in tabular format, which is equivalent to Oracle 11*g* Release 1 or earlier versions of the crs_stat -t command.

To retrieve permission for a cluster resource:

```
#./crsctl getperm resource ora.prod.db -g dba
Name: ora.prod.db
 [root@alpha2 bin]#
```

Here is the equivalent Oracle 10*g* command to retrieve the same information:

```
[root@alpha2 bin]# ./crs_getperm ora.prod.db -g dba
Name: ora.prod.db
r--
[root@alpha2 bin]#
To check version of  Oracle Clusterware:
[root@alpha2 bin]# ./crsctl query  crs softwareversion
Oracle Clusterware version on node [alpha2] is [11.2.0.1.0]
```

Similarly, users can query activeversion and releaseversion of Oracle Clusterware.

Deleting Resource

In previous releases, users had to unregister the cluster resource and then delete the resource profile, but with the crs_profile command in Oracle 11*g*, all this can be done in a single command, as shown here:

```
# $GRID_HOME/bin/crsctl delete resource testresource -f
```

This example will delete the resource testresource forcefully. The equivalent command to delete the resource in previous releases was as follows:

```
# $GRID_HOME/bin/crs_unregister testresource
```

clsfmt

Oracle provides scripts and tools that use this cluster format utility to format the Oracle Cluster Registry and voting disk. The root.sh script internally executes this utility to format the OCR and voting disk, after installing the binaries of Oracle Grid Infrastructure.

NOTE
Improper use of this utility will format and erase content of the OCR and voting disk and may render the cluster in an unusable state. This section lists this utility for academic purposes only.

olsnodes

Use this utility to check that all the nodes have joined the cluster. The olsnodes command syntax is shown here:

```
Usage: olsnodes [ [-n] [-i] [-s] [-t] [<node> | -l [-p]] | [-c] ] [-g] [-v]
-n print node number with the node name
-p print private interconnect address for the local node
-i print virtual IP address with the node name
<node> print information for the specified node
-l print information for the local node
-s print node status - active or inactive
-t print node type - pinned or unpinned
-g turn on logging
-v Run in debug mode; use at direction of Oracle Support only.
-c print clusterware name
```

You can check the status of Oracle CRS by executing this command without any command-line options. The output should be a listing of the nodes, confirming that CRS is up and running and that all the nodes can communicate with each other via the CRS:

```
# olsnodes
[root@alpha2 bin]# ./olsnodes
alpha1
alpha3
alpha2
[root@alpha2 bin]#
```

Oracle has enhanced this utility in Oracle 11g, and users can use this utility to also print the name of the cluster, as shown next:

```
[root@alpha2 bin]# ./olsnodes -c
prod
[root@alpha2 bin]#
```

In previous releases of Oracle Clusterware, users had to go through multiple steps—such as creating a resource profile, updating the resource profile, and re-registering the cluster resource—but all this can be done in the same command now:

```
# crsctl modify resource testresource -attr  USR_ORA_VIP=10.11.122.23 -i
```

Oracle Cluster Diagnostic Collection Tool—diagcollection

The Oracle cluster diagnostic collection tool helps you collect the diagnostic information for all the required components, such as host, OS, cluster, and agents, at once. This tool is available in the $GRID_HOME/bin directory.

```
[root@alpha1 bin]# ./diagcollection.pl
Production Copyright 2004, 2008, Oracle.  All rights reserved
Cluster Ready Services (CRS) diagnostic collection tool
diagcollection
     --collect
[--crs] For collecting crs diag information
[--adr] For collecting diag information for ADR
[--ipd] For collecting IPD-OS data
[--all] Default.For collecting all diag information.
[--core] UNIX only. Package core files with CRS data
[--afterdate] UNIX only. Collects archives from the specified date.
Specify in mm/dd/yyyy format
[--aftertime] Supported with -adr option.
Collects archives after the specified time.
Specify in YYYYMMDDHHMISS24 format
[--beforetime] Supported with -adr option.
Collects archives before the specified date.
Specify in YYYYMMDDHHMISS24 format
[--crshome] Argument that specifies the CRS Home location
[--incidenttime] Collects IPD data from the specified time.
Specify in MM/DD/YYY24HH:MM:SS format
If not specified, IPD data generated in the past 24 hours are collected
[--incidentduration] Collects IPD data for the duration after the specified
time.  Specify in HH:MM format. If not specified, all IPD data after
incidenttime are collected

  NOTE:
  1. You can also do the following
./diagcollection.pl --collect --crs --crshome <CRS Home>
    --clean       cleans up the diagnosability
                  information gathered by this script
  --coreanalyze  UNIX only.
Extracts information from core files and stores it in a text file
```

By default, this diagnostic tool will collect whole diagnostic information, which can be controlled by using the different options shown in the preceding example. For instance, use the --crs option to collect only CRS diagnostic data.

NOTE
*Users can use undocumented option --nocore to ignore the core
data while collecting diagnostic information using the Oracle cluster
diagnostic tool.*

GPnP Tool

Oracle introduced the Grid Plug and Play profile in Oracle 11g. The Oracle Grid Plug and Play
profile management tool (gpnptool) is used to manage the Grid Plug and Play profile.

```
[root@alpha1 bin]# ./gpnptool
Oracle GPnP Tool

Usage:
 "gpnptool <verb> <switches>", where verbs are:

        create   Create a new GPnP Profile
        edit     Edit existing GPnP Profile
        getpval  Get value(s) from GPnP Profile
        get      Get profile in effect on local node
        rget     Get profile in effect on remote GPnP node
        put      Put profile as a current best
        find     Find all RD-discoverable resources of given type
        lfind    Find local gpnpd server
        check    Perform basic profile sanity checks
        c14n     Canonicalize, format profile text (XML C14N)
        sign     Sign/re-sign profile with wallet's private key
        unsign   Remove profile signature, if any
        verify   Verify profile signature against wallet certificate
        help     Print detailed tool help
        ver      Show tool version
```

Here's how to display the current GPnP profile on local node alpha1:

```
[root@alpha1 bin]# ./gpnptool get
Warning: some command line parameters were defaulted. Resulting command line:
        ./gpnptool.bin get -o-

<?xml version="1.0" encoding="UTF-8"?><gpnp:GPnP-Profile Version="1.0"
xmlns="http://www.grid-pnp.org/2005/11/gpnp-profile" xmlns:gpnp="http://
www.grid-pnp.org/2005/11/gpnp-profile" xmlns:orcl="http://www.oracle.com/
gpnp/2005/11/gpnp-profile" xmlns:xsi="http://www.w3.org/2001/XMLSchema-
instance" xsi:schemaLocation="http://www.grid-pnp.org/2005/11/gpnp-
profile gpnp-profile.xsd" ProfileSequence="7" ClusterUId="72b7d68d5c0
85f78bf11ec4d1cb135e4" ClusterName="prod" PALocation=""><gpnp:Network-
Profile><gpnp:HostNetwork id="gen" HostName="*"><gpnp:Network id="net1"
IP="172.16.194.144" Adapter="bond0" Use="public"/><gpnp:Network id="net2"
IP="172.16.194.112" Adapter="bond1" Use="cluster_interconnect"/></
gpnp:HostNetwork></gpnp:Network-Profile><orcl:CSS-Profile id="css"
DiscoveryString="+asm" LeaseDuration="400"/><orcl:ASM-Profile id="asm"
```

```
DiscoveryString="" SPFile="+ASMDAT1/prod/asmparameterfile/registry.253.727438
675"/><ds:Signature xmlns:ds="http://www.w3.org/2000/09/xmldsig#"><ds:Signed
Info><ds:CanonicalizationMethod Algorithm="http://www.w3.org/2001/10/xml-exc-
c14n#"/><ds:SignatureMethod Algorithm="http://www.w3.org/2000/09/xmldsig#rsa-
sha1"/><ds:Reference URI=""><ds:Transforms><ds:Transform Algorithm="http://www.
w3.org/2000/09/xmldsig#enveloped-signature"/><ds:Transform Algorithm="http://
www.w3.org/2001/10/xml-exc-c14n#"> <InclusiveNamespaces xmlns="http://www.
w3.org/2001/10/xml-exc-c14n#" PrefixList="gpnp orcl xsi"/></ds:Transform></
ds:Transforms><ds:DigestMethod Algorithm="http://www.w3.org/2000/09/xmlds
ig#sha1"/><ds:DigestValue>FKHv0Fqp/BzHGFaVrBAvoyHmmj8=</ds:DigestValue></
ds:Reference></ds:SignedInfo><ds:SignatureValue>iHnLSaRjNrR2WNeyDc5zGE/eZpLF/3
l2p/5zCWxcetsYIoxCTkEfq9xRQrNsnQiixcFrS02OSHyuwArM7Tv5a0HjqvQJ/rKleHprNV1fcq/
XKUzaajmsTWQKynnkwBKnfNRBPqsSpUgHZznov/O8quIWBDl7qYsiTw+RK5detxY=</
ds:SignatureValue></ds:Signature></gpnp:GPnP-Profile>
Success.
```

Oracle Interface Configuration—oifcfg

The Oracle interface configuration tool helps you to define network interface card usage in an Oracle RAC environment. This utility is useful while managing the hostname, IP address changes during datacenter migrations, or network reconfigurations that require changing IP addresses to cluster members. Here are some usage examples for this tool.

This command should return values for global public and global cluster_interconnect:

```
$ oifcfg getif
```

Here's an example:

```
en0 144.25.68.0 global public
en5 192.168.100.0 global cluster_interconnect
```

If the command does not return a value for global cluster_interconnect, enter the following commands to delete and set the desired interface:

```
# oifcfg delif -global
# oifcfg setif -global <interface name>/<subnet>:public
# oifcfg setif -global <interface name>/<subnet>:cluster_interconnect
```

Cluster Configuration Utility—clscfg

This utility is used during CRS installation. However, you should not use it unless instructed to do so under guidance from OSS (Oracle Support Services). The command "clscfg –concepts" provides a good description of some CRS concepts, including private interconnect, hostnames, node names, voting disk, ocssd, evmd, crsd, and ocr.

The following options are available with the Cluster Configuration utility:

```
[root@alpha2 bin]# ./clscfg
clscfg: EXISTING configuration version 5 detected.
clscfg: version 5 is 11g Release 2.
clscfg -- Oracle cluster configuration tool
```

This tool is typically invoked as part of the Oracle Cluster Ready Services install process. It configures cluster topology and other settings. Use -help for information on any of these modes.
Use one of the following modes of operation.

```
-install    - creates a new configuration
-add        - adds node specific configuration on the newly added node.
-upgrade    - upgrades an existing configuration
-downgrade  - downgrades an existing configuration
-local      - creates a special single-node configuration for ASM
-localadd   - creates keys in OLR for HASD
-concepts   - brief listing of terminology used in the other modes
-trace      - may be used in conjunction with any mode above for tracing
WARNING: Using this tool may corrupt your cluster configuration. Do not use
unless you positively know what you are doing.
```

Cluster Name Check Utility—cemutlo
This utility prints the cluster name information. Following is the usage syntax for this utility:

```
#$ORA_CRS_HOME/bin/cemutlo [-n] [-w]
  where:
  -n prints the cluster name
  -w prints the clusterware version in the following format:
  <major_version>:<minor_version>:<vendor_info>
#$ORA_CRS_HOME/bin/cemutlo -n
prod
#$ORA_CRS_HOME/bin/cemutlo -w
2:1:
```

This utility can be used only in Oracle 10g onward; for Oracle 9i you need to use cemutls. Note that the olsnodes utility can also be used to print the name of the cluster.

Add Node Script—addnode.sh
This script must be run when you are adding a new node to an existing cluster. For example, the following command will add alpha4 to the cluster PROD:

```
#$GRID_HOME/bin/addnode.sh -silent "CLUSTER_NEW_NOES={alpha4}"
  "CLUSTER_NEW_VIRTUAL_HOSTNAMES={alpha4-vip}"
```

More details on adding a node to an existing cluster are discussed in Appendix B.

Delete Node Script—deletenode.sh
This script needs to be run when you are deleting an existing node from a cluster. Deleting a node from the cluster is a multiple-step process. The following steps will delete alpha3 from the cluster PROD:

1. Expire the CSS lease on alpha3 by using the following command from the other cluster nodes:

```
crsctl unpin css -n alpha3
```

2. Execute the rootcrs.pl script from the $GRID_HOME/crs/install directory on alpha3:

```
$GRID_HOME/crs/install/rootcrs.pl -delete -force
```

3. Disable Oracle Clusterware applications running on alpha3. This includes the virtual IP for alpha3 also.

4. As the Oracle Grid Infrastructure owner, execute the following command from the other cluster nodes to delete alpha3 from the cluster.

```
crsctl delete node -n alpha3
```

5. As the Oracle Grid Infrastructure owner, execute the following command on alpha3 to update the node list:

```
runInstaller -updateNodeList ORACLE_HOME=/u02/11.2.0/grid
"CLUSTER_NODES={alpha3}"  CRS=TRUE -local
```

6. As the Oracle Grid Infrastructure owner, execute the following command on alpha3 to delete Oracle Home:

```
deinstall -local
```

7. As the Oracle Grid Infrastructure owner, execute the following command on the other cluster nodes (alpha1 and alpha2):

```
runInstaller -updateNodeList ORACLE_HOME=/u02/11.2.0/grid
"CLUSTER_NODES={alpha1,alpha2}"  CRS=TRUE
```

More details on deleting a node from an existing cluster are provided in Appendix B.

Administering OCR

OCR is the Oracle RAC configuration information repository that manages information about the cluster node list and instance-to-node mapping information. Processes that make up the CRS and other cluster-aware applications use this repository to share information among them. Its contents include but are not limited to the following:

■ Node membership information

■ Database instance, node, and other mapping information

■ Service characteristics

■ Characteristics of any third-party applications controlled by CRS (10*g* R2 and later)

OCR's location is specified during CRS installation. The file pointer indicating the OCR device location is in the file ocr.loc, whose location is somewhat platform dependent. For example, on

Linux systems it is located in /etc/oracle, and on Solaris it is located at /var/opt/oracle. The contents of ocr.loc follow:

```
#ocrconfig_loc=+ASMCCF1
local_only=FALSE
```

The first line offers information about the last operation performed on OCR impacting the contents of the ocr.loc file. Oracle 10*g* R2 onward provide a choice of mirroring OCR at the Oracle level or at the OS level to provides high availability.

Little day-to-day maintenance is required for OCR. However, OCR is a critical component of an HA framework, so if anything happens to the OCR you should be prepared to take corrective actions immediately. The following Oracle utilities are used to administer OCR. Practice these commands on a test system to be ready for any eventuality with the OCR:

- **ocrcheck**   Performs a quick health check on OCR and prints space usage statistics
- **ocrdump**   Dumps contents of OCR to an OS file
- **ocrconfig**   Performs export, import, add, replace, remove, restore, and show backup operations on OCR

Checking OCR Integrity

You can use the ocrcheck utility to perform a quick health check on OCR, as shown next. The command returns the OCR version, total space allocated, space used, free space, location of each device, and the result of the integrity check.

```
[root@alpha2 bin]# $GRID_HOME/bin/ocrcheck
Status of Oracle Cluster Registry is as follows :
        Version                  :          3
        Total space (kbytes)     :     262120
        Used space (kbytes)      :       3400
        Available space (kbytes) :     258720
        ID                       :  238319528
        Device/File Name         :  +ASMCCF1
Device/File integrity check succeeded
Cluster registry integrity check succeeded
Logical corruption check succeeded
```

The command also creates a log file in the directory $GRID_HOME/log/<hostname>/client; the contents of this log file reflect what is displayed in the output.

Dumping OCR Information

The Oracle-supplied utility ocrdump writes the contents of OCR to an OS file. By default it dumps the contents into a file named OCRDUMP in the current directory. Alternatively, you can specify a destination file and can also dump information in XML format. The command-line options available for this command can be viewed by using the command with the –help option.

The contents of the dump file are generally used by OSS (Oracle Support Services) to check configuration information in the OCR. The dump file is an ASCII file that you can open using any text editor. The file contains a set of key name, value type, and key value information.

Here's how to dump content of the OCR file into an XML file:

```
# $GRID_HOME/bin/ocrdump 1.xml -xml
```

Maintaining a Mirror OCR

Starting from version 10*g* Release 2, Oracle allows you to create a mirror copy of the OCR, thereby eliminating OCR as a single point of failure. It also eliminates the need for mirroring OCR using methods external to Oracle, such as storage- or array-level mirroring.

The following command adds/relocates the ocrmirror file to the specified location:

```
ocrconfig -replace ocrmirror '+ASMCCF1'
```

NOTE
Using "ocrconfig –replace" is the only way to add/relocate OCR files. Copying the existing OCR file to a new location and manually adding/ changing the file pointer in the ocr.loc file is not supported and will not work.

You can use the following command to relocate an existing OCR file:

```
ocrconfig -replace ocr '+ASMCCF1'
```

You can relocate OCR only when OCR is mirrored. To relocate OCR or a mirror to a new location, another copy of OCR should be fully functional.

NOTE
OCR mirror add/relocate operations can be performed while CRS is running and hence do not require any system downtime.

The following command can be used to remove the OCR or the ocrmirror:

```
ocrconfig -replace ocr
```

or

```
ocrconfig -replace ocrmirror
```

There is no need to specify the file location as an option on the command line. It will retrieve the file location and remove the intended file.

Administering Oracle Local Registry

Although all the commands available to manage OCR are not available to OLR, Oracle Local Registry is still managed in similar ways to how we manage the Oracle Cluster Registry. Users can use the following command to manage OLR by adding -local in the command line:

```
ocrcheck -local
ocrdump -local
```

```
ocrconfig -local -export filename
ocrconfig -local -import filename
ocrconfig -local -repair old filename
```

Administering the Voting Disk

Oracle Clusterware uses a voting disk to resolve cluster membership issues in the event of partitioned clusters. Consider an eight-node cluster experiencing a breakdown in communication between the nodes—four nodes cannot communicate with the other four nodes. Situations like this can cause serious data integrity issues. A voting disk or a quorum disk provides a mechanism to resolve such issues. In case of a break in communication and a partitioned cluster, a voting disk helps in deciding which set of nodes should survive if another set of nodes should go down.

All voting disks must be placed on shared storage to be accessible by all the nodes. A voting disk is a small file if you are using a raw device for it; a 280MB raw device should be used for each voting disk. Oracle 11*g* supports up to 32 voting disks. Having multiple voting disks removes the voting disk as a single point of failure and eliminates the need to mirror them outside Oracle. Oracle Universal Installer (OUI) allows you to specify up to three voting disks during Oracle Grid Infrastructure installation. Having three voting disks allows CRS operation to continue uninterrupted when any of the three voting disks fails. For the cluster to survive failure of *x* number of voting disks, you needs to configure (2*x*+1) voting disks.

Starting with Oracle 11*g*, voting disks can reside in Oracle ASM. Users can add, remove, or migrate voting disks in the Oracle ASM or between ASM and non-ASM file systems. Oracle will back up the voting disk in the Oracle Cluster Registry as a result of any configuration changes. Oracle will automatically restore the voting disk data into the newly added voting disk.

In a Nutshell

In this chapter we explored how using Oracle RAC services helps in workload management. Managing and administering services become easier with this Oracle-supplied package. Oracle provides various tools to create and manage services and service policies. Oracle services are a one-stop solution for configuring and managing various kinds of workloads in the clusterware.

Oracle 11*g* enhanced the clusterware management framework and provides lots of enhancements to the server control utility. Some of the functionalities provided by the CRS tools are merged with the server control utility, and the server control utility is enhanced to manage the clusterwide resources.

We also discussed various utilities for managing Oracle Cluster Ready Services, including the Oracle Cluster Registry and voting disks. Oracle Cluster Registry and voting disks are very critical components of the clusterware, and we discussed managing these components. The newly enhanced utilities make managing Oracle clusterware relatively simpler and easier.

CHAPTER
9

Oracle RAC Backup
and Recovery

n this chapter we discuss the key concepts and internals behind backup and recovery operations of Oracle Real Application Clusters (Oracle RAC) databases. Basic backup and recovery methods for the Oracle RAC database are similar to those for single-instance databases, except in Oracle RAC we have redo records from archived redo logs from multiple instances. No special considerations for media recovery or any other advanced recovery mechanisms are required for Oracle RAC, so this chapter does *not* cover generic backup (and recovery) mechanisms.

However, we discuss the recovery issues that are specific to Oracle RAC, starting from the basics and then delving deeper into Oracle RAC–based backup and recovery as well as into other information that is not easily available or accessible. *Oracle Backup and Recovery User Guide 11g* (Release 2 [11.2], Part Number E10642-03) and *Oracle Database Backup and Recovery Reference 11g* (Release 2 [11.2], Part Number E10643-03) can be used as supplemental references for basic information of backup and recovery operations.

Introduction to Backups

One of the key features of the Oracle RDBMS engine is its ability to recover from various kinds of faults, disasters, and human errors. The Oracle backup and recovery mechanism has evolved since its early days of Oracle 6 into a near "fault-tolerant" database engine that can guarantee data protection as well as recoverability more than any other database vendor's product. Transaction recovery is possible mainly due to the redo log. The structure of the redo log and its associated buffer has undergone changes since the days of Oracle 6 when it was first introduced, but it largely remains the same, and its primary purpose and importance inside Oracle both remain.

Oracle has developed its own tools/utilities (Recovery Manager, or RMAN) to perform backups and restore/recover a database in the simplest or easiest ways possible. Oracle also provides the user with the flexibility to choose between RMAN and other tools to make backups and restore data. Recovery of restored data can be done only through an Oracle interface such as SQL*Plus or RMAN.

Oracle Backup Options

Generally, Oracle's backup options can be classified based on the tools or technologies used to implement them. The following serves as a rough guide to understanding the various tools used for Oracle backups in the industry today.

Small, Noncritical Databases

These include operating system (OS) built-in utilities such as tar, cpio, and so on, that are available to Windows users. The backup media can be a tape or disk. Usually, Windows systems do not have a separate backup tool or framework. This type of backup is almost exclusively a closed-database backup, where the business operation has the luxury of performing a *cold backup*—stopping and shutting down the databases for a backup.

Medium to Large Databases

These databases may also use common utilities such as tar and cpio. DBAs generally write or borrow automated scripts to perform these backups. Servers have a fast tape drive or two connected to the database host. Automated tape libraries are used in large organizations. It is common to find backup tools such as Veritas NetBackup, HP OmniBack or Storage Data Protector, IBM Tivoli, and so on, implemented at the database level. RMAN is also widely used but with a lesser degree of integration with the third-party backup tools.

Oracle Data Guard is increasingly becoming a standard choice for disaster recovery in many types of organizations. Since Oracle 8*i*, Oracle Data Guard has presented a "near real-time switchover capability" that was not possible before with an Oracle database. Additional server hardware and disk storage (equivalent to your primary system) is required to implement Oracle Data Guard.

Enterprise Databases

These are big-spending mega corporations that use sophisticated technologies such as disk mirroring and splitting and remote geographical mirroring, which could be in conjunction with cluster technologies such as Oracle RAC. These companies may also deploy large, automated tape libraries or robotic libraries with scores of tape drives and redundancies. It has become increasing difficult for tape libraries to keep up with the rapid pace of Oracle data growth. Backup as well as recovery time is critical here. To overcome this time constraint, large enterprises employ disk mirroring as a method of quick data backup (sometimes known as *snapshots*) and also use the copy for reporting purposes or as a standby database. This comes at an extra cost, which can be millions of dollars.

NOTE
If you're using snapshot and split-mirror for database backups, the backup set should be required to be "crash consistent." Crash consistent is the state of disks equivalent to what would be found following a catastrophic failure that abruptly shuts down the system. A restore from such a shadow copy set would be equivalent to a reboot following an abrupt shutdown.

Oracle Backup Basics

Oracle backups can be taken at the physical level (hot or cold) or at the logical level. A physical backup is composed of the following:

- Datafiles
- Controlfiles
- Archived redo log files (if the database is in ARCHIVELOG mode)
- Parameter files (init.ora and SPFILE)

A physical backup is performed by taking an operating system copy of these files. Alternatively, RMAN can be used to accomplish the backup of the database files, with the exception of the init.ora file. It is a well-known fact that online redo logs need not be backed up, irrespective of the fact that a database is in ARCHIVELOG mode or NOARCHIVELOG mode. For detailed information on this topic and other basics mentioned in this chapter, refer to the *Oracle 11g Backup and Recovery Concepts User's Guide.*

Performing Backups in Oracle

Oracle databases exist in every size and shape. With terabyte-sized databases becoming as common as PlayStations and Nintendo Wii's, large organizations and corporations no longer depend on tape libraries for backups; sophisticated disk-mirroring mechanisms haven taken their place. Oracle as a database company has come up with excellent solutions, such as RMAN and Oracle Data Guard, that allow even the largest databases to be backed up. The backup scheme needs to be chosen carefully. Some like to back up to disk and then push data to tape, whereas others like to back up directly to tape.

In Oracle, full, incremental, and incremental merge backups can be performed using RMAN by itself or in combination with other third-party backup tools such as IBM Tivoli, Veritas NetBackup, and HP Storage Data Protector. If a third-party tool is to be used without RMAN integration, the traditional method of putting a database in backup mode and pulling it out is to be followed. Oracle 10*g* and above allow you to put the whole database into backup mode with a single command, whereas prior to version 10*g*, each tablespace had to be put in backup mode and pulled out at the end of a backup.

RMAN Backup for Oracle RAC Databases

RMAN is capable of handling Oracle RAC databases, and it can be configured to perform Oracle RAC database backups. Beginning with Oracle 9*i*, many of the configuration items are now persistent and need to be performed only once during the setup phase. As mentioned, RMAN should be actively considered as the backup solution even for Oracle RAC. The only consideration would be the time taken to perform the backup for large databases (larger than 500GB) when tape drives or tape libraries are used, which would be the same whether Oracle RAC is used or not. In such cases, disk-mirroring technology can be used if backup and restore time is of prime importance and/or the database size exceeds a terabyte.

Choosing the Archive Log Destination in an Oracle RAC Database

Configuring the ARCHIVELOG mode in an Oracle RAC database is a crucial decision for a DBA. Because archive logs can be placed on ASM and a Cluster File System drive (shared) or a local drive (non-shared), it has serious implications on your backup and recovery strategies. The primary consideration is to ensure that all archived redo logs can be read from every node during recovery and, if possible, even during backups, irrespective of whether RMAN is used.

The key point to understand is that when a node generates an archived redo log, Oracle always records the filename of the archived log in the controlfile of the database. If you are using RMAN with a recovery catalog, RMAN also records the archived redo log file names in the recovery catalog when a resynchronization occurs. However, archived log file pathnames do not include the node name, so RMAN expects to find the files it needs on the nodes where the channels are allocated.

The archived redo log naming scheme that you use is important because when a node writes to a log with a specific filename on its file system (or CFS), the file must be readable by any node that needs to access this archived redo log for backup and/or recovery purposes.

> **NOTE**
> *When Fast Recovery Area (known as Flash Recovery Area in earlier versions) is configured, the location and the size should be same across the databases. Fast Recovery Area simplifies the backup management and is highly recommended for Oracle RAC databases.*

The Oracle-recommended configuration for Oracle RAC is to use Automatic Storage Management (ASM) for storing the Fast Recovery Area (FRA), using a different disk group for your recovery set than for the datafiles.

The backup and recovery strategy you choose depends on how you configure the archiving destinations for each node. It doesn't matter if only one or all nodes perform archived redo log backups; you need to ensure that all archived redo logs are backed up.

If a cluster file system is used, all instances can write to a single archive log destination. Backup and recovery of the archive logs are easy because all logs are centrally located. If a cluster file system is not available, Oracle generally recommends that local archive log destinations be used for each instance with Network File System (NFS) read mount points to all other instances. This is known as the *local archive with NFS scheme*. During backup, you can either back up the archive logs from each host or select one host to perform the backup for all archive logs. During recovery, one instance may access the logs from any host without having to copy them first to the local destination. It is still crucial to provide a second archive destination to avoid single points of failure, irrespective of the scheme being used.

If RMAN parallelism is used during recovery, the node that performs the recovery must have access to all the archived redo logs in your cluster. Multiple nodes can restore archived logs in parallel. However, during recovery, only one node applies the archived logs. Therefore, the node that is performing the recovery must be able to access all of the archived logs that are needed for recovery.

Oracle Data Guard and Oracle RAC

Oracle Data Guard was first introduced in Oracle 8*i* as Standby Database and has since undergone many enhancements. Later versions of Oracle introduced Oracle Data Guard with support for Oracle Real Application Clusters. By this we mean that the primary database can be Oracle RAC and/or the standby database can be Oracle RAC. This provides for and extends the maximum availability demands that 24×7 shops place on database and other systems today. Oracle Data Guard also works seamlessly with RMAN, and this integration is helpful for creating standby databases using the DUPLICATE DATABASE command. Refer to the *Oracle Recovery Manager Reference* for more details.

Instance Recovery in Oracle RAC

Instance recovery in Oracle RAC is not radically different from the way it is performed on a single instance. Some additional steps are required because redo entries for a data block can now exist in any redo threads. Hence, global (clusterwide) coordination and synchronization is required to ensure that the consistency and reliability of data blocks are maintained, just like the Oracle recovery mechanism would in the case of a single-instance recovery.

At this juncture, it is important that you understand the subtle differences in the terms *instance recovery* and *crash recovery*. Although they generally mean the same thing in terms of operations, some minor contextual differences exist.

In a single-instance environment, the two terms are one and the same. In RAC, *crash recovery* means that all instances in the Oracle RAC database have failed and hence all instances have to be recovered or all instances may need recovery, depending on the operations they were performing. The point is, in an Oracle RAC crash recovery, all instances need to participate and are qualified candidates for recovery operations.

Instance recovery means that one or more instances in the cluster database have failed and need to be recovered by the other surviving instance. Thread recovery is applicable in both situations because a single instance is being recovered, and the term generally describes the recovery of a single thread (or instance) in a cluster database and has more relevance in an Oracle RAC database than in a single-instance scenario.

The following section looks at the key concepts of recovery operations in the Oracle RAC database. Instance recovery and media recovery involve additional steps in the Oracle RAC environment as multiple redo streams record database changes, and they should be seamlessly applied to the database during recovery in a chronological order. The following structures ensure the recovery operations in Oracle RAC databases.

Redo Threads and Streams

Redo information generated by an instance is called a *thread of redo*. All log files for that instance belong to this thread. An online redo log file belongs to a group, and the group belongs to a thread. If the database is running in ARCHIVELOG mode, the thread is nothing but all the archived redo log files. If the server is running in NOARCHIVELOG mode, then the thread is effectively the size of the online redo log files. A record in the controlfile describes each and every online redo log file. Details about the log file group and thread association details are stored in the controlfile.

A *redo stream* consists of all the threads of redo information ever recorded. The stream forms a timeline of changes performed to the database. In a single-instance database, the terms *thread* and *stream* refer to the same thing because a single instance has only one thread. Oracle RAC databases have multiple threads of redo—that is, each active instance has one active thread. In Oracle RAC, the threads are parallel timelines and together form the stream.

Redo Records and Change Vectors

When users make changes to the database, Oracle records them in the redo log file as *change vectors*. Each change vector is a description of a single change, usually to a single block. A set of change vector structures makes up the content of each redo record. A redo record contains one or more change vectors and is located by its *redo byte address (RBA)* and points to a specific location in a redo log file (or a thread). It consists of three components: a log sequence number, a block number within the log, and a byte number within the block.

Checkpoints

Checkpoints are important database events that synchronize the database buffer cache and the datafiles. Without the various checkpoint mechanisms, recovery of data would be impossible. Checkpoints are used to determine the location or point from where recovery should start. This is the most important use of checkpoints and is indispensable in instance recovery (single and Oracle RAC).

In simple but crude terms, a *checkpoint* is a framework that enables the writing of dirty blocks to disk based on a system commit number (SCN) and RBA validation algorithm and, more importantly, limits the number of blocks required for recovery.

Checkpoints ensure that data blocks that have redos generated up to a point in the redo log are written to disk. Checkpoint information is stored in a data structure called the *checkpoint structure,* which defines (points to) a specific location in a given redo log file. Checkpoint structures are stored in datafile headers and in the controlfile and are usually made up of the checkpoint SCN, checkpoint RBA, thread ID, timestamp, and some other control information. Like an RBA, these structures are used to find the starting point for reading the redo log for a redo application.

Checkpoints are triggered by a number of events (such as log switches, hot backups, and shutdowns) that in turn produce different types of checkpoints. The most important ones are briefly explained next.

Thread Checkpoint or Local Checkpoint

A thread checkpoint collects all dirty buffers in an instance that contains changes to any online datafile before a designated SCN—the thread checkpoint SCN—and writes them to disk. The SCN is associated with a specific RBA in the log, which is used to determine when all the buffers have been written. A thread checkpoint can occur at a log switch or if any of the thread checkpoint conditions are satisfied.

All blocks dirtied prior to this thread checkpoint SCN in that thread for all online datafiles are written to disk. In an Oracle RAC database, a thread checkpoint occurs independently and separately for each instance, because each has its own thread or redo. This information is recorded in a structure called the *thread checkpoint structure* and in multiple controlfile records and all online datafile headers.

Database Checkpoint or Global Checkpoint

When a database checkpoint needs to be triggered, Oracle looks for the thread checkpoint that has the lowest checkpoint SCN for all open and enabled threads (highest checkpoint SCN for all closed threads), and that itself becomes the database checkpoint. All blocks in memory that contain changes made prior to this SCN across all instances must be written out to disk. For a single-instance database, a database checkpoint is the same as a thread checkpoint. The information is recorded in several controlfile records and all online datafile headers.

Incremental Checkpoint

When data blocks are modified in the buffer cache, they are placed in a queue called the Checkpoint Queue (CKPTQ) for background writing by the DBWR process. The CKPTQ was introduced in Oracle 8. This queue is ordered by the RBA of the first log record to modify the block, which is nothing but the earliest modification record for that block. The oldest dirty blocks are the first in the queue and are waiting to be written out. Since Oracle 8i, when the touch count mechanism was introduced, some blocks may still remain in the buffer cache if it is an active buffer or a hot buffer.

The idea behind incremental checkpoints is to reduce the amount of redo that has to be read during instance recovery. This allows instance recovery time to be bounded by a DBA. To accomplish this, an "in-memory" checkpoint record is updated approximately every 3 seconds and action is also taken to ensure that the number and age of dirty data blocks in the cache are limited.

A CKPTQ enables the incremental checkpoint to avoid having a cache filled with many dirty blocks, which all must be written at once when a checkpoint occurs. Because the dirty block count is kept low, the number of blocks that need to be recovered in case of a crash is fewer, resulting in faster database recovery. The length of this list is an indicator of the amount of blocks that need recovery if the block is lost in a crash. Information on this is visible in the V$INSTANCE_ RECOVERY view.

Log History Considerations

The controlfile always maintains a record of the archived log files generated for each thread. This enables an instance that is performing media recovery to identify the archived log files that it needs regardless of which instance generated them. The number of entries that are maintained in the controlfile is determined by the value assigned with the MAXLOGHISTORY setting in the CREATE DATABASE command.

Usually, DBAs overlook or sometimes do not pay much attention to the log history until the following occurs:

- Oracle complains that more online redo log files cannot be created during an attempt to create them.
- Standby redo log files cannot be created in a physical Oracle Data Guard setup.
- The DBA is asked to generate metrics about the rate at which redo is generated.

Generally, it is recommended that MAXLOGHISTORY should not be less than the total number of archived log files that are generated across all your instances between each complete database backup. This enables a recovering instance to identify the archived log files that it requires after you restore the most recent backup.

If there are insufficient archived log entries in your controlfile, you are prompted for the required filenames when you initiate the recovery process. This can be hard to do when hundreds or maybe thousands of archived logs need to be applied. To increase the size of the MAXLOGHISTORY setting, the controlfile must be re-created.

Crash Recovery

The internal mechanics of recovery are well beyond the discussion context of this chapter, yet it is important to remind you of some important characteristics of recovering a single instance (non-OPS or Oracle RAC). As mentioned earlier, the terms *instance recovery* and *crash recovery* refer to the same recovery aspect. The only notable difference is that in Oracle RAC, crash recovery involves *all* the instances. For a single instance, crash recovery and instance recovery are the same. Some of these points are also applicable to Oracle RAC databases because the mechanisms are basically the same.

Steps in Crash Recovery (Single Instance)

When an instance failure occurs (which leads to a database crash in a single-instance database), the following is the recovery process:

1. The on-disk version of a block is the starting point for recovery. Oracle will need to consider only the block on disk, and the recovery is straightforward. Crash recovery is automatic, using the online redo logs that are current or active.

2. The starting point of a thread recovery is at most the last full checkpoint. The starting point is provided in the controlfile and compared against the same information in all datafile headers. Only the changes from a single redo thread need to be applied.

3. The block specified in the redo log is read into the cache. If the block has the same timestamp as the redo record (SCN match is satisfied), the redo is applied. The block is then written out by a recovery checkpoint at a log switch or when aged out of the cache.

Crash Recovery in Oracle RAC

Oracle performs instance recovery automatically upon detecting that an instance has died. Instance/crash recovery is performed automatically when the database is opened for the first time after a crash or when one of the instances of an Oracle RAC database fails. In the case of Oracle RAC, a surviving instance detects the need to perform instance recovery for one or more failed instances by the following methods:

- A foreground process in a surviving instance detects an "invalid block lock" condition when an attempt is made to read a block into the buffer cache. This is an indication that another instance died while a block covered by that lock was in a potentially dirty state in its buffer cache.

- The invalid block condition is more of a suspect lock that needs to be resolved because it's in a dubious state before being accessed or its master died in the instance crash and hence a new master needs to be constructed. Therefore, the foreground process sends a notification to its instance's System Monitor (SMON) process, which begins a search for dead instances.

- The death of another instance is detected if the current instance is able to acquire that instance's redo thread locks, which is usually held by an open and active instance.

NOTE
In Oracle RAC, the SMON process in the surviving instance obtains a reliable list of dead instances together with a list of "invalid" block locks. These locks are invalid because the instance that had locked these blocks has crashed and their status remains "fuzzy" and/or unknown. The background process SMON also performs the recovery. The instance performing the recovery would then clean up these locks and make them available for normal use as soon as recovery and cleanup are complete.

Instance Recovery

The procedure used to recover from single-instance crash failures as well as failures of Oracle RAC instances is called *instance recovery*. In the case of Oracle RAC, a surviving instance recovers all the failed instances. Instance recovery aims to restore the data block changes that were in the cache of the failed instance and to close the thread that was left open. Instance recovery uses only online redo log files and current online datafiles (not restored backups).

Instance Recovery in OPS

In Oracle Parallel Server (OPS), instance recovery processes one thread at a time and recovers one instance at a time. It applies all redos (from the thread checkpoint through the end-of-thread) from each thread before starting on the next thread.

This scheme depends on the fact that only one instance at a time can have a given block modified in its cache (both single instance and OPS). In OPS, if a change is to be made to the block by other instances, the block is written to disk by the holding instance before the requesting instance can make a change. This was the ping protocol mechanism used in pre–Oracle RAC days and in some current block copy situations. You may recall that a holding instance must write the block to disk if another instance requests the same block for modification.

The recovery process uses the checkpoint structure to know where to start reading the thread in a database. When a surviving instance is recovering a failed OPS instance, a redo from only one thread (crashed instance) needs to be applied to a given block (as read from disk during instance recovery). This is because only this thread contains the most recent modification for that block. This is also the case for single-instance or crash recovery. This kind of recovery is also called *one-thread-at-a-time recovery* because one thread is recovered at a time.

Instance recovery is always done using the online redo logs. Recovery starts with the thread with the highest checkpoint SCN. It continues to recover the threads in the order of decreasing thread checkpoint SCNs. This avoids advancing the database checkpoint by each thread recovered. Once the one-thread-at-a-time procedure completes recovering all the threads, the database checkpoint is advanced at the end of recovery.

Note that for OPS, other complex recovery operations such as distributed lock manager (DLM) freeze and reconfiguration, lock invalidation and cleaning, cluster communications, and so on, are not presented here. Some of these will be discussed in the recovery steps later in this chapter.

With Oracle 9*i* and Cache Fusion Phase II, disk ping is avoided in many situations because the holding instance downgrades its lock (EXL→SHR), keeps a "past image" of the block (which cannot be modified from this point onward by this instance or any other instance), and sends the block across the interconnect to the requesting instance, which can then make the required changes to the block after being granted the required and compatible locks. This topic is discussed in "Internals of Cache Fusion Recovery", later in this chapter.

Instance Recovery in Oracle RAC

Oracle RAC introduced a few good optimization techniques in recovery, and one of them is the *thread merge* mechanism. Using this formula, redos from multiple threads are merged when crash recovery or instance recovery is performed in Oracle RAC. This is because changes from multiple instances may not have made it to the datafiles. This is termed *thread merge recovery*. Media recovery also uses the thread merge mechanism where redos from all the threads are merged and applied simultaneously. The redo records are merged in increasing SCN order. More on the thread merge mechanism is presented in "Two-Pass Recovery," later in this chapter.

Crash Recovery and Media Recovery

Some of the basic differences between crash and media recovery are presented here for completeness in understanding recovery structures:

Number	Crash Recovery	Media Recovery
1	Automatic. Uses the online redo logs that are CURRENT or ACTIVE.	Manual process. Can be performed even without ARCHIVELOG mode, if there's enough information in the online redo logs.

2	No concept of incomplete recovery unless block corruption (data or redo) is identified. This is a complicated situation and is not discussed here.	Can be complete or incomplete. Incomplete recovery requires RESETLOGS to open the database.

Bounded Recovery

Two-pass recovery was introduced in Oracle 8*i*. Its history is tightly connected to the introduction of bounded recovery. *Bounded time recovery* is a feature that enables you to control the amount of time taken for crash recovery with some predetermined limits by specifying a suitable value for DB_BLOCK_MAX_DIRTY_TARGET. This feature allows you to specify an upper bound on the time (or number of block) required for instance and crash recovery. The fewer the number of dirty buffers in the buffer cache at the time of the failure, the faster the recovery time. Remember that DB_BLOCK_MAX_DIRTY_TARGET is a hidden parameter since Oracle 9*i*.

Starting with Oracle 8*i*, the FAST_START_IO_TARGET parameter controls the target number of I/Os needed for crash recovery. DBWR writes data blocks continuously to meet this target and also writes the oldest dirty buffers first, thus ensuring that the checkpoint will progress. This is where direct control over roll forward I/O was introduced, a feature lacking in Oracle 7. Hence, since Oracle 8*i*, the definitions of LOG_CHECKPOINT_INTERVAL and LOG_CHECKPOINT_TIMEOUT have been redone and are widely documented: The incremental checkpoint should not lag the tail of the redo log by more than the LOG_CHECKPOINT_INTERVAL number of redo blocks (X$KCCLE. LEBSZ). LOG_CHECKPOINT_TIMEOUT is reinterpreted to mean that the incremental checkpoint should lag the tail of the redo log by no more than that many seconds' worth of redo records.

Block Written Record (BWR)

One of the optimization recovery mechanisms used by Oracle 9*i* and later is the writing of additional (yet critical) information into the redo log about checkpoints. Normally, the cache aging and incremental checkpoint system would write a number of blocks to disk. When Dirty Buffer Writer (DBWR) completes a data block write operation, it also adds a redo record (in the redo log file) that states that the block has been written. It basically writes the data block address along with the SCN information. DBWR can write block-written records (BWRs) in batches, although in a "lazy" fashion.

In Oracle RAC, a BWR is written when an instance writes a block covered by a global resource or when it is told that the past image (PI) buffer it is holding is no longer necessary. Recovery processes that indicate redo information for the block is not needed prior to this point use this record. The basic use of BWR is to make recovery more efficient; hence, the instance does not force a flush of the log buffer after creating it because it is not essential for ensuring the accuracy of recovery.

Past Image (PI)

PI is what makes Oracle RAC Cache Fusion version II click. It makes Oracle RAC "unbreakable" in terms of recovery and in the context of Cache Fusion. It eliminates the write/write contention problem that existed (or still does in some sites!) in many OPS databases. Because block transfers from one node's buffer cache to another's required an intermediate disk write (a ping), with associated slower I/O and network congestion, OPS's scalability in large environments was limited, particularly for online transaction processing (OLTP). In OPS, time to recover depended upon the number of nodes that touched the buffer, which is a drawback in making OPS an HA solution.

In the simplest of terms, a PI is a copy of a globally dirty block and is maintained in the database buffer cache. It can be created and saved when a dirty block is shipped across to another instance after setting the resource role to global (if it was not already set). A PI must be maintained by an instance until it or a later version of the block is written to disk. The Global Cache Service (GCS) is responsible for informing an instance that its PI is no longer needed after another instance writes a newer (a current) version of the same block. PIs are discarded when GCS posts all the holding instances that a new and consistent version of that particular block is now on disk.

Checkpoints and PI

In Cache Fusion, when an instance needs to write a block to satisfy a checkpoint request, the instance needs to check the role of the resource covering the block. If the role is global, the instance must inform GCS that it needs to write that block to disk. GCS is responsible for finding the most current block image and informing the instance holding that image to perform the block write. GCS then informs all holders of the global resource that they can release their PI copies of the block, hence allowing the global resources to be released.

Two-Pass Recovery

Oracle RAC introduced the concept of two-pass recovery, where the recovery process (SMON or the foreground process) performs a two-step "read" procedure. Basically, this limits the number of I/O reads required for recovery by recording more information in the logs (BWR). The first read builds a list of blocks that are mentioned in the redo log (all data blocks that have redo information). Some of these redo records could be BWR entries, denoting that the block mentioned is up to date until that point in the redo. Therefore, the recovery process need not "recover" this block, and it is removed from the list being built. The resultant list of this first pass is a list of blocks that have redo information but were not written to disk (because there was an instance failure). This list is called the *recovery set*.

The second read now processes only blocks from this list or set, which is smaller than the blocks touched in the redo stream in the first pass. Redo is applied in this phase and fewer data blocks are read and written in the second pass, thus offsetting the cost of reading the online redo log files twice. If the system is unable to perform two-pass recovery, it will fall back to the single pass. The alert file states the result from two-pass recovery. Two-pass crash recovery can be suppressed with the following setting:

```
_two_pass=false
```

Two-Pass Recovery in Oracle RAC

Two-pass recovery in Oracle RAC has some additional steps to be performed because multiple instances (threads) may have failed or crashed. This involves reading and merging all the redo information for a particular block from all the threads, and is called a *log merge* or a *thread merge* operation.

One of the bigger challenges in Oracle RAC recovery is that a block could have been modified in any of the instances (dead or alive). This was not the case in OPS. Hence, in Oracle RAC, getting hold of the latest version of a dirty block needs an intelligent and efficient mechanism that completes the identification of the latest version of that block and processes it for recovery. The introduction of PI images and BWRs makes it possible to significantly reduce recovery time and efficiently recover from an instance failure or crash.

First Pass

This pass does not perform the actual recovery but rather merges and reads redo threads to create a hash table of blocks that need recovery and that are not known to have been written back to the datafiles. This is where incremental checkpoint SCN is crucial because the redo byte address (RBA) denotes a starting point for recovery. All modified blocks are added to the recovery set. As BWRs are encountered, the file, DBA, and SCN of each change vector are processed to limit the number of blocks to recover in the next pass. A block need not be recovered if its BWR version is greater than the latest PI present in any of the buffer caches.

Redo threads from all failed instances are read and merged by SCN, beginning at the RBA of the last incremental checkpoint for each thread. When the first change to a data block is encountered in the merged redo stream, a block entry is added in the recovery set data structure. Entries in the recovery set are organized in a hash table.

Second Pass

In this stage, SMON rereads the merged redo stream (by SCN) from all threads needing recovery. The redo log entries are again compared against the recovery set built in the first pass, and any matches are applied to the in-memory buffers as in single-pass recovery. The buffer cache is flushed and the checkpoint SCN for each thread is updated upon successful completion. This is also the single-pass thread recovery if only one pass is to be done.

Cache Fusion Recovery

Cache Fusion recovery is applicable only in Oracle RAC. Because additional steps—GRD (re) configuration, internode communication, and so on—are required on top of the existing recovery steps, it is known as Cache Fusion recovery. The SMON from a surviving instance recovers the failed instance. If a foreground process detects instance recovery, it posts SMON. As of Oracle 9*i* and beyond, foreground processes no longer perform instance recovery.

Crash recovery is a unique case of instance recovery whereby all instances have failed. Yet, in either case, the threads from failed instances need to be merged. The only distinction being, in instance recovery, SMON performs the recovery. In crash recovery, a foreground process performs the recovery.

Let's now examine the main steps involved in Cache Fusion recovery or instance recovery. The main advantages or features of Cache Fusion recovery are as follows:

- Recovery cost is proportional to the number of failures, not the total number of nodes.
- It eliminates disk reads of blocks that are present in a surviving instance's cache.
- It prunes recovery sets based on the global resource lock state.
- The cluster is available after an initial log scan, even before recovery reads are complete.

In Cache Fusion recovery, the starting point for recovery of a block is its most recent PI version. A PI could be located in any of the surviving instances, and multiple PI blocks of a particular buffer can exist. An on-disk version is used for recovery only if no PI is available. This feature is called Cache Fusion recovery because, from Oracle 9*i* onward, the on-disk version of a block might not be the latest copy because Cache Fusion allows the shipping of copies of CURRENT blocks across the interconnect by using the PI concept.

Dynamic Reconfiguration and Affinity Remastering

Remastering is the term used to describe the operation whereby the node attempting the recovery tries to own or master the resource(s) once mastered by another instance prior to a failure. Hence, the term *remaster* is used for the operation performed during instance recovery or when a node joins or leaves a cluster.

When one instance departs the cluster, the GRD component of that instance needs to be redistributed to the surviving nodes. Similarly, when a new instance enters the cluster, the GRD portions of the existing instances need to be redistributed to create the GRD portion of the new instance.

As an optimization feature during instance recovery, remastering of all resources does not happen across all nodes. From Oracle 9*i* onward, Oracle RAC uses an algorithm called *lazy remastering* to remaster only a minimal number of resources during a reconfiguration. A minimum subset of resources is remastered to maintain consistency of the lock database. This occurs in parallel during the first pass log read where the recovery set is built. The entire Parallel Cache Management (PCM) lock space remains invalid while the DLM and SMON complete the following two crucial steps:

1. Integrated Distributed Lock Manager (IDLM) master node discards locks that are held by dead instances; the space reclaimed by this operation is used to remaster locks that are held by the surviving instance for which a dead instance was mastered.

2. SMON issues a message saying that it has acquired the necessary buffer locks to perform recovery.

While the lock domain is invalid, most PCM lock operations are frozen, making the database unavailable for users requesting a new or incompatible lock. Operations that do not require interaction with the DLM can proceed without affecting the remastering operations. If a second instance fails, its resources are remastered on the other surviving instances evenly. As resources are remastered, they are cleared of any reference to the failed instance.

In addition, the database can automatically adapt and migrate resources in the GRD, based on the affinity of a resource to a particular instance. If a single instance is identified as the sole user of a tablespace, the block resource masters for files of that tablespace are lazily and dynamically moved to that instance.

In both cases, the use of dynamic resource remastering provides the key benefit of greatly increasing the likelihood of local cache access without additional interconnect traffic. Another great advantage of the lazy remastering scheme is that instances keep many of their locks/resources during a reconfiguration, whereas in OPS 8*i*, all resources and locks were deleted from all instances. Because of this concept, many processes can resume active work during a reconfiguration because their locks/resources do not have to be moved away or deleted.

A good discussion on this topic is available in Metalink Note 139435.1.

Fast Reconfiguration in Oracle RAC

Fast reconfiguration is an enhancement feature introduced in Oracle 9*i* and designed to increase the availability time for Oracle RAC instances during instance reconfiguration. Reconfiguration of open DLM locks/resources takes place under the following conditions:

- An instance joins the cluster.
- An instance fails or leaves the cluster.
- A node is halted.

In previous versions (Oracle 7, 8, and 8*i* OPS), this operation could be relatively instantaneous or could be delayed for several minutes while *lock remastering* took place. Consider a situation in which an instance leaves a cluster. The lock-remastering process is triggered and all open global locks/resources are deleted from the departing instance and all locks/resources on all instances are *distributed evenly* across surviving instances. During this time no lock operations can occur on the database.

The amount of time that reconfiguration took primarily depended on the number of open DLM locks/resources (usually higher with fixed locking) and hardware resources such as memory, interconnect speed, and CPUs. Reconfiguration in Oracle 8*i* and earlier was prone to performance bottlenecks, as the instance would experience a hang situation until the completion of this task, and the lock database was frozen completely.

Oracle 10*g* (and 11*g* RAC) overcomes these issues with optimization techniques whereby the thrust is on decreasing the amount of time it takes to complete reconfiguration and allowing some processes to continue work (in parallel) during reconfiguration.

One of the most significant changes in Oracle RAC is that fixed locks are no longer used. Remember that fixed locks are allocated during instance startup as well as during reconfiguration in Oracle 8*i* and earlier versions. Fixed PCM locks are initially acquired in null mode. All specified fixed locks are allocated at instance startup and deallocated at instance shutdown. Fixed locks are preallocated and statically hashed to blocks at startup time. The init.ora parameter gc_files_to_lock determines the fixed PCM locks along with gc_rollback_locks.

So in Oracle RAC, fixed locks are no longer used during instance startup or reconfiguration; this speeds up startup time. Also, instead of remastering all locks/resources across all nodes, Oracle uses the lazy remastering algorithm (introduced in the preceding section) to remaster only a minimal number of locks/resources during a reconfiguration. For a departing instance (expected or unexpected), Oracle RAC tries to determine how best to distribute only the locks/resources from the departing instance and a minimal number from the surviving instances.

Let's consider a simple example of this phenomenon in Figure 9-1, although the actual resource-mastering process is quite different from this simplified one:

- Instance A masters resources 1, 3, 5, and 7.
- Instance B masters resources 2, 4, 6, and 8.
- Instance C masters resources 9, 10, 11, and 12.

Now, assume that instance B crashes (see Figure 9-2). Now resources 2, 4, 6, and 8 will be affected by the instance failure. The resources mastered in instance A and instance C are not affected by this failure.

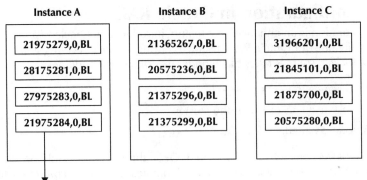

21975284: Decimal representation of the Lock Element Name as found in column
LOCK_ELEMENT_NAME in V$BH. X$KJBL.KJBLNAME2 has the full LE.
0: Class of the block as found in column CLASS# in V$BH
BL: Keyword for PCM Locks meaning **BL**ock

FIGURE 9-1   *Resource mastering example*

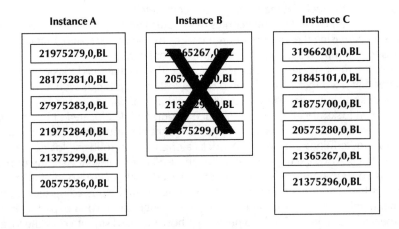

FIGURE 9-2   *Instance crash*

Now instances A and C remaster their resources. After remastering, the DLM database (GRD)
could look like this (see Figure 9-3):

■   Instance A masters resources 1, 3, 5, 7, 4, and 8.

■   Instance C masters resources 9, 10, 11, 12, 2, and 6.

So, instead of removing all resources and remastering them evenly across instances, Oracle
RAC will remaster only the resources necessary (in this case, those owned by the departing
instance), thus using a more efficient means of reconfiguration. With an instance joining the

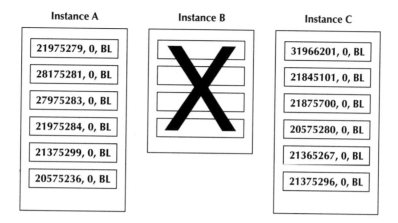

FIGURE 9-3   *Resource remastering*

cluster, Oracle RAC will remaster a limited number of resources from the other instances to the new instance.

Assume that instance B now rejoins the cluster; a minimal number of resources are remastered to instance B from the other instances. This is much faster than the 8*i* behavior of redistributing all resources. Here is the configuration after instance B rejoins the GRD:

- Instance A masters resources 1, 3, 5, and 7.
- Instance B masters resources 2, 4, 6, and 8.
- Instance C masters resources 9, 10, 11, and 12.

Fast reconfiguration is controlled by the parameter _gcs_fast_reconfig. Another parameter, _lm_master_weight, controls which instance will hold or (re)master more resources than others. Similarly, _gcs_resources is also used to control the number of resources an instance will master at a time. Each instance can have a different value.

With the concept of lazy remastering, instances retain many of their locks/resources during a reconfiguration process, whereas in previous versions, all locks were deleted from all instances. Because of this concept, many processes can resume active work during a reconfiguration because their locks/resources do not have to be moved or remastered.

Internals of Cache Fusion Recovery

As mentioned, when you recover an Oracle RAC database, additional steps are involved due to the presence of a cluster and multiple instances. When an instance fails, for example, in a two-node Oracle RAC database, the failure is detected by the surviving instance, which then performs the following recovery steps, as explained in Figure 9-4. Note that GRD reconfiguration (remastering) and single-pass recovery can be done in parallel.

The steps for GRD reconfiguration are as follows:

1. Instance death is detected by the cluster manager.
2. Requests for GRD locks are frozen.

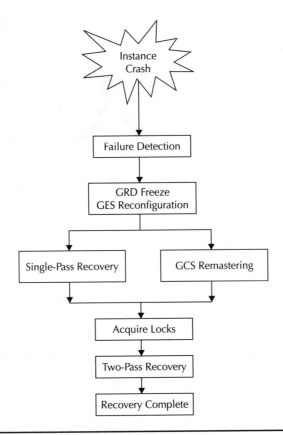

FIGURE 9-4 *Two-pass recovery in Oracle RAC*

3. Enqueues are reconfigured and made available.
4. DLM recovery is performed.
5. GCS (PCM lock) is remastered.
6. Pending writes and notifications are processed.

The steps for single-pass recovery are as follows:

1. The instance recovery (IR) lock is acquired by SMON.
2. The recovery set is prepared and built. Memory space is allocated in the SMON Program Global Area (PGA).
3. SMON acquires locks on buffers that need recovery.

The two-pass recovery steps are as follows:

1. The second pass is initiated. The database is partially available.
2. Blocks are made available as they are recovered.

3. The IR lock is released by SMON. Recovery is complete.

4. The system is available.

Global Resource Directory Reconfiguration

An instance failure is detected by the cluster manager (Cluster Group Services). The DLM reconfiguration process is started and all locks owned by the failed instance are remastered. This is when the PCM lock database is frozen and no instance can acquire a PCM lock. The reconfiguration phase (in lazy mode) can continue in parallel along with the first-pass read process. During this phase, existing PIs in any instance buffer caches are identified as potential candidates for recovery. DLM reconfiguration or recovery is performed by LMON.

First-Pass Redo Log Read

SMON acquires the IR (Instance Recovery) enqueue. By doing that, Oracle keeps multiple surviving instances from trying to recover a failed instance simultaneously and causing severe inconsistencies and more failures.

The SMON process of a surviving instance that has acquired the IR enqueue starts the first-pass log read of the failed instance's redo thread. SMON then merges the redo thread ordered by SCN to ensure that changes are written in a sequential order. The recovery set is built during this phase and contains the first dirty and last dirty version information (SCN, Seq#) of each block. SMON trims the recovery set (removes blocks no longer needed for recovery) based on the DBAs found in the redo stream because these blocks are nothing but PIs already written to disk. The BWR helps in this trimming.

The result of the first-pass log read is a recovery set (built into the PGA of SMON) that contains only blocks modified by the failed instance with no subsequent BWR to indicate that the blocks were later written. Each entry in the recovery list is ordered by the first dirty SCN to specify the order in which to acquire instance recovery locks.

The recovering SMON process will then inform each lock element's master node for each block in the recovery list that it will be taking ownership of the block and lock for recovery. Logically speaking, only the part of the database requiring recovery is locked and the rest is still available for normal operations. Note that the actual locking is done during the second-pass read.

Acquiring block buffers (and their locks) for recovery is a complex process and needs DLM (GES) messaging and coordination. Depending on the lock status of each buffer during the time of recovery, the recovery process has to perform a series of steps before an exclusive lock on the buffer can be held. A detailed description of the various lock states and eventual outcome is discussed in Metalink Note 144152.1.

Recovery Lock Claim

It is in this phase that SMON indicates to DLM (GES) that it needs IR locks on all the buffers identified in the recovery set. SMON continues to acquire locks on all buffers until it runs through the recovery set. If the master node for a resource has failed and the DLM remastering has not completed, SMON waits until the resource is made available. This also implies that DLM recovery is occurring in parallel. Now, SMON sends a clusterwide message to indicate that all required locks on buffers have been acquired. The DLM lock database is unfrozen and is available for normal operations.

Validate Global Resource Directory

After the DLM completes reconfiguration, only the resources that are locked for recovery are unavailable to foreground lock requests. Once the PCM lock database is released, other foreground processes can continue to acquire buffer locks as long as they are not requesting an "in-recovery" buffer. The GRD is globally resynchronized and flagged off as available.

Second-Pass Log Read and Redo Application

It is in this phase that redo threads of failed instances are again read and merged by SCN. Buffer space for recovery is allocated in the database buffer cache and the resources that were identified in the previous reading of the redo logs are claimed as recovery resources. This is done to prevent other instances from accessing those resources. Then, assuming that there are PIs or current images of blocks to be recovered in other caches in the cluster, the most recent PI is the starting point of recovery.

If neither the PI buffers nor the current buffer for a data block are in any of the surviving instances' caches, SMON performs a log merge of the failed instances. Then redo is applied to each buffer identified in the first pass until its SCN matches the last dirty SCN that was identified in the first pass. SMON recovers and posts DBWR to write the recovery buffer and clear the "in-recovery" state of the buffer. Soon after the write, SMON releases the recovery resources so that more blocks become available as recovery proceeds. Recovery time is determined by this phase.

After all blocks have been recovered and the recovery resources have been released, the system is again fully available. In summary, the recovered database or recovered portions of the database become available earlier and before the completion of the entire recovery sequence. This makes the system available sooner and it makes recovery more scalable.

NOTE
The performance overhead of a log merge is proportional to the number of failed instances and to the size of the redo logs for each instance.

Online Block Recovery for Cache Fusion

When a data buffer becomes corrupt in an instance's cache, the instance will initiate online block recovery. Block recovery will also occur if either a foreground process dies while changes are being applied or an error is generated during redo application. In the first case, SMON initiates block recovery and in the second case the foreground process initiates block recovery. Online block recovery consists of finding the block's predecessor and applying redo changes from the online logs of the thread in which corruption occurred. The predecessor of a fusion block is its most recent past image. If there is no past image, the block on disk is the predecessor. For non-fusion blocks, the disk copy is always the predecessor.

If the lock element of the block needing recovery is held in XL0 (Exclusive, Local, no past images) status, the predecessor will be located on disk. If the Lock Element (LE) of the block needing recovery is held in XG# (Global Exclusive) status, the predecessor will exist in another instance's buffer cache. The instance with the highest SCN PI image of the block will send a consistent read copy of the block to the recovering instance.

Backup and Recovery of the Voting Disk and OCR

The voting disk and OCR are the two critical components in Oracle Clusterware. Here we discuss the backup and recovery of the voting disk and OCR.

Oracle Clusterware backups should include the voting disk and OCR components. The voting disk is a disk partition that stores information about the status of the nodes and membership details. The OCR is a file that manages the configuration and the details about the services. We recommended mirroring the voting disk and the OCR using Oracle-provided mirroring techniques. Mirroring the voting disk and OCR can be configured during installation or at later stages dynamically.

Backup and Recovery of Voting Disks

Voting disks can be backed up by the standard operating system commands: the UNIX dd command or Windows ocopy command. Adding voting disks can be done using the CRSCTL commands. The following commands back up the voting disk in UNIX and Windows. The manual backing up of the voting disk and the restoring of voting disks are available until Oracle 11*g* Release 1 and are no longer possible from Oracle 11*g* Release 2 onward.

Here's the command for UNIX:

```
dd if=voting_disk_name of=backup_file_name
```

Here's the command for Windows:

```
ocopy voting_disk_name backup_file_name
```

Recovering Voting Disks

Voting disks can be recovered by restoring the backup file. The following commands recover the voting disks from the backup.

Here's the command for UNIX:

```
dd if=backup_file_name of=voting_disk_name
```

Here's the command for Windows:

```
copy backupfile_name voting_disk_name
```

NOTE
Starting with Oracle 11g Release 2, you no longer need to back up the voting disk. The voting disk data is automatically included with OCR backups. Upon a successful OCR restore, you can simply run the "crsctl add css votedisk" command to create new voting disks in the desired location. Manual backup of voting disks using dd or any copy command is unsupported on Oracle 11g Release 2.

Backup and Recovery of OCR

Because Oracle Cluster Registry (OCR) is very critical to the functionality of Oracle Grid Infrastructure, the clusterware automatically creates OCR backups every four hours. At any one time, Oracle always retains the last three backup copies of the OCR in the master node. Also, the CRS daemon (CRSd) process that creates the backups also creates and retains an OCR backup for each full day and at the end of each week. At any point in time you will have five successful OCR backups created automatically by the clusterware.

The default location for generating backups on UNIX-based systems is GRID_HOME/cdata/ *<cluster_name>*, where *<cluster_name>* is the name of your cluster. The Windows-based default location for generating backups uses the same path structure. By default, the second node is selected as the master node and OCR is backed up and stored in the master node.

Apart from automatic backup, you can also manually back up the OCR using the following command. This command backs up the OCR without waiting for the scheduled automatic backups. Oracle Local Registry is excluded in the automatic backup mechanism and manual backup is the only option for Oracle Local Registry.

```
ocrconfig  -manualbackup
```

To recover the OCR from automated backup, you can use the ocrconfig command. The following command lists the successful backups of the OCR. It lists both the manual and automatic backups in the target location. However, you can query the auto or manual backups using the "–showbackup manual" or "–showbackup auto" option.

```
ocrconfig -showbackup
```

OCR recovery is warranted when there is a corruption in the OCR or loss of an OCR device. Restarting the resources or removing and adding the resources back to OCR should be considered before attempting an OCR restore, because OCR requires downtime of Oracle Grid Infrastructure. You can use the ocrcheck command to check the status of the OCR before attempting the OCR restore.

To recover the OCR, you should stop Oracle Clusterware from all the nodes. This can be done by executing "crsctl stop crs" in all the nodes. If the command fails due to OCR corruption or if it returns any errors, you can use "crsctl stop crs –f" to force stop the CRS.

Once the CRS daemons are stopped in all the nodes, the following command restores the OCR:

```
ocrconfig -restore <file_name>
```

Restart Oracle Clusterware on all the nodes in your cluster by restarting each node or running the following command:

```
crsctl start crs
```

OCR can also be exported and imported. This can be an alternative recovery mechanism for OCR recovery. The following command can be used to export the contents of OCR:

```
ocrconfig -export <file_name>
```

This creates the binary copy of the OCR. This file cannot be edited by text editors. Human-readable information about OCR can be obtained by using the ocrdump command. This command dumps the contents of the OCR to a text file in the current directory.

To import the OCR, stop Oracle CRS by executing "crsctl stop crs." Once the CRS daemon is stopped in all the nodes, you can use the following command to import the OCR:

```
ocrconfig -import <file_name>
```

Optionally, you can run the cluster verification utility to verify the integrity of all the cluster nodes configured as a part of your cluster:

```
$ cluvfy comp ocr -n all -verbose
```

NOTE
The file formats and compatibility of the backup restore operations are totally different in ocrconfig –backup and ocrconfig –export. The first one is a byte-by-byte copy of the contents of the OCR, and the second is the logical copy of the OCR. If you want to recover from manual or automatic backup, you need to use the ocrconfig –restore option. If you want to import the OCR from a previously exported OCR, use the ocrcofig –import option. Extreme care should be taken while recovering the OCR.

Validating OCR Backups

OCR backups can be validated by the ocrdump utility. This utility is normally used to dump the contents of OCR to a text file. The same can be used to verify the contents and structural integrity of the OCR backups.

```
ocrdump -backupfile <backup_file_name>
```

NOTE
It is recommended that you manually back up the OCR from other nodes because the clusterware-initiated automatic OCR backup process backs up the OCR only for the master node. If the master node is down and cannot be rebooted, OCR backups are lost. Hence, it is important to integrate the OCR backup process with the regular backup schedules.

In a Nutshell

We have discussed the concepts and inner workings of Oracle RAC recovery operations. Oracle RAC backup and recovery processes are the same as single-instance backup and recovery, except for the thread merging and two-pass recovery concepts. For the exact commands and syntaxes, refer to *Oracle 11g Recovery Manager Reference*.

Oracle RAC introduced two-pass recovery to optimize media recovery. Fast reconfiguration helps make instance recovery efficient by distributing the resources from failed nodes to surviving nodes. This also helps to reduce the reconfiguration times while members are joining or leaving the clusters.

We also discussed the backup and recovery operations of the two key components of the clusterware: Oracle Clusterware Repository and the voting disk. These are automatically backed up when clusterware is running. We also discussed the manual backup and restore operation of these critical components.

CHAPTER
10

Oracle RAC Performance
Management

n this chapter we look at considerations and procedures for optimizing performance in the Oracle RAC environment, which consists of a database opened by multiple instances. Interinstance coordination and reliable communication are necessary to preserve data integrity and other database characteristics. This requires CPU, network bandwidth, and memory resources. However, this need for additional system resources should not impact the end user's transaction processing time. Techniques mentioned in this chapter should help you to identify and address user response time problems and optimize performance in an Oracle RAC environment.

Traditionally, the capacity of a database tier could be increased by adding hardware to the existing system or by replacing the system with a higher capacity system. Oracle RAC offers an alternative to this approach by allowing you to scale the database tier horizontally by adding one or more database servers to the existing machine(s). This also lets you make use of low-cost servers, including those running Linux operating systems, thereby reducing the overall cost of ownership.

Overall, the Oracle RAC database instance tuning process is similar to that of single-instance database tuning. The same principles of SQL tuning—identifying hot spots and tuning contentions—are applicable to the Oracle RAC environment. Tools used for monitoring Oracle instance and system usage are also the same.

Tuning the cluster interconnects and cache synchronization delays are some of the additional components that need to be considered while tuning Oracle RAC. Because the buffer caching and shared pool components are global in the Oracle RAC environment, another key consideration is that any issue with one instance may potentially affect the other instances. However, the good news is the enhanced wait event model and the extensive framework data collection mechanism at the global cache layer provide a great amount of information on how they are working under the hood. Automatic Workload Repository (AWR) and STATSPACK reports contain additional information required for tuning the Oracle RAC instance and database.

Oracle RAC Design Considerations

The best applications, database designs, and coding practices that are applicable to a single-instance Oracle database are also applicable to Oracle RAC. A well-tuned application in a single-instance environment on a symmetric multiprocessing (SMP) machine should run well in an Oracle RAC environment.

If an application has capacity issues, moving to the Oracle RAC environment will not solve them; at best it will provide some temporary relief until the basic design or code issues are fixed; at worst, it may actually degrade performance because Oracle RAC may amplify an existing performance flaw. So is there anything you can do to make an application run better in an Oracle RAC environment? The following sections address this question.

Oracle Design Best Practices

Let's quickly recall the Oracle design best practices for application and database layout:

■ Optimize connection management. Ensure that the middle tier and programs that connect to the database are efficient in connection management and do not log on or off repeatedly. Not retaining database connections has an impact in a single-instance environment. However, the impact is a lot higher in an Oracle RAC environment.

■ Ensure that the SQL execution is well tuned. Optimize execution plans and data access paths. Many textbooks have been devoted to this subject, and lots of tools are available to tune SQL automatically. A majority of database performance problems are due to inefficient SQL execution plans. Tools such as ADDM and SQL Tuning Advisor go a long way in pointing out SQL statements that can be optimized and how to optimize them.

■ Ensure that the application is using bind variables to minimize parsing. Introduction of the initialization parameter cursor_sharing has addressed this problem to some extent, but it still remains an important consideration for online transaction processing (OLTP) applications. For data warehouse applications, using bind variables may not be desirable.

■ Use packages and procedures in place of anonymous PL/SQL blocks and big SQL statements. Packages and procedures are compiled and stored in the database and can be reused without runtime compilation overhead.

■ Use the latest database space management features. New features such as locally managed tablespace and automatic segment space management (ASSM) improve performance and simplify database administration. These features are used by default if you are creating a database using the Database Configuration Assistant (DBCA). Upon migrating an old database, consider using these features as soon as possible.

■ If a sequence is being used frequently and by multiple concurrent sessions, ensure that a large cache is used. The default value for cache sequence is 20.

■ Avoid use of data definition languages (DDLs) in a production environment that operates during normal business hours. Use of DDLs increases invalidations of the already parsed SQL statements, and they need to be recompiled before reuse. DDLs also increase the invalidations of the buffers in the cache, which is another source of performance issues.

■ Index leaf block contention is the single largest cause of buffer busy waits in a single-instance environment and can cause buffer cache contention (gc buffer busy) in an Oracle RAC environment. Indexes are a necessary evil because they help to retrieve data access. However, they become a drag on Data Manipulation Language (DML) statements, as indexes need to be updated during insert, update, and delete operations. Consider using reverse key index and index-only tables. Partitioning tables and indexes is another effective way to minimize contention.

■ Optimize contention on data blocks by avoiding small tables with too many rows in a block. You can use the "minimize records per block" clause of the "alter table" command to restrict the number of rows per block.

Oracle RAC–Specific Design Best Practices

Following are some application design considerations that can help you optimize performance specifically in an Oracle RAC environment:

■ Do not reread the recently modified/inserted data just to validate it. There is no need to read and compare the data to confirm what has been inserted or committed. Built-in checks and balances help ensure data integrity and avoid corruptions.

- If business requirements do not dictate otherwise, consider using application partitioning. This is discussed in detail in the following section.

- Consider restricting DML-intensive users to one instance. If few users are performing DMLs on certain sets of data, allow these users to access the same instance; although not necessary, this strategy helps in reducing cache contention.

- Group read-only data together and put it in a read-only tablespace (or tablespaces). Read-only tablespaces require little resource and lock coordination. Keeping read-only and read-intensive data separate from DML-intensive data will help optimize Oracle RAC Cache Fusion performance.

- Avoid unnecessary auditing in an Oracle RAC environment. It has lots of negative side effects because it creates more shared library cache locks. Also, if required, implement auditing at the application layer.

- Use full table scans sparingly because they cause the Global Cache Service to service lots of block requests. Tuning the inefficient SQL queries and collecting system statistics for the optimizer to use CPU costing will also help. The statistics "table scans (long tables)" in V$SYSSTAT provide the number of full table scans done by the instance.

- If the application makes a large number of new session "logon storms," increase the cache value of the sys.audses$ sequence:

```
alter sequence sys.audses$ cache 10000;
```

Partitioning the Workload

In workload partitioning, a certain type of workload is executed on an instance—that is, partitioning allows users who access the same set of data to log on from the same instance. This limits the amount of data shared among the instances and therefore saves resources used for messaging and Cache Fusion data block transfer.

Whether to partition or not to partition? The decision is a fine balance between business needs and system resources conservation. You can save system resources by implementing workload partitioning in an Oracle RAC environment. If the system's processing resources are being used to their full capacity, partitioning might help. However, if the system has enough spare resources, partitioning probably isn't necessary.

Consider the following before implementing workload partitioning:

- Oracle RAC can handle buffer cache contention, and if the system CPU resources and private interconnect bandwidth is sufficient, you do not need to partition.

- At times, it might be much easier and more economical to add extra CPU power or interconnect bandwidth rather than implementing a workload partitioning scheme.

- You don't need to consider partitioning the user workload unless evidence indicates that contention is impacting performance and partitioning the workload will improve performance. Chapter 16 discusses this topic in greater detail.

- Establish baseline statistics with and without workload partitioning. If the comparison shows significant performance improvements with partitioning, consider implementing workload partitioning.

Scalability and Performance

Scalability and high availability are the two most significant advantages offered by Oracle RAC. If you were to look up the word *scalability* on Dictionary.com, you'd see the following definition: "How well a solution to some problem will work when the size of the problem increases."

A system is said to be "fully scalable" if its response time remains unchanged, whether it serves 1, 100, 1,000, or any other number of users. Consider a real-life example: If the freeways are 100-percent scalable, travel time from point A to point B will always remain the same, whether one car is on the highway or millions of cars. Are highways fully scalable? Probably not! A four-lane freeway with properly designed exit and entrance ramps might support hundreds or even thousands of cars, but if the number of cars increases beyond a limit, the drivers will have to slow down to yield and to avoid accidents. A freeway that is scalable for thousands of cars and allows them to travel at a speed of 65 mph may not be able to support the same number of trucks at that speed. Therefore, the scalability of a system not only depends on the number of users but also on the type of workload. It is reasonable to expect that the same freeway cannot support 10,000 mixed vehicles (cars, trucks, bikes, and so on).

The points to be noted are as follows:

- No real-life system is fully scalable all the time.

- Each and every system has a limit beyond which it may not be able to support additional users without compromising the response time.

- A system that is scalable for a certain number of users of some type may not be able to support the same number of a different type of users.

However, for all practical purposes, a system is assumed to be fully scalable as long as its response time does not degrade (or remains within service-level agreements) for an intended maximum number of users. With reference to Oracle RAC, scalability is generally discussed in terms of the ability to support additional user workload when a node, identical to the existing node, is added. For example, consider the following data:

$3,000$ = the number of user transactions per second processed with three nodes
$4,000$ = the number of user transactions per second processed with four nodes
Scalability = $((4,000 - 3,000) / 3,000 / 3) \times 100 = 100\%$

Here are the assumptions for this example:

- All nodes have the same hardware configuration.

- Response time and the user workload characteristics remain unchanged. Only the number of user transactions is increased.

A real-life system consists of multiple components. For a system to be scalable, each of its components needs to support the increased user workload—that is, all its components need to be scalable. For an Oracle RAC system to be fully scalable, all the following components need to be scalable:

- Application
- Network
- Database

- Operating system
- Hardware

If any of the components cannot perform for the intended number of users, the system will not be scalable.

A specific application's scalability may vary depending on several factors. In general, the scalability of an application is built during the design process by avoiding any point of serialization. An application's scalability in the Oracle RAC environment might be limited if the same data blocks are frequently needed by all the instances, thereby increasing the Cache Fusion activity. For example, if each transaction is updating a running total maintained in a row, the block containing the row needs to be updated by each transaction, thereby causing the block to travel among the instances very rapidly. This behavior would limit the application's scalability.

Choosing the Block Size for an Oracle RAC Database

Most operating systems have a buffer cache that keeps frequently used data in memory to minimize disk access. To optimize I/O efficiency, the first choice is to make the Oracle block size equal to the file system buffer size. If that is not acceptable, the Oracle block size should be set to a multiple of the OS file system cache block size. For example, if the file system buffer is 4K, then the preferred Oracle block sizes will be 4K, 8K, 16K, and so on. If the OS buffer cache is not being used or the OS being used does not have a buffer cache (as in Windows), you can choose any block size without compromising the I/O efficiency. This is achieved by using raw devices, a shared file system, or Automatic Storage Management (ASM). Therefore, you do not need to consider file system buffer size while choosing a block size for Oracle RAC.

Oracle supports multiple block sizes inside a database; therefore, different tablespaces can have different block sizes. The parameter db_block_size represents the standard block size for the database and is used by the system tablespace, temporary tablespace, auxiliary tablespace, and any other tablespace for which a different block size is not specified while it is being created.

Most of the applications use the 8K block size for the database. While designing a decision support system (DSS)/data warehouse system, consider larger block sizes. For data that is mostly read-only or retrieved using full table scans, a large block size is helpful. A large block size is also helpful when row size is larger—for example, while using large objects (LOBs) to store documents, images, and so on. Using a small block size for an index is sometimes helpful because it reduces contention on index branch blocks. Similarly, for tables with smaller row sizes, using smaller block sizes will reduce contention. Wait events such as buffer busy waits, global cache busy, buffer busy global cr, and so on, are indications of block-level contention, and moving the index/table with high contention to a tablespace with a smaller block size will help reduce contention.

Using Automatic Segment Space Management

Automatic Segment Space Management (ASSM) was introduced in Oracle 9i and is the preferred way to manage space within a segment. Oracle uses bitmaps stored within the segment to manage free space for the segment. This is a more efficient and simpler way to manage space within a segment compared to the traditional linked-list-based space management algorithm. The traditional method uses the PCTUSED, FREELISTS, and FREELIST GROUPS parameters for managing space usage for tables, indexes, and so on. Using ASSM also provides dynamic affinity of space to instances, because there is no association of extents to instances as there is while using FREELIST GROUPS. Therefore, there is no performance degradation or wasted space when instances are added or removed from an Oracle RAC environment.

To ensure that an object uses ASSM, create that object in a tablespace that has been created with the segment space management "auto" clause. The following lines of code provide the basic syntax for creating a tablespace with ASSM:

```
SQL> create tablespace data_assm
  2  datafile '$ORADATA/data_assm01.dbf' size 1000M
  3  extent management local
  4  segment space management auto ;
```

Column SEGMENT_SPACE_MANAGEMENT of the DBA_TABLESPACES data dictionary view can be queried to view this characteristic of existing tablespaces. Performance of a frequently, concurrently executed insert statement can be improved by migrating the inserted object from a tablespace with manual segment space management to ASSM. Once these objects are identified, the following methods are available to move them from one tablespace to another:

- Export/import
- alter table ... move
- alter index ... rebuild
- Online table redefinition

Select one of these methods to move the object to the desired tablespace, keeping availability requirements for the application in mind while the move operation is being performed. If the system has enough resources, consider using parallel query/DML to optimize the elapsed time for the operation.

Limitations of ASSM

Following are the limitations of the ASSM feature:

- ASSM cannot be used for a system tablespace.
- ASSM can be used only for a locally managed tablespace. If, due to any reason, a dictionary managed tablespace is created, the ASSM clause cannot be used.
- ASSM cannot be used with temporary tablespaces.
- ASSM does not offer any control over space management, because the parameters FREELISTS and FREELIST GROUPS are not available.

Introduction to the V$ and GV$ Views

The dynamic performance (V$) view contains database statistics and is commonly used for performance analysis and tuning. In the Oracle RAC environment, a global (GV$) view corresponds to each V$ view. V$ views contain statistics for one instance, whereas GV$ views contain information from all the active instances. Each GV$ view contains an INST_ID column of type NUMBER, which can be used to identify the instance associated with the row data.

When a query is issued against a GV$ view, the instance gets statistics from remote instances using the parallel query mechanism. Starting from Oracle 10g, special parallel query slaves are dedicated to this task. They are named pz98, pz99, and so on, to distinguish them from general parallel query slaves. Here's an example:

```
$ ps -ef | grep PROD
oracle    6810    1   0 Jun07 ?         00:00:59 ora_pmon_PROD2
oracle    6812    1   0 Jun07 ?         00:00:00 ora_diag_PROD2
oracle    6824    1   0 Jun07 ?         00:01:17 ora_dbw0_PROD2
<<<unwanted lines deleted from here>>>
oracle    7168    1   0 Jun07 ?         00:01:41 ora_pz99_PROD2
oracle   25130    1   0 Jun29 ?         00:00:07 ora_pz98_PROD2
```

Most of the performance-tuning tools (Oracle Enterprise Manager, AWR, ADDM) and scripts make use of these views.

V$ Views Containing Cache Fusion Statistics

Generally, an AWR report should suffice to analyze the performance in an Oracle RAC environment. Seven or eight Oracle RAC–specific segments (described later in this chapter) are included in the AWR report and provide statistical information about Cache Fusion performance. Refer to Appendix A for a discussion on some of the important V$ views that can be used to manage performance in an Oracle RAC environment.

Oracle RAC Wait Events

An *event* can be defined as an operation or a particular function that the Oracle kernel performs on behalf of the user session or its own background process. Tasks such as reading and writing data blocks to and from datafiles, receiving data from other instances' memory, and waiting for the permission to read and acquire the block from the resource master are known as *database events,* and they have specific names. But why are these events called *wait events?*

All sessions accessing Oracle database instances need resources to perform their tasks concurrently and independently. A resource may be a data buffer, a latch, an enqueue (lock), or a piece of code to be executed exclusively. Some of these resources are serialized by access, and at any point in time only one process can have exclusive access; the others wanting the resource must wait in the queue. Whenever a session has to wait for something, the wait time is tracked and charged to the event that is associated with that wait. For example, a session that needs a block that is not in the current instance's cache makes a read call to the operating system to be delivered from another instance's cache and waits for the block. The wait time is charged to the waiting session's account. If the block is read from the disk, the wait time is charged to the requesting instance's "db file sequential read" wait event. If the block is coming from the other instance's cache, the wait time is charged against "global cache" wait events. Another session may have completed the last instruction and is now waiting for user input. This is generally termed an *idle wait,* and the wait time is charged to the "SQL*Net message from client" event. In short, when a session is not using the CPU, it may be waiting for a resource, for an action to complete, or simply for more work. Events that are associated with all such waits are known as *wait events*.

Wait events are further classified by their type—Cluster, User I/O, System I/O, or Network, for example. Table 10-1 lists different wait classes and the number of wait events in each class. Note that even though more than 1,118 wait events are available in Oracle Database 11g R2 and they are divided into 13 different categories, you would normally deal with fewer than 50 events while analyzing Oracle RAC performance.

Understanding Cluster Waits

When a session requests access to a data block in CR/CUR (Consistent Read/Current) mode, it sends a request to the lockmaster for proper authorization. However, whether it will receive the block via the Cache Fusion mechanism or a permission to read from the disk is not known until the request is satisfied. Two placeholder events—"gc cr request" and "gc current request"—keep track of the time a session spends in this state. For example, in a two-node cluster, when a session sends a request for a CR block, its wait time is counted against "gc cr request." Let's assume that the lockmaster grants the lock to the requestor, thereby authorizing it to read the block from the disk so all the wait time is now logged against the wait event "gc cr grant 2-way." Similarly, the wait time would be logged against "gc cr block 2-way" if the requesting instance receives the CR copy of the block from the master. In the end, there should not be any wait time logged against these two placeholder wait events.

Wait Class	Number of Wait Events in the Class
Commit	2
Scheduler	7
Queuing	9
Application	17
Configuration	24
System I/O	30
Concurrency	32
Network	35
User I/O	45
Cluster	50
Administrative	54
Idle	94
Other	719

TABLE 10-1 *Wait Classes in Oracle Database 11g R2*

Two-Way and Three-Way Wait Events

Oracle 10*g* and later versions track whether a lock request was satisfied with just two-way communication between requestor and master/holder. In two-way events, the master instance is also the current holder of that block and is able to send the needed CR/current copy of the block via Cache Fusion to the requestor. This is the typical case in two-node cluster environments. In the case of three-way events, the master forwards the request to the holder. The holder in turn sends the CR/current copy of the block as desired by the requestor. Three-way waits and messages are seen at clusters with more than two nodes. Any kind of messaging and block transfer will be completed in at most three hops, irrespective of the number of nodes in the cluster.

Figure 10-1 explains the typical processing of a global cache wait and its potential outcome based on the status of the block in any other instance's cache. Depending on the caching status/availability the outcome of the wait will be a block transfer or message grant.

The cluster wait events belong to one of the following categories:

- Block-oriented waits
- Message-oriented waits

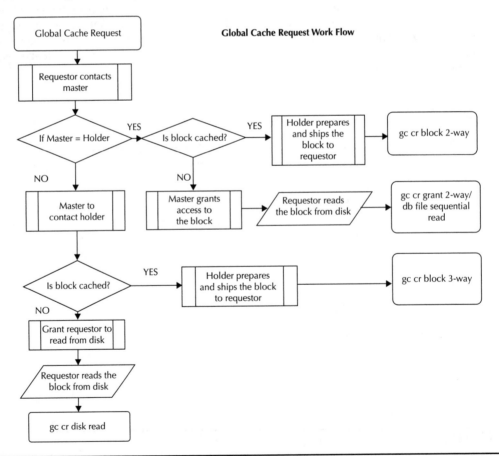

FIGURE 10-1 *Global cache processing workflow*

- Contention-oriented waits
- Load-oriented waits

Block-Oriented Waits

Block-oriented waits are the most common wait events in the cluster wait events. The block-oriented wait event statistics indicate that the requested block was served from the other instance. In a two-node cluster environment, a message is transferred to the current holder of the block and the holder ships the block to the requestor. In a cluster environment with more than two nodes, the request for the block is sent to the holder of the block through the resource master and includes an additional message.

These events are usually the most frequent in the absence of block contention, and the length of the wait is determined by the time it takes on the physical network, the time to process the request in the serving instances, and the time it takes for the requesting process to wake up after the block arrives.

The average wait time and the total wait time should be considered when being alerted to performance issues where these particular waits have a high impact. Usually, either interconnect or load issues or SQL execution against a large shared working set can be found to be the root cause.

The following are the most common block-oriented waits:

```
gc current block 2-way
gc current block 3-way
gc cr block 2-way
gc cr block 3-way
```

Message-Oriented Waits

The message-oriented wait event statistics indicate that no block was received because it was not cached in any instance. Instead, a global grant was given, allowing the requesting instance to read the block from disk or modify it. These waits are normally followed with a disk read event such as "db file sequential read" or "db file scattered read."

If the time consumed by these events is high, it may be assumed that the frequently executed SQL causes a lot of disk I/O (in the event of the cr grant) or that the workload inserts a lot of data and needs to find and format new blocks frequently (in the event of the current grant).

The following are the most common message-oriented waits:

```
gc current grant 2-way
gc current grant 3-way
gc cr grant 2-way
gc cr grant 3-way
```

Contention-Oriented Waits

The contention-oriented wait event statistics indicate that a block was received that was pinned by a session on another node, was deferred because a change had not yet been flushed to disk, or was deferred because of high concurrency, and therefore could not be shipped immediately. This typically happens with concurrent DMLs on index blocks where the other instance is waiting for the current block to add the index entry while the index block is busy in the holder. In this case, the contention-oriented wait "gc current block busy" will be followed by the "gc current split" or "gc buffer busy" event.

A buffer may also be busy locally when a session has already initiated a Cache Fusion operation and is waiting for its completion when another session on the same node is trying to read or modify the same data. These waits can occur with Oracle 11*g* when a foreground process is waiting for an antilock broadcast to update a read-mostly object. Read-mostly locks and reader bypass optimizations are discussed in the next chapter.

High service times for blocks exchanged in the global cache may exacerbate the contention, which can be caused by frequent concurrent read and write accesses to the same data.

The following are the most common contention-oriented waits.

```
gc current block busy
gc cr block busy
gc current buffer busy
```

Wait event "block busy" suggests that a *single* session required access to a specific block that is deemed "busy" on a remote node (for various reasons stated earlier). A "buffer busy" indicates that *multiple* sessions are waiting for a block that is deemed "busy" on a remote node. In other words, dealing with a "buffer busy" situation involves multiple sessions contending for the same block and requires tuning that is similar to dealing with "buffer busy waits" or "read by other sessions," albeit in an Oracle RAC environment.

Load-Oriented Waits

The load-oriented wait events indicate that a delay in processing has occurred in the GCS, which is usually caused by high load, by CPU saturation, and would have to be solved by additional CPUs, load balancing, or offloading processing at different times or to a new cluster node. For the events mentioned, the wait time encompasses the entire roundtrip from the time a session starts to wait after initiating a block request until the block arrives.

Whenever a request for any block transfer or message transfer waits for more than 1 ms in the internal queue after the interprocess communication (IPC) layer, the system is considered "overloaded." This could typically happen when an LMS process is not able to catch up with the arrival rate and the messages are queued for LMS processing.

You should seldom see the congested waits in a well-balanced cluster environment. The following are the most common load-oriented waits, and existence of these waits indicates that the system is overloaded or underpowered:

```
gc current block congested
gc cr block congested
gc current grant congested
gc cr grant congested
```

We will describe the important Oracle RAC wait events and the possible action plan when a wait event appears in the "Top 5 Timed Wait Events" section of the AWR report. We will also look at messages and data flow during some of the important global cache wait events.

gc current block 2-way

As indicated in Figure 10-2, an instance requests authorization for a block to be accessed in current mode to modify the block. The instance mastering the corresponding resource receives the request. The master has the current version of the block and sends the current copy of the block to the requestor via the Cache Fusion mechanism. This event indicates write/write contention.

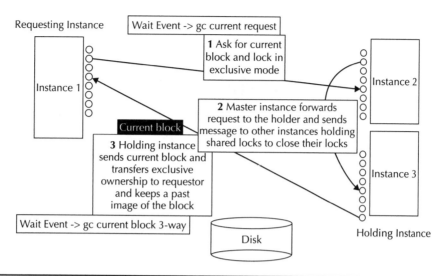

FIGURE 10-2 *Wait event: gc current block 2-way*

NOTE
The appearance of gc current block 2-way and the following three events in the "Top 5" event section doesn't necessarily indicate performance issues. It merely indicates that the instances are accessing copies of data present in each other's cache and that the Cache Fusion mechanism is being used to transfer copies of the data among the instances. However, if the average wait time for each event is very high, it might be impacting performance and needs further analysis.

If this wait event appears in the "Top 5" timed events, do the following:

- Analyze the contention. Segments in the "Current Blocks Received" section of the AWR report should help you identify the top contentious objects.
- Ensure that good database object design practices, database object layout, and space management practices are being followed for the top contentious objects.
- Optimize the application contention by using an appropriate application-partitioning scheme.
- Look at "Tips for Avoiding Oracle RAC Wait Events" at the end of this section.

gc current block 3-way
Figure 10-3 shows this wait event. An instance requests authorization for a block to be accessed in current mode. The instance mastering the corresponding resource receives the request and forwards the message to the current holder, telling it to relinquish ownership. The holding instance sends a copy of the current version of the block to the requestor via the Cache Fusion

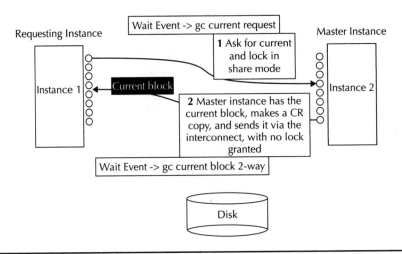

FIGURE 10-3 *Wait event: gc current block 3-way*

mechanism and transfers the exclusive lock to the requesting instance. This event indicates write/ write contention.

If this wait event appears in the "Top 5" timed events list, your plan of action should be similar to that for a gc current block 2-way event.

gc cr block 2-way

Figure 10-4 shows a pictorial representation of the event. An instance requests authorization for a block to be accessed in CR mode. The instance mastering the corresponding resource receives the request. The master has the current version of the block. It makes a CR copy using the current block and undo data it has and sends the CR copy of the block to the requestor via the interconnect. This event indicates write/read contention.

If this wait event appears in the "Top 5" timed events, then do the following:

■ Analyze the contention. The "Segments by CR Blocks Received" section of the AWR report should help you to identify the top contentious objects.

■ Optimize the application contention by using an appropriate application-partitioning scheme.

■ Look at "Tips for Avoiding Oracle RAC Wait Events" at the end of this section.

gc cr block 3-way

Figure 10-5 shows a pictorial representation of this event. An instance requests authorization for a block to be accessed in CR mode. The instance mastering the corresponding resource receives the request. The master forwards the request to the current holder of the block. The holding instance sends a CR copy of the block to the requestor via the Cache Fusion mechanism. This event indicates write/read contention.

If this wait event appears in the "Top 5" timed events list, the plan of action should be similar to that for the gc current block 2-way event.

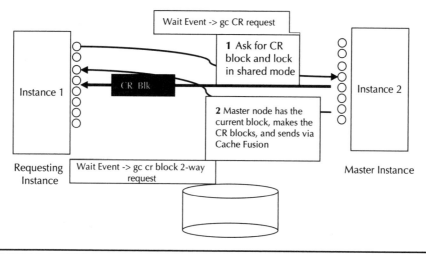

FIGURE 10-4   *Wait event: gc cr block 2-way*

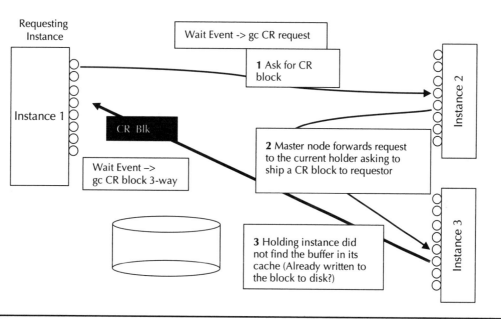

FIGURE 10-5   *Wait event: gc cr block 3-way*

gc current grant 2-way

Figure 10-6 shows a pictorial representation of this event. When an instance needs a block in current mode, it sends the request to the master instance. The master instance finds that currently no instances, including self, has any lock on the requested block. It sends a message back to the requesting instance granting it the shared lock on the block. The requesting instance then reads the block from the disk. This event doesn't indicate any contention.

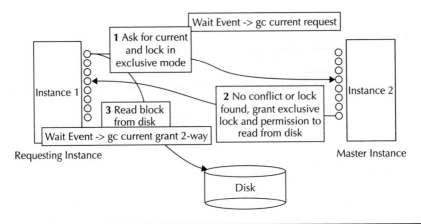

FIGURE 10-6 *Wait event: gc current grant 2-way*

The presence of this event in the "Top 5" list indicates that the instance is spending a significant amount of time in obtaining the locks. Here's a list of what you should do:

- Tune the SQL to optimize the number of blocks accessed by the application, thereby reducing the number of blocks it is requesting.
- Look at "Tips for Avoiding Oracle RAC Wait Events" at the end of this section.

gc current block busy

When a request needs a block in current mode, it sends a request to the master instance. The requestor eventually gets the block via Cache Fusion transfer; however, the block transfer is delayed due to either of the following reasons:

- The block was being used by a session on another instance.
- The block transfer was delayed because the holding instance could not write the corresponding redo record to the online redo log file immediately.

You can use the session-level dynamic performance views V$SESSION and V$SESSION_ EVENT to find the programs or sessions causing the most waits on this event:

```
select e.sid, e.time_waited, s.program, s.module
from v$session_event e, v$session s
where s.sid=e.sid
and e.event='gc current block busy'
order by e.time_waited;
```

To drill down further, you can use the following query to find out the module- or program-level details:

```
select st.sid, st.value, s.program, s.module
from v$sesstat st, v$session s, v$statname n
where s.sid=st.sid
```

```
and st.statistic#=n.statistic#
and n.name = 'gc CPU used by this session'
order by st.value;
```

Care should be taken to interpret the results of this query because the longer a session has been running, the larger the values are for total wait times and statistics. To eliminate this fallacy, you should run the query a couple of times, spaced by a few seconds, and compare the difference (that is, not the absolute values). After identifying some candidate sessions for causing performance problems, your analysis should focus on all wait events and statistics for those sessions.

This event indicates significant write/write contention. If the event appears in the "Top 5" list of the AWR report, do the following:

- Ensure that the Log Writer (LGWR) is tuned. Refer to the *Oracle Performance Tuning Guide* for information about tuning the LGWR performance.

- Use appropriate application partitioning to avoid contention.

- Look at "Tips for Avoiding Oracle RAC Wait Events" at the end of this section.

gc cr disk read

Figure 10-7 shows a pictorial representation of the gc cr disk read event. This wait event is returned when an instance receives a request to send a CR buffer, but the buffer is not cached locally. The requester waits on gc cr request, and when the read disk status is returned, the requester reads the block requested from disk. This typically happens during long-running queries

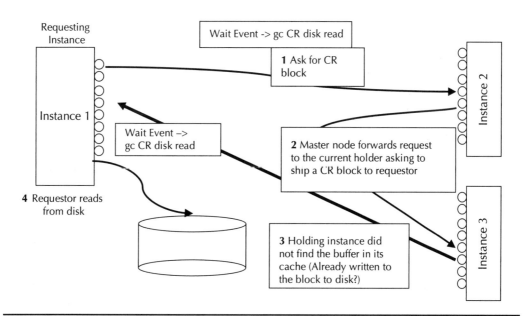

FIGURE 10-7 *Wait event: gc cr disk read*

that do not find undo blocks in the local cache of the instance that owns the undo segment, or in any other cache in the global cache.

We get this event when the node, which we hoped to be able to serve the CR block, did not have the block on cache, because it may be still reading the block from disk or because the block might be just pushed out of cache. However, this is a very rare occurrence and not a common performance issue.

To get further information about this event, you can set the 10708 event to level 5. It should dump the lock element covering the resource and other information, so you may be able to find which objects are causing this event as well as how you ended up hitting this event. It is usually recommended that you set the event at the process level or session level rather than the instance level because this tracing would produce a huge amount of trace files.

Buffer Busy Global CR

When an instance needs to generate a CR version of the current block, the block can be in either the local cache or a remote cache. If the latter, then LMS on the other instance will try to create the CR block; when the former, the foreground process executing the query will perform the CR block generation. When a CR version is created, the instance (or instances) needs to read the transaction table and undo blocks from the rollback/undo segment that are referenced in the active transaction table of the block. The details of the CR block fabrication and the role of transaction tables are discussed in the next chapter.

Sometimes this cleanout/rollback process may cause several lookups of local and remote undo headers and undo blocks. The remote undo header and undo block lookups will result in a "global cache cr request." Because undo headers are frequently accessed, a buffer wait may also occur. Until the CR image can be generated, the process will wait for the event "buffer busy global CR."

gc cr failure

Failure is not an option in cluster communications because lost messages or blocks may potentially trigger node evictions. This wait event is triggered when a CR block is requested from the holder of the block and a failure status message is received from the requestor. This happens only when there is an unforeseen event such as lost block or checksum or an invalid block request or when the holder cannot process the request. You will see multiple timeouts for the placeholder wait (like gc cr request) before receiving the gc cr failure event. This is also one of the events you should very rarely notice in the production environment. Immediate attention is required. You can query the system statistics view V$SYSSTAT for "gc blocks lost" or "gc claim blocks lost."

The most common reasons for the block failures at the global cache layer can be any of the following. However, the causes for the blocks lost are not known to Oracle. We need to investigate the hardware and network layers (using netstat or OS logs, for example) to find clues.

- Lost blocks during transfer
- Checksum errors
- Invalid format or SCN in the block

If you notice the gc blocks lost wait event frequently, you should engage the system administrator and network administrator to investigate the hardware and network layers. The following discussion lists some possible problem areas to consider while investigating this issue.

Interconnect-Related Issues

Oracle Global Cache and Global Enqueue performance and stability are greatly dependent on the interconnect for synchronization. Any potential delay in communication or disruption will affect the stability of the cluster.

Large UDP datagrams may be fragmented and sent in multiple frames based on Maximum Transmission Unit (MTU) size. These fragmented packets need to be reassembled on the receiving node. High CPU utilization (sustained or frequent spikes) as well as inadequate reassembly of buffers and UDP buffer space can cause packet reassembly failures. Fragmented packets have a time-to-live for reassembly. Packets that are not reassembled are dropped and requested again. If there is no buffer space for arriving fragments, they are silently dropped.

Also look for misconfiguration in the bonding driver or jumbo frames. While using jumbo frames, you should configure the entire I/O path (NIC cards, switches, and routers) for an MTU of 9000. Also, if there are mismatches in the interconnect communication path or a duplex mode mismatch in the NIC cards, you will find packets lost.

If the CPU is saturated at the host level, you might see the delays in network transfer latencies. Similarly, if the interconnect is saturated, you will notice dropped packets. Check the following section to estimate the interconnect traffic. If the interconnect is running at full capacity, upgrading the interconnect to a higher bandwidth (for example, from GigE to 10GigE or InfiniBand). If the hardware does not support higher capacity interconnect, consider bonding the NIC cards for additional capacity.

The "netstat -s" output for the IP layer will look like the following, and you must pay close attention to the "packets dropped" or "packet assembly failed" statistic. Also, check the firmware updates for network interface cards (NICs), although diagnosis of this layer requires OS/hardware vendor intervention.

```
Ip:
    26290871 total packets received
    12 with invalid addresses
    0 forwarded
    0 incoming packets discarded
    19983565 incoming packets delivered
    18952689 requests sent out
    8 fragments dropped after timeout
    6924738 reassemblies required
    766457 packets reassembled ok
    8 packet reassembles failed
    522626 fragments received ok
    3965698 fragments created
```

NOTE
On some platforms, the extended statistics for the interconnect are available from the internal view X$KSXPIF. This view contains the interface statistics, such as send_errors, receive_errors, packets_ dropped, and frame_errors at the interface level. You can use this information in analyzing network errors.

gc cr block busy

This event is the same as a "gc current block busy" event, except in this case the requesting instance has requested the block in CR mode.

gc current buffer busy

This event is also similar to the "gc current block busy" event. In this case, the session does not wait because the transfer from another instance was delayed, but because another session on the same instance has already initiated the lock request and is waiting for the response from the master instance. Thus, multiple sessions on the local instance are accessing the same block simultaneously. This event indicates local contention for the block.

If this wait event appears in the "Top 5" list in the AWR report, tune the SQL statements to optimize the number of blocks touched by the application, thereby reducing the number of blocks being requested.

gc current block congested

When an instance needs a block in current mode, it sends the request to the master instance. The requestor gets the block via Cache Fusion; however, the block-transfer process is delayed due to heavy workload on Cluster Group Services (GCS). As we have seen earlier, if any of the message or block transfers wait for more than 1 ms in the IPC queue before being picked up by the LMS process, you will see a congested wait.

This event doesn't indicate any concurrency or contention at the block level. However, it does indicate that GCS is heavily loaded and the background processes involved with its work need more CPU time. Lack of CPU resources on the holding instance might cause this to happen. Adding more LMS processes also sometimes helps to overcome this situation.

If this wait event appears in the "Top 5" list of the AWR report, consult the "Tips for Avoiding Oracle RAC Wait Events" section.

gc cr block congested

This event is the same as the "gc current block congested" event, except that in this case the requesting instance has requested the block in CR mode.

Tips for Avoiding Oracle RAC Wait Events

Following are some generic quick checks for avoiding excessive waits on the global cache:

- Ensure that the system has enough CPU resources. Monitor the average run queue length to make sure it stays below 1 in order to avoid CPU starvation for critical Oracle RAC–related processes, such as LMS.

- Interconnect network transfer speed and bandwidth should not impact the Cache Fusion data transfer. Have a look at the AWR report, including how much network traffic is generated by each instance. Ensure that the overall network traffic is well below the bandwidth of the private interconnect.

- If multiple Oracle RAC database instances are running on each node, evaluate the network bandwidth against the sum total of traffic generated by all instances. Refer to the "Tuning the Cluster Interconnect" section near the end of this chapter.

- Ensure that the socket send and receive buffers are configured appropriately. Refer to the platform/protocol information available from Oracle.

Global Cache Statistics

Global cache statistics are accounted for across the cluster level. Like a well-audited financial statement, all the numbers for blocks served from the source instance should be equal to the blocks received at the target instance(s). The statistics also include blocks lost and blocks retransmitted during failures. In the following sections we will take a close look at the most common Oracle RAC–related system statistics and their significance in analyzing performance issues.

gc current blocks received

This statistic represents the number of current blocks received through the interconnect from other instances. This counter is incremented by a foreground or background process when a request for a current block or a "global cache cr request" results in the shipping of a current block at the other instance. On the other side, the sender increments the "gc current blocks served" statistic.

gc current blocks served

This counter is incremented when the LMS processes are instructed by the GCS to send the current block to the requesting instance. When there is a request for the current block, the holding instance receives a BAST (blocking asynchronous system trap) to release the ownership on the block and sends a data block as a result. However, sometimes the holder can ignore the request and continue working on the block up to _gc_defer_time, when some critical operation such as block cleanout is pending.

   This gives additional buffer time to respond to the request while allowing local processes to finish the job. However, the holder must flush the pending redo on the block to disk and write the block written record (BWR) to disk. Block written records are discussed in Chapter 9.

gc cr blocks served

This statistic represents the number of the CR block requests served by the instance. When a CR block is requested, the holder clones the buffer into its local buffer cache and applies the undo information to make the buffer a point-in-time copy and ships the block to the requesting instance.

   Because the undo for that block is cached locally, it is normally efficient in building the CR version at the holding instance. The serving of a CR block is usually a very fast operation and is not blocked. However, sometimes it may include the flushing of a pending redo to disk, if a current block is shipped for CR.

   In some cases, a complete block CR version may involve reading data or an undo block from the disk or from the other instance's cache. In these cases, the incomplete copy is sent to the requestor. The requestor will be given the block version with all the changes, which could be rolled out on the holder side, and can then resume the CR block creation itself.

   The CR block fabrication process is discussed in Chapter 11.

gc cr blocks received

This counter is incremented in a foreground or background process when a search for a consistent read version of a block fails to find a local buffer with the required snapshot of the data. It also means that the current version for that particular block is not cached locally. Therefore, an attempt is made to get the block from a remote instance. The holder may ship either a CR or a current version of the block; the receiver copies it as a CR buffer. The block may be cached with exclusive access rights in another instance if it was recently modified there, or with shared access rights.

gc prepare failures

When a remote cache request is initiated, a request handle and a BID (buffer ID) are allocated in the PGA of the requestor. Moreover, a buffer is allocated in the SGA for remote DMA (Direct Memory Access). The number of buffers that can be allocated is port specific, depending on the characteristics of the underlying IPC protocol. If a buffer cannot be allocated because too many buffers are allocated already, the allocation is retried immediately. Under normal circumstances, buffers are prepared and unprepared all the time, so that the probability of failure is very low.

Some background processes such as SMON and PMON may prepare a lot of buffers for transaction or instance recovery, respectively. The occurrence of failures is normally very low, but is sometimes observed during recovery of large recovery sets. Usually, no intervention is required.

gc blocks lost

This is a very important statistic and should be 0 or close to 0. This counter is incremented when the message for the block has arrived and the actual block has not arrived. This could happen when there is contention in the network or hardware errors in the network layer. You will notice this error sometimes when the public network is used for cluster communication.

gc blocks corrupt

Before a block is shipped, a checksum is computed and stored in the buffer header. When the block is received, the checksum will be recomputed and compared to the stored value. If the checksum does not match, the block will be ignored, the request cancelled, the receive buffer freed ("unprepared"), and the statistic incremented. The request will then be retried.

The occurrence of corrupt blocks indicates that the block was damaged during the transfer, usually owing to network transmission or adapter problems. A retry is attempted. By default, the checksum is computed. In order to save CPU cycles, sometimes the following setting is used to turn off the checksum function

```
_interconnect_checksum = FALSE
```

Turning off the checksum function is only advisable for use in benchmarks and when reliable IPC protocols such as RDG are used. Do *not* disable interconnect checksum in production environments.

Global Cache Statistics Summary

Table 10-2 summarizes the global cache–related statistics discussed so far, their related statistics and wait events, and the V$views containing additional details and initialization parameters influencing the behavior of the statistics.

Global Cache Service Times

The Global Cache Services layer also tracks the various latencies for most of the service times associated with the block transfers. The timing mechanism is well instrumented and provides a wealth of information about the performance of Cache Fusion at the global level. We will be discussing the most important service times in the global cache layer and their significance in performance management of Oracle RAC.

Global Cache Statistic	Related Statistics and Wait Events	Related Views and Initialization Parameters
gc current blocks received	gc current blocks served gc current block 2-way gc current block 3-way gc current block busy gc current block congested gc current block receive time	V$INSTANCE_CACHE_TRANSFER V$SEGMENT_STATISTICS V$SQLAREA _gc_global_lru
gc current blocks served	gc current blocks received gc current block busy	V$CURRENT_BLOCK_SERVER _gc_defer_time
gc cr blocks served	gc cr block flush time gc cr block build time gc cr block send time	V$CR_BLOCK_SERVER _fairness_threshold _cr_grant_local_role
gc cr blocks received	gc cr blocks received gc cr block 2-way gc cr block 3-way gc cr block busy gc cr block congested	V$CR_BLOCK_SERVER V$SEGMENT_STATISTICS V$SQLAREA V$INSTANCE_CACHE_TRANSFER
gc blocks lost	cr request retry	gcs_server_processes _lm_lms OS utilities such as netstat
gc blocks corrupt		_interconnect_checksum _reliable_block_sends

TABLE 10-2 *Global Cache Statistics with Their Associated Wait Events and Parameters*

gc current block receive time

Like any other Oracle kernel calls, when one instance makes a request for a resource, the kernel starts a timer to measure the service times. Each individual request is timed from the point when the request is made until it completes. This statistic represents the cumulated end-to-end elapsed time or latency for a current block request.

The start time of the request is stored in a global cache structure representing the state of a cached data block. The average request time (end-to-end roundtrip time for an average current block receive time) can be obtained by the following formula:

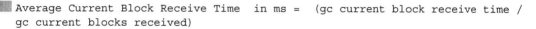

```
Average Current Block Receive Time  in ms =  (gc current block receive time /
gc current blocks received)
```

NOTE
The Oracle kernel instruments the timing in centiseconds (1/100th of a second) and we multiply the number by 10 to convert it to milliseconds (1/1000th of a second).

The very same calculation that is used in the "Cache Fusion Statistics" section of the AWR report is displayed as "Avg global cache current block receive time (ms)."

gc cr block receive time

This statistic represents the accumulated end-to-end elapsed time or latency for a request to receive a CR block from other instances' cache. Because CR requests are never blocked, the latency component is just processing and messaging times.

The average request time (end-to-end roundtrip for an average cr block receive time) can be obtained by the following formula:

```
Average time per CR block in ms =  (gc cr block receive time /
gc cr blocks received) * 10
```

gc current block flush time

The current block flush time is part of the processing time for a current block. When there is a request (usually BAST) for a current block from the master, the pending redo *must* be flushed to the log file by LGWR before LMS sends the block to the requestor. However, the operation is asynchronous in that LMS queues the request, posts LGWR, and continues processing. LMS would check its log flush queue for completions and then send the block, or go to sleep and be posted by LGWR. The performance of the redo log writes and redo log sync time can influence the overall service time significantly.

The average time for gc current block flush time can be obtained by the following formula:

```
Average time for gc current block flush time = (gc current block flush time /
V$CURRENT_BLOCK_SERVER.(FLUSH1+FLUSH10+FLUSH100+FLUSH1000+FLUSH1000) ) *10
```

NOTE
All current block transfers do not require a log flush. If the block is not modified or the redo is already written to disk, the block can be shipped directly to the other instance.

gc current block pin time

The pin time indicates how much elapsed time is required to process a BAST. It does not include the flush time and the send time, but it does include the time for which a release is deferred. Normally a very high average pin time indicates contention on current blocks and requires tuning to reduce the block-level concurrency. In some cases this is associated with a high incidence of deferring the block shipping (sometimes until _gc_defer_time) of the hot block and is commonly observed on index blocks.

The average global cache current block pin time (ms) can be obtained by the following formula:

```
Avg global cache current block pin time (ms) =  (gc current block pin time /
gc current blocks served) *10
```

gc current block send time

The send time is measured when a block is handed to the IPC layer to be sent. The requests are queued in a completion queue, and the send time is measured from when a block is handed off to the IPC layer until the system call returns a completion. The average latency is usually small and expected to be in the microsecond range.

gc cr block flush time

The CR block flush time is part of the service time for a CR buffer and is similar to processing for a current buffer. A normal CR buffer processing does not include the "gc cr block flush time" because CR processing is designed for highest efficiency. However, in some cases a log flush for a CR block transfer is required when a CR buffer is cloned from a current buffer that has redo pending. A high percentage is indicative of hot blocks with frequent read after write access.

The average global cache cr block flush time (ms) can be obtained by the following formula:

```
Avg global cache cr block flush time (ms) =  ( gc cr block flush time /
V$CR_BLOCK_SERVER.FLUSHES) *10
```

gc cr block build time

The cr block build time shows the accumulated time from the point when the database cache layer is notified of a CR request until it is either sending it or needs to wait for a log flush for that block. This is the time it takes to find or construct the read-consistent version of a block. The build time is mostly CPU time incurred scanning the cache for CR versions of blocks and/or creating CR copies.

The process of building or finding the block should never be blocked and never require non-local memory or disk accesses. This is known as the "lightwork rule." Also, an instance can refuse to ship CR blocks if it was asked for too many copies of the same CR block. In this case, the instance will disown the ownership of that block and the requestor can go and read the block from disk after appropriate grants from the master. Additional details about CR block fabrication and lightwork rule are provided in Chapter 11.

Global Cache Service Times Summary

Table 10-3 summarizes the Global Cache Service time-related statistics discussed so far, their related statistics and wait events, and the V$views containing additional details and initialization parameters influencing the behavior of the statistics.

Enqueue Tuning in Oracle RAC

Oracle RDBMS preserves the integrity of user data during simultaneous use of the same data block by using GCS. In addition to data blocks, end users can concurrently access many other shared resources. Oracle uses a queuing mechanism to ensure proper use of these shared resources. In an Oracle RAC environment, Global Enqueue Services (GES) protects and regulates access to these shared resources.

Enqueue wait is the time spent by a session waiting for shared resources. A user's response time and hence the database performance might be negatively impacted if a user session spends a long time waiting for a shared resource (or an enqueue). Waiting for the updating of the control file (CF enqueue), of an individual row (TX enqueue), and of an exclusive lock on a table (TM enqueue) are all examples of enqueue waits.

In an Oracle RAC environment, some enqueues are similar to single-instance counterparts and need to be coordinated only at the instance level. However, many of the enqueues need to be coordinated globally. GES is responsible for coordinating the global enqueues. Due to global coordination, some enqueues might have higher performance impacts in the Oracle RAC environment.

Global Cache Service Time Statistic	Related Statistics and Wait Events	Related Views and Initialization Parameters
gc current block receive time	gc current block pin time gc current block flush time gc current block send time	V$CURRENT_BLOCK_SERVER _gc_defer_time
gc cr block receive time	gc cr block flush time gc cr block build time gc cr block send time	V$CR_BLOCK_SERVER
gc current block flush time	Redo write time Log file sync	V$CURRENT_BLOCK_SERVER
gc current block pin time		V$CURRENT_BLOCK_SERVER
gc current block send time	msgs sent queue time on ksxp (ms) msgs sent queued on ksxp	
gc cr block flush time	Redo write time msgs sent queue time on ksxp (ms) msgs sent queued on ksxp gc cr block busy log file sync	
gc cr block build time	gc cr block ship time log file sync	V$CR_BLOCK_SERVER _fairness_threshold

TABLE 10-3 *Global Cache Service Statistics with Associated Wait Events and Parameters*

The number of enqueue resources allocated during the instance startup is calculated as

```
GES Resources = DB_FILES + DML_LOCKS + ENQUEUE_RESOURCES
        + PROCESSES + TRANSACTIONS + 200) × (1 + (N - 1) / N)
```

where *N* is the number of Oracle RAC instances.

Dynamic performance view V$RESOURCE_LIMIT contains the initial allocation, current_utilization, max_utilization, and limit_value statistics for enqueues. The following SQL session output shows enqueue-related statistics from V$RESOURCE_LIMIT:

```
SQL> column current_utilization heading CURRENT
SQL> column MAX_UTILIZATION heading MAX_USAGE
SQL> column  INITIAL_ALLOCATION heading INITIAL
SQL> column resource_limit format a23
SQL>select * from v$resource_limit;
RESOURCE_NAME             CURRENT   MAX_USAGE INITIAL    LIMIT_VALU
----------------------- ---------- ---------- ---------- ----------
processes                     35         44        150        150
sessions                      40         49        170        170
enqueue_locks                 16         35       2261       2261
enqueue_resources             16         52        968  UNLIMITED
ges_procs                     33         41        320        320
```

```
ges_ress                    0          0       4161   UNLIMITED
ges_locks                   0          0       6044   UNLIMITED
ges_cache_ress            346       1326          0   UNLIMITED
ges_reg_msgs               46        225       1050   UNLIMITED
ges_big_msgs               22        162        964   UNLIMITED
ges_rsv_msgs                0          0        301         301
gcs_resources            7941      10703      13822       13822
<<<output lines not relevant are deleted >>>>
```

Oracle AWR Report

AWR is Oracle's mechanism for gathering and preserving statistics useful for performance analysis. Oracle 10g introduced a new background process, MMON (Manageability Monitor), to do this work. Every 15 minutes, it takes a snapshot of statistics needed for performance tuning and diagnostics. Snapshots older than one week are automatically purged. Snapshot data is stored in a set of tables in the SYSAUX tablespace; these tables are owned by SYS. AWR is fully Oracle RAC aware and is active by default on all the instances. One of the MMON processes acts as the master and coordinates snapshots on all the active instances. AWR takes concurrent snapshots on all the instances and statistics from all the instances stored in the AWR repository with the same snap_id. The column inst_id is used to differentiate statistics for different instances from the same snapshot.

The package DBMS_WORKLOAD_REPOSITORY is available for managing snapshots manually. You can use this package to create, drop, and modify snapshots. This package can also be used to establish baseline snapshots. Following are some sample commands using this package.

The following command takes an immediate snapshot and archives the data in the repository:

```sql
sql> execute DBMS_WORKLOAD_REPOSITORY.CREATE_SNAPSHOT ();
```

To modify the snapshot retention interval to 30 days (43,200 minutes) from its default setting of 7 days, you can use the following command:

```sql
sql> execute DBMS_WORKLOAD_REPOSITORY.MODIFY_SNAPSHOT_SETTINGS
( retention => 43200);
```

You can also change the default snapshot interval of 60 minutes to any other desired value. The following command changes the snapshot interval to 4 hours (240 minutes):

```sql
sql> execute DBMS_WORKLOAD_REPOSITORY.MODIFY_SNAPSHOT_SETTINGS
( interval => 240);
```

A baseline snapshot is a snapshot that is taken when the database instances and the application are running at the optimal performance level. Baseline snapshots are used for comparative analysis. To mark a range of snapshots as baseline snapshots, use the following command:

```sql
sql> execute DBMS_WORKLOAD_REPOSITORY.CREATE_BASELINE
(start_snap_id => 20, end_snap_id => 25, baseline_name => 'normal  baseline');
```

Baseline snapshots are not removed during normal purge operations and need to be removed manually using the DROP_BASELINE procedure as follows:

```
sql> execute DBMS_WORKLOAD_REPOSITORY.DROP_BASELINE
(baseline_name => 'optimal baseline', cascade => FALSE);
```

Even though AWR is Oracle RAC aware and snapshots are taken simultaneously on all the active instances, reporting and analysis need to be done at the individual instance level. The script $ORACLE_HOME/rdbms/admin/awrrpt.sql is used to create an AWR report. Here is a sample session to generate an AWR report:

```
SQL> @awrrpt.sql
Current Instance
~~~~~~~~~~~~~~~~
   DB Id        DB Name      Inst Num Instance
 -----------   ------------  -------- ------------
 3553717806      PROD             2   PROD2
Specify the Report Type
~~~~~~~~~~~~~~~~~~~~~~~~~
Would you like an HTML report, or a plain text report?
Enter 'html' for an HTML report, or 'text' for plain text
Defaults to 'html'
Enter value for report_type:text

<<<lines for other snapshots deleted from here>>>
                         1384 30 Jul 2005 10:00       1
                         1385 30 Jul 2005 11:00       1
Specify the Begin and End Snapshot Ids
~~~~~~~~~~~~~~~~~~~~~~~~~~~~~~~~~~~~~~~~~
Enter value for begin_snap: 1384
Begin Snapshot Id specified: 1385
Specify the Report Name
~~~~~~~~~~~~~~~~~~~~~~~~~
The default report file name is awrrpt_2_1384_1385.txt. To use this
name, press <return> to continue, otherwise enter an alternative.

Enter value for report_name:PROD2_SAT_JULY3005_10to11.txt
```

TIP
Instead of accepting the default name for the report file, give it a name that includes the instance name, the day and date, and the interval for which the report is generated. This will make the report comparison and tracking easy.

Interpreting the AWR Report

Oracle performance tuning is a complex and evolved subject—books have been written about it. It is not possible to explain the contents of an AWR report in a few paragraphs here. However, we will attempt to familiarize you with the structure of the report and point out some important Oracle RAC–specific statistics to which you should pay attention.

An AWR report generated in an Oracle RAC environment contains the following Oracle RAC–specific sections, which are not present in an AWR report generated in a single-instance database environment:

- Number of instances
- Instance global cache load profile
- Global cache efficiency percentage
- GCS and GES—workload characteristics
- Messaging statistics
- Service statistics
- Service wait class statistics
- Top 5 CR and current blocks segments

Number of Instances Section
This section lists the number of instances at the beginning and end of the AWR report interval.

```
RAC Statistics  DB/Inst: PROD/PROD1  Snaps: 2239-2240
                              Begin   End
                              ----- -----
          Number of Instances:     3    3
```

Global Cache Load Profile Section
This section contains information about the interinstance Cache Fusion data block and messaging traffic.

```
Global Cache Load Profile
~~~~~~~~~~~~~~~~~~~~~~~~~~~           Per Second      Per Transaction
                                     -----------      ---------------
    Global Cache blocks received:      312.73              12.61
    Global Cache blocks served:        230.60               9.30
     GCS/GES messages received:        514.48              20.74
    GCS/GES messages sent:             763.46              30.78
    DBWR Fusion writes:                 22.67               0.91
```

The first two statistics indicate the number of blocks transferred to or from this instance. If the database does not contain tablespaces with multiple block sizes, you can use these statistics to calculate the amount of network traffic generated by the instance. Assuming the database block size is 8K, you can calculate the amount of data sent by this instance:

$230 \times 8,192 = 1,884,160$ bytes/sec = 1.9 MB/sec

You can also calculate the amount of data received by this instance:

$313 \times 8,192 = 2,564,096$ bytes/sec = 2.5 MB/sec

To determine the amount of network traffic generated due to messaging, you first need to find the average message size. Use the following message SQL query to find the average message size:

```
select sum(kjxmsize*
(kjxmrcv+kjxmsnt+kjxmqsnt))/sum((kjxmrcv+kjxmsnt+kjxmqsnt))
from x$kjxm
where kjxmrcv > 0 or kjxmsnt > 0 or kjxmqsnt >0 ;
```

For the system from which the sample report was taken, the average message size was about 300 bytes.

Calculate the amount of messaging traffic on the network like this:

$$300 (763 + 514) = 383,100 = 0.4 \text{ MB}$$

In case the system for which the report is being analyzed is not available to determine the average message size, you can add 10 to 12 percent of the data traffic to estimate the messaging traffic. Assuming the report is from a two-node Oracle RAC environment, then calculate the total network traffic generated by Cache Fusion activity like this:

$$= 1.9 + 2.5 + 0.4 = 4.8 \text{ MBytes/sec}$$
$$= 4.8 \times 8 = 38.4 \text{ Mbits/sec}$$

To estimate the network traffic generated in an Oracle RAC environment consisting of two or more nodes, first generate an AWR report from all the instances for the same interval. Then calculate the total network traffic generated due to Cache Fusion activity:

$$= \Sigma \text{ block received} + \Sigma \text{ Msg Recd} \times \text{Avg Msg size}$$

Note that Σ block received = Σ block served, and Σ Msg Sent = Σ Msg Recd. These calculations would require an AWR report from all the instances for the same interval.

NOTE
The AWR report from Oracle Database 10g Release 2 contains an extra line that indicates the interconnect traffic generated by the instance "Estd Interconnect traffic (KB)." A quick sum of this statistic from all the instances will provide the overall interconnect traffic, thus avoiding the trouble of the aforementioned calculations.

The "DBWR Fusion writes" statistic in this section indicates the number of times the local DBWR was forced to write a block to disk due to remote instance(s). This number should be low; it is better to analyze this as a fraction of overall DBWR writes, which is available as the "Physical writes" statistics in the "Load Profile" section of the report:

```
Load Profile
~~~~~~~~~~~~
```

	Per Second	Per Transaction
Redo size:	700,266.45	28,230.88
Logical reads:	17,171.74	692.27
Block changes:	2,394.61	96.54
Physical reads:	208.42	8.40
Physical writes:	215.54	8.69
User calls:	275.03	11.09
Parses:	22.06	0.89

In this case, "DBWR Fusion writes" is approximately 10.5 percent of the overall Physical writes. Establish a baseline percentage when the performance is good. You can fine-tune this number by ensuring that instances do not step on each other's data or partitioning of the application.

Global Cache Efficiency Percentages Section

This section of the report shows how the instance is getting all the data blocks it needs.

```
Global Cache Efficiency Percentages (Target local+remote 100%)
~~~~~~~~~~~~~~~~~~~~~~~~~~~~~~~~~~~~~~~~~~~~~~~~~~~~~~~~~~~~~~~~~~~
Buffer access -   local cache %:    97.19
Buffer access - remote cache %:     1.82
Buffer access -         disk %:     0.99
```

The most preferred method is to get data in the local buffer cache, followed by the remote instances' cache, and lastly from the disk. The sum of the first two rows gives the *cache hit ratio* for the instance. The value for the remote cache hit should typically be less than 10 percent. Consider implementing an application-partitioning scheme if this value is higher than 10 percent.

GCS and GES Workload Characteristics Section

This section contains timing statistics for global enqueue and global cache. The statistics are further subdivided into the following four subsections:

- Average time (in milliseconds) to obtain an enqueue
- Time the instance has to wait before receiving a block in consistent read (CR) mode or in current mode
- Amount of time/delay for an instance to process a CR request
- Amount of time/delay for an instance to process a current block request

```
Global Cache and Enqueue Services - Workload Characteristics
~~~~~~~~~~~~~~~~~~~~~~~~~~~~~~~~~~~~~~~~~~~~~~~~~~~~~~~~~~~~~~~~~
                    Avg global enqueue get time (ms):    951.5

        Avg global cache cr block receive time (ms):      3.9
   Avg global cache current block receive time (ms):      3.0

          Avg global cache cr block build time (ms):      0.7
           Avg global cache cr block send time (ms):      0.3
      Global cache log flushes for cr blocks served %:   50.5
          Avg global cache cr block flush time (ms):     10.1

      Avg global cache current block pin time (ms):       1.4
     Avg global cache current block send time (ms):       0.3
 Global cache log flushes for current blocks served %:    1.4
     Avg global cache current block flush time (ms):      4.4
```

As a rule of thumb, all timings related to a CR block should be less than 5 ms, and all timings related to current block processing should be less than 10 ms. However, nowadays close to 1–5 ms is considered acceptable due to faster networks, but these numbers are good and conservative.

I have seen these numbers at less than a millisecond in high-performance systems such as Oracle Exadata Database Machine.

GCS and GES Messaging Statistics Section

The first section contains statistics related to sending a message, and generally all these statistics should be less than 1 millisecond. The second section details the breakup of direct and indirect messages.

```
Global Cache and Enqueue Services - Messaging Statistics
~~~~~~~~~~~~~~~~~~~~~~~~~~~~~~~~~~~~~~~~~~~~~~~~~~~~~~~~~~~~
                Avg message sent queue time (ms):       0.5
         Avg message sent queue time on ksxp (ms):      1.7
            Avg message received queue time (ms):       0.2
              Avg GCS message process time (ms):        0.5
              Avg GES message process time (ms):        0.2

                      % of direct sent messages:       52.22
                    % of indirect sent messages:       46.95
                    % of flow controlled messages:      0.83
```

Direct messages are the messages sent by an instance foreground process or the user process to remote instances, whereas indirect messages are the messages that are not urgent and are pooled and then sent. Indirect messages are low-priority messages. These statistics generally depend on the nature of the workload among the instances, and not much can be done to fine-tune them. Establish a baseline for these during normal user workloads. Also, observe these statistics after any significant change in the user workload and establish a new baseline after any changes.

Service Statistics Section

Statistics in this section show the resources used by all the service instance supports.

```
Service Statistics  DB/Inst: PROD/PROD1  Snaps: 2239-2240
-> ordered by DB Time
-> us - microsecond - 1000000th of a second

                                                       Physical      Logical
Service Name           DB Time (s)   DB CPU (s)         Reads         Reads
-------------------    -----------   -----------     ----------    ----------
PROD                   1,198,708.4     17,960.0        491,498   9,998,798,201
SYS$USERS                  3,903.3        539.7        245,724       2,931,729
SYS$BACKGROUND                29.3          4.8          7,625       4,801,655
```

The instance PROD1 is serving the workload connected using the service PROD. If multiple services are configured, the breakup will appear here. There are two internal services in addition to the application services defined by the DBA. SYS$BACKGROUND is used by all background processes. SYS$USERS is the default service for user sessions that are not associated with applications services—for example, connecting as "sqlplus / as sysdba."

Service Wait Class Statistics Section

This section summarizes waits in different categories for each service. If a service response is not acceptable, these statistics can show where the service is waiting.

```
Service Wait Class Stats  DB/Inst: PROD/PROD1  Snaps: 2239-2240
-> Wait Class info for services in the Service Statistics section.
-> Total Waits and Time Waited displayed for the following wait
   classes: User I/O, Concurrency, Administrative, Network
-> Time Waited (Wt Time) in centisecond (100th of a second)

Service Name
-------------------------------------------------------------------------------

 User I/O  User I/O Concurcy  Concurcy    Admin    Admin   Network   Network
Total Wts  Wt Time Total Wts  Wt Time Total Wts  Wt Time Total Wts   Wt Time
--------- --------- --------- --------- --------- --------- --------- ---------
PROD
 2227431   4136718   3338963  95200428         0         0   1660799     15403
SYS$USERS
 2 59502    188515       274       486         0         0      1676         3
SYS$BACKGROUND
   10412      1404      4135     12508         0         0         0         0
          -------------------------------------------------------------
```

Top 5 CR and Current Blocks Segments Section

These sections contain the names of the "Top 5" contentious segments (index or tables). If a table or an index is being subject to a very high percentage of CR and current block transfers, you need to analyze its usage pattern, database layout characteristics, and other parameters that might cause contention.

```
Segments by CR Blocks Received  DB/Inst: PROD/PROD1  Snaps: 2239-2240
                                                           CR
            Tablespace                     Subobject  Obj.  Blocks
Owner       Name       Object Name         Name       Type  Received  %Total
---------- ---------- -------------------- ---------- ----- ---------- -------
ES_MAIL    ESINFREQID ES_INSTANCE                     TABLE   136,997   58.65
ES_MAIL    ESINFREQID ES_INSTANCE_IX_TYPE             INDEX    21,037    9.01
ES_MAIL    ESFREQTBL  ES_FOLDER                       TABLE    14,616    6.26
ES_MAIL    ESFREQTBL  ES_USER                         TABLE     6,251    2.68
ES_MAIL    ESSMLTBL   ES_EXT_HEADER                   TABLE     2,467    1.06
          -------------------------------------------------------------

Segments by Current Blocks Received  DB/Inst: PROD/PROD1  Snaps: 2239-2240
                                                          Current
            Tablespace                     Subobject  Obj.  Blocks
Owner       Name       Object Name         Name       Type  Received  %Total
---------- ---------- -------------------- ---------- ----- ---------- -------
ES_MAIL    ESINFREQID ES_INSTANCE                     TABLE   602,833   80.88
ES_MAIL    ESSMLTBL   ES_EXT_HEADER                   TABLE    18,527    2.49
ES_MAIL    ESINFREQID ES_INSTANCE_IX_TYPE             INDEX    13,640    1.83
ES_MAIL    ESFREQTBL  ES_FOLDER                       TABLE    11,242    1.51
ES_MAIL    ESINFREQID ES_INSTANCE_IX_FOLDE            INDEX     5,026     .67
          -------------------------------------------------------------
```

Oracle Database 10*g* R2 contains the following additional information in these sections:

```
-> Total Current Blocks Received:            2,328
-> Captured Segments account for            93.1% of Total
```

The additional information allows you to compare the top segment's activity with respect to the overall system activity in that category.

STATSPACK

AWR is intended to supersede STATSPACK. AWR is automated and works out of the box without needing customization. STATSPACK is available in the form of a package, but it is not installed automatically. Note that you need to be licensed to use AWR, whereas STATSPACK continues to be a free product.

Although AWR and STATSPACK serve similar objectives and their reports look alike, there are differences. Oracle developers and DBAs extensively use STATSPACK. When STATSPACK snapshots are taken at a level higher than the default level of 5, much more statistical information is provided. Generally, it should not be necessary to run STATSPACK at a level greater than 5. Due to the scope of this book, we will limit our discussions to the AWR report only, with a quick introduction to STATSPACK.

Refer to $ORACLE_HOME/rdbms/admin/spdoc.txt to install, configure, and use STATSPACK. Complete the following steps to install and begin using the package:

1. Execute the script spcreate.sql; this script creates the required schema and the corresponding schema objects.

2. Execute the script spauto.sql; this script configures an automatic snapshot for every hour on the hour. Execute this script on each instance.

3. Use the script spreport.sql to generate the STATSPACK report.

All these scripts are located in the $ORACLE_HOME/rdbms/admin directory.

ADDM

Automatic Database Diagnostic and Monitor (ADDM) is Oracle's major step toward making the database self-tuning. The following infrastructure components are introduced with ADDM:

- **MMON**   Manageability Monitor is a new background process that does all the work required for ADDM.

- **AWR**   Automatic Workload Repository is a set of database objects used to gather and store database performance statistics.

- **Packages**   The package DBMS_ADVISOR is available to manage ADDM.

- **Parameters**   The STATISTICS_LEVEL initialization parameter should be set either to TYPICAL or ALL for ADDM to function. The DBIO_EXPECTED parameter needs to be set to represent the average read time for a database block. Its default value is 10000 (10 milliseconds). Use the following command to set this parameter:

```
Sql> execute DBMS_ADVISOR.SET_DEFAULT_TASK_PARAMETER
('ADDM','DBIO_EXPECTED'. 30000)
```

■ **Auxiliary tablespace** Oracle uses an auxiliary tablespace (SYSAUX) as the storage space for the tools and other components (AWR, ADDM, and so on). This tablespace is created by default during database creation.

The goal of ADDM is to optimize the time spent by the database for servicing the user workload. Its sole objective is to reduce DB Time, which consists of the following two components:

■ **Wait time** Time spent by user sessions while waiting for any resources

■ **CPU time** Time spent by user sessions while processing user work

MMON analyzes the data stored in the AWR repository and uses predefined, built-in rules to suggest how DB Time can be reduced. It generates a report with recommendations but does not implement them automatically. Its findings include the following:

■ **System capacity issues** CPU, I/O subsystem usage.

■ **Instance management** Analyzes instance memory management parameters such as SGA, redo log buffers, buffer cache, and so on. Also analyzes other initialization parameters for optimal settings.

■ **Java, SQL, and PL/SQL tuning** Analyzes high resource-consuming Java, SQL, and PL/SQL statements and whether the optimal data access path is being used.

■ **Contention** In a single-instance environment, analyzes contention in single instances as well as in the Oracle RAC environment. Takes into account buffer_busy_waits and all global cache–related wait events.

■ **Database structure** Analyzes the online redo log file size, among other things.

■ **Miscellaneous** Analyzes application connection patterns.

Tuning the Cluster Interconnect

Oracle uses cluster interconnect for sending messages to coordinate data block access and for sending copies of data blocks from one instance's cache to another instance's cache to optimize disk I/O. Therefore, cluster interconnect performance is crucial to Oracle RAC performance. Its configuration and proper functioning is one of the most important parts of Oracle RAC performance tuning.

Verifying That Private Interconnect Is Used

In Oracle Database 11*g*, you can specify the private interconnect while configuring the CRS. Ensure that the private interconnect is used for Cache Fusion traffic. Also ensure that the private interconnect is not used by other network-intensive functions such as ftp and rcp commands between the cluster nodes because this might impact Oracle RAC performance.

You can use the following commands to verify that the intended private interconnect is being used for the Cache Fusion traffic:

```
SQL> oradebug setmypid

Statement processed.

SQL> oradebug ipc
```

Information written to trace file.

SQL> oradebug tracefile_name

/u02/app/oracle/diag/rdbms/alpha/alpha1/trace/alpha1_ora_3766.trc

This will dump a trace file to the user_dump_dest. The output will look something like this:

```
SSKGXPT 0xb466a1e0 flags  sockno 13 IP 10.1.0.201 UDP 42773
SKGXPGPID Internet address 10.1.0.201 UDP port number 42773
```

This indicates that IP 10.1.0.201 with a UDP protocol is being used for Cache Fusion traffic. Also, cluster interconnect information is printed in the alert.log:

```
Interface type 1 eth1 10.1.0.0 configured from GPnP Profile for use as a cluster interconnect
Interface type 1 eth0 10.1.1.0 configured from GPnP Profile for use as a public interface
```

In Oracle 11g, you can query the internal view X$KSXPIA to find out the network interface used for Cache Fusion traffic. Also, this view lists the source of the information (from where it picks the IP address, such as OCR or from the cluster_interconnects parameter). The column value for PICKED_KSXPIA is listed as OCR if it picks from the Oracle Cluster Registry and is listed as CI if it picks the address via the cluster_interconnects initialization parameter.

```
SELECT INST_ID,PUB_KSXPIA,PICKED_KSXPIA,NAME_KSXPIA,IP_KSXPIA
FROM X$KSXPIA;


INST_ID PUB_KS PICKED NAME_KSXPIA      IP_KSXPIA
------- ------ ------ --------------- ----------------
      1 N      OCR    eth1             10.1.0.201
      1 Y      OCR    eth0             10.1.1.201
```

Interconnect Latencies

Starting from Oracle 11g, the newly introduced background process "ping" periodically measures the network statistics. It wakes up periodically (about every 5 seconds) and measures the latencies for message transfers and block transfers. On every wakeup, it sends two messages to all the cluster nodes (of 500 bytes and 8192 bytes, respectively), calculates the roundtrip latencies, and maintains the information internally. AWR also uses this information to display the "Interconnect Ping Latency Stats" section of the report. The internal data is exposed via X$KSXPPING.

Be warned that the observed latencies may include the scudding latency from the operating system running the ping command. Take this data with a grain of salt because long latency could be reported when there is a long scheduling latency or high IPC latency due to host load. Because ping is not a mandatory process for the functioning of the cluster but rather a mere diagnostic process, it is not scheduled to run in real time. Scheduling the ping process in real time would potentially overcome the aforementioned issues; however, this is not recommended due to the importance (or unimportance) of the process. It is advisable to run the ping process in default time-sharing schedule mode.

As always, it is recommended that you establish baseline statistics when the cluster is performing normally and compare the interconnect latencies from X$KSXPPING when you notice a performance issue.

NOTE
*A known bug (6511290) with the ping process was generating
unexpectedly high network traffic, resulting in high CPU usage on
11.1.0.7. If you notice the ping process consuming a lot of the CPU
processing, you can turn off the process by setting the parameter
_ksxp_ping_enable to FALSE.*

The internal view X$KSXPCLIENT provides the total overview network traffic generated by the other diagnostic processes in the Oracle 11g RAC environment. You can look up the network traffic generated by the ping process by using the following SQL query:

```
select * from X$KSXPCLIENT where name ='ping';

ADDR             INDX INST_ID NAME BYTES_SENT  BYTES_RCV
---------------- ------ ------- ---- ---------- ----------
00000000907CC0E8      9       1 ping     650904     650904
```

Verifying That Network Interconnect Is Not Saturated

As mentioned in the preceding sections, you can use the AWR report to analyze the following:

- Network traffic generated by Oracle instances. Ensure that at no point in time the traffic generated is saturating the private interconnect.

- Whether the network delays and latency, as indicated in the AWR report, are excessive. In Oracle Database 11g R2, you can use the OEM to monitor the interconnect traffic.

Consider upgrading the network interconnect to a higher capacity when you see the interconnect traffic is reaching about 50 percent of its theoretical capacity.

In a Nutshell

Performance tuning in the Oracle RAC environment is similar to tuning in a single-instance environment, with a few additional considerations for Oracle RAC. Applications partitioning and newly introduced performance features such as ASSM also help greatly in Oracle RAC. Caching frequently used sequences and choosing the right block size each has a big positive impact on performance.

New wait events and enhanced statistics-collection tools are available with Oracle Database 11g. Oracle RAC wait events and system statistics provide the fine-grained diagnostic information about the block transfers and interinstance messaging. New optimization techniques and improved statistics-collection metrics at the global cache and enqueue services layers take performance analysis to the next level.

Automatic Workload Repository (AWR) is the performance warehouse for Oracle databases, and AWR reports provide tremendous information related to Oracle RAC performance. AWR and ADDM reports are an excellent place to start analyzing performance in an Oracle RAC environment. Analyzing Oracle RAC performance is simplified with these tools. In the next chapter, we look at resource management in an Oracle RAC environment.

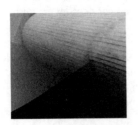

PART IV

Advanced Concepts in Oracle RAC

CHAPTER
11

Global Resource Directory

elcome to the world of resource management and administration in a parallel computing environment. This chapter provides a detailed discussion about resource management and locking issues as well as the interinstance coordination activities that take place in the cluster. Understanding the internal workings of locking will help you in architecting Oracle RAC solutions and administering the Oracle RAC. Be warned that the concepts discussed here are specific to the current versions of Oracle and may not be applicable to past or future versions.

The Oracle RAC environment includes numerous resources, such as multiple versions of data block buffers in buffer caches in different modes. Oracle uses different types of locking and queuing mechanisms within a cluster to coordinate lock resources, data, and interinstance data requests. We will examine how Oracle coordinates these resources to maintain the integrity of shared data and resources.

Coordination of concurrent tasks within a cluster is called *synchronization*. Resources such as data blocks and locks must be synchronized between the nodes because nodes within a cluster acquire and release ownership of them frequently. The synchronization provided by the Global Resource Directory (GRD) maintains clusterwide concurrency of the resources and in turn ensures the integrity of shared data. The amount of synchronization depends on the amount of resources and the number of users and tasks working on them. Little synchronization may be needed to coordinate a small number of concurrent tasks, but with many concurrent tasks, significant synchronization is required.

Synchronization is also required for buffer cache management because it is divided into multiple caches, and each instance is responsible for managing its own local version of the buffer cache. Copies of data blocks may be exchanged between the nodes in the cluster. This concept is sometimes referred to as the *global cache,* although in reality each node's buffer cache is separate and copies of blocks are exchanged through traditional distributed locking mechanisms. Global Cache Services (GCS) maintains the cache coherency across the buffer cache resources. Global Enqueue Services (GES) controls the resource management across the clusters' non-buffer cache resources.

Resources and Enqueues

A *resource* is an identifiable entity—that is, it has a name or reference. The referenced entity is usually a memory region, a disk file, a data block, or an abstract entity; the name of the resource *is* the resource. A resource can be owned or locked in various states, such as *exclusive* or *shared*. By definition, any shared resource is lockable. If it is not shared, no access conflict can occur. If it is shared, access conflicts must be resolved, typically with a lock. Although the terms *lock* and *resource* refer to separate objects, they are often used interchangeably. A global resource is visible and used throughout the cluster. A local resource is used by only one instance. It may still have locks to control access by the multiple processes of the instance, but no access to it is available from outside the instance.

Each resource can have a list of locks, called the *grant queue,* that are currently granted to users. A *convert queue* is a queue of locks that are waiting to be converted to particular modes.

Conversion is the process of changing a lock from the mode it currently holds to a different mode. Even if the mode is NULL, it is regarded as holding a lock without any conflicts of interest on that resource.

Acquiring a lock (known as a *grant* on that resource) is the process of acquiring a lock on a resource that currently does not have a lock (mode = no-lock). In addition, a resource has a lock value block (LVB) that can contain a small amount of data.

Figure 11-1 shows the grant and convert queue representation for a block and the structure. The data block resource (also known as *PCM resource*) is identified using the following format:

```
[LE] [Class] [BL]
[0x10000c5][0x1],[BL]
Grant Queue
Convert Queue
Lock Value Block
```

- ■ **LE**   Lock element that denotes the data block address (DBA—not to be confused with the other DBA, database administrator). It is visible in V$BH.LOCK_ELEMENT_ADDR.
- ■ **Class**   Class of the block. Visible in V$BH.CLASS# (data, undo, temp, and so on).
- ■ **BL**   Buffer cache management locks (or buffer locks).

Data buffer cache blocks are the most obvious and most commonly used global resource. Other data item resources are also global in the cluster, such as transaction enqueues and library cache and shared pool data structures.

The data buffer cache blocks are handled by the GCS (Parallel Cache Management, or PCM). The non–data block resources are handled by GES (non–Parallel Cache Management, or non-PCM). The Global Resource Manager (GRM, the old DLM) keeps the lock information valid and correct across the cluster.

The evaluation of a vendor-supplied DLM to Oracle Clusterware was discussed in Chapter 2.

Grants and Conversions

Locks are placed on a resource grant or convert queue. If the lock mode changes, it is moved between the queues. If several locks exist on the grant queue, they must be compatible. Locks of the same mode are not necessarily compatible with each other.

NOTE
Lock conversation and the compatibility matrix of DLM locks were discussed in Chapter 2. We discuss the management of GES locks later in this chapter.

```
[0x10000c5][0x1],[BL]
Grant Queue
Convert Queue
Lock Value Block
```

FIGURE 11-1   *Grant queue and convert queue*

A lock leaves the convert queue under any of the following conditions:

■ The process requests the lock termination (that is, removes the lock).

■ The process cancels the conversion; the lock is moved back to the grant queue in the previous mode.

■ The requested mode is compatible with the most restrictive lock in the grant queue and with all the previous modes of the convert queue, and the lock is at the head of the convert queue.

Figure 11-2 shows the lock conversion mechanisms. Convert requests are processed in a First In, First Out (FIFO) fashion.

The grant queue and convert queue are associated with each and every resource that is managed by the GES. The sequence of operations is discussed in detail in the following example with respect to the compatibility of lock modes. This is an example of a resource getting locks placed on its grant or resource queues:

1. A shareable read lock is granted.

2. Another shareable read lock is granted. They are compatible and can reside on the grant queue.

3. Another shareable read lock is placed on the grant queue.

4. One lock converts to shareable NULL. This conversion can be done in place because it is a simple downgrade.

5. Another lock attempts to convert to exclusive write. It has to be placed on the convert queue.

Figure 11-3 shows the interested resource's grant and convert queue structure in all five stages.

Locks and Enqueues

Enqueues are basically locks that support queuing mechanisms and can be acquired in different modes. An enqueue can be held in exclusive mode by one process, and others can be held in non-exclusive mode depending on the type. Enqueues in Oracle RAC are the same as the enqueues used in a single instance of the Oracle RDBMS, except for the scope. Few enqueues are local to the instance and few are global. A transaction is protected by a TX (transaction) enqueue

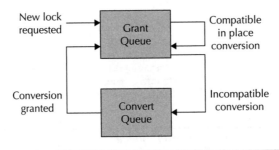

FIGURE 11-2 *Lock conversion*

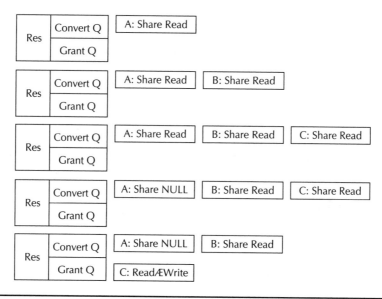

FIGURE 11-3   *Grant and convert queue operations*

irrespective of whether it is for a single instance or a clustered environment. However, the temporary tablespace enqueue is local to the instance where it is held.

Cache Coherency

In *cache coherency,* the contents of the caches in different nodes are in a well-defined state with respect to each other. Cache coherency identifies the most up-to-date copy of a resource, also called the *master copy.* In case of node failure, no vital information is lost (such as a committed transaction state) and atomicity is maintained. This requires additional logging or copying of data but is not part of the locking system.

Cache coherency is the mechanism by which multiple copies of an object are kept consistent between Oracle instances. Parallel Cache Management (PCM) ensures that a master copy of a data block is stored in one buffer cache and consistent copies of the block are stored in other buffer caches. The background process LCKx is responsible for this important task. This process dialogues with LMD0 to synchronize access to resources.

The lock and resource structures for instance locks reside in the GRD (also called the Distributed Lock Manager, or DLM), a dedicated area within the shared pool. The GRD maintains information about the shared resources such as data blocks.

Details about the data block resources and cached versions are maintained by GCS. Additional details—such as the location of the most current version, state of the buffer, role of the data blocks (local or global), and ownership details such as most current versions—are maintained by GES.

Each instance maintains a part of the GRD in its System Global Area (SGA). The GCS and GES nominate one instance, called the *resource master,* to manage all information about a particular resource. Each instance knows which instance masters which resource. GCS maintains cache coherency by using the Cache Fusion algorithm.

GES manages all non–Cache Fusion interinstance resource operations and tracks the status of all Oracle enqueue mechanisms. The primary resources of the GES controls are dictionary cache locks, library cache locks, and standard enqueues. GES also performs deadlock detection of all deadlock-sensitive enqueues and resources.

Global Enqueue Services

GES coordinates the requests of all global enqueues (any non-buffer cache resources). This is the single point of contact for lock management in the Oracle RAC. It is also involved in deadlock detection and request timeouts. During normal operation, it manages caching and performs the cleanup operation during cluster reconfiguration.

Latches and Enqueues

The two types of local locks are latches and enqueues. Latches are instance specific and do not affect database-wide operations. Latches do not affect the global operations of clustered environments. Enqueues, however, can be both local to an instance and global to a cluster.

Latches are lightweight, low-level serialization mechanisms that protect in-memory data structures in the SGA. They do not support queuing and do not protect database objects such as tables or datafiles. They are atomic and are held for a very short time. They do not support multiple levels and are always acquired in exclusive mode. Because latches are synchronized within a node, they do not facilitate internode synchronization.

Enqueues are shared structures that serialize access to database resources. Enqueues support multiple modes and are held longer than latches. They have a database-wide scope because they protect persistent objects such as tables or library cache objects. For example, if you update a row in a block, no one from any other instance should be able to update the same row. A transaction (TX) enqueue protects the update for your operation; this enqueue is a global lock in Oracle RAC.

Enqueues are associated with a session or transaction, and Oracle can use them in any of the following modes:

- Shared or protected read
- Exclusive
- Protected write
- Concurrent read
- Concurrent write
- NULL

Depending on the operation on the resource, an enqueue lock is obtained on that resource. The following listing provides the most common locking modes for the associated operations:

```
Operation                 Lock Mode LMODE Lock Description
------------------------- --------- ----- ----------------
  Select                    NULL      1     null
  Lock For Update           SS        2     sub share
  Select for update         SS        2     sub share
  Insert/Delete/Update      SX        3     sub exclusive
```

```
Lock Row Exclusive          SX      3       sub exclusive
Create Index                S       4       share
Lock Share                  S       4       share
Lock Share Row Exclusive    SSX     5       share/sub exclusive
Alter/Drop/Truncate table   X       6       exclusive
Drop Index                  X       6       exclusive
Lock Exclusive              X       6       exclusive
Truncate table              X       6       exclusive
```

The following explains the compatibility matrix of the enqueue modes:

Compatible	NULL	SS	SX	S	SSX	X
NULL	Yes	Yes	Yes	Yes	Yes	Yes
SS	Yes	Yes	Yes	Yes	Yes	No
SX	Yes	Yes	Yes	No	No	No
S	Yes	Yes	No	Yes	No	No
SSX	Yes	Yes	No	No	No	No
X	Yes	No	No	No	No	No

Lock Modes

Enqueues are acquired in various lock modes. Table 11-1 summarizes each lock mode and provides a detailed description; this information is common to both single-instance and multi-instance databases.

NOTE
For a complete and detailed discussion on the fundamentals of locking, refer to Oracle document Oracle Database Concepts (Oracle 11g Release 2; Part Number E16508-05), Chapter 9, "Data Concurrency and Consistency," under the topic "Overview of the Oracle Database Locking Mechanisms."

Global Locks Database and Structure

Each node holds directory information for a set of resources. To locate a resource, the directory service uses a hashing function on the resource name to determine which nodes hold the directory tree information for the resource. The lock request is sent directly to the holding node. The GRD also stores information on resource locks and the converter and granter queues. When a process requests a lock that is owned by the same node, the structure is created local to the node. In this case, the directory node is the same as the master node.

The GES layer in Oracle RAC synchronizes global locks among all active instances in a cluster. Global locks are mainly of two types:

- Locks used by the GCS for buffer cache management. Those locks are called Parallel Cache Management (PCM) locks.

- Global locks, such as global enqueues, that Oracle synchronizes within a cluster to coordinate non-PCM resources. These locks are used to protect the enqueue structures (and are managed by GES). They are called *non-PCM locks*.

Mode	Summary	Description
NULL	Null mode. No lock is on the resource.	Conveys no access rights. Typically, a lock is held at this level to indicate that a process is interested in a resource, or it is used as a placeholder. Once created, NULL locks ensure the requestor always has a lock on the resource; there is no need for the DLM to create and destroy locks constantly when ongoing access is needed.
SS	Subshared mode (concurrent read). Read—there may be writers and other readers.	The associated resource can be read in an unprotected fashion; other processes can read and write the associated resource. This lock is also known as an RS (row share) table lock.
SX	Shared exclusive mode (concurrent write). Write—there may be other readers and writers.	The associated resource can be read or written to in an unprotected fashion: other processes can both read and write to the resource. This lock is also known as an RX (row exclusive) table lock.
S	Shared mode (protected read). Read—no writers are allowed.	A process cannot write to the associated resource, but multiple processes can read it. This is the traditional shared lock. Any number of users can have simultaneous read access to the resource. Shared access is appropriate for read operations.
SSX	Subshared exclusive mode (protected write). One writer only—there may be readers.	Only one process can hold a lock at this level. This allows a process to modify a resource without allowing other processes to modify the resource at the same time. Other processes can perform unprotected reads. This traditional update lock is also known as an SRX (shared row exclusive) table lock.
X	Exclusive mode. Write—no other access is allowed.	When a lock is held at this level, it grants the holding process exclusive access to the resource. Other processes cannot read or write to the resource. This is the traditional exclusive lock.

TABLE 11-1   *Lock Mode Summary*

GES tracks the status of all Oracle locks and their corresponding resources. Global locks are allotted and created during instance startup, and each instance owns or masters some set of resources or locks.

Global locks are held by background processes within instances rather than by transactions. An instance *owns* a global lock that *protects* a resource, such as a data block or data dictionary entry, when the resource enters the instance's SGA. The GES manages locking only for resources accessed by more than one instance. In the following sections we discuss non-PCM coordination (non-PCM locks) only.

GES Locks
Many non-PCM locks control access to datafiles and controlfiles and also serialize interinstance communication. They also control library caches and dictionary caches. These locks protect datafiles, not the datafile blocks inside the file. Examples of these are Data Manipulation Language (DML) enqueues (table locks), transaction enqueues, and Data Definition Language (DDL) locks or dictionary locks. The System Change Number (SCN) and the mount lock are global locks, not enqueues.

Transaction Locks or Row-Level Locks

Oracle's row-level locking is one of the most sophisticated features in the RDBMS; it is also one of the least understood topics. Row-level locks protect selected rows in a data block during a transaction. A transaction acquires a global enqueue and an exclusive lock for each individual row modified by one of the following statements: INSERT, UPDATE, DELETE, or SELECT with the FOR UPDATE clause.

These locks are stored in the block, and each lock refers to the global transaction enqueue. Because they are stored in the block level, their scope is wider at the database level. A transaction lock is acquired in exclusive mode when a transaction initiates its first change. It is held until the transaction does a COMMIT or ROLLBACK. SMON also acquires it in exclusive mode when recovering (undoing) a transaction. Transaction locks are used as a queuing mechanism for processes awaiting the release of an object locked by a transaction in progress.

Internal Implementation of Row-Level Locks

Every data block in the datafile, with the exception of the temp and rollback segments, will be created with a predefined number of transaction slots. (Undo segments have different types of transaction slots, called *transaction tables*.) These transaction slots are called *interested transaction lists (ITLs)* and are controlled by the INITRANS parameter. The default value for INITRANS is 2 for tables and 3 for index segments.

Every transaction slot occupies 24 bytes of free space in the variable part of the data block header. The maximum number of transaction slots is controlled by the MAXTRANS parameter. However, the size of the variable part of the database block header cannot exceed 50 percent of the data block size. This limits the total number of transaction slots in the data block.

ITL slots are acquired for every DML lock that affects that data block. An ITL contains the transaction ID (XID), which is the pointer to an entry in the transaction table of a rollback segment. Another transaction can always read the data from the rollback segment. If new transactions want to update the data, they must to wait until the current transaction commits or rolls back.

Any transaction that is interested in performing a DML lock on the rows belonging to that block *must* get an ITL slot before proceeding. An ITL entry consists of the XID, the undo byte address (UBA), the flags indicating the transaction status (Flag), and the lock count (Lck) showing the number of rows locked by this transaction within the block and the SCN at which the transaction is updated. The XID uniquely identifies the transaction and provides the information about the undo for that transaction. Figure 11-4 shows the relational links between the block and ITL and the transaction tables.

Transaction Table

The transaction table is the data structure within the rollback segment that holds the transaction identifiers of the transactions using that rollback segment. The number of rows in the transaction table is equal to the number of transaction slots in that rollback segment and is visible via the internal view X$KTUXE (available only when logged in as SYS).

A transaction ID (XID) is the three-part information that consists of the undo segment number, the undo segment slot number, and the wrap number in the undo segment (USN. SLOT#.WRAP#). The dynamic performance view V$TRANSACTION can be queried to get more details on that particular transaction.

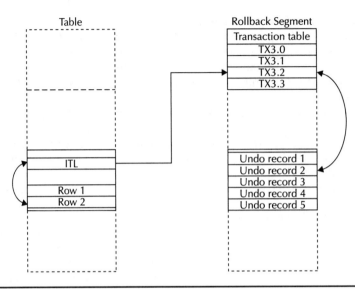

FIGURE 11-4 *Internal implementation of row-level locks*

While the transaction commits, Oracle completes the bare minimum requirements for the transaction commit operation as the system is optimized for higher throughput. This involves updating the flag in the transaction table in the rollback segment, and the block is not revisited. This process is known as *fast commit*. During this time, the ITL in the data block (called *open ITL*) is still pointing to the transaction table of the corresponding rollback segments. If the instance crashes before the transaction is committed (or rolled back), transaction recovery is performed while opening the database the next time by the data from the rollback segments.

If at the same time or a later time another transaction visits the data block, which has an open ITL, to get a consistent-read copy (CR), the transaction looks up the transaction table to find the status of the transaction. If the transaction is uncommitted, the second transaction creates a copy of the data or index block in memory, gets the UBA from the ITL, reads the data from the undo, and uses it to roll back the change defined by the undo. If the undo does not populate the ITL with an SCN, or the SCN is too old, another copy of the data block is made and the undo is read from the undo block once again to undo the next change. The UBA in the transaction table is used to roll back the entire transaction as a result of a rollback command, process failure, or shutdown immediate command.

If the status of the transaction in the table is committed, the transaction is deemed committed. Now the rows are no longer locked by the transaction, but the lock byte in the row header is not cleared until the next time DML is performed on the block. The lock byte cleanout is piggy-backed with the DML operation. The block cleanout is delayed by some discrete time interval because of the fast commit—this is called *delayed block cleanout*. This cleanout operation closes the open ITLs for the committed transactions and generates the redo information, because a block cleanout may involve updating the block with a new SCN. This is why you see the redo generation for some select statements.

Table Locks

Table locks (TM) are DML locks that protect entire tables. A transaction acquires a table lock when a table is modified by one of the following statements: INSERT, UPDATE, DELETE, SELECT with the FOR UPDATE clause, or LOCK TABLE. A table lock can be held in any of several modes: null (N), row share (RS), row exclusive (RX), share lock (S), share row exclusive (SRX), or exclusive (X).

Messaging in Oracle RAC

The synchronization effort to achieve parallel processing among nodes ideally uses a high-speed interconnect linking the parallel processors. For parallel processing within a single node, messaging is not necessary; shared memory is used instead. The DLM handles messaging and locking between nodes. Interrupts are used when more than one process wants to use the processor in a uniprocessor architecture. Shared memory and semaphores are used when more than one process wants to communicate in a symmetric multiprocessing (SMP) system.

In Oracle RAC, GES uses messaging for interinstance communication. The implementation of interprocess/internode communication is done by messages and asynchronous traps (ASTs). Messaging is used for both intra-instance communication (between the processes of the same instance on the same node) and interinstance communication (between processes on other nodes).

The LMON process of an instance communicates with the other LMON processes on other servers and uses the same messaging framework. Similarly, the LMD process from one instance communicates with other LMD processes using messages. Any process's lock client performs direct sends. Although the GRD has been a part of the RDBMS kernel, processes requiring the lock handle on the resource do not directly access the resource directory. This is done by a background message from the requesting instance's LMD to the master instance. Once the message is received, the lock handle in the GRD is updated with the new information. The returning message confirms the acknowledgment of the grant for a set of operations on that resource and management of those resources. This helps in deadlock detection and avoidance. The messaging traffic information can be obtained from the fixed view V$GES_MISC.

Three-Way Lock Messages

Messaging is used by GES for interinstance and interprocess communication. Interinstance messaging is used between the LMON process from one instance and the LMON process of another instance. Intra-instance or interprocess communication is used when LMON wants to communicate with the LMD process.

In interinstance messaging, a maximum of three parties is involved. Let's look at typical three-way communication. The three-way lock message involves up to a maximum of three nodes—namely, the master (M) instance, holding (H) instance, and requesting (R) instance. The sequence of messages is shown in Figure 11-5, where requesting instance R is interested in block B1 from holding instance H. The resource is mastered in master instance M.

1. Instance R gets the ownership information about a resource from the GRD, which maintains details such as lock ownership and current state. Instance R then sends the message to master instance M, requesting access to the resource. This message is sent by a direct send because it is critical.

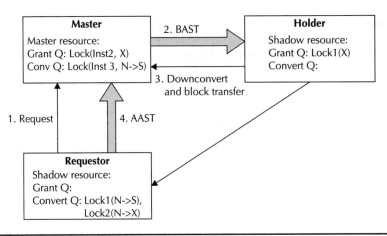

FIGURE 11-5   *Three-way lock messages*

2. Instance M receives the message and forwards that request to holding instance H. This message is also sent by a direct send message. This message to the holder is known as a *blocking asynchronous trap (BAST)*, which is discussed in the next section.

3. Instance H sends the resource to instance R. It uses high-speed interconnect to transfer the resource. The resource is copied to the requesting instance's memory.

4. Upon receipt of the resource and lock handle on that resource, instance R sends an acknowledgment to instance M. This message is queued for propagation; it is not a critical message. This is called *acquisition asynchronous trap (AAST)* and is discussed in the next section.

Asynchronous Traps

When a process requests a lock on a resource, the GES sends a blocking AST (BAST) to notify the holder, another process that currently owns locks on that resource in incompatible modes. When the holder receives the BAST from the requestor, owners of locks can relinquish them to permit access by the requester. When a lock is obtained, an acquisition AST (AAST) is sent to tell the requester that it now owns the lock. ASTs are delivered by LMD or LMS to the process that has submitted a lock request. This is done by sending all messages to the LMD on the remote node, which then forwards the messages to the actual waiting process in earlier versions.

TX Enqueue Affinity Optimization

Starting with Oracle 11*g*, an instance that starts the transaction will become the master of the TX enqueue for it by mastering those resources. This optimization is introduced to reduce the TX enqueue waits on the node running active transactions. This resource mastership optimization is an exception to the hashing-based resource mastership. The optimization currently works with 16 nodes, and when there are more than 16 nodes, the optimization is turned off. However, you can enable this by increasing _lm_tx_delta to the higher value to suit the total of instances. There are no known issues on increasing that value.

Messaging Deadlocks

Deadlocks can occur if one process (A) is waiting to send a BAST to another process to acquire a lock, and another process (B) is waiting on the lock that the waiting process holds. In this condition, the first process (A) will not be checking on BASTs, so it will not see that it is blocking another process. Because too many writers are trying to send messages (known as *BAST-only messages)* and no one is reading messages to free up buffer space, a deadlock occurs.

Message Traffic Controller (TRFC)

GES totally depends on messages for resource management. These messages are typically small in size (128 bytes) and interconnect plays a great role if the number of messages is high, depending on the number of resources. The interconnect is also expected to be lightweight or low latency so that it can reduce deadlocks. To streamline the messaging traffic and to avoid deadlocks, the message traffic controller introduces the ticketing mechanism for a smooth flow of messages.

Normally, messages are sent with the message sequence number along with tickets that control the message flow. This way, the receiver ensures that all the messages are received from the sender. The TRFC is used to control the DLM traffic between all the nodes in the cluster by buffering sender sends (in case of network congestion) and making the sender wait until the network window is large enough to accommodate the traffic.

The traffic controller will keep a predefined number of tickets in the reserve pool. The size of the ticket pool is dependent on the function of the network send buffer size. Any process that sends messages should acquire a ticket before sending and return the ticket to the pool once the message is sent. Used tickets are released back to the pool by the receivers (LMS or LMD), according to the remote receiver report of how many messages the remote receiver has received. This is similar to the transaction slot entry in the data blocks, where any DML lock should get the ITL slot before modifying the block. If no tickets are available, the messages are buffered at the sender side and sent when a ticket is available. The number of tickets can be manually controlled by the hidden parameter _lm_tickets, for which no tweaking is required unless a big send queue is affecting system performance.

The ticket availability and send queue details can be obtained from V$GES_TRAFFIC_ CONTROLLER. A node relies on messages to return from the remote node to release tickets for reuse. This ticketing mechanism allows for a smooth flow of messages.

The following query provides a snapshot of ticket usage details:

```
SQL> SELECT LOCAL_NID LOCAL ,REMOTE_NID REMOTE,TCKT_AVAIL AVAILABILITY,
  2  TCKT_LIMIT LIMIT,SND_Q_LEN SEND_QUEUE,TCKT_WAIT WAITING
  3  FROM V$GES_TRAFFIC_CONTROLLER;
```

LOCAL	REMOTE	AVAILABILITY	LIMIT	SEND_QUEUE	WAITING
0	1	750	1000	0	NO
0	1	750	1000	0	NO
0	1	750	1000	0	NO

Another mechanism is implemented to help avoid running out of tickets. If the number of available tickets goes below 50, the active send backing is enabled for aggressive messaging. This helps the traffic controller maintain speed. The number of tickets that triggers active send back is configurable via the _lm_ticket_active_sendback parameter. This query can be run to monitor ticket usage and availability. Pay particular attention to the TCKT_WAIT column, which shows YES when messages are waiting for tickets. If it is waiting for tickets, you need to check the TCKT_ LIMIT and TCKT_AVAIL columns, which show the ticket limit and ticket availability at that time, respectively.

In extreme situations, the preceding query may hang, because to get information about ticket availability, tickets are required. Under those conditions, the sessions will be waiting for the "KJCTS: client waiting for tickets" wait event. Alternatively, using the lkdebug -t option to oradebug can also dump the ticket information to the trace files:

```
oradebug setmypid
oradebug unlimt
oradebug lkdebug -t
```

Global Cache Services

GCS also uses locks to coordinate shared data access by multiple instances. These are different from the enqueue locks used by GES. These GCS locks protect only data blocks in the global cache (previously known as *parallel cache,* and the locks were known as *PCM locks).*

A GCS lock can be acquired in shared mode or in exclusive mode. Each lock element can have the lock role set to either local or global. If the lock role is local, the block can be handled as it is usually handled in a single instance. Local mode reads the block from the disk if it is not seen in the buffer cache and can write the block to disk when it holds the lock mode X.

In a global role, three lock modes are possible—shared, exclusive, and null. The instance can modify the block only with the exclusive (X) mode. When the lock role is global, the instance cannot read the block from the disk as it does in the single-instance mode. It has to go through the master and can write to or read from the disk only when directed by the master. Otherwise, it has to wait for the buffer from the other instance.

GCS maintains the lock and state information in the SGA. It is stored in an internal data structure called *lock elements*. It also holds a chain of cache buffer chains that are covered by the corresponding lock element. The lock elements are exposed as fixed table view V$LOCK_ ELEMENT, which shows the lock element, the buffer class, and the state of the buffer.

Lock Modes and Lock Roles

A lock mode describes the access rights to a resource. The compatibility matrix is clusterwide. For example, if a resource has an S lock on one instance, an X lock for that resource cannot exist anywhere else in the cluster. A lock role describes how the resource is to be handled. The treatment differs if the block resides in only one cache.

Cache Fusion changes the use of PCM locks in the Oracle server and relates the locks to the shipping of blocks through the system via IPC. The objectives are to separate the modes of locks from the roles that are assigned to the lock holders, and to maintain knowledge about the versions of past images of blocks throughout the system.

Global Lock Modes

GCS locks use the following modes: exclusive (X), shared (S), and null (N). An instance can acquire a global lock that covers a set of data blocks in either shared or exclusive mode, depending on the access type required.

Exclusive (X) lock mode is used during UPDATE or any of the DML operations. DML operations require that the blocks be in exclusive mode. If one instance needs to update a data block that is owned by another instance in an incompatible mode, the first instance asks GES to request that the second instance disown the global lock.

Shared (S) lock mode allows the instance to read (SELECT) blocks. Multiple instances can own a global lock in shared mode as long as they are reading the data. All instances can read the block without any change in the lock state of the other instance. This means instances do not have to disown global locks to allow another instance to read the data block. In other words, reading does not require any explicit locking or lock conversion, whether it is a single instance or cluster implementation of Oracle.

Null (N) lock mode allows instances to keep a lock without any permission on the block(s). This mode is used so that locks need not be continually created and destroyed. Locks are simply converted from one mode to another.

Lock Roles

Lock roles are introduced to handle the Cache Fusion functionality. A lock role can be either local or global. The lock role for a resource is local if the block is dirty only in the local cache. The role becomes global if the block is dirty in a remote cache or in several caches.

Initially, a block is acquired in a local lock role with no past images. If the block is modified locally and other instances express interest in the block, the instance holding the block keeps a past image (PI) and ships a copy of the block, and then the role becomes global.

A PI represents the state of a dirty buffer. Initially, a block is acquired in a local role, with no PIs present. The node that modifies the block keeps PIs, as the lock role becomes global, only after another instance expresses interest in this block. A PI block is used for efficient recovery across the cluster and can be used to satisfy a CR request, remote or local.

The node must keep a PI until it receives notification from the master that a write to disk has completed covering that version. The node then logs a block written record (BWR). The BWR is not necessary for the correctness of recovery, so it need not be flushed.

When a new current block arrives on a node, a previous PI is kept untouched because some other node might need it. When a block is pinged out of a node carrying a PI and the current version, it might or might not be combined into a single PI. At the time of the ping, the master tells the holder whether a write is in progress that will cover the older PI. If a write is not in progress, the existing current block replaces the older PI. If a write is in progress, this merge is not completed and the existing current block becomes another PI. An indeterminate number of PIs can exist.

Local and Global Roles

In the local role, only S and X modes are permitted. All changes are on the disk version, except for any local changes (mode X). When requested by the master instance, the holding instance serves a copy of the block to others. If the block is globally clean, this instance's lock role remains local. If the block is modified by this instance and passed on dirty, a PI is retained and the lock role becomes global. The lock mode reads from disk if the block is not in the cache and may write to the block if the lock mode is X.

The local role states that the block can be handled similarly to the way it is handled in single-instance mode. In the local role, the lock mode reads from disks and writes the dirty block back to disk when it ages out without any further DLM activity.

In the global lock role, the possible lock modes are N, S, and X. When the lock role for a block is global, that block may be dirty in any of the instances and the on-disk version may be obsolete. Therefore, interested processes can modify the block only with mode X. The instance cannot read from disk because it is not known whether the disk copy is current. The holding instance may send a copy to others when instructed by the master. The instance may write a block in X mode or the PI, and the write requests must be sent to the master.

Lock Elements

A lock element (LE) holds lock state information (converting, granted, and so on). LEs are managed by the lock processes to determine the mode of the locks. LEs also hold a chain of cache buffers that are covered by the LE and allow the Oracle database to keep track of cache buffers that must be written to disk in case an LE (mode) needs to be downgraded (X → N)

Figure 11-6 shows the LEs and hash chains.

LEs protect all the data blocks in the buffer cache. The following describes the classes of the Oracle data blocks, which are managed by the LEs using GCS locks. The class of the lock elements directly maps to X$BH.CLASS. The column state of X$BH can contain one of the following values:

- 0 or FREE
- 1 or EXLCUR
- 2 or SHRCUR
- 3 or CR
- 4 or READING

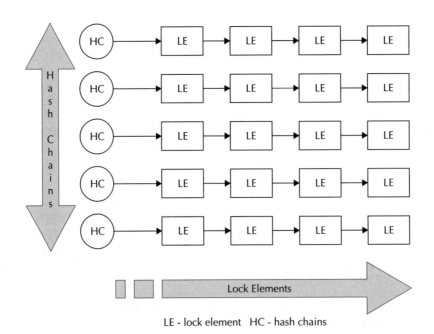

LE - lock element   HC - hash chains

Number of hash buckets = Number of hash chains = LPRIM (_db_block_buffers)

FIGURE 11-6 *Hash chains and lock elements*

- 5 or MRECOVERY
- 6 or IRECOVERY
- 7 or WRITING
- 8 or PI

GCS manages PCM locks in the GRD. PCM locks manage the data blocks in the global cache. Because the buffer cache is global, if a buffer is not found in the local cache, a block may be cached in the other instance's buffer cache. If the block is not found in any of the instances, the GCS instructs the requesting instance for a disk read. The GCS monitors and maintains the list and mode of the blocks in all the instances. Based on the request and availability, the GCS asks the holding instance to ship the block to the requesting instance, or instructs the requesting instance to read the block from the disk. All types of blocks are copied between instances in a coherent manner, and requests can be for write or read.

The database blocks from the shared database can be cached in the buffer cache of any instance that is used by the application. A local cache miss will consult the GCS to determine whether a requested block is cached by another instance. If the block is in cache, the GCS will inform the instance which node holds a lock on the block (the potential holder) of the request. If that node still has the block in its cache, it will send a copy of the block to the requestor. If the block is not in the node's cache, the GCS will grant an access right to the requestor and the block will be read from disk into the requestor's cache. The frequency and distribution of these events depends on the application.

Each database block has a master instance, where the complete lock state of the block is known. Each instance will be a master for some data blocks. Resource instances and master instances have a one-to-one relation. One resource cannot be mastered in more than one instance, but one instance can master more than one resource.

Although more than one instance may use the same set of resources in the Oracle RAC, only one instance is allowed to modify a block. GCS ensures cache coherency by requiring that instances acquire a lock before modifying or reading a database block. GCS locks are *not* to be confused with the row-level locks in single-instance environments. Row-level locks are still used in conjunction with PCM locks.

Row-level locks are independent of GCS locks. GCS locks ensure the block is used by only one instance, and row-level locks manage blocks at the row level. GCS ensures that the current mode buffer is exclusive for one instance and pre-images are allowed for other instances in shared mode.

If another instance needs to read a block, the current version of the block may reside in many buffer caches under shared locks. Thus, the most recent copy of the block in all SGAs contains all changes made to that block by all instances, regardless of whether any transactions on those instances have been committed.

At the same time, if a data block is updated in one buffer cache, the cached copies in other buffer caches are no longer current. New copies can be obtained after the modification operation completes. This is called *CR block fabrication*. Normally CR building occurs when a request is made for a block in that mode for a query. In simple terms, if a query wants a copy of a modified block, a CR copy is built. The process is quite simple and straightforward in a single-instance environment because the process can find all the required information in the local cache. In Oracle RAC, additional processing and messaging take place to have the buffer cache synchronization occur across all the nodes.

In CR building, the master of a block may be the local instance where the request is made, the instance where the block is cached, or any other instance. In clusters with only two nodes, blocks cached in another instance can be accessed after two hops, because the master is on the requesting mode or the caching node. In clusters with more than two nodes, a block access may require at most three hops but may complete in two hops if the master is the local node or the caching node. If the block is not cached anywhere, the request will complete after two hops.

> **NOTE**
> *Block access between instances is done on a per-block basis. When an instance locks a block in exclusive mode, other instances cannot access the block in the same mode. Every time Oracle tries to read a block from the database, it must obtain a global lock. Ownership of the lock is thus assigned to the instance. Block lock is also known as BL type enqueues.*

Consistent Read Processing

Readers do not block writers, and SELECT does not require any lock in the Oracle RDBMS. This means readers never block writers. The consistent read (CR) mechanism in the RDBMS kernel enables read consistency across the instances. Read consistency ensures that the behavior of data returned by a query or transaction is consistent with respect to the start of the query to the end of the query or transaction. At the same time, the transaction sees its own committed and uncommitted changes. Read consistency is guaranteed with the help of undo segments. The consistent read version of blocks is called *CR blocks,* and its processing is called *CR processing.*

During the start of the query or transaction, the Snap SCN (SCN of the block during that particular point in time) along with the UBA is obtained. During the transaction, any time the other interested session is looking for the CR buffer, the block version at a particular point in time is obtained from the undo segments. The interested process clones the buffer and scans the undo chain to construct the CR copy of the buffer at a particular point in time. Sometimes the process has to loop to take the buffer back to the required point in time. The information to go back to a previous point in time is available from the undo segments. The CR building process is the same for single-instance and Oracle RAC.

During CR processing, one ITL is scanned during every pass and the undo records are applied to the cloned buffer. Sometimes applying undo information may involve block cleanout. Once the block is cleaned or no open ITLs are listed, or when the SNAP SCN is less than or equal to the query SCN, the block is deemed valid and that buffer is returned as a CR buffer. But a few regulations are implemented to make the CR building efficient in both single-instance and Oracle RAC. A buffer cannot be cloned an infinite number of times, because a built-in mechanism limits the number of CR copies per DBA. This controls the CR versions of a hot object filling the buffer cache. The hidden parameter _db_block_max_cr_dba limits the number of CR copies per DBA on the buffer cache.

In a multi-instance environment, when a buffer is transferred to another instance during Cache Fusion transfer, the past image buffer is kept in the home instance. Undo records can also be applied on top of this PI buffer during CR processing. CR processing does not generate any redo information.

This process becomes a little complex when the block is held in the other instance's cache. When the requestor wants a CR copy, it sends a message to the holder of the block. On receipt of the CR request, the holder walks through the undo block(s), constructs the CR copy, and ships the block to the requesting instance. Figure 11-7 shows the steps in the CR fabrication process.

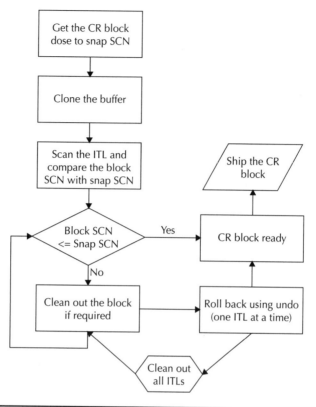

FIGURE 11-7 *CR block fabrication process*

Sometimes creating a CR block to the Snap SCN may involve too much work for the holder, going back too far in time or reading the blocks from disk; in that case, the holder may not construct the CR block because it will be too expensive. After all, the holder does a "favor" for the requestor by constructing the CR block and sending it. In this case, the holder just ships the block to the requesting instance and CR fabrication is done at the requestor's instance.

Holder construction of CR copies to the requesting instances sometimes impacts the equilibrium of the instances, if one instance is always used for queries. In this case, the reading instance always has the privilege of getting all the required blocks to its cache, because CR fabrication is done by another instance. Because CR fabrication can be expensive when the fabricator has to scan through the chain of undo blocks and read the blocks from disks, a couple of optimization techniques are used to avoid CR request thrashing. One such technique is the *lightwork rule,* which prevents the LMS processes going to disk while responding to CR requests for data, undo, or undo segment header blocks. This rule can prevent the LMS process from completing its response to the CR request.

Lightwork Rule and Fairness Threshold
When too many CR requests arrive for a particular buffer, the holder can disown the lock on the buffer and write the block to the disk. Then the requestor can read the block from the disk after

acquiring the required lock on the object. The process of disowning the block is technically known as *fairness downconvert*. The number of consecutive requests after the holder converts the lock elements is configurable via the _fairness_threshold parameter. This parameter defaults to 4, which is usually enough for most instances. However, it requires a special setting when one instance in the cluster is always used for queries.

The lightwork rule is invoked when CR construction involves too much work and no current block or PI block is available in the cache for block cleanouts. Any additional disk I/O to serve the CR block will kick the lightwork rule. The lightwork statistics are recorded in X$KCLCRST.LIGHT1, whereas X$KCLCRST.LIGHT2 is incremented when the buffer is in instance recovery mode.

The number of times the instance performs a fairness downconversion and the lightwork rule is invoked is shown in the V$CR_BLOCK_SERVER view. The V$CR_BLOCK_SERVER view also lists details about the CR request processing and the distribution of block requests:

```
V$CR_BLOCK_SERVER
Name                            Type        Notes
------------------------------  ---------   ------------------------
CR_REQUESTS                     NUMBER      CR+CUR =Total Requests
CURRENT_REQUESTS                NUMBER
DATA_REQUESTS                   NUMBER
UNDO_REQUESTS                   NUMBER
TX_REQUESTS                     NUMBER      DATA+UNDO+TX= CR+CUR
CURRENT_RESULTS                 NUMBER
PRIVATE_RESULTS                 NUMBER
ZERO_RESULTS                    NUMBER
DISK_READ_RESULTS               NUMBER
FAIL_RESULTS                    NUMBER
FAIRNESS_DOWN_CONVERTS          NUMBER      # of downconverts from X
FAIRNESS_CLEARS                 NUMBER      # of time Fairness counter cleared
FREE_GC_ELEMENTS                NUMBER
FLUSHES                         NUMBER      Log Flushes
FLUSHES_QUEUED                  NUMBER
FLUSH_QUEUE_FULL                NUMBER
FLUSH_MAX_TIME                  NUMBER
LIGHT_WORKS                     NUMBER      # of times light work rule evoked
ERRORS                          NUMBER
```

The number of times a downconvert occurs and the lightwork rule is invoked from the instance startup can be obtained using the following query:

```
SQL> SELECT CR_REQUESTS, LIGHT_WORKS ,DATA_REQUESTS, FAIRNESS_DOWN_CONVERTS
  2 FROM
  3 V$CR_BLOCK_SERVER;

CR_REQUESTS LIGHT_WORKS DATA_REQUESTS FAIRNESS_DOWN_CONVERTS
----------- ----------- ------------- ----------------------
      80919        5978         80918                  17029
```

When the data request to downconvert ratio is more than 40 percent, lowering the _fairness_ threshold value may improve the performance and greatly reduce the interconnect traffic for the

CR messages. This parameter can be set to 0 when the systems are used for query purposes only. Setting _fairness_threshold to 0 disables the fairness downconverts. This parameter can be altered only with the consent of Oracle Support.

Lost Block Optimization

Global Cache Services detects lost blocks using side channel messages. Lost blocks and retransmits for the lost blocks may increase the load significantly, especially when the system is loaded fully and the lost blocks are part of a multiblock request. The side channel batch timeout is handled by the new parameter _side_channel_batch_timeout_ms, which defaults to 500 ms in Oracle 11g. In previous versions this was controlled by the parameter _side_channel_batch_ timeout with a 6-second default value.

In Oracle 11g, lost blocks handling has been improved to eliminate false lost blocks resulting from scheduling delays. Also, side channel batching has been improved to accommodate the increase in logical side channel messages. A new algorithm has been added to favor disk reads over CR serving once a block has been lost. This will quickly reduce the network congestion from lost block retries. The scheme is gradually switched back to CR serving based on load, I/O rate, and CR receive time.

GCS Resource Mastering

GRD is like a central repository for locks and resources. It is distributed in all the nodes, and no single node has information about all the resources. Only one node maintains complete information about one resource, and that node is called the *master node* for that resource. Other nodes need to maintain information only about locally held locks on that resource. The process of maintaining information about the resources is called *lock mastering* or *resource mastering*.

GCS resources and locks share one-to-many relationships in the GRD. There is one "resource" initiated for every data block address (DBA) present in the global cache, and more than one lock can be allocated for that resource. Each instance that has a copy of the block in its cache may hold a lock on that resource.

In other words, the GCS lock structure is physically located on each node of the cluster interested in that data block. The resource lock is allocated only in the master node. The master node is responsible for synchronizing access on that resource to the other nodes, and the master node for the resource is known as the *resource master*.

Resource Weight

The "weight" of an instance can be defined as the number of resources it is "willing to master." By default, this weight is the number of resources an instance can accommodate in its SGA with respect to the other instances. It is computed during startup and broadcast to the member nodes as well as published in the LMON trace files. This discussion is purely for academic purposes because Oracle RAC handles the resource allocations automatically and seamlessly. The following is an extract from LMON trace showing the publication of the resource weight.

```
Name Service frozen
kjxgmcs: Setting state to 0 1.
kjxgrdecidever: No old version members in the cluster
kjxgrssvote: reconfig bitmap chksum 0x6694d07e cnt 1 master 1 ret 0
kjfcpiora: published my fusion master weight 39280
kjfcpiora: published my enqueue weight 64
```

```
kjfcpiora: publish my flogb 3
kjfcpiora: published my cluster_database parameter=0
kjfcpiora: publish my icp 1
```

The following formula is used to calculate the GCS resources. A minimum of 2,500 resources are allocated in the shared pool if the calculated resources are less than 2,500:

```
nres = (pcmlocks + pcmlocks/10);
        if (nres <= 2500)
           nres = 2500;
```

You can query gv$resource_limit to find out the details about the GCS resources:

```
SQL> SELECT RESOURCE_NAME,LIMIT_VALUE
     FROM GV$RESOURCE_LIMIT
     WHERE RESOURCE_NAME='gcs_resources';
```

The default relative weight can be described by the following function; the value of the relative weight is between 0 and 1:

```
                           SizeInBlocksOfCache(Local)
Relative Weight (i) =   ----------------------------
                          ∑  SizeInBlocksOfCache(Global)
```

If the initialization parameters for SGA are the same across all the instances, all the instances will have the same relative weight. When the relative weight is the same, the resources in the GCS layer are evenly mastered. If the buffer cache and shared pool settings are different from one another, the relative weight will be different and the number of resources they master will also be different.

Resource Master

The rule used to assign the mastership is a composite HASH*MAP integer function that associates the data block address (DBA) with instance numbers. Under normal conditions, each active instance of the cluster will receive the mastership of a number of resources proportional to the weight it has, as shown here:

```
Instance = MAP(HASH(M,RESOURCE)) = n
```

In this case, M is a number that is a multiple of N, and N is the maximum number of instances, as specified by cluster_database_instances. MAP is a discrete function specified by an array.

The construction of MAP(.) is done by taking into account the relative weight of each instance.

Modifying the Mastership Distribution

Normally, the number of resource "slots" preallocated is proportional to the number of cache buffers defined for the local cache. This simple rule guarantees that globally there will be enough resource slots preallocated to accommodate all the possible resources that will protect the DBAs present in the global cache during the activity. Actually, the total number of resources is 10 percent greater than the total number of buffers defined in the global cache. When modifying the default distribution, we will need to take into account this aspect to avoid excessive recourse to free lists in the shared pool.

It is possible to force the number of resource slots a node publishes and hence remodulate the WEIGHT function using the parameter _gcs_resources, which otherwise defaults to the number of local buffers in the cache. Setting _gcs_resources to 0 totally disables resource mastering for that particular node.

Read-Mostly Locking

Starting with Oracle 11g, a new and improved locking mechanism was introduced to optimize the performance of the applications with very little read-write contention. Most of the lock requests on an object (or partition) known for reads can be handled better at the GCS layer by pregranting read access to all the blocks. This will greatly reduce the locking overhead associated with shared read access. This also reduces the messaging and CPU costs associated with block grants. However, current block (write) access on these objects mastered by this protocol would come up slightly additional cost than the standard cache fusion transfers. This new optimization is called *read-mostly locking*.

Internals of Read-Mostly Locking

The Global Cache Layer maintains the object-level statistics for Shared and Exclusive lock requests and invokes the read-mostly policy for the objects for the standard Dynamic Resource Mastering protocol. Theoretically an object can transform into a read-mostly object in as short as 10 minutes based on the access, and it can be taken out of read-mostly status within the next 10 minutes if the access pattern changes. If the object is a standard read-only object, it is always better to place it into the read-only tablespace. Placing the object in the regular read-only tablespace totally eliminates the GCS locking overhead and yields better performance than read-mostly locking.

When an object becomes read-mostly, any instance can just go ahead and read the blocks belonging to that object without waiting for grants from the master because the shared (S-affinity) access on that object is pregranted to all the nodes. This reduces the lock requests, grant messages, and block transfers on that object. The read-mostly status of the object is dissolved when there is a write request on the object, and this is done through the newly introduced lock element called *anti-lock*.

When a write request is requested on the read-mostly object, GCS broadcasts a message to all instances asking them to open an anti-lock on the object. When an anti-lock is present on an object, all access to that block will be controlled through the standard Cache Fusion protocol, even if the object is read-mostly. Anti-locks are dissolved when the object is taken out of read-mostly status.

Keep in mind that when the object is read-mostly, you will see an increase in disk I/O because the blocks on that object are *always* read from disk although they are cached in another instance's buffer cache. Therefore, if your system is I/O bound, read-mostly locking will complicate the situation, so it is recommended that you turn off the read-mostly feature. You can disable the read-mostly feature by setting the parameter _gc_read_mostly_locking to FALSE.

Resource Affinity and Dynamic Resource Remastering

Global Resource Directory includes a feature called *resource affinity,* which allows for the resource mastering of the frequently used resources on its local node. It uses dynamic resource remastering to move the location of the resource masters. This technique optimizes the system for situations in which certain transactions are always being executed on one instance. This happens in an application-partitioning environment or an activity-based, load-balancing environment. When activity shifts to another instance, the resource affinity will correspondingly move to the new instance. If activity is not localized, the resource ownership is distributed to the instances equitably.

Dynamic resource remastering is the ability to move the ownership of a resource between instances of Oracle RAC during runtime without affecting availability. When one resource or set of resources is frequently accessed by one node more than the other nodes, it would be better to have that resource mastered by the frequently requesting instance. In normal conditions, a resource can be mastered only during instance reconfiguration. This happens when an instance joins or leaves the cluster. Other than a node joining or leaving the cluster, the ownership is remastered from one node to another node (outside the reconfiguration jurisdiction) based on the frequency of the usage. This kind of online resource mastership change is called *dynamic remastering*.

Few applications do the application partitioning, and a set of requests is always directed to one particular node. This happens when application partitioning is implemented or where some third-party load balancers are employed to route the connections based on the user or application type.

In these situations, one node may always be requesting a particular subset of resources. During these situations it will be beneficial to have those resources mastered at the same instance. This greatly reduces interconnect messaging traffic as the resources are mastered by the requesting instance. The resource can be of an object or file based on the version of Oracle being used. Currently remastering occurs at the object level, which helps fine-grained object remastering. For example, table partitions will have a different object ID and can be remastered to different instances. Figure 11-8 shows dynamic remastering.

Dynamic Resource Mastering Policy

Note that remastering is done only under very stringent conditions. The resources and their access patterns are evaluated in a predefined time interval. Moreover, only resources that are heavily

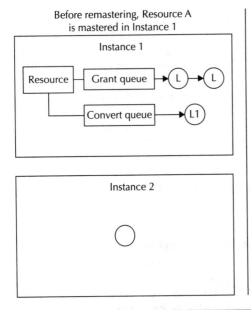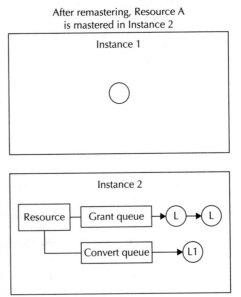

FIGURE 11-8 *Dynamic remastering*

accessed are considered candidates for resource mastering. Once the resources are identified as hot resources or frequently used resources, they are eligible for remastering evaluation. The following parameters influence the DRM protocol.

- **_gc_policy_time**

  This parameter controls the DRM window for candidate selections. On every window of _gc_policy_time, the object-level statistics are sampled to select the candidates for remastering. The access patterns are analyzed at this interval and objects are moved to the DRM queue. The decisions to establish or dissolve read-mostly locking are also evaluated at this interval. This parameter defaults to 10 minutes, and this is usually good for most of the systems. However, if you notice the DRM happening too frequently, consider increasing this to a higher value. Setting this parameter to 0 disables the object affinity and read-mostly policy enablement, which essentially disables the remastering in practical terms.

- **_gc_affinity_ratio**

  This parameter works as a filter condition during object selection. To get into the selection queue, a node must access the object more than the number of times specified by this parameter. This parameter defaults to 50, which essentially defines that a node should access an object 50 times more than the other node to master the interested resource. This essentially simulates the application partitioning at the resource directory.

- **_gc_policy_minimum**

  This parameter works in conjunction with _gc_affinity_ratio during object selection. It defines the minimum number of global cache operations per minute to qualify for affinity or read-mostly selection. It defaults to 1500 global cache operations (open, convert, and close) per minute, essentially helping to pick the hot objects in the GRD. Depending on the access distribution of objects in the GRD, you may want to increase or decrease the number. Increasing this to a higher number reduces the number of objects evaluated for DRM. In Oracle 10*g* this was controlled by _gc_affinity_minimum.

- **_gc_read_mostly_locking**

  This parameter defaults to TRUE, which means the read-mostly policy evaluation is to be considered during the DRM window. Any changes to this parameter should be carefully benchmarked.

- **_gc_transfer_ratio**

  This parameter works in conjunction with _gc_read_mostly_locking. An object can be considered read-mostly when the number of block transfer is less than 50 percent of the number of disk reads. This parameter defaults to 2 (which is 50 percent), and changing this to a lower value usually reduces the likelihood of an object becoming read-mostly.

- **_lm_drm_max_requests**

  At the DRM policy evaluation interval, if the objects selected for affinity or read-mostly are less than 100, they are processed in a single batch. If more than 100 objects are queued for evaluation, they are handled in batches and this parameter limits the number of objects per batch. This parameter defaults to 100, and there is no need to change it unless recommended by Oracle Support.

Object Affinity Statistics

GRD maintains the object-level statistics in the SGA, and you can query the X$OBJECT_POLICY_
STATISTICS. You can query them anytime to find out the global cache operations on a particular
object. The statistics are maintained by the LCK0 and used for read-mostly and object affinity
evaluation. The same information is available in X$OBJECT_AFFINITY_STATISTICS in Oracle 10g.
However, in Oracle 10g this information is a cumulative average from the instance startup.

In Oracle 11g this information is refreshed in every policy interval, which is 10 minutes. So
when you query the X$OBJECT_POLICY_STATISTICS, the value you see is the object affinity
statistics from the last policy evaluation, which is less than or equal to 10 minutes. The v$view
V$GCSPFMASTER_INFO can be queried to list the objects under the DRM protocol (affinity and
read-mostly). The following shows the interesting columns for DRM analysis:

```
Name                                    Null?    Type
--------------------------------------  -------- ------------------------
INST_ID                                          NUMBER
FILE_ID                                          NUMBER
DATA_OBJECT_ID                                   NUMBER
GC_MASTERING_POLICY                              VARCHAR2(11)
CURRENT_MASTER                                   NUMBER
PREVIOUS_MASTER                                  NUMBER
REMASTER_CNT                                     NUMBER
```

DATA_OBJECT_ID can be joined with DBA_OBJECTS.DATA_OBJECT_ID to get the object_name.
When _gc_undo_affinity and _gc_undo_affinity_locks are set to TRUE (the default), undo segments
are also listed in this view. Undo segments will have an object ID value of 4294950912+USN. For
example, undo segment 8 will have the object ID 4294950920 in the DATA_OBJECT_ID.

The GC_MASTERING_POLICY will have the type of mastering policy (affinity or read-mostly).
CURRENT_MASTER and PREVIOUS_MASTER list the current and previous masters of that object,
respectively. When the value of CURRENT_MASTER is 32767, the object has dissolved its affinity
or read-mostly during the latest policy evaluation. A value of 32767 for PREVIOUS_MASTER
means the object has never been in the object affinity table in the evaluation period.

REMASTER_CNT lists the number of times the object was remastered. Please take this statistic
with a grain of salt because it was not working as documented in earlier versions. However in
11g, a little care should be taken while interpreting the remaster count because the count is reset
to 0 when the affinity is dissolved and the value lists the number of times it was remastered from
the previous affinity dissolution. This view does not keep the record of dissolved objects, and the
statistics are reset when they are removed from the affinity table.

Dynamic resource remastering requires the acquisition of the RM (remastering) enqueue at
the exclusive level. The RM enqueue is a single-threaded enqueue, and only one enqueue exists
per database. So at any point in time, only one node can be performing the remastering
operation, and the other node has to wait for the current node to complete the operation. Once
the node acquires the RM enqueue, it broadcasts the message to all other nodes and starts the
remastering of resources selected based on the candidate selection algorithm. If too many
resources are queued for remastering, the remastering occurs in batches. Up to 100 resources are
selected for remastering after acquisition of the RM enqueue. The LMD processes from all the
instances request the corresponding LMON process on the respective instances to remaster the
resource, and the GRD is updated to reflect the current resource ownership.

Figure 11-9 explains the remastering process.

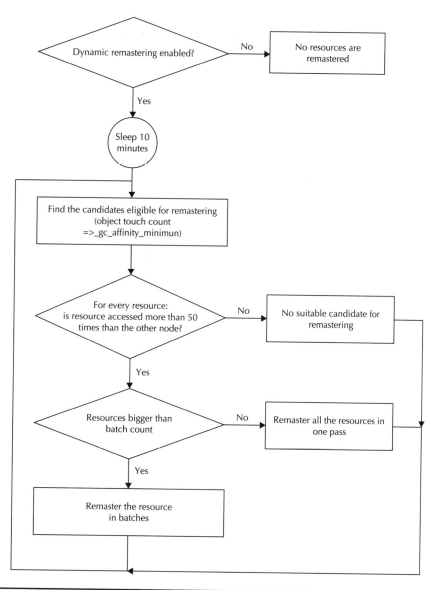

FIGURE 11-9 *Flowchart of dynamic remastering*

Disabling Dynamic Remastering

Resources are initially mastered to instances based on the simple hashing algorithm. But resource remastering is quite expensive in terms of the messages and resource ownership transfers to the other instances in a busy environment. For benchmarks or an application-partitioned environment that does not require dynamic remastering, you can disable it using the hidden parameter _lm_dynamic_remastering. Setting the hidden parameter _lm_file_affinity disables dynamic remastering for the objects belonging to those files. Setting _gc_policy_time to 0 also disables dynamic remastering.

In a Nutshell

Congratulations! You have just completed learning about the foundations of resource management in Oracle Real Applications Clusters. Global Resource Directory consists of Global Enqueue Services and Global Cache Services, and it is the central reference in resource management in Oracle Real Applications Clusters.

Messaging plays an important role in the lock management and conversion operations. Resources are queued in grant and convert queues, and the traffic controllers avoid message traffic deadlocks with the ticketing mechanism. This chapter also looked at Oracle's implementation of row-level locks and its CR block fabrication process.

Affinity and read-mostly mechanisms in Dynamic Resource Mastering help GCS to master the resources close to the operation. We have explored the algorithms as well as the inner workings and references of Dynamic Resource Mastering. Next, we will take a closer look at Cache Fusion, which is the foundation for high performance in Oracle RAC systems.

CHAPTER
12

A Closer Look
at Cache Fusion

scalable high-performance system should spend the least amount of time in message transits and should use the most efficient communication methods for I/O processing. Cache Fusion makes this possible. In this chapter we look under the hood of Cache Fusion to understand the internal operations of various kinds of block transfers that occur between instances. Understanding the internal operations of the block transfers will help you appreciate the intelligence built into this component of Real Application Clusters and help in designing scalable database applications.

We also take a look at how and why Oracle moves data blocks from one instance to another instance in an Oracle RAC environment. We also explain concepts closely associated with the Cache Fusion technology and wherever possible provide relevant database instance statistics.

Oracle RAC appears to merge the database buffer cache of multiple instances so that the end user sees only a single large buffer cache. In reality, the buffer caches of each node remain separate; copies of data blocks are shared through distributed locking and messaging operations. A data block present in an instance's buffer cache can be copied to another instance's buffer cache over the high-speed interconnect, thereby eliminating a reread from disk by other instance(s). Figure 12-1 depicts the notion of a single large buffer cache spread across all the database instances among the nodes of a cluster.

Starting with version 8.1.5, Oracle introduced the framework of sharing data using the private interconnects between the nodes, which was used only for messaging purposes in previous versions. This protocol is known as Cache Fusion Protocol. Data blocks are shipped throughout the network similar to messages, thus reducing the most expensive component of data transfer— disk I/O—to data sharing.

Using the private interconnect greatly increases performance and scalability while preserving availability benefits of the classic implementation of a shared disk architecture in which the disk is the medium of data sharing. Simply put, while the basic data sharing and coherency mechanisms remain largely the same (distributed locks and messaging), copies of data blocks can now be passed from one node to another with one high-speed network hop instead of the two relatively slow hops required for a disk ping.

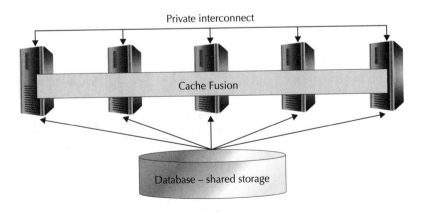

FIGURE 12-1 *Cache Fusion creates merged buffer caches of participating instances.*

The Cache Fusion technology has evolved and has been refined to run applications efficiently without any specific changes to those applications. As one would expect, with every release of Oracle RDBMS, Oracle has introduced newer concepts and improved efficiency. Table 12-1 shows the history of Cache Fusion and the evaluation of the related technologies along with the newer releases of Oracle RAC.

Key Components in Cache Fusion

The following sections cover a few terms and concepts used in the discussion of Cache Fusion. In simple terms, every resource in the global cache (such as data blocks, index blocks, and undo blocks) has potentially handled up to three parties. At startup, the simple hashing algorithm divides the management role of the resources into available instances. Each instance controls the access to the resources, and their role is resource "master" for the resources. Any instance that has acquired the permission (to read or modify) is the current "owner" of the resource. Someone else requesting access on that resource can be a "requestor" of that resource. This explanation is over-simplified, but relevant to the context of this discussion.

Ping

The transfer of a data block from one instance's buffer cache to another instance's buffer cache is known as a *ping*. Whenever an instance needs a block, it sends a request to the master of the resource to obtain a lock in the desired mode. If another lock resides on the same block, the master will ask the current holder to downgrade/release the current lock. As you learned in an earlier chapter, this process is known as a *blocking asynchronous trap (BAST)*. When an instance receives a BAST, it downgrades the lock as soon as possible. However, before downgrading the

Oracle Release	Feature	Description
Prior to 8.1.5	Oracle Parallel Server (OPS)	OPS used disk-based pings.
8.1.5	Cache Fusion I or Consistent Read Server	Consistent read version of the block is transferred over the interconnect.
9i	Cache Fusion II (write/write cache fusion)	Current version of the block is transferred over the interconnect.
10g R1	Oracle Cluster Ready Services (CRS) and Automatic Storage Management (ASM)	CRS eliminates the need for third-party clusterware, although it can be used.
10g R2	Oracle CRS for High Availability	CRS provides high availability for non-Oracle applications.
11g R1	Read-Mostly and Reader Bypass	Improved Cache Fusion protocol to reduce the read-mostly application locking overheads.
11g R2	CRS Server Pools and ASM Cluster File System	ASM can be used for OCR and voting disks; ACFS can be used as a generic file system.

TABLE 12-1   *History of Cache Fusion*

lock, it might have to write the corresponding block to disk. This operation sequence is known as *disk ping* or a *hard ping*.

> **NOTE**
> *The definitions of AST and BAST used in this book are based on Oracle context. Various implementations (such as VMS) use different definitions for AST and BAST.*

Starting with Oracle 9i, disk pings have been reduced because blocks are transferred from one instance's buffer cache to another instance's buffer cache via the private interconnect in many cases. This type of transfer is known as *Cache Fusion block transfer*. Some amount of block transfers in the Oracle RAC environment is healthy because it indicates sharing of data among the instances and minimizes disk I/O. However, excessive block transfers can impact performance, consuming CPU and network resources.

As discussed in Chapter 10, the amount of data sent and received by an instance via Cache Fusion can be viewed in the Automatic Workload Repository (AWR) report in the Global Cache Load Profile section.

Deferred Ping

Oracle uses various mechanisms to mitigate pinging. When BAST is received by an instance, it might defer sending the block or downgrading the lock by tens of milliseconds. This extra time might allow the holding instance to complete an active transaction and mark the block header appropriately. This will eliminate any need for the receiving instance to check the status of the transaction immediately after receiving/reading a block. Checking the status of an active transaction is an expensive operation that might require access (and pinging) to the related undo segment header and undo data blocks as well. Prior to Oracle 9i, you could use the parameter gc_defer_time to define the duration by which an instance deferred downgrading a lock. In Oracle versions 9i and later, this parameter has been replaced by the hidden parameter _gc_defer_time.

Past Image (PI) Blocks

PI blocks are copies of blocks in the local buffer cache. Whenever an instance has to send a block it has recently modified to another instance, it preserves a copy of that block, marking it as PI. An instance is *obliged* to keep PIs until the current owner of the block writes that block to the disk. PIs are discarded after the latest version of the block is written to disk. When a block is written to disk and is known to have a global role, indicating the presence of PIs in other instances' buffer caches, Global Cache Services (GCS) informs the instance holding the PIs to discard them. With Cache Fusion, a block is written to disk to satisfy checkpoint requests and so on, not to transfer the block from one instance to another via disk.

When an instance needs to write to a block—to satisfy a checkpoint request, for example—the instance checks the role of the resource covering the block. If the role is global, the instance must inform the GCS of the write requirement. The GCS is responsible for finding the most current block image and informing the instance holding that image to perform the block write. The GCS then informs all holders of the global resource that they can release the buffers holding the PI copies of the block, allowing the global resources to be released.

A block written record (BWR) is placed in its redo log buffer when an instance writes a block covered by a global resource or when it is told it can free up a PI buffer. Recovery processes to indicate that redo information for the block is not needed for recovery prior to this point use this record. Although the BWR makes recovery more efficient, the instance does not force a flush of the log buffer after creating it because it is not essential for accurate recovery.

The fixed table X$BH can be used to find the number of past image blocks present in the buffer cache:

```
SQL> select state, count(state) from X$BH group by state;
     STATE   COUNT(STATE)
---------- ------------
         1  403
         2  7043
         8  15
         3  659
```

There are 15 past image blocks indicated in the STATE column (with a value of 8) of the X$BH table.

Lock Mastering

The memory structure where GCS keeps information about a data block (and other sharable resources) usage is known as the *lock resource*. The responsibility of tracking locks is distributed among all the instances, and the required memory also comes from the participating instances' System Global Area (SGA). Due to this distributed ownership of the resources, a master node exists for each lock resource. The master node maintains complete information about current users and requestors for the lock resource. The master node also contains information about the PIs of the block.

Whenever an instance needs a data block, it must contact the master of lock resources corresponding to that data block. The master instance for the required lock resource could be local or remote. If local, fewer messages or no messages need to be sent over the interconnect to obtain the required lock for that block. (For more information, see Chapter 11.)

Types of Contention

Contention of a resource occurs when two or more instances want the same resource. If a resource such as a data block is being used by an instance and is needed by another instance at the same time, a contention occurs. There are three types of contention for data blocks:

- **Read/read contention** Read/read contention is never a problem because of the shared disk system. A block read by one instance can be read by other instances without the intervention of GCS. Also, when the object is read-mostly, any instance can read the block(s) without additional messages from/to GCS.

- **Write/read contention** Write/read contention was addressed in Oracle 8*i* by the consistent read. The holding instance (most of the time) constructs the CR block and ships the requesting instance using interconnects.

- **Write/write contention** Write/write contention is addressed by the Cache Fusion technology. Since Oracle 9*i*, cluster interconnect is used in some cases to ship data blocks among the instances that need to modify the same data block simultaneously.

It is important to note that although the interconnect is the route for the current block to be shipped, the locking information is stored in the GRD to avoid corruptions in the blocks in memory due to conflicting access. There is no user- or application-level tuning or modification for this.

In the following sections, we look at how these components work seamlessly in a real-world situation. We explore how these contentions were addressed before Cache Fusion was introduced and how they work with Cache Fusion.

Cache Fusion I or Consistent Read Server

Cache Fusion I (also known as *consistent read server*) was introduced in version 8.1.5. Oracle keeps a list of recent transactions that have changed a block. The original data contained in the block is preserved in the undo segment, which can be used to provide consistent read versions of the block to other readers or to recover an uncommitted transaction after an instance or a process crash.

Generally, when a transaction is committed, the server process places a flag in the undo segment header indicating the transaction status as "committed." To save time, it does not stamp each and every block it has modified with a commit flag. Thus, in the future, whenever another process reads that block and finds an active transaction in the block, the reader refers to the corresponding undo segment header to determine whether the transaction has been committed. If the undo segment header indicates that the transaction has been committed, the reader updates the block with the System Commit Number (SCN) in the transaction layer of the block to signify the commit and moves on to read the block. However, if the transaction has not yet been committed, the reader locates the undo block where the original data is stored and makes a consistent read image of the block for its use.

This discussion leads us to infer the following:

- When a reader reads a recently modified block, it might find an active transaction in the block.

- The reader will need to read the undo segment header to decide whether the transaction has been committed or not.

- If the transaction is not committed, the process creates a consistent read (CR) version of the block in the buffer cache using the data in the block and the data stored in the undo segment.

- If the undo segment shows the transaction is committed, the process has to revisit the block and clean out the block and generate the redo for the changes.

In an Oracle RAC environment, if the process of reading the block is on an instance other than the one that has modified the block, the reader will have to read the following blocks from the disk:

- **Data block**   To get the data and/or transaction ID and Undo Byte Address (UBA)
- **Undo segment header block**   To find the last undo block used for the entire transaction
- **Undo data block**   To get the actual undo record to construct a CR image

Before these blocks can be read, the instance modifying the block will have to write those blocks to disk. This will result in at least six disk I/O operations. The number of I/O operations can be optimized if the modifying instance, knowing that an instance needs a CR copy of the block it recently modified, can construct a CR copy of the block and send it to the requesting instance. It is highly probable that the data block, undo segment header block, and undo block will still be in this instance's buffer cache. Thus, by making a CR copy and sending it over the private interconnect, potentially six disk I/Os have been replaced by a single data block transfer over the interconnect.

Prior to Cache Fusion, whenever an instance needed to modify a data block that had been recently modified by another instance, the sequence of operation shown next and in Figure 12-2 occurred:

1. An instance sends a message to the lock manager requesting a shared lock on the block.

2. Following are the possibilities in the global cache:

   ■ If there is no current user for the block, the lock manager grants the shared lock to the requesting instance.

   ■ If another instance has an exclusive lock on that block, the lock manager asks the owning instance to downgrade the lock.

3. Based on the result, either of the following can happen:

   ■ If the lock is granted, the requesting instance reads the block from the disk.

   ■ The owning instance writes the block to disk and disowns the lock on that resource.

4. The owning instance also informs the lock manager and the requesting instance that it has released the lock.

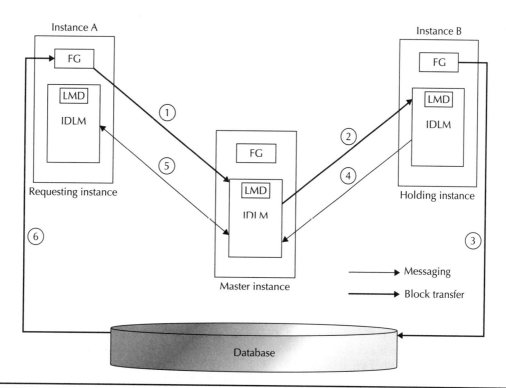

FIGURE 12-2 *Write/read contention before Cache Fusion*

5. The requesting instance now has the lock granted. The lock manager updates the IDLM with the new holders of that resource.

6. The requesting instance reads the block from disk. If it is looking for the previous version of the block, it can proceed with the regular CR block fabrication in its own buffer cache.

CR fabrication can be an expensive operation, especially when the undo information is cached in the remote node. The requesting instance has to make a few additional disk I/Os to get the blocks to its own cache. Because the disk is used as a data transfer medium, latency issues will crop up and application scalability and performance will degrade when the data is not partitioned across the instances.

If the CR block fabrication occurs at the holding instance, part of the disk I/O can be avoided because the data blocks and undo blocks are local to that instance. Upon undo block fabrication, the holder can ship the *processed* block to the requestor. Read/write contention is avoided by building CR in the holding instance, and this is the first phase in Cache Fusion.

Following is the sequence of operations with the implementation of the CR server engine in Oracle 8*i*. The newly introduced background process—the Block Server Process (BSP)—makes the CR fabrication at the holder's cache and ships the CR version of the block across the interconnect. The sequence of operations is shown in Figure 12-3.

1. An instance sends a message to the lock manager requesting a shared lock on the block.

2. Following are the possibilities in the global cache:
   - If there is no current user for the block, the lock manager grants the shared lock to the requesting instance.
   - If another instance has an exclusive lock on that block, the lock manager asks the owning instance to build a CR copy and ship it to the requesting instance.

3. Based on the result, either of the following can happen:
   - If the lock is granted, the requesting instance reads the block from disk.
   - The owning instance creates a CR version of the buffer in its own buffer cache and ships it to the requesting instance over the interconnect.

4. The owning instance also informs the lock manager and the requesting instance that it has shipped the block.

5. The requesting instance now has the lock granted. The lock manager updates the IDLM with the new holders of that resource.

While making a CR copy needed by another instance, the holding instance may refuse to do so if either of the following occurs:

- It doesn't find any of the needed blocks in its buffer cache. It will not perform a disk read to make a CR copy for another instance.

- It is repeatedly asked to send a CR copy of the same block. After sending CR copies of the same block four times, it will voluntarily relinquish the lock, write the block to disk, and let other instances get the block from disk. The number of copies it will serve before it does so is governed by the hidden parameter _fairness_threshold.

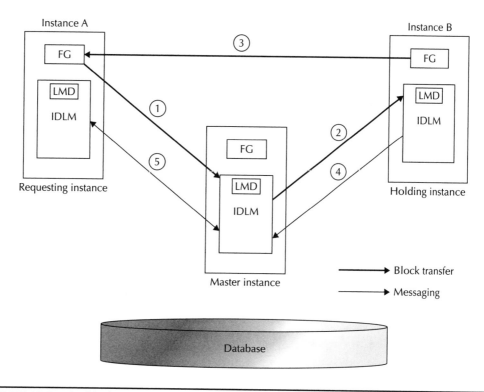

FIGURE 12-3 *CR block transfer in Cache Fusion*

While downgrading the lock and writing the block to disk, the holding instance will send a copy of the block it has constructed so far, and the requesting instance will continue the construction of the CR copy needed by it. This is known as the *lightwork rule*. Refer to Chapter 11 for a detailed discussion on the lightwork rule and fairness threshold.

Cache Fusion II or Write/Write Cache Fusion

The CR server addressed read/write contention in the first phase of Cache Fusion. The second phase of Cache Fusion, introduced in Oracle 9i, implements the framework for current block transfers for write/write contention. Prior to Oracle 9i, whenever an instance needed to modify a data block that had been recently modified by another instance, the following sequence of operations would take place, as illustrated in Figure 12-4:

1. An instance sends a message to the lock manager requesting an exclusive lock on the block.

2. Following are the possibilities in the global cache:

   ■ If there is no current user for the block, the lock manager grants the exclusive lock to the requesting instance.

   ■ If another instance has an exclusive lock on that block, the lock manager asks the owning instance to release the lock.

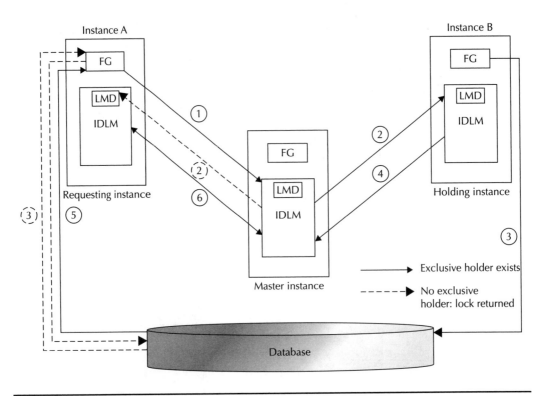

FIGURE 12-4 *Write/write contention in pre–Cache Fusion*

3. Based on the result, either of the following can happen:

   ■ If the lock is granted, the requesting instance reads the block from the disk.

   ■ The owning instance writes the block to disk and disowns the lock on that resource.

4. The owning instance also informs the lock manager and the requesting instance that it has released the lock.

5. The requesting instance now has the exclusive lock. It can read the block from disk and proceed with the intended changes to the block.

6. The lock manager updates the resource directory with the new information about the holder.

Often, the requesting instance will find an active transaction in the active transaction list of the block, and it might need the corresponding undo block header and undo data block to clean out the block. Thus, multiple disk I/Os might be needed before the requesting instance can modify the block. Cache Fusion makes this operation relatively efficient and fast, as shown in Figure 12-5:

1. The instance sends a message to the lock manager to request an exclusive lock on the block.

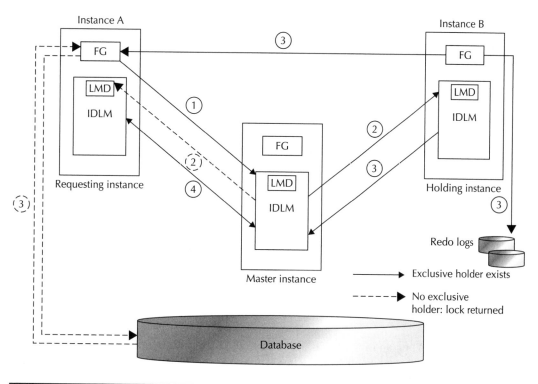

FIGURE 12-5   *Cache Fusion current block transfer*

2. Following are the possibilities in the global cache based on whether any other user is holding the lock:

- If there is no current user for the block, the lock manager grants the exclusive lock to the requesting instance.
- If another instance has an exclusive lock on that block, the lock manager asks the owning instance to release the lock.

3. Based on the result, either of the following can happen:

- If the lock is granted, the requesting instance reads the block from the disk.
- The owning instance sends the current block to the requesting instance via the high-speed interconnects. To guarantee recovery in the event of instance death, the owning instance writes all the redo records generated for the block to the online redo log file. It will keep a past image of the block and inform the master instance that it has sent the current block to the requesting instance.

4. The lock manager updates the resource directory with the current holder of the block.

Cache Fusion in Operation

Before we get into Cache Fusion operation, here's a quick recap of GCS resource roles and modes. A GCS resource can be *local* or *global*. It is local if it can be acted upon without consulting other instances. It is global if it cannot be acted upon without consulting or informing remote instances. GCS is used as a messaging agent to coordinate manipulation of a global resource.

Depending on the type of operation an instance intends to do on a block (resource), an instance will acquire the block in shared or exclusive mode. When an instance needs a block to satisfy a query request, it requires the block to be in consistent read mode or in shared mode. When an instance needs a block to satisfy a DML (update, insert, delete) request, it needs the block in exclusive mode. The Null (N) mode indicates that the instance does not currently hold the resource in any mode. This is the default status for each instance.

An instance having a resource with a local role can have the resources in X, S, or N mode. The following table denotes the different states of a resource:

Mode/Role	Local	Global
Null: N	NL	NG
Shared: S	SL	SG
Exclusive: X	XL	XG

- **SL**   When an instance has a resource in SL form, it can serve a copy of the block to other instances and it can read the block from disk. Because the block is not modified, there is no need to write to disk.

- **XL**   When an instance has a resource in XL form, it has sole ownership and interest in that resource. It also has the exclusive right to modify the block. All changes to the blocks are in its local buffer cache, and it can write the block to disk. If another instance wants the block, it will contact the instance via GCS.

- **NL**   An NL form is used to protect consistent read blocks. If a block is held in SL mode and another instance wants it in X mode, the current instance will send the block to the requesting instance and downgrade its role to NL.

- **SG**   In SG form, a block is present in one or more instances. An instance can read the block from disk and serve it to other instances.

- **XG**   In XG form, a block can have one or more PIs, indicating multiple copies of the block in several instances' buffer caches. The instance with the XG role has the latest copy of the block and is the most likely candidate to write the block to disk. GCS can ask the instance with the XG role to write the block to disk or to serve it to another instance.

- **NG**   After discarding PIs when instructed by GCS, the block is kept in the buffer cache with NG role. This serves only as the CR copy of the block.

Consider the following: a four-instance Oracle RAC environment, with instances A, B, C, and D. Instance D is the master of the lock resources for the data block BL. In this example, we'll work with only one block (BL) to begin with, and it will reside on disk at SCN 987654.

We will choose a three-letter code for the lock state: The first letter will indicate the lock mode: N = Null, S = Shared, and X = Exclusive. The second letter will indicate the lock role: L = Local and G = Global. The third letter will be a digit indicating the past image: 0 = block does not have any past image, and 1 = a PI of the block.

The following examples will undergo a sequence of operations to help you understand the current block and CR block transfers from the instances. These scenarios include reading from disk, reading from cache, getting the block from cache for update, performing an update on a block, performing an update on the same block, reading a block that was globally dirty, performing a rollback on a previously updated block, and reading the block after commit. Although these examples do not cover all the functionalities of Cache Fusion, they are the most common operations in a real-world environment.

Example 1: Reading a Block from Disk

In this example, instance C wants to read the block. It will request a lock in shared mode from the master instance.

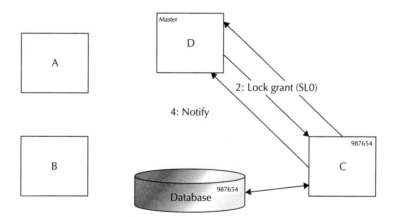

1. Instance C requests the block by sending a shared lock request (S, C) to master instance D. (S represents the type of the lock requested and C represents the requesting instance.)

2. The block has never been read into the buffer cache of any instance and it is not locked. Master instance D grants the lock to instance C. The lock granted is SL0, indicating that it is a shared lock with local interests, and no past images of this block exist.

3. Instance C reads the block from the shared disk in to its buffer cache.

4. Instance C has the block in shared mode. The lock manager updates the resource directory.

Example 2: Reading a Block from the Cache

We begin at the end of example 1. Instance B wants to read the same block that is cached in instance C.

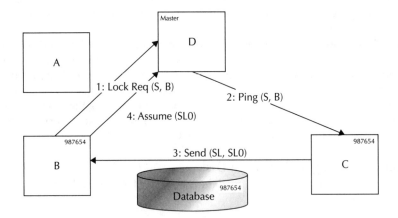

1. Instance B sends a shared lock request, Lock Req (S, B), to master instance D.

2. The lockmaster at instance D knows that the block may be available at instance C and hence sends a ping message to instance C.

3. Instance C sends the block to instance B over the interconnect. Along with the block, instance C also indicates that instance B should take the current lock mode and role from instance C.

4. Instance B sends a message to instance D that it has assumed the SL lock for the block. This message is not critical (yet it is important) for the lock manager; hence, this message is sent asynchronously.

Example 3: Getting a (Cached) Clean Block for Update

We begin at the end of example 2. Instance A wants to modify the same block that is already cached in instances B and C.

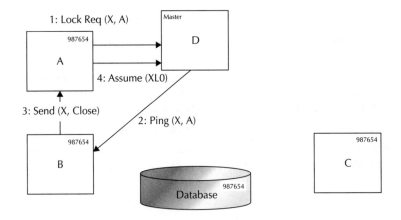

1. Instance A sends an exclusive lock request, Lock Req (X, A), to master instance D.

2. The lockmaster at D knows that the block may be available at instance B in SCUR mode and at instance C in CR mode. It also sends a ping message to the shared lock holders. The most recent access was at instance B, and instance D sends a BAST message to instance B.

3. Instance B sends the block to instance A over the interconnect and closes its shared (SCUR) lock. The block may still be in its buffer to be used as CR; however, it releases any lock on it.

4. Instance A now has the block in exclusive mode and sends an assume message to instance D. Instance A holds the lock in XL0 mode.

5. Instance A modifies the block in its buffer cache. The changes are not committed and the block has not yet been written to disk; therefore, the SCN on disk remains at 987654.

Example 4: Getting a (Cached) Modified Block for Update and Commit

This example begins at the end of example 3. Instance C now wants to update the block BL. Note that instance A has already updated the block and the block has an open transaction on it. If instance C tries to update the same row, it will wait for the previous update to commit or roll back. However, in this case, instance C updates a different row and after the update, it issues a commit.

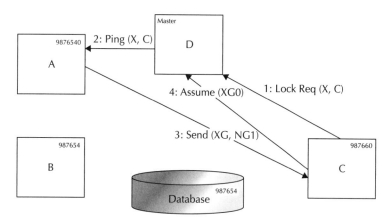

1. Instance C sends an exclusive lock request, Lock Req (X, C), to master instance D.

2. The lockmaster at D knows that instance A holds an exclusive lock on the block and hence sends a ping message to instance A.

3. Instance A sends the dirty block to instance C over the interconnect. It downgrades the lock on the buffer from XCUR to NULL. It keeps a PI version of the block and disowns any lock on that buffer. Before shipping the block, instance A has to create a PI image and flush any pending redo for the block changed. The block mode on instance A is now NG1.

4. Instance C sends a message to instance D indicating it now has the block in exclusive mode. The block role G indicates that the block is in global mode and if it needs to write the block to disk it must coordinate it with the other instances that have past images of that block. Instance C modifies the block and issues a commit. This takes the SCN to 987660.

NOTE
Row-level locks and block locks operate independently in the Oracle RAC environment. In this example, we update the same block in two different instances, but not the same row. Refer to Chapter 11 for a detailed discussion of Oracle's implementation of row-level locking. Row locks (known as enqueue type TX) and GCS buffer locks (known as enqueue type BL) can run in parallel for a transaction.

Example 5: Commit the Previously Modified Block and Select the Data

Now instance A issues a commit to release the row-level locks held by the transaction and flush the redo information to the redo log files. Global locks on the resources remain the same.

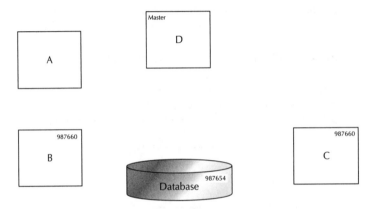

1. Instance A wants to commit the changes. Commit operations do not require any synchronous modifications to the data block.

2. The lock status remains the same as the previous state and change vectors for the commits are written to the redo logs.

Example 6: Write the Dirty Buffers to Disk Due to Checkpoint

Continuing at the end of example 5, instance B writes the dirty blocks from the buffer cache due to a checkpoint.

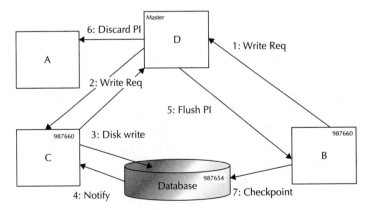

1. Instance B sends a write request to master D with the necessary SCN.

2. The lockmaster at D knows that the most recent copy of the block may be available at instance C and hence sends a message to instance C asking to write.

3. Instance C initiates a disk write and writes a BWR into the redo log file.

4. Instance C gets the write notification that the write is completed.

5. Instance C notifies the master that the write is completed.

6. On receipt of the notification from C, master instance D tells all PI holders to discard their PIs, and the lock at instance C writes the modified block to the disk.

7. All instances that have previously modified this block will also have to write a BWR. The write request by instance C has now been satisfied, and instance C can now proceed with its checkpoint as usual.

Example 7: Master Instance Crash

This example continues from example 6.

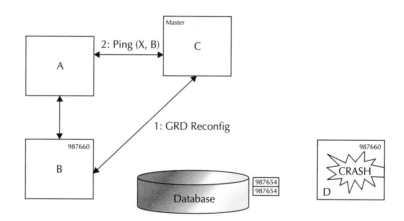

1. The master instance D crashes.

2. The Global Resource Directory (GRD) is frozen momentarily and the resources held by master instance D will be equally distributed in the surviving nodes.

NOTE
Mode details on the GRD are discussed in Chapter 11, and GRD and fast reconfiguration after node failure are discussed in Chapter 9.

Example 8: Select the Rows from Instance A

Now instance A queries the rows from that table to get the most recent data.

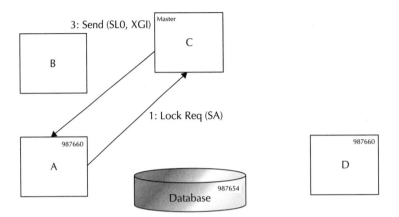

1. Instance A sends a shared lock request, Lock Req (S, D), to master instance C.
2. Master instance C knows that the most recent copy of that block may be in instance C (which is the current master) and asks the holder to ship the CR block to instance A.
3. Instance C ships the CR block to instance A over the interconnect.

Sequence of Operations

Table 12-2 lists the sequence of operations on the nodes and corresponding modes of the buffers in various caches.

Cache Fusion Walkthrough

In the following Cache Fusion example, we will use the V$SEGMENT_STATISTICS, X$BH, XLE, XKJBL, V$DLM_RESS, and V$GES_ENQUEUE views to trace blocks and the lock status in a four-node environment. We will use the EMP table contained in the SCOTT schema. The EMP table can be created using the script demobld.sql contained in the $ORACLE_HOME/sqlplus/demo directory. For this example, a primary key on column EMPNO was added to make it more selective for the retrieval. We also manually master the EMP table to instance D for demonstration purposes. The following command can be used to remaster an object to one instance manually:

```
oradebug lkdebug -m pkey <objected>
```

Run the following SQL script as any DBA user to get the data_object_id for the EMP table owned by the user *SCOTT:*

```
GET_OBJECT_ID.SQL
```

The data dictionary view dba_objects contains details about all the objects in the database. We query this view to get details about the data_object_id for the EMP table:

```
REM We get the object id of the EMP table
column owner format a10
```

Example	Operation on Node A	Operation on Node B	Operation on Node C	Operation on Node D	Buffer Status A	B	C	D
1			Read the block from disk.				SCUR	
2		Read the block from cache.				CR	SCUR	
3	Update the block.				XCUR	CR	CR	
4			Update the same block.		PI	CR	XCUR	
5	Commit the changes.				PI	CR	XCUR	
6		Trigger checkpoint.				CR	XCUR	
7				Instance crash.				
8	Select the rows.				CR		XCUR	

TABLE 12-2   *Sequence of Operations on Nodes and Buffer Status in Examples 1 through 8*

```
column data_object_id format 999999
column object_name format a15
select owner, data_object_id, object_name
from dba_objects
where owner='SCOTT'
and object_name='EMP';

SQL> @GET_OBJECT_ID

OWNER         DATA_OBJECT_ID OBJECT_NAME
----------    -------------- ----------------
SCOTT                  51151 EMP
```

The dictionary view dba_extents keeps storage detail information for all segments in the database. We can get the details about the file_id and block_id of the EMP table by querying this view:

SEG_DETAILS.SQL

You can query the dba_extents view or use the dbms_rowid package to get the details:

```
REM We get the File ID, Starting Block ID for EMP Table
col owner format a8
```

```
col segment_name format a12
select owner,segment_name,file_id,block_id,blocks
from dba_extents
where owner='SCOTT'
and segment_name='EMP'

SQL> @GET_SEGMENT_DETAILS
OWNER      SEGMENT_NAME    FILE_ID    BLOCK_ID     BLOCKS
--------   ------------    --------   ----------   ---------
SCOTT      EMP                    4          25           8
```

Alternatively, we can get the details about the file number and block number of the rows from the EMP table using the following method. The rowid is the physical address of the row inside the database and uniquely identifies a row in the database.

```
SQL> select rowid,empno,ename from scott.emp where empno in(7788,7876);
ROWID                    EMPNO ENAME
------------------       ---------- ----------
AAAMfPAAEAAAAAgAAH        7788 SCOTT

AAAMfPAAEAAAAAgAAK        7876 ADAMS

SQL> select
  2  dbms_rowid.rowid_block_number('AAAMfPAAEAAAAAgAAH') Block_No
  3  from dual;
  BLOCK_NO

----------


      32
SQL> select
  2  dbms_rowid. rowid_relative_fno('AAAMfPAAEAAAAAgAAH') File_no
  3  from dual;
  FILE_NO
----------

       4
```

Queries Used to Get the Lock and Buffer Status
Following is a quick explanation of the queries used to get the lock and buffer status information. The following four queries were used, and they need to be run in a session logged in with SYS as *sysdba*—a few of them reference the internal views and they are visible only to SYS users.

GET_SEGMENT_STATS.SQL
The dynamic performance view v$segment_statistics contains statistics for each segment, such as number of reads, writes, row lock waits, and ITL waits. This view is used to get information about how data blocks belonging to the EMP table are received by the instances.

```
column stat format a35
column value format 99999
```

```
select STATISTIC_NAME stat, value val
from v$segment_statistics
where value > 0
and OWNER='SCOTT' and OBJECT_NAME='EMP';
```

GET_BUFFER_STAT.SQL

The internal view X$BH contains the status of the block in the buffer cache. We can get the status of any cached buffer in the buffer cache from this view. The predicate obj=51151 is used to restrict our interest on the EMP table. To get the status of the block that contains the rows of EMPNO 7788 and 7369, dbablk=32 is used. The last condition in the predicate, class=1, is used to get the details about the data blocks of the EMP table.

```
SELECT
state, mode_held, le_addr, dbarfil, dbablk, cr_scn_bas, cr_scn_wrp
FROM x$bh
WHERE obj=51151
AND dbablk=32
AND class=1;
```

Column STATE of X$BH contains information about the mode of the block in the buffer cache. You can also query V$BH to get the same information. However, querying V$BH may be an expensive operation in production because it accesses all buffers (joining with X$LE) and may consume a large amount of CPU cycles. Hence, it is always better to query X$BH whenever you access the buffer cache information.

The following table contains information about the various block statuses in the buffer cache:

State	Explanation
0	Buffer is free, unused.
1	Buffer current, locked in X mode.
2	Buffer current, locked in S mode.
3	Consistent read buffer.
4	Buffer being read.
5	Buffer under media recovery.
6	Buffer under instance recovery.
7	Write clone buffer.
8	Past Image buffer.

State values 1, 2, 3, and 8 are the most commonly seen buffers modes in the buffer cache; we will use these values in our demo example.

GET_RESOURCE_NAME.SQL

The GCS resource name to be used in the query GET_RESOURCE_STAT was retrieved using the following query:

```
column hexname format a25
column resource_name format a15
```

```
select
b.kjblname hexname,b.kjblname2 resource_name,
b.kjblgrant,b.kjblrole,b.kjblrequest
from
X$LE a, X$KJBL b
where a.le_kjbl=b.kjbllockp
and a.le_addr=(select le_addr from
x$bh where dbablk=32 and obj=51151
and class=1 and state! =3);
```

```
SQL> @GET_RESOURCE_NAME
HEXNAME                         RESOURCE_NAME    KJBLGRANT   KJBLROLE KJBLREQUE
------------------------        ---------------  ---------   -------- ---------
[0x20][0x40000],[BL]            32,262144,BL     KJUSEREX           0 KJUSERNL
```

The kjblname column in the internal view X$KJBL provides the resource name in hexadecimal format, and kjblname2 provides the resource name in decimal format. We will be using the hex format *([id1],[id2],[type])* to query the resource in the V$GC_ELEMENT and V$DLM_RESS views.

GET_RESOURCE_STAT.SQL
The following query was used to monitor the resource allocated to the data block from the EMP table:

```
column resource_name format a22
column state format a8
column mast format 9999
column grnt format 9999
column cnvt format 9999
select
a.resource_name,b.state,a.master_node mast,a.on_convert_q cnvt ,
a.on_grant_q grnt,b.request_level,b.grant_level
from v$dlm_ress a,
V$ges_enqueue b
where upper(a.resource_name)=upper(b.resource_name1)
and a.resource_name like '%[0x20][0x40000],[BL]%';
```

```
SQL> @GET_RESOURCE_STAT

RESOURCE_NAME           STATE     MAST  CNVT  GRNT REQUEST_L GRANT_LEV
---------------------   --------  ----  ----  ---- --------- ---------
[0x20][0x40000],[BL]    GRANTED      3     0     1 KJUSERNL  KJUSERPR
[0x20][0x40000],[BL]    GRANTED      3     0     1 KJUSERNL  KJUSERPR
```

Sample Operation Details
We will perform a sample operation. At the end of each SQL operation, we'll take a snapshot using the aforementioned four queries to monitor the status change in blocks and locks in the participating instances. User statements should be run as *SCOTT,* and monitoring queries should be run as user *SYS* because they refer to internal views.

The sequence of operations is as follows:

1. Select instance C to get the row with EMPNO=7788 from the EMP table:

    ```
    SELECT EMPNO, ENAME, SAL from EMP where EMPNO=7788;
    ```

2. Select the same row on instance B:

    ```
    SELECT EMPNO, ENAME, SAL from EMP where EMPNO=7788;
    ```

3. Update the row on instance A:

    ```
    UPDATE EMP SET SAL=SAL+1000 where EMPNO=7788;
    ```

4. Update a new row (EMPNO=7369) in instance C:

    ```
    UPDATE EMP SET SAL=SAL*2 where EMPNO=7369;
    ```

5. Commit the changes in instance A:

    ```
    COMMIT;
    ```

6. Write the changes to the disk because of a checkpoint in instance B:

    ```
    ALTER SYSTEM CHECKPOINT; ALTER SYSTEM SWITCH LOGFILE;
    ```

7. A master node crash occurs.

8. Select the data from instance A and verify the status of the current master:

    ```
    SELECT EMPNO,ENAME,SAL FROM EMP WHERE EMPNO IN (7788,7369)
    ```

At the beginning of the example, the buffer cache does not contain any block belonging to the EMP table:

```
Lock status queries run on instance A at the beginning
$sqlplus '/as sysdba'

SQL*Plus: Release 11.2.0.1.0 Production on Thu Aug 19 00:54:09 2010
Copyright (c) 1982, 2009, Oracle.  All rights reserved.
Connected to:
Oracle Database 11g Enterprise Edition Release 11.2.0.1.0 - 64bit Production
With the Partitioning, Real Application Clusters, Automatic Storage Management, OLAP,
Data Mining and Real Application Testing options
SQL> @GET_SEGMENT_STATS
no rows selected
SQL>@GET_BUFFER_STAT
no rows selected
SQL> @GET_RESOURCE_NAME
no rows selected
SQL>@GET_RESOURCE_STAT
no rows selected

Lock status queries run on instance B at the beginning
$sqlplus '/as sysdba'
SQL*Plus: Release 11.2.0.1.0 Production on Thu Aug 19 00:54:09 2010
Copyright (c) 1982, 2009, Oracle.  All rights reserved.
Connected to:
Oracle Database 11g Enterprise Edition Release 11.2.0.1.0 - 64bit Production
```

```
With the Partitioning, Real Application Clusters, Automatic Storage Management, OLAP,
Data Mining and Real Application Testing options
SQL> @GET_SEGMENT_STATS
no rows selected
SQL>@GET_BUFFER_STAT
no rows selected
SQL> @GET_RESOURCE_NAME
no rows selected
SQL>@GET_RESOURCE_STAT
no rows selected

Lock status queries run on instance C at the beginning
$sqlplus '/as sysdba'
SQL*Plus: Release 11.2.0.1.0 Production on Thu Aug 19 00:54:09 2010
Copyright (c) 1982, 2009, Oracle.  All rights reserved.
Connected to:
Oracle Database 11g Enterprise Edition Release 11.2.0.1.0 - 64bit Production
With the Partitioning, Real Application Clusters, Automatic Storage Management, OLAP,
Data Mining and Real Application Testing options
SQL> @GET_SEGMENT_STATS
no rows selected
SQL>@GET_BUFFER_STAT
no rows selected
SQL> @GET_RESOURCE_NAME
no rows selected
SQL>@GET_RESOURCE_STAT
no rows selected

Lock status queries run on instance D at the beginning
$sqlplus '/as sysdba'
SQL*Plus: Release 11.2.0.1.0 Production on Thu Aug 19 00:54:09 2010
Copyright (c) 1982, 2009, Oracle.  All rights reserved.
Connected to:
Oracle Database 11g Enterprise Edition Release 11.2.0.1.0 - 64bit Production
With the Partitioning, Real Application Clusters, Automatic Storage Management, OLAP,
Data Mining and Real Application Testing options
SQL> @GET_SEGMENT_STATS
no rows selected
SQL>@GET_BUFFER_STAT
no rows selected
SQL> @GET_RESOURCE_NAME
no rows selected
SQL>@GET_RESOURCE_STAT
no rows selected
```

As you can see, the buffer cache does not contain any block belonging to the table EMP. Because no blocks are in the buffer cache, no resources are needed to keep track of them. Therefore, no rows are returned by the queries. The table EMP is mastered by instance D, and every request on the table will be routed through instance D.

Example 1: Retrieve the Data from Disk

The first example retrieves the data from disk and monitors the resource movements between master and holder instances. To start, we'll query the data from the EMP table on instance C.

Connect as *SCOTT* and run the following query to load a buffer from disk to the buffer cache of instance C. Instance D is the master of the resource. You can query the X$KJBR.KJBRMASTER view to find the master node for a particular resource.

```
REM Let us query the EMP data from instance C
REM This query is run as user SCOTT

SQL> select empno,ename,sal from emp
  2  where empno=7788;
     EMPNO ENAME            SAL
---------- ---------- ----------
      7788 SCOTT           3000
```

Now we run the lock status queries on instance C. We run the monitoring queries as user *SYS*, because we query the internal tables. These queries yield the following results:

```
REM #### Result of lock queries on instance C,
REM after a select from emp table on instance C
REM This query is run as user SYS
SQL> @get_segment_stats
OBJECT_NAM STAT                                   VALUE
---------- ------------------------------------ -------
EMP        physical reads                             1

SQL> @get_resource_name
HEXNAME                      RESOURCE_NAME    KJBLGRANT    KJBLROLE KJBLREQUE
------------------------     ---------------  ---------  ---------- ---------
[0x20][0x40000],[BL]         32,262144,BL     KJUSERPR            0 KJUSERNL
SQL> @get_resource_stat
no rows selected
SQL> @get_buffer_stat
STATE  MODE_HELD      FILE#      BLOCK#   SCN_BASE   SCN_WRAP
-----  ----------  ----------  ----------  ----------  ----------
    2           0           4          32           0           0
```

Observe the following:

■ The block was retrieved from disk, indicated by "physical reads" for the segment in the v$segment_statisics view.

■ The block is held in the current shared mode, as indicated by 2 in the STATE column of the x$bh table. X$BH STATE is 2 (SCUR).

■ The master node is node 3 (where instance D is running; the node numbering starts with 0).

■ A protected read lock (shared read), as indicated by KJUSERPR, has been granted on this resource.

■ The row data resides in the File# 4 and Block# 32 in the database. The following excerpt from the block dump shows that all 14 rows of the EMP table reside in the same block. The block dump output has been edited for brevity:

```
Start dump data blocks tsn: 4 file#: 4 minblk 32 maxblk 32
buffer tsn: 4 rdba: 0x01000020 (4/32)
scn: 0x0000.000adca3 seq: 0x01 flg: 0x04 tail: 0xdca30601

Block header dump: 0x01000020
 Object id on Block? Y
 seg/obj: 0xc7cf  csc: 0x00.adca2  itc: 2  flg: E  typ: 1 - DATA
     brn: 0  bdba: 0x1000019 ver: 0x01 opc: 0
     inc: 0  exflg: 0

Itl          Xid                 Uba      Flag  Lck      Scn/Fsc
0x01  0x0014.017.00000102  0x01400239.0023.06  C---  0  scn 0x0000.000a9cb9
0x02  0x000a.012.000001ea  0x0080118f.00d1.11  C-U-  0  scn 0x0000.000ad663
data_block_dump,data header at 0x64c6664
===============
tsiz: 0x1f98
hsiz: 0x2e
pbl: 0x064c6664
bdba: 0x01000020
      76543210
flag=--------
ntab=1
nrow=14
```

In this block dump, nrow=14 shows that all 14 rows are stored in the same block. The data block address (bdba) is 0x01000020; this will be used later to verify the block written records in the redo logs.

The block dump belongs to the EMP table and the object ID of the block is shown as seg/obj:0xc7cf, where the object ID 51151 is represented as 0xc7cf.

Here's the result of lock queries on master instance D after a select from EMP table on instance A:

```
REM Lock status on the Master Node D
SQL> @get_segment_stats
no rows selected
SQL> @get_buffer_stat
no rows selected
SQL> @get_resource_name
no rows selected
SQL> @get_resource_stat
RESOURCE_NAME          STATE     MAST  CNVT  GRNT  REQUEST_L  GRANT_LEV
---------------------- --------  ----- ----- ----- ---------  ---------
[0x20][0x40000],[BL]   GRANTED     3     0     1   KJUSERNL   KJUSERPR
```

Observe the following:

■   There is no physical read or logical read on the EMP table in the master node. The query GET_SEGMENT_STATS on V$segment_statistics confirms this.

■   Because there is no read on the EMP table, no blocks from the EMP table are cached in the master node.

■   Because no blocks are cached, no resource is allocated to protect that block in instance D.

■   The query GET_RESOURCE_STAT tells us that the resource is granted on a protected read level.

Example 2: Read the Block from Cache

Continuing from example 1, we run the same query from instance B. The data is already cached in instance C and we should get the block from instance C. The block was read to instance C from disk by the disk read, and the block is not changed yet. The on-disk version and the cache version are the same because no modifications were made from instance C.

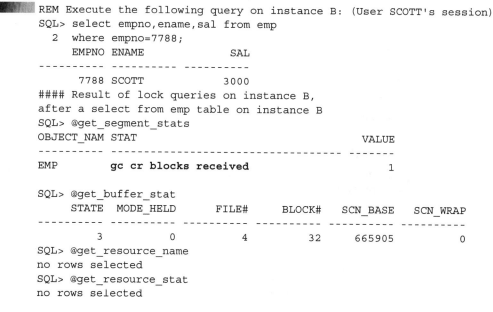

```
REM Execute the following query on instance B: (User SCOTT's session)
SQL> select empno,ename,sal from emp
  2  where empno=7788;
     EMPNO ENAME            SAL
---------- ---------- ----------
      7788 SCOTT           3000
#### Result of lock queries on instance B,
after a select from emp table on instance B
SQL> @get_segment_stats
OBJECT_NAM STAT                                        VALUE
---------- ------------------------------------ -------
EMP        gc cr blocks received                         1

SQL> @get_buffer_stat
     STATE  MODE_HELD      FILE#      BLOCK#   SCN_BASE   SCN_WRAP
---------- ---------- ---------- ---------- ---------- ----------
         3          0          4         32     665905          0
SQL> @get_resource_name
no rows selected
SQL> @get_resource_stat
no rows selected
```

Observe the following:

■   The block was retrieved from the cache and not from the disk, as indicated by "gc cr blocks received" for the segment in the v$segment_statisics view.

■   The block is held in the current shared mode as indicated by 3 in the STATE column of the x$bh table. X$BH.STATE is 3 (CR).

■   Because the buffer is CR state, it does not require any locks to protect it, and no resources are allocated for that buffer in the master node.

■   Master node is node 3 (where instance D is running, the node numbering starts with 0).

Now we will look at the change in lock status in the master instance D and the instance served the block, which is instance C.

Here are lock statistics in the master instance:

```
SQL> @get_resource_stat
RESOURCE_NAME            STATE      MAST  CNVT  GRNT  REQUEST_L GRANT_LEV
----------------------- --------- ----- ----- ----- --------- ----------
[0x20][0x40000],[BL]     GRANTED     3     0     1  KJUSERNL  KJUSERPR

#### Result of lock queries on instance C
after a select from emp table on instance B

SQL> @get_buffer_stat
STATE   MODE_HELD       FILE#      BLOCK#     SCN_BASE   SCN_WRAP
----- ---------- ---------- ---------- ---------- ----------
   2          0          4          32          0          0
SQL> @get_resource_name
HEXNAME                       RESOURCE_NAME   KJBLGRANT   KJBLROLE KJBLREQUE
----------------------------- --------------- --------- ---------- ---------
[0x20][0x40000],[BL]          32,262144,BL    KJUSERPR           0 KJUSERNL
```

Observe the following:

- The master instance granted the shared access to instance C.
- The SCUR lock mode is compatible with another CR mode without any conflicts.
- Instance C shipped the block to instance B over the interconnect as instructed by master instance D.
- The column KJBLGRANT shows KJUSERPR for the lock in SCUR mode in instance C.
- No additional locks are required to protect the CR buffer in instance A, so no lock status changes are in the master instance.
- A block present in the buffer cache in CR mode can be used locally by the instance for the query. However, it cannot be used for update and cannot be served to other instances; hence, the block does not require a lock.

At the end of example 2, the global cache has two copies of the buffer in two of its caches. Instance C has the buffer in SCUR mode, and instance B has the buffer in CR mode. The buffer is still in the local role, no one has yet updated the block, and there is no past image in any of the caches.

Example 3: Update the Row in Instance A

The block that holds the data about user *SCOTT* (EMPNO=7788) is now cached in instances B and C. Instance C reads the block from disk and serves it to instance B via the interconnect. Then instance A updates the data and makes the buffer incompatible. Instance A does not commit the changes.

Now let's update the block on instance A:

```
REM Let us update DML on instance A:

UPDATE EMP SET SAL=SAL+1000 WHERE EMP=7788;
```

```
#### Result of lock queries on instance A

SQL> @get_segment_stats
OBJECT_NAM STAT                                          VALUE
---------- ----------------------------------- -------
EMP  gc current blocks received                          1

SQL> @get_buffer_stat
STATE  MODE_HELD      FILE#       BLOCK#    SCN_BASE    SCN_WRAP
----- ---------- ---------- ---------- ---------- ----------
    1           0          4         32          0          0

SQL> @get_resource_name
HEXNAME                          RESOURCE_NAME   KJBLGRANT   KJBLROLE KJBLREQUE
------------------------  --------------- --------- ---------- ---------
[0x20][0x40000],[BL]      32,262144,BL    KJUSEREX           0 KJUSERNL
SQL> @get_resource_stat
no rows selected
```

Observe the following:

■ State 1 in x$bh shows that the block is held by the instance A in exclusive mode in the current state.

■ Statistics "gc current blocks received" indicates that the block is obtained from the global cache through Cache Fusion and not from the disk.

■ Column KJBLGRANT has a value of KJUSEREX, indicating that an instance has an exclusive lock on this resource.

■ Instance A has upgraded its lock from Null to X mode.

```
REM Lock and Block statistics from node B and C

REM Buffer Status in Node B (After Instance A updated the Block)
SQL> @get_buffer_stat
STATE  MODE_HELD      FILE#       BLOCK#    SCN_BASE    SCN_WRAP
----- ---------- ---------- ---------- ---------- ----------
    3           0          4         32     669341          0
SQL> @get_resource_name
no rows selected

SQL> @get_resource_stat
no rows selected

REM  Buffer Status from Node C
SQL> @get_buffer_stat
STATE  MODE_HELD      FILE#       BLOCK#    SCN_BASE    SCN_WRAP
----- ---------- ---------- ---------- ---------- ----------
    3           0          4         32     669340          0
```

```
SQL> @get_resource_name
no rows selected

SQL> @get_resource_stat
no rows selected

REM Resource Statistics from Master Node
SQL> @get_resource_stat
RESOURCE_NAME            STATE     MAST  CNVT  GRNT  REQUEST_L  GRANT_LEV
--------------------     --------  ----- ----- ----- ---------  ---------
[0x20][0x40000],[BL]     GRANTED      3     0     1  KJUSERNL   KJUSEREX
```

Observe the following:

- Instance C downgraded its lock from SCUR to Null mode and has the buffer in CR mode only.
- The buffer status in instance C is changed from 2 (SCUR) to 3 (CR).
- Instances B and C no longer have any lock on the resource. A block present in the buffer cache in CR mode can be used locally by the instance for query. However, the block cannot be used for update and cannot be served to other instances, so it does not require any lock.
- The master instance shows the lock covering the resource is granted in exclusive mode.
- Instance A has the most recent block in the buffer cache. Now any instance requesting the block will be served by instance A.

Example 4: Update a New Row (in the Same Block) in Instance C

Continuing from example 3, we update the same block from another instance, but here we update a different row. Updating the same row will cause waits for TX enqueue, because we are working with a single instance. The buffer holding block 32 is held exclusively by instance A and protected by a BL enqueue. Row-level locks in an Oracle RAC instance operate similarly to those in a single instance. In this example, we update the same block but a different row.

Let's update the same block on instance C. The block already has an open transaction operating on empno 7788.

```
REM On instance C's scott session:
UPDATE EMP SET SAL = SAL*2 WHERE EMPNO=7369;
COMMIT;

Result of lock queries on instance C, after an update to emp table on instance C
SQL> @get_segment_stats
OBJECT_NAM STAT                                      VALUE
---------- -----------------------------------       -------
EMP        physical reads                             1
EMP        gc current blocks received                 1

SQL> @get_buffer_stat
```

```
STATE  MODE_HELD       FILE#      BLOCK#    SCN_BASE   SCN_WRAP
-----  ----------  ----------  ----------  ----------  ----------
    1          0           4          32           0           0
SQL> @get_resource_name
HEXNAME                          RESOURCE_NAME   KJBLGRANT   KJBLROLE KJBLREQUE
------------------------------   -------------   ---------   -------- ---------
[0x20][0x40000],[BL]             32,262144,BL    KJUSEREX           0 KJUSERNL

SQL> @get_resource_stat
no rows selected
```

Observe the following:

- The statistic "gc current blocks received . . .1" indicates that the instance received one block belonging to this segment (table) from a remote instance via GCS.
- A value of 1 in the STATE column of the X$BH view on instance C indicates that the block is current and is locked exclusively by this instance.
- The resource is held in exclusive mode as shown as KJUSEREX in the third query.

Now let's query the master node to see lock statistics:

```
REM Statistics from Master Node (Instance D)

SQL> @get_resource_stat
RESOURCE_NAME          STATE     MAST  CNVT  GRNT REQUEST_L GRANT_LEV
---------------------  --------  ----- ----- ----- --------- ---------
[0x20][0x40000],[BL]   GRANTED      3     0     1 KJUSERNL  KJUSEREX
[0x20][0x40000],[BL]   GRANTED      3     0     1 KJUSERNL  KJUSERNL
```

Now we will go back to the instance that served the block to this instance. Instance A served the current block to instance C:

```
REM Resource statistics in node A
SQL> @get_buffer_stat
     STATE  MODE_HELD       FILE#      BLOCK#    SCN_BASE   SCN_WRAP
---------- ----------  ----------  ----------  ----------  ----------
         8          0           4          32           0           0

SQL> @get_resource_name
HEXNAME                          RESOURCE_NAME   KJBLGRANT   KJBLROLE KJBLREQUE
------------------------------   -------------   ---------   -------- ---------
[0x20][0x40000],[BL]             32,262144,BL    KJUSERNL          0 KJUSERNL
```

Note the following:

- Instance A downconverts the block from XCUR to PI (STATE equals 8).
- A Null mode lock as indicated by KJUSERNL protects the PI.
- Master node D shows the locks covering instance C as exclusive (KJUSEREX) and the lock covering instance A (KJUSERNL) for the PI image.

■ The master keeps track of the PI images across the buffer cache. All these instances will be asked to discard the PI copies once the current block is written to disk.

If you look at examples 3 and 4 closely, you can understand that the buffer locks are independent of row-level locks. When the block is updated in instance C, a row-level lock is placed in the block. When the block is updated again, another row-level lock is placed in the block.

The block-level storage parameter INITRANS controls the initial number of row-level locks that can be taken on that block. As demand grows, the number of row-level locks in the block grows as long as the block has enough space to record the transaction information. Refer to Chapter 11 for a better understanding of Oracle's internal implementation of row-level locks.

Example 5: Commit the Block in Instance A and Select the Rows

Now the process operating on instance A decides to commit the changes. Commit operations in the Oracle RAC environment work the same as operations in a single-instance environment as far as transactional locks are concerned. In the global cache, level commits do not make any lock status changes in the lock management layer. Now we will explore the query results after issuing a commit in instance A:

```
REM Let us commit our update done in example 3
REM In SCOTT's session, we will issue a commit.
COMMIT;
```

The following are the results in instance A after issuing a commit:

```
Resource statistics in node A
SQL> @get_buffer_stat
      STATE  MODE_HELD      FILE#     BLOCK#    SCN_BASE   SCN_WRAP
   ---------- ----------  ---------- ---------- ---------- ----------
         8          0           4        32          0          0
SQL> @get_resource_name
HEXNAME                     RESOURCE_NAME    KJBLGRANT   KJBLROLE KJBLREQUE
-------------------------- ---------------- ---------- ---------- ---------
[0x20][0x40000],[BL]        32,262144,BL     KJUSERNL            0 KJUSERNL


SQL> @get_segment_stats
OBJECT_NAM STAT                                          VALUE
---------- ----------------------------------------- -------

EMP        gc current blocks received                     1

REM Resource Statistics in  Instance C
SQL> @get_segment_stats

OBJECT_NAM STAT                                          VALUE
---------- ----------------------------------------- -------

EMP        physical reads                                 1
EMP        gc current blocks received                     1
```

```
SQL> @get_buffer_stat
STATE  MODE_HELD      FILE#      BLOCK#     SCN_BASE   SCN_WRAP
-----  ----------  ----------  ----------  ----------  ----------
   1        0          4          32           0          0
SQL> @get_resource_name
HEXNAME                       RESOURCE_NAME    KJBLGRANT    KJBLROLE KJBLREQUE
----------------------        ---------------  ---------    -------- ---------
[0x20][0x40000],[BL]          32,262144,BL     KJUSEREX            0 KJUSERNL

REM Statistics from Master Node (Instance D)
SQL> @get_resource_stat
RESOURCE_NAME            STATE     MAST  CNVT  GRNT  REQUEST_L  GRANT_LEV
--------------------     --------  ----- ----- ----- ---------  ---------
[0x20][0x40000],[BL]     GRANTED    3     0     1    KJUSERNL   KJUSEREX
[0x20][0x40000],[BL]     GRANTED    3     0     1    KJUSERNL   KJUSERNL
```

Observe the following:

■ Commits do not make any major changes in the global cache locks.

Example 6: Disk Writes Due to a Checkpoint

Continuing from example 5, the modified buffer from instance C is written to disk due to a checkpoint. We will explore the resource statistics after the checkpoint.

```
REM Let us trigger a checkpoint in Instance C
SQL> alter system checkpoint global;
System altered.

REM Resource Statistics in Instance A
SQL> @get_buffer_stat
STATE  MODE_HELD      FILE#      BLOCK#     SCN_BASE   SCN_WRAP
-----  ----------  ----------  ----------  ----------  ----------
   3        0          4          32         669387        0
SQL> @get_resource_name
no rows selected
SQL> @get_resource_stat
no rows selected

REM Resource Statistics in  Instance C
SQL> @get_segment_stats
OBJECT_NAM STAT                                   VALUE
---------- ----------------------------------     -------

EMP        physical reads                            1
EMP        gc current blocks received                1

SQL> @get_buffer_stat
STATE  MODE_HELD      FILE#      BLOCK#     SCN_BASE   SCN_WRAP
-----  ----------  ----------  ----------  ----------  ----------
   1        0          4          32           0          0
```

```
SQL> @get_resource_name
HEXNAME                            RESOURCE_NAME   KJBLGRANT   KJBLROLE KJBLREQUE
-----------------------------      ------------- ----------  ---------- ---------
[0x20][0x40000],[BL]               32,262144,BL    KJUSEREX            0 KJUSERNL


Statistics from Master Node (Instance D)


SQL> @get_resource_stat
RESOURCE_NAME                   STATE     MAST  CNVT  GRNT  REQUEST_L GRANT_LEV
--------------------------      --------  ----- ----- ----- --------- ---------
[0x20][0x40000],[BL]            GRANTED      3     0     1 KJUSERNL   KJUSEREX
```

Here are some observations:

- The checkpoint request from instance C to the master does not change any lock status in the current node.

- The PI from node A is discarded and the buffer is changed to CR mode. Hence, the status of the buffer is changed from 8 to 3.

- Because the PI buffer is changed to CR, there is no need for the master to protect that resource. Therefore, the KJUSERNL lock is destroyed.

- Instance C also generates a BWR and writes it to redo log files. The BWR dump is shown here:

```
Block Written Record Dump in Redo Log File of Instance C

CHANGE #1 MEDIA RECOVERY MARKER SCN:0x0000.00000000 SEQ:  0 OP:23.1
   Block Written - afn: 4 rdba: 0x01000020 BFT:(1024,16777248) non-BFT:(4,32)
                   scn: 0x0000.001778e1 seq:0x01 flg:0x00


REDO RECORD - Thread:1 RBA: 0x000006.00004d4a.0010 LEN: 0x0070 VLD: 0x06
SCN: 0x0000.00178185 SUBSCN:  1 08/19/2010 22:36:35
CHANGE #1 MEDIA RECOVERY MARKER SCN:0x0000.00000000 SEQ:  0 OP:23.1
```

Example 7: Instance Crash

At this time, instance D (the master instance for our interested resource EMP) crashes. Here is the reconfiguration information from the alert log of instance A:

```
Reconfiguration started (old inc 8, new inc 10)
List of instances:
 1 2 3 (myinst: 1)
 Global Resource Directory frozen
 * dead instance detected - domain 0 invalid = TRUE
 Communication channels reestablished
Thu Aug 19 00:57:32 2010
 * domain 0 not valid according to instance 3
 * domain 0 not valid according to instance 2
 Master broadcasted resource hash value bitmaps
 Non-local Process blocks cleaned out
```

```
Thu Aug 19 00:57:34 2010
 LMS 0: 1 GCS shadows cancelled, 0 closed, 0 Xw survived
 Set master node info
 Submitted all remote-enqueue requests
 Dwn-cvts replayed, VALBLKs dubious
 All grantable enqueues granted
 Post SMON to start 1st pass IR
Thu Aug 19 00:57:36 2010
Instance recovery: looking for dead threads
Thu Aug 19 00:57:36 2010
Setting Resource Manager plan DEFAULT_MAINTENANCE_PLAN via parameter
Beginning instance recovery of 1 threads
 Submitted all GCS remote-cache requests
 Post SMON to start 1st pass IR
 Fix write in gcs resources
Reconfiguration complete
```

Example 8: Select the Data from Instance A

After instance reconfiguration, we select the data from instance A. Here are the resource statistics on the master node:

```
SQL> @get_segment_stats
OBJECT_NAM STAT                                        VALUE
---------- ----------------------------------- -------
EMP          gc cr blocks received                        1
EMP          gc current blocks received                   1

SQL> @get_buffer_stat

      STATE  MODE_HELD      FILE#     BLOCK#    SCN_BASE    SCN_WRAP
---------- ---------- ---------- ---------- ---------- ----------
         3          0          4         32     670125           0
SQL> @get_resource_name
no rows selected
SQL> @get_resource_stat
no rows selected
```

Upon instance recovery, the EMP table is remastered in instance C. We query X$KJBR with the resource name and confirm the resource is remastered in instance C. Alternatively, oradebug lkdebug -a <pkey> can be used to determine the details about the master of that resource.

```
REM Resource Statistics from the (new) master node
SQL> @get_master_info
    INST_ID KJBRNAME                       KJBRROLE KJBRMASTER
---------- --------------------- ---------- ----------

         3 [0x20][0x40000],[BL]                   0          2
```

```
SQL> @get_resource_stat
RESOURCE_NAME            STATE       MAST   CNVT   GRNT  REQUEST_L  GRANT_LEV
----------------------   --------    -----  -----  ----- --------   ---------
[0x20][0x40000],[BL]     GRANTED       3      0      1   KJUSERNL   KJUSEREX
```

Observe the following:

■ Instance ID 3 is instance C, because instance numbers for the INST_ID start from 1.
   KJBRMASTER shows 2 because for KJBR the numbering starts from 0.

■ Upon the master instance crash, the resources are equally distributed to the surviving
   nodes and the sample object (obj=51151, EMP) is remastered to instance C.

Resource Mastering and Remastering

If you have carefully read the concepts of Cache Fusion so far, the following should be clear:

■ Resource usage (including locks on the data blocks) is tracked by GCS. GCS resources
   and responsibilities are equally distributed among all the instances.

■ Every resource has a master, and the master instance knows the complete lock state of
   the resource at any point in time.

■ When an instance needs a resource, it requests the desired lock from the master instance
   by sending a message.

■ Based on the current status of the resource, the master grants access to the resource or
   asks the holder to disown the lock on that resource.

■ If one instance accesses a particular resource more often than the others, it would be
   beneficial to master the resource to that instance to reduce the number of messages on
   ownership transfers.

■ At any point in time a resource can be accessed at the maximum of three hops. This is
   true irrespective of the number of instances because only three parties are involved in
   any resource management operation.

■ If the application's data access patterns are such that a set of data blocks is generally
   accessed by only one instance, then making the local instance the master of those
   resources can optimize the amount of messages sent to remote instances. Oracle keeps
   track of data block access patterns by instances and remasters the resources to optimize
   the messaging. By default, the Oracle kernel invokes the remastering algorithm every
   10 minutes.

■ Starting from Oracle 11*g*, the objects with a high number of read lock requests are
   treated specially with the "read-mostly" locking protocol. Object affinity for read-mostly
   and dynamic remastering can be controlled by the _gc_affinity_locking parameter. This
   parameter defaults to TRUE, which enables read-mostly and object remastering validation
   periodically.

■ In Oracle 11*g*, undo affinity and object affinity are enabled by default. However, undo
   affinity can be disabled by setting _gc_undo_affinity=false and object affinity can be
   disabled by setting _gc_affinity_locking=false individually. However, you can disable the
   affinity locks for undo and object affinity by setting _gc_affinity_locks=false.

- The undocumented initialization parameter _gc_read_mostly_locking controls the read-mostly policy evaluation periodically. Setting _gc_read_mostly_locking=false disables the read-mostly policy evaluation. You can manually force an object to be read-mostly using the following command:

```
oradebug lkdebug -m pkey_readmostly <obj#>
```

And you can dissolve the read-mostly status for an object using this command:

```
oradebug lkdebug -m dpkey <obj#>
```

Background Process and Cache Fusion

The following sections describe the functions performed by each background process as it relates to GCS.

LMON: Lock Monitor Process

LMON maintains GCS memory structures. It handles the abnormal termination of processes and instances. Reconfiguration of locks and resources when an instance joins or leaves the cluster are handled by LMON. Activities that occur during instance reconfigurations are tracked by it in its trace file. In versions 10g R2 and later, LMON is responsible for executing dynamic lock remastering every 10 minutes. In current versions, LMON is known as the Global Enqeueue Services monitor.

LMS: Lock Manager Server

LMS is the most active Oracle RAC background process; it can become very active, consuming significant amounts of CPU time. Oracle recommends that this process be allocated the needed CPU time by increasing its priority. Starting from 10g R2, Oracle has implemented a feature to ensure that the LMS process does not encounter CPU starvation. It is also known as the Global Cache Service (GCS) process in current versions.

This process is responsible for receiving remote messages and executing the desired GCS requests, which include the following operations:

- Retrieves requests from the server queue queued by LMD to perform requested lock operations.
- Rolls back any uncommitted transactions for any blocks that are being requested for consistent read by the remote instance.
- Copies blocks from the holding instance's buffer cache and sends a read-consistent copy of the block to the requesting foreground process on the requesting instance to be placed into the buffer cache.

LMS also sends messages to remote instances that are not sent by the user processes. Each Oracle RAC instance can have two or more LMS processes. The internal view X$KJMSDP contains statistics for the work performed by each LMS process for the instance.

The number of LMS processes can also be set with the init parameter GCS_SERVER_PROCESSES. Oracle has been optimizing the default number of LMS processes, which varies from version to version. In most of the versions, the default value is as follows:

```
MIN(CPU_COUNT/2, 2))
```

However, starting with 10g R2, in a single CPU machine, only one LMS process is started. You can consider increasing the value of this parameter if global cache activity is very high.

LMD: Lock Manager Daemon Process (LMDn)

The LMD process performs global lock deadlock detection. It also monitors for lock conversion timeouts. It manages lock manager service requests for GCS resources and sends them to a service queue to be handled by the LMSn process. This process primarily handles lock requests for Global Enqueue resources. The internal view X$KJMDDP contains statistics for the work done by each LMD process for the instance.

LCKn: Lock Process (LCK0)

This process manages instance resource requests and cross-instance calls for shared resources. During instance recovery, it builds a list of invalid lock elements and validates lock elements.

DIAG: Diagnostic Daemon (DIAG)

The diagnostic daemon process was introduced in Oracle 10g as a part of the new enhanced diagnosability framework. It regularly monitors the health of the instance. It also checks for instance hangs and deadlocks. Most importantly, it captures the vital diagnostics data for instance and process failures.

In a Nutshell

Cache Fusion contributes to the extreme performance of Oracle Database RAC. In this chapter, you saw examples of how it actually works and what happens "under the hood" to enable the transparency of the sessions and connected applications. Understanding the workings of Cache Fusion will help you to appreciate the functionalities and enable designing highly scalable system architectures.

Past Image (PI) blocks and block written records (BWR) optimize the block transfer between instances and guarantee faster block recovery during instance failures in high-concurrency environments. Newly improved dynamic remastering and read-mostly affinity algorithms reduce the messages between master and requestor on some specific conditions.

The background processes Lock Manager Demon (LMD) and Global Cache Services (GCS) handle the block and lock transfers between the instance and play a major role in the implementation of Cache Fusion between the instances. The DIAG process enhances diagnosability, and the LCK processes play a major role in Cache Fusion recovery.

CHAPTER
13

Workload and Connection Management

he fundamental features of a good, scalable database management system include connection and workload balancing of database connections. Efficient management of these connections, once established, is very important, especially for providing database as a service for big enterprise applications. Fault-tolerant services must be provided by the database engine so that users can take appropriate actions as alternatives to failures and errors.

In a large installation, potentially thousands of users could log on or off from a database within a short span of time. An efficient database engine ensures minimal delays in processing their requests and managing the resources used by these connections. Complex installations are required on external hardware and/or software mechanisms to aid them in integrating messaging and notifications within the cluster when a failure occurs in a cluster service such as an Oracle RAC instance, network interfaces, disks, and so on.

Workload Distribution and Load Balancing

Workload distribution can sometimes be called *load balancing*. *Workload distribution* is the management of user connections in such a way that the work they perform is distributed uniformly across Oracle RAC nodes or cluster database instances. It does not necessarily mean that the *work itself* is evenly spread between nodes due to this mechanism. The distribution of work is an indirect result of the connection distribution.

The workload distribution strategy must be determined during the test implementation phase of application deployment (if not earlier) to make it clear how the application is actually going to connect to the various nodes and database instances. Designers and architects should work out the application behavior with adequate testing to understand how the system performs under a given workload; this information provides a benchmark for the live implementation.

Workload distribution can occur on a per-connection basis, based on server-CPU load or on application/module usage. Certain strategies may be more appropriate than others, depending on the implementation and type of usage. The implementation architecture also plays a crucial role in the performance of the system as well as the way the workload is distributed.

Consider, for example, a four-node Oracle RAC database running Oracle E-Business Suite R12*i*. Multiple applications and web servers on the system may or may not be clustered. A total of 8,000 users (connections) access the database via a dedicated server mechanism, and no external, intelligent network devices route the connection request(s) to a particular Oracle RAC instance based on some predetermined criteria.

Using Oracle's workload distribution mechanism, you can ensure that about 2,000 clients connect to each Oracle RAC node, thereby ensuring that the *connections* are balanced—but not necessarily the *work* these connections perform. In this system, one particular node is more heavily loaded than the others, because the users connected to that node are firing many batch jobs, while the other nodes are running user modules—Inventory, Payables, GL, and the like. Nevertheless, you would like these connections to perform equal units of work, thereby achieving the ever-elusive and mirage-like *load-balanced* system. But one of the most difficult tasks to achieve is a complete and perfectly balanced system—unless the application behavior is very well analyzed, the users are well educated, and the application access is restricted to one node, ensuring a uniform usage pattern. This is easier said than done, however, as many of us may have discovered over the years. If only one database server responds to all the incoming requests, the capacity of the server will not be able to handle high volumes of incoming traffic once the workload increases. Needless to say, application as well as database response time takes a beating—and so do the DBAs. An increase in work and connections to the database server can lead to a point at which upgrading the server hardware will no longer be cost effective.

To achieve server scalability, more servers need to be added to distribute the load among the cluster. Distributing the load among these clustered servers is known as *load balancing*.

Such situations are nothing new for someone who has been in the IT industry since the early 1990s, when clustered solutions took off like a rocket. Load balancing and clustering go hand in hand and can be applied to various types of applications such as Internet web servers, telecom applications, and network information servers.

Generic load balancing can become a highly technical and complicated topic and is best treated by network and systems professionals who operate large networks. Load balancing is decided at the system architecture design level, although the implementation mechanisms and methods could differ, depending on the application and type of load balancing being done. In this discussion, we look at load balancing particularly from an Oracle perspective.

In Oracle database applications, load balancing is the attempt to achieve a balanced number of database connections across all the database servers. Load balancing also distributes the services across all the nodes in a cluster implementation. Load balancing can be accomplished using a hardware device or by using Oracle's own software mechanism, as you will learn in the following few sections.

Oracle attempts load balancing by introducing the workload distribution principle. By ensuring a uniform set of connections across all the nodes, we can hope that all the servers are equally loaded to achieve maximum scalability, of course depending on many other factors—too many to discuss here. We can hope that each user will perform equivalent amounts of work, irrespective of the node to which each user is logged in.

Application designers and implementers like to restrict usage of an application/module to a particular node only in hopes of achieving balance. For example, if we have deployed General Ledger, Payables, Accounts Receivable, and Inventory in our organization on a four-node cluster for 8,000 users, we might restrict usage of General Ledger and Payables to nodes 1 and 2, respectively. Nodes 3 and 4 can run only Accounts Receivable and Inventory, respectively. This method—commonly known as *application partitioning*—can sometimes cause an imbalanced cluster. In such cases, each node accepts a maximum of 2,000 connections, and a node runs only one application at a time.

Using this method, we could end up in a situation where nodes 1 and 2 are loaded evenly and the other two nodes are heavily loaded. It is also possible that between the last two nodes, node 4 could be running at near 100-percent CPU and memory utilization due to the intense workload generated by the Inventory users. Therefore, it is quite possible that an acceptable approach such as application partitioning can sometimes yield unexpected or undesirable results.

Overcoming these challenges is one of the best things about working in clustered environments. See Chapter 16 for more information about this topic.

Problems occur because the work patterns and resource usage of each application can be different. The way they scale and their behavior with increased workload can be vastly different. Hence, it is extremely crucial to test and measure workload profile and performance statistics *before* implementing an application and/or before deploying soft load balancing (application partitioning).

NOTE
Designers and architects should also work out whether a policy-managed database or an administrator-managed database would suit the workload. A policy-managed database suits big installations where multiple cluster databases are running from the same Oracle Grid Infrastructure, whereas an administrator-managed database suits small installations where the DBA can decide the placement of the cluster database instance resources within the cluster.

Hardware and Software Load Balancing

The deciding factors for choosing one method of load balancing over another depends on the requirements, available features, complexity of implementation, and cost. We will consider hardware- and software-based load balancing here, because they are more applicable to the Oracle database application.

Hardware load-balancing devices can route TCP/IP packets to various servers in a cluster. These types of load balancers provide a robust topology with high availability but come at a much higher cost. On one hand, this method uses a circuit-level network gateway to route traffic. However, its implementation is more expensive than software implementations.

The most commonly used load balancers are software based and are used mainly as additional/optional features of software applications such as web servers. Oracle provides some form of load balancing as an integrated component of its database software. Software-based load balancers are cheaper than their hardware counterparts. Software is more configurable based on requirements, and it can incorporate intelligent routing based on multiple input parameters. On the other hand, additional hardware can be needed to isolate the load-balancing application.

Let's look at some of the features Oracle provides in terms of load balancing connections to the database.

Load Balancing and Oracle Net Services

Many applications like to balance their workloads across all the instances of an Oracle RAC database. Usually, load balancing with Oracle (excluding the parallel feature) meant connection load balancing—that is, the connections to the database are balanced on a "round-robin" basis, CPU load, or session count at connect time. With Oracle Net Services, there are two types of connection load balancing: one on the client side and the other on the server side.

NOTE
The discussion about connect-time load balancing is for dedicated connections only. Shared server connections can also take advantage of these features but are not discussed here.

Client-Side Load Balancing

Oracle's client-side load balancing feature enables clients to randomize connection requests among all the available listeners. Oracle Net Services progresses through the list of protocol addresses in a round-robin sequence, balancing the load on various listeners. This normally is referred to as *client-side connect-time load balance*. Without client-side load balancing, Oracle

Net Services progresses through the list of protocol addresses sequentially until one succeeds. Figure 13-1 illustrates client-side load balancing.

Client-side load balancing is defined in the client connection definition file (tnsnames.ora) by setting the parameter LOAD_BALANCE = ON. When this parameter is set to ON, Oracle Net Services progresses through the list of listener addresses in a random sequence, balancing the load on the various listeners. When it's set to OFF, the addresses are tried sequentially until one succeeds. This parameter must be correctly specified in the Net Services name (connect descriptor). By default, this parameter is set to ON for the DESCRIPTION_LIST.

When using SCAN (Single Client Access Name) in the connection definition, the Oracle database randomly connects to one of the available SCAN listeners in a round-robin fashion and balances the connections on the three SCAN listeners. Here is a sample tnsnames.ora (client and server) configuration for a four-node Oracle RAC database using SCAN:

```
RAC =
  (DESCRIPTION =
    (ADDRESS = (PROTOCOL = TCP)(HOST = SCAN-HOSTNAME)(PORT = 1701))
    (CONNECT_DATA =
      (SERVICE_NAME = RAC)
    )
  )
```

Upon receiving a connection request from the users using the preceding connection details, SCAN will connect to one of the SCAN listeners defined by SCAN in a round-robin fashion. Once SCAN is connected to a SCAN listener, the SCAN listener will identify the least-loaded cluster database instance providing the requested service. Once the least-loaded instance is identified, the SCAN listener will redirect the client to the local listener of the cluster node running the least-loaded cluster database instance. The local listener will connect the client to the database instance.

NOTE
Oracle does not load balance when the client connects to the database using EZConnect.

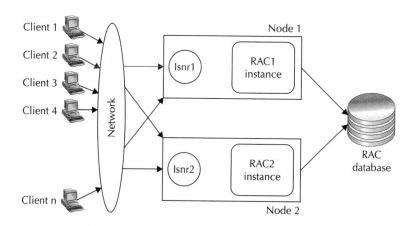

FIGURE 13-1 *Client-side load balancing*

Load balancing can also be specified for an ADDRESS_LIST or associated with a set of addresses or set descriptions. If you use ADDRESS_LIST, LOAD_BALANCE = ON should be within the (ADDRESS_LIST =) portion. If you do not use ADDRESS_LIST, LOAD_BALANCE = ON should be within the (DESCRIPTION =) portion. Here is a sample tnsnames.ora (client and server) configuration for a four-node Oracle RAC database:

```
RAC =
  (DESCRIPTION =
    (LOAD_BALANCE = ON)
    (ADDRESS = (PROTOCOL = TCP)(HOST = node1-vip)(PORT = 1541))
    (ADDRESS = (PROTOCOL = TCP)(HOST = node2-vip)(PORT = 1541))
    (ADDRESS = (PROTOCOL = TCP)(HOST = node3-vip)(PORT = 1541))
    (ADDRESS = (PROTOCOL = TCP)(HOST = node4-vip)(PORT = 1541))
    (CONNECT_DATA = (SERVICE_NAME = RAC)
  ))
```

Alternatively, you can configure it in another way. Since LOAD_BALANCE is ON by default, the reference is not needed unless you want to turn it off. Most examples show LOAD_BALANCE= ON when the Oracle Connection Manager is being used.

```
RAC =
  (DESCRIPTION =
    (ADDRESS_LIST =
      (ADDRESS = (PROTOCOL = TCP)(HOST = node1-vip)(PORT = 1541))
      (ADDRESS = (PROTOCOL = TCP)(HOST = node2-vip)(PORT = 1541))
      (ADDRESS = (PROTOCOL = TCP)(HOST = node3-vip)(PORT = 1541))
      (ADDRESS = (PROTOCOL = TCP)(HOST = node4-vip)(PORT = 1541))
    )
    (CONNECT_DATA = (SERVICE_NAME = RAC)
  ))
```

The listener.ora file on *each* node will look like this NODE1 file:

```
LISTENER=(DESCRIPTION=(ADDRESS_LIST=
(ADDRESS=(PROTOCOL=IPC)(KEY=LISTENER))))                      # line added by Agent
LISTENER_SCAN3=(DESCRIPTION=(ADDRESS_LIST=
(ADDRESS=(PROTOCOL=IPC)(KEY=LISTENER_SCAN3))))               # line added by Agent
LISTENER_SCAN2=(DESCRIPTION=(ADDRESS_LIST=
(ADDRESS=(PROTOCOL=IPC)(KEY=LISTENER_SCAN2))))               # line added by Agent
LISTENER_SCAN1=(DESCRIPTION=(ADDRESS_LIST=
(ADDRESS=(PROTOCOL=IPC)(KEY=LISTENER_SCAN1))))               # line added by Agent
ENABLE_GLOBAL_DYNAMIC_ENDPOINT_LISTENER_SCAN1=ON             # line added by Agent
ENABLE_GLOBAL_DYNAMIC_ENDPOINT_LISTENER_SCAN2=ON             # line added by Agent
ENABLE_GLOBAL_DYNAMIC_ENDPOINT_LISTENER_SCAN3=ON             # line added by Agent
ENABLE_GLOBAL_DYNAMIC_ENDPOINT_LISTENER=ON                   # line added by Agent
```

The listener.ora on each node will define three SCAN listeners and one local listener, as shown in the preceding listener.ora.

The tnsnames.ora on each node (as well as your client PCs or other hosts) may also contain the individual entries for each of the Oracle RAC instances, as shown next. This is useful when a client program wants to connect to a specific node.

```
RAC1 =
  (DESCRIPTION =
    (ADDRESS_LIST =
      (ADDRESS = (PROTOCOL = TCP)(HOST = NODE1-vip)(PORT = 1541))
    )
    (CONNECT_DATA =
      (SERVICE_NAME = RAC)
      (INSTANCE_NAME = RAC1)
    ))

RAC2 =
  (DESCRIPTION =
    (ADDRESS_LIST =
      (ADDRESS = (PROTOCOL = TCP)(HOST = NODE2-vip)(PORT = 1541))
    )
    (CONNECT_DATA =
      (SERVICE_NAME = RAC)
      (INSTANCE_NAME = RAC2)
    ))

RAC3 =
  (DESCRIPTION =
    (ADDRESS_LIST =
      (ADDRESS = (PROTOCOL = TCP)(HOST = NODE3-vip)(PORT = 1541))
    )
    (CONNECT_DATA =
      (SERVICE_NAME = RAC)
      (INSTANCE_NAME = RAC3)
    ))

RAC4 =
  (DESCRIPTION =
    (ADDRESS_LIST =
      (ADDRESS = (PROTOCOL = TCP)(HOST = NODE4-vip)(PORT = 1541))
    )
    (CONNECT_DATA =
      (SERVICE_NAME = RAC)
      (INSTANCE_NAME = RAC4)
    ))
```

Starting from Oracle 11g, Oracle automatically sets the value for the LOCAL_LISTENER database parameter, so there is no need to set this parameter manually. The LOCAL_LISTENER database parameter allows the database instance to know about the local listener.
   Here is a sample value for the LOCAL_LISTENER database parameter:

```
(DESCRIPTION=(ADDRESS_LIST=(ADDRESS=(PROTOCOL=TCP)(HOST=NODE1-VIP)(PORT=1541))))
```

In this way, the tnsnames.ora on each node should be able to resolve its local listener, and listeners on each cluster node know about each other. With this, the configuration is complete; now when clients start to connect using the Oracle RAC service name (which matches the init. ora/SPFILE parameter SERVICE_NAME) from a client terminal using SQL*Plus or any other front-end application, the connections are randomly sent to each of the active nodes. This is the round-robin feature mentioned earlier. An "lsnrctl services" command can reveal the statistics for each node.

Note that provisioning a "random" method of a database connection mechanism can also be done using a hardware device that is configured appropriately. Cost is a major factor to be considered, and if the *database instance* is down for some reason, the hardware device has no way of knowing it, even though it has the intelligence to recognize that the node is up and running. This lack of *database knowledge* can cause delays or timeouts for connections. Oracle helps you overcome these limitations with its simple client-side load-balancing feature.

One of the disadvantages of the client-side method of load balancing is that client connections won't be able to gauge the load and other resource consumption factors on the instance/node to which they are trying to connect. Hence, timeouts can also occur if the node being attempted for connection is heavily loaded and unable to respond quickly.

In any load-balancing scheme, regardless of the connection method, once a connection is established, that connection continues to stay on that instance (until it terminates) and does not migrate to other less heavily loaded nodes in case the usage spikes up. This is an important misconception that even many DBAs and application technologists hold on to.

Server-Side Load Balancing

Server-side load balancing is also known as *listener-connection load balancing*. This feature improves connection performance by balancing the number of active connections among multiple dispatchers and instances. In a single-instance environment (when shared servers are used), the listener selects the least-loaded dispatcher to handle the incoming client requests.

The core of server-side load balancing is the Dynamic Service Registration, which is a feature where listeners on all the cluster nodes register themselves with other listeners in the cluster to know the database instances and services provided by the databases in the cluster. Dynamic service registration is implemented by PMON, where a listener is always aware of all instances and dispatchers regardless of their locations. Depending on the load information, a listener decides to which instance and, if a shared server is configured, to which dispatcher the incoming client request will be sent. Figure 13-2 illustrates typical server-side load balancing.

In a shared server configuration, a listener selects a dispatcher in the following order:

1. Least-loaded node
2. Least-loaded instance
3. Least-loaded dispatcher for that instance

In a dedicated server configuration, a listener selects an instance in the following order:

1. Least-loaded node
2. Least-loaded instance

If a database service has multiple instances on multiple nodes, the listener chooses the least-loaded instance on the least-loaded node. If a shared server is configured, the least-loaded dispatcher of the selected instance is chosen.

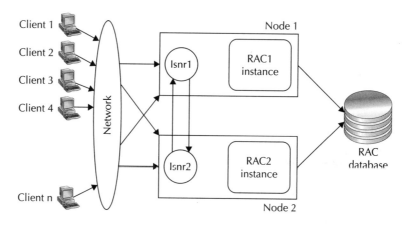

FIGURE 13-2 *Server-side load balancing*

As mentioned, the initialization parameter remote_listener is used to enable listener-connection load balancing. The entry on every node would look like this:

```
*.remote_listener='SCAN:<port>'
```

Oracle sets the remote_listener database parameter.

The listener considers the current workload being executed on all the available instances for the requested database service. With server-side load balancing, the listener routes incoming client connections to instances on the least-loaded nodes. The listener determines the connection distribution based on profile statistics that are dynamically updated by PMON. The higher the node load, the more frequently PMON updates the load profile. Updates occur in as little as 3 seconds on heavily loaded nodes and may take up to 10 minutes on lightly loaded nodes.

The service updates are printed to the listener log as follows:

```
19-DEC-2010 18:07:25 *
(CONNECT_DATA=(SERVICE_NAME=PROD)(INSTANCE_NAME=PROD1)(CID=(PROGRAM=)(HOST=erpa
s2)(USER=applprod))) * (ADDRESS=(PROTOCOL=tcp)(HOST=130.188.1.214)
(PORT=48604))
* establish * PROD * 0
19-DEC-2010 18:07:27 * service_update * PROD2 * 0
19-DEC-2010 18:07:29 * service_update * PROD1 * 0
19-DEC-2010 18:10:12 *
(CONNECT_DATA=(SERVICE_NAME=PROD)(INSTANCE_NAME=PROD1)(CID=(PROGRAM=)(HOST=erpd
b1)(USER=applprod))) * (ADDRESS=(PROTOCOL=tcp)(HOST=130.188.1.215)
(PORT=47933))
* establish * PROD * 0
19-DEC-2010 18:10:12 *
(CONNECT_DATA=(SERVICE_NAME=PROD)(INSTANCE_NAME=PROD1)(CID=(PROGRAM=)(HOST=erpd
b1)(USER=applprod))) * (ADDRESS=(PROTOCOL=tcp)(HOST=130.188.1.215)(PORT=47934))
```

```
* establish * PROD * 0
19-DEC-2010 18:12:13 * service_update * PROD2 * 0
19-DEC-2010 18:12:15 * service_update * PROD1 * 0
19-DEC-2010 18:12:24 * service_update * PROD1 * 0
19-DEC-2010 18:13:42 * service_update * PROD1 * 0
```

Depending on the load information sent by each PMON process, the listener, by default, redirects the incoming connection request to the listener of the least-loaded instance on the least-loaded node. By default, Oracle uses the run queue length to distribute the load. To trace the load balancing, you can set the debug event 10237 in the init.ora file, and the PMON trace file in diagnostic_dest can be examined to confirm the load balancing:

```
event="10257 trace name context forever, level 16"
```

If you want to guarantee that the listener redirects the connection request based on session load, set PREFER_LEAST_LOADED_NODE_[listener_name] to OFF in the listener.ora file. This is suited for applications that use connection pools.

In summary (without external hardware) Oracle provides two different types of load balancing: namely, client-side and server-side load balancing. Here are some points to keep in mind:

- Client-side load balancing is affected by setting a parameter in tnsnames.ora. It simply distributes the sessions pretty much uniformly across all the available instances, regardless of whether a specific session exerts too much of the load or a specific instance is already heavily loaded.

- Server-side load balancing is affected by the remote_listener parameter in init.ora. This takes into account the instance that is loaded, not just the count of the sessions in each.

- Both can be used concurrently. Therefore, it's possible that client-side load balancing directs a connection to a specific listener, but that listener may direct the connection to an instance on a different node.

Table 13-1 summarizes the overall details about the different types of load balancing, with their advantages and disadvantages.

Transparent Application Failover

Transparent Application Failover (TAF) enables an application user to reconnect to a database automatically if a connection fails. Active transactions roll back, but the new database connection, achieved using a different node, is identical to the original node. This is true regardless of how the connection fails.

TAF notifications are used by the server to trigger TAF callbacks on the client side. TAF is configured using either a client-side-specified Transparent Network Substrate (TNS) connect string or using server-side service attributes. However, if both methods are used to configure TAF, the server-side service attributes will supersede the client-side settings, because the server-side service attributes are the preferred way to set up TAF.

	Hardware Load Balancing (Switch)	Software Load Balancing (Server)	Software Load Balancing (Client)
Implementation	Implemented at the network level. Depending on the address, the connection is routed to a specific node.	Implemented at server level. Based on the CPU usage of the server, the connection is accepted or forwarded to another node.	Implemented using client configuration files. Connections distributed to different nodes from the list of nodes.
Operation Parameters	At network level. Network address of the incoming connection.	Implemented at OS level; CPU usage statistics from OS.	Application level; from the application or module.
Cost	Additional cost involved, as it requires additional hardware.	No additional cost.	No additional cost.
Optimization for Logon Storms	Well optimized for logon storms—huge number of connection requests during very short time.	Not optimized for logon storms. All connections may land in one node.	Partial optimization for logon storms as requests are distributed to nodes on a round-robin basis.

TABLE 13-1   *Types of Load Balancing*

When a failure occurs, callback functions are initiated on the client-side via Oracle Call Interface (OCI) callbacks. This will work with standard OCI connections as well as connection pool and session pool connections.

TAF Considerations

TAF works very well for the reporting and query-only applications, without requiring any additional code changes at the application layer. However, it does not fail over or protect the following elements:

- Active insert, update, and delete transactions
- PL/SQL server-side package variables
- Applications not using OCI 8

Even with Oracle 11g R2, TAF supports only failover of SELECT statements and client applications built using OCI. Custom application code may be required to trap errors or exceptions and perform alternative actions. Any application written using OCI 8 or later can take advantage of TAF. Many Oracle tools use OCI transparently; therefore, SQL*Plus, the Pro*C precompiler, the ODBC driver, and the thick Java Database Connectivity (JDBC) driver all work with TAF.

For an application to utilize the TAF feature, it must incorporate the appropriate OCI 8 (or later) usages and provide certain network configuration information. This requires the manual configuration of the tnsnames.ora and listener.ora files. It is possible to utilize TAF in a configuration where connected clients are performing update transactions; however, additional coding is required to achieve this.

Uncommitted changes at the time of failure are automatically rolled back by the database. To ensure that the application does not think that changes still exist, an error is returned to the application, which can then trigger the application to execute its own rollback statement. The application can then retry the transaction. In most cases, the application will receive another error during the rollback phase, indicating that the connection has been lost. This error must be trapped, but it can be ignored because the database will have already undone any transactional changes active during the failover.

Alternatively, Oracle Net Services can also preconnect users to a second node. If the primary node dies, the second connection already will be in place, bypassing network bottlenecks at reconnect time.

Configuring TAF

For a client to use TAF, it can either connect to the database using a connect descriptor that contains a FAILOVER_MODE portion or use server-side TAF defined for a service created using the SRVCTL utility. An example of a tnsnames.ora entry for a four-node Oracle RAC database follows:

```
RAC =
  (DESCRIPTION =
    (ADDRESS = (PROTOCOL = TCP)(HOST = NODE1-vip)(PORT = 1541))
    (ADDRESS = (PROTOCOL = TCP)(HOST = NODE2-vip)(PORT = 1541))
    (ADDRESS = (PROTOCOL = TCP)(HOST = NODE3-vip)(PORT = 1541))
    (ADDRESS = (PROTOCOL = TCP)(HOST = NODE4-vip)(PORT = 1541))
    (CONNECT_DATA =
      (SERVICE_NAME = RAC)
      (FAILOVER_MODE=(TYPE=SELECT)(METHOD=BASIC))
  ))
```

It is assumed that the SERVICE_NAME parameter in init.ora or SPFILE is accurately configured. Services can also be configured using the Server Control utility (SRVCTL), DBCA, or Enterprise Manager. Most importantly, the service entries have to be updated in the OCR repository. The tnsnames.ora files should be configured as shown earlier in the chapter. Initialization parameters such as local_listener and remote_listener should also be accurately configured.

Note that we have not used FAILOVER=ON. This default parameter is set to ON if you use DESCRIPTION_LIST, DESCRIPTION, or ADDRESS_LIST in tnsnames.ora. FAILOVER=ON/TRUE/ YES provides for connect-time failover, where Oracle Net Services tries the first address in the list and if that fails, it fails over to the next one in the address list. Without this, Oracle would try only one address (if LOAD_BALANCE=ON, a random address is selected or else the first one in the list is used for a connection attempt) from the list and report an error on connection failure.

This type of service configuration for the service RAC tells Oracle Net Services to fail over to another instance providing the service RAC only when the instance to which we are currently connected fails.

TAF Configuration Options

The notable part of TAF configuration is shown here:

```
(FAILOVER_MODE=(TYPE=SELECT)(METHOD=BASIC))
```

The TYPE parameter can take any of the following three values:

- **SESSION** Set to failover the session. If a user's connection is lost, a new session is automatically created for the user on the backup node using the service name specified in tnsnames.ora. This type of failover does not attempt to recover selects.

- **SELECT**   Set to enable users with open cursors to continue fetching on them after a failure. Using this mode can incur overhead on the client side in normal select operations.

- **NONE**   This is the default. No failover functionality is used. This can also be explicitly specified to prevent failover from happening.

The METHOD parameter can accept either of the following two values and basically determines which method of failover takes place on instance failure from the primary node to the secondary:

- **BASIC**   Set to establish connections at failover time. This option requires almost no work on the backup server until failover time.

- **PRECONNECT**   Set to pre-established connections. This means that a separate database connection to the secondary (backup instance) is maintained all the time while there is a connection to the primary instance. This provides faster failover but requires that the backup instance be able to support all connections from every supported instance. Note that the "BACKUP=" clause is mandatory when using the PRECONNECT method of failover.

Here is a sample configuration with connect-time failover, connection load balancing, and TAF for a four-node Oracle RAC database:

```
RAC =
(DESCRIPTION=
(LOAD_BALANCE=ON)
(FAILOVER=ON)
(ADDRESS=(PROTOCOL=tcp)(HOST=NODE1)(PORT=1541))
(ADDRESS=(PROTOCOL=tcp)(HOST=NODE2)(PORT=1541))
(ADDRESS=(PROTOCOL=tcp)(HOST=NODE3)(PORT=1541))
(ADDRESS=(PROTOCOL=tcp)(HOST=NODE4)(PORT=1541))
(CONNECT_DATA=
(SERVICE_NAME=RAC)
(FAILOVER_MODE=(TYPE=select)(METHOD=basic)(BACKUP=RAC2)))
```

The BACKUP=RAC2 clause is crucial here to avoid failover-related issues. Assume that we are connected to an instance and a failure occurs on that instance. When TAF is triggered, Oracle Net Services tries to fail over to another instance as per the TNS configuration. It will try connecting using the service name RAC and can attempt to reconnect to the failed node itself because Oracle RAC is a service being offered by *n* number of nodes. Although Oracle Net Services would fail over to another address in the list due to the FAILOVER=ON parameter (which provides connect-time failover), we can avoid unnecessary connect-time delays and errors. With the BACKUP= RAC2 clause, Oracle Net Services will ensure that once TAF is triggered, the connection request is only sent to the BACKUP=RAC2 node, and this is done immediately without any other address being tried.

It is recommended that TAF be configured using the BACKUP parameter in the CONNECT_ DATA of the connect string; this makes it obvious which connect string will be used for failover. Without the BACKUP parameter, failover can still occur, but you may see some strange effects, such as disconnected sessions returning to the same node from which they were disconnected.

The "BACKUP" TNS alias is not actually verified to be a valid node of an Oracle RAC cluster that connects to the same database as the main connection. Therefore, it is possible to set BACKUP to a totally different machine and database with different schema objects. This could cause some confusion, such as a failed-over select returning "ORA-942: Table or view does not exist" if the table does not exist at the BACKUP connection. This is the most common failover mechanism used in Oracle Data Guard environments.

Oracle 11*g* Release 2 allows server-side TAF configuration. The TAF configuration mentioned in this section can also be configured on the server side on an Oracle Net Service using the SRVCTL utility.

Here is an example of creating a service called RACSRV with the TAF configuration explained in this section:

```
SRVCTL ADD SERVICE -d RAC -s RACSRV -r RAC1,RAC2,RAC3,RAC4
SRVCTL START SERVICE -d RAC -s RACSRV
SRVCTL MODIFY SERVICE -d RAC -s RACSRV -q TRUE -P BASIC -e SELECT
```

Users can use other options of the SRVCTL utility to configure various other TAF configurations for a service such as failover delays, failover retries, AQ HA notifications, and so on.

When a service is created with the PRECONNECT policy, Oracle internally creates another PRECONNECT service, but it does not remove this internally created service when the user changes the policy of the Oracle Net Service to something other than PRECONNECT. There is an open bug (10128981). The easy workaround to this issue is to manually delete these internally created resources using the CRSCTL utility.

Refer to the *Oracle 11g Real Application Clusters Administration and Deployment Guide* available on the Oracle Technology Network website for the complete syntax of the SRVCTL utility.

Validating the Failover

To check whether your TNS entries are working correctly and if TAF is indeed being triggered, use the following set of steps. (Ensure that this is a test system or that your database is running in ARCHIVELOG mode if data protection is important.)

1. Log into the primary node as *SYS* where a user connection is made using the new TAF-enabled TNS service entry:

```
col sid format 999
col serial# format 9999999
col failover_type format a15
col failover_method format a15
col failed_over format a12

SQL> select instance_name from v$instance ;

INSTANCE_NAME
----------------
RAC1

SQL> select sid, serial#, failover_type, failover_method, failed_over
```

```
from v$session where username = 'SCOTT';
       SID     SERIAL# FAILOVER_TYPE FAILOVER_METHOD FAILED_OVER
---------- ---------- ------------- --------------- -----------
        26          8 SELECT        BASIC           NO
```

This shows that the user *SCOTT* has logged into instance RAC1. You could also use the following method:

```
SQL> select inst_id, instance_name from gv$instance ;

INST_ID INSTANCE_NAME
------- -------------
      1 RAC1
      2 RAC2
      3 RAC3
      4 RAC4


SQL> select inst_id, sid, serial#, failover_type, failover_method,
failed_over from gv$session where username = 'SCOTT';

INST_ID       SID    SERIAL# FAILOVER_TYPE FAILOVER_METHOD FAILED_OVER
------- --------- ---------- ------------- --------------- -----------
      1        26          8 SELECT        BASIC           NO
```

2. As user *SCOTT,* run a long query that would last for a period of 45 seconds or more. Here's a commonly used query:

```
SQL> select count(*) from
(select * from dba_source
union
select *  from dba_source
union
select *  from dba_source
union
select *   from dba_source
union
select *   from dba_source)
```

At this juncture, you can "SHUTDOWN ABORT" the instance on which *SCOTT* is running the query—which is instance RAC1 in this case. *SCOTT's* user screen (SQL*Plus) should hang for a few seconds or more, depending on various factors such as cluster communication and node failure detection, network delays, and timeout parameters.

3. After the failover is completed internally by Oracle, the screen should return to normal and the query should continue to process and display results, as follows:

```
COUNT(*)
----------
    128201
```

(Note that the resultant value 128201 is an example; the exact value you get depends on the number of objects in your system.)

4. As user *SYS,* run the query to find out if *SCOTT'*s session was indeed failed over to the other node. The advantage of using GV$ views is that you don't need to log into each instance and query them individually to find out if *SCOTT* has been transferred there.

```
SQL> select inst_id, sid, serial#, failover_type, failover_method,
failed_over from gv$session where username = 'SCOTT';

INST_ID      SID    SERIAL# FAILOVER_TYPE FAILOVER_METHOD FAILED_OVER
-------   --------- --------- ------------- --------------- -----------
      3       16        10 SELECT        BASIC           YES
```

The YES for FAILED_OVER specifies that *SCOTT'*s session did fail over to instance RAC3 when RAC1 failed due to a shutdown abort.

Troubleshooting TAF Issues

Oracle use a resource type of ora.service.type for each Oracle Net Service configured in the cluster database. Oracle Clusterware also manages the virtual IPs (VIPs) on which the listeners listen. If a node goes down, the service and VIPs that are managed by CRS will fail over to a surviving node. By having the listener listen on the VIPs, we can avoid waiting for a TCP timeout if a node goes down. Connections will be routed to surviving nodes and will be able to resume their work when the failover is completed. When troubleshooting TAF issues, it is important to look at the CRS layer, the network layer, and the database layer to identify where a problem may reside.

To check whether TAF is working, we can analyze the output of crs_stat once failover has happened. Here is an excerpt from the crs_stat output:

```
[node2]/> $ORA_CRS_HOME/bin/./crsctl stat res -t
--------
NAME=ora.RAC.ERP.svc
TYPE=ora.service.type
TARGET=ONLINE
STATE=ONLINE on node2
NAME=ora.LISTENER_SCAN1.lsnr
TYPE=ora.scan_listener.type
TARGET=ONLINE
STATE=ONLINE on node1

NAME=ora.LISTENER_SCAN2.lsnr
TYPE=ora.scan_listener.type
TARGET=ONLINE
STATE=ONLINE on node2

NAME=ora.LISTENER_SCAN3.lsnr
TYPE=ora.scan_listener.type
TARGET=ONLINE
STATE=ONLINE on node3
NAME=ora.node1.LISTENER_RAC1.lsnr
TYPE=application
TARGET=ONLINE
STATE=OFFLINE
```

```
NAME=ora.node1.vip
TYPE= =ora.cluster_vip_net1.type
TARGET=ONLINE
STATE=ONLINE on node2

NAME=ora.node2.LISTENER_RAC2.lsnr
TYPE=application
TARGET=ONLINE
STATE=ONLINE on node2

NAME=ora.node2.vip
TYPE= =ora.cluster_vip_net1.type
TARGET=ONLINE
STATE=ONLINE on node2

[node2]/> srvctl status service -d RAC -s ERP
   Service ERP is running on instance(s) RAC2
```

Looking at the highlighted sections, you can see that node1's virtual IP and the ERP service failed over to node2. Compare this output with the earlier one and you can understand what has happened. The ocssd.log and crsd.log files located under $GRID_HOME/log/<hostname>/cssd and $GRID_HOME/log/<hostname>/crsd also provide detailed output about the CRS reconfiguration and node membership details.

Relocation of Failed Service(s)

Once a set of services fails over to another surviving instance and eventually when the failed instance is restarted, all the migrated services do not automatically come back to the restarted instance. For instance, in Oracle 11*g* RAC, once the failed node restarts, it reclaims its own VIP, which was temporarily taken over by node2.

Services have to be manually relocated. An example of the ERP service is provided next, in which the service is relocated from node2 back to node1:

```
[node1]/> srvctl relocate service -d RAC -s ERP -i RAC2 -t RAC1
```

Workload Management

Workload management enables users to manage the distribution of workloads to provide optimal performance for users and applications. Workload management comprises the following:

- **Services**   Oracle uses services to manage workload. You can define services in Oracle RAC databases that enable you to group database workloads and route work to the optimal instances that are assigned to offer those services.

- **Load Balancing Advisory**   Provides information to applications about the current service levels being supplied by the database and its instances, and provides recommendations to applications about where to direct application requests to obtain the best service based on the defined policy.

- **High Availability Framework**   Enables the Oracle database application to maintain components in a running state at all times.

Oracle Services

To manage workloads, you can define and assign services to a particular application or to a subset of an application's operations. You can also group other types of work under services. For example, online users can be a service, batch processing can be another, and reporting can be another service type. It is recommended that all users who share a service have the same service-level requirements. You can define specific characteristics for services, and each service is a separate unit of work. A service is the building block that can be used to divide work into logical workloads.

Services allow applications to benefit from the reliability of the redundant parts of the cluster. The services hide the complexity of the cluster from the client by providing a single system image for managing work.

Each service represents a workload with the following:

- Globally unique name
- Common service-level policies—performance, HA, and so on
- Common priority
- Common function and footprint

Services supply many benefits. They provide a single system image to manage competing applications, and they allow each workload to be managed in isolation and as a unit. Using standard user interfaces in DBCA, NetCA, SRVCTL, and Oracle Enterprise Manager (OEM) with services, a workload is configured, administered, enabled and disabled, and measured as a single entity. OEM supports viewing and operating services as a whole, with the ability to drill down to the instance level when needed. A service can span one or more instances of an Oracle database or multiple databases in a global cluster, and a single instance can support multiple services. The number of instances offering the service is transparent to the application.

Services enable the automatic recovery of work. This is achieved according to business rules. Following outages, the service is recovered quickly and automatically at the surviving instances. When instances are later repaired, services that are not running are restored quickly and automatically by CRS. Immediately, the service changes state—up or down, and a notification is available for applications using the service—to trigger immediate recovery and load-balancing actions.

Services are dynamic and tightly integrated with Oracle Resource Manager. The resources assigned to a service can be augmented when the load increases, and they can be reduced when the load declines. This dynamic resource allocation provides a cost-effective solution for meeting demands as they occur. For example, services are measured automatically and the performance is compared to service-level thresholds. Performance violations are reported to OEM, allowing the execution of automatic or scheduled solutions.

A number of RDBMS features act in concert to support services. The Automatic Workload Repository (AWR) collects a service's performance metrics, recording the service performance, including SQL execution times, wait classes, and resources consumed by the service. AWR alerts you when service response time thresholds are exceeded. The dynamic views V$SERVICE STAT and V$SERVICE_EVENT report the current service status with one hour of history, as configured by default.

NOTE
Oracle 11g has integrated services with data dictionary, AWR, Database Resource Manager, Parallel Query, Streams, Scheduler, and even Oracle Data Guard to keep primary services available across sites.

Configuring Services

Use SRVCTL to configure services. For backward compatibility, services are also created implicitly when the service_names parameter is set for the instance. To configure the service-level thresholds and Database Resource Manager for services, use OEM or SRVCTL

Available and Preferred Instances

There is no need to define the available and preferred instances for policy-managed Oracle RAC databases because Oracle will manage the placement of services automatically, but you can define the available and preferred instances for an administrator-managed Oracle RAC database using DBCA, SRVCTL, or Oracle Enterprise Manager.

This definition process creates a number of high availability (HA) resources that are managed by the clusterware to keep the services available. The DBCA and SRVCTL interfaces for a service ask the administrator to enter the list of instances that are the preferred locations for the service, plus any additional instances that are available to support the service in the event of an outage or planned operation. Once the service is created, Database Resource Manager can be used to create consumer groups that control the priority of the service.

When you define a service for an administrator-managed Oracle RAC database, you define which instances will normally support that service. These are known as the *preferred* instances. You can also define other instances to support a service if the service's preferred instance fails. These are known as *available* instances.

When you specify the preferred instances, you are specifying the number of instances on which a service will initially run. For example, on a three-node cluster, the preferred configuration may offer the Payroll service from instance 1 and the ERP service from instances 2 and 3.

The number of preferred instances also sets the initial cardinality for that service, which means that the service will start on at least a number of database instances equal to the number of preferred instances. For example, if a service is configured with two preferred instances, Oracle Clusterware will set the cardinality for this service to 2, which means Oracle will always try to keep this service running on two database instances when the preferred instance fails.

Afterward, due either to instance availability or planned service relocations, a service may be running on an available instance. When a service moves to an available instance, Oracle does not move the service back to the preferred instance when the preferred instance comes back online. This is because the service is already running on the desired number of instances. All this provides a higher level of continual service availability and avoids a second service outage due to failback processing.

Oracle Net Services provides connection load balancing that lets you to spread user connections across all of the instances that are supporting a service. Oracle RAC uses FAN (Fast Application Notification) to notify applications about configuration changes and the current service level that is provided by each instance where the service is enabled.

The easiest way to use FAN is to use the Oracle clients that have Fast Connection Failover (FCF), which means the clients have been integrated with the HA FAN events. These include JDBC, OCI, and ODP.NET. OCI clients can include clients with TAF enabled. For OCI and ODP. NET, you must enable the service to send FAN high availability events—in other words, set AQ_HA_NOTIFICATIONS to TRUE.

By default, when you create a database, Oracle defines one special database service for your Oracle RAC database. The default database service is always available on all instances in an Oracle RAC environment, unless the instance is in restricted mode. You cannot alter this service or its properties.

Workload Balancing

When it comes to workload balancing, connection placement uses connection load balancing and work request placement uses runtime load balancing. The benefit of managing work across multiple servers as a single unit is that it increases the utilization of the available resources. Work requests can be distributed across instances offering a service according to the current service performance. Balancing work requests occurs at two different times—at *connect time* and at *runtime*.

Connection Pooling and Load Balancing Advisory

Historically, load balancing within a pool of connections was based on the initial load information provided by Oracle to the middle tier. So the load information was outdated in no time because the workload on the system was bound to increase as more users connected. Hence, load balancing involved distributing an even number of connections across all the Oracle RAC instances. When an application asked for a connection, it was given a random connection (to an instance) from a set of inactive connections in the pool. There was no way of knowing how loaded the instance was before connecting to it.

Oracle 10*g* R2 introduced connection pool load balancing—also called the Load Balancing Advisory. With this new feature configured, an Oracle RAC database will periodically send load information and the current service level to the connection pool. The information is collated from all active instances and sent as a FAN to the connection pool manager in the middle tier. Because there is a periodic update about the service information and the listener is able to route connections based on intelligence, this is also referred to as *runtime load balancing*.

Oracle RAC's Load Balancing Advisory monitors the work for each service in an instance and provides a percentage value of how much of the total workload should be sent to this instance as well as a service quality flag. The feedback is provided as an entry in the AWR and a FAN event is published.

Well-designed and well-built applications generally tend to make good use of connection pools built into the middle tier of an application. For example, applications using Common Object Request Broker Architecture (CORBA), BEA WebLogic, and other Java-based applications can take advantage of the connection pooling mechanism in the middle layer. This mechanism is not new to Oracle 11*g* but has existed since the early days of TP monitors and the evolution of large-scale OLTP application deployment.

In simple terms, the connection pool is a named group of identical connections to the database. Applications borrow connections from the connection pool and use the connections to perform database calls. When that work is complete, the connection channel is released back to the connection pool to be reused.

Connection caching or pooling is used to preserve connections and minimize the overhead of creating new connections at the OS level. By maintaining the connection(s) for a long time, the OS does not need to spend time allocating process space, CPU time, and so on, every time a connection is made. Even disconnection from the database requires quite a bit of OS coordination, such as database lock cleanup and other housekeeping activities that can be avoided by using connection pooling.

Standard architectures that can use the Load Balancing Advisory include connection load balancing, TP monitors, application servers, connection concentrators, hardware and software load balancers, job schedulers, batch schedulers, and message queuing systems. All of these applications can allocate work.

The Load Balancing Advisory is deployed with key Oracle clients, such as Listener, JDBC Implicit Connection Cache 11*g*, and ODP.NET Connection Pool. The Load Balancing Advisory is also open for third-party subscription by way of Oracle Notification Service.

Connection Load Balancing

Good applications connect once to the database server and stay connected. This is a best practice for all applications—connection pools, client/server, and server side. Because connections are relatively static, the method for balancing connections across a service should not depend on metrics that vary widely during the lifetime of the connection.

Three metrics are available for the listeners to use when selecting the best instance:

- **Session count by instance**   For symmetric services and the same capacity nodes, the absolute session count evenly distributes the sessions.

- **Run queue length of the node**   For asymmetric services or different capacity nodes, the run queue length places more sessions on the node with the least load at the time of connection.

- **Goodness of service**   For all services and any capacity nodes, the goodness of the service is a ranking of the quality of service experienced at an instance. The ranking compares the service time to the service's threshold value. It also considers states such as whether access to an instance is restricted. Examples of goodness ratings are excellent, average, violating, and restricted. To avoid a listener routing all connections to the excellent instance between updates to the goodness values, each listener adjusts its local ratings by a delta as connections are distributed. The delta value used is the resource consumed by each connection using a service.

Oracle also introduced changes to connection load balancing on the server side. When services are created using the DBMS_SERVICE.CREATE_SERVICE package, you also need to specify a connection load-balancing goal using the parameter CLB_GOAL. It accepts two values, CLB_GOAL_LONG or CLB_GOAL_SHORT. LONG is the default value, which means connections are held for longer periods, based on session count.

To specify a method of load balancing, a database service needs to be created. Here's an example:

```
EXECUTE DBMS_SERVICE.CREATE_SERVICE(service_name=>'rac.acme.com',-
network_name=>'rac.acme.com',-
goal=>dbms_service.goal_service_time,-
clb_goal=>dbms_service.clb_goal_short);
```

With CLB_GOAL_SHORT, connection load balancing uses the Load Balancing Advisory, when it is enabled (either GOAL_SERVICE_TIME or GOAL_THROUGHPUT). When CLB_GOAL_NONE (no Load Balancing Advisory) is used, connection load balancing uses an abridged advice based on CPU utilization.

With CLB_GOAL_LONG, connection load balancing balances the number of connections per instance using session count per service. This setting is recommended for applications with long connections such as SQL*Forms. This setting can be used with Load Balancing Advisory when connection pools are used. As the name suggests, CLB_GOAL_LONG creates long-lived connections and CLB_GOAL_SHORT creates connections of short duration.

The parameter goal=>dbms_service.goal_service_time is concerned with connection pool load balancing or runtime load balancing, which also requires the configuration of database services and configuration of Oracle Net Services connection load balancing. This feature is described in the next section.

So, when an application requests a connection, the connection pool is able to provide a connection to the instance that will best service the client request. This load-balancing algorithm is able to route work requests based on a defined policy. When database services are created, a goal is specified along with it, which can be GOAL_THROUGHPUT, GOAL_SERVICE_TIME, or GOAL_NONE.

GOAL_THROUGHPUT means that the load balancing will be based on the rate that work is completed in the service plus the available bandwidth. If GOAL_SERVICE_TIME is specified, load balancing is based on the elapsed time for work done in the database service plus the available bandwidth to the service.

For a detailed discussion on the basics and configuration steps, refer to the Oracle document "Oracle Clusterware and Oracle Real Application Clusters Administration and Deployment Guide" (10g Release 2 [10.2], Part No: B14197-01).

If the connection pool load-balancing feature is used, the GOAL_* parameters are set using DBMS_SERVICE and CLB_GOAL is ignored. Having PREFER_LEAST_LOADED_NODE_[listener_name] in listener.ora will disable/override new functionality.

Runtime Load Balancing

Runtime load balancing (RLB) is used when selecting connections from connection pools. For connection pools that act on services at one instance only, the first available connection in the pool is adequate. When connection pools act on services that span multiple instances, for runtime load balancing, a metric is needed that is responsive to the current state of each service at each instance.

The AWR measures the response time, CPU consumption, and service adequacy for each service and is integrated with the Load Balancing Advisory. The views V$SERVICE_METRICS and V$SERVICE_METRICS_HISTORY contain the service time for every service and are updated every 60 seconds with 1 hour of history. These views are available to applications to use for their own runtime load balancing. For example, a middle-tier application using connection pools can use the service metrics when routing the runtime requests to instances offering a service.

The Database Resource Manager maps services (in place of users) to consumer groups, thereby automatically managing the priority of one service relative to others. The Oracle RAC high availability features keep the services available, even when some or all components are unavailable. The Oracle Data Guard Broker, in conjunction with Oracle RAC, is capable of migrating the primary service across various Oracle Data Guard sites for disaster tolerance.

Using Service Time for Load Balancing

Using the service time for load balancing is a major improvement over earlier approaches that use round robin or run queue length. The run queue length metric does not consider sessions that are blocked in wait—for example, interconnect wait, IO wait, and application wait—and unable to execute. Run queue length and session count metrics also do not consider session priority.

Using service time for load balancing recognizes machine power differences, sessions that are blocked in wait, failures that block processing, and competing services of different importance. Using service time prevents sending work to nodes that are overworked, hung, or failed.

The Load Balancing Advisory takes into consideration different-sized nodes, and in cases where a node is heavily loaded, the connection pool is capable of removing connections for that instance from the pool (as they become inactive or hung). The connection pool is then able to create new connections to another instance, providing better service levels.

The response times DB time and CPU time are available for each service at each instance in V$SERVICE_METRICS_HISTORY. Just as the listener uses this data to deal connections across the service, the connection pool algorithm can use the data when selecting connections from the connection pool. Using this approach distributes the work across instances that are serving the service well and avoids sending work to slow, hung, failed, and restricted instances.

Assuming that an ODP.NET-based application uses connection pooling with the grid runtime load-balancing attribute enabled, an ODP.NET connection pool registers for an RLB notification with a particular service in an Oracle RAC or grid environment. If the environment is properly configured, the service periodically sends notifications to ODP.NET with information on the responsiveness of each service member.

For optimal performance, ODP.NET dispenses connections to service members based on information received about their responsiveness. This attribute can be used only against Oracle instances within an Oracle RAC database. Its value is also ignored if pooling=False.

The grid runtime load-balancing attribute is enabled by setting the grid runtime load-balancing connection string attribute to True. The default is False. The following connection string enables the grid runtime load-balancing attribute:

```
"user id=apps;password=apps;data source=erp;grid runtime load" + "balancing=true;"
```

Measuring Workloads by Service

If configured, the AWR maintains performance statistics, including response times, resource consumption, and wait events, for all services and for all the work that is being done in the system. Selected metrics, statistics, wait events, and wait classes, plus SQL level traces, are maintained for the service, optionally augmented by module and action names. The statistics aggregation and tracing by service are new in their global scope for Oracle RAC and in their persistence across instance restarts and service relocation for both Oracle RAC and single-instance Oracle.

By default, statistics are collected for the work attributed to every service. Each service can be further qualified by module name and action name to identify the important transactions within the service. This eliminates the hard work associated with measuring the time for all calls for the service. The service, module, and action name provide a user explicable unit for measuring elapsed time per call and for setting and resource consumption thresholds.

As most programmers know by now, the module and action can be set with the following:

```
DBMS_APPLICATION_INFO.SET_MODULE(module_name => 'add_customer',
action_name => 'CUST_ADD');
```

The module and action are visible in V$SESSION. This naming format is a way of tying a portion of the application code to the database work done on its behalf. The module name is set to a user-recognizable name for the program that is currently executing (script or form). The action name is set to a specific action that a user is performing within a module (such as reading mail or entering new customer data). Setting these tags using OCI in 11*g* does not result in additional roundtrips to the database.

We can use the DBMS_MONITOR package to control the gathering of statistics that quantify the performance of services, modules, and actions. DBMS_MONITOR is also used for tracing services, modules, and actions.

High Availability Features

For HA clients connected to an Oracle RAC database, HA event notification can provide a best-effort programmatic signal to the client in the event of a failure. Client applications can register a callback on the environment handle to signal interest in this information. When a significant failure event occurs (which applies to a connection made by this client), the callback is invoked, with information concerning the event (the event payload) and a list of connections (server handles) that were disconnected as a result of the failure.

The HA event notification mechanism improves the response time of the application in the presence of failure. In the past, a failure would result in the connection being broken only after the TCP timeout expired, which could take minutes. With HA event notification, standalone, connection pool, and session pool connections are automatically broken and cleaned up by OCI, and the application callback is invoked within seconds of the failure event. If any of these server handles are TAF enabled, failover will also automatically be engaged by OCI.

Applications must connect to an Oracle RAC instance to enable HA event notification. Furthermore, these applications must initialize the OCI environment in OCI_EVENTS mode. Then these applications can register a callback that is invoked whenever an HA event occurs.

Grid Connection Recovery: ODP.NET

When the grid connection recovery attribute is enabled, the ODP.NET connection pool subscribes to an Oracle RAC FAN event. FAN notifies ODP.NET whenever a node or a service is down. This allows ODP.NET to properly clean up resources from connections that have been severed and establish new connections to healthy service members. This provides better availability with minimal application management, and applications can quickly recover from downed nodes or services.

The grid connection recovery attribute is enabled by setting the grid connection recovery connection string attribute to True. The default is False. The grid connection recovery attribute can be used only against Oracle instances within an Oracle RAC or grid environment. The attribute value is ignored if pooling=False. The following connection string enables the grid connection recovery attribute:

```
"user id=apps;password=apps;data source=erp;grid connection recovery=true;"
```

Notifications and FAN

One of the main principles of a highly available application is that it be able to receive fast notification when the status of a critical resource or component changes. This resource or component could be within a cluster or outside, but it is critical to the functioning of the application. The Fast Application Notification (FAN) feature provides a framework to achieve higher levels of availability and reliability for a cluster database. FAN is always aware of the current configuration of the server pools in the cluster, so Oracle always try to make an application connection to the database instances that are able to respond. Oracle posts a FAN event on any state change in the cluster.

Using notifications, applications are able to perform some form of retaliatory action or handle this event (by executing a program or script) so that application availability is not compromised or a certain set of predetermined actions are taken to minimize the impact of this status change known as an event.

The timely execution of these handler programs minimizes the impact of cluster component failures by avoiding connection timeouts, application timeouts, and reacting to cluster resource reconfiguration in both planned and unplanned scenarios.

Event-based Notification

The concept of event-based notification is not new. Customers who have deployed Oracle Enterprise Manager or monitored enterprise IT resources using third-party management console products that rely on low-overhead protocols such as SNMP are already familiar with the usage and benefits of receiving component up, down, or threshold violation alerts from the database layer. Production sites may also implement their own polling mechanisms by capturing events and delivering proper notifications to higher application layers.

Traditionally, client or mid-tier applications connected to the database have relied on connection timeouts, out-of-band polling mechanisms, or other custom solutions to realize that a system component has failed. This approach has huge implications in application availability, because downtimes are extended and more noticeable.

The other area where the traditional approach falls short is in the management of complex database cluster environments, because of the exponential growth in the number of server-side components, both horizontally (across all cluster nodes) and vertically (across cluster node components such as listeners, instances, and application services). Furthermore, with the introduction of grid computing to the enterprise, such levels of component complexity must be interconnected, monitored, and managed in a proactive and automated way.

When the state of an Oracle database service changes (up, down, restart failure), the new status is posted or relayed to interested subscribers through FAN events. Applications can use these events to achieve very fast failure detection and re-create, reestablish, and balance a connection pool following a failure as well as failback detection to restore normal services.

A FAN event is issued whenever a service becomes available, whenever it becomes unavailable, and whenever it is no longer being managed by CRS. The notification events occur for status changes in resources under CRS for services, service members, databases, and instances. Databases and instances are included to accommodate applications that depend on these resources directly. The notification event is used to eliminate the HA problems of sessions waiting to time out when blocked in receive and/or are wasting time processing in think-time after their service has terminated. This is done by providing a notification in the form of an out-of-band event to the client side. In this way, sessions are notified quickly when the application changes state.

Because important HA events are pushed as soon as they are detected, this method results in a more efficient use of existing computing resources and in better integration with enterprise applications, including mid-tier connection managers or IT management consoles such as trouble ticket loggers and e-mail/paging servers.

FAN is a distributed system that is enabled on each participating node. This makes it reliable and fault tolerant because the failure of one component is detected by another one. Therefore, event notification can be detected and pushed by any of the participating nodes.

FAN events are tightly integrated with Oracle Data Guard Broker, Oracle JDBC implicit connection cache, and Oracle Enterprise Manager. Starting from Oracle Database 10g, JDBC applications managing connection pools do not need custom code development. They are automatically integrated with the Oracle Notification Service (ONS) if implicit connection cache and fast connection failover are enabled. Figure 13-3 shows the FAN architecture.

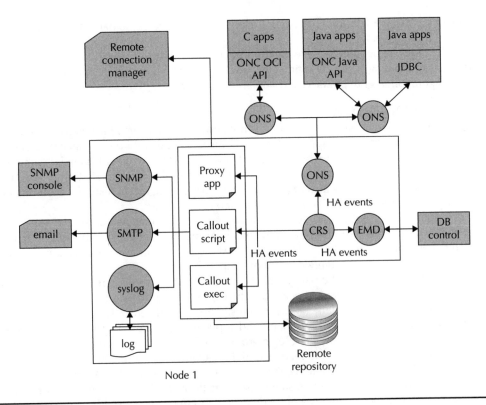

FIGURE 13-3 *FAN architecture ONS*

Application Failure Issues

When a service goes down in a cluster, applications end up wasting time trying one or some of these activities:

- ■ Waiting for a TCP/IP timeout when a node fails without closing sockets and open additional sockets for every subsequent connection while that particular IP is down.

- ■ Attempting to connect when services are down and not connecting when services resume.

- ■ Attempting to execute work on slow, hung, or dead nodes.

The existing mechanisms in Oracle do not allow for these types of problems to be reported, so accounting for downtime or performance issues caused by them is not possible or at best is an estimation.

When a node fails without closing the network sockets, all sessions that are blocked in an I/O use the transport layer configuration (tcp_keepalive) for a predefined period before timing out. The problem could be worse for sessions that are processing something at the client end and are not aware that the server is down. The status is known only after the last result set is to be fetched or processed. This causes severe delays or timeouts.

For cluster configuration changes, the RAC HA framework publishes a FAN event immediately when a state change occurs in the cluster. Instead of waiting for the application to poll the database and detect a problem, applications receive FAN events and can react immediately to them.

On receipt of a FAN event, applications can abort sessions in communication with the failed instance or node, relocate them to another node, notify sessions waiting to resume operations, and reorganize incoming work on the fly as additional resources become available or lost. For example, if a service is down, a DOWN event is published. For DOWN events, the disruption to the application can be minimized because sessions to the failed instance or node can be terminated. Incomplete transactions are terminated and the application user is immediately notified. Application users who request connections are directed to available instances only.

You can also use server-side callouts to do the following:

- Page DBAs or open support tickets when resources fail to start.

- Automatically start dependent external applications that need to be co-located with a service.

- Change resource plans or shut down services when the number of available instances decreases—for example, if nodes fail.

- Automate the failback of a service to PREFERRED instances if needed.

For UP events, when services and instances are started, new connections can be created so that the application can immediately take advantage of the extra resources.

FAN also publishes Load Balancing Advisory events. Applications can take advantage of the Load Balancing Advisory FAN events to direct work requests to the instance in the cluster that is currently providing the best service quality.

Using FAN

FAN can be used in three ways. First, applications can take advantage of FAN without programmatic changes by utilizing an integrated Oracle client. The integrated clients for FAN events include Oracle Database JDBC, Oracle Database Oracle Data Provider for .NET (ODP. NET), OCI Connection Pool, and Connection Manager.

Second, applications can use the ONS API to subscribe to FAN events and execute event-handling actions upon receipt. Third, applications can implement FAN server-side callouts on the database tier.

Applications can also enable the Oracle JDBC implicit connection cache and let FAN events be handled by the Oracle JDBC libraries directly. Oracle implicit connection cache is deprecated and has been replaced with Universal Connection Pool. Using this method, you no longer need to write any custom Java or C code to handle FAN events, nor do you need to invoke the ONC API directly. They are automatically integrated with ONS if implicit connection cache and fast connection failover are enabled. Consider this as an out-of-the-box integration with the ONS.

A typical Java application using FAN would require the application developer to download the current FAN jar (known as simplefan.jar) from the following location:

www.oracle.com/technetwork/database/enterprise-edition/jdbc-112010-090769.html

The developer would then add this jar file in the CLASSPATH of the application. There is no need to start any ONS daemon to use Oracle Universal Connection Pool on the client side because having this jar file in the CLASSPATH is sufficient. The application developer would need to instantiate the FanManager class and use methods provided by this class to configure and use FAN.

Please refer to the Oracle JDBC Developer Guide for detailed steps for implementing FAN:

http://download.oracle.com/docs/cd/E11882_01/java.112/e16548/toc.htm

FAN Events and Notification

FAN events consist of a header and payload information delivered as a set of name-value pairs accurately describing the name, type, and nature of the cluster event. Based on this payload, the event recipient can take concrete management, notification, or synchronization steps. These could include actions such as shutting down the application connection manager, rerouting existing database connection requests, refreshing stale connection references, logging trouble tickets, and sending a page to the database administrator. The objective is to deliver FAN events so that they precede any other polling intervals or connection timeouts.

Notification is the first step in the processes for application recovery, service recovery, offline diagnosis, and fault repair. Notification occurs in several forms:

- **In-band notification** Using strong and weak dependencies in CRS and special CRS events for check and fail actions, dependent resources receive an in-band notification to start and stop. These events occur as a result of starting or stopping interdependent resources, and as a result of dependent resources failing and restarting. These notifications are considered "in-band" because they are posted and processed synchronously as part of CRS managing the system.

- **Out-of-band notification** FAN provides callouts, events, and paging; e-mail from the enterprise console, status changes, fault notifications, and fault escalation are forwarded to invoke repair and to interrupt applications to respond to the service change. These FAN events are considered "out-of-band" because they are issued asynchronously through gateway processes out of RAC/HA to listeners, enterprise console, and callouts.

- **Error and event logs** When a fault occurs in any layer, details of the error are reported to persistent event logs. This is the case for all error conditions, including those that are automatically recovered by the CRS system. For expediency, all event logs should have a consistent format and should be logged to a consistent location. Data collection is essential to ensure that a root cause for the condition can be found early. Once the problem is identified, a resolution can be produced.

Three categories of events are currently supported in FAN:

- Service events, which include both application services and database services
- Node events, which include cluster membership states and native join/leave operations
- Load balancing events sent from the Oracle RAC Load Balancing Advisory

In addition to application services, Oracle RAC standardizes the generation, presentation, and delivery of events pertaining to managed cluster resources, which include these event types:

Event Type	Description
SERVICE	Primary application service event
SRV_PRECONNECT	Shadow application service event (mid-tiers and TAF using primary and secondary instances)
SERVICEMEMBER	Application service on a specific instance event
DATABASE	Oracle database event
INSTANCE	Oracle instance event
ASM	Oracle ASM instance event
NODE	Oracle cluster node event

This table describes the event status for each of these managed cluster resources:

Event Status	Description
status=up	Managed resource comes up.
status=down	Managed resource goes down.
status=preconn_up	Shadow application service comes up.
status=preconn_down	Shadow application service goes down.
status=nodedown	Managed node goes down.
status=not_restarting	Managed resource cannot fail over to a remote node.
status=restart_failed	Managed resource fails to start locally after a discrete number of retries.
status=unknown	Unrecognized status.

The event status for each managed resource is associated with an event reason. The reason further describes what triggered the event, as shown in the following table:

Event Reason	Activity Type	Event Trigger
reason=user	Planned	User-initiated commands such as srvctl and sqlplus.
reason=failure	Unplanned	Managed resource polling checks detected a failure.
reason=dependency	Unplanned	Dependency of another managed resource that triggered a failure condition.
reason=unknown	Unhandled	Unknown or internal application state when event is triggered.
reason=autostart	CRS boot	Initial cluster boot (managed resource has profile attribute AUTO_START=1, and was offline before the last CRS shutdown).
reason=boot	CRS boot	Initial cluster boot (managed resource was running before the last CRS shutdown).

Other event payload fields further describe the unique cluster resource whose status is being monitored and published. They include the following:

Event Resource Identifier	Description
VERSION=<n.n>	Event payload version (currently VERSION=1.0)
timestamp=<eventDate> <eventTime>	Server-side date and time when the event was detected
service=<serviceName.dbDomainName>	Name of the (primary or shadow) application service (excluded from NODE events)
database=<dbName>	Name of the Oracle RAC database (excluded from NODE events)
instance=<sid>	Name of the Oracle RAC instance (excluded from SERVICE, DATABASE, and NODE events)
host=<hostName>	Name of the cluster node as returned by the clusterware (excluded from SERVICE and DATABASE events)
card=<n>	Service membership cardinality (excluded from all events except "SERVICE status=up")

The combination of all these attributes and types result in a FAN event with the following payload structure:

```
<Event_Type> VERSION=<n.n>
service=<serviceName.dbDomainName>
[database=<dbName> [instance=<sid>]] [host=<hostname>]
status=<Event_Status> reason=<Event_Reason> [card=<n>]
timestamp=<eventDate> <eventTime>
```

Here's an example:

```
Service events:
SERVICE VERSION=1.0 service=homer.simpsons.com database=BART status=up
reason=user card=4 timestamp=16-Feb-2010 21:09:15

SERVICEMEMBER VERSION=1.0 service=barney.simpsons.com database=BEER
instance=DRAUGHT host=moesplace status=down reason=user
timestamp=16-Mar-2010 19:01:34

DATABASE VERSION=1.0 service=skywalker.starwars.com database=STARS
host=galaxy status=up reason=boot timestamp=08-Mar-2010 15:31:00

INSTANCE VERSION=1.0 service=robinhood.thieves.com database=RANSOM
instance=SCOTLAND host=locksley status=down reason=failure
timestamp=12-Mar-2010 17:25:09
ASM VERSION=1.0 instance=ASM1 host=apps status=down reason=failure
timestamp=12-Mar-2010 11:54:46
Node events:

NODE VERSION=1.0 host=sales status=nodedown timestamp=16-Mar-2010 13:54:51
```

Configuring Server-Side Callouts

Server-side callouts are executables that Oracle executes upon the posting of a FAN event. These executables are stored in the $GRID_HOME/racg/usrco directory on each cluster node. Users can store any number of executables in this directory, but Oracle does not guarantee that it will execute them in order. However, Oracle does guarantee that all the executables in the $GRID_HOME/racg/usrco directory will be executed. It is not a good practice to use multiple callouts; instead, use a single callout script that parses the FAN events and calls the respective executable store at another location.

Here is a sample parsing callout:

```
#!/bin/bash
FAN_LOGFILE=/tmp/FAN.log
EVENT_TYPE=$1
shift
for ARGS in $@ ; do
        PAYLOAD_PROPERTY=`echo $ARGS | awk -F"=" '{print $1}'`
        VALUE=`echo $ARGS | awk -F"=" '{print $2}'`
        case $PAYLOAD_PROPERTY in
                VERSION|version)        EVENT_VERSION=$VALUE ;;
                SERVICE|service)        EVENT_SERVICE=$VALUE ;;
                DATABASE|database)      EVENT_DATABASE=$VALUE ;;
                INSTANCE|instance)      EVENT_INSTANCE=$VALUE ;;
                HOST|host)              EVENT_HOST=$VALUE ;;
                STATUS|status)          EVENT_STATUS=$VALUE ;;
                REASON|reason)          EVENT_REASON=$VALUE ;;
                CARD|card)              EVENT_CARD=$VALUE ;;
                TIMESTAMP|timestamp)    EVENT_TIMESTAMP=$VALUE ;;
                ??:??:??)               EVENT_LOGTIME=$PAYLOAD_PROPERTY ;;
        esac
done

# Stat Event Handler Section
# Write your event specific actions here.
# End Event Handler Section
```

You have to create an executable script with the preceding contents and place this script under $GRID_HOME/racg/userco directory on each cluster node. Whenever Oracle posts a FAN event, this executable script will be called. This script will parse the event payload properties and call event-specific tasks from the event handler section.

In a Nutshell

Oracle was one of the first commercial databases to foresee the need for an efficient mechanism to deal with a large user population and workload distribution in a single-instance database as well as Oracle RAC environments. Workload distribution is very critical for an Oracle RAC environment to have balanced resource utilization among the cluster nodes and for optimal performance.

The Transparent Application Failover (TAF) feature helps the connected sessions seamlessly migrate to another instance during an unexpected instance failure. Complex applications and applications not supported by TAF configurations can utilize the Fast Application Notification (FAN) feature discussed in this chapter. End-user applications can subscribe to FAN notifications and take appropriate actions based on the FAN events.

Oracle started providing load balancing and simple failover with version 7.3 and enhanced these features as it progressed to version 11g. With so many rich features and flexible options in load balancing and connection management, the user has plenty of choices for managing the connections.

CHAPTER
14

Oracle RAC
Troubleshooting

revious chapters in this book provided comprehensive information for understanding the architecture, functionalities, and processes of Oracle Real Application Clusters 11*g* Release 2. How efficiently and effectively you can troubleshoot this mammoth depends on your level of understanding of Oracle Real Application Clusters and the associated Oracle Grid Infrastructure components. In this chapter we look into the details of debugging Oracle Real Application Clusters, from simple startup problems to complex system hang or crash problems.

As a single piece of software, Oracle RDBMS is one of the most complex commercial products in the world, with lots of changes incorporated into Oracle RAC 11*g* Release 2. Troubleshooting the Oracle RAC database involves analyzing the debug information of Oracle Grid Infrastructure and database instances. But with the help of a solid and extensive diagnostics framework, you can usually diagnose even complex problems simply by viewing and interpreting Oracle's detailed debug trace files.

Each database instance in a cluster has its own alert log stored inside the $DIAG_DESTINATION/rdbms/<dbname>/SID/trace directory, which will be the first and foremost thing to examine whenever a problem is reported. Alert logs show detailed information about the basic settings of the database, including the nondefault parameters used.

Alert logs also contain information about startup and shutdown as well as details of nodes joining and leaving, with timestamps.

Just like a database instance's alert log, each cluster node has a clusterware alert log (alert<hostname>.log) stored inside the $GRID_HOME/log/<hostname> directory. This will be the first log file to analyze if the database alert log file has reported symptoms/incidents related to Oracle Clusterware or ASM. Before getting into details on how to troubleshoot, it is very important to know the location of all debug files required to diagnose different processes and components of the Oracle RAC database.

Installation Log Files

Installing Oracle RAC involves the installation of software and executing post-installation configuration scripts, such as root.sh, so you will be analyzing different types of debug log files depending on which stage of the installation failure has occurred. Oracle stores software installation log files inside the logs directory of Oracle central inventory, where the location of central inventory is specified by the oraInst.loc file. This file is stored at /etc/oracle on the Linux operating system and at /var/opt/oracle on other UNIX operating systems. Oracle records all actions performed by Oracle Universal Installer in the log file named Install Actions<*timestamp*>.log.

Oracle stores the debug log file for the root.sh configuration script under the $GRID_HOME/cfgtools/crsconfig directory. Oracle records actions performed by the root.sh configuration script in the rootcrs_<hostname>.log debug log file.

NOTE
My Oracle Support Bulletin ID 810394.1, "RAC and Oracle Clusterware Starter Kit and Best Practices," from the Oracle RAC Assurance Support Team, provides the latest information on generic and platform-specific best practices for implementing an Oracle RAC cluster.

Log Directory Structure in the Oracle RDBMS

Starting with Oracle 11g, Oracle stores all diagnostic data, such as trace files, core files, and the alert logs, inside a common directory structure called Automatic Diagnostic Repository (also known as the ADR). The ADR has a unified directory structure across multiple database instances, and all major components involved in the Oracle RAC database, such as ASM, CRS, and database instances, store their diagnostic files inside their own dedicated directory inside the ADR. Using a unified directory structure to store all diagnostic data in a common place allows Oracle support tools such as ADRCI to collect and analyze diagnostic data across multiple databases and ASM instances.

The location of the ADR is specified by the database initialization parameter diagnostic_dest, which by default points to a location specified by the operation system environment variable $ORACLE_BASE. In case both the environment variable ORACLE_BASE and the database initialization parameter diagnostic_dest are not defined, Oracle by default uses $ORACLE_HOME/log as the Automatic Diagnostic Repository. ADR contains one top directory named diag as well as subdirectories for technology components of the Oracle RAC database to store their diagnostic files. In a typical Oracle Database 11g installation, you will see the following subdirectories inside the $ADR_BASE/diag directory:

- asm
- clients
- crs
- diagtool
- lsnrctl
- netcman
- ofm
- rdbms
- tnslsnr

In an Oracle RAC 11g Release 2 installation, where a separate user owns Oracle Grid Infrastructure and the Oracle RAC database, you may notice that the directories (except for rdbms, clients, and diagtool) are empty, because the software owner of Oracle Grid Infrastructure has its own dedicated ORACLE_BASE and the diagnostic_dest parameter is not configured. The database view V$DIAG_INFO can be queried to display the ADR locations. This view provides important information about ADR locations as well as the number of active incidents and problems reported inside the ADR.

NOTE
Users can use the ADR command-line interface tool ADRCI to view and package diagnostic data stored inside the ADR. Refer to My Oracle Support Note 443529.1 for details on how to use ADRCI.

On a database instance, the rdbms/<dbname>/<SID> subdirectory has the following important subdirectories that store the diagnostic files for the respective database instances:

- **cdump**   This directory contains core dumps.

- **trace**   This directory stores the database alert log and trace files of the foreground and background database processes.

- **alert**   This directory stores the XML alert log.

- **hm**   This directory stores the health check output files.

- **incident**   This directory stores the incident directory created by critical errors, and each incident directory is named as the ID of the incident.

- **metadata**   This directory contains the diagnostic metadata.

Log Directory Structure in Oracle Grid Infrastructure

In the Oracle 11*g* Release 2 RAC installation, a cluster node consists of a Grid home and an Oracle RDBMS home. The Grid home is where Oracle Grid Infrastructure is installed and is commonly known as GRID_HOME. Diagnostic log files for Oracle Clusterware and ASM are stored under the $GRID_HOME/log/<hostname> directory. Each component in the Oracle Grid Infrastructure stack has its respective directories created under the $GRID_HOME/log/<hostname> directory. Unlike earlier releases of Oracle Clusterware, Oracle Grid Infrastructure stores all Oracle Clusterware–related debug log files under the $GRID_HOME/log directory. In a typical Oracle 11*g* Release 2 Grid Infrastructure home, you will find the following directories containing debug log files for different components of Oracle Grid Infrastructure:

- **$GRID_HOME/log**   This is the main directory for storing trace and diagnostic log files of Oracle Clusterware and ASM on each cluster node.

- **$GRID_HOME/log/<hostname>**   Contains trace and diagnostic log files of Oracle Clusterware and ASM for the local node only. Each cluster node has its own dedicated log directory inside its own GRID_HOME. This directory contains individual subdirectories for each component of Oracle Grid Infrastructure.

- **$GRID_HOME/log/<hostname>/agent**   Contains trace and diagnostic log files for oraagent, orarootagent, oracssdagent, and oracssdmonitor for the CRSD and OHASD daemons.

- **$GRID_HOME/log/<hostname>/client**   Contains trace and diagnostic log files for various Oracle Grid Infrastructure clients, such as CLSCFG, GPNP, OCRCONFIG, OLSNODES, and OIFCFG.

- **$GRID_HOME/log/<hostname>/crfmond**   Contains trace and diagnostic log files recorded by the System Monitor Service provided by Oracle Cluster Health Monitor (Oracle CHM).

- **$GRID_HOME/log/<hostname>/cssd**   Contains Cluster Synchronization (CSS) logs, containing actions such as reconfigurations, missed check-ins, connects, and disconnects from the client CSS listener. In some cases, the logger logs messages with the category of auth.crit for the reboots done by Oracle. This could be used for checking the exact time when the reboot occurred.

- **$GRID_HOME/log/<hostname>/cvu**   Contains the trace and debug log files generated by the Oracle Cluster Verification utility.

- **$GRID_HOME/log/<hostname>/evmd**   Contains the trace and diagnostic files for the Event Volume Manager (EVM) and evmlogger daemons. This is not used as often for debugging as the CRSD and CSSD directories.

- **$GRID_HOME/log/<hostname>/gnsd**   Contains the trace and debug log files to troubleshoot problems related to the Oracle Grid Naming Service, which is introduced in Oracle Grid Infrastructure.

- **$GRID_HOME/log/<hostname>/mdnsd**   Contains the trace and diagnostic log files to troubleshoot the Multicast Domain Name Service. The Oracle Grid Naming Service uses this service to manage name resolution and service discovery.

- **$GRID_HOME/log/<hostname>/racg**   Contains the trace and debug log files for each Oracle RACG executable.

- **$GRID_HOME/log/<hostname>/crflogd**   Contains the trace and diagnostic log files recorded by Cluster Logger Services provided by the Oracle Cluster Health Monitor (Oracle CHM).

- **$GRID_HOME/log/<hostname>/crsd**   Contains the trace and diagnostic log files of the Oracle CRSD daemon and is a good point to start with any Oracle Clusterware issues.

- **$GRID_HOME/log/<hostname>/ctssd**   Contains the debug log files to troubleshoot the Oracle Cluster Time Synchronization Service introduced in Oracle Grid Infrastructure to synchronize the clocks on the cluster nodes.

- **$GRID_HOME/log/<hostname>/diskmon**   Contains the debug log files to troubleshoot the Oracle Disk Monitor daemon.

- **$GRID_HOME/log/<hostname>/giplcd**   Contains the debug and trace files to troubleshoot the Oracle Grid Interprocess Communication daemon.

- **$GRID_HOME/log/<hostname>/gpnpd**   Contains the log and output files of the Oracle Grid Plug and Play daemon.

- **$GRID_HOME/log/<hostname>/ohasd**   Contains the log and output files of the Oracle High Availability Services daemon. The OHASD log files are really important to diagnose cluster startup issues in Oracle 11g onward.

- **$GRID_HOME/log/<hostname>/srvm**   Contains log files for the Oracle Server Manager service.

Troubleshooting a Failed Oracle Grid Infrastructure Installation

Troubleshooting a failed Oracle RAC install starts with analyzing different sets of log files, depending upon the stage of the install where the failure has occurred. For example, to troubleshoot an installation failure that has occurred prior to executing the root.sh configuration script, completing most of the prerequisites in the installation documentation and fixing the errors reported by OUI in the Perform Prerequisites Checks screen ensures that the installation will succeed. However, there may be scenarios where the installation still fails even after you've ensured the prerequisites. In such cases, you review the installation log files stored inside the log subdirectory of the Oracle Central Inventory. Oracle Universal Installer records each install action in the installation log file, and reviewing this log file shows you the actual action that Oracle Universal Installer was performing when the installation failed.

Oracle Universal Installer is a Java program, and advance Java trace can be enabled to trace detail debug information about actions being performed by Oracle Universal Installer. Chapter 4 explains the procedure to enable advanced Java tracing for Oracle Universal Installer. You have to cancel the existing installation session and restart the Oracle Universal Installer with advanced Java trace options if you wish to debug. Once enabled, the trace file provides the exact commands being executed by Oracle Universal Installer, along with the command's output. After reviewing this trace file, you can narrow down the command or action that causes the installation to fail and take the appropriate measures to resolve the underlying issue. Once the underlying issue is resolved, you can either proceed with the current installation or restart the Oracle Universal Installer, depending on at which stage the error occurred—the OUI offers "retry" options where it can.

Sometimes an Oracle RAC installation fails while executing a post-installation configuration script, such as root.sh, especially when Oracle Grid Infrastructure is being installed. The root.sh configuration script configures and starts the Oracle Clusterware and ASM if the OCR and voting files are stored inside the ASM. The root.sh script validates permissions on the file system and configures network resources, such as creating virtual IPs for configuring storage, creating the ASM disk group to store OCR and voting files, and establishing a link between third-party clusterware and Oracle Clusterware, if third-party clusterware is used. In most cases, misconfiguration of the network and shared storage are the main reasons behind failure of the root.sh configuration script—unless you are encountering an unwelcome Oracle bug.

Inside the root.sh configuration script, you can see that it executes rootmacro.sh, rootinstall.sh, setowner.sh, rootadd_rdbms.sh, rootadd_filemap.sh, and rootcrs.pl. In this case, rootcrs.pl is the main configuration script, and performs most of the configuration done by root.sh, and other configuration scripts only validate permissions and create the required directories on the file system. It is very easy to fix a failure of the root.sh script if it is happening in a script other than rootcrs.pl.

Oracle records all actions performed by the rootcrs.pl configuration script in the rootcrs_<hostname>.log file, stored in the $GRID_HOME/cfgtools/crsconfig directory, and this is the first file to be analyzed to identify the action/command that's causing root.sh failure. Once the failed configuration item is known, further diagnostic log files must be reviewed to identify the root cause of the failure. For example, if the rootcrs_<hostname>.log file is reporting a failure on starting the Cluster Synchronization Service daemon, then you review the diagnostic log file for the OCSSD daemon stored at $GRID_HOME/log/<hostname>/cssd/ocssd.log to identify the root cause of the failure. Once the root cause is identified, the root.sh configuration script can be rerun because starting with Oracle Grid Infrastructure 11*g* Release 2 (11.2.0.2), the configuration script root.sh is restartable on the failed node.

To rerun root.sh in Oracle Grid Infrastructure 11*g* Release 2 (prior to 11.2.0.2), deconfigure the cluster by executing the following two scripts as the *root* user.

Run the following script on all cluster nodes except the last node:

```
$GRID_HOME/crs/install/rootcrs.pl -verbose -deconfig -force
```

Run the following script on the last cluster node. This script will erase data from the OCR and voting disk:

```
$GRID_HOME/crs/install/rootcrs.pl -verbose -deconfig -force -lastnode
```

You should be very patient and calm while troubleshooting a root.sh failure because sometimes simply overlooking the available information can delay the overall troubleshooting response time. For example, the root.sh fails with the following error on the terminal:

```
PROT-1: Failed to initialize ocrconfig
Command return code of 255 (65280) from command:
/u01/11.2.0/app/grid/bin/ocrconfig  upgrade oragrid oinstall
Failed to create Oracle Cluster Registry configuration, rc 255
```

As shown next, after reviewing the rootcrs_<hostname>.log file, you know that the root.sh configuration script is using software user *oragrid* to create and configure OCR inside the ASM, but the ASMLib drivers were configured using the software owner *oracle*.

```
Executing as oragrid: /u02/11.2.0/app/grid/bin/asmca -silent
-diskGroupName DATA -diskList ORCL:ASMD1,ORCL:ASMD2
-redundancy EXTERNAL -configureLocalASM
Creating or upgrading OCR keys
Command return code of 255 (65280) from command:
/u01/app/11.2.0/grid/bin/ocrconfig -upgrade oragrid oinstall
```

In this example, the install issue is resolved after you reconfigure the ASMLib with the *oragrid* user and rerun root.sh successfully.

Oracle introduced lots of new features in Oracle Grid Infrastructure 11*g* Release 2, especially in 11.2.0.2, which added more prerequisites to be met prior to installing Oracle Grid Infrastructure. Starting with Oracle Grid Infrastructure 11.2.0.2, multicasting must be enabled on the private network because Oracle uses multicasting to provide Highly Available IP (HAIP) to implement redundancy of the private interconnect using the Oracle stack; if multicasting is not enabled, the root.sh configuration script succeeds on the first cluster node but fails on subsequent cluster nodes to start Cluster Synchronization Services in clustered mode.

Oracle uses multicasting to establish the initial connection/link with other cluster nodes, and if multicasting is not enabled, other cluster nodes cannot join an existing cluster, which root.sh starts when executed on the first node. Oracle provides a program to validate whether multicasting on the private network is enabled or not. Refer to My Oracle Support Note 1212703.1, which details this new requirement of enabling multicast for the private network. Sometimes root.sh fails to start Cluster Synchronization Services in clustered mode even when multicasting is enabled on the private network. This may happen if IGMP snooping is enabled and is rejecting the multicast network packets on the private network, so ensure that IGMP snooping is configured appropriately to allow multicast networking.

Apart from the obvious reasons, certain bugs may cause root.sh to fail. For example, one such unpublished bug (8670579) causes root.sh to fail while the OLR is being created. This bug is documented in My Oracle Support Note 1068212.1. Another unpublished bug (8979500) causes root.sh to fail on the Solaris platform because CRS clients are not able to connect to the ASM instance. Therefore, it is always a good practice to search the knowledge base and bug database to see if you are encountering a known bug to speed up the resolution process.

Inside the Database Alert Log

The directory where the install software for Oracle RDBMS is stored is known as ORACLE_HOME. The log files stored are related to each of the database instances running out of this Oracle home. Suppose, for example, that you have a database called TEST with a database instance called TEST1. All its background process trace files, along with alert.log, would be available in the $ORACLE_BASE/diag/rdbms/test/TEST1/trace directory; that's the default location Oracle 11*g* database

Let's take a closer look at staring up an instance in a two-node Oracle RAC cluster running version 11.2.0.2. We use SQL*Plus to issue the startup command on node1 and then on node2. The sequence of events follows, with additional explanations added as required.

Please note that the IP addresses are masked in the following examples because they are taken from live databases.

```
SQL> startup nomount;

<from the alert log>
Cluster communication is configured to use the following interface(s) for this
instance
  169.254.222.55
cluster interconnect IPC version:Oracle UDP/IP (generic)
IPC Vendor 1 proto 2
Tue Jan 25 16:37:47 2011
PMON started with pid=2, OS id=10254
```

As shown in this extract of an actual alert log for an Oracle RAC 11.2.0.2 database, Oracle uses Highly Available IP as the interconnect from the reserved IP range 169.254.X.X. The correct interconnect must be used for the Cache Fusion traffic. Some may choose the public network for the interconnect traffic, but doing so will bring the database to its knees. To identify the network used for Cache Fusion or a private traffic, you can do any of the following:

```
# ./oifcfg getif
bond0   173.21.17.127  global  public
bond1   173.21.17.0    global  cluster_interconnect
#
```

As you can see, bond1 is used as the cluster interconnect, and the private virtual IP 169.254.222.55 is configured and running on this network interface, which is evident from the following command:

```
# /sbin/ifconfig bond1:1
# /sbin/ifconfig bond1:1
bond1:1   Link encap:Ethernet   HWaddr 00:17:A4:77:0C:8E
          inet addr:169.254.222.55  Bcast:169.254.255.255  Mask:255.255.0.0
          UP BROADCAST RUNNING MASTER MULTICAST  MTU:1500  Metric:1
```

Depending on the source of the information, PICKED_KSXPIA is populated with the values GPnP, OSD, OCR, and CI. If the cluster_interconnects parameter is set in the SPFILE, the query will return the following output:

```
SQL> select INST_ID,PUB_KSXPIA,PICKED_KSXPIA,NAME_KSXPIA,IP_KSXPIA
from x$ksxpia where PUB_KSXPIA = 'N';;
```

```
INST_ID P PICK NAME_KSXPIA  IP_KSXPIA
--------- - ---- ------------ ----------------
        1  N GPnP   bond1:1        169.254.222.55
```

Another option is the conventional method of finding the interconnect information from an Interprocess Communications (IPC) dump. This was the only method available in Oracle versions prior to 10*g*, but this method is also possible in Oracle 10*g* onward. Starting from Oracle 10*g* R2, X$KSXPIA is exposed as GV$CONFIGURED_INTERCONNECTS.

Log in to the database as user SYS:

```
SQL> oradebug setmypid
SQL> oradebug tracefile_name
SQL> oradebug ipc
```

This will dump a trace file to DIAGNOSTIC_DIR/diag/rdbms/<dbname>/SID/trace. The output will look something like this:

```
SKGXP:[2b1b8d37ba58.44]{ctx}:  SSKGXPT 0x2b1b8d37d180 flags 0x5 { READPENDING }
sockno 5 IP 169.254.222.55 UDP 50842 lerr 0
SKGXP:[47397333351000.44]{ctx}:
```

You can see that we are using IP 169.254.222.55 with a User Datagram Protocol (UDP). To change the network that Oracle RAC uses, you can change the order of the networks in the operating system–dependent network configurations using the cluster_interconnects parameter.

The moment the first instance is started, its alert log gets populated with important information. The first thing to notice in the preceding example after the list of nondefault parameters is the IP address used for the interconnect. Ensure that you see the correct protocol that you have configured for interconnect usage. The supported interconnect protocols with respect to various operating systems are listed in Chapter 3.

```
lmon registered with NM - instance number 1 (internal mem no 0)
Reconfiguration started (old inc 0, new inc 6)
List of instances:
 1 2 (myinst: 1)
 Global Resource Directory frozen
* allocate domain 0, invalid = TRUE
 Communication channels reestablished
 * domain 0 not valid according to instance 2
 * domain 0 valid = 0 according to instance 2
 Master broadcasted resource hash value bitmaps
 Non-local Process blocks cleaned out
 LMS 0: 0 GCS shadows cancelled, 0 closed, 0 Xw survived
 LMS 1: 0 GCS shadows cancelled, 0 closed, 0 Xw survived
 Set master node info
 Submitted all remote-enqueue requests
 Dwn-cvts replayed, VALBLKs dubious
 All grantable enqueues granted
 Post SMON to start 1st pass IR
 Submitted all GCS remote-cache requests
```

```
Post SMON to start 1st pass IR
Fix write in gcs resources
Reconfiguration complete
```

When an instance starts up, it's the Lock Monitor's (LMON) job to register with the Node Monitor (NM). That's what we see in the alert.log with the instance ID that is getting registered. When any node joins or leaves a cluster, the global resource directory undergoes a reconfiguration event. We see the start of the reconfiguration event along with the old and new incarnation. Next, we see the number of nodes that have joined the cluster. Because this was the first node to be started up, in the list of nodes we see only one node listed, and the number starts with 0. A reconfiguration event is a seven-step procedure, and upon completion the "reconfiguration complete" message is logged to alert.log.

The messages logged in alert.log are summaries of the reconfiguration event. The LMON trace file would have more information about the reconfiguration. Following are the contents of the LMON trace file:

```
kjxgmrcfg: Reconfiguration started, reason 1
kjxgmcs: Setting state to 0 0.
```

Here, you can see the reason for the reconfiguration event. The most common reasons would be 1, 2, and 3. Reason 1 means that the NM initiated the reconfiguration event, as typically seen when a node joins or leaves a cluster. A reconfiguration event is initiated with reason 2 when an instance death is detected. How is an instance death detected? Every instance updates the controlfile with a heartbeat through its Checkpoint (CKPT) process. If heartbeat information is not present for x amount of time (normally 30 seconds in UNIX variants), the instance is considered to be dead and the Instance Membership Recovery (IMR) process initiates reconfiguration. This type of reconfiguration is commonly seen when significant time changes occur across nodes, the node is starved for CPU or I/O time, or some problems occur with the shared storage.

A reason 3 reconfiguration event is due to a communication failure. Communication channels are established between the Oracle processes across the nodes. This communication occurs over the interconnect. Every message sender expects an acknowledgment message from the receiver. If a message is not received for a timeout period, then a "communication failure" is assumed.

This is more relevant for protocols such as UDP, as Reliable Shared Memory (RSM), Reliable DataGram protocol (RDG), and Hyper Messaging Protocol (HMP) do not need it, because the acknowledgment mechanisms are built into the cluster communication and protocol itself. When the block is sent from one instance to another using wire, especially when unreliable protocols such as UDP are used, it is best to get an acknowledgment message from the receiver.

The acknowledgment is a simple side channel message that is normally required for most of the UNIX systems, where UDP is used as the default IPC protocol. When user-mode IPC protocols such as RDG (on HP Tru64 UNIX TruCluster) or HP HMP are used, the additional messaging can be disabled by setting _reliable_block_sends to TRUE.

NOTE
The hidden database parameter _reliable_block_sends is by default set to TRUE in an Oracle 11g RAC database.

For Windows-based systems, it is always recommended to leave the default value as is:

```
Database mounted in Shared Mode (CLUSTER_DATABASE=TRUE).
Completed: alter database mount
```

Because this is an Oracle RAC database, every instance mounts the database in shared mode. Sometimes you want to mount the database in exclusive mode, as in completing the actions of a patchset application. Checking the alert log is one way to confirm that:

```
Tue Jan 25 16:38:04 2011
alter database open
```

This instance was first to open. In earlier versions such as Oracle 9*i*, every commit System Commit Numbers (Commit SCN) is broadcasted to all the nodes, and the log writer is held up until all the pending redos are written to the disk. Starting with Oracle 10*g*, the wait is greatly reduced because the broadcast and commit are asynchronous. This means the system waits until it is sure that all nodes have seen the Commit SCN. Any message with an SCN greater than Commit SCN is deemed sufficient.

Before doing a broadcast, the process checks whether it has already received a higher SCN from that instance. It used the same SCN to determine whether a foreground or an LMS has to be posted. With Oracle 10*g*, this is decoupled: an SCN is needed to release foregrounds and an SCN is needed for shipping buffers. The init.ora parameter "_lgwr_async_broadcasts = true" can be used to change the broadcast method.

NOTE
*The database parameter max_commit_propagation_delay is obsolete in Oracle 11*g *RAC.*

RAC ON and OFF

In some cases, you may want to disable the Oracle RAC options for testing purposes—perhaps to run a benchmark or to convert the Oracle RAC binaries to single-instance binaries.

In such a case, you can use the following procedure to convert the Oracle RAC installation to non–Oracle RAC. Disabling and enabling Oracle RAC options are available only for UNIX platforms. Windows installations do not support relinking binaries with Oracle RAC ON and OFF.

Use the following steps to disable Oracle RAC (known as RAC OFF):

1. Log in as the Oracle software owner (which is typically the UNIX account *oracle*) in all nodes.

2. Shut down all the instances from all the nodes using a NORMAL or IMMEDIATE option.

3. Change the working directory to $ORACLE_HOME/lib:

   ```
   cd $ORACLE_HOME/lib
   ```

4. Run the following "make" command to relink the Oracle binaries without the Oracle RAC option:

   ```
   make -f ins_rdbms.mk rac_off
   ```

   This normally runs for a few minutes and should not pose any errors.

5. Now relink the Oracle binaries:

   ```
   make -f ins_rdbms.mk ioracle
   ```

Now the Oracle binaries are relinked with the RAC OFF option. You may have to edit the init.ora or SPFILE parameters accordingly. If errors occur in step 4, you may need to contact Oracle Support and log a service request with the trace and log files.

Use the following steps to enable Oracle RAC (known as RAC ON):

1. Log in as the Oracle software owner (typically the UNIX account *oracle*) in all nodes.

2. Shut down all the instances from all the nodes using a NORMAL or IMMEDIATE option.

3. Change the working directory to $ORACLE_HOME/lib:

   ```
   cd $ORACLE_HOME/lib
   ```

4. Run the following "make" command to relink the Oracle binaries without the RAC option:
   ```
   make -f ins_rdbms.mk rac_on
   ```

   This normally runs for a few minutes and should not pose any errors.

5. Now relink the Oracle binaries:
   ```
   make -f ins_rdbms.mk ioracle
   ```

Now the Oracle binaries are relinked with the RAC ON option. You may need to edit the init.ora or SPFILE parameters accordingly. If any errors occur in step 4, you may need to contact Oracle Support and log a service request with the trace and log files.

Database Performance Issues

Oracle RAC databases have more than one instance using the same set of resources, and a resource may be requested by more than one instance. Resource sharing is well managed by Global Cache Services (GCS) and Global Enqueue Services (GES). However, in some cases, the resource management operations could run into a deadlock situation and the entire database may hang because of serialization issues. Sometimes, software bugs also cause database-hang issues, and these situations almost always require the intervention of Oracle Support in the form of a service request.

Database-hang issues can be placed in the following categories:

- Hung database
- Hung session(s)
- Overall instance/database performance
- Query performance

We will examine only the hung database because that is more critical and complex than the others and also related to our point of interest. Detailed texts are available for analyzing the database and query performance.

Hung Database

Oracle Support defines a "true" database hang as "an internal deadlock or a cyclical dependency between two or more processes." When dealing with DML locks (that is, enqueue type TM), Oracle is able to detect this dependency and roll back one of the processes to break the cyclical condition. On the other hand, when this situation occurs with internal kernel-level resources (such as latches or pins), Oracle is usually unable to automatically detect and resolve the deadlock.

If you encounter a database-hang situation, you need to take system state dumps so that Oracle Support can begin to diagnose the root cause of the problem. Whenever you take such dumps for a hang, it is important to take at least three of them a few minutes apart, on all instances of your database. That way, evidence shows whether a resource is still being held from one time to the next.

The maxdump file size should be set to unlimited, as this will generate bigger and larger trace files, depending on the size of the System Global Area (SGA), the number of sessions logged in, and the workload on the system. The SYSTEMSTATE dump contains a separate section with information for each process. Normally, you need to take two or three dumps in regular intervals. Whenever you make SYSTEMSTATE dumps repetitively, make sure you reconnect every time so that you get a new process ID and also the new trace files. Expect HUGE trace files!

Starting with Oracle Database 10g, a SYSTEMSTATE dump includes session wait history information. If you are using Oracle 10g or later, you don't need to take multiple system state dumps. The SYSTEMSTATE dump can be taken by any of the following methods.

From SQL*Plus:

```
alter session set max_dump_file_size = unlimited;
alter session set events 'immediate trace name systemstate level 10';
```

Using oradebug:

```
oradebug setmypid
oradebug unlimit
oradebug dump systemstate 10
```

When the entire database is hung and you cannot connect to SQL*Plus, you can try invoking SQL*Plus with the prelim option if you're using Oracle 10g or later. This attaches the process to the Oracle instance and no SQL commands are run. No login triggers or pre-processing is done, and no SQL queries are allowed to run. See the change in banner from normal sqlplus and prelim sqlplus:

```
$sqlplus -prelim
SQL*Plus: Release 11.2.0.2.0 Production on Mon Nov 8 15:16:37 2010
Copyright (c) 1982, 2010, Oracle.  All rights reserved. / as sysdba
SQL>
```

Alternatively, oradebug allows you to dump the global system state by connecting to one node. The following shows the global SYSTEMSTATE dump from oradebug:

```
oradebug -g all dump systemstate 10
```

The –g option is used for Oracle RAC databases only. This will dump system states for all the instances. The SYSTEMSTATE dump/trace file can be found in the user_dump_dest directory on the instance where the dump was generated.

Hanganalyze Utility

A severe performance problem can be mistaken for a hang. This usually happens when contention is so bad that it *seems like* the database is completely hung. Usually, a SYSTEMSTATE dump is used to analyze these situations. However, if the instance is large with more than a few gigabytes of SGA and with a heavy workload, a SYSTEMSTATE dump may take an hour or more and often fails to dump the entire SGA and lock structures. Moreover, a SYSTEMSTATE dump has the following limitations when dealing with hang issues:

- Reads the SGA in a "dirty" manner, so it may be inconsistent when the time to dump all of the process is long.

- Usually dumps a lot of information (most of which is not needed to determine the source of the hang), which makes it difficult to determine quickly the dependencies between processes.

- Does not identify "interesting" processes on which to perform additional dumps (ERRORSTACK or PROCESS STATE).

- Often very expensive operation for databases that have large SGAs. A SYSTEMSTATE dump can take hours, and taking a few continuous dumps within an interval of a few minutes is nearly impossible.

To overcome the limitations of the SYSTEMSTATE dump, a new utility called hanganalyze was introduced in Oracle 8*i*. In Oracle 9*i*, the hanganalyze command was enhanced to provide clusterwide information in Oracle RAC environments on a single shot. This uses the DIAG daemon process in the Oracle RAC process to communicate between the instances. Clusterwide, hanganalyze will generate information for all the sessions in the cluster regardless of the instance that issued the command.

Hanganalyze can be invoked from SQL*Plus or through oradebug (which is available when you connect as *SYS* in the SQL*Plus utility). The following syntax can be used to get a hanganalyze trace when connected to SQL*Plus:

```
alter session set events 'immediate trace name hanganalyze level <level>';
```

Or when logged in as *SYS*:

```
oradebug hanganalyze <level>
```

Clusterwide, hanganalyze can be obtained like so:

```
oradebug setmypid
oradebug setinst all
oradebug -g def hanganalyze <level>
```

The <level> sets the amount of additional information that will be extracted from the processes found by hanganalyze (ERROSTACK dump) based on the STATE of the node. The following table describes the various levels and the trace information emitted when they are set:

Level	Trace Information
1–2	Only hanganalyze output. No process dump at all.
3	Level 2 + Dump only processes thought to be in a hang (IN_HANG state).
4	Level 3 + Dump leaf nodes (blockers) in wait chains (LEAF, LEAF_NW, IGN_DMP state).
5	Level 4 + Dump all processes involved in wait chains (NLEAF state).
10	Dump all processes (IGN state).

Hanganalyze uses internal kernel calls to determine whether a session is waiting for a resource and reports the relationships between blockers and waiters. In addition, it determines which processes are "interesting" to be dumped, and it may perform automatic PROCESS STATE dumps and ERRORSTACKs on those processes, based on the level used while executing hanganalyze.

NOTE
Hanganalyze is not intended to replace a SYSTEMSTATE dump, but it may serve as a roadmap to interpret a system state while diagnosing complex issues. Performance issues related to row cache objects, enqueues, and latches can be analyzed only with hanganalyze and/ or a SYSTEMSTATE dump. The process state information in these dumps provides an accurate snapshot of the locks/latches held by each process or session. It also tells us which event the process was waiting for and if any TM locks were held for a transaction. Problems associated with DDL statement locks and row cache lock issues can be debugged using only these dumps.

Debugging Node Eviction Issues

One of the most common and complex issues in Oracle RAC is performing the root cause analysis (RCA) of the node eviction issues. Oracle evicts a node from the cluster mainly due to one of the following three reasons:

- The node is not able to complete the network heartbeat (NHB).
- The node is not able to complete the disk heartbeat (DHB).
- The node does not have enough CPU to perform either of the heartbeat operations.

The whole troubleshooting theory to debug node evictions in Oracle Clusterware revolves around the aforementioned reasons. You must read the previous chapters in this book to understand how Oracle performs network and disk heartbeats—it is very important to understand this process before you attempt to troubleshoot node evictions. The node eviction process is reported as Oracle error ORA-29740 in the alert log and LMON trace files. To determine the root cause, first look at the Oracle Clusterware alert_hostname.log.

The first step is to establish the reason why the failed node is evicted from the cluster. Was it not able to perform network heartbeat (NHB) or disk heartbeat (DHB)? Which process was responsible for evicting the failed node? Was there an infrastructure problem or was the failed node just busy? To know the exact reason of the node eviction, you will review the clusterware alert log file, which has details of why the failed node was evicted and which process caused the failed node to be evicted from the cluster. Here is an example from the clusterware alert log of a failed cluster node:

```
reboot advisory message from host: racnode01, component: cssagent,
with timestamp: L-2010-11-05-10:03:25.340
reboot advisory message text: Rebooting after limit 28500 exceeded;
disk timeout 27630, network timeout 28500,
```

```
last heartbeat from CSSD at epoch seconds 1241543005.340,
4294967295 milliseconds ago based on invariant clock value of 93235653
```

As you can see in this example, the CSSDAGENT caused the failed node to reboot, so now you can look into the diagnostic log file of the CSSDAGENT process to get more details on why CSSDAGENT failed and rebooted the node. The CSSDAGENT process is responsible for spawning and monitoring the OCSSD process, and CSSDAGENT can cause a cluster node to be evicted if the cluster node is very busy and the OCSSD process cannot be scheduled on the failed cluster node.

Starting with Oracle 11*g* Release 2, Oracle evicts a cluster node as a last resort because it will first try killing the processes on the failed node that are capable of performing I/O and then stopping the clusterware on the failed node rather than simply rebooting the failed node.

Here is an example of the clusterware alter log from Oracle Grid Infrastructure 11.2.0.2 showing how Oracle Clusterware is restarting the CSSD process on the problematic cluster node rather than rebooting the node:

```
CRS-1652:Starting clean up of CRSD resources.
...
CRS-1654:Clean up of CRSD resources finished successfully.
CRS-1655:CSSD on node racnode02 detected a problem and started to shutdown.
...
CRS-1713:CSSD daemon is started in clustered mode
```

Rebootless Node Fencing in Oracle RAC 11.2.0.2

In Oracle Grid Infrastructure 11.2.0.2, if one of the cluster nodes hangs or the cluster node does not perform the network or disk heartbeat on time, Oracle first tries killing the processes responsible for I/O operations on the failed node, such as the database writer, archiver, and so on. If Oracle succeeds in killing the processes responsible of performing I/O, it updates the ohasdrun cluster controlfile stored in the /etc/oracle/scls_scr/<hostname>/root directory and with "restart" flag; subsequently OHASD restarts Oracle Clusterware on the failed node.

Regardless of whether Oracle Clusterware reboots or just restarts the clusterware, the Oracle Clusterware alert log will record the important messages about the possible reason behind the Oracle Clusterware restart or node reboot. If the node is not able to complete the network heartbeat (NHB) on time, you must check the private network between the cluster nodes because sending and receiving packets over the private network performs the network heartbeat.

Oracle starts writing informational messages into the Clusterware alert log if it is not able to complete the network heartbeat, even after waiting for half of the time period specified by the miscount parameter of Oracle Clusterware—which is, by default, set to 30 seconds and must not be changed without consulting Oracle Support. You may observe the following messages in the Oracle Clusterware alert log when Oracle is not able to complete the network heartbeat:

```
Network communication with node rac1 (1) missing for 50% of timeout interval.
Removal of this node from cluster in 14.920 seconds
...
```

```
Network communication with node rac1 (1) missing for 90% of timeout interval.
Removal of this node from cluster in 2.900 seconds
This node is unable to communicate with other nodes in the cluster
and is going down to preserve cluster integrity
```

Oracle has continuously provided toolsets to proactively collect the diagnostics information to troubleshoot node evictions, because in the absence of historical diagnostics information, it is impossible to identify the cause of a node eviction. Oracle Clusterware Health Monitor collects diagnostics information to perform root-cause analysis in such situations. Clusterware Health Monitor can be installed in pre–11.2.0.2 Grid Infrastructure by downloading software from the following location:

www.oracle.com/technetwork/database/clustering/downloads/ipd-download-homepage-087212.html

Cluster Health Monitor

Cluster Health Monitor (CHM) is a subsequent version of the Instantaneous Problem Detector for Clusters, or IPD/OS. Cluster Health Monitor is designed to proactively collect the diagnostics information for detecting and analyzing various problems in Oracle Grid Infrastructure, including node evictions. Cluster Health Monitor continuously tracks the OS resource consumption at each node, process, and device level. Cluster Health Monitor can be configured for real-time monitoring, and when thresholds are hit, an alert can be sent to the operator. For root-cause analysis, historical data can be replayed to understand what was happening at the time of failure.

The use of the divide-and-conquer policy is suggested for debugging node eviction issues because there could be various reasons from OS resource contention—from a faulty network to clock synchronization. You should analyze these possible reasons carefully, one by one. Cluster Health Monitor can be useful to provide the historical data from the time when a particular node was evicted. As mentioned, there could be various reasons for a node eviction, but the following items could provide a quick win:

- Check the clock synchronization between cluster nodes. Ensure that NTP is configured correctly on all cluster nodes.

- Check the network connectivity between cluster nodes. Use the following command to test the network connectivity between the cluster nodes on the public and private interface:

```
ping -s <size of MTU> -c 10 -l <Public IP of local node>
<Public IP of another cluster node>
ping -s <size of MTU> -c 10 -l <Private IP of local node>
<Private IP of another cluster node>
```

If the cluster node is evicted because it could not access more than half of the number of voting disks or create and complete the disk heartbeat in time, then in a two-node cluster you may see the following messages in the Oracle Clusterware alert log file, which show that the cluster node is having some problem accessing the shared storage:

```
No I/O has completed after 90% of the maximum interval.
Voting file ORCL:OCR_VOTE2 will be considered not functional in 19750 milliseconds
```

The number of voting files available (1) is less than the minimum number of voting files required (2), resulting in CSSD termination to ensure data integrity.

Analyze the output of the preceding test and ensure 100 percent of the packets is being received for the public and private interface for all cluster nodes.

- Check and ensure that all cluster nodes can access the shared storage where the OCR and voting disks are stored.

- Check that there are enough OS resources (such as CPU and memory) available even when there is peak activity in the Oracle RAC database. Cluster Health Monitor will be helpful in analyzing the historical CPU data.

To get into deeper levels of the node-eviction process, you need to understand the basics of node membership and Instance Membership Recovery (IMR), also referred to as *Instance Membership Reconfiguration*.

Instance Membership Recovery

IMR is the basic framework that handles the split-brain resolution in the earlier versions, where the cluster foundation was provided by vendor clusterware. The functionality is still in the database kernel, but is handled outside the RDBMS layer because the Oracle Grid Infrastructure stack is more tightly integrated with the hardware layer.

Instance Membership Recovery

When a communication failure occurs between the instances, or when an instance is not able to issue the heartbeat information to the controlfile, the cluster group may be in danger of possible data corruption. In addition, when no mechanism is present to detect the failures, the entire cluster will hang. To address the issue, IMR was introduced in Oracle 9*i* and improved in Oracle 10*g*. IMR removes the failed instance from the cluster group. When a subset of a cluster group survives during failures, IMR ensures that the larger partition group survives and kills all other smaller groups.

IMR is a part of the service offered by Cluster Group Services (CGS). LMON is the key process that handles many of the CGS functionalities. As you know, cluster software (known as Cluster Manager, or CM) can be a vendor-provided or Oracle-provided infrastructure tool. CM facilitates communication between all nodes of the cluster and provides information on the health of each node—the node state. It detects failures and manages the basic membership of nodes in the cluster. CM works at the cluster level and not at the database or instance level.

Inside Oracle RAC, the Node Monitor (NM) provides information about nodes and their health by registering and communicating with the CM. NM services are provided by LMON. Node membership is represented as a bitmap in the GRD. A value of 0 denotes that a node is down, and a value of 1 denotes that the node is up. There is no value to indicate a "transition" period such as during bootup or shutdown. LMON uses the global notification mechanism to let others know of a change in the node membership. Every time a node joins or leaves a cluster, this bitmap in the GRD has to be rebuilt and communicated to all registered members in the cluster.

Node membership registration and deregistration is done in a series of synchronized steps—a topic beyond the scope of this chapter. Basically, cluster members register and deregister from a group. The important thing to remember is that NM always communicates with the other instances in the cluster about their health and status using the CM. In contrast, if LMON needs to send a message to LMON on another instance, it can do so directly without the help or involvement of CM. It is important to differentiate between cluster communication and Oracle RAC communication.

A simple extract from the alert log file about member registration is provided here:

```
Thu Jan 1 00:02:17 1970
alter database mount
Thu Jan 1 00:02:17 1970
lmon registered with NM - instance id 1 (internal mem no 0)
Thu Jan 1 00:02:17 1970
Reconfiguration started
List of nodes: 0,
 Global Resource Directory frozen
```

Here you can see that this instance was the first to start up and that LMON registered itself with the NM interface, which is a part of the Oracle kernel.

When an instance joins or leaves the cluster, the LMON trace of another instance shows the reconfiguration of the GRD:

```
kjxgmpoll reconfig bitmap: 0 1 3
*** 1970-01-01 01:20:51.423
kjxgmrcfg: Reconfiguration started, reason 1
```

You may find these lines together with other lines asking SMON to perform instance recovery. This happens when any instance crash occurs or when an instance departs the cluster without deregistering in a normal fashion:

```
Post SMON to start 1st pass IR
*** 1970-01-01 01:20:51.423
kjxgmpoll reconfig bitmap: 0 1 3
*** 1970-01-01 01:20:51.423
kjxgmrcfg: Reconfiguration started, reason 1
kjxgmcs: Setting state to 2 0.
*** 1970-01-01 01:20:51.423
 Name Service frozen
```

The CGS is present primarily to provide a coherent and consistent view of the cluster from an OS perspective. It tells Oracle the number of nodes that are in the cluster. It is designed to provide a synchronized view of the cluster instance membership. Its main responsibility involves regular status checks of the members and measuring whether they are valid in the group—and very importantly, it detects split-brain scenarios in case of communication failures.

Specific rules bind together members within the cluster group, which keeps the cluster in a consistent state:

- Each member should be able to communicate without any problems with any other registered and valid member in the group.

- Members should see all other registered members in the cluster as valid and have a consistent view.

- All members must be able to read from and write to the controlfile.

So, when a communication failure occurs between the instances, or when an instance is not able to issue the heartbeat information to the voting disk, IMR is triggered. Other than IMR, there is no mechanism to detect failures that could result in a hang of the entire cluster.

Member Voting

The CGS is responsible for checking whether members are valid. To determine periodically whether all members are alive, a voting mechanism is used to check the validity of each member. All members in the database group vote by providing details of what they presume the instance membership bitmap looks like. As mentioned, the bitmap is stored in the GRD. A predetermined master member tallies the vote flags of the status flag and communicates to the respective processes that the voting is done; then it waits for registration by all the members who have received the reconfigured bitmap.

How Voting Happens

The Checkpoint (CKPT) process updates the controlfile every 3 seconds in an operation known as the *heartbeat*. CKPT writes into a single block that is unique for each instance; therefore, intra-instance coordination is not required. This block is called the *checkpoint progress record*.

All members attempt to obtain a lock on a controlfile record (the *result record)* for updating. The instance that obtains the lock tallies the votes from all members. The group membership must conform to the *decided (voted)* membership before allowing the GCS/GES reconfiguration to proceed. The *controlfile vote result record* is stored in the same block as the heartbeat in the controlfile checkpoint progress record.

In this scenario of dead instances and member evictions, a potentially disastrous situation could arise if pending I/O from a dead instance is to be flushed to the I/O subsystem. This could lead to potential data corruption. I/O from an abnormally departing instance cannot be flushed to disk if database integrity is to be maintained. To "shield" the database from data corruption in this situation, a technique called *I/O fencing* is used. I/O fencing implementation is a function of CM and depends on the clusterware vendor.

I/O fencing is designed to guarantee data integrity in the case of faulty cluster communications causing a split-brain condition. A split-brain occurs when cluster nodes hang or node interconnects fail, and as a result, the nodes lose the communication link between them and the cluster. Split-brain is a problem in any clustered environment and is a symptom of clustering solutions and not Oracle RAC. Split-brain conditions can cause database corruption when nodes become uncoordinated in their access to the shared datafiles.

For a two-node cluster, split-brain occurs when nodes in a cluster cannot talk to each other (the internode links fail) and each node assumes it is the only surviving member of the cluster. If the nodes in the cluster have uncoordinated access to the shared storage area, they would end up overwriting each other's data, causing data corruption because each node assumes ownership of shared data. To prevent data corruption, one node must be asked to leave the cluster or should be forced out immediately. This is where IMR comes in, as explained earlier in the chapter.

Many internal (hidden) parameters control IMR and determine when it should start. If a vendor clusterware is used, split-brain resolution is left to it and Oracle would have to wait for the clusterware to provide a consistent view of the cluster and resolve the split-brain issue (10 minutes), This can potentially cause a delay (and a hang in the whole cluster) because each node can potentially think it is the master and try to own all the shared resources. Still, Oracle relies on the clusterware for resolving these challenging issues.

Note that Oracle does not wait indefinitely for the clusterware to resolve a split-brain issue, but a timer is used to trigger an IMR-based node eviction. These internal timers are also controlled using hidden parameters. The default values of these hidden parameters are not to be touched because that can cause severe performance or operational issues with the cluster.

An obvious question that pops up in your mind might be, Why does a split-brain condition take place? Why does Oracle say a link is down, when my communication engineer says it's fine? This is easier asked than answered because the underlying hardware and software layers that support Oracle RAC are too complex, and it can be a nightmare trying to figure out why a cluster broke in two when things seem to be normal. Usually, configuration of communication links and bugs in the clusterware can cause these issues.

As mentioned time and again, Oracle completely relies on the cluster software to provide cluster services, and if something is awry, Oracle, in its overzealous quest to protect data integrity, evicts nodes or aborts an instance and assumes that something is wrong with the cluster.

Cluster reconfiguration is initiated when NM indicates a change in the database group or when IMR detects a problem. Reconfiguration is initially managed by the CGS, and after this is completed, IDLM (GES/GCS) reconfiguration starts.

Cluster Reconfiguration Steps

The cluster reconfiguration process triggers IMR, and a seven-step process ensures complete reconfiguration:

1. The name service is frozen. The CGS contains an internal database of all the members/ instances in the cluster with all their configuration and servicing details. The name service provides a mechanism to address this configuration data in a structured and synchronized manner.

2. The lock database (IDLM) is frozen. The lock database is frozen to prevent processes from obtaining locks on resources that were mastered by the departing/dead instance.

3. Determination of membership and validation and IMR occur.

4. Bitmap rebuild takes place, including instance name and uniqueness verification. CGS must synchronize the cluster to be sure that all members get the reconfiguration event and that they all see the same bitmap.

5. Delete all dead instance entries and republish all names newly configured.

6. Unfreeze and release the name service for use.

7. Hand over reconfiguration to GES/GCS.

Now that you know when IMR starts and node evictions take place, let's look at the corresponding messages in the alert log and LMON trace files to get a better picture. (The logs have been edited for brevity. Note that all the lines in boldface define the most important steps in IMR and the handoff to other recovery steps in CGS.)

Problem with a Node

Assume a four-node cluster (instances A, B, C, and D), in which instance C has a problem communicating with other nodes because its private link is down. All other services on this node are assumed to be working normally.

Alter log on instance C:

```
ORA-29740: evicted by member 2, group incarnation 6
Thu Jun 30 09:15:59 2005
LMON: terminating instance due to error 29740
Instance terminated by LMON, pid = 692304
...
...
...
```

Alter log on instance A:

```
Thu Jun 30 09:15:59 2005
Communications reconfiguration: instance 2
Evicting instance 3 from cluster
Thu Jun 30 09:16:29 2005
Trace dumping is performing id=[50630091559]
Thu Jun 30 09:16:31 2005
Waiting for instances to leave:
3
Thu Jun 30 09:16:51 2005
Waiting for instances to leave:
3
Thu Jun 30 09:17:04 2005
Reconfiguration started
List of nodes: 0,1,3,
 Global Resource Directory frozen
 Communication channels reestablished
 Master broadcasted resource hash value bitmaps
Thu Jun 30 09:17:04 2005
Reconfiguration started
```

LMON trace file on instance A:

```
*** 2005-06-30 09:15:58.262
kjxgrgetresults: Detect reconfig from 1, seq 12, reason 3
kjxgfipccb: msg 0x1113dcfa8, mbo 0x1113dcfa0, type 22, ack 0, ref 0,
stat 3
kjxgfipccb: Send timed out, stat 3 inst 2, type 22, tkt (10496,1496)
*** 2005-06-30 09:15:59.070
kjxgrcomerr: Communications reconfig: instance 2 (12,4)
Submitting asynchronized dump request [2]
kjxgfipccb: msg 0x1113d9498, mbo 0x1113d9490, type 22, ack 0, ref 0,
stat 6
kjxgfipccb: Send cancelled, stat 6 inst 2, type 22, tkt (10168,1496)
kjxgfipccb: msg 0x1113e54a8, mbo 0x1113e54a0, type 22, ack 0, ref 0,
stat 6
kjxgfipccb: Send cancelled, stat 6 inst 2, type 22, tkt (9840,1496)
```

Note that "Send timed out, stat 3 inst 2" is LMON trying to send messages to the broken instance.

```
kjxgrrcfgchk: Initiating reconfig, reason 3 /* IMR Initiated */
*** 2005-06-30 09:16:03.305
kjxgmrcfg: Reconfiguration started, reason 3
kjxgmcs: Setting state to 12 0.
*** 2005-06-30 09:16:03.449
```

Name service frozen:

```
kjxgmcs: Setting state to 12 1.
*** 2005-06-30 09:16:11.570
Voting results, upd 1, seq 13, bitmap: 0 1 3
```

Note that instance A has not tallied the vote; hence, it has received only the voting results. Here is an extract from the LMON trace file on instance B, which managed to tally the vote:

```
Obtained RR update lock for sequence 13, RR seq 13
*** 2005-06-30 09:16:11.570
Voting results, upd 0, seq 13, bitmap: 0 1 3
...
...
```

Here's the LMON trace file on instance A:

```
Evicting mem 2, stat 0x0007 err 0x0002
kjxgmps: proposing substate 2
kjxgmcs: Setting state to 13 2.
Performed the unique instance identification check
kjxgmps: proposing substate 3
kjxgmcs: Setting state to 13 3.
  Name Service recovery started
  Deleted all dead-instance name entries
kjxgmps: proposing substate 4
kjxgmcs: Setting state to 13 4.
  Multicasted all local name entries for publish
  Replayed all pending requests
kjxgmps: proposing substate 5
kjxgmcs: Setting state to 13 5.
  Name Service normal
  Name Service recovery done
*** 2005-06-30 09:17:04.369
kjxgmrcfg: Reconfiguration started, reason 1
kjxgmcs: Setting state to 13 0.
*** 2005-06-30 09:17:04.371
  Name Service frozen
kjxgmcs: Setting state to 13 1.
```

GES/GCS recovery starts here:

```
Global Resource Directory frozen
node 0
node 1
node 3
res_master_weight for node 0 is 632960
res_master_weight for node 1 is 632960
res_master_weight for node 3 is 632960
...
...
...
```

Death of a Member

For the same four-node cluster (A, B, C, and D), instance C has died unexpectedly:

```
kjxgrnbrisalive: (3, 4) not beating, HB: 561027672, 561027672
*** 2005-06-19 00:30:52.018
kjxgrnbrdead: Detected death of 3, initiating reconfig
kjxgrrcfgchk: Initiating reconfig, reason 2
*** 2005-06-19 00:30:57.035
kjxgmrcfg: Reconfiguration started, reason 2
kjxgmcs: Setting state to 6 0.
*** 2005-06-19 00:30:57.037
  Name Service frozen
kjxgmcs: Setting state to 6 1.
*** 2005-06-19 00:30:57.239
Obtained RR update lock for sequence 6, RR seq 6
*** 2005-06-19 00:33:27.261
Voting results, upd 0, seq 7, bitmap: 0 2
Evicting mem 3, stat 0x0007 err 0x0001
kjxgmps: proposing substate 2
kjxgmcs: Setting state to 7 2.
  Performed the unique instance identification check
kjxgmps: proposing substate 3
kjxgmcs: Setting state to 7 3.
  Name Service recovery started
  Deleted all dead-instance name entries
kjxgmps: proposing substate 4
kjxgmps: proposing substate 4
.kjxgmcs: Setting state to 7 4.
  Multicasted all local name entries for publish
  Replayed all pending requests
kjxgmps: proposing substate 5
kjxgmcs: Setting state to 7 5.
  Name Service normal
  Name Service recovery done
*** 2005-06-19 00:33:27.266
```

```
kjxgmps: proposing substate 6
...
...
...
kjxgmps: proposing substate 2
```

GES/GCS recovery starts here:

```
Global Resource Directory frozen
node 0
node 2
res_master_weight tor node 0 is 632960
res_master_weight for node 2 is 632960
 Total master weight = 1265920
 Dead  inst 3
Join  inst
 Exist inst 0 2
...
...
```

Advanced Debugging for Oracle Clusterware Modules

By default, Oracle records minimal debugging information in the diagnostic log files. There are situations where you require detailed information to diagnose the potential problems in Oracle Clusterware. You can instruct Oracle Clusterware to record more debugging information for different Oracle Clusterware processes and cluster resources. The CRSCTL utility is used to set the advanced debugging in Oracle Clusterware. Oracle Clusterware services such as Cluster Synchronization Services, Cluster Ready Services, and so on, have multiple modules or functions in them for which advance debugging can be enabled to a debug level between 0 and 5. Here is an example of identifying the Oracle Clusterware services and modules on which advance debugging can be enabled.

Run the following command to display the services:

```
# ./crsctl get log -h
Usage.
  crsctl get {log|trace} {mdns|gpnp|css|crf|crs|ctss|evm|gipc} "<name1>,..."
where
    mdns          multicast Domain Name Server
    gpnp          Grid Plug-n-Play Service
    css           Cluster Synchronization Services
    crf           Cluster Health Monitor
    crs           Cluster Ready Services
    ctss          Cluster Time Synchronization Service
    evm           EventManager
    gipc          Grid Interprocess Communications
    <name1>, ...    Module names ("all" for all names)
```

```
crsctl get log res <resname>
where
    <resname>        Resource name
```

The following command displays modules of Cluster Synchronization Services along with the current debug levels:

```
# ./crsctl get log css all
Get CSSD Module: CLSF   Log Level: 0
Get CSSD Module: CSSD   Log Level: 2
Get CSSD Module: GIPCCM  Log Level: 2
Get CSSD Module: GIPCGM  Log Level: 2
Get CSSD Module: GIPCNM  Log Level: 2
Get CSSD Module: GPNP   Log Level: 1
Get CSSD Module: OLR   Log Level: 0
Get CSSD Module: SKGFD   Log Level: 0
```

As shown here, Cluster Synchronization Services have eight different modules. Because setting advance debugging writes a lot of extra diagnostic information in the diagnostic file, so you must be very careful while setting advance debugging because it may adversely impact the performance of your Oracle cluster. You should only enable advance debugging on the required module rather than setting it on the whole service. For example, if you see some errors related to the Oracle Local Registry in the Oracle Clusterware alert log and you want to know more information about what's happening during the failure, you should enable advance debugging for the OLR module of the Cluster Synchronization Service as shown here:

```
# ./crsctl set log css OLR:5
Set CSSD Module: OLR   Log Level: 5
```

Similarly, you can enable advance debugging for Oracle Cluster Resources as well. Suppose you are unable to start a virtual IP resource; it would not make sense to enable advance debugging for the whole of CRS. Rather it is more efficient to just enable advance debugging for that failing cluster resource. Here is an example of enabling advance debugging for Oracle network resource ora.backup.vip:

```
#./crsctl set log res ora.backup.vip:3
Set Resource ora.alpha1.vip Log Level: 3
```

Advance debugging can be enabled from level 0 to 5, where a higher level records more diagnostic information, with the possibility that the highest debug level may reveal some source code snippets, which must be analyzed by Oracle product support because end users may get confused by such raw diagnostic information. When advanced debugging is enabled, Oracle writes lots of diagnostic information and wraps the diagnostic files. Therefore, there's a chance that the interesting diagnostic file is wrapped. To avoid losing the required diagnostic data, it is recommended that you create a custom script to move the diagnostic files to a safer location before Oracle wraps them. Here is a sample script that can be executed on the cluster node to move log files of the CRSD daemon:

```
# Shell script to move diagnostic files of the CRSD daemon
# when advance debugging is enabled.
# Change the GRID_HOME variable to specify your Oracle Clusterware Home.
```

```
GRID_HOME=/u02/11.2.0/grid
# Specify the HOST variable to define your cluster node name.
# This should not contain domain name in it.
HOST=<add your cluster node name here>
# Change the DELAY variable to specify frequency time in seconds,
# this script will move the logfiles.
# By default script will move logfiles every 200 seconds.
DELAY=200
CRSDLOGFIR=$GRID_HOME/log/$HOST/crsd
while [ 2 -ne 3 ]; do
 COMPRESSFILE = $GRID_HOME/log/$HOST/`date +m%d%y%"-"%H%M`.tar
 tar -cf $COMPRESSFILE $CRSDLOGFIR/*
 sleep $DELAY
done
exit
```

Debugging Various Utilities in Oracle RAC

Prior to Oracle Database 10g, you had to modify the srvconfig file located in the $ORACLE_HOME/bin directory to enable the advance tracing by changing the JRE options. Beginning with Oracle 10g, special environment variable SRVM_TRACE can be used to trace the SRVM files and various Java-based utilities, such as DBCA, ASMCA, CLUVFY, DBUA, and SRVCTL. Oracle displays trace data on the standard output while tracing the SRVCTL utility, whereas trace files for others are written into the file system.

By default, tracing is enabled for the Database Configuration and Database Upgrade Assistants, and their trace files are located under $ORACLE_HOME/cfgtools/dbca and $ORACLE_HOME/cfgtools/dbua, respectively. The trace file for CLUVFY is stored under the $GRID_HOME/cv/log directory. There are situations where you enable this trace file for debugging. For example, if you are unable to start a database or database instance using the SRVCTL utility and the standard error reported by the SRVCTL utility is not providing enough information, setting the SRVM_TRACE environment variable to TRUE provides more information that is helpful in debugging the problem. Here is an example of enabling a Java trace for the SRVCTL utility, which is unable to start a single-instance database called SINGLEDB in the cluster:

```
$ srvctl start database id singledb
PRCR-1013 : Failed to start resource ora.singledb.db
PRCR-1064 : Failed to start resource ora.singledb.db on node racnode02
CRS-2674: Start of 'ora.singledb.db' on 'racnode02' failed
```

Setting the SRVM_TRACE environment variable to TRUE reveals more information, and it is found that the OCR is corrupt because it is showing SINGLEDB as a cluster database and reporting a database resource placement error as well:

```
[main] [ 2010-09-10 14:04:38.414 EST ] [CRSNative.searchEntities:857]  found 1 ntities
[main] [ 2010-09-10 14:04:38.415 EST ] [DatabaseImpl.getDBInstances:1185]
riID=ora.singledb.db 1 1 result={CLUSTER_DATABASE=true, LAST_SERVER=racnode02,

USR_ORA_INST_NAME=SINGLEDB, USR_ORA_INST_NAME@SERVERNAME(racnode02)=SINGLEDB}
[main] [ 2010-09-10 14:04:38.418 EST ] [DatabaseImpl.getDBInstances:1322]  Instances:
<SINGLEDB,racnode02>
```

```
[main] [ 2010-09-10 14:04:38.419 EST ] [StartAction.executeDatabase:220]  starting db resource
[main] [ 2010-09-10 14:04:38.419 EST ] [CRSNative.internalStartResource:339]  About to start
resource: Name: ora.singledb.db, node: null, options: 0, filter null
[main] [ 2010-09-10 14:04:38.505 EST ] [CRSNativeResult.addLine:106]  callback:
ora.oemrolt2.db false CRS-2672: Attempting to start 'ora.singledb.db' on 'racnode02'
[main] [ 2010-09-10 14:05:09.275 EST ] [CRSNativeResult.addLine:106]  callback:
ora.oemrolt2.db true CRS-2674: Start of 'ora.singledb.db' on 'racnode02' failed
[main] [ 2010-09-10 14:05:09.276 EST ] [CRSNativeResult.addLine:106]  callback:
ora.oemrolt2.db true CRS-2632: There are no more servers to try to place resource
'ora.singledb.db' on that

would satisfy its placement policy
[main] [ 2010-09-10 14:05:09.278 EST ] [CRSNativeResult.addComp:162]  add comp: name
ora.singledb.db, rc 223, msg CRS-0223: Resource 'ora.singledb.db' has placement error.
[main] [ 2010-09-10 14:05:09.279 EST ] [CRSNative.internalStartResource:352]  Failed to start
resource: Name: ora.singledb.db, node: null, filter: null, msg CRS-2674: Start of
'ora.singledb.db'

on 'racnode02' failed
CRS-2632: There are no more servers to try to place resource 'ora.singledb.db' on that would
satisfy its placement policy
PRCR-1079 : Failed to start resource ora.singledb.db
CRS-2674: Start of 'ora.singledb.db' on 'racnode02' failed
CRS-2632: There are no more servers to try to place resource 'ora.singledb.db' on that would
satisfy its placement policy
```

The issue is resolved after re-registering the database SINGLEDB in the OCR using the SRVCTL utility.

In a Nutshell

This chapter provides a solid foundation for troubleshooting Oracle Grid Infrastructure—from troubleshooting a failed install to troubleshooting node evictions. Like Oracle RDBMS, Oracle Grid Infrastructure comes with a detailed diagnostic framework that helps you to quickly identify the root cause of any failures. Additional logging can be enabled whenever required, and this chapter covered the methods to enable further diagnostic logging.

Oracle Grid Infrastructure evicts the node in question when there is a communication failure either between the nodes or I/O path or between the nodes to the voting files. A node eviction or reboot is a mandatory evil to protect data integrity because whenever there is a question between database availability and avoiding database corruption, the vote goes to avoiding database corruption, which in turn triggers the node eviction.

In this chapter, you have seen the basic and advanced methods of collecting diagnostic information when a hang situation occurs. You also studied the steps in node reconfiguration and IMR internals. Most of the complex problems may require assistance from Oracle Support, and this chapter will help you when dealing with Oracle Support personnel.

PART
V

Deploying Oracle RAC

CHAPTER
15

Extending Oracle RAC for Maximum Availability

s Real Application Clusters is becoming an increasingly common solution for scalability across enterprises, it is time to think beyond the obvious. Oracle RAC is designed primarily as a scalability and availability solution that resides in a single datacenter. However, it is possible, under certain circumstances, to build and deploy an Oracle RAC system in which the nodes in the cluster are locationally isolated by great distances. Having nodes in geographically separate locations provides continuous data availability and limited disaster recovery in case of site failures.

The choice of extending Oracle RAC depends on the failure it is designed to address. To protect against multiple points of failure, a cluster must be geographically dispersed: nodes can be put in different rooms, on different floors of a building, or even in separate buildings or separate cities. Your decision as to the distance between the nodes rests on the types of disaster from which you need protection and the technology used to replicate data between the storage systems.

Modern datacenter clusters are built around high-performance storage area networks (SANs) that provide secure, reliable, and scalable data storage facilities. An effective business continuance and disaster recovery plan mandates the deployment of multiple datacenters located at optimal distances to protect against regional power failures or disasters, yet close enough for synchronous data replication without affecting the application performance. Achieving this balance for successful business continuance poses a significant challenge.

The time in which a business needs to recover during a disaster determines the type of data replication that is required. Synchronous data replication provides the least amount of downtime but requires the datacenters to be close enough so that the application performance is not affected by the latencies introduced for every I/O operation. Asynchronous or semi-synchronous replication allows for greater distance, but the datacenters are in lock step with each other, with the secondary datacenter lagging behind the primary by a fixed amount of time. This, in turn, implies that a loss of data occurs for that period of time. An optimal solution is to increase the distance between the datacenters without introducing additional latency for I/O operations.

For example, if a business has a corporate campus, the individual Oracle RAC nodes could be placed in separate buildings. This configuration provides a degree of disaster tolerance in addition to the normal Oracle RAC high availability, because a fire in one building would not bring the database down. Extended Oracle RAC, if properly set up, provides continuous data availability even during regional disasters. Figure 15-1 shows the basic architecture of an extended Oracle RAC configuration. The components used in Extended Clusters are discussed later in the chapter.

Implementing Oracle RAC on an extended cluster provides double advantages. Being able to distribute any and all work across all nodes, including running as a single workload across the whole cluster, allows for the greatest flexibility in usage of resources. Should one site fail—for example, because of a fire at a site—all work can be routed to the remaining site, which can rapidly (in less than a minute) take over the processing.

However, various other Oracle data replication technologies (such as Oracle Data Guard, Oracle Streams, and Oracle Golden Gate) work in tandem with Oracle RAC to build a *maximum availability architecture*. They require some potential changes at the application level and involve additional layers of software components to work synchronously. Moreover, they work on a primary/secondary (or primary/standby) method, which involves complex failover and failback procedures.

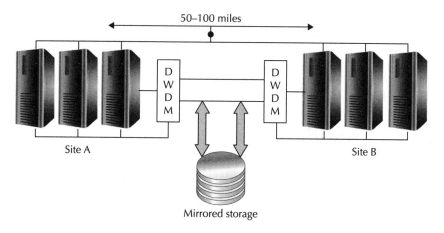

50–100 miles

Site A

Site B

Mirrored storage

FIGURE 15-1   *Extended Oracle RAC architecture*

Extending Oracle RAC to maximum availability works transparently with the existing application because networking complexities are hidden in the Oracle RAC layers and clients continue to work with available services defined in the Oracle RAC as if they are working in the regular datacenter instances.

Extended Benefits

Other than providing the usual maximum availability during the most common failures, an extended Oracle RAC configuration allows these two important benefits:

- Full utilization of resources
- Extreme rapid recovery

Full Utilization of Resources

In the extended Oracle RAC configuration, all the members of the cluster are available for processing all the time—unlike in usual primary/standby configurations, where only one half of resources is used and the other half is kept idle or near idle, expecting a disaster at the primary. This provides a tremendous advantage for customers because the resources are fully utilized, and it allows greater flexibility of scheduling the resources across the cluster nodes.

Extreme Rapid Recovery

The key advantage of extended Oracle RAC over any other failover technologies is the ability to provide extremely rapid recovery. The MTTR (Mean Time To Recover; in simple terms, the recovery time during failures) for most commonly available failover technologies is between just a few minutes to hours. However, in extended Oracle RAC, should there be any disaster in one datacenter, the existing and incoming workload can be routed to the other node in a rapid manner—in most cases, within seconds.

If the application layer is aware of Oracle RAC in terms of multiple addresses or is configured for Transparent Application Failovers (TAFs), the failover is totally transparent to the end users. No other high-availability or disaster recovery technologies currently on the market provide this amount of flexibility.

Design Considerations

Before going to the design and implementation of extended clusters, let's take a look at the key points to consider when designing a solution that involves "geo-clusters." Network infrastructure plays a major role in extending Oracle RAC, because performance is greatly impacted by roundtrip latency. An optimal solution is to increase the distance between the datacenters without introducing additional latency for I/O operations.

Speed of Light

In a vacuum, light travels at 186,282 miles per second. To make the math simpler, we can round that off to 200,000 miles per second, or 200 miles per millisecond. In any computer communications, we require confirmation for any message, so we must use roundtrip distances for our calculations. Light can travel up to 100 miles away and back in 1 millisecond (ms), but the actual transit time is longer. This is in part because the speed of light is slowed by about 30 percent through an optical fiber and because straight lines rarely occur in global communications situations, but also because delays are introduced when the signal passes through an electronic switch or signal regenerator.

In considering all the factors, such as the inevitable switch delays, the conservative rule of thumb is that it takes 1 millisecond for every 50 miles of distance roundtrip. Therefore, 500 miles adds 10 milliseconds to the latency of a disk access. Given the normal disk access latency of 8 to 10 milliseconds, this distance merely doubles the total latency; however, the shadowing software layer can cope with that. But if the latency is more than double, the software might think the disk at the other end has gone offline and will incorrectly break the shadow set. Therefore, the speed of light becomes the limiting factor due to the latency caused by the distance between the datacenters, even with the use of dark fiber.

Network Connectivity

Network interconnect has a great impact on performance in a normal Oracle RAC environment. It has even greater impact in an extended Oracle RAC environment. Planned redundancy should be introduced at every component level to avoid failures and interconnect. In addition, SAN and IP networking need to be kept on separate dedicated channels.

A scalable and reliable lightweight and protocol-independent network is required for extended Oracle RAC. Traditional networks are limited to about 6 miles before repeaters are needed. Repeaters and any other intermediate switches introduce inevitable delays via latency between the switches. Dark fiber networks allow the communication to occur without these repeaters across a much greater distance. Dark fiber networks with dense wavelength-division multiplexing (an optical technology used to increase bandwidth over existing fiber-optic backbones) provide low-latency/high-bandwidth communication over longer distances.

Dense Wavelength Division Multiplexing

In optical communications, wavelength-division multiplexing (WDM) technology multiplexes multiple optical carrier signals on a single optical fiber by using different wavelengths of laser light to carry different signals. This allows for a multiplication in capacity and makes it possible to perform bidirectional communications over one strand of fiber.

WDM technology is further divided into two market segments—dense and coarse WDM. Systems with more than eight active wavelengths per fiber are generally considered dense WDM (DWDM) systems, whereas those with fewer than eight active wavelengths are classed as coarse WDM (CWDM).

CWDM and DWDM technologies are based on the same concept of using multiple wavelengths of light on a single fiber, but the two technologies differ in the spacing of the wavelengths, the number of channels, and the ability to amplify signals in the optical space.

CWDM is also used in cable television networks, where different wavelengths are used for the downstream and upstream signals. DWDM works by combining and transmitting multiple signals simultaneously at different wavelengths on the same fiber. In effect, one fiber is transformed into multiple virtual fibers that provide the extended bandwidth. With this over-bandwidth extension, single fibers have been able to transmit data at speeds up to 400 Gbps (gigabits per second).

A key advantage to DWDM is that it is protocol and bit-rate independent. DWDM-based networks can transmit data in IP, ATM, SONET/SDH, and Ethernet and can handle bit rates between 100 Mbps (megabits per second) and 2.5 Gbps. Therefore, DWDM-based networks can carry different types of traffic at different speeds over an optical channel.

Cache Fusion Performance

As we have seen, the secret recipe behind the extreme performance of Oracle Real Application Clusters is Cache Fusion. The Cache Fusion is built under the assumption that the nodes are connected through the high-speed local network. With extended Oracle RAC separating the nodes by miles, a great penalty was introduced to Cache Fusion performance. The local interconnect latencies are always in the order of 1–2 ms, and any additional latency beyond these provides a great threat to the application scalability.

Oracle Corporation, along with various hardware partners, tested the extended Oracle RAC setup with different configurations and observed the preceding behaviors and illustrated them in the following figure. Figure 15-2 shows the effects of distance on I/O latency for reading from a physical disk.

Data Storage

The next important factor in designing an extended Oracle RAC solution is the storage for the data files across the clusters. The storage should be concurrently available with both the instances, yet at the same time should be continuously synchronized in real time. *Synchronous replication* means that I/O is not complete until both sides acknowledge its completion.

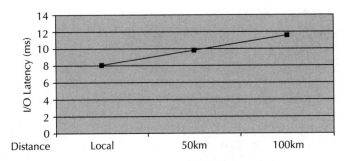

FIGURE 15-2 *Distance effect on I/O latency*

Although it is possible to implement Oracle RAC on extended distance clusters with storage at only one site, if the site with the storage should fail, the storage is no longer available to any surviving nodes and the whole cluster becomes unavailable. This defeats the purpose of having had Oracle RAC nodes at different locations. Hence, we mirror the storage in both the sites, and nodes use the storage at their respective sites transparently. In addition, to maintain consistency of data, every write to the primary storage is written over to the secondary storage in the same sequence before the application writes are considered successful. This method helps ensure that data stored at both sites is always consistent; the only data that could be lost in the event of a failure is the data that was not committed or was being transmitted at the time of the failure.

Figure 15-3 shows the components involved in the physical implementation of the extended Oracle RAC cluster.

Common Techniques for Data Mirroring

A couple of mirroring techniques are most commonly used in the industry. However, the choice of storage is totally dependent on the hardware—some hardware configurations support array-based mirroring and a few support host-based mirroring.

Array-Based Mirroring

In array-based mirroring, all the writes are forwarded to one site and then mirrored to the other node using the disk technologies. Array-based mirroring means having a primary/secondary site setup. Only one set of disks is always used, and all the reads and writes are serviced by that storage. If the node or site fails, all the instances will crash and need to be restarted after the secondary site is brought to life.

Array-based mirroring is quite simple to implement, because the mirroring is done by the storage system and is transparent to the database applications. If the primary site fails, all access to the primary disks is lost. An outage may be incurred before the system can switch to the secondary site. Figure 15-4 explains the architecture of array-based mirroring.

Host-Based Mirroring

Host-based mirroring, as the name suggests, mirrors at the host level. It requires closely integrated clusterware and Logical Volume Manager (LVM). The underlying Cluster Logical

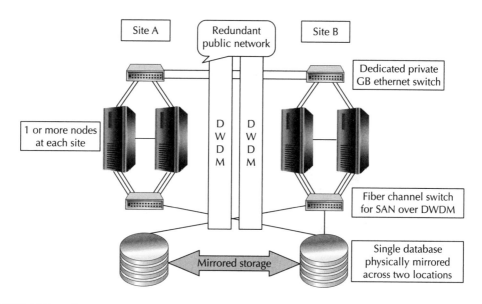

FIGURE 15-3 *Extended Oracle RAC component architecture*

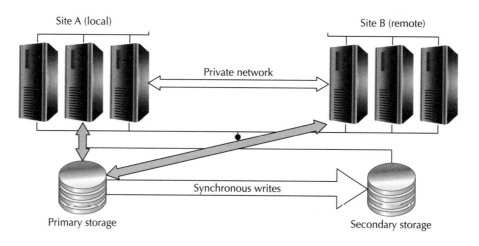

FIGURE 15-4 *Array-based mirroring*

Volume Manager (CLVM) mirrors the writes to both nodes synchronously. But from the database or operating system point of view, only one set of disks exists. The disk mirroring is done transparently to the database.

Oracle Automatic Storage Management (ASM) 11*g* can be used to mirror the storage with its ability to mirror the data using fail groups. A disk group can be double- or triple-mirrored using the fail groups. However, the voting disk and Oracle Cluster Registry (OCR) cannot be mirrored using Oracle Clusterware.

Figure 15-5 explains the architecture of host-based mirroring.

Table 15-1 summarizes the pros and cons of array-based mirroring and host-based mirroring.

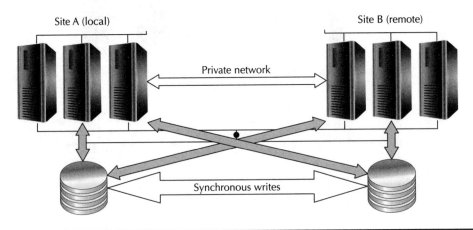

FIGURE 15-5 *Host-based mirroring*

Description	Array-Based	Host-Based
Write propagation	Disk writes are always sent to one site and changes are synchronously propagated to another node using disk-mirroring techniques.	Writes are always sent to both nodes. Both nodes service user requests all the time.
Primary/ secondary setup	Requires primary/secondary site setup. If the primary site fails, all access to primary disks is lost. An outage may be incurred before one can switch to secondary.	No primary/secondary setup is required, because writes are propagated in both sides. Similarly, reads also can be serviced from both nodes.
Storage appearance to the nodes	Storage system appears as two sets, and at any point in time only one set of storage is being used.	Storage is transparent to the application. The OS or the Storage Software (ASM) hides the underlying storage structure, and the application does not know the dual nature of the storage.
Failover during failures	Delay in recovery. The secondary site should be manually switched to active status during failures. This includes downtime.	Instant failure to surviving arrays. The surviving instance continues to run without downtime.

TABLE 15-1 *Array-Based Mirroring vs. Host-Based Mirroring*

Description	Array-Based	Host-Based
Advantage	Data mirroring is done at the storage (disk array) level. The host CPU is not used for data mirroring.	Both nodes can be used concurrently all the time.
Disadvantage	Only one set of mirroring is used at a time. Failover is not instant.	The nodes do mirroring, and overhead is passed to the CPU.
Uniform performance	A node close to the primary storage always performs better than the secondary one.	Because the I/O requests are serviced from all the nodes, close to uniform performance is expected in all the nodes. Also, when ASM with the "preferred read" option is used, the reads are serviced by the physically closest node.
Single-vendor storage requirement	Both the sites should have the same storage (physical, architectural, and logical) because proprietary block mirroring techniques are implemented at the storage layer.	Storage can be from different vendors/ different types because the mirroring is handled by the application.
Example	EMC (SDRF) Symmetric Remote Data Facility	Oracle ASM, HP OpenView storage mirroring, IBM HACMP

TABLE 15-1 *Array-Based Mirroring vs. Host-Based Mirroring* (continued)

ASM Preferred Read

With the growing use of Extended Oracle RAC under Oracle Automatic Storage Management (ASM), the new features introduced with 11*g* greatly improve the performance of read operations. The newly introduced "ASM preferred read" allows you to choose the extents physically closest to the node, even if that extent is a secondary extent for reads.

You can configure ASM to read from a secondary extent if that extent is closer to the node instead of ASM reading from the primary copy, which might be farther from the node. Using preferred read failure groups is most beneficial in an extended cluster.

The initialization parameter ASM_PREFERRED_READ_FAILURE_GROUPS can be used to specify a list of failure group names as preferred read disks. It is recommended that you configure at least one mirrored extent copy from a disk that is local to a node in an extended cluster. However, a failure group that is preferred for one instance might be remote to another instance.

Challenges in Extended Clusters

A few challenges are normally seen in extended clusters that are not expected in normal clusters. The first important thing is the cost and complexity of the network connectivity between the nodes. The private interconnect plays a more important role in the extended clusters than in normal clusters because the distance between the nodes adds an important and expensive component to the overall performance—network latency. Network latency should be taken into consideration because every message and every block transfer includes this additional delta time.

The second important thing is the mirroring technique used for the storage replication. The choice of mirroring technique makes a difference, because from the application layer, the Oracle kernel should see the storage as a single storage and the abstraction should be provided from the lower layers. The choice of mirroring also plays an important role in manual restart during node failures.

The third important thing to be considered during the design is the quorum. A third site for the quorum device is recommended to maximize availability in an extended cluster environment. The third site acts as arbitrator as to which site will survive during communication failures. This is worthwhile only when third-party clusterware is used. Oracle's clusterware uses the quorum device during regular operations (versus only during a cluster reconfig event) and therefore no advantage is gained by having it at a third location.

Normally, with the support of the mirrored voting disk, this problem can be overcome in the regular clusters. However, for the stretch clusters, another level of redundancy can be set up using a third site as a quorum site. This will enable the cluster to be functional if a disturbance occurs between the communications channels from the nodes. The choice of quorum plays an important role in tie-breaking during split-brain situations. The third site can be a simple workstation to act as an arbitrator in case of failures, as shown in Figure 15-6.

Extended Oracle RAC Limitations

Oracle RAC on extended clusters is a very specific solution for customers who want to build business applications on extended clusters. However, it does not work well for long distances. Extended clusters have not been tested for distances greater than 100 miles. If the distance between the nodes is greater than 100 miles, the system should be carefully tested and prototyped before being implemented.

Extended clusters *require* a dedicated point-to-point high-speed network. They cannot use the public network, and setting up a DWDM or dark fiber may cost hundreds of thousands of dollars. Extended Oracle RAC clusters are not suitable for unstable networks. A slight interruption in network service will cause node eviction and failures.

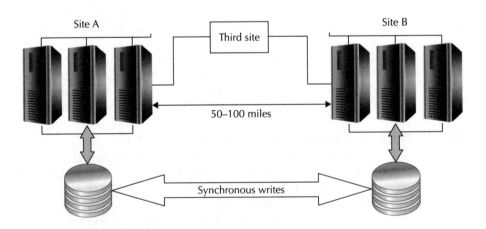

FIGURE 15-6 *Third site as quorum in a three-node structure*

Extended Oracle RAC vs. Oracle Data Guard

Extended Oracle RAC is a high availability solution that can be used as a limited disaster recovery solution. It does not replace the functionalities of Oracle Data Guard, which is a true disaster recovery solution. If you are looking for a true disaster recovery solution, Oracle Data Guard can be considered in conjunction with extended Oracle RAC. Oracle Data Guard can be used to overcome the intrinsic limitations imposed by the extended Oracle RAC. It also offers the following advantages over extended Oracle RAC:

- **Network efficiency**   Oracle Data Guard does not require expensive DWDM or dark fiber technologies for mirroring. It uses normal TCP/IP for communication and does not require additional protocol converters. Oracle Data Guard transmits only redo data or incremental changes. It does not ship block images unless traditional hot backups are used.

- **No distance limitation**   Fiber-based mirroring solutions have an intrinsic distance limitation and they cannot be deployed over thousands of miles. They also require additional protocol converters that indirectly add to the cost, complexity, and latency.

- **Data protection**   Oracle Data Guard protects from logical corruptions as the database is recovered from the primary. It validates the redo records from the archive logs of the primary database before applying to the secondary database. Both SQL apply and redo apply do not simply mirror the block images like storage mirroring, thus providing a better protection against physical and logical corruptions.

- **Better flexibility and functionality**   Oracle Data Guard uses commodity hardware and storage. It does not restrict you to specific storage vendors using proprietary mirroring technology. Remote mirroring solutions typically need identically configured storage from the same vendor. You cannot have a scaled-down version of the disaster recovery site. Oracle Data Guard can also be deployed in asynchronous mode. It provides a variety of protection methods and a graceful handling of network connectivity issues.

Deploying Oracle RAC on extended clusters requires careful architectural planning and deployment practices. Correctly implemented extended Oracle RAC clusters can also be used as a limited disaster recovery solution. Oracle Data Guard and Oracle RAC are designed for different kinds of failure scenarios. They do not compete with each other but rather complement each other when used correctly.

In a Nutshell

Extended Oracle RAC configurations are very special within the clustering technologies, with the member nodes spread across geographic locations. The "speed of light" factor plays the most important role in the latency between member nodes and puts a practical limitation on the distance between the nodes. Approximately 1 millisecond of latency is introduced for every 50 miles, which limits the extended clusters to being less than a few hundred miles apart.

Mirroring the storage for extended Oracle RAC can be done using two methods: host mirroring and storage mirroring. Oracle ASM uses the host-mirroring approach, and storage vendors use storage-mirroring techniques. The newly introduced ASM preferred read feature takes advantage of local storage for reading and greatly increases the performance for reads.

In summary, Oracle RAC on extended distance clusters is an attractive alternative architecture that allows scalability, rapid availability, and even some limited disaster recovery protection with all nodes fully active. This architecture can provide great value when used properly, but it is critical that its limitations are well understood.

CHAPTER
16

Developing Applications
for Oracle RAC

racle Real Application Clusters can be used to scale most database applications—from custom to commercial off-the-shelf (COTS). An application that runs on a single-instance environment can be directly ported to the Oracle RAC platform without needing any major architecture or code changes when it is designed optimally, and almost all packaged applications can be ported to Oracle RAC when scalability or availability of the application is in question.

In simplest terms, an application vendor could install Oracle RAC on a cluster, install the application on top of it, and run the application without any loss in business functionality due to changes in database status (single instance to multiple instances). That means that your order-entry form or balance sheet report will not go missing from the application menu just because your database has been clustered.

Although any application developed on a single-instance database can run against an Oracle RAC database without modification, the performance of some apps may be suboptimal in Oracle RAC as compared to a single instance. That might be true for well-designed and well-performing applications (on a single instance) because even though Oracle RAC is scalable, that's not necessarily the case for every application. Scalability of the underlying application is critically important for scaling applications running on Oracle RAC.

With this background, many technologists, architects, and managers *assumed* that Oracle RAC could solve all their scalability and performance problems. Suddenly, Oracle RAC was the much-anticipated panacea for a badly performing application on a single node. This created a large potential market for Oracle RAC, from small shops to large enterprises. What it also created, eventually, was much chagrin among users because Oracle RAC did not perform as it was "supposed" to. Like many new software products, Oracle RAC encountered many challenges in the beginning, but its technical prowess, robust features, and performance have always been its greatest strengths.

Oracle RAC is part of a high availability option that customers can exercise when maximum availability is a primary criterion. Using Oracle RAC for the sole purpose of improving system scalability and performance may or may not pay off because such improvements depend on many factors. Key among these factors are application design and scalability.

NOTE
It is worth mentioning, at this point, the highly commendable work of many stalwarts in the field of application performance and scalability through education of the masses about the challenges, pitfalls, and techniques in achieving real-world scalability. Their books, whitepapers, articles, and web links are widely known in the Oracle world, and a good scan of their repertoire is more than enough for Oracle users to help them through the maze of scalability and performance issues.

A well-designed and tuned database that services an equally well-designed application could scale admirably on Oracle RAC with multiple nodes, as compared to a single symmetric multiprocessing (SMP) box. This scalability in terms of the number of concurrent users, workload achieved, and performance has been proven many times by hardware and application vendors on various platforms and different types of applications. Reliable figures and facts are available from individual companies and analysts to prove the scalability of Oracle RAC on multiple nodes. (For more information on the latest results, visit www.tpc.org. Oracle regularly publishes results of large TPC benchmarks on Oracle E-Business Suite and other well-known applications using Oracle RAC.)

Application performance in Oracle RAC depends on how well the application performs on a single instance. Even though no changes are required to run an application in Oracle RAC, specific issues must be considered when an application moves to Oracle RAC, because these issues could hinder the performance of the application or the overall system. More insight on these best practices is provided throughout this chapter.

Comparison of application and database performance and scalability on single-node SMP boxes versus scalability in clustered systems is tricky and sometimes inconclusive due to the complex nature of the various software layers involved and database/application characteristics. For example, a batch job to reconcile all accounts in a banking application may perform 25 transactions per second and consume 4,500 seconds to complete. Of the total 4,500 seconds, 4,000 seconds is CPU time on an eight-CPU box, at 90-percent utilization (7.2 CPUs fully utilized). For this example, consider the 500 seconds' worth of latency-related issues such as I/O waits, locking, and so on. Also assume that no other job or process is running when this batch is executed.

If the job needs to be completed in half the time—2,250 seconds—then a generic solution would be to double the CPU capacity on the same box. Theoretically, a 16-CPU box should complete the same job in 2,250 seconds at 25 transactions per second and 90-percent utilization (14.5 CPUs fully utilized). This is assuming that nothing much can be done about reducing the wait time of 500 seconds and that the application is well tuned.

Without going deeper into any scalability formulas, queuing models, and theorems (which are critical, vital, and indispensable tools for architects, designers, and developers), and all the other technical complexities that accompany scalability challenges, can we provide a confident answer whether a single-instance database with higher CPU capacity would scale? Is it possible to achieve the same scalability (completing the job in 2,250 seconds) if we deploy a two-node Oracle RAC with eight CPUs each?

A straightforward and simple answer would be difficult to provide without knowing factors such as these:

- How much time are we spending waiting on a single instance for I/O, locks, and so on? Can that be reduced?

- Can the application work exactly the same way, with the same throughput of 25 transactions per second, without modifications in Oracle RAC?

- Can the application perform the same without running into locking/concurrency issues when deployed on Oracle RAC?

- What would be the application throughput with lock mastering overhead when Oracle RAC is used?

- Do we have enough parallel streams/processes within the application logic to take advantage of extra CPU resources?

- What about the cost factor? Which model is cheaper?

This is just the beginning of a long discussion that will take the consideration of many more factors before a useful answer results. All that could prove useless, however, if the application testing results on both single-node and Oracle RAC are not considered.

Nevertheless, we have seen that with a given set of characteristics and metrics, significant trends can be observed and recorded in single-node as well as Oracle RAC systems to provide effective and meaningful data for analysts and designers. This data can be used in conjunction with further testing results to make decisions or take positive actions. It would be rather naive to act solely upon individual data (such as just single-node SMP results) to make a decision on the best model for scaling and achieving the required performance.

This chapter is by no means a complete lesson on application scalability and performance, how to achieve it, and how not to. The aim is to provide some best-practice solutions and suggestions for an application running on an Oracle RAC database that can fit a wide variety of applications, from pure online transaction processing (OLTP) environments to a mix of data warehousing and online systems. Applications such as traditional enterprise resource planning, banking/insurance, general finance, customer relations, telecom billing, manufacturing, web applications, Internet stores, and data warehouses can apply these best practices according to their environments. As always, testing is mandatory because a generic recommendation that suits all requirements doesn't exist. The so-called "one size fits all" formula is a myth and fails more often than not.

These best practices and guidelines have been drawn from experience at various sites on different platforms and breeds of applications, from Oracle's own experiences and knowledge base, from debates and discussions with users, and from technologists and Oracle RAC enthusiasts across the globe. The guidelines are intended to reduce overall contention for resources such as data/index blocks, latches and locks, memory, and CPU cycles in an Oracle RAC environment.

Let's now examine some of the factors that affect application performance and scalability on an Oracle RAC database. No particular order of priority has been established, but they all deserve equal attention and probably more in certain situations, depending on the complexity and urgency of the problems/challenges being faced.

Even though this chapter is not an exhaustive list of all the factors that need careful consideration and analysis, it includes some of the most contentious issues that affect Oracle RAC databases of all versions and sizes.

Application Partitioning

To start, consider reading *Oracle 8i Parallel Server Administration, Deployment and Performance for Release 2 (8.1.6) (Part No.A76970-01)*, available online on the Oracle Technology Network site at http://download.oracle.com/docs/cd/A87860_01/doc/index.htm.

Although it is more than a decade old, this manual is an excellent primer about the basic problems applications could face in a parallel-server environment and the types of partitioning schemes that can be adopted to overcome them. Subsequent releases of Oracle documentation have eliminated much of this foundational material, which was deemed unnecessary from Oracle 9i RAC onward. Yet a review of Chapters 5 and 6 in particular would do the reader a lot of good, especially if you are new to Oracle RAC and its traditional problem areas.

In Oracle Parallel Server (OPS), application partitioning was necessary to scale applications. This scheme had to be adopted to avoid block pings across all participating instances in the parallel database. One of the stumbling blocks in OPS 8i in certain implementations was the disk pinging effect and its need for a *forced block write* of a dirty block to the disk by a holding instance when another instance requested the same block for modification. Remember that Cache Fusion I minimized the need to write blocks to disk even for a consistent read (CR) block. But when multiple instances required the same block for modification, application scalability was limited because increased requests for the same block caused an increase in disk writes. This also increased global locking activity—interconnect traffic as well as heavy CPU usage. A lot of special care and attention was needed to tune such parameters as GC_FILES_TO_LOCK, which was almost the only way to control locking at the block level.

Contention occurs when the same application with the same transaction pattern is run on multiple nodes at the same time. Hence, the application needs the same set of blocks for Data Manipulation Language (DML) operations as they touch or operate on the same set of tables. This is called *table overlap* and occurs when the same table or set of tables are accessed by two or more application components concurrently. For example, a transaction table could be simultaneously queried and updated by both Receivables and Payments modules. This creates more chances of contention for a block or set of blocks, depending on the type of transaction.

A high INSERT rate into the same table from different nodes has the potential to cause contention for the block being affected and also for the bitmapped blocks (BMBs; in the ASSM tablespace). If indexes are present for that table, this may also cause contention for the index branch/leaf blocks. The use of database sequences for the generation of key values increases the chances of buffer contention.

If the database used freelist-managed segments, the master freelist in the segment header block would come under tremendous pressure. Tuning experience has shown that increasing FREELIST GROUPS and FREELISTS will help alleviate these issues, which in most cases requires you to re-create the objects, especially with groups. Large UPDATE requests on the same table, when submitted from two or more instances, can cause the same type of effect, although they may not necessarily fight for segment headers. However, data block contention is quite possible. There may also be some enqueue problems that we won't discuss here.

Cache Fusion II minimized some of the forced disk write effect by directly transmitting a copy of the current block across the high-speed interconnect to the requesting instance in some circumstances. However, a copy of the buffer has to be shipped to the requesting instance through the interconnect constantly between the instances.

Best Practice: Application Partitioning Schemes

To reduce these effects, application-partitioning schemes were introduced in OPS 8*i* and continued to be used until Oracle 11g. These schemes are definitely not obsolete in Oracle 11g and can still provide increased performance and scalability. However, application partitioning is not a requirement for Oracle RAC database installations, although many sites are known to use it effectively.

Application partitioning refers to the following:

- Identification of the main functional business components of the application and segregation

- Scheduling an application or a component of the application to run on a specific node or nodes only, thereby restricting access to that application through a particular node (or nodes)

For example, a production manufacturing application could run Inventory on node 1, BOM on node 2, Payments on node 3, and Receivables on node 4. It is rather difficult to avoid table overlaps in most of these types of applications, in which multiple modules share the same set of tables. By running an application module on a single node or a maximum of two, you can minimize block pinging effects. This is a partial solution when tables cannot be split (so that each application module uses its own tables and indexes) and when data partitioning is not possible. In the next section, you'll see how data partitioning can be used to overcome this problem.

Application partitioning can reduce the chances of block pinging. The fewer the number of common tables across modules, the better the application performance. Oracle 11*g* RAC can also leverage this basic type of partitioning—in OLTP as well as batch/decision support system (DSS) types of environments.

Read-Mostly Locking

Oracle 11*g* also introduces a new locking mechanism called *read-mostly locking*. This is implemented in the form of a new locking element called *anti-lock*. The anti-lock element controls the behavior of the "read mostly" locking scheme by granting Shared read (S affinity lock) globally to all the nodes. With a global S access to an object, all nodes are pre-granted read access to all the blocks for the object, which eliminates the locking overhead associated with read access. Any read access on the objects covered by the read-mostly locking scheme can bypass the standard Cache Fusion protocol for block transfers between instances. However, the write access on the objects strictly follows the regular Cache Fusion mechanism and might come with higher cost than reads.

This new locking protocol is further optimized for application-partitioning schemes, especially in a carefully partitioned application with very little read-write contention between objects, and if most of the access is for SELECTs.

Data Partitioning

Data segment partitioning has been available in Oracle since version 8. The benefits of data partitioning are well known to users, and many large databases have reaped rich rewards by implementing the many schemes introduced in each successive release of the Oracle server. (Note that partitioning requires Oracle Enterprise Edition, which is an extra cost option.)

Partitioning data as well as indexes needs liberal consideration and a well-planned approach in Oracle RAC environments. Partitioning can help minimize a lot of contention for data and index blocks, provided the right partitioning strategy is chosen. Data partitions can have a much bigger impact on performance in Oracle RAC since starting from 10*g* lock mastering (and dynamic remastering) is handled at the segment level.

Also when Automatic Segment Space Management (ASSM) is used, the bitmap blocks manage the free space allocation (known as the L2 bitmaps) and the bitmap blocks have instance affinity. Instance affinity in L2 bitmaps greatly helps the local node to grow (or access) the local L1 bitmap blocks without going to global cache during segment space allocation. Each segment has its own L1 and L2 bitmap blocks, and L3 bitmaps (often) are stored in segment header blocks.

Interval Partitioning

Oracle 11*g* introduces a new partitioning strategy called *interval partitioning*. Interval partitioning overcomes the previous limitations built into range partitioning, where a specific range value or limit is specified by the DBA creating the partitions for the table. Technically this is an extension to the existing range partitioning, where Oracle creates a partition automatically when the inserted value does not meet the insertion criteria for all other existing partition ranges within the table.

Range partitioning requires at least one range partition that is specified during table creation. Once the range partitioning key is given for the value of the range partition, this transition point is used as the baseline to create interval partitions compared to this point.

The type of environment/application is a crucial factor in choosing the type of partitions to create. This means that the application could be a straightforward OLTP system or a mix of OLTP and batch processing. Some environments are pure batch or DSS in nature, sometimes referred to as *data warehouses*. Each of these environments has a predominant "type" or "nature" of transaction. It could be INSERT intensive, UPDATE intensive, or SELECT intensive, or a mixture of these. It is common to see OLTP applications that do a lot of all three types of activities, including DELETEs. Some applications also have lots of DDL embedded in their systems. Transaction volume (rate of inserts, updates, and deletes) is another critical factor that needs to be considered while you're choosing the correct partitioning strategy.

Most of the discussion in data partitioning and buffer-busy problems is restricted to large INSERT-related issues because they are the most common.

Best Practice: Guidance Systems

The data is guided or directed into each partition based on the data set that will be used for processing on that node/instance. This may also be broadly referred to as *workload characterization* and can be used in conjunction with application partitioning.

For example, the data is inserted using a guidance system to ensure that the data is processed from a particular node only. Assume a four-node Oracle RAC database with each node processing data for one region only. When data arrives for insert, the guidance system routes the data such that node 1 inserts Western region data only, node 2 inserts Eastern region data, and so on.

The guidance system can be application logic or a combination of software (for example, Data Dependent Routing in Tuxedo) and intelligent devices with algorithms built in. Data is usually routed through these systems. Telecom applications make extensive use of guidance systems, although the usage is far more complicated and extensive.

In certain cases, the data arriving (from an external system, flat files, and so on) could be presorted and guided to an instance such that no intelligence or guidance is required at the application end during the insert into a node. Once the data is in, the application on node 1 will process data from partition 1 to partition 25. Node 2 (running the same or another module) will process data from partition 26 to 50, and so on. User data is not shared between the nodes during processing, except in certain unavoidable circumstances. This creates an affinity between nodes and data/index blocks. Therefore, the application is more likely to find a block or set of blocks in its local cache, thereby effectively reducing cross-instance communication and block transfers.

In typical OLTP environments, the number of blocks that are generally visited per query or DML operation is small. This is because data selection is driven mostly by primary or unique key lookups. Large-range scans are less likely, unless the application requires them, is not well designed, or suffers from various types of "over-indexing" and architectural issues.

In contrast, batch operations that select lots of data (data mining, reporting, DML) need hundreds of thousands of blocks to be visited to satisfy the query. Without partitioning and proper guidance, intense competition for data/index blocks among instances will cause block contention, which is visible as one or a combination of the following wait events:

```
'buffer busy waits',
'read by other session',
'global cache cr request',
'gc cr buffer busy',
'gc current block busy'
```

Application changes may be required to guide this data using a key value such as instance ID or the equivalent. Data structure changes are also required because a column will be added to the table(s). This column identifies the instance from which this row was inserted (or in some cases last updated). For example, if the table is to be range partitioned on order_date, the partition key can be (order_date, instance_id). Some designers like to use a different column name that identifies each guided row and binds it to a particular instance or table partition. As mentioned before, guidance into each instance/partition is done using some predetermined algorithm. This column will also form a part of the partition key (order_date, <column name>). Further, we could also have index partitions based on this column.

Using this key value, data is inserted or updated into the correct partition, which will later be processed by the application on a particular node only. This scheme can significantly reduce contention for data blocks, bitmap blocks, and index leaf blocks (when indexes are partitioned).

The following extract from Oracle documentation "Oracle 9i Real Application Clusters Deployment and Performance" (Release 2 [9.2], Part No. A96598-01) summarizes this strategy in a very lucid manner:

> Cache Fusion eliminates most of the costs associated with globally shared database partitions by efficiently synchronizing this data across the cluster. However, object partitioning, without changing your application, can sometimes improve performance for hot blocks in tables and indexes. This is done by re-creating objects as hash or composite partitioned objects.

> For example, consider a table that has a high insert rate which also uses a sequence number as the primary key of its index. All sessions on all nodes access the right-most index leaf block. Therefore, unavoidable index block splits can create a serialization point that results in a bottleneck. To resolve this, rebuild the table and its index, for example, as a 16-way hash partitioned object. This evenly distributes the load among 16 index leaf blocks.

Buffer Busy Waits/Block Contention

This particular subject has been covered extensively in almost every Oracle tuning book and in many articles and whitepapers since time immemorial. In Oracle 8i OPS days, reducing data block contention (mainly during inserts) was possible using FREELISTS and FREELIST GROUPS. If application designers, developers, and DBAs are able to work out the correct settings for these two parameters, it is still a valid and effective approach to reduce contention for data blocks significantly as well as segment header waits in Oracle RAC environments when concurrent inserts are used. Performance tests with large concurrent inserts have shown that using these parameters can provide the same or better benefits when compared to using ASSM tablespaces. Needless to say, end users would have to use locally managed tablespaces in Oracle 10g and above, along with accurately sized extents and other segment management clauses. Free space management is done using FREELISTS and FREELIST GROUPS in manual segment space management based tablespaces and using bitmap blocks in Automatic Segment Space Management (ASSM) tablespaces.

The segment header block can be a point of great contention between instances. Freelist groups alleviate the contention for the segment header block because they move the point of contention away from the segment header to dedicated blocks of master freelists. Each freelist group can be associated with an instance, provided the numbers of freelist groups is equal to or greater than the number of instances.

Hot Blocks and X$KSLHOT

Starting from Oracle 10g, you no longer have to write multiple and repeated queries on V$BH or X$BH or dump data/index blocks to find hot blocks that are generally chased by applications. A new view called X$KSLHOT has been added to simplify the identification of hot blocks. To use this feature, you need to set the little-known hidden parameter _db_block_hot_tracking to true.

This table has a sample of the RDBAs that are responsible for contention. The kslhot_id column is the RDBA, and the kslhot_ref column is a count of the relative number of times it was encountered. A higher kslhot_ref implies the corresponding kslhot_id is a bright candidate for a hot buffer.

Be warned, that the clustering_factor of indexes is influenced by using multiple freelists (not freelist groups) as data gets scattered among more blocks. This sometimes increases the I/O cost of the table access by index as the index keys are widely scattered among more blocks.

Oracle 9i introduced ASSM, which is an effective "auto" method of reducing block contention, because it randomizes inserts by trying to pick a different block for insertion for each process. There is no guarantee that each time it will behave in the same way, but the chances that the same block will be picked by two or more inserting processes are low in ASSM. Hence, this random factor tilts the balance in favor of ASSM, especially in Oracle RAC.

When the FREELIST parameter is used, Oracle maps a process to a freelist using the following formula:

```
mod(oracle process_id, no. of process freelists) + 1
```

In ASSM, it uses the process ID to guide itself to a space map block, and even choosing a block is based on the process ID. As we have seen earlier, one of the key benefits of using ASSM tablespaces is that Level 2 BMBs have an affinity to an instance. Hence, they are normally not sent across the interconnect. In addition, the blocks that they manage also have an affinity to the same instance as the Level 2 BMBs.

Using ASSM can also have an extreme effect on the clustering_factor of an index (although it is not a symptom that is repeated every time), because the data is distributed across many blocks. Application development teams should test their applications on ASSM with high inserts and analyze the trend because no silver-bullet solution exists for all situations. Also, using ASSM can cause performance problems during full table scans because the tables are generally larger than non-ASSM tables.

Index Partitioning

One of the most glaring mistakes at many sites is to partition the table and not partition related indexes. Index partitioning is equally or more important than table partitioning—index blocks have a tendency to get hotter than the table blocks because of high concurrency at the block level due to the smaller row length of index keys. The following techniques can be implemented to alleviate index block contention issues.

Buffer Busy Waits: Index Branch/Leaf Blocks Contention

In an application where the loading or batch processing of data is a dominant business function, there are more chances of performance issues affecting response times due to the overhead of index maintenance during large volume inserts. Depending on the access frequency and the number of processes concurrently inserting data, indexes can become hot spots and contention can be exacerbated by frequent leaf block splits, ordered and monotonically increasing key values in the index (usually generated using a sequence), and sometimes due to a low tree depth.

A leaf or branch block split can become an important serialization point if the particular leaf block or branch of the tree is concurrently accessed. The following wait events are typical indicators of this kind of block contention issue:

- `gc buffer busy`
- `gc current block busy`
- `gc current split`

In an Oracle RAC environment, the transaction splitting a leaf block and the transactions waiting for the split to complete are affected if the data required for the operation is not locally cached. Before and during a split operation, the transaction performing the split will have to execute a series of global locking operations before a pin is acquired on the target block. These operations are expensive, especially in Oracle RAC, where the latencies adversely affect application performance during large inserts. *Blocking asynchronous trap (BAST)* processing during a branch/leaf split has additional impact on the time taken to complete the split.

Note that periodic index rebuilding for so-called "performance improvement" in the Oracle RAC environment could be counterproductive. As a matter of fact, Oracle B-tree indexes are balanced by design, and under normal conditions, rebuilding the indexes at periodic intervals is not required. Rebuilding indexes makes the index blocks more compact and reduces the free space. In other words, we need to consider Oracle RAC implications not just for design or development issues, but for maintenance activities, too.

The challenge is to minimize the chances of multiple instances inserting (data and index) into the same block concurrently. This can be done by using hash or range partitions with appropriate changes in the application code or database structure. The partition scheme is dependent on the suitability to the application.

A right-growing index experiences increased contention for the leaf blocks mostly due to the fact that keys are generated in order of increasing sequence. Therefore, the leaf blocks tend to heat up quite often. This is known as *buffer busy wait*. Moreover, frequent splitting of indexes may introduce further serialization points.

Distributing the access to the leaves over multiple index partitions alleviates the hot spots. Apart from a significant reduction of contention, local cache affinity improves because leaf blocks are retained in a local cache longer and are more available for local users.

Best Practice: Index Partitioning

Partitioning of indexes provides huge improvements in OLTP as well as batch-type environments. The choice between local or global indexes is highly dependent on the application and how the data is queried, whether index lookups are unique key (or PK) based or index range scans. Partition maintenance and performance are also key points to consider while choosing an index partition type.

Global indexes are good for OLTP environments, where performance is generally high on the wish list, and for applications that like to perform unique key lookups. Oracle 10*g* R2 and onward support hash partitioning of global indexes, which provides more flexibility for handling partitioned indexes.

In Oracle 9*i*, the only way to partition an index by hash was to partition the corresponding table as well. In Oracle 10*g* and above, it is possible to partition only the index independent of the table, and it becomes simpler if contention is limited to index blocks.

It is worth mentioning at this point, however redundant it might be, that SQL statements must make use of the partition key in their WHERE clause for partition elimination/pruning to happen. Note that partition elimination works only for range or list partitions. Index range scans can be disastrously slow without restrictive predicates based on partitioned and indexed columns. These columns should be the partition key or part of it to leverage on partition pruning. The type of predicate (=, >, <) has the potential to make or break the query.

Reducing Leaf Block Contention with Reverse Key Index

Some applications benefit from reverse key indexes (high INSERT environments) in terms of performance, but they are notorious for generating high I/O. Because the actual (nonreversed) values of the index are not stored sequentially in the index, index range scans cannot be performed. Generally, fetch-by-key and full index scans can be performed on a reverse key index. If the reverse key index is built on a single column, an index range scan will not be used by the Cost Based Optimizer (CBO). If the reverse key index is built on multiple columns, it will be used by CBO for a range scan operation when the equality predicate is used on the leading columns of the index.

Note that the clustering_factor of a reverse key index will incline more toward the number of rows because the index points to table rows that are scattered over different or many blocks. This will influence the CBO toward choosing an execution plan without the reverse key index.

Sometimes, a combination of reverse key indexes and an adequately cached database sequence that generates the key values can provide immense relief for databases with acute index leaf block contention.

You can attain great benefits (that are offset at times due to side effects) with the usage of reverse key indexes, but be careful while implementing reverse key indexes where the application performs index range scans. Designers and developers should also consider these options while choosing indexing and partitioning strategies.

One of the undesirable side effects of using reverse key indexes is that they must be constantly rebuilt with 50 percent or more free space to be beneficial, because a large number of block splits can and will take place in an active table.

Global Cache Defers and Reverse Key Indexes

Although reverse key indexes and hash partitioning help greatly in combating the waits for the objects with high concurrency, they require an additional tweak to work flawlessly. Oracle provides multiple optimization techniques to overcome a problem, and some of them are counterproductive while working together. Reverse key indexes is one of the features that needs careful execution.

When there is high concurrency at the block level, it is often beneficial to keep the blocks in a holding instance for an extended time and allow the lock processes to continue the work than to repeatedly send and receive the block. When high concurrency is observed at the block level, the new optimization technique called *Global Cache Defer* is implicitly invoked and suspends all the send requests for some time. This has an adverse effect on performance when hash partitioning or reverse key indexes are used to cure the same issue.

The Global Cache Defer mechanism used to be very aggressive in earlier versions of Oracle. The Global Cache Defer time is controlled by the parameter _gc_defer_time, which defaults to 3 centiseconds. Disabling Global Cache Defers should be carefully benchmarked before rolling out to production.

Sorted Hash Clusters

Oracle offers several optional methods for storing table data, including clusters and hash clusters. *Sorted hash clusters* are particularly suitable for systems requiring very high data insertion and retrieval rates.

This table structure better supports first-in first-out (FIFO) data processing applications, where data is processed in the order it was inserted. Such applications are typically found in the telecommunications and manufacturing environments. For example, consider the call detail record (CDR) data structure that is common in telecommunication environments. For billing and auditing purposes, each call is to be recorded and associated with its origin. Usually, calls are stored as they arrive from the switch. This data can be retrieved later in FIFO order or a customized order when customer bills are generated.

Although it is common practice to capture this data in two standard tables, a sorted hash cluster is a better solution because it allows inexpensive access to the sorted list of call records for any given subscriber and allows the billing application reading the call records to walk through the sorted list in a FIFO manner. Any application in which data is always consumed in the order in which it is inserted will see tremendous performance improvements by using this type of optimized table structure.

The key is to partition the data and indexes as required by the application. Store your data the way the application needs it and queries it. If the algorithm selects customers in a descending order, explore the possibilities of storing customers in a descending order and use an index created in descending order of customers. There might be potential overhead in using this method because it would require constant table/index rebuilding, loading of data, and other associated administrative work. But with automated tasks, the benefits of using methods like these can sometimes outweigh the overhead.

In Oracle RAC environments, the application must build the intelligence to process data from a defined set of data/index partitions only. This reduces the chances of block contention and the "ping-pong" effect of repeated blocks traveling between instances.

Working with Sequences

Database sequences are useful for generating numbers that grow or increase sequentially in an order that is configurable. Application designers need not use "home-grown" sequence generators using a database table and update it using local logic. Such sequences are not very scalable, especially in Oracle RAC environments with high inserts, when they are used with specific clauses. Yet, in certain cases, these customized and non-Oracle sequences are the only way to achieve certain goals that cannot be achieved using Oracle's own sequences.

A select from a sequence is an update to the data dictionary when it is not cached. So every select internally invokes a DML and commit, which is expensive in Oracle RAC, because system commit numbers (SCNs) must be synchronized across the cluster when sequences are used extensively.

In Oracle RAC environments, performance degradation due to heavy use (or abuse) of sequences and a high insert rate can manifest in different ways:

- Contention for the SV enqueue. If you see contention for the SV enqueue, the problem is complicated and Oracle Support Services might be required.

- Buffer busy waits for various classes of blocks such as data, index leaves, or segment headers.

- TX enqueue waits on the index blocks may also be visible.

- In certain cases, ITL waits are also possible when a sufficient number of transaction slots is not reserved or available. This could be due to a very low setting for PCTFREE combined with a default value for INITRANS or artificially limiting transaction slots using MAXTRANS.

CACHE and NOORDER

The CACHE option speeds up selection and processing of sequences and minimizes the writes to SEQ$. Note that the CACHE option is usable only if an application is able to accept gaps in the sequence, irrespective of whether you use Oracle RAC.

From a performance and scalability perspective, the best way of using sequences is to use the CACHE and NOORDER options together. The CACHE option ensures that a distinct set of numbers is cached in each instance after the first use of the sequence. The NOORDER option specifies that the sequence numbers may not be in order. For applications that perform large concurrent inserts from multiple instances concurrently and a key value like the primary key is generated using the sequence, the NOORDER option along with CACHE option provides the best throughput.

In a high insert environment, tables that have their key values generated from sequences tend to have hot blocks for both data and indexes, because the block where inserts are going is wanted by every instance. Without partitioning the table and the applicable indexes, these blocks would become a major point of contention. Hence, partitioning of data and indexes should be one of the first steps in reducing this type of contention. Along with partitioning, using an additional column along with the key value is critical to avoid contention.

These hot blocks are generally visible as "buffer busy waits" or "read by other session," depending on the mode being waited for. There would also be an increase in the number of CR and CUR mode blocks transferred between instances, sometimes even with partitioning implemented.

One of the disadvantages of the NOORDER option is that the key values may not be in order. So if an invoice number, customer number, or account number is generated using this sequence and regulatory norms require you to maintain the order of numbers, NOORDER cannot be used. An abnormal instance shutdown or a crash will introduce gaps in sequences. Cached sequences may be lost during a shared pool flush or rollback. Sequences do not support rollback because a sequence, once fetched, remains fetched and the number is deemed consumed forever.

CACHE and ORDER

If you need sequences for which the ordering of numbers needs to be guaranteed, you can specify the CACHE option with the ORDER clause. This ensures the ordering of numbers, because each instance caches the same set of numbers, unlike the NOORDER option.

Note that the Oracle documentation wrongly states that the CACHE and ORDER options do not work together. Both Oracle 9i and 10g RAC support this feature, however. These two options may not be as scalable as the CACHE and NOORDER method, but they ensure that sequences are in order, although gaps can still occur across instance startup and shutdown.

NOCACHE and ORDER

This option is used when an application requires all sequence values in an order and without gaps. Using NOCACHE and ORDER has the biggest performance impact on Oracle RAC environments, and designers must understand the inherent scalability limitations before choosing this model.

To overcome buffer busy waits for data blocks while using sequences to generate the key value, specify FREELISTS if segment management is manual or use ASSM tablespaces. In addition, the segment header block is also subject to heavy contention in Oracle RAC environments. To reduce that, use FREELIST GROUPS.

Best Practice: Use Different Sequences for Each Instance

A good practice in Oracle RAC is to use different sequences for each instance to avoid a single point of contention. Each inserting process on a particular node uses its own sequence to select monotonically increasing key values. Selecting from a different sequence for high inserts can be a great solution, but it requires a change in the application.

In Oracle RAC environments, to overcome buffer busy waits for index leaves where the key values are generated using sequences, do the following:

- Use ASSM tablespaces. Partition the table and its relevant indexes. Guide the data into the table partitions using additional columns, if necessary. Remember to analyze the effects on the clustering_factor of your indexes.
- Cache large values of the sequence and use NOORDER if possible.

With caching, the difference between sequence values generated by different instances increases; thus, newer index block splits would create an effect called an *instance affinity* to index leaf blocks. This seems to work only when CACHE and NOORDER are used together.

For example, if we use a sequence cache of 20, instance 1 would insert values 1, 2, 3, and so on, and instance 2 would concurrently insert 20, 21, 22, and so on. If the difference between the values is a lot smaller than the number of rows in the block, the two instances will continue to modify the same index block as sequence values increase.

If we set a value of 5000 for the sequence cache, instance 1 would insert values 1, 2, 3, and so on, while instance 2 concurrently inserts 5001, 5002, 5003, and so on. At the beginning of the inserts, both instances would write to the same leaf block, but subsequent block splits would cause the inserts to be distributed across different blocks because the difference in sequence values causes the inserts to map to different blocks.

There is no such thing as a best value for the CACHE option in sequences. Generally, developers should consider the rate of insert per second/per instance as a guide to setting the cache value. Sequences may not be the best scalable solution, especially when an instance is used for the generation of ordered and gapless sequence numbers at a very high rate.

Connection Management

Applications that do not use transaction monitors are generally guilty of poor database connection management. Efficient management of database connections is critical in single-instance databases and in Oracle RAC databases.

Some applications disconnect from the database and then reconnect repeatedly. This is a common problem with stateless middleware applications such as Shell/Perl scripts and precompiler programs that exit on error and tend to use the AUTO_CONNECT option to reestablish the connection. Even in precompiler programs such as Pro*C, application architecture and design would force an unnecessary "connection-disconnection-reconnection" to the database, thus impeding scalability and performance.

Connecting to the database incurs operating system costs associated with creating a new process or thread. Many recursive SQL statements also need to be executed during the process of establishing a new connection to the database. Because the session is new, these recursive SQL statements require a soft parse. This adds to the load on the library cache latches. Data file operations require operating system coordination, and this adds to the overhead of maintaining the process.

All these types of overhead can be avoided by retaining database connections as long as they are required. Usually, applications built with a transaction monitor such as BEA Tuxedo do not suffer from these issues because a database connection is maintained consistently.

The Pro*C/C++ connection pooling and OCI session pooling features help maintain connections to the database. These features can be deployed in applications built using Pro*C/OCI and when transaction monitors such as BEA Tuxedo, CORBA, and WebSphere are not used. Stateless connection pooling improves the scalability of the mid-tier applications by multiplexing the connections.

Full Table Scans

Repetitive full table scans in Oracle RAC can impede performance and scalability as the private interconnect is used for transferring blocks, and that can eat into network bandwidth. This would cause a delay for other required and important blocks such as index blocks, undo blocks, header blocks, and any messages. The goal is to reduce interconnect traffic and bring down latency. With a lot of full table scans, interconnects could get overloaded, thereby flooding the private network.

Another very important factor to be considered with full table scans is an appropriate value for DB_FILE_MULTIBLOCK_READ_COUNT, also known as MBRC. Not only does this parameter have a charming influence on the optimizer to lean toward a full table scan (irrespective of Oracle RAC or non–OracleRAC), but achieving interconnect saturation is easy if high values are used for this parameter.

Experience has shown that 16 can be a high MBRC value for an application such as Oracle E-Business Suite 11i. Many such systems experience severe performance degradation with an MBRC of 16 while running in Oracle RAC mode. Lowering the value to 8 immediately brings the performance back to acceptable or normal levels.

With a high MBRC value in Oracle RAC, when Oracle performs multiblock reads and the data is transferred across instances, the interconnect tends to get flooded with large number of blocks flowing from one end to the other. Using a lower value for MBRC (such as 8) is a good starting point for applications on Oracle RAC databases.

Full table scans are not necessarily evil, and in some cases they are the best data access method for a particular process. But they are a common issue in many Oracle RAC performance problems, especially with custom applications. You can easily identify the full table scans in the database using any of the following techniques.

Identifying Full Table Scans

Automatic Workload Repository is one of the most common tools used to monitor most databases. You can easily spot and conclude from the top wait events whether full table scans are the problem. Existence of the "db file scattered read" wait event in the top five wait events is a quick and early indicator of a full table scan problem.

Other than Statspack, v$sysstat can be queried for the table scan statistic. You can run the following query on v$sysstat to check the number of times data is accessed using the full table scan method:

```
select name, value from v$sysstat
where name like 'table scan%'
```

A Statspack report quickly followed by a query on v$sysstat can confirm whether full table scans are a problem. Normally, performance monitoring tools or scripts built on using v$session_ wait will quickly detect the full scans if they find the excessive waits on the "db file scattered read." A "db file scattered read" wait event lists the file# and block# along with the number of blocks it is reading (typically less than or equal to the MBRC value) during the full scan. These are displayed as p1, p2, and p3 values for the "db file scattered read" wait event. For a known file# and block#, you can use the following query to get the name of the table that is being accessed via full table scans:

```
select distinct owner, segment_name,segment_type
from dba_extents where file_id=<file#> and
<block#> between  block_id and block_id+blocks -1;
```

Other than querying v$sysstat or v$session_wait, you can implement numerous techniques to detect full table scans if you suspect they are a problem. For example, if the PHYSBLKRDS is significantly higher than the PHYRDS in the V$FILESTAT, there is a good chance of full scans on the segment residing in that datafile. Also, blocks read by full table scans are not subject to normal LRU processing in the buffer cache. A special flag is set in the buffer cache (X$BH.FLAG), and if the state is 0×80000, you know the block is read using the full scans.

After identifying the table scans, you need to confirm whether they are expected or unreasonable. You can query either v$session_longops or v$sql_plan to confirm that. Any of the following queries can be employed for this purposes, and using the hash_value, you can identify and turn the offending SQL queries for efficiency:

```
select sid,username,opname,target,totalwork,sofar,sql_hash_value.
from v$session_longops
where opname='table scan'
and totalwork>sofar

select object_owner,object_name,hash_value
from v$sql_plan
where operation='TABLE ACCESS'
and options='FULL'
```

A distinct advantage of these views over v$session_wait is that the values are not quickly overwritten and they are cached for an extended period of time. You can even query at a later time and confirm the activity. The v$session_longops view is quite important here, because it also lists the other expensive operations in the database, such as hash joins, sorting, and RMAN operations.

Interconnect Protocol

Choosing the appropriate protocol to carry your blocks across the high-speed interconnect is a crucial decision. So are the configuration and settings for the protocol.

Oracle 9*i* made the first definitive shift toward the User Datagram Protocol (UDP), a connectionless protocol. With 10g R1, Oracle has actively suggested the use of UDP on all platforms, even though hardware vendors have developed some exciting and lighting-fast technologies for transfer of data across high-speed interconnects. Prominent among them are Digital Equipment's (aka Compaq, aka HP) Reliable DataGram (RDG), HP's Hyper Messaging Protocol (HMP), and Veritas' Low Latency Transport (LLT).

Each of these protocols uses its own proprietary hardware interconnects based on fiber-optic or Gigabit Ethernet technology with very low network latency. Yet, each one of them has its own problems with Oracle RAC—except for RDG, which seems to perform and scale wonderfully well on Tru64 systems with minimal fuss.

What makes the crucial difference in interconnect performance (and subsequently application response time and scalability) is choosing the right values for the internal layers of each of these protocols, especially UDP. The receive and send buffer size is usually left at default values on many installation sites. The Oracle kernel uses its own default values (128K for UDP on all UNIX platforms). If the OS tunable parameters for UDP have been configured, the Oracle kernel uses those values to set its buffer sizes.

Default values are seldom adequate for applications that support hundreds or thousands of users. The number of connections and concurrent users may not always be a good yardstick for workload measurement. Some applications have less user count but a large transaction volume and cause a lot of internode traffic. Using the default UDP settings, Oracle RAC databases/applications that tend to have highly active internode block transfers may not scale when the workload increases.

A value of 64K (65,536 bytes) for udp_sendspace can be used while tuning this layer. Any value above that is most likely useless because the lower layer (IP) cannot process more than 64K. A value that is 10 times that of udp_sendspace is a good setting for udp_recvspace. Usually, recommendations suggest setting both these parameters to 1MB each, which is also valid in many cases, yet 1MB is more of a generic tuning guideline as compared to the 64K practice, which is derived and calculated based on UDP and IP behavior.

An interesting relationship that UDP shares with FTS is that low or "untuned" values for UDP buffer sizes can cause timeouts when CR blocks are requested by remote instances. Timeouts are visible in the "gc cr multi block" wait event or in a trace file generated via SQL Trace or a 10046 event setting. A look into V$SYSTEM_EVENT can provide the ratio of timeouts versus waits for the CR request event:

Event	Waits	Timeouts	Total Wait Time (s)	Avg wait (ms)	Waits /txn
gc cr multi block	12,852	**3,085**	612	47	3.6

A large value for MBRC can exacerbate the situation. Hence, proper care must be taken while choosing values for UDP buffers as well as MBRC.

Ethernet Frame Size

Other than the protocol, the frame size also has significant impact on the interconnect performance. The most common data block size in Oracle is 8192 bytes, and the default frame size for the Ethernet is 1500 bytes. A data block that is sent from one instance to another instance through the interconnect is shipped in at least four packets, and they are assembled back at the other instance. Although the default frame size is quite good for most of the Cache Fusion messages, for efficient block transfers it is strongly recommended to use the jumbo frames that support 9K frame size.

While using jumbo frames, you need to ensure that the complete data transfer path—from the NIC to switches—supports jumbo frames. With jumbo frames, there is no fragmentation of packets during the data transfer and thus less latency and low CPU usage compared with smaller frame sizes.

Library Cache Effect in the Parsing

As in single-instance environments, it is best to avoid excessive and unnecessary parsing of SQL statements and PL/SQL code in Oracle RAC. Additional overhead is incurred in Oracle RAC for parsing because many locks are now global. In old parlance, library cache–related locks fall under the non-PCM locks category.

- Library cache load and pin lock acquisition on a library object such as a PL/SQL procedure, package, or function requires global coordination by Global Enqueue Services (GES).

- Although parsing of SELECT statements does not require global lock coordination, Data Definition Language (DDL) statements do need messages to be sent across to master nodes for synchronization and lock grants.

Note that if the same SQL statement is sent for parsing on all nodes, these statements are individually parsed and executed on each node and probably with different execution plans due to potentially varying init.ora or SPFILE parameters.

When many objects are compiled or parsed, even reparsed due to invalidations, it can give rise to delays and have significant impact on performance. Application developers must take care while using DDL statements, including GRANT and REVOKE commands, because these statements invalidate all objects that are referred to or by the PL/SQL object.

Repeated hard parsing and parse failures can severely limit scalability and harm the application performance. Tuning methodologies followed on single-instance databases are also applicable in Oracle RAC and should be rigorously implemented.

Commit Frequency

Certain wait events have multiple effects in Oracle RAC. For example, a "log file sync" wait event is associated with excessive commits, and application designers/developers usually are advised to reduce the frequency of their commits to reduce the burden on LGWR and reduce the number of LGWR writes to a log file. A close associate of "log file sync" is "log file parallel write."

In Oracle RAC environments, log file sync has more implications because each commit or rollback needs SCN propagation and global synchronization, and may also require controlfile synchronization. Hence, extra caution must be exercised in Oracle RAC environments when you are choosing a commit interval or frequency. Some business applications may need to commit more often than other applications require. Developers and users must be aware of the performance tradeoff that accompanies a high commit rate.

In a single-instance database, when a user commits or rolls back a transaction, the process waits on log file sync, and the background Oracle process (LGWR) will wait on a log file parallel write. On an Oracle RAC database, in addition to the latency created by these usual suspects, time consumed in SCN-related communication and controlfile writes will also need to be considered while you are calculating the cost of commit/rollback.

NOTE
Excessive cross-instance requests for changed or dirty blocks will cause more redo generation because all changes made to a block need to be written out before a copy of the block is transferred across to the requesting instance. In this case, LMS initiates the log synchronization and waits on a log file sync. Once log writing is complete, LMS can go ahead and ship the copy of the block to the requestor.

In a Nutshell

As noted at the beginning of the book, Oracle RAC can be compared to a stereo amplifier. If the original music is good, you will hear good music with Oracle RAC. If the original music has a lot of noise, Oracle RAC will amplify that noise and the outcome is sometimes unpleasant. A well-performing application in a single-instance environment will perform equally well or outperform when implemented on Oracle RAC.

Developing applications for Oracle RAC does not require any major changes other than the few considerations explained in this chapter. Other than a few exceptions, all single-instance application design best practices are applicable to Oracle RAC databases as well.

Good luck in designing and deploying a highly scalable application on Oracle RAC!

PART
VI
Appendixes

APPENDIX
A

Oracle RAC Reference

he Oracle database is very rich in terms of providing diagnostic data and statistics. It provides an enormous amount of statistics about most of the internal operations, which are exposed through a group of underlying views maintained by the database server. These views are normally accessible to the database administrator user *SYS*. They are called *dynamic performance views* because they are continuously updated while a database is open and in use, and their contents relate primarily to performance.

These views are built on the set of internal memory structures commonly known as *x$views*. These internal and undocumented views expose the runtime statistics of the relative data structures in a tabular format. Although these views appear to be regular database tables, they are not. You can select from these views, but you cannot update or alter them because the definitions are not stored in the dictionary.

The catalog.sql script (which is executed automatically by the Database Configuration Assistant during database creation) creates the public synonyms for the dynamic performance views. After installation, only user *SYS* or anyone with the DBA role has access to the dynamic performance tables.

In this appendix, we explore the important v$views that are used in Oracle Real Application Clusters for diagnostics and troubleshooting. These views contain the system-level statistics from the instance startup, and the contents are reset when the instance is shut down because the data structures containing the data are reset during the instance shutdown. All of the information is cached in the System Global Area (SGA) of the respective instances.

For clusterwide information, you can query GV$ views. For every v$view, a corresponding GV$ view exists. When you query the GV$ view, the data from other instances are retrieved by parallel query mechanisms, and the initialization parameter parallel_max_servers should be set to a minimum of 2 for GV$ views to work.

Global Cache Services and Cache Fusion Diagnostics

The following views can be queried to get the details about the buffer cache contents and Global Cache Services (GCS) operations. Cache Fusion diagnostic information can also be obtained from these views.

V$CACHE

This view contains information about every cached block in the buffer cache. It also keeps the relevant details about the cached block to the database object. This view is a good source of information about cached blocks in local instances in Oracle RAC environments. Table A-1 shows information about columns and data types in this view.

Table A-2 shows block classes and descriptions. Table A-3 defines the buffer states.

Column	Data Type	Description
FILE#	Number	Datafile ID (FILE# from V$DATAFILE or FILE_ID in DBA_DATA_FILES).
BLOCK#	Number	Block number of the cached block.
CLASS#	Number	Class number (see Table A-2).
STATUS	Varchar2 (6)	Status of the block in SGA (see Table A-3).
XNC	Number	Number of times PCM locks were converted from X to null lock mode.
FORCED_READS	Number	Number of times the block was reread from cache because another instance forced it out by requesting this block in exclusive mode.
FORCED_WRITES	Number	Number of times GCS had to write the block to cache because this instance used the block and another instance requested a lock on the block in conflicting mode.
NAME	Varchar2 (30)	Name of the database object to which the block belongs.
PARTITION_NAME	Varchar2 (30)	Name of the partition. The column is null if the object is not partitioned.
KIND	Varchar2 (15)	Type of object (table, view procedure, and so on).
OWNER#	Number	Number of owner.
LOCK_ELEMENT_ADDR	Raw (4|8)	Address of lock element that contains the PCM lock covering the buffer.
LOCK_ELEMENT_NAME	Number	Name of lock element that contains the PCM lock covering the buffer.

TABLE A-1   *V$CACHE Information*

Class	Explanation
1	Data
2	Sort segment
3	Save undo block
4	Segment header
5	Save undo segment header
6	Freelist block
7	Extent map
8	Space management bitmap block
9	Space management index block

TABLE A-2   *Block Class and Descriptions*

State	Explanation
0	Buffer free, unused
1	Buffer current, locked in X mode
2	Buffer current, locked in S mode
3	Consistent read buffer
4	Buffer being read
5	Buffer under media recovery
6	Buffer under instance recovery
7	Write clone buffer
8	Past Image buffer

TABLE A-3 *Buffer States*

V$CACHE_TRANSFER

This Oracle RAC view is similar to V$CACHE, which contains information from block headers in SGA that have been pinged at least once by the current instance relative to the database object.

Column	Data Type	Description
FILE#	Number	Datafile ID (FILE# from V$DATAFILE or FILE_ID in DBA_DATA_FILES).
BLOCK#	Number	Block number.
CLASS#	Number	Class number (see Table A-2).
STATUS	Varchar2 (6)	Status of block in SGA (see Table A-3).
XNC	Number	Number of times PCM locks were converted from X to null lock mode.
FORCED_READS	Number	Number of times the block was reread from cache because another instance forced it out by requesting this block in exclusive mode.
FORCED_WRITES	Number	Number of times GCS had to write this block to cache because this instance had used the block and another instance had requested a lock on the block in a conflicting mode.
NAME	Varchar2 (30)	Name of the database object to which this block belongs.
PARTITION_NAME	Varchar2 (30)	Name of the partition. This is null if the object is not partitioned.
KIND	Varchar2 (15)	Type of object.
OWNER#	Number	Owner number.
GC_ELEMENT_ADDR	Raw (4|8)	Address of the lock element containing the PCM lock covering the buffer.
GC_ELEMENT_NAME	Number	Name of the lock element that contains the PCM lock covering the buffer.

TABLE A-4 *V$CACHE_TRANSFER Information*

V$INSTANCE_CACHE_TRANSFER

This view keeps information about the transfer of cache blocks through interconnect. These statistics can be used to find the number of blocks transferred from one instance to another instance using Cache Fusion. This view also shows how many block transfers incurred a delay or congestion (see Table A-5).

Column	Data Type	Description
INSTANCE	Number	Instance number transferring the block.
CLASS	Varchar2 (18)	Class of cache block being transferred.
LOST	Number	Number of blocks that were sent by another instance but never arrived in this instance.
LOST_TIME	Number	Time waited for blocks that were sent by another instance but never arrived in this instance.
CR_BLOCK	Number	CR block transfers not affected by remote processing delays.
CR_BLOCK_TIME	Number	Total time waited for CR blocks from a particular instance.
CR_2HOP	Number	Number of CR blocks received by this instance from a particular instance after a two-way roundtrip.
CR_2HOP_TIME	Number	Time waited for CR blocks received by this instance from a particular instance after a two-way roundtrip.
CR_3HOP	Number	Number of CR blocks received by this instance from a particular instance after a three-way roundtrip.
CR_3HOP_TIME	Number	Time waited for CR blocks received by this instance from a particular instance after a three-way roundtrip.
CR_BUSY	Number	CR block transfers affected by remote contention.
CR_BUSY_TIME	Number	Time waited for CR blocks received by this instance from a particular instance and were delayed by a log flushed on the sending instance.
CR_CONGESTED	Number	CR block transfers affected by remote system load.
CR_CONGESTED_TIME	Number	Time waited for CR blocks received by this instance from a particular instance and were delayed because LMS was busy.
CURRENT_BLOCK	Number	Current block transfers not affected by remote system delays.
CURRENT_BLOCK_TIME	Number	Total time waited for current blocks from a particular instance.
CURRENT_2HOP	Number	Number of current blocks received by this instance from a particular instance after a two-way roundtrip.
CURRENT_2HOP_TIME	Number	Time waited for current blocks received by this instance from a particular instance after a two-way roundtrip.
CURRENT_3HOP	Number	Number of current blocks received by this instance from a particular instance after a three-way roundtrip.
CURRENT_3HOP_TIME	Number	Time waited for current blocks received by this instance from a particular instance after a three-way roundtrip.

TABLE A-5 *V$INSTANCE_CACHE_TRANSFER Information*

Column	Data Type	Description
CURRENT_BUSY	Number	Current block transfers affected by remote contention.
CURRENT_BUSY_TIME	Number	Time waited for current blocks received by this instance from a particular instance and were delayed by a log flushed on the sending instance.
CURRENT_CONGESTED	Number	Current block transfers affected by remote system load.
CURRENT_CONGESTED_TIME	Number	Time waited for current blocks received by this instance from a particular instance and were delayed because LMS was busy.

TABLE A-5   *V$INSTANCE_CACHE_TRANSFER Information* (continued)

V$CR_BLOCK_SERVER

This view keeps statistics about CR block transfer across the instances (see Table A-6). Global Cache Service Process (LMS) from the holding instance constructs the CR block for the requesting instance and ships the CR version of the block using the interconnect. CR building is discussed in more detail in Chapter 11.

Column	Data Type	Description
CR_REQUESTS	Number	Number of CR blocks served due to remote CR block requests.
CURRENT_REQUEST	Number	Number of current blocks served due to remote CR block requests.
DATA_REQUEST	Number	Number of CR or current requests for data blocks.
UNDO_REQUESTS	Number	Number of CR requests for undo blocks.
TX_REQUESTS	Number	Number of CR requests for undo segment header blocks. Total number of requests would be equal to the sum of DATA_REQUEST, UNDO_REQUESTS, and TX_REQUESTS column.
OTHER_REQUESTS	Number	Number of CR requests for other types of blocks.
CURRENT_RESULTS	Number	Number of requests when no changes were rolled out of the block returned to the requesting instance.
PRIVATE_RESULTS	Number	Number of requests when changes were rolled out of the block returned to the requesting instance and only the requesting transaction can use the CR block.
ZERO_RESULTS	Number	Number of requests when changes were rolled out of the block returned to the requesting instance and only zero-XID transactions can use the block.
DISK_READ_RESULTS	Number	Number of requests when the requesting instance had to read the block from disk.

TABLE A-6   *V$CR_BLOCK_SERVER Information*

Column	Data Type	Description
FAIL_RESULTS	Number	Number of requests failed and the requesting transaction reissued the request.
STALE	Number	For internal use only.
FAIRNESS_DOWN_CONVERTS	Number	Number of times the instance receiving request has down-converted an X lock on a block because it was not modifying the block.
FAIRNESS_CLEARS	Number	Number of times the "fairness counter" was cleared. This counter tracks the number of times a block was modified after it was served.
FREE_GC_ELEMENTS	Number	Number of times a request was received from another instance and X lock had no buffers.
FLUSHES	Number	Number of times LMS flushed the logs.
FLUSHES_QUEUED	Number	Number of flushes queued by LMS.
FLUSH_QUEUE_FULL	Number	Number of occasions the flush queue was full.
FLUSH_MAX_TIME	Number	Maximum flush time.
LIGHT_WORKS	Number	Number of times the lightwork rule was evoked (see Chapter 11).
ERRORS	Number	Number of occasions an error was signaled by the LMS process.

TABLE A-6   *V$CR_BLOCK_SERVER Information* (continued)

V$CURRENT_BLOCK_SERVER

This view keeps statistics about the current block transfer across the instances (see Table A-7). The GCS Process (LMS) from the holding instance ships the current block to the requesting instance after flushing the required recovery information to the redo log buffer. This view provides the most important information about how long the holding instance waited to flush the information before sending the block to the requestor.

Column	Data Type	Description
PIN1	Number	Number of pins taking less than 1ms
PIN10	Number	Number of pins taking 1ms to 10ms
PIN100	Number	Number of pins taking 10ms to 100ms
PIN1000	Number	Number of pins taking 100ms to 1000ms
PIN10000	Number	Number of pins taking 1000ms to 10000ms
FLUSH1	Number	Number of flushes taking less than 1ms

TABLE A-7   *V$CURRENT_BLOCK_SERVER Information*

Column	Data Type	Description
FLUSH10	Number	Number of flushes taking 1ms to 10ms
FLUSH100	Number	Number of flushes taking 10ms to 100ms
FLUSH1000	Number	Number of flushes taking 100ms to 1000ms
FLUSH10000	Number	Number of flushes taking 1000ms to 10000ms
WRITE1	Number	Number of writes taking less than 1ms
WRITE10	Number	Number of writes taking 1ms to 10ms
WRITE100	Number	Number of writes taking 10ms to 100ms
WRITE1000	Number	Number of writes taking 100ms to 1000ms
WRITE10000	Number	Number of writes taking 1000ms to 10000ms

TABLE A-7   *V$CURRENT_BLOCK_SERVER Information* (continued)

V$GC_ELEMENT

This view displays one-to-one information for each global cache resource used by the buffer cache (see Table A-8). There is an entry for each global cache resource in this view, used by a buffer cache.

Column	Data Type	Description
GC_ELEMENT_ADDR	Raw (4|8)	Address of the PCM lock element containing the PCM lock covering the buffer; if more than one buffer has the same address, these buffers are covered by the same PCM lock.
INDX	Number	Platform-specific lock manager identifier; can be joined with the V$CACHE_LOCK view.
CLASS	Number	Platform-specific lock manager identifier; can be joined with the V$CACHE_LOCK view.
GC_ELEMENT_NAME	Number	Name of the lock element that contains the PCM lock covering the buffer; if more than one buffer has the same address, these buffers are covered by the same PCM lock.
MODE_HELD	Number	Value for the lock mode held. This is often 3 for share and 5 for exclusive.
BLOCK_COUNT	Number	Number of blocks covered by the PCM lock.
RELEASING	Number	Nonzero if the PCM lock is downgraded.
ACQUIRING	Number	Nonzero if the PCM lock is upgraded.
INVALID	Number	Would be nonzero upon PCM lock failure.
FLAGS	Number	Process-level flags for the lock element.

TABLE A-8   *V$GC_ELEMENT Information*

Global Enqueue Services Diagnostics

The following views can be queried to get the details about statistics for Global Enqueue Services. Few of these views are extensively used in single-instance environments to query enqueue statistics.

V$LOCK

This view maintains information about locks held within a database and outstanding requests for locks or latches (see Table A-9). Table A-10 shows the lock modes.

Column	Data Type	Description
ADDR	Raw (4 | 8)	Address of the lock state object
KADDR	Raw (4 | 8)	Address of the lock
SID	Number	Session identifier holding the lock
TYPE	Varchar2 (2)	Type of resource, which could be user or system type
ID1	Number	Resource identifier 1
ID2	Number	Resource identifier 2
LMODE	Number	Lock mode held (see Table A-10)
REQUEST	Number	Mode of lock requested (see Table A-10)
CTIME	Number	Time since the current mode was granted
BLOCK	Number	1 if the lock is blocking another lock; 0 otherwise

TABLE A-9   *V$LOCK Information*

Lock Mode	Description
0	none
1	null (NULL)
2	row-S (SS)
3	row-X (SX)
4	share (S)
5	S/row-X (SSX)
6	exclusive (X)

TABLE A-10   *Lock Modes*

V$GES_BLOCKING_ENQUEUE

This view maintains information about locks that are being blocked or are blocking others as well as locks that are known to the lock manager (see Table A-11). The content of this view is a subset of V$GES_ ENQUEUE because this view maintains information only about blocked locks, whereas V$GES_ ENQUEUE maintains all locks known to the lock manager.

Column	Data Type	Description
HANDLE	(Raw 4 | 8)	Pointer to the lock
GRANT_LEVEL	Varchar2 (9)	Level granted to the lock
REQUEST_LEVEL	Varchar2 (9)	Level requested for the lock
RESOURCE_NAME1	Varchar2 (30)	Resource name of the lock
RESOURCE_NAME2	Varchar2 (30)	Resource name of the lock
PID	Number	Process identifier holding the lock
TRANSACTION_ID0	Number	Lower 4 bytes of the transaction identifier the lock belongs to
TRANSACTION_ID1	Number	Upper 4 bytes of the transaction identifier the lock belongs to
GROUP_ID	Number	Group identifier of the lock
OPEN_OPT_DEADLOCK	Number	1 if the DEADLOCK option is set; otherwise 0
OPEN_OPT_PERSISTENT	Number	1 if the PERSISTENT option is set; otherwise 0
OPEN_OPT_PROCESS_OWNED	Number	1 if the PROCESS_OWNED option is set; otherwise 0
OPEN_OPT_NO_XID	Number	1 if the NO_XID option is set; otherwise 0
CONVERT_OPT_GETVALUE	Number	1 if the GETVALUE convert option is set; otherwise 0
CONVERT_OPT_PUTVALUE	Number	1 if the PUTVALUE convert option is set; otherwise 0
CONVERT_OPT_NOVALUE	Number	1 if the NOVALUE convert option is set; otherwise 0
CONVERT_OPT_DUBVALUE	Number	1 if the DUBVALUE convert option is set; otherwise 0
CONVERT_OPT_NOQUEUE	Number	1 if the NOQUEUE convert option is set; otherwise 0
CONVERT_OPT_EXPRESS	Number	1 if the EXPRESS convert option is set; otherwise 0
CONVERT_OPT_ NODEADLOCKWAIT	Number	1 if the NODEADLOCKWAIT convert option is set; otherwise 0
CONVERT_OPT_ NODEADLOCKBLOCK	Number	1 if the NODEADLOCKBLOCK convert option is set; otherwise 0
WHICH_QUEUE	Number	Which queue the lock is currently located in: 0 for Null Queue, 1 for Granted Queue, 2 for Convert Queue
STATE	Varchar2 (64)	State of the lock
AST_EVENT0	Number	Last know AST event
OWNED_NODE	Number	Node identifier owning the lock
BLOCKED	Number	1 if the lock request is blocked by others; otherwise 0
BLOCKER	Number	1 if the lock is blocking others; otherwise 0

TABLE A-11 *V$GES_BLOCKING_ENQUEUE Information*

V$ENQUEUE_STATISTICS

This view displays details about enqueue statistics in the instance (see Table A-12). Most of the enqueues are global in nature and are visible across instances. Table A-13 shows enqueue types and descriptions.

Column	Data Type	Description
EQ_NAME	Varchar2 (64)	Name of the enqueue that the request is for
EQ_TYPE	Varchar2 (2)	Type of enqueue (see Table A-13)
REQ_REASON	Varchar2 (64)	Reason for the enqueue request
TOTAL_REQ#	Number	Total number of times the enqueue was requested or converted
TOTAL_WAIT#	Number	Number of times the enqueue request or conversion resulted in a wait
SUCC_REQ#	Number	Number of times the enqueue request or conversion was granted
FAILED_REQ#	Number	Number of times the enqueue request or conversion failed
CUM_WAIT_TIME	Number	Amount of time (in milliseconds) spent waiting for the enqueue or conversion
REQ_DESCRIPTION	Varchar2 (4000)	Description of the enqueue request
EVENT#	Number	Number for the event

TABLE A-12 *V$ENQUEUE_STATISTICS Information*

Name	Enqueue Type	Enqueue Description
AB	ABMR process initialized	Lock held to ensure that the ABMR process is initialized.
AB	ABMR process start/stop	Lock held to ensure that only one ABMR is started in the cluster.
AD	allocate AU	Synchronizes accesses to a specific ASM disk AU.
AD	deallocate AU	Synchronizes accesses to a specific ASM disk AU.
AD	relocate AU	Synchronizes accesses to a specific ASM disk AU.
AE	lock	Prevents dropping an edition in use.
AF	task serialization	This enqueue is used to serialize access to an advisor task.
AG	contention	Synchronizes generation use of a particular workspace.
AM	ASM Password File Update	Allows one ASM password file update per cluster at a time.
AM	client registration	Registers the DB instance to the ASM client state object hash.

TABLE A-13 *Enqueue Types and Descriptions*

Name	Enqueue Type	Enqueue Description
AM	shutdown	Prevents the DB instance registration during ASM instance shutdown.
AM	rollback COD reservation	Reserves a rollback COD entry.
AM	background COD reservation	Reserves a background COD entry.
AM	ASM cache freeze	Starts the ASM cache freeze.
AM	ASM ACD Relocation	Blocks the ASM cache freeze.
AM	group use	Client group use.
AM	group block	ASM group block.
AM	ASM File Destroy	Prevents same file deletion race.
AM	ASM User	Prevents a user from being dropped if it owns any open files.
AM	ASM Amdu Dump	Allows only one AMDU dump during a block read failure.
AM	ASM file descriptor	Serializes access to the ASM file descriptors.
AM	ASM disk-based alloc/dealloc	Synchronizes disk-based allocations/deallocations.
AM	block repair	Serializes block repairs.
AM	ASM reserved	Checks id1 of a call for a specific purpose.
AM	disk offline	Synchronizes disk offline operations.
AO	contention	Synchronizes access to objects and scalar variables.
AS	service activation	Synchronizes new service activation.
AT	contention	Serializes alter tablespace operations.
AV	volume relocate	Serializes relocating volume extents.
AV	AVD client registration	Serializes inst registration and first DG use.
AV	add/enable first volume in DG	Serializes taking the AVD DG enqueue.
AV	persistent DG number	Prevents DG number collisions.
AW	user access for AW	Synchronizes user accesses to a particular workspace.
AW	AW$ table lock	Global access synchronization to the AW$ table.
AW	AW state lock	Row lock synchronization for the AW$ table.
AW	AW generation lock	In-use generation state for a particular workspace.
AY	contention	Affinity Dictionary test affinity synchronization.
BB	2PC across RAC instances	2PC distributed transaction branch across Oracle RAC instances.
BF	PMON Join Filter cleanup	PMON bloom filter recovery.
BF	allocation contention	Allocates a bloom filter in a parallel statement.
BR	multisection restore section	Lock held to serialize section access during multisection restore.
BR	proxy-copy	Lock held to allow cleanup from backup mode during an RMAN proxy-copy backup.
BR	file shrink	Lock held to prevent file from decreasing in physical size during RMAN backup.

TABLE A-13 *Enqueue Types and Descriptions* (continued)

Name	Enqueue Type	Enqueue Description
BR	space info datafile hdr update	Lock held to prevent multiple processes from updating the headers at the same time.
BR	request autobackup	Lock held to request controlfile auto-backups.
BR	perform autobackup	Lock held to perform a new controlfile auto-backup.
BR	multisection restore header	Lock held to serialize file header access during multisection restore.
CA	contention	Synchronizes various IO calibration runs.
CF	contention	Synchronizes accesses to the controlfile.
CI	contention	Coordinates cross-instance function invocations.
CL	drop label	Synchronizes accesses to label cache when a label is being dropped.
CL	compare labels	Synchronizes accesses to label cache for label comparison.
CM	instance	Indicates the ASM disk group is mounted.
CM	gate	Serializes access to the instance enqueue.
CM	diskgroup dismount	Serializes an ASM disk group dismount.
CN	race with init	During descriptor initialization.
CN	race with txn	During registration.
CN	race with reg	During a transaction commit to see concurrent registrations.
CO	master slave det	Enqueue held by Master in Cleanout Optimization.
CQ	contention	Serializes access to cleanup client query cache registrations.
CR	block range reuse ckpt	Coordinates fast block range reuse checkpoint.
CT	reading	Lock held to ensure that change-tracking data remains in existence until a reader is done with it.
CT	global space management	Lock held during change-tracking space management operations that affect the entire tracking file.
CT	local space management	Lock held during change-tracking space management operations that affect just the data for one thread.
CT	CTWR process start/stop	Lock held to ensure that only one CTWR process is started in a single instance.
CT	state	Lock held while enabling or disabling change tracking, to ensure that it is only enabled or disabled by one user at a time.
CT	change stream ownership	Lock held by one instance while change tracking is enabled, to guarantee access to thread-specific resources.
CT	state change gate 2	Lock held while enabling or disabling change tracking in Oracle RAC.
CT	state change gate 1	Lock held while enabling or disabling change tracking in Oracle RAC.
CU	contention	Recovers cursors in case of death while compiling.

TABLE A-13   *Enqueue Types and Descriptions* (continued)

Name	Enqueue Type	Enqueue Description
CX	Index Specific Lock	Index-specific lock on CTX index.
DB	contention	Synchronizes the modification of database-wide supplemental logging attributes.
DD	contention	Synchronizes local accesses to ASM disk groups.
DF	contention	Enqueue held by foreground or DBWR when a datafile is brought online in Oracle RAC.
DG	contention	Synchronizes accesses to ASM disk groups.
DL	contention	Lock to prevent index DDL during direct load.
DM	contention	Enqueue held by foreground or DBWR to synchronize database mount/open with other operations.
DN	contention	Serializes group number generations.
DO	startup of MARK process	Synchronizes startup of MARK process.
DO	Staleness Registry create	Synchronizes Staleness Registry creation.
DO	disk online recovery	Synchronizes disk online operations and their recovery.
DO	disk online operation	Represents an active disk online operation.
DO	disk online	Synchronizes disk online operations and their recovery.
DP	contention	Synchronizes access to LDAP parameters.
DR	contention	Serializes the active distributed recovery operation.
DS	contention	Prevents a database suspend during LMON reconfiguration.
DT	contention	Serializes changing the default temporary tablespace and user creation.
DV	contention	Synchronizes access to lower-version Diana (PL/SQL intermediate representation).
DW	contention	Serializes in-memory dispenser operations.
DX	contention	Serializes tightly coupled distributed transaction branches.
FA	access file	Synchronizes accesses to open ASM files.
FB	contention	Ensures that only one process can format data blocks in auto-segment space managed tablespaces.
FC	open an ACD thread	LGWR opens an ACD thread (ACD is Active Change Directory, a data structure like redo logs for ASM Instance).
FC	recover an ACD thread	SMON recovers an ACD thread.
FD	Flashback on/off	Synchronization.
FD	Marker generation	Synchronization.
FD	Tablespace flashback on/off	Synchronization.
FD	Flashback coordinator	Synchronization.
FD	Restore point create/drop	Synchronization.
FD	Flashback logical operations	Synchronization.

TABLE A-13 *Enqueue Types and Descriptions* (continued)

Name	Enqueue Type	Enqueue Description
FE	contention	Serializes flashback archive recovery.
FG	serialize ACD relocate	Only one process in the cluster may do ACD relocation in a disk group.
FG	LGWR redo generation enq race	Resolves a race condition to acquire Disk Group Redo Generation Enqueue.
FG	FG redo generation enq race	Resolves a race condition to acquire Disk Group Redo Generation Enqueue.
FL	Flashback db command	Enqueue used to synchronize Flashback Database and deletion of flashback logs.
FL	Flashback database log	Synchronization.
FM	contention	Synchronizes access to global file mapping state.
FP	global fob contention	Synchronizes various File Object (FOB) operations.
FR	recover the thread	Waits for lock domain detach.
FR	use the thread	Indicates this ACD thread is alive.
FR	contention	Begins recovery of the disk group.
FS	contention	Enqueue used to synchronize recovery and file operations or synchronize dictionary check.
FT	disable LGWR writes	Prevents LGWR from generating a redo in this thread.
FT	allow LGWR writes	Allows LGWR to generate a redo in this thread.
FU	contention	This enqueue is used to serialize the capture of the DB Feature Usage and High Watermark statistics.
FX	issue ACD Xtnt Relocation CIC	ARB relocates ACD extent.
HD	contention	Serializes accesses to ASM SGA data structures.
HP	contention	Synchronizes accesses to queue pages.
HQ	contention	Synchronizes the creation of new queue IDs.
HV	contention	Lock used to broker the high watermark during parallel inserts.
HW	contention	Lock used to broker the high watermark during parallel inserts.
ID	contention	Lock held to prevent other processes from performing a controlfile transaction while NID is running.
IL	contention	Synchronizes accesses to internal label data structures.
IM	contention for blr	Serializes block recovery for In Memory Undo (IMU) transaction.
IR	contention	Synchronizes instance recovery.
IR	contention 2	Synchronizes parallel instance recovery and shutdown immediate.
IS	contention	Enqueue used to synchronize instance state changes.

TABLE A-13 *Enqueue Types and Descriptions* (continued)

Name	Enqueue Type	Enqueue Description
IT	contention	Synchronizes accesses to a temp object's metadata.
JD	contention	Synchronizes dates between the job queue coordinator and slave processes.
JI	contention	Lock held during materialized view operations (such as refresh and alter) to prevent concurrent operations on the same materialized view.
JQ	contention	Lock to prevent multiple instances from running a single job.
JS	wdw op	Lock got when doing a window open/close.
JS	job run lock - synchronize	Lock to prevent a job from running elsewhere.
JS	aq sync	Scheduler event code and AQ synchronization.
JS	evt notify	Lock got during event notification.
JS	contention	Synchronizes accesses to the job cache.
JS	evtsub drop	Lock got when dropping subscriber to event queue.
JS	evtsub add	Lock got when adding subscriber to event queue.
JS	q mem clnup lck	Lock obtained when cleaning up queue memory.
JS	sch locl enqs	Scheduler of nonglobal enqueues.
JS	queue lock	Lock on internal scheduler queue.
JS	job recov lock	Lock to recover jobs running on crashed Oracle RAC instance.
JX	cleanup of queue	Releases SQL statement resources.
JX	SQL statement queue	Statement.
KD	determine DBRM master	Determines DBRM master.
KM	contention	Synchronizes various Resource Manager operations.
KO	fast object checkpoint	Coordinates fast object checkpoint.
KP	contention	Synchronizes data pump process startup.
KQ	access ASM attribute	Synchronization of ASM cached attributes.
KT	contention	Synchronizes accesses to the current Resource Manager plan.
MD	contention	Lock held during materialized view log DDL statements.
MH	contention	Lock used for recovery when setting Mail Host for AQ e-mail notifications.
MK	contention	Changing values in enc$.
ML	contention	Lock used for recovery when setting Mail Port for AQ e-mail notifications.
MN	contention	Synchronizes updates to the LogMiner dictionary and prevents multiple instances from preparing the same LogMiner session.
MO	contention	Serializes MMON operations for restricted sessions.
MR	contention	Lock used to coordinate media recovery with other uses of datafiles.

TABLE A-13   *Enqueue Types and Descriptions* (continued)

Name	Enqueue Type	Enqueue Description
MR	standby role transition	Lock used to disallow concurrent standby role transition attempt.
MS	contention	Lock held during materialized view refresh to set up MV log.
MV	datafile move	Held during online datafile move operation or cleanup.
MW	contention	This enqueue is used to serialize the calibration of the manageability schedules with the Maintenance window.
MX	sync storage server info	Lock held to generate a response to the storage server information request when an instance is starting up.
OC	contention	Synchronizes write accesses to the outline cache.
OD	Serializing DDLs	Lock to prevent concurrent online DDLs.
OL	contention	Synchronizes accesses to a particular outline name.
OQ	xsoqhiFlush	Synchronizes access to OLAPI history flushing.
OQ	xsoq*histrecb	Synchronizes access to OLAPI history parameter CB.
OQ	xsoqhiAlloc	Synchronizes access to OLAPI history allocation.
OQ	xsoqhistrecb	Synchronizes access to OLAPI history globals.
OQ	xsoqhiClose	Synchronizes access to OLAPI history closing.
OT	Generic Lock	CTX generic locks.
OW	termination	Terminates the wallet context.
OW	initialization	Initializes the wallet context.
PD	contention	Prevents others from updating the same property.
PE	contention	Synchronizes system parameter updates.
PF	contention	Synchronizes accesses to the password file.
PG	contention	Synchronizes global system parameter updates.
PH	contention	Lock used for recovery when setting Proxy for AQ HTTP notifications.
PI	contention	Communicates remote Parallel Execution Server Process creation status.
PL	contention	Coordinates plug-in operation of transportable tablespaces.
PR	contention	Synchronizes process startup.
PS	contention	Parallel Execution Server Process reservation and synchronization.
PT	contention	Synchronizes access to ASM Partner Status Table (PST) metadata.
PV	syncshut	Synchronizes instance shutdown_slvstart.
PV	syncstart	Synchronizes slave start_shutdown.
PW	perwarm status in dbw0	DBWR 0 holds enqueue indicating prewarmed buffers present in cache.

TABLE A-13 *Enqueue Types and Descriptions* (continued)

Name	Enqueue Type	Enqueue Description
PW	flush prewarm buffers	Direct Load needs to flush prewarmed buffers if DBWR 0 holds enqueue.
RB	contention	Serializes ASM rollback recovery operations.
RC	Result Cache: Contention	Coordinates access to a resultset.
RD	RAC load	Updates Oracle RAC load info.
RE	block repair contention	Synchronizes block repair/resilvering operations.
RF	DG Broker Current File ID	Identifies which configuration metadata file is current.
RF	FSFO Primary Shutdown suspended	Records when FSFO Primary Shutdown is suspended.
RF	FSFO Observer Heartbeat	Captures recent Fast-Start Failover Observer heartbeat information.
RF	RF - Database Automatic Disable	Means for detecting when database is being automatically disabled.
RF	synchronization: critical AI	Synchronizes critical apply instance among primary instances.
RF	new AI	Synchronizes selection of the new apply instance.
RF	synchronization: AIFO master	Synchronizes apply instance failure detection and failover operation.
RF	atomicity	Ensures atomicity of log transport setup.
RF	synch: DG Broker metadata	Ensures read /write atomicity of DG configuration metadata.
RK	set key	Wallet master key rekey.
RL	RAC wallet lock	Oracle RAC wallet lock.
RN	contention	Coordinates nab computations of online logs during recovery.
RO	contention	Coordinates flushing of multiple objects.
RO	fast object reuse	Coordinates fast object reuse.
RP	contention	Enqueue held when resilvering is needed or when data block is repaired from mirror.
RR	contention	Concurrent invocation of DBMS_WORKLOAD_* package API.
RS	prevent file delete	Lock held to prevent deleting file to reclaim space.
RS	prevent aging list update	Lock held to prevent aging list update.
RS	record reuse	Lock held to prevent file from accessing while reusing circular record.
RS	file delete	Lock held to prevent file from accessing during space reclamation.
RS	write alert level	Lock held to write alert level.
RS	read alert level	Lock held to read alert level.
RS	persist alert level	Lock held to make alert level persistent.
RT	contention	Thread locks held by LGWR, DBW0, and RVWR to indicate mounted or open status.

TABLE A-13 *Enqueue Types and Descriptions* (continued)

Name	Enqueue Type	Enqueue Description
RT	thread internal enable/disable	Thread locks held by CKPT to synchronize thread enable and disable.
RU	waiting	Results of rolling migration CIC.
RU	contention	Serializes rolling migration operations.
RW	MV metadata contention	Lock held by CREATE/ALTER/DROP materialized view while updating materialized view flags in detail tables.
RX	relocate extent	Synchronizes relocating ASM extents.
SB	table instantiation	Synchronizes table instantiation and EDS operations.
SB	logical standby metadata	Synchronizes Logical Standby metadata operations.
SE	contention	Synchronizes transparent session migration operations.
SF	contention	Lock used for recovery when setting Sender for AQ e-mail notifications.
SH	contention	Should seldom see this contention because this enqueue is always acquired in no-wait mode.
SI	contention	Prevents multiple streams table instantiations.
SJ	Slave Task Cancel	Serializes cancelling a task executed by a slave process.
SK	contention	Serializes shrink of a segment.
SL	get lock for undo	Sends lock request for undo to LCK0.
SL	get lock	Sends lock request to LCK0.
SL	escalate lock	Sends lock escalate to LCK0.
SO	contention	Synchronizes access to Shared Object (PL/SQL Shared Object Manager).
SP	contention 1	(1) Due to one-off patch.
SP	contention 2	(2) Due to one-off patch.
SP	contention 3	(3) Due to one-off patch.
SP	contention 4	(4) Due to one-off patch.
SQ	contention	Lock to ensure that only one process can replenish the sequence cache.
SR	contention	Coordinates replication/streams operations.
SS	contention	Ensures that sort segments created during parallel DML operations aren't prematurely cleaned up.
ST	contention	Synchronizes space management activities in dictionary-managed tablespaces.
SU	contention	Serializes access to SaveUndo segment.
SW	contention	Coordinates the 'alter system suspend' operation.
TA	contention	Serializes operations on undo segments and undo tablespaces.
TB	SQL Tuning Base Cache Update	Synchronizes writes to the SQL Tuning Base Existence Cache.

TABLE A-13 *Enqueue Types and Descriptions* (continued)

Name	Enqueue Type	Enqueue Description
TB	SQL Tuning Base Cache Load	Synchronizes writes to the SQL Tuning Base Existence Cache.
TC	contention 2	Lock of setup of a unique tablespace checkpoint in null mode.
TC	contention	Lock held to guarantee uniqueness of a tablespace checkpoint.
TD	KTF dump entries	KTF dumping time/SCN mappings in SMON_SCN_TIME table.
TE	KTF broadcast	KTF broadcasting.
TF	contention	Serializes dropping of a temporary file.
TH	metric threshold evaluation	Serializes threshold in-memory chain access.
TK	Auto Task Slave Lockout	Serializes spawned Autotask Slaves.
TK	Auto Task Serialization	Lock held by MMON to prevent other MMON spawning of Autotask Slave.
TL	contention	Serializes threshold log table read and update.
TM	contention	Synchronizes accesses to an object.
TO	contention	Synchronizes DDL and DML operations on a temp object.
TP	contention	Lock held during purge and dynamic reconfiguration of fixed tables.
TQ	TM contention	TM access to the queue table.
TQ	DDL-INI contention	Streams DDL on the queue table.
TQ	INI contention	TM access to the queue table.
TQ	DDL contention	TM access to the queue table.
TS	contention	Serializes accesses to temp segments.
TT	contention	Serializes DDL operations on tablespaces.
TW	contention	Lock held by one instance to wait for transactions on all instances to finish.
TX	allocate ITL entry	Allocates an ITL entry in order to begin a transaction.
TX	index contention	Lock held on an index during a split to prevent other operations on it.
TX	row lock contention	Lock held on a particular row by a transaction to prevent other transactions from modifying it.
TX	contention	Lock held by a transaction to allow other transactions to wait for it.
UL	contention	Lock used by user applications.
US	contention	Lock held to perform DDL on the undo segment.
WA	contention	Lock used for recovery when setting the watermark for memory usage in AQ notifications.
WF	contention	This enqueue is used to serialize the flushing of snapshots.
WG	lock fso	Acquires lobid local enqueue when locking file system object (FSO).

TABLE A-13   *Enqueue Types and Descriptions* (continued)

Name	Enqueue Type	Enqueue Description
WG	delete fso	Acquires lobid local enqueue when deleting file system Object (FSO).
WL	RAC-wide SGA contention	Serializes access to Oracle RAC–wide SGA.
WL	RFS global state contention	Serializes access to RFS global state.
WL	contention	Coordinates access to redo log files and archive logs.
WL	Test access/locking	Tests redo transport access/locking.
WM	WLM Plan activation	Synchronizes new WLM Plan activation.
WP	contention	This enqueue handles concurrency between purging and baselines.
WR	contention	Coordinates access to logs by Async LNS and ARCH/FG.
XC	XDB Configuration	Lock obtained when incrementing XDB configuration version number.
XD	ASM disk OFFLINE	Serialize OFFLINE Exadata disk operations.
XD	ASM disk ONLINE	Serialize ONLINE Exadata disk operations.
XD	ASM disk drop/add	Serialize Auto Drop/Add Exadata disk operations.
XH	contention	Lock used for recovery when setting No Proxy Domains for AQ HTTP notifications.
XL	fault extent map	Keeps multiple processes from faulting in the same extent chunk.
XQ	recovery	Prevents relocation during _recovery_asserts checking.
XQ	relocation	Waits for recovery before doing relocation.
XQ	purification	Waits for relocation before doing block purification.
XR	database force logging	Lock held during database force logging mode.
XR	quiesce database	Lock held during database quiesce.
XY	contention	Lock used for internal testing.
ZA	add std audit table partition	Lock held to add partition to standard audit table.
ZF	add fga audit table partition	Lock held to add partition to fine grained access (FGA) audit table.
ZG	contention	Coordinates file group operations.
ZH	compression analysis	Synchronizes analysis and insert into compression$ as well as prevents multiple threads analyzing the same table during a load.
ZZ	update hash tables	Lock held for updating global context hash tables.

TABLE A-13   *Enqueue Types and Descriptions* (continued)

V$LOCKED_OBJECT

This view displays information about DML locks acquired by different transactions in databases with their mode held (see Table A-14). It also keeps the transaction's ID (transaction ID is XIDUSN.XIDSLOT.XIDSQN).

Column	Data Type	Description
XIDUSN	Number	Number of the undo segment
XIDSLOT	Number	Number of the slot
XIDSQN	Number	Sequence number of the transaction
OBJECT_ID	Number	ID of object being locked by this transaction
SESSION_ID	Number	Session ID responsible for this transaction and lock hold
ORACLE_USERNAME	Varchar2 (30)	Oracle user name
OS_USER_NAME	Varchar2 (30)	OS user name
PROCESS	Varchar2 (14)	OS process ID
LOCKED_MODE	Number	Lock mode; same as LMODE column of V$LOCK

TABLE A-14 *V$LOCKED_OBJECT Information*

V$GES_STATISTICS

This view displays miscellaneous statistics for GES (see Table A-15).

Column	Data Type	Description
STATISTIC#	Number	Statistic ID
NAME	Varchar2 (64)	Name of statistic
VALUE	Number	Value attached with this statistic

TABLE A-15 *V$GES_STATISTICS Information*

V$GES_ENQUEUE

This view displays information about all locks known to the Lock Manager (see Table A-16). It also keeps the grant level, request level, and other related information.

Column	Data Type	Description
HANDLE	(Raw 4 | 8)	Pointer to the lock
GRANT_LEVEL	Varchar2 (9)	Level granted to the lock
REQUEST_LEVEL	Varchar2 (9)	Level requested for the lock
RESOURCE_NAME1	Varchar2 (30)	Resource name of the lock
RESOURCE_NAME2	Varchar2 (30)	Resource name of the lock
PID	Number	Process ID holding the lock
TRANSACTION_ID0	Number	Lower 4 bytes of the transaction ID to which lock belongs
TRANSACTION_ID1	Number	Upper 4 bytes of the transaction ID to which lock belongs
GROUP_ID	Number	Group ID of the lock
OPEN_OPT_DEADLOCK	Number	1 if the DEADLOCK option is set; otherwise 0
OPEN_OPT_PERSISTENT	Number	1 if the PERSISTENT option is set; otherwise 0
OPEN_OPT_PROCESS_OWNED	Number	1 if the PROCESS_OWNED option is set; otherwise 0
OPEN_OPT_NO_XID	Number	1 if the NO_XID option is set; otherwise 0
CONVERT_OPT_GETVALUE	Number	1 if the GETVALUE convert option is set; otherwise 0
CONVERT_OPT_PUTVALUE	Number	1 if the PUTVALUE convert option is set; otherwise 0
CONVERT_OPT_NOVALUE	Number	1 if the NOVALUE convert option is set; otherwise 0
CONVERT_OPT_DUBVALUE	Number	1 if the DUBVALUE convert option is set; otherwise 0
CONVERT_OPT_NOQUEUE	Number	1 if the NOQUEUE convert option is set; otherwise 0
CONVERT_OPT_EXPRESS	Number	1 if the EXPRESS convert option is set; otherwise 0
CONVERT_OPT_NODEADLOCKWAIT	Number	1 if the NODEADLOCKWAIT convert option is set; otherwise 0
CONVERT_OPT_NODEADLOCKBLOCK	Number	1 if the NODEADLOCKBLOCK convert option is set; otherwise 0
WHICH_QUEUE	Number	Tells in which queue the lock is currently located: 0 for Null Queue, 1 for Granted Queue, 2 for Convert Queue
STATE	Varchar2 (64)	State of the lock
AST_EVENT0	Number	Last known AST event
OWNED_NODE	Number	Node ID owning the lock
BLOCKED	Number	1 if the lock request is blocked by others; otherwise 0
BLOCKER	Number	1 if the lock is blocking others; otherwise 0

TABLE A-16   *V$GES_ENQUEUE Information*

V$GES_CONVERT_LOCAL

This view maintains information about all local GES operations (see Table A-17). It displays such information as average convert time, count, and number of conversions. Lock Conversion types are listed in Table A-18

Column	Data Type	Description
INST_ID	Number	Instance ID
CONVERT_TYPE	Varchar2 (64)	Conversion type (see Table A-18)
AVERAGE_CONVERT_TIME	Number	Average conversion time for each lock in hundredths of a second
CONVERT_COUNT	Number	Number of conversions

TABLE A-17 *V$GES_CONVERT_LOCAL Information*

Type	Description
NULL -> SS	NULL mode to subshared mode
NULL-> SX	NULL mode to shared exclusive mode
NULL -> S	NULL mode to shared mode
NULL -> SSX	NULL mode to subshared exclusive mode
NULL -> X	NULL mode to exclusive mode
SS -> SX	Subshared mode to shared exclusive mode
SS -> S	Subshared mode to shared mode
SS -> SSX	Subshared mode to subshared exclusive mode
SS-> X	Subshared mode to exclusive mode
SX -> S	Shared exclusive mode to shared mode
SX -> SSX	Shared exclusive mode to subshared exclusive mode
SX -> X	Shared exclusive mode to exclusive mode
S -> SX	Shared mode to shared exclusive mode
S -> SSX	Shared mode to subshared exclusive mode
S -> X	Shared mode to exclusive mode
SSX -> X	Subshare mode exclusive to exclusive mode

TABLE A-18 *GES Lock Conversion Types*

V$GES_CONVERT_REMOTE

This view maintains information about all remote GES operations (see Table A-19). It displays such information as average convert time, count, and number of conversions.

Column	Data Type	Description
INST_ID	Number	Instance ID
CONVERT_TYPE	Varchar2 (64)	Conversion type
AVERAGE_CONVERT_TIME	Number	Average conversion time for each lock in hundredths of a second
CONVERT_COUNT	Number	Number of conversions

TABLE A-19 *V$GES_CONVERT_REMOTE Information*

V$GES_RESOURCE

This view maintains information about all resources known to the lock manager (see Table A-20). It keeps the information about the master node for that particular resource.

Column	Data Type	Description
RESP	Raw (4 | 8)	Pointer to the resource
RESOURCE_NAME	Varchar2 (30)	Resource name in hexadecimal format for the lock
ON_CONVERT_Q	Number	1 if on convert queue; otherwise 0
ON_GRANT_Q	Number	1 if on convert queue; otherwise 0
PERSISTENT_RESOURCE	Number	1 if it is a persistent resource; otherwise 0
MASTER_NODE	Number	Node ID mastering this resource
NEXT_CVT_LEVEL	Varchar2 (9)	Next lock level to be converted on global convert queue
VALUE_BLK_STATE	Varchar2 (32)	State of value block
VALUE_BLK	Varchar2 (64)	First 64 bytes of value block

TABLE A-20 *V$GES_RESOURCE Information*

Dynamic Resource Remastering Diagnostics

Dynamic resource remastering is a key feature of Oracle RAC that masters the frequently accessed resources to the local node. More information on dynamic remastering is available in Chapter 11.

V$HVMASTER_INFO

This view maintains information about current and previous master instances of GES resources in relation to the hash value ID of resource (see Table A-21).

Column	Data Type	Description
HV_ID	Number	Hash value ID of the resource
CURRENT_MASTER	Number	Instance currently mastering the resource
PREVIOUS_MASTER	Number	Previous instance that mastered this resource
REMASTER_CNT	Number	Number of times this resource has remastered

TABLE A-21 *V$HVMASTER_INFO Information*

V$GCSHVMASTER_INFO

This view displays the same kind of information for GCS resources that V$HVMASTER_INFO displays for GES resources (see Table A-22). Both views display information about the number of times remastering has occurred for resources. This view does not display information about resources belonging to files mapped to a particular master.

Column	Data Type	Description
HV_ID	Number	Hash value ID of the resource
CURRENT_MASTER	Number	Instance currently mastering this PCM resource
PREVIOUS_MASTER	Number	Previous instance that mastered this PCM resource
REMASTER_CNT	Number	Number of times this resource has remastered

TABLE A-22 *V$GCSHVMASTER_INFO Information*

V$GCSPFMASTER_INFO

This view displays information of the current and previous masters about GCS resources belonging to files mapped to a particular master, including the number of times the resource has remastered (see Table A-23). File-based remastering was introduced in Oracle 10g R1; starting with Oracle 10g R2, remastering is done by object level, which allows fine-grained remastering.

Column	Data Type	Description
FILE_ID	Number	File ID
OBJECT_ID	Number	Object ID
TYPE	Number	Type of object
CURRENT_MASTER	Number	Instance currently mastering this file
PREVIOUS_MASTER	Number	Previous instance that mastered this file
REMASTER_CNT	Number	Number of times this file has remastered

TABLE A-23   *V$GCSPFMASTER_INFO Information*

Cluster Interconnect Diagnostics

Starting from Oracle 10g, the cluster interconnect information is available from the v$views. In previous versions, you had to query the alert log or invoke an IPC dump to get details about the interconnects used. The following views provide information about the interconnects configured and used in Oracle RAC.

V$CLUSTER_INTERCONNECTS

This view displays information about interconnects being used for cluster communication (see Table A-24). This view also lists details about the source of the information because interconnect information is also stored in the Oracle Cluster Registry (OCR) and can be configured using the initialization parameter.

Column	Data Type	Description
NAME	Varchar2 (15)	Name of the interconnect—eth0, eth1, and so on.
IP_ADDRESS	Varchar2 (16)	IP address of the interconnect.
IS_PUBLIC	Varchar2 (4)	Yes if the interconnect is public, No if the interconnect is private. Could be null if the type of interconnect is unknown to the cluster.
SOURCE	Varchar2 (31)	Indicates where the interconnect was picked up; interconnect information is available from OCR, OSD software, or the CLUSTER_INTERCONNECTS parameter.

TABLE A-24   *V$CLUSTER_INTERCONNECTS Information*

V$CONFIGURED_INTERCONNECTS

This view's display is the same as V$CLUSTER_INTERCONNECTS, but this view displays information for all configured interconnects of which Oracle is aware, instead of those being used (see Table A-25).

Column	Data Type	Description
NAME	Varchar2 (15)	Name of the interconnect—eth0, eth1, and so on.
IP_ADDRESS	Varchar2 (16)	IP address of the interconnect.
IS_PUBLIC	Varchar2 (4)	Yes if the interconnect is public, No if the interconnect is private. Could be null if the type of interconnect is unknown to the cluster.
SOURCE	Varchar2 (31)	Indicates where the interconnect was picked up.

TABLE A-25   *V$CONFIGURED_INTERCONNECTS Information*

APPENDIX
B

Adding and Removing Cluster Nodes

racle RAC is a highly scalable solution that allows users to add/remove nodes on demand in the existing cluster without affecting the availability of the active database services. Whereas Oracle RAC 10*g* extended the capacity to add and remove the nodes online, Oracle RAC 11*g* Release 2 has introduced new features such as RACONE node, which can be transparently converted to an Oracle RAC database. Nodes should be homogeneous and should have the same computing capacity. Though adding a node with higher or lower capacity than the members is technically possible, it is usually not recommended because it creates a logical imbalance between the nodes.

Adding a Node

Adding a node to an existing cluster is similar to installing the Oracle RAC environment. You must complete all prerequisites explained in the installation chapters of this book. There are mainly two different ways to add a new node into the existing cluster—either clone an existing grid home or use the addNode.sh script. You can clone an existing grid home either by executing the clone.pl script manually or using Oracle Enterprise Manager. Oracle Enterprise Manager provides a graphical user interface to clone an existing grid home but underneath uses the clone.pl script. Though you can add another node via cloning, most users use the addNode.sh script. We will also use the addNode.sh script to explain the procedure to add a new node to the existing cluster.

Regardless of the option chosen to add a new node, typically you will need to complete the following prerequisites:

1. Configure the public and private networks, and ensure that multicasting is enabled for the private network. Also, the network interface name must be the same as that of other nodes in the cluster.

2. Configure the operating system and make sure that the system is configured exactly the same as the other nodes in the cluster. For example, you must ensure that the kernel parameters are set the same, that the same directory structure to store software binaries is created, that users and groups are created with same names and IDs, that shell limits are configured, and that user equivalence have been set up for software owners.

3. Configure shared storage as mentioned in Chapter 4. If you are using ASM, you install and configure ASM libraries on the new node but do not create ASM disks on the new node because ASM disks are already created. You will need to scan the ASM disks on the new node and make sure that ASM disks are detected on the new node.

In the following example, we add a new node to the cluster ORARAC, which has three nodes: RAC1, RAC2, and RAC3. The Oracle instance on each node will be called ORARAC1, ORARAC2, and ORARAC3, respectively. The newly added node will be called RAC4, and the Oracle instance on it will be named ORARAC4. The following walkthrough shows the process of adding the node RAC4 to the cluster ORARAC.

Pre-install Checking

The Cluster Verification utility can be used to verify that the system has been configured properly for Oracle Grid Infrastructure. The following command can be used to verify the readiness of the new node. The Cluster Verification utility can be run either from the staging directory or from any of the existing nodes. The following command in the node RAC1 invokes the Cluster

Verification utility and performs the post-hardware and operating system check for Oracle Grid Infrastructure:

```
$ ./runcluvfy.sh stage - pre crsinst -n rac1,rac2,rac3,rac4 -r 11gR2
$ ./runcluvfy.sh stage -pos hwos -n rac4
```

Alternatively, the following command runs the Cluster Verification utility from the existing nodes:

```
$ cluvfy stage -pos hwos -n rac4
```

Once this post-hardware test has passed, you can compare the system configuration of the new node with any existing node in the cluster to ensure that the new node has been configured the same way other nodes in the cluster are configured. The following command in the node RAC1 invokes the Cluster Verification utility and compares the system configuration of the rac1 and rac4 nodes, assuming that the Oracle Inventory group is oinstall and that the OS dba group is asmdba:

```
$cluvfy comp peer -refnode rac1 -n rac4 -orainv oinstall -osdba asmdba -r 11gR2
```

The Cluster Verification utility in Oracle 11*g* RAC provides another test to verify the integrity of the cluster and the new node being added. This stage test should be executed, and the output of this test must be analyzed carefully before the addNode.sh script is executed. The following command invokes the Cluster Verification utility and executes the pre-nodeadd test:

```
$cluvfy stage -pre nodeadd -n rac4
```

The addNode.sh script internally performs this check, so make sure the preceding test succeeds prior to executing addNode.sh. The Cluster Verification utility should be successful before installation begins. If any error is reported during the verification, it must be fixed before you proceed with the Cluster Ready Services installation.

Executing the addNode.sh Script

The addNode.sh script performs most of the work to add a node into the existing cluster by distributing the Oracle Grid Infrastructure binaries from the existing cluster node to the node being added to the cluster. This script also relinks the binaries on the new node being added. The addNode .sh script can be executed on the GUI in silent mode, whereas GUI mode would require the user to set the DISPLAY variable before invoking the addNode.sh script. Mostly users execute this script in silent mode because doing so provides more options for automation by scripting the node-addition process in large organizations. Once all the prerequisites mentioned in the previous section are met, execute the addNode.sh script located in the $GRID_HOME/oui/bin directory to add the new node:

```
$addNode.sh -silent "CLUSTER_NEW_NODES={rac4}" "CLUSTER_NEW_VIRTUAL_
HOSTNAMES={rac4-vip}"
```

If you are using GNS, you need not provide the virtual hostname for the new node because Oracle GNS will allocate the virtual hostname and IP address automatically. You will execute the following command to add a new node if GNS is configured:

```
$addNode.sh -silent "CLUSTER_NEW_NODES={rac4}"
```

The addNode.sh script internally performs various checks to verify the readiness of the node being added to the cluster and invokes the Oracle Universal Installer in silent mode to distribute the Oracle Grid Infrastructure binaries.

NOTE
The Cluster Verification utility has a historical trend of not verifying the shared storage properly, and you may find that the addNode.sh script fails complaining about shared storage. If you are sure that the shared storage is configured properly, you can set the environment variable IGNORE_PREADDNODE_CHECKS to the value Y. This will avoid the addNode.sh script performing the prenode check, which internally checks for the shared storage.

Installing the Oracle Database Software

After you have installed the Oracle Grid Infrastructure, you can install the Oracle software. Installation of the Oracle database software can also occur from any of the existing nodes. The shell script addNode.sh in the $ORACLE_HOME/oui/bin directory calls the OUI and copies the software to the new node. The following process installs the Oracle software to the newly added node.

Log in as the *oracle* user on any of the cluster nodes and set the environment variables. Invoke addNode.sh in silent mode from $ORACLE_HOME/oui/bin:

```
$./addNode.sh -silent "CLUSTER_NEW_NODES={rac4}"
```

This command executes the OUI in silent mode and copies the database software to the new node and asks you to run the root.sh script at the end. Run the script on the newly added node as specified. If the existing cluster database is a policy-managed database, then the root.sh script will add this new node to the Free Pool, and whenever you increase the cardinality of the database server pool, Oracle will assign an Oracle RAC database instance on the rac4 node and add this rac4 node to the database server pool. For a policy-managed database, you need not follow any more steps to add a node to the existing Oracle RAC database; however, you should follow the remaining steps to create a database instance on the RAC4 node if you are adding this node to an administrator-managed database.

Creating a Database Instance

Now follow these steps on the first node to create the database instance in the new node:

1. Log in as the user *oracle* on RAC4, set the environment to the database home, and invoke the Database Creation Assistant (DBCA):

   ```
   $ORACLE_HOME/bin/dbca
   ```

2. In the Welcome screen, choose Oracle Real Application Clusters Database to create the instance and then click Next.

3. Choose Instance Management and click Next.

4. Choose Add Instance and click Next.

5. Select ORARAC (or the cluster database name you have set up) as the database and enter the SYSDBA username and password at the bottom of the screen. Click Next.

6. You will see a list of the existing instances. Click Next, and on the following screen enter **ORARAC4** as the instance name and choose RAC4 as the node name.

7. This creates a database instance called ORARAC4 (on RAC4). Click Next in the Database Storage screen. During creation, you will be asked whether the ASM instance should be extended to RAC4. Choose Yes.

Removing a Node

Oracle stores vital information in the Oracle Inventory about Oracle products configured and running on the node, and it is very important to update the Oracle Inventory while removing a node so that Oracle Inventory contains current information. Removing a cluster node in Oracle RAC 11*g* Release 2 is very easy because logically unpinning a cluster node from the cluster and shutting it down will separate the node from the cluster, and then you can use the unpinned node for any other purpose. However, if the cluster node being unpinned hosts the Oracle database running on 11*g* Release 1 or an earlier version and you want to completely remove the node from the cluster, you need to follow these steps to completely remove the node from the cluster:

1. Delete the database instance on the node to be deleted.

2. Remove the node from the database.

3. Remove the node from the clusterware.

Deleting the Instance on the Node to Be Deleted

You can delete the instance using the Database Creation Assistant ($ORACLE_HOME/bin/dbca). Invoke the DBCA and choose the Oracle RAC database. In this screen, choose Instance Management and then choose Delete Instance. You will see a screen with the database name. At the bottom of the screen, enter the SYSDBA user and password. Then choose the instance to delete and confirm the deletion.

Alternatively, you can delete the database instance using Oracle Enterprise Manager. Navigate to the cluster database target page and then navigate to Server and click the Delete Instance link, which will take you to the Delete Instance page. Provide the database login information and follow the instructions to delete the database instance.

Removing the Node from the Database

Starting with Oracle Database 11*g* Release 2, Oracle has introduced a new utility called Deinstall to uninstall the Oracle software. It is highly recommended that you uninstall Oracle database or grid home using this utility. Refer to the Oracle database installation guide for complete and detailed instructions to use this utility. For your quick reference, you can access the official documentation about this utility from the following web page:

http://download.oracle.com/docs/cd/E11882_01/install.112/e16763/remove_oracle_sw .htm#BABHGAAB

Removing the RAC4 Node from the Clusterware

Do the following to remove the RAC4 node from the cluster, assuming you are not using GNS:

1. Run the following command as the *root* user from the RAC1 node or any other node that will remain in the cluster to end the lease of the RAC4 node:

```
$cd $GRID_HOME/bin
$./crsctl unpin css -n RAC4
```

Make sure that the CSS is running on the RAC4 node before expiring the lease on this node because the preceding command will fail if CSS is not running on the node being deleted.

2. Execute the rootcrs.pl script as the *root* user on the RAC4 node from the $GRID_HOME/crs/ install directory to disable the cluster resources. You run this only on the nodes to be deleted.

```
$cd $GRID_HOME/crs/install
$./rootcrs.pl -delete -force
```

You must stop cluster resources manually if this script fails.

3. Execute the following command as the *root* user from any node in the cluster that will remain in the cluster:

```
$cd $GRID_HOME/bin
$./crsctl delete node -n RAC4
```

4. As the software owner, execute the following command to update the Oracle Inventory:

```
$cd $GRID_HOME/oui/bin
$./runInstaller -updateNodeList ORACLE_HOME=$GRID_HOME
"CLUSTER_NODES={rac4}" CRS=TRUE -local
```

5. Execute the following command to deinstall the Oracle Grid Infrastructure home. You don't delete the physical Oracle home from the node being deleted if it is a shared Oracle home, but you will update Oracle Inventory to detach the grid home from the node being deleted.

If the RAC4 node is using the shared grid home, execute the following command from the $GRID_HOME/oui/bin directory to update the Oracle Inventory:

```
$cd $GRID_HOME/oui/bin
$./runInstaller -detachHome ORACLE_HOME=$GRID_HOME
```

Otherwise, execute the following command as the software owner to delete the grid Oracle home:

```
$cd $GRID_HOME/deinstall
$./deinstall -local
```

6. Execute the following command as the software owner to update the Oracle Inventory on all the nodes remaining in the cluster:

```
cd $GRID_HOME/oui/bin
 ./runInstaller -updateNodeList ORACLE_HOME=$GRID_HOME
"CLUSTER_NODES={rac1,rac2,rac3}" CRS=TRUE
```

If you are using Grid Naming Services (GNS), you only need to follow steps 2, 3, and 6 in this process.

APPENDIX
C

References

e have made every effort to provide you with a list of all the materials used as references in this book. Any omissions from this list are purely unintentional.

Chapter 1

Dictionary.com. http:/www.dictionary.com.

Peterson, Erik. "RAC at a Distance." Oracle OpenWorld Conference, San Francisco, 2005.

Oracle Database High Availability Overview. 11*g* Release 2 (11.2). Part Number E17157-05.

Oracle Database High Availability Best Practices. 10*g* Release 2 (10.2). Part Number B25159-01.

"Implementing HA with Oracle Real Application Clusters." Oracle World Presentation, 2005.

Oracle Database New Features Guide. 11*g* Release 2 (11.2). Part Number E17128-04.

Chapter 2

Pfister, Gregory F. *In Search of Clusters, 2nd Ed.* Prentice Hall PTR, 1997.

Slee, Roland. "Oracle RAC 10*g* Value Proposition." October 2004. http://www.oracleracsig.org.

*Oracle8*i *Parallel Server Concepts and Administration.* Release 8.1.5. Part Number A67778-01.

*Oracle8*i *Parallel Server Setup and Configuration Guide.* Release 8.1.5. Part Number A67439-01.

*Oracle9*i *Real Application Clusters Administration.* Release 2 (9.2). Part Number A96596-01.

Oracle Database New Features Guide. 11*g* Release 2 (11.2). Part Number E17128-04.

Oracle Real Application Clusters Administration and Deployment Guide. 11*g* Release 2 (11.2). Part Number E16795-08.

Chapter 3

Oracle Corporation. Metalink forum and support notes. http://metalink.oracle.com.

Vaidyanatha, Gaja Krishna, Kirtikumar Deshpande, and John A. Kostelac. *Oracle Performance Tuning 101.* McGraw-Hill/Professional, 2001.

*Oracle9*i *Real Application Clusters Concepts.* Release 2 (9.2). Part Number A96597-01.

Oracle Database Reference. 11*g* Release 2 (11.2). Part Number E17110-05.

Oracle Database Concepts. 10*g* Release 2 (10.2). Part Number B14220-02.

Oracle Clusterware Administration and Deployment Guide. 11*g* Release 2 (11.2). Part Number E16794-09.

Oracle Real Application Clusters Administration and Deployment Guide. 11*g* Release 2 (11.2). Part Number E16795-08.

Oracle Database Release Notes. 11*g* Release 2 (11.2) for Linux. Part Number E16778-08.

Oracle Automatic Storage Management Administrator's Guide. 11*g* Release 2 (11.2). Part Number E16102-07.

Oracle Database Performance Tuning Guide. 11*g* Release 2 (11.2). Part Number E16638-04.

Chapter 4

Gopalakrishnan, K. "Tracing Universal Installer." *SELECT Journal*. Quarter 4, 2005.

Oracle Database Oracle Clusterware and Oracle Real Application Clusters Installation Guide. 10*g* Release 2 (10.2) for Linux. Part Number B14203-07.

Oracle Clusterware Administration and Deployment Guide. 11*g* Release 2 (11.2). Part Number E16794-09.

Oracle Real Application Clusters Installation Guide. 11*g* Release 2 (11.2) for Linux and UNIX. Part Number E17214-08.

Oracle Database New Features Guide. 11*g* Release 2 (11.2). Part Number E17128-04.

Oracle Real Application Clusters Administration and Deployment Guide. 11*g* Release 2 (11.2). Part Number E16795-08.

Oracle Automatic Storage Management Administrator's Guide. 11*g* Release 2 (11.2). Part Number E16102-07.

Oracle Database Release Notes. 11*g* Release 2 (11.2) for Linux. Part Number E16778-08.

Oracle Grid Infrastructure Installation Guide. 11*g* Release 2 (11.2) for Linux. Part Number E17212-10.

Chapter 5

Oracle Corporation. Metalink forum and support notes. http://metalink.oracle.com.

Oracle Database Oracle Clusterware and Oracle Real Application Clusters Installation Guide. 10*g* Release 2 (10.2) for Linux. Part Number B14203-07.

Oracle Grid Infrastructure Installation Guide. 11*g* Release 2 (11.2) for Linux. Part Number E17212-10.

Oracle Real Application Clusters Installation Guide. 11*g* Release 2 (11.2) for Linux and UNIX. Part Number E17214-08.

Oracle Clusterware Administration and Deployment Guide. 11g Release 2 (11.2). Part Number E16794-09.

Oracle Database Patch Set Notes. 10g Release 1 (10.1.0.4). Patch Set 2 for Linux x86.

Oracle Database New Features Guide. 11g Release 2 (11.2). Part Number E17128-04.

Oracle Database Release Notes. 11g Release 2 (11.2) for Linux. Part Number E16778-08.

Chapter 6

Oracle Corporation. Metalink forum and support notes. http://metalink.oracle.com.

Oracle Database Oracle Clusterware and Oracle Real Application Clusters Installation Guide. 10g Release 2 (10.2) for Linux. Part Number B14203-07.

Oracle Grid Infrastructure Installation Guide. 11g Release 2 (11.2) for Linux. Part Number E17212-10.

Oracle Clusterware Administration and Deployment Guide. 11g Release 2 (11.2). Part Number E16794-09.

Oracle Real Application Clusters Administration and Deployment Guide. 11g Release 2 (11.2). Part Number E16795-08.

Oracle Automatic Storage Management Administrator's Guide. 11g Release 2 (11.2). Part Number E16102-07.

Oracle Database Release Notes. 11g Release 2 (11.2) for Linux. Part Number E16778-08.

Oracle Database New Features Guide. 11g Release 2 (11.2). Part Number E17128-04.

Chapter 7

Oracle Database Concepts. 10g Release 2 (10.2). Part Number B14220-02.

Oracle Clusterware Administration and Deployment Guide. 11g Release 2 (11.2). Part Number E16794-09.

Oracle Grid Infrastructure Installation Guide. 11g Release 2 (11.2) for Linux. Part Number E17212-10.

Oracle Database Quick Installation Guide. 11g Release 2 (11.2) for Linux x86-64. Part Number E16768-04.

Oracle Real Application Clusters Administration and Deployment Guide. 11g Release 2 (11.2). Part Number E16795-08.

Oracle Automatic Storage Management Administrator's Guide. 11g Release 2 (11.2). Part Number E16102-07.

Oracle Database Administrator's Guide. 10g Release 2 (10.2). Part Number B14231-02.

Oracle Database New Features Guide. 11*g* Release 2 (11.2). Part Number E17128-04.

Oracle Database Reference. 10*g* Release 1 (10.1). Part Number B10755-01.

Chapter 8

Oracle Clusterware Administration and Deployment Guide. 11*g* Release 2 (11.2). Part Number E16794-09.

Oracle Database Net Services Administrator's Guide. 10*g* Release 2 (10.2). Part Number B14212-01.

Oracle Database Reference. 10*g* Release 1 (10.1). Part Number B10755-01.

Oracle Database Application Developer's Guide: Fundamentals. 10*g* Release 2 (10.2). Chapter 15. Part Number B14251-01.

Oracle Database PL/SQL Packages and Types Reference. 10*g* Release 2 (10.2). Part Number B14258-01.

Oracle Real Application Clusters Administration and Deployment Guide. 11*g* Release 2 (11.2). Part Number E16795-08.

Chapter 9

Oracle Database Backup and Recovery Basics. 10*g* Release 2 (10.2). Part Number B14192-03.

Oracle Database Oracle Clusterware and Oracle Real Application Clusters Installation Guide. 10*g* Release 2 (10.2) for hp Tru64. Part Number B14206-01.

Oracle Database Backup and Recovery User's Guide. 11*g* Release 2 (11.2). Part Number E10642-04.

Oracle Database New Features Guide. 10*g* Release 2 (10.2). Part Number B14214-02.

Oracle Database Concepts. 11*g* Release 2 (11.2). Part Number E16508-05.

*Oracle8*i *Parallel Server Concepts and Administration.* Release 8.1.5. Part Number A67778-01.

*Oracle9*i *Real Application Clusters Concepts.* Release 2 (9.2). Part Number A96597-01.

Oracle Database Oracle Clusterware and Oracle Real Application Clusters Installation Guide. 10*g* Release 2 (10.2) for Linux. Part Number B14203-07.

Oracle Clusterware Administration and Deployment Guide. 11*g* Release 2 (11.2). Part Number E16794-09.

Oracle Real Application Clusters Administration and Deployment Guide. 11*g* Release 2 (11.2). Part Number E16795-08.

Chapter 10

Deshpande, Kirtikumar, Richmond Shee, and K. Gopalakrishnan. *Oracle Wait Interface: A Practical Guide to Performance Diagnostics & Tuning*. McGraw-Hill/Professional, 2004.

Oracle Database Performance Tuning Guide. 11*g* Release 2 (11.2). Part Number E16638-04.

Oracle Database New Features Guide. 11*g* Release 2 (11.2). Part Number E17128-04.

Oracle Database Concepts. 11*g* Release 2 (11.2). Part Number E16508-05.

*Oracle9*i *Real Application Clusters Administration*. Release 2 (9.2). Part Number A96596-01.

*Oracle8*i *Parallel Server Concepts and Administration*. Release 8.1.5. Part Number A67778-01.

*Oracle9*i *Real Application Clusters Concepts*. Release 2 (9.2). Part Number A96597-01.

Oracle Real Application Clusters Administration and Deployment Guide. 11*g* Release 2 (11.2). Part Number E16795-08.

Oracle Database Reference. 11*g* Release 2 (11.2). Part Number E17110-05.

Chapter 11

Deshpande, Kirtikumar, Richmond Shee, and K. Gopalakrishnan. *Oracle Wait Interface: A Practical Guide to Performance Diagnostics & Tuning*. McGraw-Hill/Professional, 2004.

E-mail discussions in the comp.databases.oracle.server and oracle-l mailing lists.

Oracle Database Concepts. 11*g* Release 2 (11.2). Part Number E16508-05.

*Oracle9*i *Real Application Clusters Real Application Clusters Guard I: Concepts and Administration*. Release 2 (9.2). Part Number A96601-01.

*Oracle8*i *Parallel Server Concepts and Administration*. Release 8.1.5. Part Number A67778-01.

*Oracle9*i *Real Application Clusters Concepts*. Release 2 (9.2). Part Number A96597-01.

Oracle Real Application Clusters Administration and Deployment Guide. 11*g* Release 2 (11.2). Part Number E16795-08.

Oracle Database Reference. 11*g* Release 2 (11.2). Part Number E17110-05.

Chapter 12

Demel, Sohan. "Oracle Real Application Clusters: Cache Fusion Delivers Scalability." Oracle whitepaper. February 2002.

E-mail discussions in the comp.databases.oracle.server and oracle-l mailing lists.

Oracle Database Concepts. 11*g* Release 2 (11.2). Part Number E16508-05.

Oracle9i Real Application Clusters Real Application Clusters Guard I: Concepts and Administration. Release 2 (9.2). Part Number A96601-01.

Oracle8i Parallel Server Concepts and Administration. Release 8.1.5. Part Number A67778-01.

Oracle9i Real Application Clusters Concepts. Release 2 (9.2). Part Number A96597-01.

Chapter 13

E-mail discussions in the comp.databases.oracle.server and oracle-l mailing lists.

Oracle Database Net Services Administrator's Guide. 11*g* Release 2 (11.2). Part Number E10836-06.

Oracle Database Performance Tuning Guide. 11*g* Release 2 (11.2). Part Number E16638-04.

Oracle Database Net Services Reference. 11*g* Release 2 (11.2). Part Number E10835-05.

Oracle8i Parallel Server Concepts and Administration. Release 8.1.5. Part Number A67778-01.

Oracle9i Real Application Clusters Concepts. Release 2 (9.2). Part Number A96597-01.

Chapter 14

E-mail discussions in the comp.databases.oracle.server and oracle-l mailing lists.

Oracle Database Concepts. 11*g* Release 2 (11.2). Part Number E16508-05.

Oracle8i Parallel Server Concepts and Administration. Release 8.1.5. Part Number A67778-01.

Oracle9i Real Application Clusters Concepts. Release 2 (9.2). Part Number A96597-01.

Oracle Database Reference. 11*g* Release 2 (11.2). Part Number E17110-05

Oracle Database New Features Guide. 11*g* Release 2 (11.2). Part Number E17128-04.

Chapter 15

Peterson, Frik. "RAC at a Distance." Oracle OpenWorld Conference, San Francisco, 2005. E-mail discussion in Oracle-l mailing list.

E-mail discussions in the comp.databases.oracle.server and oracle-l mailing lists.

HP/Oracle CTC web page. http://www.hporaclectc.com.

Oracle Maximum Availability Architecture (MAA). http://www.oracle.com/technology/deploy/availability/htdocs/maa.htm.

Oracle Automatic Storage Management Administrator's Guide. 11*g* Release 2 (11.2). Part Number E16102-07.

Chapter 16

E-mail discussions in the comp.databases.oracle.server and oracle-l mailing lists.

Oracle Database Concepts. 11*g* Release 2 (11.2). Part Number E16508-05.

Oracle Database Reference. 11*g* Release 2 (11.2). Part Number E17110-05.

Oracle Database Application Developer's Guide: Fundamentals. 10*g* Release 2 (10.2). Part Number B14251-01.

*Oracle8*i *Parallel Server Concepts and Administration.* Release 8.1.5. Part Number A67778-01.

*Oracle9*i *Real Application Clusters Concepts.* Release 2 (9.2). Part Number A96597-01.

Oracle Real Application Clusters Administration and Deployment Guide. 11*g* Release 2 (11.2). Part Number E16795-08.

Oracle Database Performance Tuning Guide. 11*g* Release 2 (11.2). Part Number E16638-04.

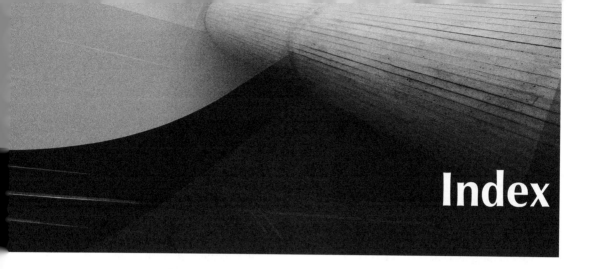

Index

H

I

Q

R

T

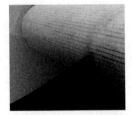

GET YOUR FREE SUBSCRIPTION TO *ORACLE MAGAZINE*

Oracle Magazine is essential gear for today's information technology professionals. Stay informed and increase your productivity with every issue of *Oracle Magazine*. Inside each free bimonthly issue you'll get:

- Up-to-date information on Oracle Database, Oracle Application Server, Web development, enterprise grid computing, database technology, and business trends
- Third-party news and announcements
- Technical articles on Oracle and partner products, technologies, and operating environments
- Development and administration tips
- Real-world customer stories

If there are other Oracle users at your location who would like to receive their own subscription to *Oracle Magazine*, please photocopy this form and pass it along.

Three easy ways to subscribe:

① Web
Visit our Web site at **oracle.com/oraclemagazine**
You'll find a subscription form there, plus much more

② Fax
Complete the questionnaire on the back of this card and fax the questionnaire side only to **+1.847.763.9638**

③ Mail
Complete the questionnaire on the back of this card and mail it to **P.O. Box 1263, Skokie, IL 60076-8263**

ORACLE®

Want your own FREE subscription?

To receive a free subscription to *Oracle Magazine*, you must fill out the entire card, sign it, and date it (incomplete cards cannot be processed or acknowledged). You can also fax your application to **+1.847.763.9638. Or subscribe at our Web site at oracle.com/oraclemagazine**

O **Yes, please send me a FREE subscription** *Oracle Magazine*.   O No.

O From time to time, Oracle Publishing allows our partners exclusive access to our e-mail addresses for special promotions and announcements. To be included in this program, please check this circle. If you do not wish to be included, you will only receive notices about your subscription via e-mail.

O Oracle Publishing allows sharing of our postal mailing list with selected third parties. If you prefer your mailing address not to be included in this program, please check this circle.

If at any time you would like to be removed from either mailing list, please contact Customer Service at +1.847.763.9635 or send an e-mail to oracle@halldata.com. If you opt in to the sharing of information, Oracle may also provide you with e-mail related to Oracle products, services, and events. If you want to completely unsubscribe from any e-mail communication from Oracle, please send an e-mail to: unsubscribe@oracle-mail.com with the following in the subject line: REMOVE [your e-mail address]. For complete information on Oracle Publishing's privacy practices, please visit oracle.com/html/privacy.html

X
signature (required)   date

name   title

company   e-mail address

street/p.o. box

city/state/zip or postal code   telephone

country   fax

Would you like to receive your free subscription in digital format instead of print if it becomes available? O Yes O No

---

YOU MUST ANSWER ALL 10 QUESTIONS BELOW.

① WHAT IS THE PRIMARY BUSINESS ACTIVITY OF YOUR FIRM AT THIS LOCATION? (check one only)

- ☐ 01 Aerospace and Defense Manufacturing
- ☐ 02 Application Service Provider
- ☐ 03 Automotive Manufacturing
- ☐ 04 Chemicals
- ☐ 05 Media and Entertainment
- ☐ 06 Construction/Engineering
- ☐ 07 Consumer Sector/Consumer Packaged Goods
- ☐ 08 Education
- ☐ 09 Financial Services/Insurance
- ☐ 10 Health Care
- ☐ 11 High Technology Manufacturing, OEM
- ☐ 12 Industrial Manufacturing
- ☐ 13 Independent Software Vendor
- ☐ 14 Life Sciences (biotech, pharmaceuticals)
- ☐ 15 Natural Resources
- ☐ 16 Oil and Gas
- ☐ 17 Professional Services
- ☐ 18 Public Sector (government)
- ☐ 19 Research
- ☐ 20 Retail/Wholesale/Distribution
- ☐ 21 Systems Integrator, VAR/VAD
- ☐ 22 Telecommunications
- ☐ 23 Travel and Transportation
- ☐ 24 Utilities (electric, gas, sanitation, water)
- ☐ 98 Other Business and Services _____

② WHICH OF THE FOLLOWING BEST DESCRIBES YOUR PRIMARY JOB FUNCTION? (check one only)

CORPORATE MANAGEMENT/STAFF
- ☐ 01 Executive Management (President, Chair, CEO, CFO, Owner, Partner, Principal)
- ☐ 02 Finance/Administrative Management (VP/Director/ Manager/Controller, Purchasing, Administration)
- ☐ 03 Sales/Marketing Management (VP/Director/Manager)
- ☐ 04 Computer Systems/Operations Management (CIO/VP/Director/Manager MIS/IS/IT, Ops)

IS/IT STAFF
- ☐ 05 Application Development/Programming Management
- ☐ 06 Application Development/Programming Staff
- ☐ 07 Consulting
- ☐ 08 DBA/Systems Administrator
- ☐ 09 Education/Training
- ☐ 10 Technical Support Director/Manager
- ☐ 11 Other Technical Management/Staff
- ☐ 98 Other

③ WHAT IS YOUR CURRENT PRIMARY OPERATING PLATFORM (check all that apply)

- ☐ 01 Digital Equipment Corp UNIX/VAX/VMS
- ☐ 02 HP UNIX
- ☐ 03 IBM AIX
- ☐ 04 IBM UNIX
- ☐ 05 Linux (Red Hat)
- ☐ 06 Linux (SUSE)
- ☐ 07 Linux (Oracle Enterprise)
- ☐ 08 Linux (other)
- ☐ 09 Macintosh
- ☐ 10 MVS
- ☐ 11 Netware
- ☐ 12 Network Computing
- ☐ 13 SCO UNIX
- ☐ 14 Sun Solaris/SunOS
- ☐ 15 Windows
- ☐ 16 Other UNIX
- ☐ 98 Other
- 99 ☐ None of the Above

④ DO YOU EVALUATE, SPECIFY, RECOMMEND, OR AUTHORIZE THE PURCHASE OF ANY OF THE FOLLOWING? (check all that apply)

- ☐ 01 Hardware
- ☐ 02 Business Applications (ERP, CRM, etc.)
- ☐ 03 Application Development Tools
- ☐ 04 Database Products
- ☐ 05 Internet or Intranet Products
- ☐ 06 Other Software
- ☐ 07 Middleware Products
- 99 ☐ None of the Above

⑤ IN YOUR JOB, DO YOU USE OR PLAN TO PURCHASE ANY OF THE FOLLOWING PRODUCTS? (check all that apply)

SOFTWARE
- ☐ 01 CAD/CAE/CAM
- ☐ 02 Collaboration Software
- ☐ 03 Communications
- ☐ 04 Database Management
- ☐ 05 File Management
- ☐ 06 Finance
- ☐ 07 Java
- ☐ 08 Multimedia Authoring
- ☐ 09 Networking
- ☐ 10 Programming
- ☐ 11 Project Management
- ☐ 12 Scientific and Engineering
- ☐ 13 Systems Management
- ☐ 14 Workflow

HARDWARE
- ☐ 15 Macintosh
- ☐ 16 Mainframe
- ☐ 17 Massively Parallel Processing
- ☐ 18 Minicomputer
- ☐ 19 Intel x86(32)
- ☐ 20 Intel x86(64)
- ☐ 21 Network Computer
- ☐ 22 Symmetric Multiprocessing
- ☐ 23 Workstation Services

SERVICES
- ☐ 24 Consulting
- ☐ 25 Education/Training
- ☐ 26 Maintenance
- ☐ 27 Online Database
- ☐ 28 Support
- ☐ 29 Technology-Based Training
- ☐ 30 Other
- 99 ☐ None of the Above

⑥ WHAT IS YOUR COMPANY'S SIZE? (check one only)

- ☐ 01 More than 25,000 Employees
- ☐ 02 10,001 to 25,000 Employees
- ☐ 03 5,001 to 10,000 Employees
- ☐ 04 1,001 to 5,000 Employees
- ☐ 05 101 to 1,000 Employees
- ☐ 06 Fewer than 100 Employees

⑦ DURING THE NEXT 12 MONTHS, HOW MUCH DO YOU ANTICIPATE YOUR ORGANIZATION WILL SPEND ON COMPUTER HARDWARE, SOFTWARE, PERIPHERALS, AND SERVICES FOR YOUR LOCATION? (check one only)

- ☐ 01 Less than $10,000
- ☐ 02 $10,000 to $49,999
- ☐ 03 $50,000 to $99,999
- ☐ 04 $100,000 to $499,999
- ☐ 05 $500,000 to $999,999
- ☐ 06 $1,000,000 and Over

⑧ WHAT IS YOUR COMPANY'S YEARLY SALES REVENUE? (check one only)

- ☐ 01 $500, 000, 000 and above
- ☐ 02 $100, 000, 000 to $500, 000, 000
- ☐ 03 $50, 000, 000 to $100, 000, 000
- ☐ 04 $5, 000, 000 to $50, 000, 000
- ☐ 05 $1, 000, 000 to $5, 000, 000

⑨ WHAT LANGUAGES AND FRAMEWORKS DO YOU USE? (check all that apply)

- ☐ 01 Ajax
- ☐ 02 C
- ☐ 03 C++
- ☐ 04 C#
- ☐ 05 Hibernate
- ☐ 06 J++/J#
- ☐ 07 Java
- ☐ 08 JSP
- ☐ 09 .NET
- ☐ 10 Perl
- ☐ 11 PHP
- ☐ 12 PL/SQL
- ☐ 13 Python
- ☐ 14 Ruby/Rails
- ☐ 15 Spring
- ☐ 16 Struts
- ☐ 17 SQL
- ☐ 18 Visual Basic
- ☐ 98 Other

⑩ WHAT ORACLE PRODUCTS ARE IN USE AT YOUR SITE? (check all that apply)

ORACLE DATABASE
- ☐ 01 Oracle Database 11*g*
- ☐ 02 Oracle Database 10*g*
- ☐ 03 Oracle9*i* Database
- ☐ 04 Oracle Embedded Database (Oracle Lite, Times Ten, Berkeley DB)
- ☐ 05 Other Oracle Database Release

ORACLE FUSION MIDDLEWARE
- ☐ 06 Oracle Application Server
- ☐ 07 Oracle Portal
- ☐ 08 Oracle Enterprise Manager
- ☐ 09 Oracle BPEL Process Manager
- ☐ 10 Oracle Identity Management
- ☐ 11 Oracle SOA Suite
- ☐ 12 Oracle Data Hubs

ORACLE DEVELOPMENT TOOLS
- ☐ 13 Oracle JDeveloper
- ☐ 14 Oracle Forms
- ☐ 15 Oracle Reports
- ☐ 16 Oracle Designer
- ☐ 17 Oracle Discoverer
- ☐ 18 Oracle BI Beans
- ☐ 19 Oracle Warehouse Builder
- ☐ 20 Oracle WebCenter
- ☐ 21 Oracle Application Express

ORACLE APPLICATIONS
- ☐ 22 Oracle E-Business Suite
- ☐ 23 PeopleSoft Enterprise
- ☐ 24 JD Edwards EnterpriseOne
- ☐ 25 JD Edwards World
- ☐ 26 Oracle Fusion
- ☐ 27 Hyperion
- ☐ 28 Siebel CRM

ORACLE SERVICES
- ☐ 28 Oracle E-Business Suite On Demand
- ☐ 29 Oracle Technology On Demand
- ☐ 30 Siebel CRM On Demand
- ☐ 31 Oracle Consulting
- ☐ 32 Oracle Education
- ☐ 33 Oracle Support
- ☐ 98 Other
- 99 ☐ None of the Above

0801 4004